Films by Genre

For
Nicky and Daniel Andrés

Films by Genre

775 Categories, Styles, Trends and Movements Defined, with a Filmography for Each

by

Daniel Lopez

McFarland & Company, Inc., Publishers
Jefferson, North Carolina, and London

, 63139176X

British Library Cataloguing-in-Publication data are available

Library of Congress Cataloguing-in-Publication Data

Lopez, Daniel, 1945–
    Films by genre : 775 categories, styles, trends and movements
defined, with a filmography for each / by Daniel Lopez.
        p.   cm.
    Includes bibliographical references and index. ∞
    ISBN 0-89950-780-8 (lib. bdg. : 50# alk. paper)
    1. Motion pictures — Catalogs.   2. Film genres.   I. Title.
PN1998.L63   1993
791.43′75 — dc20   92-56661
                                                            CIP

Manufactured in the United States of America

McFarland & Company, Inc., Publishers
    Box 611, Jefferson, North Carolina 28640

PN
1998
.L63
1993

Table of Contents

v

Preface

Reproduction of the "moving image" from celluloid began in the late 19th century. Soon these "moving pictures" started to make worldwide impact, and there arose the need to meet an ever-increasing demand for the new product. Many early filmmakers used subject matter already in circulation; others improved on it, introduced variations, or created new story angles; many films started to resemble each other and fall into types. Hence the emergence of film genres. Through the years films have continued to be classified into groupings, types, and genres for critical appraisal, easy identification of subject matter, or just to give a quick clue or reference as to their nature. Thus, the intention of this guide is basically to provide a quick referral to the numerous film genres, movements, styles, categories, and trends into which films may readily be classified.

This guide is essentially an alphabetical listing of entries with a brief description of the genre, subgenre, trend, or film grouping alluded to in the entry heading, which may include in brackets synonymous or related words. There follows a sample of films which may best exemplify it.[1] Representative films may range from the earliest offerings of filmmakers to a few as recent as 1992. Bibliographical references for further reading or references which supply filmographies are, in some instances, indicated in the body of the entry or in the references, which begin on page 393.

Although this book is primarily concerned with film, some entries and definitions dealing only with television or video have been included for the sake of completeness.

Abbreviations of Places

(As of 1990)

Afg	Afghanistan	**IvC**	Ivory Coast
Alg	Algeria	**J**	Japan
Arg	Argentina	**Jam**	Jamaica
Aus	Austria	**Ken**	Kenya
Aust	Australia	**Leb**	Lebanon
Belg	Belgium	**Liech**	Liechtenstein
Berm	Bermuda	**Lux**	Luxembourg
Bol	Bolivia	**Maurit**	Mauritania
Braz	Brazil	**Mex**	Mexico
Bulg	Bulgaria	**Mon**	Monaco
Can	Canada	**Mor**	Morocco
Chn	China	**NZ**	New Zealand
Col	Colombia	**Nic**	Nicaragua
CR	Costa Rica	**Nig**	Nigeria
Cyp	Cyprus	**Nor**	Norway
Cz	Czechoslovakia	**Pan**	Panama
Den	Denmark	**Phil**	Philippines
Dom.R	Dominican Republic	**Pol**	Poland
		Port	Portugal
Ecua	Ecuador	**PR**	Puerto Rico
EG	East Germany	**Q**	Quebec (Canada)
Egy	Egypt	**Rum**	Rumania
F	France	**Sen**	Senegal
Fin	Finland	**SA**	South Africa
G	Germany/W. Ger.	**Sp**	Spain
Gab	Gabon	**Sw**	Sweden
GB	Great Britain	**Swiz**	Switzerland
Gr	Greece	**Syr**	Syria
HK	Hong Kong	**Tai**	Taiwan
Hol	Holland	**Thai**	Thailand
Hung	Hungary	**Tun**	Tunisia
Icel	Iceland	**Tur**	Turkey
Ind	India	**US**	United States
Indon	Indonesia	**USSR**	Union of Soviet Socialist Republics
Ire	Ireland		
Isr	Israel	**Ven**	Venezuela
It	Italy	**Yug**	Yugoslavia

xxiii

Note to Film Listings

Abbreviations

ABC American Broadcasting Company
BBC British Broadcasting Corporation
CBS Columbia Broadcasting System
ITV Independent Television (GB)
NBC National Broadcasting Company

aka also known as (additional title or titles)
Cf Compare with
Comp Compiled by
MCTV made-for-cable TV
Prod Producer; Produced by
[rel. in 44] released in 1944
TV film made for television
v version

The film listings include in the following order:

Original title or titles.
Film's nationality (if not from the U.S.), year
    of production (or instead, copyright year or year
    of release) and if it is made for television
    or cable TV.
Director(s)/Filmmaker(s)
Additional titles, e.g. working title (title or
    titles used during production), transla-
    tion of title, re-release title, etc.

Films by Genre

A-Level Title *see* **VIDEO**

A-PICTURE ("A" Property, First Feature)   The term A-picture or first feature was used to designate the main attraction in a double program and refers to a high quality, high-budget film in contrast to a lower-budgeted or B-picture exhibited as the second feature of a double bill. *See also* **B-MOVIE.**

"A" Property *see* **A-PICTURE**

Absolute Film *see* **ABSTRACT FILM**

Abstract Animated Films *see* **ANIMATED FILM**

ABSTRACT FILM (Concrete Film, Nonobjective Film)   Abstract films avoid narrative and instead convey sensitive impressions and emotions by way of color, rhythm and movement. They began as experimental films made by the avant-garde in the 1920s in France and Germany and have continued to be made by filmmakers and artists using the film medium as a means of artistic expression. Abstract films, mostly shorts, are made in many countries. They include animated films consisting of drawings, splashes of color, lines and shapes forming diverse configurations; computer films; and films in which abstraction is achieved by working on the film itself by scratching, drawing or painting on its surface. New possibilities for making abstract films continue to emerge. Abstract films are also made by photographing objects in the usual manner. The term *abstract film* also refers to any nonrepresentational film. *See* Malcolm Le Grice, *Abstract Film and Beyond* (London: Studio Vista, 1977). *See also* **AVANT-GARDE.**

Rhythmus 21 (G 21) Hans Richter *aka Film ist Rhythmus / Film Is Rhythm / Rhythm 21.* *Le Rétour à la raison* (F 23) Man Ray. *Rhythmus 23* (G 23) Hans Richter *aka Rhythm 23.* *Symphonie diagonale* (G 23-24) Viking Eggeling *aka Diagonale Symphonie / Diagonalsymphonien / Diagonal Symphony* *Le Ballet mécanique* (F 24) Fernand Léger *aka Images Mobile.* *Rhythmus 25* (G 25) Hans Richter *aka Rhythm 25.* *H₂O* (29) Ralph Steiner. *Light Rhythms* (30) Francis Bruguière, Oswell Blakeston. *Colour Box* (GB 35) Len Lye. *Komposition in Blau* (G 35) Oskar Fischinger *aka Composition in Blue.* *Trade Tatoo* (GB 37) Len Lye. *Motion Painting #1* (46-47) Oskar Fischinger. *Begone Dull Care / Caprice en couleurs* (Can 49) Norman McLaren, Evelyn Lambart. *Bells of Atlantis* (52) Len Lye. *Serenal* (Can 59) Norman McLaren. *Allures* (61) Jordan Belson. *Lines-Horizontal / Lignes-Horizontales* (Can 61) Norman McLaren, Evelyn Lambart. *Lapis* (63-66) James Whitney. *Per. mu.ta.tion.s / Permutations* (67) John Whitney. *The Text of Light* (74) Stan Brakhage.

——**Absolute Film**   May be an abstract film of a nonrepresentational nature or a film that expresses a poetic rather than a concrete reality; as such, it may include impressionistic "city symphony" films like *Rien que les heures* (1926) directed by Alberto Cavalcanti and *Regen* (1929) directed by

Joris Ivens, or surrealist films like *Le Sang d'un poète* (1930) directed by Jean Cocteau.

Rien que les heures (F 26) Alberto Cavalcanti *aka Nothing But the Hours*
Melodie der Welt (G 29) Walter Ruthman *aka Melody of the World.* **Regen**
(Hol 29) Joris Ivens *aka Rain.* **Le Sang d'un poète** (F 30) Jean Cocteau *aka*
The Blood of a Poet / La Vie du poète. **Allegretto** (36) Oskar Fischinger
aka Radio Dynamics.

——**Cinéma Pur (Pure Cinema)** A theory put into practice by Henri
Chomette (1891–1941) in three short films: *Jeux de reflets et de vitesse* (1923),
A quoi rêvent les jeunes filles (1925), *Cinq minutes de cinéma pur* (1925).
He advocated the filming of cadence, rhythmic movement and purely visual
elements rather than dramatic narrative. The term has been used mostly for
what is better known as abstract film.

Jeux de reflets et de vitesse (F 23-25) Henri Chomette *aka Jeux de reflets et*
de la vitesse / Jeux de reflets, de lumière et de vitesse / Reflets de lumière et
de vitesse. **A quoi rêvent les jeunes filles** (F 25) Henri Chomette. **Cinq**
minutes de cinéma pur (F 25-26) Henri Chomette.

——**Graphic Films** Graphic film is P. Adams Sitney's general term for
what is otherwise known as abstract film. It represents a trend in avant-
garde and independent filmmakers that extends from the early works of
Hans Richter (*Filmstudie 25,* 1925-26), Viking Eggeling, Marcel Duchamp
(*Anémic Cinema,* 1925), and Fernand Léger to Len Lye, Harry Smith,
Robert Breer, as well as to some underground films of the 1960s and
beyond.

Anémic Cinema (F 25) Marcel Duchamp *aka Anaemic Cinema.* **Filmstudie**
25 (G 25-26) Hans Richter *aka Filmstudie / Film Study.* **Rainbow Dance**
(GB 36) Len Lye. **No. 7** (51) Harry Smith. **Form Phases I** (52) Robert Breer.

——**Pattern Film** An abstract film that uses as its subject matter archi-
tectural designs, objects, or the rhythm and shapes of machines in movement.

Vormittagsspuk (G 27-28) Hans Richter *aka Ghosts Before Breakfast /*
Ghosts Before Noon. **De Brug** (Hol 28) Joris Ivens *aka The Bridge.* **La**
Marche des machines (F 28) Eugène Deslaw *aka The March of the Machines*
N.Y., N.Y. (52-57) Francis Thompson.

——**Synthetic Films (Hand Made Films)** These are films made without a
camera (painted-on films, scratch films, collage films) by painting, scratching, collage, or other similar methods applied to the surface of the film
celluloid itself. The first synthetic films are attributed to Len Lye, a New
Zealander who moved to England and made *Colour Box* (1935), the first
example of abstract expressionism on film. *See also* **Cameraless Animated**
Films in **ANIMATED FILM.**

Colour Box (GB 35) Len Lye. **Love on the Wing** (GB 37-39) Norman
McLaren. **Fiddle-de-dee** (Can 47) Norman McLaren. **Free Radicals** (58)
Len Lye. **Heaven & Earth Magic & Feature** (50-62) Harry Smith *aka The*
Magic Feature / No. 12.

Absurd Comedy *see* **ANARCHIC COMEDY;** *see also* **FARCE**

Acid Film *see* **DRUG FILM: Psychedelic Films**

ACTION FILM   A film in which the action predominates and becomes the main concern in the picture's composition. Action or action-adventure are labels very much in use in catalogues, magazines, movie guides, and video rental outlets (also on video cassette covers) to highlight and gather together films whose content tends to emphasize fast moving action characterized by car chases, crashes, explosions, gunplay, and violent fights. As such, the action film appears in many diverse genres, e.g. the martial arts film (q.v.). *See also* **ACTION-ADVENTURE FILM** below.

Birds of Prey (US / Can 73 TV) William A. Graham.   *Charley Varrick* (73) Don Siegel.   *Hard Times* (75) Walter Hill *aka The Streetfighter*.   *Jaguar Lives!* (79) Ernest Pintoff.   *Southern Comfort* (81) Walter Hill.   *48 Hours* (82) Walter Hill.   *Silent Rage* (82) Michael Miller.   *Savage Streets* (84) Danny Steinmann.   *Sloane* (Phil / US 84) Daniel Rosenthal.   *African Rage* (85) Peter Collinson.   *Certain Fury* (US / Can 85) Stephen Gyllenhaal. *Code of Silence* (85) Andrew Davis.   *Commando* (85) Mark L. Lester.   *Invasion U.S.A.* (85) Joseph Zito.   *Stand Alone* (85) Alan Beattie.   *The Big Easy* (86) Jim McBride.   *Top Gun* (86) Tony Scott.   *Silent Assassins* (87) Lee Doo Young, Scott Thomas.   *Above the Law* (88) Andrew Davis *aka Nico / Nico Above the Law*.   *Deadly Pursuit* (US / Can / GB 88) Roger Spottiswoode *aka Shoot to Kill*.   *Die Hard* (88) John McTiernan.   *Midnight Run* (88) Martin Brest.   *Hard to Kill* (89) Bruce Malmuth.   *Road House* (89) Rowdy Herrington.   *Air America* (90) Roger Spottiswoode.   *Another 48 HRS* (90) Walter Hill.   *Die Hard 2* (90) Renny Harlin *aka Die Hard 2: Die Harder*.   *New Jack City* (91) Mario Van Peebles.

ACTION-ADVENTURE FILM (Actioner, Action Film)   An extremely popular form that keeps reappearing in the guise of new genres. Action implies movement, speed, and a fighting spirit; hence, films of action are fast-paced with fights, duels, or shoot-outs. The genres in which action films predominate have traditionally been the Western, the war film, the gangster film, the swashbuckler, the peplum (epic film) and, more recently, the spy film (James Bond variety), the samurai film, the Chinese swordplay movie, the kung-fu film, and the disaster film. All these genres are treated independently. *See also* **ADVENTURE FILM.**

The Three Musketeers (48) George Sidney.   *King Solomon's Mines* (50) Compton Bennett, Andrew Marton.   *The Vikings* (58) Richard Fleischer. *The Naked Prey* (US / SA 65) Cornel Wilde.   *The Dirty Dozen* (US / GB 67) Robert Aldrich.   *If He Hollers, Let Him Go!* (68) Charles Martin *aka Night Hunt*.   *The Mercenaries* (GB 68) Jack Cardiff *aka Dark of the Sun*. *Billy Jack* (71) T. C. Frank (Tom Laughlin).   *Deliverance* (72) John Boorman. *Gold* (GB 74) Peter Hunt.   *The Wind and the Lion* (75) John Milius. *Radiers of the Lost Ark* (81) Steven Spielberg.   *Treasure of the Four Crowns / El tesoro de las cuatro coronas* (US / Sp 82) Ferdinando Baldi *aka Seeing Is Believing*.   *High Road to China* (US / GB / Yug 83) Brian G. Hutton. *Indiana Jones and the Temple of Doom* (84) Steven Spielberg *aka Indy II / Indiana Jones and the Temple of Death*.   *Romancing the Stone* (84) Robert

Zemeckis. *The Emerald Forest* (GB / US 85) John Boorman. *The Jewel of the Nile* (85) Lewis Teague. *Remo Williams: The Adventure Begins...* (85) Guy Hamilton *aka Remo Unarmed and Dangerous.* *Big Trouble in Little China* (86) John Carpenter. *Florida Straits* (86 MCTV) Mike Hodger. *Cannibal Women in the Avocado Jungle of Death* (88) J. D. Athens. *"Crocodile" Dundee II / Crocodile Dundee II* (US / Aust 88) John Cornell. *The Further Adventures of Tennessee Buck* (88) David Keith. *Indiana Jones and the Last Crusade* (89) Steven Spielberg.

Action Beaver *see* **HARD-CORE PORNO FILM**

Action Films *see* **EXPANDED CINEMA**

Action Melodrama *see* **MELODRAMA**

Action News *see* **TELEVISION NEWS**

Actioner, Action Film *see* **ACTION-ADVENTURE FILM**

Activist Documentary *see* **DOCUMENTARY: Committed Documentary**

Actor's Film *see* **AUTEUR FILM**

Actualité *see* **ACTUALITY**

Actualities *see* **ACTUALITY** *see also* **TELEVISION NEWS**

ACTUALITY (ACTUALITÉ, ACTUALITIES, ACTUALITY FILM, DOCUMENTAIRE, EDUCATIONAL, INTEREST FILM, NEWS FILM, NEWS ITEM, TOPICAL) The filming of "actual" events or the normal activities of people at work or at leisure may be traced back to the Lumière brothers. They filmed many short subjects of about one minute or less focusing on people leaving work (*La Sortie des usines Lumière,* 1894), arrivals and departures of trains and people (*L'Arrivée d'un train en gare,* 1895; *Arrivée des congressistes,* 1895) and the feeding of a baby (*Repas de bébé,* 1895). These early films heralded the soon-to-come news films and newsreels or *films d'actualités* as they are known in France, and as filmmakers ventured further afield than their immediate surroundings, expedition films, travel films or travelogues. The actuality film is an early form of the documentary film.

The difference between an early actuality, a topical and an interest film is that an actuality shows something that happened at the time of filming as, for instance, the arrival of a train at the station or workers leaving a factory (see above); a topical film records an event that is newsworthy — a coronation, a horse race, and so forth. An interest film implies some measure of interpretation of its subject by the maker of the film.

La Sortie des usines Lumière (F 1894) Louis Lumière *aka La Sortie des usines / Departure of the Workers of the Lumière Factory.* *L'Arrivée d'un train en gare* (F 1895) Louis Lumière *aka Arrivée d'un train à La Ciotat / L'Arrivée d'un train en gare de La Ciotat / Arrival of a Train / The Arrival of a*

Train at the Station. Arrivée des Congressistes (F 1895) Louis Lumière *aka Arrivée des Congressistes à Neuville-sur-Saône, Lyon / Débarquement / Le Débarquement des Congressistes / Excursion of the French Photographic Society at Neuville. Répas de bébé* (F 1895) Louis Lumière *aka Le Déjeuner de bébé / Le Goûter de bébé / Feeding the Baby.*

Actuality Drama *see* **DOCUDRAMA**

ADAPTATION (Film Adaptation) The term is applied to films which are based on an already existing literary, dramatic, or musical source. Most adaptations are from novels, novelettes, short stories, or plays. Other forms of literary composition have also been inspirational for adaptation, e.g., poems. Most musicals are adaptations from stage musical comedy or from operas and operettas. Adaptations onto the screen from other media are equally common, for example, radio and television.[2]

——**Adaptations from Novels (Novel into Film)** Adaptations from novels are extremely abundant and they may vary from a more or less faithful rendering (not necessarily the best option) of the original narrative to a personal interpretation by scriptwriter and director. Films have also departed completely from the literary work to which the producers have bought the rights, with the result that the ensuing product will remind us of its source by its title only. For instance, the film *Everything You Always Wanted to Know About Sex But Were Afraid to Ask* (1972) kept the title of the original pseudo-sex book and little else.

Symptomatic of any adaptation of a novel is the need to condense the original narrative to a manageable time limit. It is only through serialization, as is done today by television networks, that a measure of the novel's creative potential can be transferred to the screen without having to carve out too much material from the original work.

David Copperfield (35) George Cukor. *Gone with the Wind* (39) Victor Fleming (uncredited: George Cukor, Sidney Franklin, Sam Wood) *aka GWTW / Tomorrow Is Another Day / The Wind. The Moon and Sixpence* (42) Albert Lewin. *Frenchman's Creek* (44) Mitchell Leisen. *The Postman Always Rings Twice* (45) Tay Garnett. *The Fountainhead* (48) King Vidor. *The Carpetbaggers* (63) Edward Dmytryk. *Lucky Jim* (GB 57) John Boulting. *The Brothers Karamazov* (58) Richard Brooks. *Lolita* (US / GB 61) Stanley Kubrick. *Tom Jones* (GB 63) Tony Richardson. *The Graduate* (67) Mike Nichols. *Ulysses* (US / GB 67) Joseph Strick. *Bratya Karamazovy* (USSR 68) Ivan Pyriev *aka The Brothers Karamazov / The Murder of Dmitri Karamazov. Il Conformista / Le Conformiste* (It / F / G 69) Bernardo Bertolucci *aka The Conformist. Catch-22* (70) Mike Nichols. *Morte a Venezia / Morte à Venise* (It / F 70) Luchino Visconti *aka Death in Venice. A Clockwork Orange* (GB 71) Stanley Kubrick. *Everything You Always Wanted to Know About Sex, but Were Afraid to Ask* (72) Woody Allen. *A Portrait of the Artist as a Young Man* (GB 77) Joseph Strick. *Lady Chatterley's Lover / L'Amant de Lady Chatterley* (GB / F 81) Just Jaeckin. *The Razor's Edge* (84) John Byrum. *Castaway* (GB 86) Nicolas Roeg. *The Mosquito Coast* (86) Peter Weir. *Tempos difíceis, este tempo / Hard Times* (Port / GB 88) João Botelho.

——**Adaptations from Plays (Stage-to-Film Adaptations, Stage-to-Screen Adaptations)**   Adaptations from plays vary a great deal; at first, sound film adaptations followed the original play closely, but as filmmaking techniques progressed, films reinterpreted or readapted the original stage plays to the requirements of the film medium. Roger Manvell includes six degrees of adaptation in his *Theater and Film* (Rutherford, Madison, NJ: Fairleigh Dickinson University Presses, 1979, pp. 36–37), which go from mere recordings of stage productions to complete transformations of the original play. *See also* **SHAKESPEARE FILM**.

Journey's End (30) James Whale. *Dangerous Corner* (34) Phil Rosen. *The Women* (39) George Cukor. *The Devil and Daniel Webster* (40) William Dieterle *aka All That Money Can Buy / Daniel and the Devil / Daniel Webster and the Devil / Here Is a Man*. *The Little Foxes* (41) William Wyler. *I Remember Mama* (48) George Stevens. *Fröken Julie* (Sw 50) Alf Sjöberg *aka Miss Julie*. *Death of a Salesman* (51) Laslo Benedeck. *A Streetcar Named Desire* (51) Elia Kazan. *The Importance of Being Earnest* (GB 52) Anthony Asquith. *The Actress* (53) George Cukor. *Huis Clos* (F 54) Jacqueline Audry *aka No Exit*. *Herr Puntila und sein Knecht Matti* (Aus 55) Alberto Cavalcanti *aka Herr Puntila and His Servant Matti*. *Cat on a Hot Tin Roof* (58) Richard Brooks. *Look Back in Anger* (GB 58) Tony Richardson. *The Balcony* (62) Joseph Strick. *The Miracle Worker* (62) Arthur Penn. *The Night of the Iguana* (64) John Huston. *Dutchman* (GB / US 66) Anthony Harvey. *Marat-Sade* (GB 66) Peter Brook *aka The Persecution and Assassination of Jean-Paul Marat as Performed by the Inmates of the Asylum of Charenton Under the Direction of the Marquis de Sade*. *Who's Afraid of Virginia Woolf?* (66) Mike Nichols. *Medea / Médée* (It / F / G 69) Pier Paolo Pasolini. *Rhinoceros* (US / Can 73) Tom O'Horgan. *Die Wildente* (G / Aus 76) Hans W. Geissendörfer *aka The Wild Duck*. *Betrayal* (GB 82) David Jones. *The Dumb Waiter* (89) Robert Altman.

Adaptations from Classics   *see*   **HARD-CORE PORNO FILM**

Adaptations from Comedies   *see*   **MUSICAL**

Adaptations from Novels, Adaptations from Plays   *see*   **ADAPTATION**

Adaptations of Broadway Musical Comedies   *see*   **MUSICAL**

Admag   *see*   **TELEVISION COMMERCIAL**

Adult Cartoons   *see*   **CARTOON FILM**

Adult Film   *see*   **HARD-CORE PORNO FILM**

Adult Western   *see*   **WESTERN: Psychological Westerns**

ADVENTURE FILM   Adventure films run parallel to action-adventure films. They are basically the same genre. The only difference between the two forms is one of emphasis. In adventure stories, action is not necessarily the dominant element of the story, while in the action-adventure film, the emphasis is on the action, which constitutes the essence of the adventure.

Adventure films cover an even greater field than that of the action movie, and they subdivide into a great variety of genres and subgenres. Because the field is so vast, it is sometimes useful to be more precise when talking about the adventure film and word combinations that abound: adventure melodrama, costume adventure, romantic adventure, romantic adventure drama, science fiction adventure movie, and many more.

The term is also employed for a type of family picture in which the outdoors, nature and wild life play a predominant role, e.g., *The Adventures of the Wilderness Family* (1975). Quite a few Walt Disney films fall under this category.

Tarzan and His Mate (34) Cedric Gibbons, Jack Conway. *She* (35) Irving Pichel, Lansing C. Holden. *The Adventures of Marco Polo* (38) Archie Mayo. *The Adventures of Tom Sawyer* (38) Norman Taurog. *Captain Fury* (39) Hal Roach. *Reap the Wild Wind* (42) Cecil B. DeMille *aka Cecil B. DeMille's Reap the Wild Wind*. *Scott of the Antarctic* (GB 48) Charles Frend. *Robinson Crusoe* (Mex 52) Luis Buñuel *aka The Adventures of Robinson Crusoe*. *Appointment in Honduras* (53) Jacques Tourneur. *The Naked Jungle* (53) Byron Haskin. *Soldier of Fortune* (53) Edward Dmytryk. *The Sundowners* (60) Fred Zinnemann. *Swiss Family Robinson* (60) Ken Annakin. *Those Magnificent Men in Their Flying Machines* (GB / US 65) Ken Annakin *aka Those Magnificent Men in Their Flying Machines; or How I Flew from London to Paris in 25 Hours and 11 Minutes*. *The Darwin Adventure* (GB 71) Jack Couffer. *The Light at the Edge of the World* (US / Sp / Liech 71) Kevin Billington. *Dersu Uzala / Deresu Usara* (USSR / J 74) Akira Kurosawa, Teruyo Nogami, Vladimir Vasiliev. *The Dove* (74) Charles Jarrott. *The Adventures of the Wilderness Family* (75) Stewart Raffill. *Caravans* (US / Iran 78) James Fargo. *Ashanti* (Isr / US / Swiz 79) Richard Fleischer *aka Ashanti: Land of No Mercy*. *Cuba* (79) Richard Lester. *Ingenjör Andrées iuftfärd / Ingenjör Andrées inftfärd* (Sw / Nor / G 82) Jan Troel *aka (The) Flight of the Eagle*. *Dance of the Dwarfs* (US / Phil 83) Gus Trikonis *aka Jungle Heat*. *Hosszú vágta / Brady's Escape* (Hung / US 83) Pál Gabor *aka The Long Ride*. *Tai-Pan* (US / HK 86) Daryl Duke *aka James Clavell's Tai-Pan*. *Crusoe* (88) Caleb Deschanel.

Adventure-Process Film *see* **CAPER FILM**

Adventure War Films *see* **WAR FILM**

Adventurer Detective Films *see* **PRIVATE DETECTIVE FILM**

Advertising Film *see* **FACTUAL FILM**

Advertising Magazine *see* **TELEVISION COMMERCIAL: Admag**

Advertising Pod *see* **TELEVISION COMMERCIAL**

Aerial Combat Movie, Aerial War Movie *see* **WAR FILM: Aviation War Films**

Afterlife Film *see* **FILM BLANC**

Agitprop *see* **PROPAGANDA FILM**

Agricultural Film *see* **FACTUAL FILM: Educational Film**

Air Combat Movie *see* **WAR FILM: Aviation War Films**

Air Movie, Airplane Film *see* **AVIATION FILM**

ALEATORY FILM   In an aleatory film, the technique consists in leaving the filmmaking and the development of subject matter open to chance and on-the-spot improvisation rather than a predetermined shooting plan. Aleatory techniques are mostly used in *cinéma vérité* and direct cinema documentaries and in some films like Robert Altman's *A Wedding* (1978).

ALLEGORY (Film Allegory)   Film allegories are films in which the plot, action, and characters have a correlative meaning on the symbolic level. In allegories, the story is presented on two levels, the concrete and the symbolic, which are separate but interdependent. Allegories usually draw attention to some fundamental truth about human existence, the nature of the world, the power of good and evil, or some other abstraction. The film medium and its genres have proved to be very adaptable to allegory and some very fine examples of the form exist.

Everywoman (19) George H. Melford. *Outward Bound* (30) Robert Milton. *No Greater Glory* (34) Frank Borzage. *Strange Cargo* (40) Frank Borzage. *Alias Nick Beal* (49) John Farrow *aka The Contact Man.* *The Night of the Hunter* (55) Charles Laughton. *Moby Dick* (56) John Huston. *Det Sjunde inseglet* (Sw 56) Ingmar Bergman *aka The Seventh Seal.* *Lord of the Flies* (GB 61) Peter Brook. *Whistle Down the Wind* (GB 61) Bryan Forbes. *Suna no onna* (J 63) Hiroshi Teshigahara *aka Woman in the Dunes / Woman of the Dunes.* *Hell in the Pacific* (68) John Boorman *aka The Enemy / Two Soldiers—East and West.* *2001: A Space Odyssey* (US / GB 68) Stanley Kubrick *aka Journey Beyond the Stars / Space Odyssey.* *Auch Zwerge haben klein angefangen* (G 69-70) Werner Herzog *aka Even Dwarfs Started Small.* *Leo the Last* (GB 70) John Boorman. *Magasiskola* (Hung 70) István Gaál *aka The Falcons.* *El Topo* (Mex 70) Alexandro Jodorowsky *aka The Mole.* *Savages* (71) James Ivory. *Greaser's Palace* (72) Robert Downey. *Majstor i Margarita / Il Maestro e Margherita* (Yug / It 72) Aleksandar Petrovic *aka The Master and Margarita.* *O Lucky Man!* (GB 73) Lindsay Anderson. *Die Halde* (G 74 TV) Rainer Erler *aka The Rubbish Tip.* *Travolti da un insolito destino nell'azzurro mare d'agosto* (It 74) Lina Wertmüller *aka Swept Away ... by an Unusual Destiny in the Blue Sea of August.* *Furtivos* (Sp 75) José Luis Borau *aka The Poachers.*

All-Star Movie Revue *see* **MUSICAL: Film Revues**

All-Star War Effort Musicals *see* **MUSICAL**

Alternative Cinema *see* **INDEPENDENT PRODUCTION**

Amateur Detective Films *see* **PRIVATE DETECTIVE FILM**

AMATEUR FILM (Home Movie)   A film made by anyone who is not professionally connected with the film industry. Amateur films may be made by aspiring filmmakers or students who at times enlist the help of friends and family in making their films, or they may consist of family shots or scenes filmed while on holiday; this latter type is better known as home movies. Amateur filmmakers usually use cameras and projectors equipped for 16mm or 8mm gauges, but, lately, video cameras have simplified the making of amateur movies. Amateur films, although normally not accessible to the public at large, are a very important branch of the film industry.

Ambient Video   *see*   **MUSIC VIDEO**

American Civil War Film   *see*   **WAR FILM: Civil War Films**

AMERICANA   Films which reflect an intrinsically characteristic or typical American way of life and its culture, real or idealized, past or present, are often referred to as Americana.

Judge Priest (34) John Ford.   *State Fair* (33) Henry King.   *Ah, Wilderness* (35) Clarence Brown.   *The Human Comedy* (42) Clarence Brown.   *Meet Me in St. Louis* (44) Vincente Minnelli.   *A Letter to Three Wives* (49) Joseph L. Mankiewicz.   *The Sun Shines Bright* (53) John Ford.   *Come Next Spring* (56) R. G. Springsteen.   *Moochie of the Little League* (59) William Beaudine [originally shown on TV in two parts].   *The Music Man* (62) Morton Da Costa.   *The Reivers* (69) Mark Rydell.   *Americana* (73) David Carradine [rel. in 81].   *Nashville* (75) Robert Altman.   *Melvin and Howard* (80) Jonathan Demme.   *Raggedy Man* (81) Jack Fisk.   *Grandview U.S.A.* (84) Randal Kleiser.   *Hoosiers* (86) David Anspaugh.   *Something Wild* (86) Jonathan Demme.   *A Winner Never Quits* (86 TV) Mel Damski.   *Mr. North* (88) Danny Huston.   *Roger & Me* (89) Michael Moore.

Analytical Documentary   *see*   **DOCUMENTARY**

Analytical Film   *see*   **REVOLUTIONARY FILM**

Anamorphic Film   *see*   **WIDE SCREEN**

ANARCHIC COMEDY (Absurd Comedy, Crazy Comedy, Gag Comedy, Zany Comedy)   Anarchic comedy is perhaps the best label to describe the kind of madness that surrounded the shenanigans and wisecracks of the Marx Brothers (Chico, Groucho, Harpo, and Zeppo).[3] They originated a type of non sensical comedy full of non sequitur scenes, and saturated with nihilistic, iconoclastic furor. They poked fun at everything in satiric sketches and parodies. It is a unique style of comedy in which very few comedians have been able to excel. Some films of W. C. Fields qualify as anarchic and so does the work of the British Monty Python group. Apart from these exceptions, only a few films have achieved the kind of madness typical of anarchic comedy.

The Marx Bros.: The Cocoanuts (29) Joseph Santley, Robert Florey.   *Animal Crackers* (30) Victor Heerman.   *Horse Feathers* (31) Norman Z. McLeod.   *Monkey Business* (31) Norman Z. McLeod.   *Duck Soup* (33) Leo McCarey.

W. C. Fields: The Dentist (32) Leslie Pearce.   *Million Dollar Legs* (32) Edward Cline.   *The Barber-Shop* (33) Arthur Ripley.   *The Fatal Glass of Beer* (33) Clyde Bruckman.   *The Pharmacist* (33) Arthur Ripley.

Monty Python: Monty Python and the Holy Grail (GB 74) Terry Gilliam, Terry Jones. *Monty Python's Life of Brian* (GB 79) Terry Jones *aka Life of Brian.* *Monty Python Live at the Hollywood Bowl* (GB 82) Terry Hughes, "Monty Python". *Monty Python's The Meaning of Life* (GB 83) Terry Jones. *Also: Hellzapoppin'* (41) H. C. Porter.

ANCIENT FILM (Film About Antiquity)   "Ancient" films or films which deal with antiquity are an amalgam of historical films, costumers, epics, religious films, adventure films, musicals, comedies, romances, even horror films exploiting ancient myths. They are based on Greek and Roman history and mythology, or the Old and New Testaments, or are set in Babylon, Egypt, Persia, and the Orient. They are examined by Jon Solomon in *The Ancient World in the Cinema* (South Brunswick and New York: A. S. Barnes, 1978) as a collective genre of over 400 films. The different genres into which the "ancient" films may be sub-divided have been treated under separate entries, e.g., **EPIC, PEPLUM, RELIGIOUS FILM**.

ANIMAL PICTURE   Animal actors have figured in many films, from the silent period to the present time. Quite often, they have dominated the action or, as it is sometimes said, they have stolen the show. In many cases, the film is built around them. This is specially so in family-oriented adventure films in which the animal adventures consist usually in making friends with children and younger members of a family or in making strange bedfellows of other inhabitants of the animal kingdom; e.g., *Sequoia* (1934) features a puma and a deer as best pals.
The earliest animal star on record to appear in a series of movies is a British collie known by the screen name of Rover. His first movie, *Rescued by Rover* (1905) was a box-office success. Famous major animal actors have included such well-known personalities as Rin Tin Tin (Rinty), Lassie, Flipper, and Francis, the talking mule, some of which, besides acting in films and starring in their own series, also made their way into long-running television series. For horse stories, see **HORSE PIC**. "Animal films" in which the animals (rats, ants, birds, frogs, bats, dogs) attack human beings as a result of an imbalance of nature or supernatural happenings are better classified under science fiction, disaster, or horror.

Rescued by Rover (GB 05) Lewin Fitzhamon. *Sequoia* (34) Chester M. Franklin *aka Malibu.* *Lassie Come Home* (43) Fred M. Wilcox [Lassie has featured in 10 films (43-78)]. *The Adventures of Rusty* (45) Paul Barnfold [Rusty has featured in 8 films (45-49)]. *Bill and Coo* (47) Dean Riesner. *The Return of Rin Tin Tin* (47) Max Nosseck [Rinty has appeared in several films and 5 serials (23-47)]. *Francis* (49) Arthur Lubin [7 films (49-56) in the "Francis" series]. *Bedtime for Bonzo* (51) Frederick de Cordova. *Rhubarb* (51) Arthur Lubin. *Old Yeller* (57) Robert Stevenson. *Perri* (57) N. Paul Kenworthy, Jr. *Flipper* (63) James B. Clark. *The Incredible Journey* (US / Can 63) Fletcher Markle. *Clarence, the Cross-Eyed Lion* (65) Andrew Marton. *Fluffy* (65) Earl Bellamy. *That Darn Cat!* (65) Robert Stevenson. *Zebra in the Kitchen* (65) Ivan Tors. *Gentle Giant* (67) James

Neilson. *Charlie, the Lonesome Cougar* (68) no director credited. *The Doberman Gang* (72) Byron Chudnow [sequels: *The Daring Dobermans* (73) Byron Chudnow and *The Amazing Dobermans* (76) David Chudnow and Byron Chudnow]. *Jonathan Livingston Seagull* (73) Hall Barlett. *Benji* (74) Joe Camp [4 "Benji" films (74-87)]. *For the Love of Benji* (US / Gr 77) Joe Camp. *The Cat from Outer Space* (78) Norman Tokar. *White Dog* (82) Samuel Fuller *aka Trained to Kill*. *Koneko monogatari* (J 86) Masanori Hata *aka The Adventures of Milo and Otis* (J / US 89).

Animals-on-the-Rampage Movie *see* **HORROR FILM: Other Denizens of Horror Movies**

Animated Cartoon *see* **CARTOON FILM**

Animated Collage Films *see* **ANIMATED FILM**

ANIMATED FILM (Animation)   An animated film is one which, by the use of some animation technique, creates the illusion of movement in inanimate objects, drawings, photographs, paper or cardboard cut-outs, puppets, plasticine, and the like. It generally makes use of stop-motion photography (photographing the film one frame at a time), but not exclusively, e.g., pixilated films, films made entirely of still photographs.

Animation is an important branch of cinematography which precedes the invention of moving pictures. The telling of a story by way of a succession of drawings goes back to ancient Egypt and Greece. As well, the projection of shadows on a screen by silhouette puppets (*ombres chinoises*) was an early instance of the capability of animation to captivate an audience.

Emyle Reynaud (1844–1918) combined his Praxinoscope with a projector to show animated "films" of a duration of up to 15 minutes in the Théâtre Optique at the Musée Grévin in Paris in 1892.

The characteristic difference between the animated film and the live-action film is that instead of a standardized continuous speed of 24 frames per second, the animated film is generally constructed by photographing frame by frame. There are, of course, other techniques of animation (drawing or painting directly on film, pixilation by editing, graphics films) that by-pass the conventional way of creating movement in the animated film, but the stop-frame system is the method most commonly employed. Most animated films fit the short category, lasting from a few seconds to several minutes. Feature-length animated films, requiring a much greater effort in their production, are not the norm. However, a world pool of several hundred animated features exists.[4]

The vast field of animation is not restricted to entertainment or commercial cinema alone. Animated films are more and more frequently used in public relations and advertising, as tools of instruction and research, and as a bona fide medium of self-expression in the arts and experimentation.

——**Abstract Animated Films**   Abstract animated movies had their beginning with the avant-garde in Europe in the twenties; they continue to be made and now fall under the headings of experimental or expanded cinema. Abstract film has no story, no narrative, no plot, just visual and audio harmony. *See also* **ABSTRACT FILM.**

> *Composition 5* (59) Dwinell Grant. *Blazes* (61) Robert Breer. *Mosaic / Mosaïque* (Can 65) Norman McLaren, Evelyn Lambart. *Synchromy / Synchromie* (Can 71) Norman McLaren.

——**Animated Collage Films (Collage Animation Films)**   Collage films are achieved by mixing diverse materials — photographs, newspaper clippings, illustrations, woodcuts, engravings — gathered from a variety of sources like old catalogues, magazines and books. Some very fine animated films are achieved by using the collage technique. *See also* **Collage Films** in **UNDERGROUND FILM.**

> *What Who How* (55) Stan VanDerBeek. *Jamestown Baloos* (57) Robert Breer. *Duo Concertantes* (61-64) Larry Jordan. *Frank Film* (74) Frank Mouris.

——**Animated Stills (Filmograph, Films Made Entirely of Stills, Still Animation)**   A series of still photographs, each held by the camera for a number of frames, or a number of related photographs moving so fast that the viewer scarcely has time to focus on them, have an appearance of mobility and have been used to tell a story, the history of a nation, or a man's life. It is a related form of animation. A filmograph is a film made of still photographs or the technique of making such films.

> *House* (55) Charles Eames, Ray Eames. *City of Gold / Capitale de l'or* (Can 57) Wolf Koenig, Colin Low. *La Jetée* (F 62) Chris Marker *aka La Jetée: Un photo-roman / The Jetty / The Pier. The Ballad of Crowfoot* (Can 68) Willie Dunn.

——**Animation of Still Paintings and Drawings (Graphics Films)**   Drawings, paintings, or photographs may seem to become animated when the camera roams over them. This is achieved by camera movement (zooms, pans), and it is a technique frequently used when illustrating the art work of a particular artist or when detailing an historical subject by the use of old prints or photographs.

> *C'est l'aviron* (Can 44) Norman McLaren [in the series: *Chants populaires*] *aka Chants populaires no. 5 / Chants populaires no. 6. Poet and Painter Series No. 4* (GB 51) John Halas *aka 4: John Gilpin* [series of 4 films]. *The Axe and the Lamp* (GB 63) John Halas.

——**Cameraless Animated Films (Direct-Animation Films, Drawn on Films, Graphic Animation, Hand-Drawn Films, Noncamera Films, Out-of-Camera Films)**   Direct drawing, painting, or scratching on celluloid is a technique which does not require a camera. It was initiated by Oskar Fischinger (1900–1967) and Len Lye (1901–1980) and later developed by Norman McLaren while he was at the National Film Board of Canada. It is done by working on individual frames or by working on the strip of film ignoring the frames; during projection, the movement of the projector will create the desired effect.

No. 1 (ca. 39) Harry Smith [*Note: Early Abstractions* (39-53) is made of *Nos. 1-5*, No. 7 and No. 10]. **Dollar Dance** (Can 43) Norman McLaren. **Begone, Dull Care / Caprice en couleurs** (Can 49) Norman McLaren, Evelyn Lambart. **Ere erea baleibu icik subua aruaren** (Sp 68-70) José Antonio Sistiaga *aka Scope, Colour, Muda 75* [1st feature-length film painted directly onto film]

——Cartoon Films   *see*   separate **CARTOON FILM** entry

——**Computer-Animated Films (Computer Films, Computer-Generated Films, Computer Graphics, Computer-Made Films)**   Computers have been used, and are used more and more frequently, for the production of animated films. They are time-saving devices which, at the same time, simplify the process of making an animated film. In the past, the only drawbacks were the lack of sophistication and the absence of a personal touch in the finished product. However, most of these initial shortcomings are being remedied as more advanced computer systems become operational. The degree of sophistication of present-day computer-generated films is very high.[5]

Poem Field no. 1 (67) Stan VanDerBeek, Ken Knowlton. **Meta Data** (Can 71) Peter Foldès. **Hunger / La Faim** (Can 72) Peter Foldès. **Matrix III** (72) John Whitney, J. Citron. **Dream Flight** (Can 82) P. Bergeron, Nadia Magnenat-Thalmann, Daniel Thalmann. **Tony de Peltrie** (Can 82-86) Pierre Lachapelle, Philippe Bergeron, Pierre Robidoux, Daniel Langlois.

——**Cut-Out Animation Films**   Besides the silhouette films which use cut-out black shapes and figures with jointed limbs, two other forms of cut-outs have been used in animated films to create a most engaging effect. They are painted cut-outs with jointed limbs and painted cut-outs mounted on sticks. The cut-outs or components may be re-arranged to suit the requirements of the picture.

L'Idée (F 31) Berthold Bartosch *aka The Idea*. **Rhythmetic** (Can 56) Norman McLaren. **Byl sobie raz** (Pol 57) Jan Lenica *aka Once Upon a Time*. **Le Merle** (Can 58) Norman McLaren. **Canon** (Can 64) Norman McLaren, Grant Munro.

——**Mixed-Media Films (Combined Live Action and Animation)**   Live-action films including animated sequences or characters, or animated films with live characters are an old form which has been used repeatedly in musicals, fantasy films, and other genres. The mixed-media films have encompassed the use of cartoons, puppets, objects, or a combination of different forms of animation. Model animation is frequently used in exotic adventure stories, e.g., *King Kong* (1933), in fantasy films, e.g., the films featuring the work of Ray Harryhausen, and in science fiction films like *2001: A Space Odyssey* (1968), or space operas like *Star Wars* (1977). There is virutally no field of filmmaking in which a combination of both types of cinematography cannot be put to use.

Gertie the Dinosaur (09) Windsor McCay *aka Gertie the Trained Dinosaur*. **Novii Gulliver** (USSR 35) Alexander Ptuschko *aka The New*

Gulliver. *Anchors Aweigh* (44) George Sidney. *The Three Caballeros* (44) Norman Fergusson. *Song of the South* (46) Wilfred Jackson (animation), Harve Foster. *The Four Poster* (52) Irving Reis. *Poklad ptaciko ostrava* (Cz 52) Karel Zeman *aka The Treasure of Bird's Island.* *Vynalez zkazy* (Cz 58) Karel Zeman *aka The Deadly Invention / The Diabolical Invention / The Fabulous World of Jules Verne / An Invention for Destruction / Invention of Destruction / Weapons of Destruction.* *Mary Poppins* (64) Robert Stevenson. *The Daydreamer* (66) Jules Bass. *20,000 ans à la française* (F 65-67) Jacques Forgeot *aka 20,000 Years in France.* *The Phantom Tollbooth* (69) Chuck Jones, Abe Levitow (animation). *Bedknobs and Broomsticks* (71) Robert Stevenson, Ward Kimball (cartoon sequences). *Funnyman* (71) John Korty. *Allegro non troppo* (It 76) Bruno Bozzetto *aka Allegro ma non troppo.* *Moonwalker* (88) Jerry Kramer, Colin Chilvers. *Who Framed Roger Rabbit?* (88) Robert Zemeckis.

——**Object Animation Films** Almost any object can be animated using the stop-motion technique, and the earliest example is a film by Albert E. Smith, *The Humpty Dumpty Circus* (1898?), in which he used toy circus figures and animated them by moving their position slightly from frame to frame. Since then, all sorts of objects have been used in animation: matchsticks, tin soldiers, pieces of furniture, skeletons. When using clay, the terms claymation and sculptmation are sometimes used for clay animation.

The Humpty Dumpty Circus (1898?) Albert E. Smith. *Pianissimo* (63) Carmen D'Avino. *Renaissance* (F 63) Walerian Borowczyk. *Closed Mondays* (74) Will Vinton, Bob Gardiner. *Bead Game / Histoire de perles* (Can 77) Ishu Patel. *Le Château de sable / The Sand Castle* (Can 77) Co Hoedeman. *The Adventures of Mark Twain* (85) Will Vinton. *The Magic Portal* (Aust 89) Lindsay Fleay.

——**Pin Screen Animation Films (Pin-Board Animation, Pinhead Animation)** Alexander Alexeïeff (1901–1979) invented a type of animation technique called pin-board, pin screen or pinhead animation. It consists of a board (called *l'écran d'épingles* or pin screen) with thousands of pins in rows which can be pressed in or out to form patterns. When illuminated from the side, the pin patterns cast shadows which result in pictures. Stop-motion photography is used to capture them. Alexeïeff made several films using his technique, which he also employed in the prologue of Orson Welles' *Le Procès / The Trial* (1962).

Une Nuit sur le mont chauve (F 33) Alexander Alexeïeff, Claire Parker *aka A Night on Bald Mountain.* *Le Nez* (F 63) Alexander Alexeïeff. *Pictures at an Exhibition* (72) Alexander Alexeïeff, Claire Parker. *Mindscape / Le Paysagiste* (Can 76) Jacques Drouin.

——**Pixilated Films (Pixilation)** In a pixilated film, the movement is broken as people jerk or jump in speeded-up motion. The effect can be achieved by editing live-action shots so that unnecessary frames are discarded, or by positioning people and photographing them once, then repeating the process until the film is completed. A third method is to follow the live action and snap one picture at a time. The result of pixilation in the finished film is not unlike a series of jump-cuts.

Neighbours / Voisins (Can 52) Norman McLaren. *Chairy Tale / Il était une chaise* (Can 57) Norman McLaren. *Pravda* (Yug 62) Ante Babaja *aka Justice*.

——**Puppet Films (Animated Puppet Films, Puppet-Animation Films)**   In puppet films, three-dimensional figures are used which may be assembled from a great variety of materials. Thus puppet films have used figures made of plasticine, plastic wire, metal, glass, paper, wood, cloth and wool. Like graphic animation, puppet films are an important form of animated films, and some true masterpieces of the genre have been created, both in feature-length and short formats. Puppet films have also often included live actors.

Le Roman du renard (F 25-36) Ladislas Starewitch *aka The Story of the Fox. Alice in Wonderland / Alice au pays des merveilles* (US / F / GB 48) Dallas Bower. *Bajaja* (Cz 50) Jirí Trnka *aka Prince Bayaya. Sen noci svatojanské* (Cz 59) Jirí Trnka *aka A Midsummer Night's Dream. Joseph Sold by His Brothers* (Isr 61) Alina Gross, Yoram Gross. *Kiberneticka babicka* (Cz 62) Jirí Trnka *aka Cybernetic Grandmother / Grandmother Cybernetics. Tatsu, no ko Taro* (J 66) Ichiro Michibayashi *aka Taro, the Son of Dragon. Pollux et le chat bleu / Dougal and the Blue Cat* (F / GB 70) Serge Danot.

——**Silhouette Films**   In direct descent from the *ombres chinoises*, the silhouette film is best represented by the work of Lotte Reiniger (1899–1981) who made in this genre the first European feature-length animated film in 1926. The silhouette film is a form of cut-out animation using black paper and filmed frame by frame. An early silhouette film was *The Clown and His Donkey* (1910) made by the British Charles Armstrong.

The Clown and His Donkey (GB 10) Charles Armstrong. *Inbad the Sailor* (15) C. Allan Gilbert. *Die Abenteuer des Prinzen Achmed* (G 26) Lotte Reiniger, Carl Koch *aka Die Geschichte des Prinzen Achmed / Adventures of Prince Achmed. The Gallant Little Tailor* (GB 54) Lotte Reiniger. *Shaka no shagai* (J 61) Nobuo Ofugi *aka The Life of Buddha.*

Animated Film Musicals   *see*   **MUSICAL**

Animated Puppet Film   *see*   **ANIMATED FILM: Puppet Films**

Animated Stills, Animation, Animation of Still Paintings and Drawings *see*   **ANIMATED FILM**

Anthology   *see*   **TELEVISION SERIES**

Anthology Film   *see*   **EPISODE FILM**

Anthropological Film   *see*   **DOCUMENTARY: Ethnographic Film**

Antidrug Film   *see*   **DRUG FILM**

Antiestablishment Film   *see*   **UNDERGROUND FILM**

Antifascist Film   *see*   **WAR FILM: Anti-Nazi War Films**

Antigenre Film   *see*   **GENRE FILM**

Anti-Heimatfilm   *see*   **HEIMATFILM: Critical Heimat Films**

Anti-Indian Picture   *see*   **WESTERN: Indian Films**

Anti-Nazi Film   *see*   **SOFT-CORE SEX-EXPLOITATION FILM: Nazi-Sadist Pictures**

Anti-Nazi War Films   *see*   **WAR FILM**

Antiracist Film   *see*   **RACIST FILM**

Antireligious Films   *see*   **RELIGIOUS FILM**

Anti-Semitic Film   *see*   **RACIST FILM**

Antisexist Film   *see*   **FEMINIST FILM**

Antisuffrage Film   *see*   **FEMINIST FILM: Women's Suffrage Films**

Antiwar Film   *see*   **WAR FILM: Pacifist Films**

Antiwesterns   *see*   **WESTERN**

Ape Movies   *see*   **JUNGLE FILM**

Aquacade-Type Film   *see*   **MUSICAL: Aqua-Musicals**

Arabian Nights Fantasy Films   *see*   **FANTASY FILM**

ARBEITERFILM (Proletarian Film, Worker Film)   In German cinema, *Arbeiterfilm* (worker film) is a designation that groups together a few films which examine the German social order in relation to the lower or working class. This short-lived genre manifested itself mainly during the period of 1970 to 1976 and was characterized by its realistic approach, at times bordering on naturalism. The films were mainly produced and broadcasted by West German television. The *Arbeiterfilm* has been documented in Richard Collins and Vincent Porter, *WDR and the Arbeiterfilm* (London: BFI, 1981).

Ich heiße Erwin und bin 17 Jahre (G 70) Erika Runge *aka My Name Is Erwin and I'm 17.   Liebe Mutter, mir geht es gut* (G 71) Christian Ziewer *aka Dear Mother, I'm OK (Fine).   Der Angestellte* (G 71-72) Helma Sanders *aka The White-Collar Worker.   Acht Stunden sind kein Tag* (G 72, TV) Rainer Werner Fassbinder *aka Eight Hours Are Not a Day* [5 episodes: *Jochen und Manon, Oma und Gregor, Franz und Ernst, Harald und Monika, Irmgard und Rolf*].   *Der lange Jammer* (G 73) Max Willutzki *aka The Long Lamentation / The Wailing Wall.   Lohn und Liebe* (G 74) Marianne Lüdcke, Ingo Kratisch *aka Love and Wages / Wages and Love.   Schneeglöckchen blühn im September* (G 74) Christian Ziewer *aka Snowdrops Bloom in September.   Familienglück* (G 75) Marianne Lüdcke, Ingo Kratisch *aka Wedded Bliss.   Flöz Dickebank* (G 75) Johannes Flütsch, Klau Helle, Marlies Kallweit *aka We've Woken Up in the Meantime.   Der aufrechte Gang* (G 76) Christian Ziewer *aka Walking Tall / Walking Upright.*

ARCHETYPE (Archetypal Film)   In motion pictures, a movie which has most of the elements that will typify later films patterned on the original model. For example, the 1920 silent film *Dr. Jekyll and Mr. Hyde* starring John Barrymore in the dual role of Jekyll and Hyde is the archetype of many other films about the good and evil doctor, and Alfred Hitchcock's *Psycho* (1960) as an archetype spawned many similar movies. Archetypes are found at the origin of every film genre. *See also* **SEMINAL FILM.**

> *Dr. Jekyll and Mr. Hyde* (20) John S. Robertson. *Psycho* (60) Alfred Hitchcock.

Architectonic Film   *see*   **UNDERGROUND FILM: Mythopoetic Film**

ARK FILM   A term that has been used to define a film in which a group of assorted characters interact while confined in an enclosed space such as a room, a hotel, a shop, a plane.

> *Street Scene* (31) King Vidor.   *Grand Hotel* (32) Edmund Goulding.   *Union Depot* (32) Alfred E. Green *aka Gentleman for a Day*.   *International House* (33) A. Edward Sutherland.   *Weekend at the Waldorf* (45) Robert Z. Leonard.   *The High and the Mighty* (54) William Wellman.   *Airport* (69) George Seaton, Henry Hathaway [followed by *Airport 1975* (74) Jack Smight; *Airport '77* (77) Jerry Jameson; and *Concorde . . . Airport '79 / Airport '80 The Concorde* (US / F 79) David Lowell Rich *aka Airport '79 / Airport '80*]. *The Poseidon Adventure* (72) Ronald Neame (uncredited: Irwin Allen).

Armed Forces Comedy, Army Comedy   *see*   **WAR FILM: Comedy War Films**

Art Cinema Film   *see*   **ART FILM**

ART FILM (Art Cinema Film, Quality Film)   This label was current in the fifties and sixties to distinguish between films with an artistic claim or purpose and the merely commercial product or genre films patterned on the Hollywood tradition. They were usually the work of established foreign directors or film *auteurs*, and they were shown by film societies, film clubs, or exhibited in small cinemas or "art houses." Many European films, some by American independent filmmakers, together with a selected few from Japan, India, and other countries, qualified as art films. Most of them had been presented in some International Film Festival or other. At present, the term as indicative of a class of film set apart from the commercial film, is losing its currency. For art film from the standpoint of genre, *see* William Charles Siska, *Modernism in the Narrative Cinema* (New York: Arno Press, 1980). *See also* Steve Neale's "Art Cinema as Institution." *Screen* 22.1 (1981):11–39.

> *Father Panchali* (Ind 55) Satyajit Ray *aka Pather Panchali / Song of the Little Road / Saga of the Road / Song of the Road* [1st of the "Apu" trilogy which includes *Aparajito / The Unvanquished* (56) and *Apur Sansar / The World of Apu* (58)].   *Jungfrukällan* (Sw 59) Ingmar Bergman *aka The Virgin Spring*. *L'Avventura* (It / F 59-60) Michelangelo Antonioni *aka The Adventure*.   *A Taste of Honey* (GB 61) Tony Richardson.   *David and Lisa* (62) Frank Perry.   *Nóz w wodzie* (Pol 62) Roman Polánski *aka Knife in the Water / The Long Sunday / The Young Lover*.   *The Cool World* (63) Shirley Clarke.   *Suna*

no onna (J 63) Hiroshi Teshigahara *aka Woman in the Dunes / Woman of the Dunes.*   **Tystnaden** (Sw 63) Ingmar Bergman *aka The Silence* [1st of a trilogy which includes *Såsom i en spegel / Through a Glass Darkly* (61) and *Nattvardsgästerna / The Communicants / Winter Light* (62)].   **Obchod na korze** (Cz 64) Ján Kadár, Elmar Klos *aka The Shop in the High Street / The Shop on Main Street / The Shop on High Street.*   **One Potato, Two Potato** (64) Larry Peerce.   **La Guerre est finie / Kriget är slut** (F /Sw 65) Alain Resnais *aka The War Is Over.*   **The Pawnbroker** (65) Sidney Lumet. *Ulysses* (US / GB 67) Joseph Strick.   **The Draughtsman's Contract** (GB 82) Peter Greenaway *aka Death in the English Garden.*

Art Film   *see*   **FILM ABOUT ART;**   *see also*   **INDEPENDENT PRODUCTION**

Arthurian Film   *see*   **SWASHBUCKLER: Chivalric Films**

Artists' Video   *see*   **VIDEO ART**

Atmospheric Film   *see*   **PERIOD FILM: Period Thrillers**

AUTEUR FILM (Author's Film, Director's Picture, Film d'Auteur) Motion pictures are considered to be collective efforts in which many people collaborate. They require, however, someone capable of assuming leadership and able to channel the team's creative energies. This person is normally the director. Most directors are craftsmen of considerable ability, and most Hollywood films are made by these directors. Normally, they are assigned a film to direct by a film production company. They are on call, so to speak. They shift from one type of film to another as is required and have little control over the final product.[6] An *auteur*, on the other hand, has a high degree of control over the film. In many cases, he is not only responsible for the dialogue and direction, but he may take part in other functions such as producing and editing. The best among them write their own screenplays or closely supervise the writing of them, and they consistently follow a theme or themes which are discernible in the overall context of their work. These *auteur* filmmakers may combine at times "author" filmmaking with conventionally made commercial films as a financial expediency. They include directors like Fernando Arrabal, Ingmar Bergman, Walerian Borowczyk, Luis Buñuel, André Delvaux, Carl Dreyer, Marco Ferreri, Jean-Luc Godard, Miklós Jancsó, Alexandro Jodorowsky, Joseph Losey, Dusan Makavejev, Pier Paolo Pasolini, Roman Polanski, Alain Robbe-Grillet, Barbet Shroeder, and many others. Their films are films d'auteur or auteur's films.

The American film critic Andrew Sarris elevated to the high status of "auteur" directors many Hollywood filmmakers previously not thought to fit into this category. *See* his *The American Cinema* (New York: E. P. Dutton, 1968).

Author's Film   *see*   **AUTEUR FILM**

AUTOBIOGRAPHICAL FILM   The general term for writing about oneself, one's own surroundings, family or intimate friends is autobiography. When a filmmaker expresses his impressions by filming his life or part of it, the end-product is known as an autobiographical film. Autobiographical films may take the form of self-portraits, diaries, travel experiences, or confessions. Whatever the approach or the mode (documentary, avant-garde, dramatic), the films will reflect the filmmaker's feelings in relation to himself and his world. Although some filmmakers obtain financial assistance or grants, most autobiographical films are independently made. For an appraisal of the autobiographical film, *see Autobiography*, ed. by John Stuart Katz (Toronto: Art Gallery of Ontario, 1978).

> *Le Sang d'un poète* (F 30) Jean Cocteau *aka The Blood of a Poet / La Vie du Poète. Le Testament d'Orphée ou ne me demandez pas pourquoi / Il testamento di Orfeo* (F / It 59) Jean Cocteau *aka The Testament of Orpheus. David Holzman's Diary* (67) Jim McBride. *Fuses* (67) Carolee Schneemann [Part 1 of *Autobiographical Trilogy*]. *Scenes from Under Childhood* (67-70) Stan Brakhage [4 films: *Section No. 1* to *Section No. 4*]. *Coming Home* (Can 71) Bill Reid. *Film Portrait* (71) Jerome Hill. *Testament* (74) James Broughton. *Not a Pretty Picture* (75) Martha Coolidge. *Lost Lost Lost* (76) Jonas Mekas. *In This Life's Body* (Aust 83) Arthur Cantrill, Corinne Cantrill.

Automobile Racing Film, Auto-Racing Film *see* **MOTORCAR RACING FILM**

AVANT-GARDE (Avant-Garde Film)   Avant-garde is a term in art that groups together individuals and movements which search, by means of experimentation, for new ways of expression and artistic creation. Most often, it implies a rejection of and a revolt against established traditional canons. In motion pictures, the notion of the avant-garde surfaced after World War I in France and Germany; it covered roughly the years 1918 to 1930 and consisted of diverse cinematic movements which were in opposition to commercial cinema and the dictates attached to narrative content. It expressed itself in the work of film impressionists (Louis Delluc, German Dulac, Marcel L'Herbier, Jean Epstein, and others); film abstractionists (Viking Eggeling, Walter Ruttman, Henri Chomette, Fernand Léger); and the work of dadaist and surrealist filmmakers (Man Ray, Luis Buñuel, Jean Cocteau). It also included futurist and other artistic manifestations of the time that sought to extend themselves into the field of filmic expression. The idea of the film avant-garde soon spread to the Soviet Union, the United States, Great Britain, and other countries. Today, it is still very much alive, even if it may manifest itself under different labels. *See* **ABSTRACT FILM, IMPRESSIONIST FILM,** and **SURREALIST FILM.**

> *La Fête espagnole* (F 19) Germaine Dulac. *Fièvre* (F 20) Louis Delluc *aka La Boue. Horizontal-Vertical Orchestra* (G 20-22) Viking Eggeling [sometimes referred to as: *Vertikal-Horizontale Messe / Horizontal-Vertical Mass*]. *Fait-Divers* (F 23) Claude Autant-Lara. *Le Ballet mécanique* (F 24) Fernand Léger *aka Images Mobile. L'Inhumaine* (F 25) Marcel L'Herbier *aka The Inhuman Woman / The New Enchantment. Cinq Minutes de*

cinéma pur (F 26) Henri Chomette.   *Ménilmontant* (F 26) Dimitri Kirsanov *aka Les Cent Pas.   Charleston* (F 27) Jean Renoir *aka Sur un air de Charleston / Charleston-Parade.   La Chute de la maison Usher* (F 28) Jean Epstein *aka The Fall of the House of Usher.   L'Etoile de mer* (F 28) Man Ray *aka The Starfish / Star of the Sea.   Un Chien andalou* (F 28) Luis Buñuel *aka El marista en la ballesta / Es peligroso asomarse al exterior / Un perro andaluz / An [The] Andalusian Dog.*

Avant-Garde   *see also*   **UNDERGROUND FILM**

AVIATION FILM (Air Movie, Airplane Film, Flying Film)   Aircraft have figured in countless pictures, but it is when flying, flyers, or the aircraft itself is at the center of the story that we can speak of the aviation film proper. Into this category of films fit many war movies, sports movies (air racing, aerobatics, barnstorming, stunt flying) and, indeed, adventure and action movies portraying the exploits of aviators or solo flyers.

The themes of aviation films are varied, and the pictures themselves may be sectioned into some important groups; foremost among them would be films of the fighter pilots or aces of World War I. Another important group deals with flying in World War II. Films dealing with the achievements of airmail flyers, the opening up of airways for pioneer passenger flying, and record breaking (speed, distance, or altitude) flights have also been favorite subjects. Of late, disaster films focusing on the dangers that might beset jumbo jets or supersonic airliners have had their moment. One particular film — *Blue Thunder* (1982) — has for its star a super helicopter equipped for police surveillance and apprehension of criminals in the modern city. For a discussion of aviation films, *see* Stephen Pendo's *Aviation in the Cinema* (Metuchen, NJ: Scarecrow, 1985). Betil Skogsberg, in *Wings of the Screen* (San Diego: A. S. Barnes, 1981), includes an extensive list of air movies in the index section of his book. *See also* **Aviation War Films** in the **WAR FILM** section.

Hell's Angels (30) Howard Hughes.   *Air Mail* (32) John Ford.   *Ceiling Zero* (35) Howard Hawks.   *L'Equipage* (F 35) Anatole Litvak *aka The Crew / Flight into Darkness.   China Clipper* (36) Ray Enright.   *D III 88* (G 39) Herbert Maisch (airborne sequences: Hans Bertram) *aka D III, Die neue deutsche Luftwaffe greft an / D III 88, The New German Air Force Attacks.   Only Angles Have Wings* (39) Howard Hawks *aka Plane No. 4.   Esquadrilla* (Sp 41) Antonio Román *aka Squadron.   Quax, der Bruchpilot* (G 41) Kurt Hoffman *aka Quax, the Unlucky Star Pilot.   Jet Pilot* (50) Josef von Sternberg [rel. in 57].   *The Sound Barrier* (GB 52) David Lean *aka Breaking the Sound Barrier.   The Dam Busters* (GB 54) Michael Anderson.   *The Man in the Sky* (GB 56) Charles Crichton.   *Reach for the Sky* (GB 56) Lewis Gilbert. *The Spirit of St. Louis* (57) Billy Wilder.   *The Flight of the Phoenix* (65) Robert Aldrich.   *Those Magnificent Men in Their Flying Machines* (GB / US 65) Ken Annakin *aka Those Magnificent Men in Their Flying Machines; or How I Flew from London to Paris in 25 Hours and 11 Minutes.   Keylja* (USSR 66) Larisa Sjepitkos *aka Wings.   Der Stern von Afrika* (G 56) Alfred Weidenmann *aka The Star of Africa.   Airport 1975* (74) Jack Smight.   *The Great Waldo Pepper* (75) George Roy Hill.   *Solo* (Aust / NZ 77) Tony Williams.

Cloud Dancer (78) Barry Brown [rel. in 80]. *The Winds of Kitty Hawk* (78 TV) E. W. Swackhamer. *Airplane!* (80) Jim Abrahams, David Zucker, Jerry Zucker *aka Flying High*. *Blue Thunder* (82) John Badham. *Top Gun* (86) Tony Scott. *Air America* (90) Roger Spottiswoode.

Aviation War Films *see* **WAR FILM**

Award Presentations *see* **TELEVISION SHOW: TV Award Show**

B-Feature *see* **B-MOVIE**

B-Level Title *see* **VIDEO**

B-MOVIE (B-Feature, Grade-B Picture, Low-Budget Production, Second Feature). The term properly corresponds to movies made on a shoestring budget. These low-budget features were the result of the double bill programming system operating in the U.S.A. from the early 1930s to the 1950s. To complete the billing or to fill the lower half of the double bill (the main feature was known as an "A" property, a film produced with a large budget) a second, inexpensive feature was needed, hence the emergence of the B-picture, made cheaply and supplied mainly by what is known today as the Poverty Row studios (such as PRC, Republic, Monogram and, since the 1950s, American International Pictures). These B-movies featured minimal casting and sets, poor to bad acting in many cases, extensive use of stock footage and they were finished in short shooting schedules. They were genre films—mostly Westerns, crime films, science fiction and horror films—and included most film series (Tarzan films, Dr. Kildare films).

B-movies since the mid-fifties have been known as "exploitation" films and they are no longer made as co-features destined to the lower part of a double bill. They have broadened their scope and made inroads into the hitherto untapped profitability of the youth-oriented film, the sex film, and the black feature film. Today, the made-for-television film is considered (at least by some) to be the B-picture successor. The B-film sported a royal monarch: in the fifties, Roger Corman, American producer and director, was crowned "King of the Bs" for his vast output of cheaply made films. His *The Little Shop of Horrors* was shot in 1960 in two-and-a-half days.[7] *See also* **CO-FEATURE, EXPLOITATION FILM, QUICKIE, Z PICTURE.**

The Son of Kong (33) Ernest B. Schoedsak *aka Jamboree*. *Five Came Back* (39) John Farrow. *The Biscuit Eater* (40) Stuart Heisler. *Stranger on the Third Floor* (40) Boris Ingster. *Among the Living* (41) Stuart Heisler. *Confessions of Boston Blackie* (41) Edward Dmytryk. *The Face Behind the Mask* (41) Robert Florey. *Whistling in the Dark* (41) S. Sylvan Simon. *Kid Glove Killer* (42) Fred Zinnemann. *The Body Snatcher* (43) Robert Wise [rel. in 45]. *Good Morning, Judge* (43) Jean Yarbrough. *The Seventh Victim* (43) Mark Robson. *Bluebeard* (44) Edgar G. Ulmer. *The Mask of Dimitrios* (44) Jean Negulesco. *San Diego I Love You* (44) Reginald LeBorg. *When Strangers Marry* (44) William Castle *aka Betrayed*. *Detour* (45) Edgar G.

Ulmer. *My Name Is Julia Ross* (45) Joseph H. Lewis. *She Gets Her Man* (45) Erle C. Kenton. *So Dark the Night* (46) Joseph H. Lewis. *The Narrow Margin* (52) Richard Fleischer. *Tarantula* (55) Jack Arnold. *Thunder Road* (58) Arthur Ripley. *The Little Shop of Horrors* (60) Roger Corman *aka The Passionate People Eater. I Saw What You Did* (65) William Castle.

B-Westerns *see* **WESTERN**

Background Film *see* **FACTUAL FILM**

Backstage Musicals *see* **MUSICAL**

Badfilm, Bad Movie *see* **TURKEY**

BALLET FILM   Ballet has been filmed repeatedly, often as a record of a ballet dancer or of a staged ballet production, but also, at times, as a ballet directly created for the film or television medium. Needless to say, this latter category of ballet films is the most noteworthy and the most artistically gratifying. However, ballet does not blend too well with film, and the masterpieces of the genre are few. The following types of ballet films are possible: film records of dancers and ballets, films with ballet sequences (e.g., Hollywood musicals), melodramas with a ballet background, films with ballet settings, films of ballet performances specially staged for the camera, original film ballets, television ballet films. *See also* **Ballet Films** in the entry for **MUSICAL.**

The Mad Genius (31) Michael Curtiz.   *La Mort du cygne* (F 37) Jean Benoît-Lévy, Marie Epstein *aka Ballerina.   Gaîté parisienne* (F 41) Jean Negulesco *aka Gay Parisian.   The Specter of the Rose* (46) Ben Hecht *aka Spectre of the Rose.   The Unfinished Dance* (47) Henry Koster.   *The Red Shoes* (GB 48) Michael Powell, Emeric Pressburger.   *The Moor's Pavane* (50) Walter V. Strate.   *Limelight* (52) Charles Chaplin.   *The Ballet of Romeo and Juliet* (USSR 54) Lev Arnshtam, Leonid Lavrosky *aka Romeo and Juliet. Dance Little Lady* (GB 54) Val Guest.   *Meet Me in Las Vegas* (56) Roy Rowland *aka Viva Las Vegas.   A Dancer's World* (57 TV) Peter Glushanok.   *Luna de Miel* (Sp 58) Michael Powell *aka Honeymoon.   The Very Eye of the Night* (58) Maya Deren.   *Der Schwanensee* (G 66) Truck Branss *aka Swan Lake. The Turning Point* (77) Herbert Ross.   *Nijinsky* (GB 80) Herbert Ross. *Nutcracker* (GB 82) Anwar Kawadri *aka Nutcracker Sweet.   Nutcracker, the Motion Picture* (86) Carroll Ballard *aka Nutcracker.   Dancers* (87) Herbert Ross.

Ballet Musicals *see* **MUSICAL**

Band Clip *see* **MUSIC VIDEO**

Bandit Gangster Film *see* **GANGSTER FILM: Outlaw Gangster Films**

BASEBALL MOVIE   Surprisingly, not many movies have been made on the subject of baseball. This most genuine of American sports has mainly inspired comedies and biographies of ball players suitably fictionalized according to the Hollywood canon of rearranged truth. For a chronological rundown of baseball in films, *see* Jack Spears, "Baseball on the Screen," chap. 8 in *Hollywood: The Golden Era* (New York: A. S. Barnes, 1971).

Elmer the Great (33) Mervyn LeRoy. *Alibi Ike* (35) Ray Enright. *The Pride of the Yankees* (42) Sam Wood. *It Happens Every Spring* (49) Lloyd Bacon. *The Stratton Story* (49) Sam Wood. *The Jackie Robinson Story* (50) Alfred E. Green. *Kill the Umpire* (50) Lloyd Bacon. *Angels in the Outfield* (51) Clarence Brown *aka Angels and the Pirates*. *Rhubarb* (51) Arthur Lubin. *Fear Strikes Out* (57) Robert Mulligan. *Damn Yankees* (58) George Abbott, Stanley Donen *aka What Lola Wants*. *Bang the Drum Slowly* (73) John Hancock. *It's Good to Be Alive* (74 TV) Michael Landon. *The Bad News Bears* (76) Michael Ritchie [followed by *The Bad News Bears in Breaking Training* (77) Michael Pressman; *The Bad News Bears Go to Japan* (78) John Berry]. *The Bingo Long Traveling All-Stars and Motor Kings* (76) John Badham. *A Love Affair: The Eleanor and Lou Gehrig Story* (78 TV) Fielder Cook. *Aunt Mary* (79 TV) Peter Werner. *The Kid from the Left Field* (79 TV) Adell Aldrich. *Tiger Town* (83 MCTV) Alan Shapiro. *The Natural* (84) Barry Levinson. *A Winner Never Quits* (86 TV) Mel Damski. *Long Gone* (87 MCTV) Martin Davidson. *Bull Durham* (88) Ron Shelton. *Eight Men Out* (88) John Sayles. *Field of Dreams* (89) Phil Alden Robinson. *Major League* (89) David S. Ward.

BASKETBALL PICTURE   An American sport, basketball is a popular game which has served as the basis for a few sports movies. Mostly, basketball films are campus comedies combining students' high jinks with the thrills of the game.

Go, Man, Go (54) James Wong Howe. *Tall Story* (60) Joshua Logan. *Drive, He Said* (70) Jack Nicholson. *Shirts/Skins* (73 TV) William Graham. *One on One* (77) Lamont Johnson. *Coach* (78) Bud Townsend. *Fast Break* (79) Jack Smight. *Inside Moves* (80) Richard Donner *aka The Guys from Marx's Bar*. *Hoosiers* (86) David Anspaugh.

Battle Film   *see*   **WAR FILM**

Beach-Blanket Film, Beach-Blanket Party Picture, Beach-Bunny Film, Beach Party Movie   *see*   **TEEN MOVIE: Beach Films**

Beaver Film   *see*   **HARD-CORE PORNO FILM**

Bedroom Farce   *see*   **SEX COMEDY**

Beefcake Film   *see*   **HARD-CORE PORNO FILM**

Bergfilm   *see*   **MOUNTAIN FILM**

Bestial Invocation Film   *see*   **NUCLEAR FILM**

Bible Film, Bible-Inspired Film   *see*   **RELIGIOUS FILM: Biblical Films**

Biblical Epics   *see*   **EPIC**

Big Bug Movie   *see*   **HORROR FILM: Other Denizens of Horror Movies**

Big-Caper Film   *see*   **CAPER FILM**

Big City Comedy   *see*   **URBAN COMEDY**

Big House Movies   *see*   **PRISON FILM**

Big-Top Movie   *see*   **CIRCUS FILM**

Bike Movie, Biker Film   *see*   **MOTORCYCLE MOVIE**

Bio, Biog   *see*   **BIOGRAPHICAL FILM**

BIOGRAPHICAL FILM (Bio, Biog, Biography, Biopic, Film Biography, Screen Biography)   The biographical film centers generally on the life, on the formative years, or on the most relevant period of a well-known individual. Biographical films have mostly been about historical figures (rulers, conquerors, revolutionaries, politicians, courtesans, explorers, war heroes, spies, outlaws, religious leaders), scientists (doctors, inventors), artists (painters, writers, composers, entertainers), and sportsmen.

Film biographies fall into two clearly defined divisions. On the one hand, there are the numerous Hollywood or studio versions which are made of highly fictionalized and fabricated facts meant to suit dramatic content; and on the other hand, there are the few films which try to adhere to known facts and follow detail as accurately as knowledge permits.

Another tendency has been to film pseudobiographies or biographies of fictitious characters and biographies which change the names of the characters, issuing disclaimers that the stories have no resemblance to known or living persons, but which are, however, based on real people.[8]

There are still not many independent studies on biographical films; one exception is the field of show business, a subcategory of the bio pic (see below). Biographical films are also discussed under the film genres to which they may belong — gangster picture, war film, musical, Western.

Rasputin and the Empress (32) Richard Boleslawsky *aka Rasputin — the Mad Monk.   Rembrandt* (GB 36) Alexander Korda.   *The Story of Louis Pasteur* (36) William Dieterle.   *The Life of Emile Zola* (37) William Dieterle *aka Emile Zola.   Victoria the Great* (GB 37) Herbert Wilcox.   *Sixty Glorious Years* (GB 38) Herbert Wilcox *aka Queen of Destiny.   Dr. Ehrlich's Magic Bullet* (39) William Dieterle *aka The Story of Dr. Ehrlich's Magic Bullet.   Juarez* (39) William Dieterle.   *The Story of Alexander Graham Bell* (39) Irving Cummings *aka The Modern Miracle.   Abe Lincoln in Illinois* (40) John Cromwell *aka Spirit of the People.   Edison, the Man* (40) Clarence Brown.   *Young Tom Edison* (40) Norman Taurog.   *The Great Moment* (42) Preston Sturges [rel. in 44].   *Devotion* (43) Curtis Bernhardt [rel. in 46].   *Madame Curie* (43) Mervyn LeRoy.   *The Magic Bow* (GB 46) Bernard Knowles.   *The Magic Box* (GB 51) John Boulting.   *The Wings of Eagles* (57) John Ford.   *Freud* (62) John Huston *aka Freud Secret Passion / The Secret Passion.   Lawrence of Arabia* (GB / US 62) David Lean.   *Young Winston* (GB 72) Richard Attenborough.   *Aloïse* (F 74) Liliane de Kermadec.   *Reds* (US / GB 81) Warren Beatty.   *Gandhi* (GB / Ind / US 82) Richard Attenborough.   *Amadeus* (US / Cz 84) Milos Forman.   *The Sicilian* (87) Michael Cimino.   *Vincent: The Life and Death of Vincent van Gogh* (Aust 87) Paul Cox *aka Vincent.*

——**Show Business Biographical Films (Showbiz Biography, Showbiz Biopic)**   They comprise film biographies of show-business personalities:

songwriters, bandleaders, singers, actors, dancers, comedians. This sub-genre of the biographical film has been documented by Robert Milton Miller in *Star Myths* (Metuchen, NJ: Scarecrow, 1983). His filmography, pp. 362–87, includes 129 titles.

The Mighty Barnum (34) Walter Lang. *The Great Ziegfeld* (36) Robert Z. Leonard. *The Story of Will Rogers* (52) Michael Curtiz. *The Glen Miller Story* (54) Anthony Mann. *I'll Cry Tomorrow* (55) Daniel Mann. *Man of a Thousand Faces* (57) Joseph Pevney. *Your Cheating Heart* (64) Gene Nelson. *Isadora* (GB 68) Karel Reisz *aka The Loves of Isadora*. *Lenny* (74) Bob Fosse. *Fear on Trial* (74 TV) Lamont Johnson. *The Night That Panicked America* (75 TV) Joseph Sargent. *Bound for Glory* (76) Hal Ashby. *The One and Only Phyllis Dixey* (GB 78 TV) Michael Tuchner *aka Peek-a-Boo: The One and Only Phyllis Dixey*. *Coal Miner's Daughter* (80) Michael Apted. *Haywire* (80 TV) Michael Tuchner. *Marilyn: The Untold Story* (80 TV) John Flynn, Jack Arnold, Lawrence Schiller. *Moviola* (80 TV) John Erman [3 films: *This Year's Blonde* (*aka The Secret Love of Marilyn Monroe*), *The Scarlett O'Hara War, The Silent Lovers*]. *Leave 'Em Laughing* (81 TV) Jackie Cooper. *The Patricia Neal Story* (81 TV) Anthony Harvey, Anthony Page.

Biographical War Films   *see*   **WAR FILM**

Biographical Westerns   *see*   **WESTERN**

Biography, Biopic   *see*   **BIOGRAPHICAL FILM**

Biology Film   *see*   **FACTUAL FILM: Educational Film**

Birth Control Film   *see*   **VICE FILM**

Black Action Picture, Black Action-Adventure Film   *see*   **BLACK FILM: Blaxploitation Movies**

Black Cinema   *see*   **BLACK FILM;**   *see also*   **FILM NOIR**

BLACK COMEDY (Dark Comedy, Gallows Humor, Murder Comedy, Sick Comedy, Sick Humor)   Black comedy is a comic mode that relies on a type of humor which treats lightly, or pokes fun at, serious taboo subjects like death, murder, or necrophilia. It is often presented as farce or satire and, in most cases, it offers social comment.

Black comedy as a comic mode fits any genre that will accommodate its macabre or grotesque subject matter. Thus many black comedies happen to be science fiction, murder stories, or even horror pictures. Traditional black comedies have presented murder as a logical expedient on the part of its perpetrator to overcome difficulties or promote his own interests. Corpses turning up by the dozen in unexpected places are the norm.

A typical example of murder for profit in a black comedy is the one which portrays a bluebeard-type who kills women dexterously for their riches with the utmost ease and without any conscious feeling of guilt or wrongdoing — a character often based on historical fact. A more recent example of black comedy is a subspecies usually cast in the horror mold or fitted into the gangster genre which presents an apparently inoffensive person (or persons) breaking loose in a series of refined murders, the next always more contrived or gruesome than the previous one, intent on avenging the death of a dear one or some wrong that has been done to him. Black comedy, very popular in the sixties, keeps evolving into new subject matter. The British are characteristically keen on the form, and a great many good black comedies are due to them.

Arsenic and Old Lace (41) Frank Capra [rel. in 44]. *Monsieur Verdoux* (47) Charles Chaplin *aka A Comedy of Murders*. *L'Auberge rouge* (F 51) Claude Autant-Lara *aka The Red Inn*. *The Trouble with Harry* (55) Alfred Hitchcock. *La vida criminal de Archibaldo de la Cruz* (Mex 55) Luis Buñuel *aka The Criminal Life of Archibaldo de la Cruz / Rehearsal for a Crime*. *Dr. Strangelove: Or, How I Learned to Stop Worrying and Love the Bomb* (GB / US 63) Stanley Kubrick. *The Loved One* (64) Tony Richardson. *Cul-de-Sac* (GB 65) Roman Polanski *aka When Katelback Comes / Riri*. *The Anniversary* (GB 67) Roy Ward Baker. *M*A*S*H* (69) Robert Altman *aka MASH*. *Mumsy, Nanny, Sonny, & Girly* (68-69) Freddy Francis *aka Girly*. *Catch-22* (70) Mike Nichols. *Loot* (GB 70) Silvio Narizzano *aka Loot ... Give the Money, Honey! Where's Poppa?* (70) Carl Reiner *aka Going Ape*. *Theatre of Blood* (GB 71) Douglas Hickox *aka Much Ado about Murder*. *Harold and Maude* (71) Hal Ashby. *La Grande Bouffe / La grande abbuffata* (F / It 73) Marco Ferreri *aka Blow-Out*. *Homebodies* (74) Larry Yust. *Les Grands Moyens* (F 75) Herbert Cornfield. *Mother Jugs and Speed* (76) Peter Yates. *The End* (78) Burt Reynolds. *De Vierde Man* (Hol 79) Paul Verhoeven *aka The Fourth Man*. *Eating Raoul* (81) Paul Bartel. *The King of Comedy* (82) Martin Scorsese [rel. in 83]. *Prizzi's Honor* (85) John Huston. *Throw Momma from the Train* (87) Danny DeVito. *Heathers* (88) Michael Lehman.

Black Documentary *see* **BLACK FILM: Black Genre Movies**

Black Exploitation Film *see* **BLACK FILM**

BLACK FILM (Black-Oriented Film) Black feature films came into prominence in the late sixties and early seventies. By 1975, they had reached a peak and had prompted a sudden output of books and studies on the "new" black cinema. As an ethnic manifestation, black pictures in the USA with an all-black cast go as far back as 1912 when short comedies started to appear. However, the first full-length black feature, *The Colored American Winning His Suit*, had its premiere at Jersey City in 1916; it was a five-reeler produced by the Frederick Douglas Film Co. The first all-black feature-length talking picture was *Hallelujah!* (1929). Black films with an all-black or mixed black and white cast have continued to be made since the silent era, but it was during the sudden boom of the sixties and seventies, when they were produced in sizeable numbers, that they reached world-wide audiences. They did not necessarily include an all-black cast, and they started to be seriously considered as a distinct genre.[9]

Black film is a handy term in the American context to designate those films that, besides including black actors, present an approach to life and society in the United States or elsewhere which clearly reflects the point of view of the black Americans and their cultural background, and are able to convey it to the audience. These pictures are mainly geared toward their black audiences, but "crossover" films are also able to reach white audiences. In many instances this cultural background offers a vivid contrast with white America, even if the plots and situations portrayed in many of the black films have been lifted virtually intact from all-white movies; this is especially true of the black exploitation ("blaxploitation," for short) films. Some are straight remakes of their white counterparts.

With the emergence of black Africa, black motion pictures started to be produced by the newly independent African nations, but these films are best considered as a manifestation of a national cinema, not necessarily as part of an all-embracing genre.

Among the various ways of classifying black films is that of determining their casts and noting to what audiences they address themselves. Thus, there are films with an all-black cast for black audiences and films with an all-black cast for general audiences. There are films with blacks in major or minor roles in white films, and even white films about blacks in which the black part is played by a white actor. In contemporary films, black and white actors may be integrated or they may have a predominantly black cast. They may also address themselves to black audiences or "crossover" to white ones. For such groupings, *see* James L. Limbacher, "Blacks on Film: A Selected List of Films Available for 16mm Rental (And Some Which are Not but Should Be)," *The Journal of Popular Film* 4 (1975): 358–78. A filmography of about 3,000 film items is provided in Phyllis Rauch Klotman, *Frame by Frame: A Black Filmography* (Bloomington: Indiana University Press, 1979).

Amid the glut of black films that flooded the American market in the seventies, two general divisions can clearly be made. The first division comprises the "serious" films that try to carry forward in a creative way the manner of expression genuine to black cinema. The second division is formed by the black exploitation pictures which comprise the great majority. In this blaxploitation group, many black films have adopted the formula of well-known Hollywood genres.

——**Black Genre Movies**   Black films fit into many other genres or into sub-genres in relation to the black genre. Among the most popular are the black musical, the social drama, the black documentary (including the rock and jazz documentary), the religious folk-drama, the black pastoral (sometimes combined with the musical) and the picaresque.

> *The Colored American Winning His Suit* (16) Prod. Rev. W. S. Smith.   *The Scar of Shame* (27) Frank Peregini, (Al Lignori).   *Hallelujah!* (29) King Vidor [1st all-black feature-length talking picture].   *Hearts in Dixie* (29) Paul Sloane.   *The Emperor Jones* (33) Dudley Murphy.   *Dark Manhattan* (37) George Randol.   *Harlem on the Prairie* (37) Sam Newfield *aka Bad Man of Harlem* [1st all-black Western].   *The Bronze Buckaroo* (38) Richard Kahn.

Broken Strings (40) Bernard B. Ray. *The Blood of Jesus* (41) Spencer Williams. *Bright Road* (53) Gerald Mayer. *Porgy and Bess* (59) Otto Preminger. *The Cool World* (63) Shirley Clarke. *Nothing But a Man* (64) Michael Roemer. *Dutchman* (GB / US 66) Anthony Harvey. *Putney Swope* (69) Robert Downey. *Brother John* (71) James Goldstone *aka Kane. The Bus Is Coming* (71) Wendell James Franklin. *Black Girl* (72) Ossie Davis. *The Book of Numbers* (72) Raymond St. Jacques. *Sounder* (72) Martin Ritt. *Wattstax* (73) Mel Stuart. *The Autobiography of Miss Jane Pittman* (74 TV) John Korty. *Conrack* (74) Martin Ritt. *The Education of Sonny Carson* (74) Michael Campus. *Let's Do It Again* (75) Sidney Poitier. *Fingers* (78) James Toback. *She's Gotta Have It* (86) Spike Lee. *Do the Right Thing* (89) Spike Lee. *Boyz N the Hood* (91) John Singleton. *New Jack City* (91) Mario Van Peebles. *Jungle Fever* (91) Spike Lee. *Straight Out of Brooklyn* (91) Matty Rich.

——**Blaxploitation Movies (Black Action Pictures, Black Action-Adventure Films, Blacksploitation Films)**   As the self-explanatory composite word indicates, these films added to the black element the sensationalism characteristic of exploitation movies that, in order to make a quick return, employ shock tactics by emphasizing acts of violence, acts of revenge, and by portraying explicit sex. The start of the cycle of "blaxploitation" movies can be dated back to 1970, and it was almost over by 1973. They created in pictures the new image of the black as superspade or superstud. For a filmography, *see* James Robert Parish and George H. Hill, *Black Action Films* (Jefferson, NC: McFarland, 1989).

Black Angels (70) Laurence Merrick *aka Black Bikers from Hell. Ganja and Hess* (70) Bill Gunn [rel. in 73] *aka Blood Couple / Double Possession / Vampires of Harlem. Sweet Sweetback's Baadasssss Song* (71) Melvin van Peebles. *Shaft* (71) Gordon Parks [3 "Shaft" films (1971-73) and a TV series (1974): 7 films]. *Blackenstein* (72) William A. Levey *aka Black Frankenstein / Blackenstein the Black Frankenstein. Blacula* (72) William Crain. *Cool Breeze* (72) Barry Pollack. *Hit Man* (72) George Armitage. *The Legend of Nigger Charley* (72) Martin Goldman. *The Mack* (72) Michael Campus *aka The Mack and His Pack. Melinda* (72) Hugh A. Robertson. *Slaughter* (72) Jack Starrett. *Super Fly* (72) Gordon Parks Jr. *aka Superfly. Coffy* (73) Jack Hill. *Abby* (74) William Girdler *aka The Blackorcist. The Black Street Fighter* (74) Timothy Galfas *aka Black Fist* (77) / *Bogard II / Homeboy. Foxy Brown* (74) Jack Hill. *The Black Gestapo* (75) Lee Frost. *Black Lolita* (75) Stephen Gibson *aka Bad Lolita. Friday Foster* (75) Arthur Marks. *Dr. Black, Mr. Hyde* (76) William Crain *aka Dr. Black and Mr. White / The Watts Monster. Avenging Godfather* (79) J. Robert Wagoner *aka Avenging Disco Godfather / Disco Godfather. Black Shampoo* (76) Greydon Clark. *Vigilante* (82) William Lustig *aka Street Cop / Street Gang. The Big Score* (83) Fred Williamson.

Black Gangster Films   *see*   **GANGSTER FILM**

Black Genre Movies   *see*   **BLACK FILM**

Black Ghetto Film   *see*   **EXPLOITATION FILM**

Black Magic Film   *see*   **HORROR FILM: Demonic Films**

Black Musicals   *see*   **MUSICAL**

Black Pastoral   *see*   **BLACK FILM: Black Genre Movies**

Black Sox Movie   *see*   **HARD-CORE PORNO FILM**

BLACK-AND-WHITE FILM (Monochrome Film)   Films produced in black and white or, more precisely, in shades of grey, headed the world's production output of motion pictures until the mid–1950s when films shot in color gradually took over. Nowadays, although films are still being made in black and white for a variety of reasons, they are the exception rather than the rule. Filmmakers still choose to film in black and white occasionally, but they mainly do so for aesthetic purposes, to better express certain atmospheric conditions, to catch an over-all mood, or to give the picture a nostalgic effect. *See also* **COLOR FILM**.

> *The Last Picture Show* (71) Peter Bogdanovich.   *Paper Moon* (73) Peter Bogdanovich.   *Young Frankenstein* (74) Mel Brooks.   *Manhattan* (79) Woody Allen.   *Raging Bull* (80) Martin Scorsese.   *Broadway Danny Rose* (84) Woody Allen.   *Down by Law* (86) Jim Jarmusch.   *Az én XX századom* (Hung / G 88) Ildikó Enyedi *aka My 20th Century*.   *Nijusseiki shonen dokuhon* (J 89) Kaizo Hayshi *aka Circus Boys*.   *Storia di ragazzi e di ragazze* (It 89) Pupi Avati *aka Story of Boys and Girls*.

Black-Oriented Film   *see*   **BLACK FILM**

Blacksploitation Film   *see*   **BLACK FILM: Blaxploitation Movies**

BLOCKBUSTER (Superspectacular)   This is a trade term that has been in current usage since the mid-fifties when the blockbuster era began with a continuous flow of this type of picture. It was a time when the Hollywood studios were trying to boost their flagging box-office returns with new ideas and marketing concepts. The term applies to a superspectacular, usually filmed in a big screen process (CinemaScope, Todd-AO, Panavision), and having a long screen running time. Another characteristic of the blockbuster (a film trying to bust into the mass-paying public) is its high cost, which oscillated from $13 million spent in filming and promoting *The Ten Commandments* (1956) to a top of $44 million for *Cleopatra* (1963). Needless to say, such a high expenditure does not ensure success at the box-office, and many of these superspectaculars have proved themselves to be flops. The term has also been used for any movie that shows a substantial commercial profit.

> *Around the World in 80 Days* (US / GB 56) Michael Anderson *aka Michael Todd's Around the World in 80 Days*.   *The Ten Commandments* (56) Cecil B. DeMille.   *55 Days at Peking / 55 días en Pekín* (US / Sp 62) Nicholas Ray, Guy Green.   *Giant* (55) George Stevens.   *War and Peace / Guerra e pace* (US /It 55) King Vidor, Mario Soldati.   *Sodoma e Gomorra / Sodom and Gomorrah / Sodome et Gomorrhe* (It / US / F 61) Robert Aldrich, Sergio Leone *aka The Last Days of Sodom*.   *Mutiny on the Bounty* (62) Lewis Milestone, Carol Reed; (some scenes by George Seaton, Billy Wilder & Fred Zinneman).   *The Carpetbaggers* (63) Edward Dmytryk.   *Cleopatra* (GB /

US 63) Joseph L. Mankiewicz, Rouben Mamoulian. *Hawaii* (66) George Roy Hill. *Doctor Doolittle* (67) Richard Fleischer. *Patton* (69) Franklin J. Schaffner *aka Patton — Blood & Guts / Patton: Lust for Glory / Patton: Salute to a Rebel*. *Darling Lili* (70) Blake Edwards. *Fiddler on the Roof* (71) Norman Jewison. *A Bridge Too Far* (GB / US 77) Richard Attenborough. *Superman* (GB / US 78) Richard Donner *aka Superman the Movie* [4 films in the series up to 1986]. *Star Trek — The Motion Picture* (79) Robert Wise *aka Star Trek* [6 films in the series up to 1991].

Blood-and-Gore Thriller, Blood Film, Blood 'n' Gore Movie *see* **GORE FILM**

Blue-Collar Film *see* **LABOR FILM**

Blue Film *see* **HARD-CORE PORNO FILM**

Blue Movie *see* **STAG MOVIE**

Blurb *see* **TELEVISION COMMERCIAL**

Body-Count Movie *see* **SLASHER FILM**

Body Horror, Body-Horror Film *see* **HORROR FILM**

Boer War Films *see* **WAR FILM**

Bomb *see* **TURKEY**

Bond Film *see* **SPY FILM: James Bond Films**

Bonding Film *see* **BUDDY FILM**

Bordello Films *see* **HOOKER FILM**

Borderline Musicals *see* **MUSICAL**

Borsch Western *see* **SPAGHETTI WESTERN**

Boudoir Comedy *see* **SEX COMEDY**

"BOUREKA" FILM   A popular Israeli film genre mostly comprising comedies but also including melodramas. "Bourekas" were so called after a type of popular Sephardic pastry. They made use of ethnic humor and folklore, stereotyping and contrasting the cultural discrepancies and different backgrounds which clearly distinguish the Sephardim (Oriental Jews) and the Ashkenazim (Eastern European Jews), the two principal population groups in present-day Israel. The "Bourekas" were most popular in the 1960s and 1970s. The term "boureka" is also used for films emphasizing Ashkenazi ghetto humor and folklore. On the subject of "bourekas," *see* chapter 3, "The 'Bourekas' and Sephardi Representation," in Ella Shohat's *Israeli Cinema* (Austin: University of Texas Press, 1989).

Sallah Shabbati (Isr 64) Ephraim Kishon *aka Sallah*. *Fortuna* (Isr 66) Menahem Golan. *HaShoter Azulay* (Isr 71) Ephraim Kishon *aka The Cop / The*

Policeman / The Policeman Azulay. **Malkot hakvish** (Isr 71) Menahem Golan *aka Highway Queen / Queen of the Road.* **Lupo be New York** (Isr 76) Boaz Davidson *aka Lupo in New York.* **Mishpakhat Tzan'ani** (Isr 76) Boaz Davidson *aka Tzan'ani Family.* **Millionaire beTzarot** (Isr 78) Yoel Zilberg *aka A Millionaire in Trouble.* **HaDoda meArgentina** (Isr 83) George Ovadia *aka The Aunt from Argentina.* **Sapar Nashim** (Isr 83) Ze'ev Revah *aka Hairstylist for Women.* **Banot** (Isr 85) Nadav Levitan *aka Girls / You're in the Army Girls.*

BOXING PICTURE (Fight Flick, Prize-Fight Film) Boxing, an old sport which can be traced back to the Sumerians, an ancient people who 5,000 years ago lived in what is now Iraq, appeared early in the cinema. Since then it has been the most popular and important branch of the sports genre as witnessed by its public acceptance and the number of fight films produced throughout the years. Early memorable boxing pictures belong to the world of comedy in its slapstick variety, e.g., the two-reeler Charlie Chaplin masterpieces *The Knockout* (1914) and *The Champion* (1915). Since then, boxing films have appeared regularly. An outstanding success in the late seventies and early eighties was the Rocky series — *Rocky* (1976), *Rocky II* (1979), *Rocky III* (1982) — which continue to show that this type of movie is still appreciated by film audiences.

The boxing milieu is at times a twilight world permeated by organized crime, marred by bribes, payoffs, prearranged deals and fixes. The movies have portrayed it accurately. The struggle of a boxer to keep out of shady deals and underworld pressures has figured prominently in boxing pictures that, at their best, are fine drama and also pack a great deal of suspense as the spectator watches the outcome of a prizefight. Some boxing films qualify as film noir, gangster movies, prison films, or even musicals and Westerns.

The Knockout (14) Charles Avery *aka Counted Out / The Fighting Demon / The Pugilist.* *The Champion* (15) Charlie Chaplin *aka Battling Charlie / Champion Charlie.* *Battling Butler* (26) Buster Keaton. *The Ring* (GB 27) Alfred Hitchcock. *The Champ* (31) King Vidor. *The Life of Jimmy Dolan* (33) Archie Mayo *aka The Kid's Last Fight.* *The Prizefighter and the Lady* (33) W. S. Van Dyke II *aka Every Woman's Man.* *Palooka* (34) Benjamin Stoloff *aka The Great Schnozzle / Joe Palooka.* *The Milky Way* (36) Leo McCarey. *Kid Galahad* (37) Michael Curtiz *aka Battling Bellhop.* *Golden Boy* (39) Rouben Mamoulian. *City for Conquest* (40) Anatole Litvak. *Gentleman Jim* (42) Raoul Walsh. *The Kid from Brooklyn* (46) Norman Z. McLeod. *Killer McCoy* (47) Roy Rowland. *The Set-Up* (48) Robert Wise. *Champion* (49) Mark Robson. *Right Cross* (50) John Sturges. *The Fighter* (51) Herbert Kline. *The Ring* (52) Kurt Neumann. *Somebody Up There Likes Me* (56) Robert Wise. *Requiem for a Heavyweight* (62) Ralph Nelson *aka Blood Money.* *Walkower* (Pol 65) Jerzy Skolimowski *aka Walkover.* *The Legendary Champions* (68) Harry Chapin. *The Great White Hope* (70) Martin Ritt. *Fat City* (71) John Huston. *Hard Times* (75) Walter Hill *aka The Streetfighter.* *Rocky* (76) John G. Avildsen. *Rocky II* (79) Sylvester Stallone. *Raging Bull* (80) Martin Scorsese. *Rocky III* (82) Sylvester Stallone. *Rocky IV* (85) Sylvester Stallone. *Homeboy* (88) Michael Seresin. *Rocky V* (90) John G. Avildsen.

Boxing Gangster Films *see* **GANGSTER FILM**

Breakfast Television Show *see* **TELEVISION NEWS**

Breakthrough Film *see* **SEMINAL FILM**

BRECHTIAN CINEMA   Bertolt Brecht (1898–1956), the German poet and playwright, developed a system of theories and techniques that he applied to his idea of epic theater.[10] Most important is his notion of the *Verfremdungseffekt* or Alienation effect which simply means that the spectator must be "alienated" or "estranged" from what takes place on stage (or on screen, for that matter) by the use of theatricality, rather than being involved emotionally as in realistic theater. Filmmakers who have adapted Brecht's ideas to the cinema also believe that the spectator should be a detached observer rather than a passive witness who strongly identifies with the actors or is mesmerized by the action on the screen, as is the case with conventional cinema. It is through aesthetic distance that the spectator or viewer is expected to become aware of social, historical, or economic realities and thus be able to arrive at his/her own critical assessment. Jean-Luc Godard and René Allio are two filmmakers who have engaged in the making of Brechtian cinema, while neo–Brechtian cinema is exemplified by the German directors Alexander Kluge, the late Rainer Werner Fassbinder and others.

Les Camisards (F 71) René Allio. *Tout va bien* (F 72) Jean-Luc Godard, Jean-Pierre Gorin. *Rude journée pour la reine* (F / Swiz 73) René Allio. *Fontane Effi Briest* (G 72-74) Raine Werner Fassbinder *aka Effi Briest. Milestones* (75) Robert Kramer. *Der starke Ferdinand* (G 75-76) Alexander Kluge *aka Strong Man Ferdinand. Hitler, ein Film aus Deutschland* (G 77) Hans Jürgen Syberberg [in 4 parts] *aka Our Hitler / Our Hitler – A Film from Germany. Deutschland bleiche Mutter* (G 79) Helma Sanders-Brahms *aka Germany, Pale Mother. Lili Marleen* (G 80) Rainer Werner Fassbinder. *Die Sehnsucht der Veronika Voss* (G 81) Rainer Werner Fassbinder *aka Veronika Voss.*

BRITISH EMPIRE FILM (Empire-Building Picture, Empire Film, Film of Empire, Imperial Film)   The films of Empire include those films which deal directly with the destiny of the British Empire, or which express the ideals or attitudes of the men that served it. As such, they cover a broad range of genres and types—family sagas, love stories, adventure films, thrillers, biographies. What they have in common is the unity of purpose and the manner in which they present the British way of life (usually idealized) and follow the conduct of the English at home or abroad. These films always show the upright, stiff-upper-lip British gentleman as he dutifully upholds the ideals of the Empire through self-sacrifice, by fulfilling his role as civil servant and soldier, or by just being merely the perfect ambassador of his country. Here, emphasis is given to two of the genre's more representative categories: the colonial film and the public school film. A description of the many films that can be included in the genre is given by Jeffrey Richards in *Visions of Yesterday.*[11]

Counterbalancing these pro–British Empire films is a group of films that seek to denounce or expose the attitudes prevalent during the days of the Empire or that seek to satirize the films themselves; an example of the former is Tony Richardson's *The Charge of the Light Brigade* (1967); of the latter, Marty Feldman's *The Last Remake of Beau Geste* (1977).

Disraeli (29) Alfred E. Green. *Journey's End* (US / GB 30) James Whale. *Java Head* (GB 34) J. Walter Ruben. *The Lost Patrol* (34) John Ford. *O.H.M.S.* (GB 36) Raoul Walsh *aka You're in the Army Now*. *Farewell Again* (GB 37) Tim Whelan *aka Troopship*. *The Great Barrier* (GB 37) Milton Rosmer, Geoffrey Barkas *aka Silent Barriers*. *Victoria the Great* (GB 37) Herbert Wilcox. *Wee Willie Winkie* (37) John Ford. *The Drum* (GB 38) Zoltan Korda *aka Drums*. *Four Men and a Prayer* (38) John Ford. *Sixty Glorious Years* (GB 38) Herbert Wilcox *aka Queen of Destiny*. *Stanley and Livingstone* (39) Henry King. *Enchantment* (48) Irving Reis. *The Mudlark* (GB /US 50) Jean Negulesco.

———**Colonial Films**   These films show the District Officer doing his job in order to preserve law and order, exerting his authority in the lands he rules as a representative of the Empire; or they show soldiers and officers quelling rebellions in far off frontiers in the name of Queen and Country.

The Flag Lieutenant (GB 32) Henry Edwards. *The Last Outpost* (35) Louis Gasnier, Charles Barton. *The Lives of a Bengal Lancer* (35) Henry Hathaway. *Sanders of the River* (GB 35) Zoltan Korda *aka Bosambo*. *The Charge of the Light Brigade* (36) Michael Curtiz. *Old Bones of the River* (GB 38) Marcel Varnel. *The Four Feathers* (GB 39) Zoltan Korda. *Gunga Din* (39) George Stevens. *The Life and Death of Colonel Blimp* (GB 43) Michael Powell, Emeric Pressburger *aka Colonel Blimp*. *Kim* (50) Victor Saville. *Soldiers Three* (51) Tay Garnett. *North West Frontier* (GB 59) J. Lee Thompson *aka Flame Over India*. *Zulu* (GB 63) Cy Endfield. *The Charge of the Light Brigade* (GB 67) Tony Richardson. *The Man Who Would Be King* (75) John Huston. *The Last Remake of Beau Geste* (77) Marty Feldman. *Kim* (84 TV) John Davies.

———**Public School Films**   Public schools were essential for the building up of character in the elitist group that supposedly would lead the nation and serve the Empire; hence the movies portraying life in these schools form part of the British Empire film. Although a minor branch of the genre, they are nevertheless highly important in fathoming the essence of the British Imperial men and their motivation in serving the Empire. Not all these films are, of course, pro–Empire, and of late some have tried to debunk the system, e.g., *If. . .* (1968).

Housemaster (GB 38) Herbert Brenon. *Goodbye, Mr. Chips* (US /GB 39) Sam Wood. *Tom Brown's Schooldays* (39) Robert Stevenson *aka Adventures at Rugby*. *Tom Brown's Schooldays* (GB 50) Gordon Parry. *If. . .* (GB 68) Lindsay Anderson *aka Crusaders*. *Goodbye, Mr. Chips* (69) Herbert Ross.

British Social Realism   *see*   **KITCHEN SINK FILM**

Broadway-to-Hollywood Musical   *see*   **MUSICAL: Adaptations of Broadway Musical Comedies**

Brothel Film   *see*   **HOOKER FILM: Bordello Films**

Buddy-Cop Films   *see*   **POLICE FILM**

BUDDY FILM (Bonding Film, Buddy-Buddy Film)   In the late sixties and early seventies, a rash of films emphasizing male camaraderie and friendship raised an outcry from feminists. They proclaimed that women were being ignored on the screen and that such films created a vacuum of worthwhile roles for actresses. Films which emphasize the world of men and their friendship for each other came to be known as "buddy" or "bonding" films. It is not a new type of movie. Whenever men have found themselves in isolated environments or in situations of danger, a bond has sprung up among them. This bond is usually between two men, but a relationship among three or more men is also possible; it is found as a matter of course in Westerns, war or adventure films, in all of which camaraderie thrives. A characteristic of these films is that they present men in strong emotional relationships since obviously men are able to feel great affection for each other and sometimes they prefer their own company to that of women. This is reflected in "buddy" films. Female bonding films are practically non-existent, although a few recent films, e.g., *Julia* (1977), qualify as such.

Flesh and the Devil (26) Clarence Brown.   *A Girl in Every Port* (28) Howard Hawks.   *Test Pilot* (38) Victor Fleming.   *Only Angels Have Wings* (39) Howard Hawks.   *Boom Town* (40) Jack Conway.   *Adieu l'ami / Due sporche carogne-tecnica di una rapina* (F /It 67) Jean Herman *aka Farewell, Friend / Honor Among Thieves.*   *Butch Cassidy and the Sundance Kid* (69) George Roy Hill.   *Midnight Cowboy* (69) John Schlesinger.   *Husbands* (70) John Cassavetes.   *Wild Rovers* (71) Blake Edwards.   *Deliverance* (72) John Boorman.   *Scarecrow* (73) Jerry Schatzberg.   *The Sting* (73) George Roy Hill.   *Thunderbolt and Lightfoot* (74) Michael Cimino.   *The Choirboys* (77) Robert Aldrich.   *Julia* (GB / US 77) Fred Zinnemann.   *Semi-Tough* (77) Michael Ritchie.   *The Turning Point* (77) Herbert Ross.   *Heartbreakers* (84) Bobby Roth.

Bullfighter Film   *see*   **BULLFIGHTING MOVIE**

BULLFIGHTING MOVIE (Bullfight Film, Bullfighter Film)   A penniless urchin's passion for bullfighting which he practices as a street game with other would-be bullfighters, is the driving force that will eventually lead him to the bullring. This rags-to-riches-and-fame underlying theme is found in many bullfighter films. Bullfighting is Spain's national sport, and bullfighter movies have been a minor local staple for many decades. The subject transcends borders, however, and some bullfighting movies have also been produced outside Spain or Mexico, the two major producers of bullfighting films. It is a minor genre.

Blood and Sand (22) Fred Niblo.   *Blood and Sand* (41) Rouben Mamoulian.   *Ni sangre ni arena* (Mex 41) Alejandro Galindo.   *La hora de la verdad* (Mex 44) Norman Foster.   *The Brave Bulls / Los toros bravos* (US /Mex 51) Robert Rossen.   *The Bullfighter and the Lady* (51) Budd Boetticher.   *The Magnificent Matador* (55) Budd Boetticher *aka The Brave and the Beautiful.*

¡Torero! (Mex 55) Carlo Velo *aka Bullfighter.* **The Brave One** (56) Irving Rapper. *Los clarines del miedo* (Sp / Mex 58) Antonio Román *aka The Bugles of Fear.* *El niño de las monjas* (Sp 58) Ignacio F. Iquino. *Tommy the Toreador* (GB 59) John Paddy Carstairs. *El toro negro* (Mex 59) Benito Alazraki *aka El juego de la muerte.* *A las cinco de la tarde* (Sp 60) Juan Antonio Bardem *aka At Five o'Clock in the Afternoon.* *Aprendiendo a morir* (Sp 62) Pedro Lazaga *aka Learning to Die.* *I due toreri / Dos toreros de aúpa* (It / Sp 64) Giorgio Simonelli. *Cabriola* (Sp 65) Mel Ferrer *aka Every Day Is a Holiday.* *Il momento della verità / El momento de la verdad* (It / Sp 65) Francisco Rosi *aka The Moment of Truth.* *Arruza* (US / Mex 68) Budd Boetticher [rel. in 71]. *El relicario* (Sp 70) Rafael Gil. *Sangre y arena* (Sp 89) Javier Elorrieta *aka Blood and Sand.*

Burlesque *see* **PARODY**

Burlesque Film *see* **SEX EXPLOITATION FILM**

Busby Berkeley Musical Extravagances *see* **MUSICAL**

Bushranger Film *see* **BUSHRANGING FILM**

BUSHRANGING FILM (Bushranger Film) In Australian speech, the bush is the countryside in general, and bushrangers were the local bandits or outlaws that roamed the bush engaged in armed robbery and other criminal activities. The bushranging films are a minor but historically important, indigenous genre depicting the life and exploits of these bandits. *The Story of the Kelly Gang* (1906) was both the first bushranging venture and Australian feature-length film and is also considered the world's first full-length film.[12] It gave impetus to this type of locally popular adventure film. Bushranging films were banned in New South Wales from 1912 to the 1940s for allegedly showing disrespect for the law and for their tendency to glorify banditry. Although their popularity has waned, now and then an occasional bushranger film has been made.

The Story of the Kelly Gang (Aust 06) Charles Tait [1st full length feature film]. *Robbery Under Arms* (Aust 07) Charles MacMahon. *When the Kelly's Rode* (34) Harry Sothwell. *The Glenrowan Affair* (Aust 51) Rupert Kathner. *Captain Thunderbolt* (Aust 53) Cecil Homes. *Robbery Under Arms* (GB 57) Jack Lee. *Adam's Woman* (Aust / US 69) Philip Leacock *aka Return of the Boomerang.* *Ned Kelly* (GB / Aust 70) Tony Richardson *aka Ned Kelly, Outlaw.* *Mad Dog Morgan* (Aust 75) Philippe Mora *aka Mad Dog.* *Bushranger* (Aust 76) TV Federico Chentrens. *Robbery Under Arms* (Aust 84 TV) Donald Crombie, Ken Hannam [3-part miniseries].

Business Film *see* **FACTUAL FILM: Educational Film**

Cableporn *see* **HARD-CORE PORNO FILM**

Caligarism *see* **EXPRESSIONIST FILM**

Camembert Western *see* **SPAGHETTI WESTERN**

Cameraless Animated Films *see* **ANIMATED FILM**

CAMP FILM (Camp) Camp is not created consciously, but it emerges as an end product. Camp is the effect produced by an object on its viewer or contemplator. Its main characteristic is that it is so bad that it may be watched with a certain degree of amusement. Camp is never dull. An attuned sensibility is required to appreciate and distinguish camp from what otherwise would just be a bad specimen of its kind. In the case of movies, the acting or the situations, although devised and played with a well-meaning degree of seriousness, will, contrary to what was intended in the first place, produce a result which may best be qualified as campy. Camp is the triumph of the ludicrous, and pure enjoyment rather than laughter is derived from it. Camp is found in many turkeys, and some camp films have frequently been elevated to the status of cult films.

Reefer Madness (36) Louis Gasnier *aka Assassin of Youth / The Burning Question / Dope Addict / Doped Youth / Love Madness / Tell Your Children.* *Voodoo Man* (44) William Beaudine. *Beyond the Forest* (49) King Vidor. *Robot Monster* (53) Phil Tucker *aka Monster(s) from Mars / Monster(s) from the Moon / Robot Monster from Mars.* *Sincerely Yours* (55) Gordon Douglas. *The Conqueror* (56) Dick Powell. *Plan 9 from Outer Space* (56) Edward D. Wood, Jr. *aka Grave Robbers from Outer Space* [rel. in 59]. *Beyond the Valley of the Dolls* (70) Russ Meyer. *Myra Breckinridge* (70) Michael Sarne. *The Jekyll and Hyde Portfolio* (71) Eric Jeffrey Haima. *Sebastiane* (GB 76) Derek Jarman, Paul Humfress. *Forbidden Zone* (80) Richard Elfman. *Mommie Dearest* (81) Frank Perry. *Venom* (GB 81) Piers Haggard. *Monsignor / Monsignore* (US / It 82) Frank Perry. *Cannibal Women in the Avocado Jungle of Death* (88) J. D. Adams. *Hollywood Chainsaw Hookers* (88) Fred Olen Ray. *Not of This Earth* (88) Jim Wynorski.

Campus Movie   *see*   **COLLEGE FILM**

Campus Musicals   *see*   **MUSICAL**

Canadian Western   *see*   **MOUNTIE PICTURE**

CANDID CAMERA COMEDY   It consists of filming real people in the streets or in unusual situations in order to see how they react to them. The proceedings are more or less amusing, and the unaware participants are almost always informed on-camera that they have been the object of a practical joke; in other words, that they are on Candid Camera. The form was made popular in American television by Allen Funt. A few feature-length motion pictures consisting of a string of episodes have also been made. The candid camera method is also used extensively in documentaries when the nature of the subject requires it.

What Do You Say to a Naked Lady? (68-70) Allen Funt. *Money Talks* (72) Allen Funt. *Smile When You Say "I Do"* (73 TV) Allen Funt. *It's a Funny, Funny World* (Isr 78) Zvi Shissel. *Achalta Ota* (Isr 80) Yehuda Barkan, Igal Shiloy *aka You've Been Had . . . You Turkey!*

CANNED DRAMA   An early term used by contemporary film critics and reviewers when referring to a motion picture. It emphasized the fact that early films were quite often restagings or recordings of stage plays, as with the films produced by the French *Film d'Art* (q.v.) company. Since finished motion pictures are stored in cans, the use of "canned" in the expression is logical.

Cannibal Films   *see*   **JUNGLE FILM**

Cape and Sword Film   *see*   **SWASHBUCKLER: Cloak and Sword Romances**

CAPER FILM (Big-Caper Film, Heist Film)   Stuart M. Kaminsky considers the big caper movie a subgenre of the adventure-process film.[13] It is, of course, a valid classification as caper movies are a subgenre of the crime film which, in turn, could be considered as one of the major branches of the adventure genre. Here, however, the caper movie is treated as a separate genre even if the connections with crime movies and adventure films are obvious.

What distinguishes a caper movie from any other film involving a robbery, carried out either by a cat-burglar, by gangsters, or by a bunch of assorted thieves, is the professionalism and planning involved in the caper. It is not a spontaneous action — "let's get into the bank and rob it" — but the result of a well-planned, well-thought-out process involving clockwork precision and methodology, all put together by a team of experts working in pairs or as a group. In this type of movie, the success of the caper takes precedence over any other concern. Naturally, since the effort put into the robbery scheme is considerable and the risks are high, the value of the heist has to be equally substantial and rewarding. It usually involves the theft of jewels, some object of art like a famous painting, or it entails a bank or casino robbery.

The caper or heist film got into full swing in the mid-fifties. It is a genre ideally suited to a great degree of suspense, and as developed in the fifties, the genre can be traced back to *The Asphalt Jungle*, a film by John Huston released in 1950. It is certainly the movie that helped launch the genre. *See also* **Heist Films** under the **GANGSTER** genre.

The Asphalt Jungle (49) John Huston. *The Lavender Hill Mob* (GB 51) Charles Crichton. *Touchez pas au Grisbi / Grisbi* (F / It 53) Jacques Becker *aka Don't Touch the Loot*. *Du Rififi chez les hommes* (F 54) Jules Dassin *aka Rififi*. *Bob le Flambeur* (F 55) Jean-Pierre Melville *aka Bob the Gambler*. *5 Against the House* (55) Phil Karlson. *Violent Saturday* (55) Richard Fleischer. *The Killing* (56) Stanley Kubrick. *I soliti ignoti* (It 58) Mario Monicelli *aka As Usual Unknown / Big Deal / Big Deal on Madonna Street / Person(s) Unknown / The Usual Unidentified Thieves*. *The Day They Robbed the Bank of England* (GB 59) John Guillermin. *Odds Against Tomorrow* (59) Robert Wise. *The League of Gentlemen* (GB 60) Basil Dearden. *Seven Thieves* (60) Henry Hathaway. *Mélodie en sous-sol / Colpo grosso al casinò* (F /It 62) Henri Verneuil *aka Any Number Can Win / The Big Grab / The Big Snatch*. *Topkapi* (63) Jules Dassin. *Goldfinger* (GB 64) Guy Hamilton. *The Pink Panther* (64) Blake Edwards [1st in a series of 7 films (1964-83)]. *Rotten to the Core* (GB 65) John Boulting.

Dead Heat on a Merry-Go-Round (66) Bernard Girard *aka The Big Noise /
Eli Kotch.* *Le Deuxième Souffle* (F 66) Jena-Pierre Melville *aka Second
Breath.* *Gambit* (66) Ronald Neame. *How to Steal a Million* (66) William
Wyler, Robert Swink *aka How to Steal a Million and Live Happily Ever
After.* *The Jokers* (GB 66) Michael Winner. *Ad ogni costo / Top Job /
Diamantes a go-go* (It / G / Sp 67) Giuliano Montaldo *aka Grand Slam.* *Rob
bery* (GB 67) Peter Yates. *Le Clan des Siciliens* (F 68) Henri Verneuil *aka
The Sicilian Clan.* *The Thomas Crown Affair* (68) Norman Jewison. *The
Anderson Tapes* (70) Sidney Lumet. *Perfect Friday* (GB 70) Peter Hall. *$
(Dollars)* (71) Richard Brooks *aka The Heist.* *The Hot Rock* (71) Peter
Yates *aka How to Steal a Diamond in Four Uneasy Lessons.* *La Bonne An-
née / Una donna e una canglia* (F /It 73) Claude Lelouch *aka Happy New
Year.* *The Sting* (73) George Roy Hill. *Il Harrowhouse* (GB 74) Aram
Avakian *aka Anything for Love / Fast Fortune.* *The First Great Train Rob-
bery* (GB 78) Michael Crichton *aka The Great Train Robbery.* *Sewers of
Gold* (GB 78 TV) Francis Megahy *aka The Dirty Money.*

CAPTIONED FILM   A film with superimposed titles to help the hearing impaired persons to follow the dialogue and lyrics or for everyone to
translate dialectical or foreign language films into the local language.

Car Race Movie, Car Racing Drama   *see*   **MOTORCAR RACING
FILM**

Car-Chase Action Film, Car-Chase / Car-Smash Movie, Car-Chase
Film, Car-Crash Film   *see*   **CHASE FILM**

Carmilla Films   *see*   **VAMPIRE FILM**

Carnaval Film   *see*   **CHANCHADA**

CARTOON FILM (Animated Cartoon, Cartoon, Drawn Film)   Cartoons or animated drawings have always been the most popular form of
animation. J. Stuart Blackton (1875–1941) made *The Enchanted Drawing*
in 1900, a short that shows the artist drawing a man's face which changes
expression several times and ends up smoking a cigar, an effect achieved by
stop-motion rather than frame-by-frame animation. The first cartoon film
to use true animation was Blackton's *Humorous Phases and Funny Faces*
(1906), also on the subject of an artist drawing a picture that comes alive
and moves. Since then, dozens of well-known and loved characters (Betty
Boop, Bugs Bunny, Donald Duck, Felix the Cat, Mickey Mouse, Mr.
Magoo, Pluto, Popeye, Road Runner, Sylvester and Tweety, Tom and
Jerry, Woody Woodpecker) have enchanted and delighted children and
family audiences. It is only recently that cartoons meant solely for adult audiences have also been made and openly exhibited. Besides being made for
entertainment, cartoons are also frequently designed for cinema and television advertising, for teaching and other purposes, e.g., propaganda: Walt
Disney's *Victory Through Air Power* (1943) represents an outstanding example of the latter.

Most cartoons are created by celluloid animation, a technique in which a series of drawings, each one slightly different from the next, are transferred to a cell (or cel) and painted; a separate background that is drawn and painted on plain paper is provided. The drawings and background are then photographed on the camera table, usually frame by frame. The finished cartoon may vary from a few seconds to over two hours in length.[14]

As with other forms of animation (*see* **ANIMATED FILM**), the current trend in the animated cartoon film is innovation (mixed media, new stylistic originality, new techniques) and the presentation of adult themes.

The Enchanted Drawing (00) J. Stuart Blackton. *Humorous Phases and Funny Faces* (06) J. Stuart Blackton. *Snow White and the Seven Dwarfs* (37) David Hand (supervising director) [Disney's 1st full-length animated feature]. *Fantasia* (40) Ben Sharpsteen (production supervisor) *aka Concert Feature* [1st U.S. film in stereophonic sound: Fantasound]. *Victory Through Air Power* (43) David Hand (supervising director). *Cinderella* (49) Ben Sharpsteen (production supervisor). *Animal Farm* (GB 51-54) John Halas, Joy Batchelor. *The Jungle Book* (67) Wolfgang Reitherman. *Le Théâtre de Monsieur et Madame Kabal* (F 67) Walerian Borowczyk *aka The Theater of Mr. and Mrs. Kabal*. *The Yellow Submarine* (GB 67) George Dunning. *Le Socrate* (F / G 68) Robert Lapoujade. *Adam 2* (G 69) Jan Lenica. *A Boy Named Charlie Brown* (69) Bill Melendez. *Il Cavaliere inesistente* (It 69) Pino Zac *aka The Non-Existent Knight*. *The Aristocats* (70) Wolfgang Reitherman. *shinbone alley* (70) John D. Wilson *aka archy and mehitabel*. *La Planète sauvage* (F / Cz 73) René Laloux *aka (The) Fantastic Planet / The Savage Planet*. *Robin Hood* (73) Wolfgang Reitherman. *Watership Down* (GB 78) Martin Rosen. *The Fox and the Hound* (81) Art Stevens, Ted Berman, Richard Rich. *Krysar* (Cz / G 85) Jirí Barta *aka The Pied Piper*. *Starchaser: The Legend of Orin* (85) Steven Hahn [1st animated feature in 3-D]. *Astérix chez les Bretons* (F /Den 86) Pino van Lamsweerde *aka Asterix in Britain*. *The Great Mouse Detective* (86) John Musker, Ron Clements, Dave Michener *aka Basil: The Great Mouse Detective*. *When the Wind Blows* (GB 86) Jimmy T. Murakami. *Oliver and Company* (88) George Scribner.

——**Adult Cartoons (Erotic Cartoons)**   The term "adult" has been used to distinguish those animated films not meant for children or family audiences. It is also applied to films with erotic or pornographic content. In terms of the animated film, pornography is not new, but it has circulated sub-rosa. Erotic cartoons are now shown openly in many countries.

I huvet på en gammal gubbe (Sw 68-69) Tage Danielson *aka In an Old Man's Head / Out of an Old Man's Head*. *Cleopatra* (J 70) Osamu Tezuka. *Fritz the Cat* (71) Ralph Bakshi. *Heavy Traffic* (73) Ralph Bakshi. *Cheap* (74) Charles Swenson.

Cartoons   *see*   **FANTASY FILM**

Case Study Films   *see*   **PSYCHIATRIC FILM**

Catastrophe Film   *see*   **DISASTER FILM**

CAUTIONARY FILM (Cautionary Tale)   A film which warns or cautions us to mend our ways in order to avoid some ill-fated end or imminent disaster. Cautionary films have a message. Most science fiction films warning us about the danger of the misuse of nuclear power (e.g., *The War Game*, 1965; *The Day After*, 1983; *Testament*, 1983) are clearly cautionary tales.

The War Game (GB 65 TV) Peter Watkins. *The Day After* (83 TV) Nicholas Meyer. *Testament* (83) Lynne Littman.

Cautionary Tale *see* **CAUTIONARY FILM**

CAVALCADE The linking of several short films or scenes from various films to form a program of some length. It has frequently been done with the work of well-known film comedians, e.g., Charlie Chaplin in *The Essanay-Chaplin Revue of 1916* (made up mostly of *The Tramp, His New Job* and *A Night Out*) and the British montage of several Essanay films by Langford Reed, *Chase Me Charlie* (1917). Many of these cavalcades are just inept pot-pourris with added sound effects to underscore the gags. *See* **COMPILATION FILM**.

Cavalcade has also been used as an appellation for films which chronicle events through a long period of time and also for chronicle films or films which span the years, and whose model may be found in *Cavalcade* (1933) and *The World Changes* (1933), the latter covering a time-period of more than seventy years from 1856 to 1929. *See also* **SAGA**.

The Essanay-Chaplin Revue of 1916 (16) Prod. Jesse J. Robbins. *Chase Me Charlie* (GB 17) Langford Reed [montage of 7 reels of Essanay films]. *Cavalcade* (33) Frank Lloyd. *The World Changes* (33) Mervyn LeRoy. *This Happy Breed* (GB 44) David Lean.

Cavalry Films *see* **WESTERN**

Celebrity Show *see* **TELEVISION SHOW: Game Show**

Chain Gang Movies *see* **PRISON FILM**

Chambara Film *see* **SAMURAI FILM**

Chamber Film *see* **KAMMERSPIELFILM;** *see also* **EXPRESSIONIST FILM**

CHANCHADA A strictly local Brazilian genre of musical comedy which emerged with the coming of sound to the Brazilian screen and which affirmed itself with the often cited *Alô Alô Brasil* (1935) and *Alô Alô Carnaval* (1936) featuring Carmen Miranda (1909–55), later of Hollywood fame. It was very popular until the 1950s. It consisted mostly of comedies spiced with musical interludes, dances, and carnival songs. The *chanchada* often appeared in the form of the *carnaval* film or as a satiric parody. By the 1960s, due to the increased appeal of television, the *chanchadas* had virtually ceased to exist although their influence is still felt in films like *Macunaíma* (1969) and *Quando o carnaval chegar* (1971), amongst others. A direct descendent of the *chanchada* is the *pornochanchada* of the 1970s, a local version of softcore sex comedy, which replaced musical interludes with mitigated eroticism. *See also* **CINEMA NOVO**.

Chanchadas: Alô Alô Brasil (Braz 35) Adhemar Gonzaga. *Alô Alô Carnaval* (Braz 36) Wallace Downey, Adhemar Gonzaga *aka Allo, Allo, Carnaval.* *Carnaval no fogo* (Braz 49) Watson Macedo. *Aviso aos navigantes* (Braz 50) Watson Macedo. *Carnaval Atlântida* (Braz 52) José Carlos Burle. *Dupla do barulho* (Braz 53) Carlos Manga. *Nem Sansão nem Dalila* (Braz 54) Carlos Manga *aka Neither Samson nor Delilah.* *Rico Ri à Toa* (Braz 57) Roberto Farias. *Macunaíma (O heroe sem nenhum cáracter)* (Braz 69) Joaquim Pedro de Andrade. *Quando o carnaval chegar* (Braz 71) Carlos Diegues *aka When Carnival Comes.* *Assim era a Atlântida* (Braz 75) Carlos Manga.

Pornochanchadas: Adultério à Brasileira (Braz 69) Pedro Carlos Rovai. *Al Ilha dos Paqueras* (Braz 70) Fauze Mansur. *O pornografo* (Braz 70) João Callegaro. *Luna de mel e amendoim* (Braz 71) Pedro Carlos Rovai, Fernando de Barrios. *A viúva virgem* (Braz 72) Pedro Rovai *aka The Virgin Widow.* *Com a cama na cabeça* (Braz 73) Mozael Silveira *aka Bed Maniacs.* *A virgem e o machão* (Braz 73) José Mojica Marins *aka The Virgin and the Macho.* *Al Ilha do desejo* (Braz 74) Jean Garret. *Guerra conjugal* (Braz 75) Joaquim Pedro de Andrade *aka Conjugal Warfare / Matrimonial War.* *Um soutien para papai* (Braz 75) C. A. Souza Barros *aka A Bra for Daddy.* *Bacalhau* (Braz 76) Adriano Stuart *aka Codfish.* *As taras de todos nós* (Braz 81) Guilherme de Almeida Prado.

Chapter Play *see* **SERIAL**

CHASE FILM (Chaser)   Any film in which a prolonged chase is included as a major element of its plot. The chase was a device much used in slapstick comedy. In fact, comic chase films or runaway films were a popular form of entertainment in the silent era. The Keystone Kops of Mack Sennett invariably used it; so did other comic actors from Max Linder to Charlie Chaplin to Buster Keaton. Besides being used for comic effect, the chase has also great suspense value, and many genre films such as adventure films, gangster films, Westerns, and thrillers employ it.

Some of the early silent films were all chase and little else. Today, the chase is a very important addition in action and suspense pictures, and it has come once more to the fore in car-chase action films and in car-crash films. This latter variety may also be designated as car-chase/car-smash movies or crash-and-wreck films.

Escaped Lunatic (03) A. E. Weed (cameraman). *How a French Nobleman Got a Wife Through the New York Herald Personal Columns* (04) Edwin S. Porter (cameraman). *Personal* (04) Bitzer (cameraman). *The Gentleman Highwayman* (05) G. W. Bitzer (cameraman). *Girl Shy* (24) Fred Newmeyer, Sam Taylor. *The General* (26) Buster Keaton, Clyde Bruckman. *Le Million* (F 30-31) René Clair. *Number Seventeen* (GB 32) Alfred Hitchcock. *The Runaround* (46) Charles Lamont. *The Great Chase* (62) Presented by Paul Killiam, Saul J. Turell. *It's a Mad, Mad, Mad, Mad World* (63) Stanley Kramer. *Good Neighbor Sam* (64) David Swift. *Bullitt* (68) Peter Yates. *Figures in a Landscape* (GB 70) Joseph Losey *aka The Hunted.* *What's Up Doc?* (71) Peter Bogdanovich. *Dirty Mary, Crazy Larry* (74) John Hugh. *The Sugarland Express* (74) Steven Spielberg. *The Wilby*

Conspiracy (75) Ralph Nelson. *Moving Violation* (76) Charles S. Dubin. *Grand Theft Auto* (77) Ron Howard. *Smokey and the Bandit* (77) Hal Needham [3 "Bandit" films (1977-83)]. *The Driver* (78) Walter Hill. *The Blues Brothers* (80) John Landis. *Dead Easy* (Aust 81) Bert Deling. *The Junkman* (82) H. B. Halicki *aka Gone in 60 Seconds Part II The Junkman.* *To Live and Die in L.A.* (85) William Friedkin. *Midnight Run* (88) Martin Brest.

Chaser *see* **CHASE FILM;** *see also* **SHORT**

Chat Show *see* **TELEVISION SHOW: Talk Show**

Cheap Film *see* **LOW-BUDGET FILM**

CHEAPIE A clear, expressive term that means just that: a movie cheaply made and of poor quality. Other terms associated with low-cost and low-investment production are: B-movie, co-feature, exploitation film, quickie, schlock movie, sleazy film, and Z picture (qq.v.).

CHICANO FILM (Chicano Cinema) A film which has for its subject matter the Mexican-American and which also relates to the Chicano cultural heritage in the United States. It may be said that Chicano-oriented pictures started in Mexico where a short-lived *género chicano* (Chicano genre) flourished between 1973 and 1975. However, with a few exceptions, Chicano films are best represented by films made by Chicanos who put their values onto film or tape and offer a representation of Chicano issues and culture as they stand, merge, or clash with Anglo-American society. Besides documentaries and shorts, Chicano cinema also includes feature-length dramatic works. On the subject, *see Chicano Cinema*, ed. by Gary D. Keller (Binghamton, N.Y.: Bilingual Review/Press, 1985).

The Lawless (49) Joseph Losey *aka The Dividing Line / Outrage*. *Salt of the Earth* (53) Herbert Biberman. *I Am Joaquín* (67) Rodolfo Corky. *De sangre chicana* (Mex 73) Pepito Romay *aka Of Chicano Blood*. *Please Don't Bury Me Alive / Por favor, ¡No me entierren vivo!* (76) Efrain Gutiér-rez. *Raíces de sangre* (Mex 76) Jesús Salvador Treviño *aka La Raza Unida / Root of Blood*. *Alambrista!* (77) Robert M. Young *aka Illegal*. *Only Once in a Lifetime* (78) Alejandro Grattan. *Boulevard Nights* (79) Michael Pressman. *Walk Proud* (79) Robert Collins. *Seguín* (81 TV) Jesús Salvador Treviño [1st episode of a six-part series, *"La Historia"*]. *300 Miles for Stephanie* (81 TV) Clyde Ware. *Zoot Suit* (81) Luis Valdez. *The Ballad of Gregorio Cortez* (82 TV) Robert M. Young *aka Gregorio Cortez*. *Heart-breaker* (82) Frank Zuniga.

Chicano Cinema, Chicano-Oriented Picture *see* **CHICANO FILM**

Child-Star Musicals *see* **MUSICAL**

Children's Classic Fantasies *see* **FANTASY FILM**

Children's Entertainment Film *see* **CHILDREN'S FILM**

Children's Fantasy Films *see* **FANTASY FILM: Children's Classic Fantasies**

Children's Fantasy Musicals *see* **MUSICAL**

CHILDREN'S FILM (Kiddie-Movie, Kids' Film) An important category of films is the children's entertainment film. They are made the world over with most countries producing the occasional children's film. However, in the USSR and the Eastern bloc, where the state controls (or used to control) film production, there has been a steady output of films made especially for children. Children's films are also popular in Japan, Scandinavia, and Britain where the Children's Film Foundation sponsors and supervises the production of several films a year. The definition of children's film includes films addressed to children and films addressed to adults, e.g., *Bugsy Malone* (1976). Either type may include a majority of children as actors or not, but in order to qualify as a children's film, the film has to have children as the focal point of the story. If meant for children, the film has to be mainly geared towards an audience of children.

In the films addressed exclusively to children, the approach and content may vary, but the most common films for children are animation films, fairy stories, and realistic films; in this latter type, adventure stories are the most successful among children.

Child audiences vary in age, and some countries orient their production to age groups. The films are usually made for children ages 5 to 12 and 12 to 16, although the age groups into which the films are allocated change according to individual countries.

A subsection of the children's movies addressed to adults deals with perverse or malevolent children, e.g., *Mumsy, Nanny, Sonny, & Girly* (1969) and *The Omen* (1976) which many would not consider children's films at all and which, naturally, may also be integrated into other genres. In the two examples cited, the films also fall under black comedy and demonology respectively.

Films suitable for both children and adults are better classed as family films. Otherwise, they may be referred to as films for children and films about children.

Peck's Bad Boy (21) Sam Wood. *Skippy* (31) Norman Taurog. *Zéro de conduite* (F 33) Jean Vigo *aka Nought for Behaviour / Zero for Conduct.* *Treasure Island* (34) Victor Fleming. *The Wizard of Oz* (39) Victor Fleming, King Vidor, Richard Thorpe, George Cukor. *The Little Fugitive* (53) Ray Ashley. *Les Quatre Cent Coups* (F 59) François Truffaut *aka The 400 Blows. Pollyanna* (60) David Swift. *Whistle Down the Wind* (GB 61) Bryan Forbes. *The Three Lives of Thomasina* (GB / US 64) Don Chaffey. *The Daydreamer* (66) Jules Bass. *A Pál utcai fiúk / The Boys of Paul Street* (Hung / US 68) Zoltán Fábri. *Heidi* (68 TV) Delbert Mann. *Hugo och Josefin* (Sw 68) Kjell Grede *aka Hugo and Josefin. Lost in the Desert* (SA 69) Jamie Hayes. *Mumsy, Nanny, Sonny, & Girly* (GB 69) Freddie Francis *aka Girly. The Amazing Mr. Blunden* (GB 72) Lionel Jeffries. *Alice in den Städten* (G 73) Wim Wenders *aka Alice in the Cities. From the Mixed-Up Files of Mrs. Basil E. Frankweiler* (73) Fielder Cook *aka The Hideaways. e'Lollipop* (SA 75) Ashly Lazerus *aka Forever*

Young, Forever Free / Lollipop. **Escape to Witch Mountain** (75) John Hough. **Ride a Wild Pony** (Aust / US 75) Don Chaffey *aka Sporting Proposition.* **Zimovanje u Jakobsfeldu** (Yug 75 TV) Branko Bauer *aka Wintering in Jakobsfeld.* **Bugsy Malone** (GB 76) Alan Parker. **Gus** (76) Vincent McEveety. **The Omen** (US / GB 76) Richard Donner *aka The Anti-Christ.* **Across the Great Divide** (77) Stewart Raffill. **The Glitterball** (GB 77) Harley Cockliss. **The Littlest Horse Thieves** (77) Charles Jarrott *aka Escape from the Dark.* **Black Island** (GB 78) Bel Bolt. **The Black Stallion** (US / Can 79) Carroll Ballard. **Little Lord Fauntleroy** (GB / US 80 TV) Jack Gold. **Tuck Everlasting** (80) Frederick King Keller. **Mystery Island** (81) Gene Scott. **Sesame Street Presents Follow That Bird** (85) Ken Kwapis. **The Outside Chance of Maximilian Glick** (Can 88) Allan A. Goldstein. **Crystalstone** (87) Antonio Pelaez. **Prancer** (89) John Hancock. **Treasure Island** (90 MCTV) Fraser Heston. **White Fang** (91) Randal Kleiser.

Chiller, Chiller-Diller *see* **HORROR FILM**

Chinese New Wave *see* **NEW CHINESE CINEMA**

CHINESE SWORDPLAY MOVIE (Wu Xia Pian)[15]   Popular since the sixties with Chinese audiences in the Far East and Chinatown theaters the world over, the Chinese swordplay genre is also known in the West where it reached a certain popularity in conjunction with the kung fu film, the other success-story genre to gain popularity among Western audiences. The Chinese swordplay films are an action genre which acknowledges the entertainment value of escapist adventure and the strong appeal of violence— by Western standards they are an extremely violent genre. The films are highly romanticized; they are an oriental equivalent of the western swashbuckler in terms of their historical or pseudo-historical period settings and in the skillful show of swordsmanship of their heroes and heroines.[16] As with the kung fu films, the combats are the main staple of the swordplay film. Most of these fights are exquisitely choreographed and rely on an unbelievable display of gore—dismemberments and blood baths are the order of the day as a single fighter/hero tackles literally hordes of assailants. Most swordplay movies have touches of the incredible or the fantastic but an important subgenre deals exclusively with the supernatural—ghosts, vampires, incantations, magic transformations, and other unspeakable things as their main ingredients.

An interesting characteristic of the genre is the role played by women. As a swordswoman, she matches or even outperforms in skill her male counterparts, and she figures as heroine in many films.

Golden Swallow (HK 68) Chang Cheh *aka The Girl with the Thunderbolt Kick.* **Hsia Nu** (Tai 69) King Hu (Hu Chin-Chuan) *aka A Touch of Zen.* **The Deaf and Mute Heroine** (HK 70) Wu Ma. **Hsin Tu-Pei-Tao** (HK 70) Chang Cheh *aka The New One-Armed Swordsman / Triple Irons.* **Valley of the Fangs** (HK 71) Chang Cheng Ho. **Ci ma** (HK 73) Chang Cheh *aka The Blood Brothers / Chinese Vengeance / Dynasty of Blood.* **The Magnificent Chivalry** (HK 73) Lee So. **Ch'u liu-hsiang** (HK 77) Chu Yuan *aka Clans of Intrigue.* **Sora tobu jujiken** (HK 77) Mei Chung Chang (Chang Mei Chun)

aka Dynasty / The Flying Sword / Super-Dragon. Hsiu-hua ta tao (HK 78)
Chu Yuan *aka Clan of Amazons. Pien-fu ch'uan-ch'i* (HK 78) Chu Yuan
aka Legends of the Bat. Siu ngou gongwu (HK 90) King Hu, Tsui Hark,
Ching Siu-tung (Ann Hui, Li Hui-min, Kam Yeung-wah) *aka Swordsman.*

Chivalric Epic *see* **SWASHBUCKLER: Chivalric Films**

Chop-Chop Film, Chop-'Em-Sock-'Em Flick, Chopsocky Pic *see*
KUNG FU FILM

Chop Suey Western *see* **SPAGHETTI WESTERN**

Christ-Figure Films, Christ Films *see* **RELIGIOUS FILM**

CHRISTMAS MOVIE   Christmas, this most holy of Christian festivities which celebrates the birth of Christ, has figured in many films as a time
when people rejoice, reencounter one another and, generally speaking, ex-
ult in a spirit of fellowship and good will.

Charles Dickens' *A Christmas Carol* (1843) is perhaps the most famous
Christmas story brought to the screen. The *Guinness Film Book of Movie
Facts & Feats* (1991, p. 26) lists twenty film adaptations or remakes of the
well-known tale.

Christmas films form a sizeable number, and they are mostly sentimental
stories, comedies, or musicals.

Scrooge (GB 35) Henry Edwards. *A Christmas Carol* (38) Edwin L.
Marin. *Holiday Inn* (42) Mark Sandrich. *The Cheaters* (45) Joseph Kane
aka The Castaway. Miracle on 34th Street (46) George Seaton *aka The Big
Heart / The Big Street. Bush Christmas* (GB / Aust 47) Ralph
Smart. *Scrooge* (GB 51) Brian Desmon Hurst *aka A Christmas Carol. The
Holly and the Ivy* (GB 52) George More O'Ferrall. *Scrooge* (GB 70) Ronald
Neame. *The Homecoming — A Christmas Story* (71 TV) Fielder Cook. *A
Dream for Christmas* (73 TV) Ralph Senensky. *The Gathering* (77 TV)
Randal Kleiser. *Questo si che è amore* (It 77) Filippo Ottoni *aka The Night
Before Christmas. A Christmas to Remember* (78 TV) George
Englund. *A Christmas Without Snow* (80 TV) John Korty. *A Christmas
Story* (83) Bob Clark. *A Christmas Carol* (84 TV) Clive Donner. *One
Magic Christmas* (US /Can 85) Phillip Borsos *aka Father Christmas / Joy
to the World / Once Upon a Christmas / Santa Claus. Santa Claus* (85)
Jeannot Szwarc *aka Santa Claus the Movie. Christmas Eve* (86 TV) Stuart
Cooper. *Bushfire Moon* (Aust 87) George Miller *aka The Christmas Visitor
/ Miracle Down Under. The Christmas Wife* (88 MCTV) David Jones.

Chronicle Film *see* **CAVALCADE**

Cinderella Film *see* **SLEEPER**

Cine-Eye *see* **KINO-GLAZ**

Cinéma à Clef *see* **FILM A CLEF**

Cinema Classic *see* **CLASSIC**

Cinéma Noir *see* **FILM NOIR**

CINEMA NOVO   The Cinema Novo was formed during the period from 1959 to 1962 when a group of filmmakers gathered round Nelson Pereira dos Santos and Carlos Diegues to formulate its directives. Its origins have been traced back to Pereira dos Santos' *Rio, quarenta graus* (1954) and *Rio, zona norte* (1957), but it was in the sixties that it grew to full maturity and won acclaim and prizes in the major film festivals of the world. Cinema Novo sought to renovate the national Brazilian cinema by contributing to an awareness of the many social problems existing in Brazil and other underdeveloped countries of Latin America. It spoke of hunger, injustice, colonialism, oppression, foreign economic dominance, and it questioned the traditional ideological, religious, social or political structures of Brazilian society. Influenced mainly by neorealism at its beginning, it rejected the conventional commercial cinema made up of escapist melodramas and local musical comedies (*chanchadas*) and in their place promoted an *auteur* policy. Cinema Novo is a militant, committed cinema whose demise (the group forming the movement was disbanded in December 1968) came about through public indifference, rising costs of production, the government's curtailment of freedom of expression and an increasing censorship. By 1970, it had virtually disappeared from the Brazilian scene. While it existed, it was a violent, angry cinema imbued with mysticism, legendary and folkloric characters, local paraphernalia, and an intense exoticism exploding in an amalgam of color and sound. Its main spokesman, theorist and filmmaker is Glauber Rocha.

Rio, quarenta graus (Braz 54) Nelson Pereira dos Santos *aka Rio, 40 graus.   Rio, zona norte* (Braz 57) Nelson Pereira dos Santos.   *Barravento* (Braz 61) Glauber Rocha *aka The Turning Wind.   O pagador de promessas* (Braz 61) Anselmo Duarte *aka The Given Word / Keeper of Promises.   O assalto ao trem pagador* (Braz 62) Roberto Farias.   *Cinco vezes favela* (Braz 62) Marco Farias, Miguel Borges, Carlos Diegues, Leon Hirszman, Joaquim Pedro de Andrade.   *Deus e o Diablo na terra do sol* (Braz 63) Glauber Rocha *aka Black God, White Devil.   Os fuzis* (Braz 63) Ruy Guerra *aka The Guns.   Vidas secas* (Braz 63) Nelson Pereira dos Santos *aka Barren Lives.   Seara vermelha* (Braz 63) Aberto d'Aversa *aka The Violent Land.   O desafio* (Braz 65) Cezar Saraceni *aka The Dare.   A falecida* (Braz 65) Leon Hirszman *aka The Deceased.   A grande cidade* (Braz 66) Carlos Diegues.   *Cara a cara* (Braz 67) Júlio Bressante *aka Face to Face.   Terra em transe* (Braz 66-67) Glauber Rocha *aka Earth Entranced / Land in Anguish / Land in Crisis.   O bravo guerreiro* (68) Gustavo Dahl *aka The Brave Warrior.   Brasil ano 2000* (68) Walter Lima Jr.   *Antônio das Mortes / Antonio-des-Mortes* (Braz / F 69) Glauber Rocha *aka O drãgao da maldade contra o santo guerreiro. Azyllo muito louco* (Braz 69) Nelson Pereira dos Santos.   *Desesperato* (Braz 69) Bernardes Filho.   *Os herdeiros* (Braz 69) Carlos Diegues. *Macunaíma (O heroe sem nenhum cáracter)* (Braz 69) Joaquim Pedro de Andrade.   *Cabezas cortadas* (Sp / Braz 70) Glauber Rocha.   *Os deuses e os mortos* (Braz 70) Ruy Guerra *aka Gods and the Dead.   Pecado mortal* (Braz 70) Miguel Faria Jr. *aka Mortal Sin.   Pindorama* (Braz 70) Arnaldo Jabor. *Prata Palomares* (Braz 70) André Faria.   *O capitão Bandeira contra ou doutor Moura Brasil* (Braz 71) Antonio Calmon.

Cinéma Pur *see* **ABSTRACT FILM**

Cinemagazine *see* **NEWSREEL**

Cinema Truth *see* **KINO-GLAZ**

CINEMA VERITE (Cinéma-Vérité Film) *Cinéma vérité* came into prominence with the filming of Jean Rouch and Edgar Morin's *Chronique d'un été* (1960) in France. The term itself is the French translation of Dziga Vertov's *Kino-Pravda* (film or cinema truth) of 1922. It soon became a style of filmmaking whose most discernible technique is the use of hand-held equipment to film people (most frequently non-actors) in their natural surroundings and events as they are taking place without the use of preconceived scenarios. It relies a lot on interviews and confrontations between people who, although knowing they are being filmed, supposedly carry on in total candor, unimpeded by the camera's presence or the filmmaker's active participation. *Cinéma vérité* is mostly applied to the filming of documentaries. The need for realism in motion pictures is very old. It has repeatedly emerged in one form or another—*Kino-Glaz* in Russia, Neorealism in Italy, Free Cinema in Britain. In America, a concurrent documentary movement referred to as direct cinema (q.v.) has many points of contact with *cinéma vérité*. The validity of *cinéma vérité* has been questioned as its goal of achieving truth by recording life as it unfolds conflicts with the presence of the filmmaker, who tends to make people self-aware and perhaps induces them to perform for the camera, negating *cinéma vérité*'s claim to objectivity. On the subject of *cinéma vérité see* M. Ali Issasi and Doris A. Paul's *What Is Cinéma Vérité?* (Metuchen, N.J.: Scarecrow, 1979).[17] *See* **DIRECT CINEMA.**

> *Chronique d'un été* (F 60) Jean Rouch, Edgar Morin *aka Chronicle of a Summer. Regards sur la folie* (F 61) Mario Ruspoli. *Un Coeur gros comme ça!* (F 61) François Reichenbach *aka The Winner. Les Inconnus de la terre* (F 61) Mario Ruspoli. *Lonely Boy* (Can 61) Wolf Koenig, Roman Kroitor *aka Paul Anka. Le Chemin de la mauvaise route* (F 62) Jean Herman *aka The Way of the Wrong Road. Pour la suite du monde / Moontrap* (Can 61-62) Pierre Perrault, Michel Brault *aka For Those Who Follow. La Punition* (F 62 TV) Jean Rouch *aka Liberté. Le Joli Mai* (F 63) Chris Marker. *Le Mystère Koumiko* (F 64) Chris Marker *aka The Koumiko Mystery. Warrendale* (Can 66 TV) Allan Winton King. *A Married Couple* (Can 69) Allan Winton King *aka Marriage / Un Couple marié. Hearts and Minds* (74) Peter Davis.

CinemaScope Film *see* **WIDE SCREEN**

Cinematograph Film *see* **FILM**

Cinepoem, Cine Poem *see* **FILM POEM**

Ciné-Poème *see* **CINE-ROMAN**

CINE-ROMAN (Ciné-Poème, Film-Novel, Roman-Ciné) A French term which lately has emerged as meaning either a book or film text based on a "literary" film or the film itself. In this latter context, the term *ciné-poème* has also been suggested. These *ciné-romans* are highly intellectual films made by a group of French literary authors, some former novelists, who turned to cinema from the mid-fifties on as a new way of personal expression and who sought to apply literary techniques to filmmaking rather than making mere adaptations of literary works.[18]

The term *cinéroman* had already been used in French silent cinema. It originated with the success of *Roman d'Amour* (1904), a Pathé film made by Lorent Heilbronn, which began a genre of sentimental films known as *cinéromans*. It was very much indebted to André Heuzé (1880–1942) for its development. *Cinéroman* also meant a publication that told the film's story by means of illustrations in a comic-strip manner.

La Pointe courte (F 54) Agnès Varda. *L'Enclos* (F / Yug 60) Armand Gatti *aka The Enclosure*. *Une aussi longue absence / L'inverno ti farà tornare* (F /It 60) Henri Colpi *aka The Long Absence*. *L'Immortelle / L'immortale* (F / It / Tur 62) Alain Robbe-Grillet. *La Jetée* (F 63) Chris Marker *aka The Jetty / The Pier* [subtitled: *Un photo-roman*]. *Muriel ou le temps d'un retour* (F 63) Alain Resnais *aka Muriel*. *Le Bonheur* (F 64) Agnès Varda *aka Happiness*. *Le Coup de grâce* (Can / F 64) Jean Cayrol, Claude Durand *aka Les temps héroïques*. *Mona, l'étoile sans nom* (F / Rum 66) Henri Colpi. *Je t'aime, je t'aime* (F 67) Alain Resnais. *Les Créatures / Varelserna* (F / Sw 66) Agnès Varda. *Détruire dit-elle* (F 69) Marguerite Duras. *L'Eden et après* (F / Cz 70) Alain Robbe-Grillet. *Glissements progressifs du plaisir* (F 73) Alain Robbe-Grillet. *India Song* (F 74) Marguerite Duras. *Stavisky...* / *Stavisky, il grande truffatore* (F /It 74) Alain Resnais *aka L'Empire d'Alexandre*. *Le Camion* (F 77) Marguerite Duras *aka The Lorry*.

CIRCUS FILM (Big-Top Movie) Although the ancient Romans are well-known for their gladiatorial combats, chariot races, and animal shows in Rome's Circus Maximus, the Colosseum, and other amphitheaters of the Empire, present-day circus performances originated in England in the late 18th century. The small, enclosed world of the circus offers ample opportunity for conflict amongst its people with their jealousies, rivalries, and flare-ups of passion. Filmmakers saw in the Big Top ready-made scenarios and brought the circus to the screen. Charlie Chaplin's *The Circus* (1925-27) is an early masterpiece. Circus movies are mostly of a dramatic nature with occasional inroads into the bizarre (e.g., *Freaks*, 1932) and the field of horror.

He Who Gets Slapped (24) Victor Seastrom. *Der Zirkuskönig* (Aus 24) Max Linder, E. E. Violet *aka King of the Circus / Le Roi du cirque*. *Variété* (G 25) Ewald André Dupont *aka Variétés / Variety / Vaudeville*. *The Circus* (25-27) Charlie Chaplin. *Four Devils* (28) F. W. Murnau. *Street Angel* (28) Frank Borzage. *Freaks* (32) Tod Browning *aka Barnum / Forbidden Love / The Monster Show / Nature's Mistakes*. *The Mighty Barnum* (34) Walter Lang. *At the Circus* (39) Edward Buzzell *aka Marx Brothers at the Circus*. *You Can't Cheat an Honest Man* (39) George Marshall. *Dumbo*

(41) Ben Sharpsteen (supervising director). *The Greatest Show on Earth* (51) Cecil B. DeMille. *Gycklarnas afton* (Sw 53) Ingmar Bergman *aka The Naked Lights / The Naked Night / Sawdust and Tinsel*. *Man on a Tightrope* (53) Elia Kazan. *La strada* (It 54) Federico Fellini *aka The Road*. *Lola Montés / Lola Montez* (F / G 55) Max Ophüls *aka The Sins of Lola Montes*. *Trapeze* (56) Carol Reed. *The Big Circus* (59) Joseph M. Newman. *Billy Rose's Jumbo* (62) Charles Walters *aka Jumbo*. *Yoyo* (F 65) Pierre Etaix *aka Yo Yo*. *Die Artisten in der Zirkuskuppel: ratlos* (G 68) Alexander Kluge *aka Artistes at the Top of the Big Top: Disorientated*. *I Clowns / Les Clowns / Die Clowns* (It / F / G 69 TV) Federico Fellini *aka The Clowns*. *Parade* (F 73 TV) Jacques Tati. *Stans Hetaste Porrshow* (Swiz / Den / Sw 74) Phyllis & Eberhard Kronhausen *aka The Hottest Show in Town*. *When the Circus Came to Town* (80 TV) Boris Sagal.

——**Funfair Movies (Fairground Movies)**   Closely connected with the circus world is the world of carnivals and itinerant sideshows. Funfairs and fairgrounds have figured in many films; in some, they provide the setting for the film's story. They make a good background for horror films. The same applies to waxworks exhibitions.

Sally of the Sawdust (25) D. W. Griffith. *Dante's Inferno* (35) Harry Lachman. *Poppy* (36) A. Edward Sutherland. *Road Show* (41) Hal Roach. *Nightmare Alley* (47) Edmund Goulding. *So Long at the Fair* (GB 50) Anthony Darnborough, Terence Fisher. *Gorilla at Large* (54) Harmon Jones. *The Glass Cage* (GB 55) Montgomery Tully *aka The Glass Tomb*. *Death of Ocean View Park* (79 TV) E. W. Swackhamer. *Carny* (80) Robert Kaylor. *The Funhouse* (81) Tobe Hooper *aka Funhouse: Carnival of Terror*. *Something Wicked This Way Comes* (82) Jack Clayton. *The World of Tomorrow* (84) Lance Bird, Tom Johnson.

CITY SYMPHONY (City Symphony Film)   A type of avant-garde documentary that tries to capture the heartbeat of a city by combining a kaleidoscope of images in its montage. The genre presents rhythmic views of city life usually from dawn to dusk. It was inaugurated by Alberto Cavalcanti's *Rien que les heures* (1926). In a way, the genre culminated with Dziga-Vertov's *Chelovek s kinoapparatom / Man with a Movie Camera* (1928), although other filmmakers have also persisted in giving their own panoramic interpretations of modern cities.

Rien que les heures (F 26) Alberto Cavalcanti *aka Nothing But the Hours*. *Berlin, die Sinfonie der Grosstadt* (G 27) Walther Ruttman *aka Berlin, Symphony of a City*. *Chelovek s kinoapparatom* (USSR 28) Dziga Vertov, Mikhail Kaufman (photography) *aka (The) Man with a Movie Camera*. *City Symphony* (G 29) Herman G. Weinberg. *A Propos de Nice, Point de vue documentée* (F 29) Jean Vigo. *São Paulo: Sinfonia de una Metropoli* (Braz 29) Adalbert Kemedy. *The City* (39) Willard Van Dyke, Ralph Steiner. *Människor i stad* (Sw 47) Arne Scuksdorff *aka People of the City / Rhythm of a City / Symphony of a City*. *Waverly Steps* (GB 47) John Eldridge. *Go! Go! Go!* (63) Marie Menken.

Civilian War Films, Civil War Films   *see*   **WAR FILM**

CLASSIC (Cinema Classic, Film Classic, Screen Classic)   A film which can withstand the test of time without losing its appeal or its ability to attract the viewer, or a film considered a classic by critics and experts due to its innovative craftsmanship or artistic value. All film producing countries have their quota of classics. Also, it is obvious that every film genre has within its ranks its acknowledged list of classics. For instance, *Casablanca* (1942) is a well-known World War II film classic and *The Maltese Falcon* (1941), a private-eye classic. Silent classics, all-time classics, and foreign classics are often ready-made labels for coffee-table books.[19]

The Wizard of Oz (39) Victor Fleming. *The Maltese Falcon* (41) John Huston *aka The Gent from Frisco*. *Casablanca* (42) Michael Curtiz.

Classic Comedy *see* **SLAPSTICK**

Classical Serial *see* **TELEVISION NOVELIZATION**

Classroom Film *see* **FACTUAL FILM: Educational Film**

Clay Animation, Claymation *see* **ANIMATED FILM: Object Animation Films**

Clerical Comedies, Clerical Melodramas *see* **RELIGIOUS FILM**

CLIFFHANGER The term is associated with the film serials of yesteryear, which often used to end with a cliffhanger that was resolved in the next episode. But the word cliffhanger applies equally to any film, short or feature length, in which suspense plays a major part. *See* **SERIAL**.

Clinker *see* **TURKEY**

CLIP (Film Clip) A film clip is a short piece of film, usually taken from a longer film, shown independently for its own intrinsic value, to make a point, for advertising purposes, or it may be used as an insert in a movie to make some analogy or other. *See also* **MUSIC VIDEO**.

Cloak and Dagger Drama *see* **SPY FILM**

Cloak-and-Sandal Epic *see* **PEPLUM**

Cloak-and-Sword Romances *see* **SWASHBUCKLER**

Close View Genre *see* **SHORT: Multi-Shot Film**

Closed-End Series *see* **TELEVISION SERIES**

Clown Comedy *see* **SLAPSTICK**

Cocaine Movies *see* **DRUG FILM**

CO-FEATURE A film of moderate budget usually forming part of a double bill. B-features fall under this category. *See also* **B-MOVIE**.

Cold Print *see* **HARD-CORE PORNO FILM**

Cold War Film *see* **WAR FILM**

Collage Animation Films   *see*   **ANIMATED FILM: Animated Collage Film**

Collage Films   *see*   **UNDERGROUND FILM**

College Campus Musical   *see*   **MUSICAL: Campus Musicals**

COLLEGE FILM (Campus Movie, College-Life Film, Collegiate Film, College-Oriented Movie)   This group of films has frequently focussed on university and college activities. It is an impressive body of films which clearly show that a separate genre of college movies has developed through the years. Since the twenties (although there are earlier college films), the genre has mainly included comedies, musicals, and melodramas, with the occasional "serious" drama. This latter category has been more prominent since the late sixties and early seventies when universities were in upheaval due to students' protests and demands for change in the education system. A great number of college films, especially campus comedies, fall equally under the genre of sports movies (*see* **FOOTBALL FILM**).

Among the films dealing with life on campus and with students and professors interacting, two divisions emerge — films which are set in civil institutions of higher learning and films which are set in military academies training cadets to become officers in some branch of the Armed Forces. These comprise only a small number. A survey of college-life films has been provided by Wiley Lee Umphlett in *The Movies Go to College* (Cranbury, NJ: Associated University Presses, 1984).

College (27) James W. Horne. *She Loves Me Not* (34) Elliott Nugent. *The Gladiator* (38) Edward Sedgwick. *The Male Animal* (42) Elliott Nugent. *Girl Crazy* (43) Norman Taurog. *Apartment for Peggy* (48) George Seaton. *It Happens Every Spring* (49) Lloyd Bacon. *Mr. Belvedere Goes to College* (49) Elliott Nugent. *The West Point Story* (50) Roy Del Ruth *aka Fine and Dandy*. *A Woman of Distinction* (50) Edward Buzzell. *The Strange One* (57) Jack Garfein *aka End as a Man*. *Sorority Girl* (57) Roger Corman. *Sex Kittens Go to College* (60) Albert Zugsmith *aka The Beauty and the Robot*. *The Nutty Professor* (62) Jerry Lewis. *The Sterile Cuckoo* (69) Alan J. Pakula *aka Pookie*. *Drive, He Said* (70) Jack Nicholson. *The End of the Road* (70) Aram Avakian. *R.P.M.* * (70) Stanley Kramer *aka R.P.M. / R.P.M.* * Revolutions Per Minute*. *The Paper Chase* (73) James Bridges. *Fraternity Row* (77) Thomas J. Tobin. *National Lampoon's Animal House* (78) John Landis *aka Animal House*. *Midnight Madness* (80) David Wechter, Michael Nankin. *A Population of One* (Can 80 TV) Robert Sherrinn. *An Officer and a Gentleman* (81) Taylor Hackford. *Taps* (81) Harold Becker. *The Lords of Discipline* (82) Franc Roddam. *Soulman* (86) Steve Miner.

College-Life Film   *see*   **COLLEGE FILM**

College Musicals   *see*   **MUSICAL: Campus Musicals**

College-Oriented Movie, Collegiate Film   *see*   **COLLEGE FILM**

COLONIAL FILM   All films which are set in foreign lands upon which a colonial power had or has jurisdiction and exerts its influence politically, socially or economically may be classed as colonial films. The biggest body of such films is the British Empire film (q.v.), but besides the United Kingdom and American-produced films dealing with the British Empire, other colonial powers, such as France, have maintained a substantial production of colonial films. Colonial films at present tend to expose and denounce rather than uphold and applaud former colonial practices.

Baroud (F 31) Rex Ingram, Alice Terry, André Jaeger-Schmitt *aka Les Hommes bleus / Love in Morocco.   Il grande appello* (It 36) Mario Camerini *aka Africa / Italia! / The Last Roll-Call / Rinnegato.   Sentinelle di Bronzo* (It 37) Romolo Marcellini.   *Luciano Serra pilota* (It 38) Goffredo Alessandrini. *Zulu* (GB 63) Cy Enfield.   *Lord Jim* (US /GB 65) Richard Brooks.   *Khartoum* (GB 66) Basil Dearden, Eliot Elisolen, Yakima Canutt *aka Battle for Khartoum.   Der leone have sept cabecas / Il leone a sette teste* (F / It 70) Glauber Rocha *aka The Lion Has Seven Heads.   La Victoire en chantant* (F / G / IvC 76) Jean-Jacques Annaud *aka Black and White in Colour / Black Victory / Noirs et blancs en couleurs.   Coup de torchon* (F 81) Bertrand Tavernier *aka Clean Slate.   Heat and Dust* (GB 82) James Ivory.   *A Passage to India* (GB 84) David Lean.   *Sarraounia* (F / Maurit 86) Mea Hondo.   *Kitchen Toto* (GB 87) Harry Hook.   *Camp de Thiaroye* (Sen / Alg / Tun 88) Ousmane Sembène, Thierno Faty Sow *aka Camp Thiaroye.*

Colonial Films   *see*   **BRITISH EMPIRE FILM**

Color-Converted Film   *see*   **COLOR FILM: Colorized Film**

COLOR FILM (Color Motion Picture)   The desire to reproduce natural color dates from the inception of photography and motion pictures. Very early examples of color films exist; it took, however, a great deal of research and experimentation before color motion pictures became a technically and commercially viable proposition. At the beginning of film production, black-and-white pictures were laboriously hand painted frame by frame in as many as six different colors. George Méliès' *Voyage à travers l'impossible* (1904) is a good example of a handcolored film. Later, stencil coloring processes were used but, as with hand coloring, were too expensive. Tinting and toning or a combination of both came next. Finally, additive and subtractive color processes were patented and continually improved.[20] An early two-color additive process invented by the Englishman George Albert Smith (1864–1959) was patented in 1906. His eight-minute-long Kinemacolor *A Visit to the Seaside* (1908) was the first successful film in natural color. Other films in Kinemacolor followed, including the first feature-length motion picture, *The World, the Flesh and the Devil* (1914), a melodrama chiefly remembered for its color rather than its artistry. Additive color processes were technically less efficient and the subtractive methods gained the upper hand.

In 1915, the Technicolor Motion Picture Corporation was established; it produced the first American feature-length color film, *The Gulf Between*

(1917), a five-reeler in two-color additive process. In 1922 premiered *The Toll of the Sea*, the first two-color subtractive Technicolor feature, and in 1932 the first film in three-color Technicolor, a very innovative color system, was seen in the Walt Disney cartoon *Flowers and Trees* in the "Silly Symphonies" series. The first dramatic short was *La Cucaracha* (1934) and the first feature made in the new process was Rouben Mamoulian's *Becky Sharp* (1935), a landmark film whose original Technicolor negative is no longer extant.[21] The Technicolor process dominated world markets until the advent of Eastman Color (an effective photographic system introduced to professional filmmaking in 1952) and of other similar three-color processes.[22]

Black-and-white film (q.v.) predominated until the mid–1950s in the United States and the mid–1960s in the United Kingdom; afterwards, the production of color films increased and, at present, most films produced the world over are in color. Color has been used for startling and extraordinary effects by some major filmmakers such as Federico Fellini, Michelangelo Antonioni, Luchino Visconti, Ingmar Bergman, Francis Ford Coppola, and others. With the appropriate application of color, it is possible to indicate time and place, convey atmosphere, and portray changes of mood. Many effects may be achieved by the selective use of color. A few features outstanding for their imaginative use of color are listed below.

> *Voyage à travers l'impossible* (F 04) George Méliès *aka An Impossible Voyage / Voyage Across the Impossible / Whirling the Worlds. A Visit to the Seaside* (GB 08) George Albert Smith [1st British color film]. *The World, the Flesh, and the Devil* (GB 14) F. Martin Thornton [1st feature-length film in color: Kinemacolor]. *The Gulf Between* (17) Wray Physioc. *The Toll of the Sea* (22) Chester M. Franklin [1st Technicolor feature in two-color subtractive process]. *Flowers and Trees* (32) Bert Gillett [1st film made in three-color Technicolor; 29th in Walt Disney's "Silly Symphonies" series]. *La Cucaracha* (34) Lloyd Corrigan [1st three-strip, live-action Technicolor film]. *Becky Sharp* (35) Rouben Mamoulian [1st feature in three-color Technicolor]. *Black Narcissus* (GB 46) Michael Powell, Emeric Pressburger. *Jigoku-mon* (J 52) Teinosuke Kukame Kinugasa *aka Gate of Hell. Moulin Rouge / Moulin-Rouge* (GB / F /US 52) John Huston. *Track of the Cat* (54) William Wellman. *Moby Dick* (56) John Huston. *Il gattopardo / Le Guépard / The Leopard* (F / It / US 63) Luchino Visconti. *Il deserto rosso / Le désert rouge* (It / F 63-64) Michelangelo Antonioni *aka The Red Desert. Giulietta degli spiriti / Juliette des esprits / Julia und die Geister* (F / It / G 65) Federico Fellini *aka Juliet of the Spirits. Blow-Up / Blow Up* (GB / It 66) Michelangelo Antonioni *aka Blowup. The Taming of the Shrew / La bisbetica domata* (US / It 66) Franco Zeffirelli. *Elvira Madigan* (Sw 67) Bo Widerberg. *The Godfather* (71) Francis Ford Coppola. *Morte a Venezia / Mort à Venise* (It / F 70) Luchino Visconti *aka Death in Venice. Don't Look Now / A Venezia . . . un dicembre rosso shocking* (GB / It 73) Nicolas Roeg. *Viskningar och rop* (Sw 71-73) Ingmar Bergman *aka Cries and Whispers.*

——**Colorized Film (Color-Converted Film, Colorized Version, Computer-Colored Film)**   A colorized film is simply an old black-and-white movie, often a classic, transmuted into color by the computerized process known as colorization (or color conversion). It was developed in 1978 by Ralph Weinger, an electronics engineer. Such films as *Captain Blood* (1935), *The Maltese Falcon* (1941), *It's a Wonderful Life* (1946), *Night of the Living Dead* (1968), and many others are now available in color. The trend, started in the eighties, has been denounced by those who oppose the practice as an outright desecration of original films never intended to be in color. It is indeed a kind of tampering with films that should be considered as finished works.

Captain Blood (35) Michael Curtiz. *Topper* (37) Norman Z. McLeod. *The Maltese Falcon* (41) John Huston *aka The Gent from Frisco.* *Yankee Doodle Dandy* (42) Michael Curtiz. *It's a Wonderful Life* (46) Frank Capra. *Night of the Living Dead* (67-68) George A. Romero *aka Flesh Eaters / Night of Anubis / Night of the Flesh Eaters.*

Combat Movie *see* **WAR FILM**

Combat Spectacular *see* **WAR FILM: War Spectaculars**

Combined Live Action and Animation *see* **ANIMATED FILM: Mixed-Media Films**

Comedies and Parodies *see* **WESTERN**

COMEDY (Comic Film, Film Comedy, Funny Film, Humorous Film, Light Film, Screen Comedy)   Comedy is a very complex topic whose definition has always been open to contention. There is no formal body of theoretical works or poetics explaining the nature of comedy as there is, for instance, for tragedy. Comedy has generally been categorized as a genre, but the impossibility of categorizing it as such has also been maintained, as comedy is a too broad label that encompasses too many types of comic films; and what is more to the point, it is also found within other film genres, any other genre as a matter of fact, when comicality is the overall intention of the filmmaker. Thus, there are war comedies, Western comedies, comedy musicals, horror comedies, and many other similar groupings. Perhaps, then, although it is possible to think of comedy as a mega-genre, it is better to define comedy in terms of comic form including many possible types or variants. This does not prevent the categorization of different types of comedy (slapstick, screwball comedy, comedy of manners, parody) as subgenres of the megagenre, or genres of their own if there is a large body of films that share similar characteristics. In the present work, they are given separate entries.

A distinction is possible between silent comedy, which perforce relies on and has to emphasize the visual element, and sound comedy which normally relies to a greater degree on the spoken word and sound for its comic effect.

Not all types of comedy travel well. This applies specially to ethnic or national comedy which is best understood in the ethnic group or country in which it originates; *see,* for example, Italian farcical comedy (the films of Totò, among others), the British "Carry On" series, or Australian "Ocker" comedies.

Comic films go back to the very beginning of cinematography; in fact, they may be traced back to the Lumière brothers' film *L'Arroseur arrosé* which had its premiere at the Grand Café in Paris on 28 December 1895. The film is credited with using for the first time a person in a comedy role, a real gardener in the employment of Mme Lumière at Lyons, acting the part of a gardener who, in the film, gets sprinkled when a youngster plays a prank on him by stepping on the gardener's hose interrupting the flow of water that hits the gardener in his face when the puzzled man looks at the hose's nozzle.

A further distinction could also be made between the comedy films in which a well-known comedian dominates to a large extent the film's action and those films which use the comic form per se without relying on well-known comic personalities. Still another differentiation, as indicated above, is possible between films which emphasize physical action and films which give greater importance to the spoken word. Most different types of comedy are included under generic entries of their own (e.g., Black comedy); comedies within major genres are mentioned at times under a main genre heading (e.g., Gangster film) but when this is not the case, it must be restated that any genre permits the comic form. *See* **ANARCHIC COMEDY, BLACK COMEDY, CAMP FILM, CANDID CAMERA COMEDY, COMEDY-DRAMA, COMEDY OF MANNERS,** *COMMEDIA ALL'ITALIANA,* **DOMESTIC COMEDY, EALING COMEDY, FARCE, GADGET COMEDY, LOCAL COMEDY, PARODY, POPULIST COMEDY, ROMANTIC COMEDY, RURAL COMEDY, SATIRE, SCREWBALL COMEDY, SENTIMENTAL COMEDY, SEX COMEDY, SITUATION COMEDY, SLAPSTICK, SOCIAL COMEDY, SOPHISTICATED COMEDY, STAND-UP COMEDY.**

L'Arroseur arrosé (F 1895) Louis Lumière *aka L'Arroseur est arrosé / Le Jardinier / The Hoser Hosed / The Sprayer Sprayed / Teasing the Gardener / Watering the Gardener.* **Tillie's Punctured Romance** (14) Mack Sennett *aka Dressler No. 1 / For the Love of Tillie / Marie's Millions / Tillie's Big Romance / Tillie's Nightmare* [1st full-length Hollywood comedy]. **The Gold Rush** (25) Charlie Chaplin. **It's a Gift** (34) Norman Z. McLeod. **Earthworm Tractors** (36) Ray Enright *aka A Natural Born Salesman.* **The Doctor Takes a Wife** (40) Alexander Hall. **Never Give a Sucker an Even Break** (41) Edward Cline *aka The Great Man / What a Man!* **The Bachelor and the Bobby-Soxer** (47) Irving Reis *aka Bachelor Knight.* **Jour de fête** (F 48) Jacques Tati *aka The Big Day / Jour de Fête (Day of the Fair) / The Village Fair.* **Inspector General** (49) Henry Koster. **Luci del varietà** (It 50) Alberto Lattuada, Federico Fellini *aka Lights of Variety / Limelight / Variety Lights.* **Lo sceicco bianco** (It 51) Federico Fellini *aka The White Sheikh.* **Les Vacances de M. Hulot** (F 52) Jacques Tati *aka [Monsieur] Mr.*

Hulot's Holiday. *Love in the Afternoon* (57) Billy Wilder. *No Time for Sergeants* (58) Mervyn LeRoy. *Some Like It Hot* (59) Billy Wilder. *Anonima Cocottes / Petites Femmes en haute finance* (It / F 60) Camillo Mastrocinque. *One, Two, Three* (61) Billy Wilder. *Tant qu'on a la santé* (F 65) Pierre Etaix. *Morgan — A Suitable Case for Treatment* (GB 66) Karel Reisz *aka Morgan! Alexandre le bienheureux* (F 67) Yves Robert *aka Alexandre / Very Happy Alexandre.* *Le Grand Amour* (F 68) Pierre Etaix. *Serafino / Serafino ou l'amour aux champs* (It / F 68) Pietro Germi. *M*A*S*H* (69) Robert Altman *aka MASH.* *Le Distrait* (F 70) Pierre Richard *aka The Daydreamer. Dramma della gelosia — tutti i particolari in cronaca* (It / Sp 70) Ettore Scola *aka A Drama of Jealousy (and Other Things...) / Jealousy, Italian Style / The Pizza Triangle.* *Raphaël ou le Débauché* (F 70) Michel Deville. *Per grazia ricevuta* (It 71) Nino Manfredi *aka The Cross-Eyed Saint / For Grace Received. Sex Shop / Quello che già conosci sul sesso e non prendi più sul serio* (F / It / G 72) Claude Berri. *Malizia* (It 73) Salvatore Samperi *aka Malicious. Les Valseuses* (F 73) Bertrand Blier *aka Going Places / Making It. Les Bidasses s'en vont en guerre / Die Trottel von der 3, Kompanie* (F / G 74) Claude Zidi. *Lily, aime-moi* (F 74) Maurice Dugowson. *Profumo di donna / Parfum de femme* (F / It 74) Dino Risi *aka Scent of a Woman / That Female Scent. Le Sauvage / Il mio uomo è un selvaggio* (F / It 75) Jean-Paul Rappeneau *aka Lovers Like Us / The Sauvage. Comme sur des roulettes* (F 76) Nina Companeez. *Le Jouet* (F 76) Francis Veber *aka Jack in the Box. Oh, God!* (76) Carl Reiner. *Foul Play* (78) Colin Higgins. *Up in Smoke* (78) Lou Adler. *The Jerk* (79) Carl Reiner. *The Blues Brothers* (80) John Landis. *Caddyshack* (80) Harold Ramis. *48 HRS* (82) Walter Hill. *Bianco rosso e Verdone* (It 83) Carlo Verdone *aka White Red and Green. Una gita scolastica* (It 83) Pupi Avati *aka A School Outing. Crocodile Dundee / "Crocodile" Dundee* (Aust / US 85) Peter Faiman. *Back to School* (86) Alan Metter. *Big* (88) Penny Marshall. *The Cook, the Thief, His Wife & Her Lover / Le cuisinier, le voleur, sa femme et son amant* (GB / F 89) Peter Greenaway.

Comedy Fantasy   *see*   **FANTASY: Fantasy-Comedy**

Comedy Musicals   *see*   **MUSICAL**

COMEDY OF MANNERS (Drawing-Room Comedy, High Comedy, Polite Comedy)   A comedy form and label mostly employed in theatrical parlance, but which has also its counterpart in cinema. Many types of comedy (romantic comedy, screwball comedy, sex comedy, sophisticated comedy) are in fact comedy of manners. The comedy of manners proper satirizes or criticizes the upper classes and the wealthy, but its meaning has been broadened to include any social group which adheres to or follows an affected or well-defined code of social behavior. The comedy of manners makes fun of the rituals that members of a particular social class practice. The French call it *comédie des moeurs* and they have excelled in the form.

The Marriage Circle (23) Ernst Lubitsch. *Un Chapeau de paille d'Italie* (F 27) René Clair *aka The Horse Ate the Hat / The Italian Straw Hat. Private*

Lives (31) Sidney Franklin.   *The Animal Kingdom* (32) Edward H. Griffith *aka The Woman in His House.   Our Betters* (33) George Cukor.   *The Three-Cornered Moon* (33) Elliot Nugent.   *The Awful Truth* (37) Leo McCarey.   *La Règle du jeu* (F 39) Jean Renoir *aka Les Caprices de Marianne / La Chasse en Sologne / Fair Play / The Rule of the Game /Rules of the Game.   Two-Faced Woman* (41) George Cukor.   *On Approval* (GB 44) Clive Brook.   *A Royal Scandal* (45) Ernst Lubitsch, Otto Preminger.   *La Ronde* (F / It 50) Max Ophüls *aka The Round Dance. The Importance of Being Earnest* (GB 52) Anthony Asquith.   *Sommarnattens leende* (Sw 55) Ingmar Bergman *aka Smiles of a Summer Night.   The Swan* (55) Charles Vidor. *Ma nuit chez Maud* (F 69) Eric Rohmer *aka My Night at Maud's / My Night with Maud* [3rd in the series of 6 "Contes moraux" / "Moral Tales" (1962-72)].   *Le Souffle au coeur / Soffio al cuore / Herzflimmern* (F / It / G 70) Louis Malle *aka Dearest Love / Murmur of the Heart.   A Midsummer Night's Sex Comedy* (82) Woody Allen *aka A Midsummer Night (a Sex Comedy).*

Comedy of Sexual Manners   *see*   **SEX COMEDY**

Comedy War Films   *see*   **WAR FILM**

COMEDY-DRAMA (Seriocomedy)   A film which mixes comedy and drama is often referred to as a comedy-drama. Many films share both the comic and dramatic forms, but in order to be successful, the comic and dramatic elements have to be well-integrated. Hollywood has a long-standing tradition of comedy-dramas; they are equally popular in other centers of film production.

The Social Secretary (16) John Emerson *aka Social Secretary* (24): reedited version.   *Call Her Savage* (32) John F. Dillon.   *La Femme du boulanger* (F 38) Marcel Pagnol *aka The Baker's Wife.   Love Affair* (39) Leo McCarey.   *Pardon My Past* (45) Leslie Fenton.   *The Farmer's Daughter* (47) H. C. Potter.   *People Will Talk* (51) Joseph L. Mankiewicz.   *Bus Stop* (56) Joshua Logan *aka The Wrong Kind of Girl.   El cochecito* (Sp 59) Marco Ferreri *aka The Wheelchair.   The Apartment* (60) Billy Wilder.   *Captain Newman, M.D.* (63) David Miller.   *Ostre sledované vlaky* (Cz 66) Jiri Menzel *aka A Difficult Love / Closely Observed Trains / Closely Watched Trains / A Close Watch on the Trains.   The Landlord* (70) Hal Ashby.   *César et Rosalie / E simpatico, ma gli romperei il muso* (F / It / G 72) Claude Sautet *aka Cesar and Rosalie.   The Front* (76) Martin Ritt.   *Charles et Lucie* (F 79) Nelly Kaplan.   *Educating Rita* (GB 83) Lewis Gilbert.   *The Gig* (85) Frank D. Gilroy.   *Hannah and Her Sisters* (86) Woody Allen.   *Nothing in Common* (86) Garry Marshall.   *Babettes gaestebud* (Den / Nor 86-87) Gabriel Axel *aka Babette's Feast.   Wish You Were Here* (GB 87) David Leland.   *The Accidental Tourist* (88) Lawrence Kasdan.   *Crimes and Misdemeanors* (89) Woody Allen.   *Do the Right Thing* (89) Spike Lee.   *Enemies, a Love Story* (89) Paul Mazursky.

Comedy-Thriller   *see*   **HAUNTED HOUSE COMEDY**

Comic Chase Film   *see*   **CHASE FILM**

Comic Film   *see*   **COMEDY**

Comic Pornographic Feature   *see*   **HARD-CORE PORNO FILM**

Comic Strip Superheroes Films   *see*   **FANTASY FILM**

Coming Attraction Trailer   *see*   **TRAILER**

COMING-OF-AGE MOVIE   The stage through which one must pass to attain adulthood and be socially responsible is frequently labelled coming-of-age. It may be a traumatic or sweet moment; it is always a momentous occasion as childhood dreams are left behind and new realities take over. The coming-of-age picture focuses on growing up or, in other words, reaching maturity.

Anthony Adverse (36) Mervyn LeRoy.   *The Member of the Wedding* (52) Fred Zinnemann.   *I vitelloni / Les Inutiles* (It / F 53) Federico Fellini *aka The Loafers / Spivs / The Young and the Passionate.*   *Aparajito* (Ind 56) Satyajit Ray *aka The Unvanquished* [2nd film in the Apu trilogy which includes *Pather Panchali* (Ind 55) and *Apur Sansar* (Ind 59)].   *Ostre sledované vlaky* (Cz 66) Jirí Menzel *aka A Difficult Love / Closely Observed Trains / Closely Watched Trains / A Close Watch on the Trains.*   *Le Souffle au coeur / Soffio al cuore / Herzflimmern* (F / It / G 70) Louis Malle *aka Dearest Love / Murmur of the Heart.*   *Summer of '42* (71) Robert Mulligan.   *American Graffiti* (73) George Lucas.   *The Getting of Wisdom* (Aust 77) Bruce Beresford.   *The Mango Tree* (Aust 77) Kevin Dobson.   *The Boss' Son* (78) Bobby Roth.   *Breaking Away* (79) Peter Yates.   *Tendres cousines / Zärtliche Cousinen* (F / G 80) David Hamilton *aka Cousins in Love.*   *Diner* (82) Barry Levinson.   *Tex* (82) Tim Hunter.   *Among the Cinders* (NZ 83) Rolf Haedrich.   *The Flamingo Kid* (84) Garry Marshall.   *Mitt liv som hund* (Sw 84) Lasse Hallström *aka My Life as a Dog.*   *My American Cousin* (Can 84) Sandy Wilson.   *Dutch Girls* (GB / Hol 85 TV) Giles Foster.   *Heaven Help Us* (85) Michael Dinner.   *Le Grand Chemin* (F 86) Jean-Loup Hubert *aka The Grand Highway.*   *Lucas* (86) David Seltzer.   *Square Dance* (87) Daniel Petrie *aka Home Is Where the Heart Is.*   *The Year My Voice Broke* (Aust 87) John Duigan.

Command Performance   *see*   **TELEVISION PROGRAM: Rerun**

COMMEDIA ALL'ITALIANA **(Comedy Italian Style)**   A characteristic type of Italian comedy which emerged in the late 1950s and early 1960s. It presented a distinctive fresco of Italian customs and idiosyncracies as it satirized and poked gentle fun at the aspirations and foibles of the high and low without discrimination. Through the 1960s it provided insight into the Italian character and, in the process, its humor crossed national borders and became well known and appreciated abroad. Dino Risi, Elio Petri, Mario Monicelli, Pietro Germi, Alberto Lattuada, Luigi Zampa, Luigi Comencini, Luciano Salce, and Ettore Scola are some of the directors who excelled in the form. Many actors and actresses (Marcello Mastroianni, Gian Maria Volontè, Vittorio Gassman, Nino Manfredi, Alberto Sordi, Ugo Tognazzi, Giancarlo Giannini, Monica Vitti, Catherine Spaak, Silvana

Pampanini, Stefania Sandrelli, Sandra Milo, Silvana Magnano, Sophia Loren, Sylva Koscina and others) figure among the most representative interpreters of the *commedia all'italiana*.

La grande guerra (It 59) Mario Monicelli *aka The Great War*. *Il mattatore* (It 59) Dino Risi *aka Love and Larceny*. *Il moralista* (It 59) Giorgio Bianchi. *Il vedovo* (It 59) Dino Risi. *Il vigile* (It 60) Luigi Zampa *aka The Cop*. *Divorzio all'italiana* (It 61) Pietro Germi *aka Divorce, Italian Style*. *Il federale* (It 61) Luciano Salce *aka The Fascist / The Party Official*. *Una vita difficile* (It 61) Dino Risi *aka A Difficult Life*. *Anni ruggenti* (It 62) Luigi Zampa *aka Roaring Years*. *Il commissario* (It 62) Luigi Comencini. *I compagni / Les Camarades* (It / F / Yug 62) Mario Monicelli *aka The Organizer / The Strikers*. *Mafioso* (It 62) Alberto Lattuada. *La marcia su Roma / La Marche sur Rome* (It / F 62) Dino Risi. *Il sorpasso* (It 62) Dino Risi *aka [The] Easy Life / The Overtaking*. *La voglia matta* (It 62) Luciano Salce *aka Crazy Desire / This Crazy Urge*. *La bella di Lodi* (It 63) Mario Missiroli. *Il boom* (It 63) Vittorio De Sica. *I mostri / Les Monstres* (It / F 63) Dino Risi. *La visita* (It 63) Antonio Pietrangeli. *Il disco volante* (It 64) Tinto Brass *aka The Flying Saucer*. *L'armata Brancaleone / L'Armée Brancaleone / Armada Brancaleón* (It / F / Sp 65) Mario Monicelli. *Io la conoscevo bene* (It 65) Antonio Pietrangeli *aka I Knew Her Well*. *Adulterio all'italiana* (It 66) Pasquale Festa Campanile *aka Adultery Italian Style*. *La ragazza con la pistola* (It 67) Mario Monicelli *aka The Girl with a Pistol*. *Colpo di stato* (It 68) Luciano Salce. *Infanzia, vocazione e prime esperienze di Giacomo Casanova veneziano* (It 69) Luigi Comencini *aka Casanova*. *Il merlo maschio* (It 70) Pasquale Festa Campanile *aka Secret Fantasy / The Virile Bird*. *Venga a prendere il caffé ... da noi* (It 70) Alberto Lattuada. *Telefoni bianchi* (It 75) Dino Risi *aka The Career of a Chambermaid / White Telephones*. *Basta che non si sappia in giro!* (It 76) Nanni Loy, Luigi Magni, Luigi Comencini *aka Nothing but Love*. *I nuovi mostri* (It 77) Mario Monicelli, Dino Risi, Ettore Scola.

Commedia dell'arte   *see*   **SLAPSTICK**

COMMERCIAL   Commercials—short films extolling the virtues of some product with the intention of inducing the public to buy it or offering the use of services available locally—were present at most cinemas and drive-ins before their use in film theaters started to fade in favor of advertising on television. Publicity films shown in film theaters have a duration of one to three minutes while commercials shown on television channels run from fifteen to sixty seconds. Advertising is the bread and butter of most commercial television stations which rely on the airtime bought by advertisers as their major source of revenue. Commercials have also been one of the main outlets for the work of filmmakers in the field of animation. Some commercials are so well-made that they have garnered praise and prizes at international competitions and film festivals.

Committed Documentary   *see*   **DOCUMENTARY**

COMPILATION FILM   Francis Doublier, a collaborator of the Lumière brothers, put together in 1898 a film made up of scenes from several Lumière films telling the story of the arrest and later imprisonment on Devil's Island of the Alsatian Jewish officer Alfred Dreyfus. Edwin S. Porter (1869-1941), in America, with the help of old shots of a fire department in action described the rescue of a mother and her child in *The Life of an American Fireman* (1902). These are two examples of what was to become a viable film form. Film compilations have gained momentum through the years and have covered diverse subjects in the nonfictional field and in the fictional to a much lesser extent. Compilation films have been made for instruction, information, propaganda and entertainment purposes.

The compilation film is made of already existing film footage or scenes from other films. The filmmaker reedits the material, rearranges it, and gives it new meaning. The filmmakers who specialize in this type of film have at their disposal unlimited footage of newsreels and documentaries to work with. The true compilation film relies on preexisting material; however, films like *Le Chagrin et la pitié* (1969) by Marcel Ophüls are interspersed with newly shot scenes of interviews and personal testimony pertinent to the case presented by the film. They are a successful, composite form. Fictional compilations, on the other hand, draw their material from fiction films to illustrate significant moments of a film genre or to highlight selective scenes from films by well-known screen comedians and superstars. The form is frequently used by television. Some television compilation films are excellently made and have earned high praise. An early book on the subject of the compilation film is Jay Leyda's *Films Beget Films* (New York: Hill and Wang, 1971).

Nonfiction Films: Padene dinasti Romanovikh (USSR 27) Esfir (Esther) Shub *aka The Fall of the Romanov Dynasty.* *Espagne 1937 / ¡España leal en Armas! (Madrid 1936)* (F / Sp 36) Luis Buñuel *aka Madrid 1936 or, Loyal Spain, Take Arms!* *World of Plenty* (GB 43) Paul Rotha. *The True Glory* (GB / US 45) Carol Reed, Garson Kanin. *The Pale Horseman* (46) Irving Jacoby. *Paris 1900* (F 47) Nicole Védrès. *Das Lied der Ströme* (EG 54) Joris Ivens *aka Song of the Rivers.* *Nuit et Brouillard* (F 55) Alain Resnais *aka Night and Fog.* *Mise Éire / I Am Ireland* (Ir 59) George Morrison [in Gaelic]. *Mourir à Madrid* (F 62) Frédéric Rossif *aka To Die in Madrid.* *The Great War* (GB / Can /Aust 64 TV) Sir Michael Redgrave [26 episodes]. *The Guns of August* (64) Nathan Kroll. *Le Chagrin et la pitié / Das Haus nebenan* (F / Swiz / G 69 TV) Marcel Ophüls *aka The Sorrow and the Pity.* *Le Bonheur dans 20 ans* (F 70) Albert Knobler, Michel Bouquet *aka Le bonheur dans vingt ans: Prague 1948-1968 / Happiness in Twenty Years.* *A Sense of Loss* (US / Swiz 72 TV) Marcel Ophüls. *The World at War* (GB 75 TV) Prod. Jeremy Isaacs [26 episodes].

Fiction Films: The Life of an American Fireman (02) Edwin S. Porter. *The Golden Age of Comedy* (57) Comp. Robert Youngson. *When Comedy Was King* (60) Comp. Robert Youngson. *Days of Thrills and Laughter* (61) Comp. Robert Youngson. *Harold Lloyd World of Comedy* (62) Comp. Harold Lloyd. *30 Years of Fun* (62) Comp. Robert Youngson. *Harold Lloyd Funny Side of Life* (63) Comp. Harold Lloyd *aka*

The Funny Side of Life. The Love Goddesses (64) Comp. Saul J. Turell, Graeme Ferguson. *MGM's Big Parade of Comedy* (64) Comp. Robert Youngson. *Censored* (65) Barry Mahon *aka This Picture Is Censored. The Crazy World of Laurel and Hardy* (65) Prod. Hal Roach. *Laurel and Hardy's Laughing 20s* (65) Comp. Robert Youngson. *And Now for Something Completely Different* (GB 71) Ian MacNaughton. *That's Entertainment!* (74) Jack Haley, Jr. *It's Showtime* (76) no director credited. *That's Entertainment, Part 2* (76) Gene Kelly. *It Came from Hollywood* (82) Andrew Solt, Malcolm Leo. *Terror in the Aisles* (84) Andrew J. Kuehn. *That's Dancing!* (85) Jack Haley, Jr. *Zombiethon* (86) Ken Dixon. *Dope Mania* (87) Johnny Legend, Jeff Vilencia.

Compilation Films   *see*   **SEX DOCUMENTARY**

Composite Film   *see*   **EPISODE FILM**

Computer Film, Computer-Generated Film, Computer Graphics, Computer-Made Film   *see*   **ANIMATED FILM: Computer-Animated Films**

Computer-Animated Films   *see*   **ANIMATED FILM**

Computer-Colored Film   *see*   **COLOR FILM: Colorized Film**

Concentration Camp War Films   *see*   **WAR FILM**

Concept Clip   *see*   **MUSIC VIDEO**

Concept Film   *see*   **FACTUAL FILM**

Conceptual Film   *see*   **STRUCTURAL FILM**

Conceptual Video   *see*   **MUSIC VIDEO**

Concert Film   *see*   **MUSICAL: Rock Concert Films**

Concrete Film   *see*   **ABSTRACT FILM, INDEPENDENT PRODUCTION**

CONFESSION FILM (Confession Story Genre, Fallen Woman Film)
Confession films are stories of girls gone astray and were popular in the early thirties, primarily among female audiences. This type of woman's picture portrayed heroines who easily gave up their virtue, prompted by self-sacrifice, seduced by some unscrupulous man, or tempted by the promise of an easy life. The end result was a series of heroines converted into martyrs having to atone for their sin. Often landed with babies and deserted by their seducers, they had to care alone for their offspring until, by the end of the picture, they convinced their seducer to make an honest woman of them or found a Good Samaritan who did so. *See also* **Confession Films** under **SOCIAL CONSCIOUSNESS FILM.**
The Divorcee (30) Robert Z. Leonard. *The Common Law* (31) Paul L. Stein. *The Easiest Way* (31) Jack Conway. *Possessed* (31) Clarence Brown. *Call Her Savage* (32) John F. Dillon. *Faithless* (32) Harry Beaumont.

Confession Films   *see*   **SOCIAL CONSCIOUSNESS FILM**

Confession Story Genre   *see*   **CONFESSION FILM**

Confession Tale   *see*   **SOCIAL CONSCIOUSNESS FILM: Confession Films**

CONSPIRACY FILM (Conspiracy Thriller, Conspiration Film, Paranoid Thriller, Political Conspiracy Film, Political Paranoid Thriller, Political Thriller)   The term conspiracy film covers films which deal with political or terrorist assassinations, government cover-ups and conspiracies in general. In today's society, the individual is, for the most part, helpless when made the target of unknown assailants, the hit men of government agencies, consortiums and corporations. He has become expendable. This paranoid fear that unknown enemies may strike at any time, the endangered person not even aware of what motivates the attack, or without any means of defense against the invisible threat, is the main theme governing many conspiration films. Some conspiracy films (e.g, *The Stepford Wives*, 1974) fall within the science fiction genre. For a broad discussion on conspiracy cinema, *see* Richard Dorfman, "Conspiracy City," *Journal of Popular Film and Television 7* (1980): 434–56. *See also* **POLITICAL THRILLER.**
> *The Tall Target* (51) Anthony Mann.   *Suddenly* (54) Lewis Allen.   *Intent to Kill* (GB 58) Jack Cardiff.   *Advise and Consent* (62) Otto Preminger.   *The Manchurian Candidate* (62) John Frankenheimer.   *Nine Hours to Rama* (63) Mark Robson.   *Rush to Judgement* (67) Emile de Antonio.   *The Groundstar Conspiracy / Requiem pour un espion* (US / Can 72) Lamond Johnson *aka The Plastic Man*.   *Executive Action* (73) David Miller.   *Nada / Sterminate "Gruppo Zero"* (F / It 73) Claude Chabrol *aka The Nada Gang*.   *The Parallax View* (74) Alan J. Pakula.   *The Stepford Wives* (74) Bryan Forbes.   *Three Days of the Condor* (75) Sidney Pollack.   *All the President's Men* (76) Alan J. Pakula.   *The Lincoln Conspiracy* (77) James L. Conway.   *Le Point de mire* (F 77) Jean-Claude Tramont.   *Sleeping Dogs* (NZ 77) Roger Donaldson.   *Winter Kills* (79) William Richert.   *The Kidnapping of the President* (Can 79) George Mendeluk.   *Blow Out* (81) Brian DePalma.   *Beyond the Doors* (83) Larry Buchanan.   *Edge of Darkness* (GB 85 TV) Martin Campbell [originally in 6 parts].   *La historia oficial* (Arg 85) Luis Puenzo *aka The Official Story*.   *Under Siege* (85 TV) Roger Young.   *Ground Zero* (Aust 86) Michael Pattinson, Bruce Myles.   *JFK* (91) Oliver Stone.

Conspiracy Thriller, Conspiration Film   *see*   **CONSPIRACY FILM**

Contamination-Mutation Film   *see*   **NUCLEAR FILM**

Contemporary Melodrama   *see*   **MELODRAMA**

Contemporary Western   *see*   **WESTERN: Modern Westerns**

Continental Western   *see*   **SPAGHETTI WESTERN**

Continuous Serial   *see*   **SOAP OPERA**

CONTRACT FILM   A term used for a film whose production costs, by legal agreement, are to be paid by an investor or sponsor such as a film studio or production company.

Cop Movie *see* **POLICE FILM;** *see also* **GANGSTER FILM: Cop Movies**

Copper Films *see* **POLICE FILM**

Co-Prod *see* **CO-PRODUCTION**

CO-PRODUCTON (Co-Prod) The term simply means that two or more countries have participated in the film's production by contributing finance and talent. There are official (by mutual agreement among governments) and unofficial co-productions. Seven countries intervened in the production of *Soldati svobodi* (1977), a Russian-Bulgarian-Hungarian-East German-Polish-Rumanian-Czechoslovakian co-production. There have also been a few five-country co-productions. It has been stated that multinational co-productions tend to obliterate national film identity. They have their advantages, too, as co-productions usually enjoy equal distribution rights in their respective countries. Co-productions also include films of one single country in which different companies have participated. Co-producing is common practice today.

The Call of the Wild / Ruf der Wildnis / Il richiamo della foresta / L'Appel de la forêt (GB / G / Sp / It / F 72) Ken Annakin. *Soldati svobodi* (USSR / Bulg / Hung / EG / Pol / Rum / Cz 77) Yuri Ozerov [in 4 parts] *aka Soldiers of Freedom.* *West Indies / Les Nègres marrons de la liberté* (Tun / Mali / IvC / Maurit / Alg / Sen / F 79) Med Hondo *aka West Indies Story.*

Cornerstone Film *see* **SEMINAL FILM**

Costume Drama *see* **COSTUME FILM**

COSTUME FILM (Costume Drama, Costumer, Costume Spectacle) A film in which spectacle and pageantry form an integral part of the picture's appeal. Costume pictures appeared early in the history of motion pictures (e.g., *The Execution of Mary Queen of Scots*, 1895). Film epics, adventure movies set in the past, historical films, and fantasy films that rely to a large extent on panoply (e.g., *Excalibur*, 1981) qualify as costume films.

The Execution of Mary Queen of Scots (1895) Alfred E. Clark. *The Hunchback of Notre Dame* (23) Wallace Worsley. *The House of Rothschild* (34) Alfred L. Werker. *La Kermesse héroïque / Die klugen Frauen* (F / G 35) Jacques Feyder *aka Carnival in Flanders.* *A Tale of Two Cities* (35) Jack Conway. *Marie Antoinette* (38) W. S. Van Dyke II. *The Private Lives of Elizabeth and Essex* (39) Michael Curtiz *aka Elizabeth the Queen.* *The Man in Grey* (GB 43) Leslie Arliss. *Young Bess* (53) George Sidney. *Desirée* (54) Henry Koster. *The Virgin Queen* (55) Henry Koster. *Diane* (56) David Miller. *Vanina Vanini* (It / F 64) Roberto Rossellini *aka The Betrayal.* *Cleopatra* (US / GB 63) Joseph L. Mankiewicz, Rouben Mamoulian. *Mary, Queen of Scots* (71) Charles Jarrott. *Henry VIII and His Six Wives* (GB 72) Waris Hussein. *The Three Musketeers* (Pan / Sp 73) Richard Lester *aka The Queen's Diamonds* [followed by *The Four Musketeers* (Pan / Sp 73) and *The Return of the Musketeers* (GB / F / Sp 89) also by Lester]. *Allonsanfa 'n* (It 73-74) Paolo & Vittorio Taviani *aka*

Allonsanfan. Barry Lyndon (GB 75) Stanley Kubrick. *Excalibur* (GB /
Ire 81) John Boorman *aka Knights / Knights Film / Merlin Lives. Pirates*
(F / Tun 86) Roman Polanski.

Costume Spectacle *see* **COSTUME FILM**

Costumer *see* **COSTUME FILM**

Costumer Sexers *see* **SOFT-CORE SEX-EXPLOITATION FILM**

Counter Commercial *see* **TELEVISION COMMERCIAL**

Countess Báthory Films *see* **VAMPIRE FILM**

Country-Doctor Picture *see* **HOSPITAL FILM**

Country Movie *see* **REDNECK MOVIE**

Court-Martial Dramas *see* **WAR FILM**

Court-Métrage *see* **SHORT**

Courtroom Drama, Courtroom Picture *see* **LAWYER FILM**

Courtship-Romance Musicals *see* **MUSICAL**

Coverage *see* **NEWSFILM**

Cowboy Film *see* **WESTERN**

Crash Film *see* **RAILWAY FILM**

Crash-and-Wreck Film *see* **CHASE FILM**

Crazy Comedy *see* **ANARCHIC COMEDY, SCREWBALL COM-
EDY**

Creature Feature *see* **MONSTER MOVIE**

Crime Drama *see* **CRIME FILM**

CRIME FILM (Crime Drama, Criminal Film) As the population of
cities grew, so crime grew with them. In its ramifications it reached all levels
of society and permeated the countryside as well. It was only natural that
the film industry should make it one of its major and most enduring subjects. Indeed, crime films are one of the most important genres of the
cinema. Crime is, however, a vast subject and crime film too broad a label
embracing many subgenres. Although some general surveys band together
all movies that deal with crime, it is best to treat the subgenres separately.[23]
Some of these subgenres have developed and matured into full genres (e.g.,
the gangster film), others are in the process of doing so. The following
subgenres of the criminal film dealing with the perpetration of crime are
listed as individual entries: **CAPER FILM, CONSPIRACY FILM, EX-
POSÉ FILM, FILM NOIR, GANGSTER FILM, GIALLO, LAWYER**

FILM, MOTORCYCLE MOVIE, MYSTERY FILM, POLICE FILM, PRISON FILM, PRIVATE DETECTIVE FILM, PSYCHOPATHIC THRILLER, SOCIAL CONSCIOUSNESS FILM, SPY FILM, THRILLER, VICE FILM, VIGILANTE FILM, WHODUNIT.
Early films such as Edwin S. Porter's *The Great Train Robbery* (1903), *The Great Bank Robbery* (1903), D. W. Griffith's *The Musketeers of Pig Alley* (1912) indicated a keen interest in different types of crime. This was also the case with serials dealing with kidnappings or vice films following these early movies. Since then, a great variety of subjects from cat burglars to bank robbers, from petty criminals to murders of all kinds, to enforcers of one sort of another, have all been part of the criminal film.

——**Crime of Passion Films**   A great many films focus on crimes committed by people motivated by greed, passion, lust, love, or revenge for having been betrayed by their lover, husband or wife. Although these people are not professional criminals, the films, by reason of the act perpetrated, belong to the crime genre.

> *Ossessione* (It 42) Luchino Visconti. *Double Indemnity* (43) Billy Wilder. *The Great Flamarion* (45) Anthony Mann. *The Postman Always Rings Twice* (45) Tay Garnett. *Scarlet Street* (45) Fritz Lang. *Sorry, Wrong Number* (48) Anatole Litvak. *Impact* (49) Arthur Lubin. *Make Haste to Live* (54) William A. Seiter. *Les Innocents aux mains sales / Gli innocenti dalle mani sporche / Die unschuldigen mit den schmutzigen Händen* (F / It / G 74) Claude Chabrol *aka Dirty Hands*. *Body Heat* (81) Lawrence Kasdan. *The Postman Always Rings Twice* (81) Bob Rafelson. *Dance with a Stranger* (GB 84) Mike Newell [*Cf. Yield to the Night* (GB 56) J. Lee Thompson]. *River's Edge* (86) Tim Hunter. *Murder Rap* (87) Kliff Keuhl. *An Affair in Mind* (GB 88 TV) Colin Luke.

——**Drug Movies**   A type of vice film (q.v.) which goes way back in film history. Popular since the turn of the century, they continue to be made. Any kind of addiction—morphine, heroin, marijuana, LSD—may figure as the evil source of human enslavement. Only current fashion singles out one type of drug in preference to another. *See also* **DRUG FILM.**

> *The Man with the Golden Arm* (55) Otto Preminger. *Death in Small Doses* (57) Joseph M. Newman. *A Hatful of Rain* (57) Fred Zinnemann. *Monkey on My Back* (57) Andre de Toth. *The Lineup* (57) Don Siegel. *Panic in Needle Park* (71) Jerry Schatzberg. *Coffy* (73) Jack Hill. *Drying Up the Streets* (Can 77 TV) Robin Spry *aka They're Drying Up the Streets*.

——**Hijacking Films (Highjacking Films)**   Hijacking as a criminal or terrorist activity has been portrayed in a few films. It always involves the seizure of a means of transportation by the hijackers who may want to rob goods or safe passage to a free country or to subject people and governments to some kind of coercion. The hijacking of airplanes (skyjacking), although a prevalent terrorist activity in the 1980s, has not figured too often in films.

> *Habricha El Hashemesh / Niet!* (Isr / F / G 72) Menahem Golan *aka Escape to the Sun / Niet*. *Skyjacked* (72) John Guillermin *aka Sky Terror*. *The*

Taking of Pelham One Two Three (74) Joseph Sargent *aka The Taking of Pelham 123*.   *The Delta Force* (US / Isr 85) Menahem Golan.   *The Taking of Flight 847: The Uli Derickson Story* (88 TV) Paul Wendkos *aka The Flight*.   *The Hijacking of the Achille Lauro* (89 TV) Robert Collins.   *Voyage of Terror: The Achille Lauro Affair* (US / G / F / It 90 TV) Alberto Negrin [in 2 parts].

———**Juvenile Delinquent Films**   Juvenile or young criminal heroes are found leading street gangs, rebelling against school discipline, committing petty thievery which escalates to major crimes, or they are portrayed as dope addicts, engaged in prostitution, or else incarcerated in penal institutions for the young. It is a very popular type of film, and a major branch of the youth picture as well as of the crime film. *See* **JUVENILE DELINQUENCY FILM.**

Wild Boys of the Road (33) William A. Wellman *aka Dangerous Age / Dangerous Days*.   *Boys Town* (38) Norman Taurog.   *Back Door to Heaven* (39) William K. Howard.   *Knock on Any Door* (49) Nicholas Ray.   *In Cold Blood* (67) Richard Brooks.   *Badlands* (73) Terrence Malick.   *Macon County Line* (73) Richard Compton.   *Dirty Mary, Crazy Larry* (74) John Hough.   *Pixote a lei do mais fraco* (Braz 80) Hector Babenco *aka Pixote*.

———**Master Criminal Films**   Master criminals and arch-villains dedicated to a life of crime and evil-doing have attracted numerous writers. Some of their most famous creations—Raffles, Arsène Lupin, Fantômas, Fu Manchu, Dr. Mabuse—have repeatedly appeared in films. They offer a kind of fascination unequalled by that of lesser criminals. Of all these super-criminals, the mysterious Dr. Fu Manchu, engaged in dreams of world domination, is perhaps the most evil and the most famous.

Sax Rohmer's Dr. Fu Manchu: The Mystery of Dr. Fu Manchu (GB 23) A. E. Coleby [15-film series].   *Further Mysteries of Dr. Fu Manchu* (GB 24) Fred Paul [8-film series].   *The Mysterious Dr. Fu Manchu* (29) Rowland V. Lee.   *The Return of Dr. Fu Manchu* (30) Rowland V. Lee *aka New Adventures of Dr. Fu Manchu*.   *Daughter of the Dragon* (31) Lloyd Corrigan.   *The Mask of Fu Manchu* (32) Charles Brabin, Charles Vidor.   *Drums of Fu Manchu* (40) William Witney, John English [15-chapter serial].   *El otro Fu Manchu* (Sp 45) Ramón Barreiro.   *The Face of Fu Manchu* (GB 65) Don Sharp.   *The Brides of Fu Manchu / Die Dreizehn Sklavinnen des Dr. Fu Man Chu* (GB / G 66) Don Sharp *aka Die 13 Sklavinnen des Dr. Fu Man Chu*.   *The Vengeance of Fu Manchu / Die Rache des Dr. Fu Man Chu* (GB / G 67) Jeremy Summers.   *Die Folterkammer des Dr. Fu Man Chu / El Castillo de Fu-Manchu / The Castle of Fu Manchu* (G / Sp / It / GB 68) Jesús Franco *aka Assignment Istanbul*.   *Der Todeskuß des Dr. Fu Man Chu / Fu-Manchu y el beso de la muerte / Kiss & Kill / Blood of Fu Manchu* (G / Sp / US / GB 68) Jesús Franco *aka Against All Odds / Fu Manchu and the Kiss of Death / Fu Manchu and the Keys of Death*.   *The Fiendish Plot of Dr. Fu Manchu* (GB 78) Piers Haggard *aka Fu Manchu*.

*Norbert Jacques' Dr. Mabuse: **Dr. Mabuse der Spieler / Dr. Mabuse der Grosse Spieler** (G 21-22) Fritz Lang [in 2 parts: Der Spieler—ein Bild der Zeit; Inferno—ein spiel von Menschen unserer Zeit] aka Dr. Mabuse / Dr. Mabuse the Gambler —Part I: Dr. Mabuse, the Great Gambler / The Great Gambler— Image of a Generation; Part II: Dr. Mabuse, King of Crime / Inferno-People of a Generation aka The Fatal Passion* [parts I & II abridged into a single feature]. *Das Testament des Dr. Mabuse* (G 32) Fritz Lang *aka The Crimes of Dr. Mabuse / The Last Will of Dr. Mabuse / The [Last] Testament of Dr. Mabuse. Im Stahlnetz des Dr. Mabuse / F.B.I. contro dottor Mabuse / Le Retour du Docteur Mabuse* (G / It / F 61) Harald Reinl *aka The Return of Dr. Mabuse. Die tausend Augen des Dr. Mabuse / Il diabolico dott. Mabuse / Le diabolique Dr. Mabuse* (G / It / F 60) Fritz Lang *aka Augen des Dr. Mabuse / Eyes of Evil / The Secret of Dr. Mabuse / The Shadow vs. the Thousand Eyes of Dr. Mabuse / The [1000] Thousand Eyes of Dr. Mabuse. Die unsichtbaren Krallen des Dr. Mabuse* (G 61) Harold Reinl *aka The Invisible Dr. Mabuse. Das Testament des Dr. Mabuse* (G 62) Werner Klinger *aka The Terror of Dr. Mabuse / The Testament of Dr. Mabuse. Scotland Yard jagt Dr. Mabuse* (G 63) Paul May *aka Dr. Mabuse vs. Scotland Yard / Scotland Yard Hunts Dr. Mabuse. Raggi mortali del Dottor Mabuse / Die Todesstrahlen des Dr. Mabuse / Les Rayons mortels du Docteur Mabuse* (It / G / F 64) Hugo Fregonese *aka Dr. Mabuse's Ray of Death / The Secret of Dr. Mabuse. Dr. Mabuse / Der Doktor Mabuse* (Sp / G 70) Jesús Franco.

Marcel Allain and Pierre Souvestre's Fantômas: Fantômas (F 13-14) Louis Feuillade [in 5 parts: *Fantômas; Fantômas II: Juve contre Fantômas; Fantômas III: Le mort qui tue; Fantômas IV: Fantômas contre Fantômas; Fantômas V: Le Faux Magistrat*]. *Fantômas* (20-21) Edward Sedgwick [20-part serial]. *Fantômas* (F 32) Paul Fejos. *Mr. Fantômas* (Belg 36) Ernest Moerman. *Fantômas* (F 47) Jean Sacha. *Fantômas contre Fantômas* (F 48) Robert Vernay. *Fantômas / Fantomas '70* (F /It 64) André Hunebelle. *Fantômas se déchaîne / Fantomas minaccia il mondo* (F /It 65) André Hunebelle *aka Fantômas Strikes Back / The Phantom. Fantômas contre Scotland Yard / Fantomas contro Scotland Yard* (F / It 66) André Hunebelle *aka Fantomas / Fantomas against Scotland Yard. Rencontre avec Fantômas* (F 66 TV) George Franju. *Fantômas* (F 80 TV) Claude Chabrol, Juan-Luis Buñuel [in 4 episodes].

E. W. Horming's A. J. Raffles: Raffles, the Amateur Cracksman (05) J. Stuart Blackton. *Raffles the American Cracksman* (05) G. M. Anderson. *Raffles the Amateur Cracksman* (17) George Irving. *Raffles, the Amateur Cracksman* (25) King Baggot. *Raffles* (30) Harry D'Arrast, George Fitzmaurice (uncredited). *The Return of Raffles* (GB 32) Mansfield Markham. *Raffles* (39) Sam Wood.

Maurice Leblanc's Arsène Lupin: Arsene Lupin (17) Paul Scardon. *The Teeth of the Tiger* (19) Chet Withey. *813* (20) Scott Sidney. *Arsène Lupin* (32) Jack Conway. *Arsène Lupin Returns* (38) George Fitzmaurice. *Enter Arsene Lupin* (44) Ford Beebe. *Les Aventures d'Arsène Lupin* (F 57) Jacques Becker *aka The Adventures of Arsène Lupin. Arsène Lupin contre Arsène Lupin* (F 62) Edouard Molinaro.

——Moonshine Films   These films concentrate on the activities of moonshiners who illegally distill or smuggle whiskey or other spirits. They are usually set in the American South and involve shoot-outs and fast car chases between the liquor runners and the law.

Thunder Road (58) Arthur Ripley. *Moonshine Mountain* (64) Herschell Gordon Lewis *aka White Trash on Moonshine Mountain. White Lightnin' Road* (65) Ron Ormond. *The Moonshine War* (70) Richard Quine. *White*

Lightning (73) Joseph Sargent *aka Mcklusty.*   *The Last American Hero* (73) Lamont Johnson *aka Hard Driver.*   *Hot Summer in Barefoot Country* (74) Will Zens.   *Moonrunners* (74) Gy Waldron.   *Dixie Dynamite* (76) Lee Frost.   *Bad Georgia Road* (77) John C. Broderick.   *Moonshine County Express* (77) Gus Trikonis.   *Thunder and Lightning* (77) Corey Allen.

——**Serial-Killer Films**   Jack the Ripper, the notorious and never apprehended 1888 killer of London prostitutes, is perhaps one of the better known serial killers to appear on film. However, with the exception of a few equally famous murderers, films which focus on real or fictitious serial killers were not in steady production until the 1980s. For the kind of killer featured in films of *Friday the 13th* variety and its ilk *see* **SLASHER FILM**.
Jack the Ripper (GB 58) Robert S. Baker, Monty Berman *aka The Return of Jack the Ripper.*   *The Boston Strangler* (68) Richard Fleischer.   *10 Rillington Place* (GB 70) Richard Fleischer.   *The Atlanta Child Murders* (85 TV) John Erman [in 2 parts].   *The Deliberate Stranger* (86 TV) Marvin J. Chomsky [in 2 parts].   *Henry: Portrait of a Serial Killer* (86) John McNaughton [rel. in 90].   *Manhunter* (86) Michael Mann *aka Red Dragon.*   *The Stepfather* (87) Joseph Ruben.   *White of the Eye* (GB 87) Donald Cammell.   *Jack's Back* (88) Rowdy Herrington.   *Jack the Ripper* (GB / US 88 TV) David Wickes [in 2 parts].   *Blue Steel* (89) Kathryn Bigelow.   *Criminal Law* (89) Martin Campbell.   *Manhunt: Search for the Night Stalker* (89 TV) Bruce Seth Green.   *Relentless* (89) William Lustig.   *Stepfather II* (89) Jeff Burr.   *Fear* (90 TV) Rockne S. O'Bannon.   *The Silence of the Lambs* (91) Jonathan Demme.

——**Thievery Films (Robbery Films)**   Excluding caper and gangster films, films featuring petty criminals, pickpockets, cat burglars, burglars and nonprofessionals stealing from banks are also quite common and may be included in a group of their own.
The Steel Trap (52) Andrew Stone.   *To Catch a Thief* (55) Alfred Hitchcock.   *The Burglar* (56) Paul Wendkos.   *Pickpocket* (F 59) Robert Bresson.   *Risate di gioia* (It 60) Mario Monicelli *aka The Passionate Thief.*   *Harry in Your Pocket* (73) Bruce Geller.   *Fun with Dick and Jane* (77) Ted Kotcheff.   *Straight Time* (77) Ulu Grosbard.   *Thief* (81) Michael Mann.   *Lassiter* (GB 84) Roger Young.   *Daddy's Boys* (88) Joe Minion.   *Family Business* (89) Sidney Lumet.   *Bail Jumper* (90) Christian Faber.

Crime of Passion Films, Criminal Film   *see*   **CRIME FILM**

Critical Heimat Films   *see*   **HEIMATFILM**

CROSS-DRESSING FILM (Drag Genre)   Men in drag and female impersonation in motion pictures are practices that have been going on since the silent period. Cross-dressing (also known as eonism) is used in films mainly for comic effect; however, it is not restricted to comedy alone. It figures in some horror movies (at least since *Psycho* [1960] inaugurated a new trend), in serious subjects, e.g., *The Queen* (1967), a documentary on homosexuals attending a drag Miss America contest, or in representations of impersonation and transvestism, e.g., *Outrageous!* (1977), *The Rocky Horror Picture Show* (1975). Although most films that feature female and male impersonation may be included under the general label of the cross-dressing film, those which have featured it as their main theme form an easily distinguishable group of films. *See also* **GAY FILM**. For a general discussion of the topic, *see* Rebecca Bell-Metereau's *Hollywood Androgyny* (New York: Columbia University Press, 1985).

Viktor und Viktoria (G 33) Reinhold Schünzel [French version: *Georges et Georgette* (33)]. *Silvia Scarlett* (35) George Cukor. *Charley's Aunt* (40) Archie Mayo *aka Charley's American Aunt*. *The Major and the Minor* (42) Billy Wilder. *I Was a Male War Bride* (49) Howard Hawks *aka You Can't Sleep Here*. *Where's Charley?* (GB 52) David Butler. *You're Never Too Young* (55) Norman Taurog. *Some Like It Hot* (59) Billy Wilder. *Psycho* (60) Alfred Hitchcock. *Homicidal* (61) William Castle. *The Queen* (67) Frank Simon. *Pope Joan* (GB 72) Michael Anderson *aka The Devil's Imposter*. *Triple Echo* (GB 72) Michael Apted *aka Soldier in Skirts*. *The Rocky Horror Picture Show* (GB 75) Jim Sharman. *Le Locataire / The Tenant* (F / US 76) Roman Polanski. *Outrageous!* (Can 77) Richard Benner. *La Cage aux folles / Il vizietto* (F / It 78) Edouard Molinaro *aka Birds of a Feather* [followed by *La Cage aux folles II* (F / It 80) by Molinaro and *La Cage aux folles 3* (F /It 85) Georges Lautner]. *Dressed to Kill* (80) Brian DePalma. *Angelos* (Gr 82) Yiorgios Katakouzinos *aka Angel*. *Tootsie* (82) Sidney Pollack. *Victor Victoria* (GB / US 82) Blake Edwards. *Yentl* (GB / US / Cz 83) Barbra Streisand. *Her Life as a Man* (84 TV) Robert Ellis Miller. *Just One of the Guys* (85) Lisa Gottlieb. *Too Outrageous!* (Can 87) Richard Benner.

Cross-Genre Movie   *see*   **HYBRID**

CROSS-OVER FILM   A film addressed to a particular audience or a film made for an ethnic or cultural group which is able to reach other audiences as well; e.g., Perry Henzell's *The Harder They Come* (1972), a Jamaican film which made reggae music popular with American audiences. Many black-oriented films are cross-over films.

CULT FILM   The term is applied to a film which is favored by a group of cognoscenti, the followers or admirers of a star, a film director or a theme which has popular appeal, or by a subcultural group whose members have elevated a particular film to the rank of a cult. It follows, then, that a film of any nature favored by a group of cultists would fall under the classification of a cult movie. Regardless of the social group to which they may belong, film cultists all have one thing in common: they have all seen the film they worship many times and tend to extol its worth.

According to the audiences which patronize them, cult films may be divided into popular cult, clique or coterie and subculture cult films. Examples of popular cult films are *Casablanca* (1942) and *King Kong* (1933). Cinephiles, film society members and cognoscenti tend to favor intellectual, artistic, genre, or experimental films — for instance, the Russian *Bronenosets "Potyomkin" / Potemkin* (1925), *Stagecoach* (1939), Luis Buñuel's *Un Chien andalou* (1928).

To the third group of cult films belongs the best known of all the cult pictures. Undoubtedly, this is the British film *The Rocky Horror Picture*

Show (1975), a rock opera movie which has gathered a cult following in several cities, mostly in the United States and Canada, with various adherents, organized in Rocky Horror Fan clubs, impersonating, rehearsing, and reenacting the dramatic roles of the film's main characters every Saturday night in suburban or repertory cinemas where the film is regularly shown to the midnight crowd. The gatherings at such sessions may be said to go well beyond the normal patronage of a cult film and reach instead the level of ritual. On the subject of cult films, *see* Dany Peary, *Cult Movies* (New York: Dell, 1981), *Cult Movies 2* (New York: Dell Trade Paperback, 1983) and *Cult Movies 3* (London: Sidgwick & Jackson, 1989).

   Bronenosets "Potyomkin" (USSR 25) Sergei M. Eisenstein, Grigori Alexandrov *aka The Armoured Cruiser Potemkin / Battleship Potemkin / Bronenosets Potemkin / Potemkin.*   *Un Chien andalou* (F 28) Luis Buñuel *aka An (The) Andalusian Dog / Es peligroso asomarse al exterior / El marista en la ballesta / Un perro andaluz.*   *Freaks* (32) Tod Browning *aka Barnum / Forbidden Love / The Monster Show / Nature's Mistakes.*   *King Kong* (33) Merian C. Cooper, Ernest B. Schoedsack *aka The Beast / The Eighth Wonder / The Eighth Wonder of the World / King Ape / King Kong (The Eighth Wonder of the World) / Kong* [1st feature sound film to use model animation]. *Reefer Madness* (36) Louis Gasnier *aka Assassin of Youth / The Burning Question / Dope Addict / Doped Youth / Love Madness / Tell Your Children.*   *Stagecoach* (39) John Ford.   *Casablanca* (42) Michael Curtiz.   *Laura* (44) Otto Preminger.   *Gun Crazy* (49) Joseph H. Lewis *aka Deadly Is the Female.*   *Johnny Guitar* (54) Nicholas Ray.   *Land of the Pharaohs* (54) Howard Hawks.   *Roi du coeur / Tutti pazzi meno io* (F / It 65) Philippe de Broca *aka King of Hearts.*   *Greetings* (68) Brian DePalma.   *Night of the Living Dead* (67-68) George A. Romero *aka Flesh Eaters / Night of Anubis / Night of the Flesh Eaters.*   *El Topo* (Mex 70) Alexandro Jodorowsky *aka The Mole.*   *Enter the Dragon / Lung cheng hu tou* (US / HK 72) Robert Clouse.   *Pink Flamingos* (72) John Waters.   *Emmanuelle* (F / Thai 73) Just Jaeckin.   *The Rocky Horror Picture Show* (GB 75) Jim Sharman.   *Altered States* (80) Ken Russell.   *Mommie Dearest* (81) Frank Perry.

   Current Affairs Program   *see*   **TELEVISION NEWS: Public Affairs Program**

   Current Melodrama   *see*   **MELODRAMA**

   Curry Western   *see*   **SPAGHETTI WESTERN**

   Custard-Pie Comedy   *see*   **SLAPSTICK**

   Cut-Down Feature   *see*   **SHORT**

   Cut-Out Animation Films   *see*   **ANIMATED FILM**

   Cycle Film   *see*   **MOTORCYCLE MOVIE**

   CZECH NEW WAVE (Young Czech Cinema)   Among diverse factors, the relaxation in the arts brought about by the de–Stalinization process in Czechoslovakia in the early 1960s made it possible for a group of filmmakers to break away from the rigid formulas of the official socialist-realist style which had been the norm until then. These filmmakers formed a unified movement or wave in the sense that they shared the common purpose of achieving artistic freedom and the desire to humanize socialism without betraying its principles. They concentrated on people and their feelings rather than on ideology. The wave was short-lived as it was stifled by the Russian tanks' occupation of Prague in August 1968. But from 1962 to 1968, its output was substantial and its films were acclaimed world-wide.

The filmmakers of the Czech New Wave may be grouped into two general camps: the realists (e.g., Milos Forman, Ivan Passer, Jirí Menzel) who seek to transcribe perceived reality more or less objectively and the nonrealists (e.g., Vera Chytilová, Jan Nemec, Evald Schorm, Pavel Juracek) who, by the use of allegory, symbolism, and surrealist devices, project subjective and intellectual worlds onto the screen. However, in spite of their different cinematic approaches, their films show an interrelationship and cohesiveness which are characteristic of the Czech New Wave. The standard background source for the Czech New Wave is Josef Skvorecky, *All the Bright Young Men and Women* (Toronto: Peter Martin Associates, 1971). *See also* Peter Hames, *The Czechoslovak New Wave* (Berkeley: University of California Press, 1985).

Smrt si ríká Engelchen (Cz 63) Ján Kadár, Elmar Klos *aka Death Is Called Engelchen.* *Transport z reaje* (Cz 63) Zbynek Brynych *aka Transport from Paradise.* *...A páty jezdec je strach* (Cz 64) Zbynek Brynych *aka (And) The Fifth Horseman Is Fear / The Fifth Rider Is Fear.* *Cerny Petr* (Cz 64) Milos Forman *aka Black Peter / Peter and Pavla.* *Démanty noci* (Cz 64) Ján Nemec *aka Diamonds of the Night.* *Intimní osvetlení* (Cz 65) Ivan Passer *aka Intimate Lighting.* *Lásky jedné plavovlásky* (Cz 65) Milos Forman *aka A Blonde in Love / Hallo, Blondie! / Loves of a Blonde.* *O slavnosti a hostech* (Cz 65) Jan Nemec *aka The Party and the Guests / A Report on the Party and the Guests.* *Konec srpna v hotelu Ozón* (Cz 66) Jan Schmidt *aka The End of August in Hotel Ozone / Late August at the Hotel Ozone.* *Mucedníci lásky* (Cz 66) Ján Nemec *aka The Martyrs of Love.* *Ostre sledované vlaky* (Cz 66) Jirí Menzel *aka Closely Observed Trains / Closely Watched Trains / A Close Watch on the Trains / A Difficult Love.* *Sedmikrásky* (Cz 66) Vera Chytilová *aka Daisies.* *Vrazda po cesky / Vrazda po nasem* (Cz 66) Jirí Weiss *aka The Crime / Murder Czech Style.* *Hori, má panenko! / Al fuoco, pompieri!* (Cz / It 67) Milos Forman *aka The Fireman's Ball / The Firemen's Ball / Like a House on Fire.* *Rozmarné léto* (Cz 67) Jirí Menzel *aka Capricious Summer.* *Faráruv konec* (Cz 68) Evald Schorm *aka Death of a Priest / End of a Priest / Konec faráre.* *Nejkrásnejvi vek* (Cz 68) Jaroslav Papousek *aka The Best Age / The Most Beautiful Age.* *Spalovac mrtvol* (Cz 68) Juraj Herz *aka The Cremator / The Cremator of Corpses.* *Vsichni dobrí radáci* (Cz 68) Vojtech Jasny *aka All Good Citizens / [All] My Good Countrymen.* *Vtáckovia, siroty a blazni / Les oiseaux, les orphelins et les fous* (Cz / F 68) Juraj Jakubisco *aka Birds, Orphans and Fools.* *Zert* (Cz 68) Jaromil Jires *aka The Joke.*

Dada, Dadaism *see* **SURREALIST FILM**

DANCE FILM Dance has figured in films since Georges Méliès (1861–

1938) started to make movies. The term dance film is general and includes any film whose main focus is dance or dancing; it applies also to a film in which dance sequences figure prominently, e.g., the film musicals of Fred Astaire and the Busby Berkeley films. This latter category of films, however, is better grouped with the musical genre. Films on ballet and modern dance, vaudeville, ballroom, or theatrical dance, ethnic or folk dance are variously included when alluding to the dance film. In short, a dance film is one whose main constituent is dancing, even if artistic expression is not the aim. *See* **BALLET FILM.**[24]

> *The Whirl of Life* (14) Oliver D. Bailey. *Bolero* (34) Wesley Ruggles. *Born to Dance* (36) Roy Del Ruth. *Ballerina* (50) Ludwig Berger *aka Dream Ballerina / Poor Little Ballerina.* *Invitation to the Dance* (52) Gene Kelly, Stanley Donen [rel. in 57]. *West Side Story* (61) Robert Wise, Jerome Robbins. *Pas de deux* (Can 67) Norman McLaren. *They Shoot Horses, Don't They?* (69) Sidney Pollack. *Ballet Adagio* (Can 72) Norman McLaren. *Dance of Ecstasy* (72) Brandon Chase. *Eight Jelly Rolls* (GB 74 TV) Twyla Tharp. *Roseland* (77) James Ivory. *Saturday Night Fever* (77) John Badham. *Fame* (80) Alan Parker. *Ballando Ballando / Le Bal* (It / F / Alg 81) Ettore Scola. *Bodas de sangre* (Sp 81) Carlos Saura *aka Blood Wedding.* *Carmen* (Sp 83) Carlos Saura *aka Carmen Story.* *Flashdance* (83) Adrian Lyne. *Tangos — L'Exil de Gardel / Tangos — El exilio de Gardel* (F / Arg 85) Fernando E. Solanas *aka Tangos.* *El amor brujo* (Sp 86) Carlos Saura *aka A Love Bewitched / Love, the Magician* [Saura's 3rd dance film after *Bodas de sangre* and *Carmen*]. *Dirty Dancing* (87) Emile Ardolino. *The "In" Crowd* (88) Mark Rosenthal. *Tango Bar* (PR / Arg 88) Marcos Zurinaga. *Tap* (89) Nick Castle.

Dance Films   *see*   **UNDERGROUND FILM**

Dance Musical   *see*   **MUSICAL: Courtship-Romance Musicals**

Dark Comedy   *see*   **BLACK COMEDY**

Daytime Drama, Daytime Serial Drama   *see*   **SOAP OPERA**

Deepies   *see*   **3-D FILM**

Delinquent Movie   *see*   **JUVENILE DELINQUENCY FILM**

DeMille Epics   *see*   **EPIC**

Demon Movie   *see*   **HORROR FILM: Demonic Films**

Depthies   *see*   **3-D FILM**

De Sade, De Sade Adaptation   *see*   **SOFT-CORE SEX-EXPLOITATION FILM**

Desert Warfare Movie   *see*   **WAR FILM: Desert War Films**

Detective Comedy Films, Detective Film   *see*   **PRIVATE DETECTIVE FILM**

Devil Movie   *see*   **HORROR FILM: Demonic Films**

Direct-Animation Film *see* **ANIMATED FILM: Cameraless Animated Films**

DIRECT CINEMA (Living Cinema, Uncontrolled Documentary) The American equivalent of *cinéma vérité* took shape in the early sixties as a development of television techniques and the early work of Richard Leacock and Robert Drew (later joined by D. A. Pennbaker and the Maysles brothers). As with *cinéma vérité*, direct cinema relies strongly on the use of lightweight cameras, portable sound recorders and fast film for its on-the-spot filming. It tries to render truth by the spontaneity of the situations being filmed without resorting to preexisting scripts. If a distinction is to be emphasized between the direct-cinema documentary approach (the term is due to Albert Maysles; Drew and Leacock used "Living Cinema") and *cinéma vérité,* it is that direct cinema avoids involvement on the part of the filmmaker who chooses not to take part in the action at any time and who tries to make the presence of the camera as unobtrusive as possible. It also avoids interviews and narration, practices permitted in *cinéma vérité.* In spite of the filmmaker's intention of effacing himself from the subject matter being filmed, the direct cinema approach to filmmaking has also been criticized as contrary to the goal of objectivity. In relation to direct cinema, *see* Stephen Mamber, *Cinema Verite in America* (Cambridge, Mass: MIT Press, 1974) and Louis Marcorelles, *Living Cinema* (London: George Allen & Unwin, 1973).

On the Pole (60) Richard Leacock, D. A. Pennebaker, William Ray, Abbot Mills, Albert Maysles. *Primary* (60) Richard Leacock, D. A. Pennebaker, Terence Macartney-Filgate, Albert Maysles. *Football* (61) James Lipscomb *aka Mooney vs. Fowle.* *The Chair* (62 TV) Gregory Shuker, Richard Leacock, D. A. Pennebaker [last of the "Living Camera" series (1961-63) of 10 one-hour films]. *Jane* (62) D. A. Pennebaker, Richard Leacock, Hope Ryden, Gregory Shuker, Abbot Mills. *Showman* (62) Albert and David Maysles. *Crisis: Behind a Presidential Commitment* (63 TV) Richard Leacock, James Lipscomb, D. A. Pennebaker, Hope Ryden. *Happy Mother's Day* (63) Richard Leacock, Joyce Chopra. *A Stravinsky Portrait* (64) Richard Leacock. *Don't Look Back* (66) D. A. Pennebaker, Howard and Jones Alk. *A Time for Burning* (66) William Jersey. *Birth and Death* (68) Arthur Barron, Gene Marner. *Law and Order* (69) Frederich Wiseman. *Salesman* (69) David Maysles, Albert Maysles, Charlotte Zwerin. *An American Family* (73 TV) Craig Gilbert [in 12 parts]. *Grey Gardens* (75) David Maysles, Albert Maysles, Ellen Hovde, Muffie Meyer.

Director's Picture *see* **AUTEUR FILM**

Dirty Movie *see* **HARD-CORE FILM;** *see also* **SOFT-CORE SEX-EXPLOITATION FILM**

DISABILITY PICTURE (Disease/Affliction Genre, Handicap Movie) Oscillating between melodrama and genuine drama, a group of films concentrates on the handicapped, the infirm, and the terminally ill. These films focus their attention on stories of endurance and fortitude. Some are based on true case histories. At their best, they show the human ability to surmount affliction by conquering pain or some physical or mental handicap. At their worst, they become an excuse for over-sentimentality and only seek to make the audience's tear ducts flow. A great many of these films are made for television, a medium in which they thrive as they address themselves to the whole family. These films may be grouped under the label of "disability pictures" or the "disease/affliction genre." Most of them are just tear-jerkers. On the subject, *see* Lauri E. Klobas, *Disability Drama in Television and Film* (Jefferson, NC: McFarland, 1988).

> *Brian's Song* (70 TV) Buzz Kulik. *Love Story* (70) Arthur Hiller. *Sunshine* (73 TV) Joseph Sargent. *A Love Affair: The Eleanor & Lou Gehrig Story* (77 TV) Fielder Cook. *And Your Name Is Jonah* (79 TV) Richard Michaels. *Aunt Mary* (79 TV) Peter Werner. *No Other Love* (79 TV) Richard Pearce [*Cf. Like Normal People* (79) Harvey Hart]. *Some Kind of Miracle* (79 TV) Jerrold Freedman. *Silent Victory: The Kitty O'Neil Story* (79 TV) Lou Antonio. *Walking Through the Fire* (79 TV) Robert Day. *A Cry for Love* (80 TV) Paul Wendkos. *Homeward Bound* (80 TV) Richard Michaels. *The Shadow Box* (80) TV) Paul Newman. *The Acorn People* (81 TV) Joan Tewkesbury. *The Best Little Girl in the World* (81 TV) Sam O'Steen. *Leave 'em Laughing* (81 TV) Jackie Cooper. *The Miracle of Kathy Miller* (81 TV) Robert Lewis. *Skeezer* (82 TV) Peter H. Hunt. *The Terry Fox Story / Terry Fox le coureur de l'espoir* (Can 83 MCTV) Ralph Thomas *aka The Road to Thunder Bay / Terry / Terry Fox the Movie. Heartsounds* (84 TV) Glenn Jordan. *Do You Remember Love?* (85 TV) Jeff Bleckner. *An Early Frost* (85 TV) John Erman. *A Time to Live* (85 TV) Rick Wallace. *A Winner Never Quits* (86 TV) Mel Damski. *David* (88 TV) John Erman. *My Left Foot* (Ire 89) Jim Sheridan.

Disaster   *see*   **TURKEY**

DISASTER FILM (Catastrophe Film)   The disaster film came into prominence in the early seventies with the commercial success of *The Poseidon Adventure* (1972). Its producer, Irwin Allen, hastened to follow up his initial success with *The Towering Inferno* (1974); the trend caught on. However, disaster movies are not new. They have been around since Georges Méliès started grinding his camera at the turn of the century. They come in a great variety of subjects and themes. Maurice Yacowar, in "The Bug in the Rug: Notes on the Disaster Genre," gives a broad interpretation of them; his schematization of eight basic types overlaps with many other genres.[25] A narrower interpretation of the genre would exclude those disaster films that are obviously better classified under the horror, science fiction, or peplum (epic) genres. Films that treat the disaster peripherally or as a climactic high point to a love or an adventure story should also be excluded. In the disaster film proper, the disaster (earthquake, fire, volcanic eruption, air crash, shipwreck) is the core of the film. Disaster films examine human character and behavior in situations of extreme danger and stress. During the ordeal, individuals will reveal themselves for what they really are, and at the end, the survivors will have proved their mettle.

——**Man-Made Disaster Films**   In these films, the disaster is the result of human error or mechanical failure.

Titanic (G 42) Herbert Selpin, Werner Klinger. *The High and the Mighty* (54) William A. Wellman. *A Night to Remember* (GB 58) Roy Baker. *The Poseidon Adventure* (72) Ronald Neame, Irwin Allen (uncredited). *The Towering Inferno* (74) John Guillermin, Irwin Allen. *The Hindenburg* (75) Robert Wise. *The Big Bus* (76) James Frawley. *The Cassandra Crossing / Le Pont de Cassandra / Cassandra Crossing* (GB / F / It / G 76) George Pan Cosmatos. *Airport '77* (77) Jerry Jameson. *Fire!* (77 TV) Earl Bellamy *aka Irwin Allen's Fire. Beyond the Poseidon Adventure* (79) Irwin Allen. *Airplane!* (80) Jim Abrahams, David Zucker, Jerry Zucher *aka Flying High.*

——**Natural Disaster Films**   In this type of film, the disaster is due to the vagaries of mother nature. Man is sometimes able to predict an oncoming catastrophe, but fails to act accordingly. In a way, he is responsible for not taking action.

Deluge (33) Felix E. Feist. *Krakatoa, East of Java* (68) Bernard L. Kowalski *aka Krakatoa / Volcano. Nippon chiubotsu* (J 73) Shiro Moritani *aka The Submersion of Japan [Cf. Tidal Wave* (J / US 73-75) Shiro Moritani, Andrew Meyer; a reworking of the Japanese feature]. *Earthquake* (74) Mark Robson *aka Earthquake 1980* [1st film in Sensurround; reedited & expanded for TV]. *Heat Wave!* (74 TV) Jerry Jameson. *Avalanche* (78) Corey Allen. *The Swarm* (78) Irwin Allen. *Meteor* (HK / US / J 79) Ronald Neame. *When Time Ran Out...* (79) James Goldstone *aka Earth's Final Fury / Volcano.*

Disease / Affliction Genre   *see*   **DISABILITY PICTURE**

Disnarrative Film   *see*   **NONLINEAR FILM**

Doctor Drama   *see*   **HOSPITAL FILM**

Docu   *see*   **DOCUMENTARY**

DOCUDRAMA (Actuality Drama, Docu-Drama, Documentary Drama, Drama-Documentary, Dramatization, Dramatized Documentary, Faction)   The designation docu-drama or docudrama has been in vogue since the midseventies to describe a made-for-television movie or a television mini-series which focuses on some well-known present, recent, or past event which is still fresh in the memory of its viewers. It may also apply to a fictionalized biography or to a totally fictionalized account of some current topic such as rape, homosexuality, political intrigue, corruption in high places and similar subjects. In fact, docudramas are an amalgam of fiction and truth, fiction perhaps tipping the balance. The form, popular with television audiences, has often been criticized for embellishing and disguising the true facts for the sake of dramatic impact, thus negating in part the documentary aspect of the composite term. The term docu-drama applies as well to some quickly made exploitative films on gruesome or bizarre incidents, e.g., the films of the Mexican filmmaker René Cardona, Jr., usually shot with an English sound track (*see* **EXPLOITATION FILM**). "Faction" is a neologism sometimes used for docudrama. For the origin and evolution of the documentary drama or docu-drama in America, *see* Tom W. Hoffer and Richard Alan Nelson, "Docudrama on American Television," *Journal of the University Film Association* 30.2 (Spring 1978): 21–27. The authors identify nine different categories.

> *The Helter Skelter Murders* (70) Frank Howard *aka The Other Side of Madness*. *Pueblo* (73 TV) Anthony Page. *The Missiles of October* (74 TV) Anthony Page. *Helter Skelter* (75 TV) Tom Gries. *I Will Fight No More Forever* (75 TV) Richard T. Heffron. *Three Days in Szczecin* (GB 75 TV) Leslie Woodhead. *Mivtza Yehonatan* (Isr 76) Menahem Golan *aka Entebbe: Operation Thunderbolt / Jonathan Operation / Operation Thunderbolt* [*Cf. Raid on Entebbe* (76 TV) Irvin Kershner and *Victory at Entebbe* (76 TV) Marvin J. Chomsky]. *Return to Earth* (76 TV) Jud Taylor. *21 Hours at Munich* (76 TV) William A. Graham. *The Trial of Lee Harvey Oswald* (77 TV) David Green. *El triángulo diabólico / Il triangolo delle Bermude* (It / Mex 77) René Cardona Jr. *aka The Bermuda Mystery / The Bermuda Triangle / Death Triangle*. *Death of a Princess* (GB 80 TV) Anthony Thomas. *El tesoro del Amazonas* (Mex 80) René Cardona *aka The Treasure of the Amazons*. *MurdeR in Texas* (81 TV) Billy Hale [in 2 parts]. *Cocaine: One Man's Seduction* (83 TV) Paul Wendkos. *Close to Home* (Can 85 TV) Rick Beairsto. *Evil Angels / A Cry in the Dark* (Aust / US 87) Fred Schepisi [*Cf. Who Killed Baby Azaria?* (Aust 83 TV) Judy Rymer]. *Working Girls* (86) Lizzie Borden. *Tailspin: Behind the Korean Airliner Tragedy* (US / GB 89 MCTV) David Darlow [*Cf. Shootdown* (88 TV) Michael Pressman].

Documentaire *see* **ACTUALITY**

DOCUMENTARY (Docu, Documentary Film, Factual Film, Non-Fiction Film, Realist Film)   John Grierson (1898–1972), filmmaker and theoretician, applied the term documentary to Robert Flaherty's *Moana* (1925) in a review of the film for *The New York Sun* on February 8, 1926. Its use, covering diverse types of factual films, spread quickly. There have been many filmmakers with their own definition and interpretation of what should constitute and delimit a documentary. However, in accepted parlance, the term documentary is applied to and includes a vast array of different types of nonfiction or semifictional films; it stretches from the objective presentation of factual material to the subjective use of film for propaganda purposes. The word "telementary" has been used to describe a documentary made for television. Documentaries may seek to document and inform, teach or educate on some subject or other, or simply record for posterity the doings of people and nature. On the subject of documentary films, *see* Eric Barnow, *Documentary* (New York: Oxford University Press, 1974) and Jack C. Ellis, *The Documentary Idea* (Englewood Cliffs, NJ: Prentice Hall, 1989).

> *Jazz on a Summer Day* (59) Bert Stern. *King: A Filmed Record ... Montgomery to Memphis* (70) Joseph L. Mankiewicz, Sidney Lumet. *Gizmo!* (77) Howard Smith. *Always for Pleasure* (78) Les Blank. *Who Are the Debolts and Where Did They Get 19 Kids?* (78) John Korty. *Hollywood* (GB 79 TV)

Kevin Brownlow, David Gill [in 13 parts]. *From Mao to Mozart: Isaac Stern in China* (80) Murray Lerner. *The Weavers: Wasn't That a Time!* (81) Jim Brown *aka Wasn't That a Time! Burden of Dreams* (82) Les Blank. *Mississippi Blues* (F / US 83) Bertrand Tavernier, Robert Parrish. *Mauvaise conduite* (F 84) Nestor Almendros, Orlando Jimenez Leal *aka Improper Conduct. Streetwise* (85) Martin Bell, Mary Ellen Mark, Cheryl McCall. *Mother Teresa* (86) Ann and Jeanette Petrie. *Private Conversations: On the Set of Death of a Salesman* (86) Christian Blackwood. *Buster Keaton: A Hard Act to Follow* (GB 87) David Gill, Kevin Brownlow [in 3 parts]. *Vincent: The Life and Death of Vincent Van Gogh* (Aust 87) Paul Cox *aka Vincent. Imagine: John Lennon* (88) Andrew Solt. *Common Threads: Stories from the Quilt* (89) Robert Epstein, Jeffrey Friedman. *John Huston — The Man, the Movies, the Maverick* (89 TV) Frank Martin. *Let's Get Lost* (89) Bruce Weber. *25 × 5: The Continuing History of the Rolling Stones* (89) Nigel Finch. *The Civil War* (90) Ken Burns.

———**Analytical Documentary (Film Essay)**   In the analytical documentary, the filmmaker presents an analysis of his film's subject matter; he not only observes reality but comments on it, his aim being to explain and elucidate. This type of documentary is subjective in its approach, although it tries to present unbiased factual information. Analytical documentaries may be compilation films (q.v.), *cinéma vérité* (q.v.), or a blend of both.

Mourir à Madrid (F 62) Frédéric Rossif *aka To Die in Madrid. L'Inde fantôme / Refléxion sur un voyage* (F 68-69 TV) Louis Malle [in 7 parts] *aka Calcutta / L'Inde 68 / Louis Malle's India / Phantom India. Millhouse: A White Comedy* (71) Emile de Antonio. *The Memory of Justice* (GB / G 73-75 TV) Marcel Ophüls [shorter version reedited by Lutz Becker]. *Hotel Terminus: The Life and Times of Klaus Barbie* (88) Marcel Ophüls.

———**Committed Documentary (Activist Documentary, Radical Documentary)**   From Dziga Vertov (*see* **KINO-GLAZ**) to radical American documentarists to Third World filmmakers, the committed documentary represents a continuum in politically Left documentaries that are ideologically committed and that aim to bring about popular awareness and change through their topical presentation of reality. *See* Thomas Waugh, ed., *Show Us Life: Toward a History and Aesthetics of the Committed Documentary* (Metuchen, NJ: Scarecrow, 1984).

Native Land (37-39) Paul Strand, Leo Hurwitz [rel. in 42]. *La Hora de los Hornos* (Arg 67) Fernando Solanas, Octavio Getino *aka The Hour of the Blast Furnaces / The Hour of the Furnaces. La Batalla de Chile. La lucha de un pueblo sin armas / La Bataille du Chile (La lutte d'un peuple sans armes)* (Chile / Cuba / F 73-79) Patricio Guzmán *aka The Battle of Chile: The Struggle of an Unarmed People* [in 3 parts]. *Nightcleaners* (GB 75) made by the Berwick Street Film Collective. *Ici et ailleurs* (F 70-76) Jean-Luc Godard, Anne-Marie Miéville *aka Here and Elsewhere. Harlan County, U.S.A.* (72-76) Barbara Kopple, Nancy Baker, Anne Lewis.

———**Documentary-Style Film (Fictionalized Documentary, Pseudo-Documentary, Quasi-Documentary, Semidocumentary)**   These terms have been used to describe films which combine documentary techniques with the dramatic. In some instances, documentary material is mixed with fictional scenes, or events that have taken place are reconstructed or recreated in films which resemble documentaries, e.g., Gillo Pontecorvo's *La Battaglia di Algeri* (1965). Some film exposés and neorealist films also fit into the documentary-style film.

Kameradschaft / La Tragédie de la mine (G / F 31) G. W. Pabst *aka Comradeship.*   *Toni* (F 35) Jean Renoir *aka Les Amours de Toni.*   *Western Approaches* (GB 44) Pat Jackson *aka The Raider.*   *La Bataille du Rail* (F 45) René Clement *aka (The) Battle of the Rails.*   *The House on 92nd Street* (45) Henry Hathaway *aka House of 92nd Street / Now It Can Be Told.*   *Roma Città aperta* (It 45) Roberto Rossellini *aka Città aperta / Open City / Rome, Open City.*   *Boomerang* (47) Elia Kazan.   *The Naked City* (48) Jules Dassin *aka Homicide.*   *O saisons, ô châteaux* (F 57) Agnès Varda *aka Castles through the Ages.*   *Les Quatre cent coups* (F 59) François Truffaut *aka The 400 Blows.*   *The Savage Eye* (59) Ben Maddow, Sidney Meyers, Joseph Strick.   *La Battaglia di Algeri / Maarakat Alger* (It / Alg 65) Gillo Pontecorvo *aka Battle of Algiers / The Battle of Algiers.*   *The Boston Strangler* (68) Richard Fleischer.

——**Ethnographic Film (Anthropological Film, Nature Film)**   Ethnographic films deal with the cultural and sociological aspects of different peoples. They may focus on primitive or modern societies, but they always seek to fathom the beliefs and societal systems by which the societies operate so that others may learn to understand them. In this respect, they are different from most travel films which concentrate superficially on a cultural group or on its most glamorous aspects. On the subject of anthropological film, *see Principles of Visual Anthropology*, ed. by Paul Hockings (The Hague: Mouton Publishers, 1975).

Nanook of the North (22) Robert Flaherty.   *Grass* (25) Meriam Cooper, Ernest B. Schoedsack *aka Grass: A Nation's Battle / Grass: The Epic of a Lost Tribe.*   *The Hunters* (56) John Marshall.   *Les maîtres fous* (F 54-55) Jean Rouch *aka Mad Masters / The Master Madmen.*   *Dead Birds* (US / Hol 61-63) Robert Gardner.   *Pour la suite du monde / Moontrap* (Can 61-62) Pierre Perrault, Michel Brault *aka For Those Who Follow.*   *Le Mystère Koumiko* (F 64) Chris Marker *aka The Koumiko Mystery.*   *Desert People* (Aust 66) Ian Dunlop; Richard Howe Tucker (photographer).   *The Holy Ghost People* (68) Nathan Gerrard (consultant); Peter Adair (photographer).   *The Village* (69) Walter Goldschmidt, Colin Young; Mark McCarty (photographer).   *The Nuer* (70) Hilary Harris, George Briedenbach, Robert Gardner.   *César's Bark Canoe / César et son Canot d'écorce* (Can 71) Bernard Gosselin.   *River of Sand* (74) Robert Gardner.   *To Live with Herds* (74) David MacDougall and Judith MacDougall.   *The Wedding Camels* (76) David MacDougall and Judith MacDougall [Turkana narration].   *Queros: The Shape of Survival* (78) John Cohen.   *Shamanen im blinden Land* (G 78-80) Michael Oppitz [in 2 parts] *aka Shamans of the Blind Country.*   *Land Where the Blues Began* (82) Alan Lomax.   *Forest of Bliss* (85) Robert Gardner.

——**Feminist Documentary**   As with feminist film (q.v.) in general, the concern of the feminist documentary is to present women's point of view to audiences in order to correct ingrained, common misconceptions about women. These documentaries also seek to expand on women's topics and issues to encourage self-awareness, inform, educate, or foster militancy to further the women's cause. There has been support for the feminist documentary as a new genre; it already comprises a substantial body of works. *See* Julia Lesage, "The Political Aesthetics of the Feminist Documentary Film," *Quarterly Review of Film Studies* 3(1978): 507–23.

> *The Woman's Film* (70) by the Women of San Francisco Newsreel (Louise Alaimo, Judy Smith, Ellen Souin). *The Continuous Woman* (73) Twin Cities Women's Film Collective. *Self Health* (74) by San Francisco Women's Health Collective (Allie Light, Judy Irola, Joan Musante). *Rape* (75) Jo Ann Elam. *Woman to Woman* (75) Donna Deitch. *Some American Feminists* (Can 77) Luce Guilbeault, Nicole Brossard, Margaret Wescott. *Mirror Phase* (GB 78) Carola Klein. *Daughter Rite* (78) Michelle Citron. *The Song of the Shirt* (79) Susan Clayton, Jonathan Curling. *Susana* (79) Susana Blaustein. *The Life and Times of Rosie the Riveter* (80) Connie Field.

——**Nature Film**   The term has been applied to documentaries which study plant and animal life, to films which emphasize the interaction of people and nature, e.g., Arne Sucksdorff's *Det Stora Aventyret / The Great Adventure* (1953), to films about wildlife in its natural habitat, e.g., Walt Disney's True-Life Adventure film *The Living Desert* (1953), or even to films featuring nudists or primitive peoples.

> *The Living Desert* (53) James Algar [1st feature-length True-Life Adventure film]. *Det Stora Aventyret* (Sw 53) Arne Sucksdorff *aka The Great Adventure*. *The Vanishing Prairie* (54) James Algar. *The African Lion* (55) James Algar. *Secrets of Life* (56) James Algar. *White Wilderness* (58) James Algar. *Jungle Cat* (60) James Algar [13th and last film in the True-Life Adventure series (1949-60), all but one directed by Algar]. *The Best of Walt Disney's True-Life Adventures* (75) James Algar.

——**Persuasive Documentary (Exposé Documentary)**   A type of documentary which tries to convince the viewer of its thesis. It uses exposé in its most blatant form as propaganda film (q.v.). *See also* **FACTUAL FILM.**

> *Report on Senator McCarthy* (54) Edward R. Murrow. *Harvest of Shame* (60 TV) David Lowe [CBS Reports series]. *The Selling of the Pentagon* (71 TV) Peter Davis (producer and writer) [CBS News special].

——**Romantic Documentary (Naturalist Documentary)**   The term romantic has been applied to the sort of documentary that idealizes humankind and nature, tends to praise the natural environment, or propounds the conservation of the natural habitat. It is a tendency which can be traced back to Robert J. Flaherty (1884–1951) whose films epitomize the romantic tradition. These documentaries are also at times referred to as nature films.

> *Moana of the South Seas* (25) Robert J. Flaherty, Frances Hubbard Flaherty *aka Moana*. *Man of Aran* (GB 34) Robert J. Flaherty. *Louisiana Story* (48) Robert Flaherty. *The Kon-Tiki* (Nor 51) Thor Heyerdahl. *The Sea Around Us* (53) Irwin Allen (producer and author of continuity and commentary). *Le Monde du Silence* (F 55) Jacques-Yves Cousteau, Louis Malle *aka The Silent World*. *The African Elephant* (71) Simon Trevor *aka King Elephant*. *Blue Water, White Death* (71) Peter Gimbel, James Lipscomb.

———**Sociological Documentary** A type of documentary that appeared towards the late 1920s, and that put its emphasis on some prevailing condition or factor and presented it from a sociological point of view.

Drifters (GB 29) John Grierson. *Nieuwe Gronden* (Hol 34) Jory Ivens *aka New Earth*. *The Plow That Broke the Plains* (36) Pare Lorentz. *The River* (37) Pare Lorentz.

———**War Documentary** War documentaries are best defined as nonfiction war films. They come in many forms and may be classified according to their function. World War II saw an extensive production of war documentaries and nonfiction films of various types — training films, incentive films, combat films, reconnaissance films, propaganda films. They were made to train the personnel, boost production, document the war, help to plan strategy, and to uplift the moral of the civil population and fighting men. They all helped in the war effort. The Vietnam war also drew the attention of documentarists and saw another upsurge of war documentaries, mostly denouncing American intervention. The war documentary is an old and essential variant of the documentary film. *See also* **Factual War Films** in **WAR FILM** entry.

Feuertaufe (G 40) Hans Bertram *aka Baptism of Fire*. *Listen to Britain* (GB 41) Humphrey Jennings, Stewart McAlister. *Stalingrad* (USSR 43) by the Central Newsreel Studios, edited by Leonid Varlomov *aka The City That Stopped Hitler — Heroic Stalingrad / The Story of Stalingrad*. *Let There Be Light* (46) John Huston. *Sad Song of Yellow Skin / Le Jaune en péril* (Can 70) Michael Rubbo. *Hearts and Minds* (74) Peter Davis.

See also the following separate entries: **ACTUALITY, CINEMA VERITE, CITY SYMPHONY, COMPILATION FILM, DIRECT CINEMA, DOCUDRAMA, FILM ABOUT ART, FREE CINEMA, KINO-GLAZ, MONDO FILM, NEWSREEL, PROPAGANDA FILM, SEX DOCUMENTARY, SPECULATIVE DOCUMENTARY.**

Documentary Drama *see* **DOCUDRAMA;** *see also* **TELEVISION DRAMA**

Documentary Film, Documentary-Style Film *see* **DOCUMENTARY**

Documentary War Film *see* **WAR FILM: Factual War Films**

Dog *see* **TURKEY**

DOMESTIC COMEDY (Family Comedy) Somewhat popular in the thirties, domestic comedies centered on the home and family, and the inter-relationships between its various members. They usually included awkward, embarrassing or funny situations and minor family problems which were cleared up by the end of the picture to make way for a happy ending. The shenanigans of madcap, wacky families, clearly allied to screwball comedy (q.v.) would also fit as a subspecies of domestic comedy. The domestic comedy was a forerunner of television situation comedy. The form is popular on television.

Emma (32) Clarence Brown. *The Three-Cornered Moon* (33) Elliot Nugent. *The Last Gentleman* (34) Sidney Landfield. *Life Begins at Forty* (35) George Marshall. *Wives Never Know* (36) Elliot Nugent. *Danger — Love at Work* (37) Otto Preminger. *There Goes the Groom* (37) Joseph Santley. *Blondie* (38) Frank Strayer [1st in a series of 28 "Blondie" films (1938–50)]. *Merrily We Live* (38) Norman Z. McLeod. *You're Only Young Once* (38) George B. Seitz [2nd film in the "Andy Hardy" series: 16 films (1937–58), following *A Family Affair* (37) also directed by Seitz]. *San Diego, I Love You* (44) Reginald LeBorg. *Father of the Bride* (50) Vincente Minnelli. *The Courtship of Eddie's Father* (63) Vincente Minnelli.

Domestic Melodramas *see* **MELODRAMA**

Doomsday Film *see* **SCIENCE FICTION FILM: SF Disaster Films**

Dope Film *see* **DRUG FILM**

Do's and Don'ts Film *see* **FACTUAL FILM: Jeopardy Film**

Double Bill *see* **DOUBLE FEATURE**

DOUBLE FEATURE (Double Bill, Dual)   Two full-length motion pictures at the local film theater. When it was common practice for theaters to show double bills, the programming consisted of two "A" pictures or, more frequently, of one "A" picture (the main or first feature) and one "B" picture (the supporting or second feature).

Down the Toilet, Down the Tube *see* **TURKEY**

Dracula Films *see* **VAMPIRE FILM**

Drag Genre *see* **CROSS-DRESSING FILM**

DRAMA   Drama is a major literary form not restricted to the stage. In cinematic usage, drama is a category comprising films that escape the dictates of formula, which is the basis of genre movies. Films with a high dramatic content, not of a melodramatic nature, that approach their subject matter in a "serious" manner are generally classified as drama. These films do not, or should not, conform with stereotyped situations — not that stereotyping is completely eradicated from drama. It permeates and influences the work of filmmakers all over the world, drawing, as they do, their inspiration from the vast pool of past cinematic achievements. However, stereotyping in drama, when noticeable, is more sophisticated than in genre movies and overrides any sense of cliché. The label drama seems to elevate automatically the prestige of any film production, hence it is used in word combinations (war drama, musical drama, science fiction drama, comedy-drama) to point out that a film is more than mere genre — war movie, musical, science fiction, comedy, or whatever the frame of the dramatic content may be.

Most films classified as drama rely on an already-existing source and they are adaptations of novels, plays, or other media, rather than of stories originally created for the screen. Dramatic films are sometimes presented in the format of the episodic, portmanteau, or ark film. Biography is also used etensively as a good source of drama. Many excellent dramas are found under different headings and only a minimal sample is listed below.

The Big Parade (25) King Vidor. *How Green Was My Valley* (41) John Ford. *In Which We Serve* (GB 42) Noel Coward, David Lean. *The Magnificent Ambersons* (42) Orson Welles. *The Lost Weekend* (45) Billy Wilder. *The Heiress* (49) William Wyler. *Pinky* (49) Elia Kazan. *The African Queen* (51) John Huston. *Moulin Rouge / Moulin-Rouge* (GB / F / US 52) John Huston. *East of Eden* (55) Elia Kazan. *Separate Tables* (58) Delbert Mann. *Long Day's Journey into Night* (62) Sidney Lumet. *Ship of Fools* (65) Stanley Kramer. *A Man for All Seasons* (GB 66) Fred Zinnemann. *Midnight Cowboy* (69) John Schlesinger. *Nashville* (75) Robert Altman. *One Flew Over the Cuckoo's Nest* (75) Milos Forman. *Kramer vs. Kramer* (79) Robert Benton. *The Last of England* (87) Derek Jarman. *An Angel at My Table* (NZ 90) Jane Campion.

Drama-Documentary *see* **DOCUDRAMA**

Drama Serial, Drama Series *see* **TELEVISION DRAMA**

DRAMATIC FILM   A fiction film that presents emotional involvement and conflict on the part of the protagonists and which usually follows the traditional dramatic structural pattern of exposition, rising action, climax, and resolution of the conflict.

Dramatic-Narrative Film *see* **FICTIONAL FILM**

Dramatic Reconstruction *see* **TELEVISION DRAMA: Documentary Drama**

Dramatization, Dramatized Documentary *see* **DOCUDRAMA**

Drawing-Room Comedy *see* **COMEDY OF MANNERS**

Drawn Film *see* **CARTOON**

Drawn on Film *see* **ANIMATED FILM: Cameraless Animated Film**

Drug-Abuse Film *see* **DRUG FILM**

DRUG FILM (Dope Film, Drug-Oriented Film, Narcotics Film)   The use and abuse of drugs is a topic that has featured in many films.[26] As early as 1894, a 30-second film made by W. K. Laurie Dickson for Thomas Edison titled *Chinese Opium Den* dealt with opium smoking. Drug films have been plentiful and all major psychoactive drugs from alcohol to tranquilizers have appeared in films at one time or another. Fads for a particular drug have dictated to some extent the abundance of movies dealing with that drug as compared to those dealing with other drugs. To fully qualify as a drug film, the film has to have drug consumption, addiction, or drug trafficking as its major concern. Most drug films are unsympathetic to the drug habit; they are antidrug films. Besides documentaries on drugs, a curious offshoot of the drug film is the drug-abuse film. For the most part, drug-abuse films are fictionalized short films made by an educational institution or official body to deal with the drug issue. They are mostly scare films cheaply produced with the intention of warning the public about the dangers of drug taking.[27] *See also* **VICE FILM.**

Chinese Opium Den (1894) W. K. Laurie Dickson *aka Opium Den / Opium Joint / Opium Smokers / Robetta and Doretto.* **To the Ends of the Earth** (48) Robert Stevenson. *Teen-age Menace* (53) Prod. Bill Free. **The Man with the Golden Arm** (55) Otto Preminger. *Escapement* (GB 57) Montgomery Tully *aka The Dream Machine / The Electronic Monster / Zex, the Electronic Fiend.* **Monkey on My Back** (57) Andre de Toth. **High School Confidential!** (58) Jack Arnold *aka Young Hellions.* **The Connection** (61) Sherley Clarke. **Long Day's Journey into Night** (62) Sidney Lumet. **Way Out** (66) Irvin S. Yeaworth, Jr. **Turn On, Turn In, Drop Out** (67) Robin Clark. **More** (Lux 69) Barber Schroeder. **Born to Win** (71) Ivan Passer *aka Addict.* **Dusty and Sweet McGee** (71) Floyd Mutrux. *Not Me* (71) Glenn M. Parker. *Panic in Needle Park* (71) Jerry Schatzberg. **Go Ask Alice** (72 TV) John Korty. **A Cry for Love** (80 TV) Paul Wendkos. **I'm Dancing as Fast as I Can** (82) Jack Hofsiss. **Bird** (88) Clint Eastwood. **Clean and Sober** (88) Glenn Gordon Caron. **Drugstore Cowboy** (89) Gus Van Sant, Jr.

Some drugs seem to attract the attention of filmmakers more than others. These include films dealing with marijuana, psychedelics, and cocaine.

——**Cocaine Movies**   Cocaine was the in-drug in the movie world of the silent stars and consequently featured in some films. There was also a smattering of cocaine films in the 1930s and again from the late 1940s on.

The Mystery of the Leaping Fish (16) John Emerson. **Human Wreckage** (23) John Griffith Wray. **The Pace That Kills** (28) Norton S. Parker, William A. O'Connor. *Cocaine Fiends* (35) Wm. A O'Connor *aka The Pace That Kills.* **Fall Guy** (47) Reginald Le Borg. **Sensations** (Hol 75) Alberto Ferro (Lasse Braun). *Cocaine Cowboys* (78) Ulli Lommel. **Cocaine: One Man's Seduction** (83 TV) Paul Wendkos. **Torchlight** (84) Tom Wright. *The Boost* (88) Harold Becker.

——**Marijuana Drug Films**   The perils of marijuana have been frequently pictorialized in a variety of films which range from hysterical and exploitative versions to counterculture eulogies. The late 1920s and 1930s saw a handful of marijuana films; they became more numerous from the late 1940s on.

Marihuana (36) Dwain Esper *aka Marihuana "The Weed with Roots in Hell" / The Pusher.* **Reefer Madness** (36) Louis Gasnier *aka Assassin of Youth / The Burning Question / Dope Addict / Doped Youth / Love Madness / Tell Your Children.* **Wild Weed** (49) Sherman Scott *aka The Devil's Weed / She Should'a Have Said No! / She Shoulda Said No—But She Didn't.* *Cannabis / New York–Parigi per una condanna a morte / Cannabis—Engel der Gewalt* (F / It / G 69) Pierre Koralnik *aka Mafia Wants Blood.* **The Evil Weed** (72) Prod. George Leonard. **The Sexual Effects of Marijuana** (75) [with John Holmes]. *Up in Smoke* (78) Lou Adler.

——**Psychedelic Films (Acid Films)**   Films in which the participants indulge in the hallucinations that psychedelic drugs provide became fashionable with the discovery of LSD and the advent of the flower people in the 1960s.

Chappaqua (66) Conrad Rooks. *Hallucination Generation* (66) Edward Andrew Mann *aka The Drifters / Hallucination. Movie Star, American Style;* or *LSD, I Hate You* (66) Albert Zugsmith. *The Trip* (67) Roger Corman. *The Weird World of LSD* (67) Robert Ground. *The Acid Eaters* (68) B. Ron Elliott *aka The Acid People. Psych-Out* (68) Richard Rush *aka The Love Children.*

Drug Movies *see* **CRIME FILM**

Drug-Oriented Film *see* **DRUG FILM**

Dual *see* **DOUBLE FEATURE**

Dud *see* **TURKEY**

Dystopian Films *see* **SCIENCE FICTION FILM**

EALING COMEDY   A style of English comedy made in the 1940s and 1950s by the Ealing Studios which achieved worldwide recognition and success. It formed a minor genre of comedy henceforth associated with the idea of typical British humor at its best. The Ealing comedies included sophisticated comedy, social satire, and black comedies such as the famous *Kind Hearts and Coronets* (1949) in which Alec Guinness played eight different roles.[28]

Come On George (GB 39) Anthony Kimmins. *Trouble Brewing* (GB 39) Anthony Kimmins. *Young Man's Fancy* (GB 39) Robert Stevenson. *Let George Do It* (GB 40) Marcel Varnel. *Hue and Cry* (GB 47) Charles Crichton. *Passport to Pimlico* (GB 48) Henry Cornelius. *Kind Hearts and Coronets* (GB 49) Robert Hamer. *Whisky Galore!* (GB 49) Alexander Mackendrick *aka Tight Little Island. The Lavender Hill Mob* (GB 51) Charles Crichton. *The Man in the White Suit* (GB 51) Alexander Mackendrick. *The 'Maggie'* (GB 53) Alexander Mackendrick *aka High and Dry. The Ladykillers* (GB 55) Alexander Mackendrick.

EARLY FILM   The first public screen presentation of a motion picture took place in Paris on March 22, 1895, when August and Louis Lumière showed *La Sortie des ouvriers de l'usines Lumière* (1894). Between 1896 and 1906 thousands of films were produced worldwide. Of these early films only a few have survived, the others having disintegrated or been irretrievably lost. Although the great majority of these films are no longer extant, producers' catalogues with detailed descriptions of the films and old programs listing titles of films can give an idea of their content. Early films were shorts with lengths varying from 15 ft. or less to 850 ft. or more (approximately 15 seconds' running time to over 14 minutes) with the longer lengths becoming more prevalent as the twentieth century progressed.[29] Imitation and repetition of subject matter were characteristic and the films may easily be grouped into several distinct types. The main types of early films include actuality (q.v.), topical and interest films, as well as other types like panoramic films[30] and travelogues, filmed vaudeville, trick films (q.v.), comedy and drama or story films. Early films offer the film historian a means of evaluating the development of the film medium.

Early Morning Program *see* **TELEVISION NEWS: Breakfast Television Show**

Eastern *see* **PARTISAN FILM**

Ecology Film *see* **FACTUAL FILM: Educational Film**

Educational *see* **ACTUALITY**

Educational Film *see* **FACTUAL FILM**

Eight *see* **STAG MOVIE**

Elegiac Western *see* **WESTERN: Modern Westerns**

Emmanuelle *see* **SOFT-CORE SEX-EXPLOITATION FILM**

Empire-Building Picture *see* **BRITISH EMPIRE FILM**

End-of-the-World Film *see* **SCIENCE FICTION FILM: SF Disaster Films**

Entertainment Film *see* **FICTIONAL FILM**

EPIC (Epic Film, Film Epic) Traditionally, epics were long narratives written in verse telling of the exploits of some mythical or legendary hero either defending the fatherland from its enemies or engaging in long sea voyages and land travels that would put him through a series of rugged adventures. The vagaries of destiny would test his valor and resilience, his equanimity and strength of character. If successful and worthy, he would be entitled to a place in the national pantheon of heroic figures and his deeds would be sung for time to come. Film epics also tell of such men and of their wars and adventures. They also tell of a national or collective will as the people, united in a common national or ethnic goal, strive against immense odds for survival as a nation or race, endeavor to conquer or settle untrodden lands, fight enemies or defend the fatherland. Movie epics are usually set in the historical past, but they can also deal with contemporary or even future events. Frequently, though, the setting is antiquity— mythological, biblical, Greek or Roman times—and the film sets, as a rule, are lavish and spectacular. The epic is an action genre which started in Italy in the early 1900s and quickly spread elsewhere. Film epics have been made in most film producing nations, but Italy and America account for the biggest output. In America, although there had been earlier films on epic themes, e.g., *The Life of Moses* (1909–10), the genre is greatly indebted to the contribution of two major film directors: D. W. Griffith and Cecil B.

DeMille. Griffith's *Judith of Betulia* (1913) was the first full-length American film to be categorized as epic, and his *The Birth of a Nation* (1914) was the first Hollywood-produced epic. The two major cycles in Hollywood epics took place between 1915 and 1927, and in the period stretching from the premiere of *The Robe* (1953), the first CinemaScope epic, to the completion of *Cleopatra* (1963), one of the greatest Hollywood box-office fiascoes, that took three years to make. Italy also saw a resurgence of the epic genre in the fifties and sixties when dozens of minor Italian epics were almost mass produced; they are better described as "peplums" (q.v.).

The terms epic and spectacular are very often used interchangeably and this has created a degree of confusion among critics as to how to class certain films as epics. The epic label has been broadened to include almost anything that is big or grandiose regardless of whether it was constructed according to the epic formula or not. Spectacle, costume picture, heroic film, historical film, monumental film — all these terms have variously been used for epic, but they have diverse connotations and are not restricted to epic alone. For a study of the American epic, *see* Foster Hirsch, *The Hollywood Epic* (Cranbury, NJ: A. S. Barnes, 1978). *See also* Gary A. Smith, *Epic Films: Casts, Credits and Commentary on Over 250 Historical Spectacle Movies* (Jefferson, NC: McFarland, 1991) and Derek Elley, *The Epic Film* (London: Routledge & Kegan Paul, 1984).

————**Biblical Epics (Religious Epics)**   A great many epics have a biblical or religious background; they are highly moralistic in tone and proclaim the triumph of right over wrong, dutifully rewarding the just or showing the martyr's self-sacrifice for the furtherance of divine will on earth.

The Life of Moses (09-10) J. Stuart Blackton [rel. in 5 parts].   *Quo Vadis* (It 12) Enrico Guazzoni.   *Judith of Betulia* (13) D. W. Griffith *aka* (with added footage) *Her Condoned Sin* (17).   *Ben-Hur: A Tale of the Christ* (25) Fred Niblo (plus Christy Cabanne, Ferdinand P. Earle, B. Reeves Eason).   *Noah's Ark* (28) Michael Curtiz *aka Noah's Ark and the Flood That Destroyed the World / Noah's Ark: The Story of the Deluge.   Fabiolà / Fabiola* (It / F 48) Alessandro Blasetti *aka Fabiola and the Fighting Gladiator / Fabulous Fabiola / The Fighting Gladiator.   David and Bathsheba* (51) Henry King.   *Quo Vadis?* (51) Mervyn LeRoy.   *The Robe* (53) Henry Koster [1st CinemaScope feature film].   *Salome* (53) William Dieterle.   *Demetrius and the Gladiators* (54) Delmer Daves.   *The Silver Chalice* (54) Victor Saville.   *Ben Hur* (59) William Wyler (plus Andrew Marton, Richard Thorpe) *aka Ben-Hur: A Tale of the Christ.The Big Fisherman* (59) Frank Borzage.   *Solomon and Sheba* (US / GB 59) King Vidor.   *Ester et il re / Esther and the King* (It / US 60) Raoul Walsh.   *Barabba / Barabbas* (It / US 61) Richard Fleischer.   *King of Kings / Rey de Reyes* (US / Sp 61) Nicholas Ray.   *The Greatest Story Ever Told* (65) George Stevens (plus Jean Negulesco, David Lean, Charlton Heston).   *Quo Vadis?* (It 85 TV) Franco Rossi.

————**DeMille Epics**   Cecil B. DeMille (1881–1959), known worldwide for his epics, was one of the great Hollywood directors. His pseudohistorical films became known as DeMille epics.

The Ten Commandments (22) Cecil B. DeMille. *The Sign of the Cross* (32) Cecil B. DeMille. *Cleopatra* (34) Cecil B. DeMille. *The Crusades* (35) Cecil B. DeMille. *King of Kings* (27) Cecil B. DeMille. *Unconquered* (47) Cecil B. DeMille. *Samson and Delilah* (48) Cecil B. DeMille. *The Ten Commandments* (56) Cecil B. DeMille.

——**Historical Epics**   As the name implies, they are based on past or recent history, but it is well-known that historical epics are famous for their lack of historical accuracy; rather they manipulate history for the sake of spectacle. The historical epic has also been placed in the category of propaganda. The nations and peoples of antiquity (the lands of Mesopotamia, Egypt, Greece, Rome) are a favorite subject for the historical epic.

Cabiria (It 13) Giovanni Pastrone. *Cleopatra* (17) J. Gordon Edwards. *Queen of Sheba* (21) J. Gordon Edwards. *Bronenosets "Potyomkin"* (USSR 25) Sergei M. Eisenstein, Grigori Alexandrov *aka The Armoured Cruiser Potemkin / Battleship Potemkin / Bronenosets Potemkin / Potemkin. The Last Days of Pompeii* (35) Ernest B. Schoedsack. *Triumph des Willens* (G 34-36) Leni Riefenstahl *aka The Triumph of the Will. The Egyptian* (54) Michael Curtiz. *Helen of Troy* (54) Robert Wise (plus Raoul Walsh). *Alexander the Great / Alejandro Magno* (US / Sp 56) Robert Rossen. *Spartacus* (60) Stanley Kubrick, Anthony Mann. *Lawrence of Arabia* (GB / US 62) David Lean. *Cleopatra* (GB / US 63) Joseph L. Mankiewicz, Rouben Mamoulian. *The Fall of the Roman Empire / La caída del Imperio Romano / La caduta dell'impero romano* (US / Sp / It 64) Anthony Mann (plus Andrew Marton). *Faraon* (Pol 65) Jerzy Kawalerowicz *aka The Pharaoh. Popioly* (Pol 65) Andrzej Wajda *aka Ashes / The Lost Army. Potop* (Pol / USSR 74) Jerzy Hoffman *aka The Deluge* [in 2 parts]. *Caligola / Caligula* (It / US 77) Giovanni Tinto Brass *aka Io Caligula. Hero* (GB 82) Barney Platts-Mills [1st feature film in Gaelic]. *Shue gim yan shau luk* (HK 87) Ann Hui *aka Romance of Book & Sword* [in 2 parts].

——**Moral Epics (Ethical Epics)**   They focus on the destiny of the human race and show the individual's progress through time as a rational being capable of discerning right from wrong, even if he/she is not always able to do right. They have a message to impart and show human historical development on a global or cosmic scale. They may use biblical or religious motifs.

Civilization (16) Thomas Harper Ince, Raymond B. West, Reginald Barker *aka Civilization: What Every True Briton Is Fighting For / He Who Returned. Intolerance* (14-16) D. W. Griffith *aka Intolerance, Love's Struggle Through the Ages / Intolerance, a Sun-play of the Ages / Love's Struggle Through the Ages / The Mother and the Law* [in 1919, two 7-reel expanded versions of "The Babylonian Story" and "The Modern Story" episodes were released as *The Fall of Babylon* and *The Mother and the Law* respectively]. *Metropolis — das Schicksas einer Menschheit im Jahre 2000* (G 26) Fritz Lang *aka Metropolis. Things to Come* (GB 36) William Cameron Menzies *aka The Shape of Things to Come / Whither Mankind. 2001: A Space Odyssey* (US / GB 68) Stanley Kubrick *aka Journey Beyond Space / Space Odyssey. Gandhi* (GB / Ind / US 82) Richard Attenborough.

——**Mythological Epics**   Mythology is a rich source for epic material, and surprisingly, it has not been plundered more often by the makers of epics (except the "peplums" made in Italy). This is in contrast with the horror and fantasy genres that have used mythological themes frequently in their films.

Amphitryon / Les Dieux s'amusent (G / F 35) Reinhold Schünzel, Albert Valentin *aka Aus den Wolken kommt das Glück. Ulisse / Ulysses* (It / US 53) Mario Camerini. *Atlas* (US / Gr 60) Roger Corman. *Teseo contro il minotauro* (It 60) Silvio Amadio *aka The Minotaur / The Warlord of Crete. L'ira di Achille* (It 62) Marino Girolami *aka Achilles. Perseo l'invincibile / Perseo y Medusa* (It / Sp 62) Alberto De Martino *aka Medusa vs. the Son of Hercules / Perseus Against the Monsters / El valle de los hombres de piedra. Jason and the Argonauts* (GB 63) Don Chaffey *aka Jason and the Golden Fleece. L'Odissea / L'Odyssée* (It / F / G 68 TV) Franco Rossi, Mario Bava, Piero Schivazzappa *aka L'avventura di Ulisse / The Odyssey* [in 6 parts; also as a feature]. *L'avventura di Enea / L'Eneide* (It / F / G 71 TV) Franco Rossi [in 6 parts; also as a feature]. *Das goldene Ding* (G 71) Ula Stöckl, Edgar Reitz, Alf Brustellin, Nicos Perakis *aka The Golden Thing / The Thing of Gold. Le Guerriere dal seno nudo / Les Amazones* (It / F / Sp 73) Terence Young *aka Le Amazzoni / The Amazons / War Goddess. Veiviseren* (Nor 87) Nils Gang *aka Pathfinder.*

———**National Epics** They are based on the feats of a national legendary or historical hero. They show great, decisive, national battles, the pioneer spirit of the peoples that formed a nation, or great revolutionary upheavals. They may be propagandistic (Russian epics are a good example of this), chauvinistic, or jingoistic. They are always patriotic.

The Birth of a Nation (14) D. H. Griffith *aka The Birth of the Nation; or The Clansman / The Clansman. The Covered Wagon* (23) James Cruze [1st epic Western]. *America* (24) D. W. Griffith *aka Love and Sacrifice. Die Nibelungen — ein deutsches Heldenlied* (G 22-24) Fritz Lang [2 parts: I. *Siegfried,* II. *Kriemhilds Rache*] *aka The Nibelunge Saga (Siegfried, the Vengeance of Kriemhild).* **Napoléon** (F / G / Sp / Cz / Sw / US 25-27) Abel Gance *aka Napoléon (vu par Abel Gance)* [sound versions: *Napoléon Bonaparte* (F 34-35), *Bonaparte et la Révolution* (F 69-71)]. *Aleksandr Nevskii* (USSR 38) Sergei Mikhailovitch Eisenstein, Dmitri Vasiliev *aka Alexander Newsky. Gone with the Wind* (39) Victor Fleming (uncredited: George Cukor, Sidney Franklin, Sam Wood) *aka GWTW / Tomorrow Is Another Day / The Wind. Ivan Groznyi I* (USSR 44) Sergei M. Eisenstein *aka Ivan the Terrible Part I. Ivan Groznyi: Boyarskii Zagovor* (USSR 45) Sergei M. Eisenstein *aka Ivan the Terrible, Part II: The Boyars Plot. Exodus* (60) Otto Preminger. *El Cid* (US / Sp / It 61) Anthony Mann *aka Samuel Bronston's El Cid. An-Nasr Salah ad-Din* (Egy 63) Youssef Chahine *aka Saladin. Den røde kappe / Rautha skikkjan / Den röda kappan* (Den / Icel / Sw 67) Gabriel Axel *aka Hagvard and Signe / The Red Mantle. Voyna i mir* (USSR 62-67) Sergey Bondarchuk [4 parts: *Andrey Bolkonskiy, Natasha Rostova, 1812 god, Pier Bezyukhov*]. *Tulipää* (Fin 80) Pirjo Honkasalo, Pekka Lehto *aka Flame Top.*

———**Revisionist Epics** Revisionist epics seek to correct past representations of history or to modify the stultified conventions governing the genre. In a way, they deviate from the established norm, but their epic quality and some epic elements are clearly discernible, even in those films that form part of other genres.

Il Gattopardo / Le guépard / The Leopard (It / F / US 63) Luchino Visconti. *The Charge of the Light Brigade* (GB 67) Tony Richardson. *Satyricon / Fellini-Satyricon* (It / F 69) Federico Fellini [*Cf.* Gian Luigi Polidoro's *Satyricon* (It 68)]. *Little Big Man* (70) Arthur Penn. *Medea / Médée* (It / F / G 69) Pier Paolo Pasolini. *Robin and Marian* (GB / US 76) Richard Lester.

Epic Film   *see*   EPIC

Epic Westerns   *see*   WESTERN

EPISODE FILM (Anthology Film, Composite Film, Episodic Film, Multiple Story Film, Omnibus Film, Portmanteau Film, Sketch Film)   A film composed of different parts or episodes which are in fact different stories, usually connected by an overall theme and forming a feature-length film. The segments or shorts that form the episode film may be by the same director or by a number of directors, nationally produced or co-produced by different countries. There are various types of episodic films, and the format is very popular in Europe. The episode film format is frequently used in horror movies and sex films where a common ploy is to gather a group of people together in some room or other confined area and have them tell each other their experiences or their dreams.

Sometimes, shorts made by a director or by several different directors are put together into a feature for the sole purpose of reaching a larger audience. This is the case with some experimental shorts made by underground filmmakers, university students, or porno directors.

Episode film is a term that has also been applied to the serial, as serials are basically made of episodes which have narrative continuity and a conclusion at the end of the serial. In the episode film per se, the episodes are separate and complete stories joined together by a common theme, narrative continuity or both. The terms portmanteau film and anthology film have also been used for an episode film in which different directors contribute their own segments.

Intolerance (14-16) D. W. Griffith *aka Intolerance, Love's Struggle Through the Ages / Intolerance, a Sun-play of the Ages / Love's Struggle Through the Ages / The Mother and the Law* [in 1919, two 7-reel expanded versions of "The Babylonian Story" and "The Modern Story" episodes were released as *The Fall of Babylon and The Mother and the Law* respectively]. *If I Had a Million* (32) James Cruze, Stephen S. Roberts, Norman McLeod, Norman Taurog, H. Bruce Humberston, Ernst Lubitsch, William A. Seiter, Lothar Mendes (uncredited). *Tales of Manhattan* (42) Julien Duvivier. *Flesh and Fantasy* (43) Julien Duvivier. *Dead of Night* (GB 45) Alberto Cavalcanti, Basil Dearden, Robert Hamer, Charles Crichton. *Quartet* (GB 48) Ken Annakin, Arthur Crabtree, Harold French, Ralph Smart. *Trio* (GB 50) Ken Annakin, Harold French. *Encore* (GB 51) Harold French, Pat Jackson, Anthony Pelissier. *Amore in città* (It 53) Michelangelo Antonioni, Federico Fellini, Dino Risi, Cesare Zavattini, Francesco Maselli, Alberto Lattuada,

Carlo Lizzani *aka Love in the City. Meet Me Tonight* (GB 52) Anthony
Pelissier *aka Tonight at 8:30. The Story of Three Loves* (53) Vincente Min-
nelli. *Les Lettres de mon moulin* (F 54) Marcel Pagnol *aka Letters from My
Windmill. Three Cases of Murder* (GB 54) Wendy Toye, David Eady,
George More O'Ferrall. *Rising of the Moon* (Ire / US 57) John Ford *aka
Three Leaves of a Shamrock. La Française et l'amour* (F 60) Henri Decoin,
Jean Delannoy, Michel Boisrond, René Clair, Henri Verneuil, Christian-
Jaque, Jean-Paul Le Chanois *aka Love and the French Woman. L'Amour
à vingt ans / L'amore a vent'anni / Liebe mit zwanzig / Milosc dwudziest
olaków / Hatachi no koi* (F / It / G / Pol / J 61) François Truffaut, Renzo
Rossellini, Marcel Ophüls, Andrzej Wajda, Shintaro Ishihara *aka Love at
Twenty. Tales of Terror* (61) Roger Corman *aka Poe's Tales of Terror /
Tales of Horror. Rogopag* (It / F 62) Roberto Rossellini, Pier Paolo
Pasolini, J. L. Godard, Ugo Gregoretti *aka Laviamoci il cervello / RoGoPaG
/ Rogopag (Un joyeux début à la fin du monde). Ieri, oggi, domani / Hier,
aujourd'hui et demain* (It / F 63) Vittorio De Sica *aka Yesterday, Today and
Tomorrow. Twice-Told Tales* (63) Sidney Salkow. *Woman Times Seven
/ Sept fois femme / Sette volte donne* (US / F / It 67) Vittorio De Sica *aka
Woman X 7. Le Petit Théâtre de Jean Renoir / Il teatrino di Jean Renoir*
(F / It / G 69 TV) Jean Renoir *aka The Little Theatre (Theater) of Jean
Renoir. Boccaccio '70 / Boccace 70* (It / F 62) Vittorio De Sica, Federico
Fellini, Mario Monicelli, Luchino Viscont. *Kaidan* (J 64) Masaki Kobayashi
aka Ghost Stories / Kwaidan / Weird Tales. Le Streghe (It / F 66) Luchino
Visconti, Mauro Bolognini, Pier Paolo Pasolini, Franco Rossi, Vittorio De
Sica *aka The Witches. Asylum* (GB 72) Roy Ward Baker *aka House of
Crazies. The Vault of Horror* (GB 72) Roy Ward Baker *aka Further Tales
from the Crypt / Tales from the Crypt II. The Best of the New York Erotic
Film Festival* (73) various directors [*Note:* different versions include different
shorts and the running time varies]. *From Beyond the Grave* (US / GB 73)
Kevin Connor *aka The Creature / The Creatures from Beyond the Grave /
Tales from Beyond the Grave / Tales from the Beyond / The Undead.
Trilogy of Terror* (75 TV) Dan Curtis. *Twilight Zone—The Movie* (83)
John Landis. *Cat's Eye* (84) Lewis Teague. *Aria* (GB 86-87) Nicolas Roeg,
Charles Sturridge, Jean-Luc Godard, Julien Temple, Bruce Beresford,
Robert Altman, Franc Roddam, Ken Russell, Derek Jarman, Bill Brydon.

Episodic Film *see* **EPISODE FILM**

Equine Picture *see* **HORSE PIC**

Eroduction *see* **HARD-CORE PORNO FILM**

Erotic Cartoon *see* **CARTOON FILM: Adult Cartoons**

EROTIC FILM   The term applies to a film which gives expression to
any form of eroticism. In cinematic parlance, erotic film has a broad accep-
tation. It includes films with daring, risqué or explicit love scenes, films in
which there is partial or extensive nudity, and films in which sexual deviations are hinted at or depicted. The erotic content, and even what is considered erotic, have varied throughout the history of the motion picture.
However, the erotic matter in films has traditionally consisted of nudity
(although nudity per se is often enough unerotic), partial nudity in

its many variants (stolen glimpses of bare flesh, dishabille, seductive un-dressing), certain physical attributes in women (breasts, well-rounded but-tocks, narrow hips, slender legs), the sex-appeal of some female and male stars (vamps, sexpots, sex kittens, seducers, macho types), and many other instances of erotic expression. A major difference between erotic films and other films that deal with sex is that erotic films do not have to be sex ex-ploitation pictures or pornographic movies. Mainstream, very respectable films featuring major stars among their cast can be termed erotic films: witness *Women in Love* (1969), *Ultimo Tango a Parigi / Last Tango in Paris* (1972), *The Sailor Who Fell from Grace with the Sea* (1976). Eroticism in films or in life is a way of sexual self-expression, and it is thus understood by whoever is responsive to its message. In films it goes as far back as the late 19th century.

Bain de la mondaine (F 1895) Henry Joly. *Après le bal—le tub* (F 1897) Georges Méliès *aka After the Ball / Après le bal le tub ou le bain de la pari-sienne.* **Foolish Wives** (20-21) Eric von Stroheim. **Greed** (23-24) Eric von Stroheim. **Casanova** (F / It 26) Alexander Volkoff. *The Wedding March* (26-27) Eric von Stroheim [2 parts; *The Honeymoon* is a version shown in Europe with material from the second part which was never finished]. *Die Büchse der Pandora* (G 28) G. W. Pabst *aka Lulu / Pandora's Box.* *Der Blaue Engel / The Blue Angel* (G / US 30) Joseph von Sternberg. *Extase / Ekstase* (Cz / Aus 32) Gustav Machaty *aka Ecstasy / Symphonie der Liebe.* *Hon dansade en sommar* (Sw 51) Arne Mattson *aka One Summer of Happiness / She Danced One Summer.* *Sommaren med Monika* (Sw 52) Ingmar Bergman *aka Monika / The Story of a Bad Girl / Summer with Monika.* **Baby Doll** (56) Elia Kazan. *Les Amants* (F 58) Louis Malle *aka The Lovers.* *Les Liaisons dangereuses / Relazioni pericolose* (F / It 59) Roger Vadim *aka Dangerous Liaisons 1960 / Liaisons dangereuses 1960. Ini-tiation au cinéma* (Belg 60) Léo Dohmen. *Massacre pour une orgie* (Lux 66) Jean-Loup Grosdard. *Femina ridens* (It 69) Piero Schivasappa *aka The Laughing Woman / Woman Laughs.* *Women in Love* (GB / US 69) Ken Russell. *Che? / Quoi? / Was?* (It / F / G 72) Roman Polanski *aka Diary of Forbidden Dreams / Forbidden Dreams / What? Ultimo Tango a Parigi / Le Dernier Tango à Paris* (It / F 72) Bernardo Bertolucci *aka Last Tango in Paris. Malizia* (It 73) Salvatore Samperi *aka Malicious. Ai no koriida / L'Empire des sens* (J / F 76) Nagisa Oshima *aka Ai no Corrida / (The) Em-pire of the Senses / In the Realm of the Senses / The Realm of the Senses. Casanova & Company / 13 Femmes pour Casanova / Casanova und Co.* (It / F / Aus / G 76) François Legrand (Franz Antel) *aka Casanova & Co. / The Rise and Rise of Casanova / Some Like It Cool. The Sailor Who Fell from Grace with the Sea* (GB 76) Lewis John Carlino. *Miele di donna / Pensione Desiderio* (It / Sp 81) Gianfranco Angelucci *aka Honey.*

ESCAPE FILM   Any film which elaborates on the preparation for the attempted or successful escape of one or more prisoners from a prison, detention facility, POW camp, or concentration camp. Prisoner-of-war escape films are very numerous (*see* **WAR FILM**). For other films dealing with escapes, *see* **PRISON FILM**.

Escape (40) Mervyn LeRoy.   *Escape* (GB 48) Joseph L. Mankiewicz.   *Un Condamné à mort s'est éhappé* (F 56) Robert Bresson *aka Un condamné à mort s'est échappé ou le vent souffle où il veut / A Man Escaped / A Man Escaped, or The Wind Bloweth Where It Listeth.*   *Breakout* (75) Tom Gries *aka The Ten-Second Jailbreak.*   *Escape from Iran — The Canadian Caper / Les Evadés d'Iran* (Can 81 TV) Lamont Johnson.   *La Fuga de Segovia / Segoviako ihesa* (Sp 81) Imanol Uribe *aka Escape from Segovia* [in Spanish and Basque].   *Night Crossing* (US / GB / G 81) Delbert Mann.   *Escape from Sobibor* (US / Yug 87 TV) Jack Gold.

ESCAPIST FILM   The kind of film that seeks only to amuse and entertain, obliterates the need to ponder too deeply on its subject matter, and allows us to relax and forget our daily worries.

Espionage Film   *see*   **SPY FILM;** *see also* **WAR FILM: Spy War Films**

Ethical Epic   *see*   **EPIC: Moral Epics**

Ethnic Comedy   *see*   **COMEDY**

ETHNIC FILM (Race Film)   Although the term ethnic film may refer to movies in which ethnic groups are stereotyped, it is more aptly applied to films made by or addressed to a country's ethnic and cultural minorities. It also applies to films which look at the characteristics of a particular race or ethnic group, or examine the cultural interrelationship existing amongst different cultures. The most active ethnic group in the making of ethnic films in America is obviously the black community which has been making films since 1912. Yiddish films have also been made for the Jewish cultural group, and recently some Asian-American films (e.g., Wayne Wang's *Chan Is Missing*, 1981) have emerged.[31]

Any film made in a language other than the officially recognized language or languages spoken in a country may be labelled an ethnic or race film. *Ljubav i strast / Love and Passion* (32) Frank Melford [in Serbo-Croat].   *The Underworld* (37) Oscar Micheaux.   *A Brivele der Mamen* (38) Joseph Green *aka A Letter to Mother* [in Yiddish].   *Di Klyatshe / The Dobbin* (39) Edgar G. Ulmer *aka Fishke der Krumer (Fishke the Lame) / Die Klatsche / The Light Ahead* [in Yiddish].   *Amerikaner Schadchen / The Marriage Broker* (40) Edgar G. Ulmer *aka Amerikaner Shadkhn / American Matchmaker* [in Yiddish].   *Golden Gate Girl* (41) Esther Eng [in Chinese].   *Juke Joint* (47) Spencer Williams.   *A Majority of One* (61) Mervyn LeRoy.   *Gone Are the Days!* (63) Nicholas Webster *aka The Man from C.O.T.T.O.N./ Purlie Victorious.*   *Zorstoki svitanki* (Can 64-66) John Krasnozony *aka Cruel Dawn* [in Ukrainian].   *Tears of Happiness* (72) Sarky Mouradian [in Armenian].   *Jama Masjid Street Journal* (79) Mira Nair.   *Dakh-Brusil* (Belg 80) Samy Szlingerbaum *aka Brussels-Transit / Shelter Brussels* [in Yiddish].   *Chan Is Missing* (81) Wayne Wang [1st Chinese-American feature].   *Los dos mundos de Angelita / The Two Worlds of Angelita* (82) Jane Morrison [in Spanish].   *Dim Sum: A Little Bit of Heart* (84) Wayne Chang [in Chinese & English].   *Ping Pong* (GB 86) Po Chih Leong [in Cantonese].

Ethnographic Film *see* **DOCUMENTARY**

European Western *see* **SPAGHETTI WESTERN**

Exclusive *see* **RELEASE**

Exhibition Film *see* **EXPO MOVIE**

Exotic Film *see* **SOUTH SEAS PICTURE**

Exotic Locale Musicals *see* **MUSICAL**

EXPANDED CINEMA (Expanded Film) Expanded cinema is a general term which is applied to the kind of independent filmmaking and film activity that seeks to expand the notion of film and film art. Expanded cinema seeks to go beyond the screen and even the film itself. It is a cinema open to all sorts of experimentation and new approaches which may or may not be combined with other activities. These novel approaches to film, which started to proliferate in the sixties (although some go as far back as the silents), include multiple-screen projection, projection of film onto places (walls, people) other than the screen, the use of computers to generate images, mixed-media environmental presentations with direct participation of individuals, the use of television and videotape (singly or in combination with film), films examining the role of light, time, and space in cinematic art, holography, and anything, for that matter, that offers the possibility of expansion in terms of cinema. Some expanded films do not fall into any easy classification; others do, being oriented towards a common goal. The appellation expanded cinema is due to Gene Youngblood; *see* his *Expanded Cinema* (New York: E. P. Dutton, 1970). *See also* **EXPO MOVIE**.

> *Per.mu.ta.tion.s / Permutations* (67) John Whitney. *Sugar Daddies* (68) Hans Scheugl. *Moon 69* (69) Scott Bartlett. *Paradise Now* (70) Sheldon Rochlin.

——**Action Films (Object Films)** A particular type of film centered on actions which are meant to confront the audience. Some of these films are based on "happenings" performed on human bodies by a group of Austrian artists and filmmakers with the intention of shocking or nauseating according to one's own reaction to the "happening" (*Materialaktion*).

> *6/64 Mama und Papa (Material-Aktion Muehl)* (Aus 64) Kurt Kren. *9/64 O Tannenbaum (Material-Aktion Muehl)* (Aus 64) Kurt Kren. *Sodoma* (Aus 64) Otto Muehl. *Bodybuilding* (G 65-66) Ernst Schmidt.

——**Kinaesthetic Films** Avant-garde films which explore the aesthetics of motion by displaying imagery made of abstract or concrete configurations. Some are computer-generated films.

> *Yantra* (50-55) James Whitney. *Lapis* (63-66) James Whitney. *Collideoscope* (66) Stan VanDerBeek, Kenneth Knowlton. *Samadhi* (66-67) Jordan Belson.

——**Multiple-Screen Projection Films** Films projected on two or more screens (Charles Eames's *Think* was projected on eleven screens at the New York World Fair in 1964) also represent an extension of film and form part of expanded cinema.

Think (64-65) Charles and Ray Eames *aka View from the People Wall* (single screen version). *The Chelsea Girls* (66) Andy Warhol [filmed in 16mm dual screen]. *Panels for the Walls of the World* (67) Stan VanDerBeek. *Wide Point* (69) John Chamberlain [projected simultaneously on 7 screens].

Expanded Film *see* **EXPANDED CINEMA**

Expedition Film *see* **TRAVEL FILM**

EXPERIMENTAL FILM (Noncommercial Film) Some current terms with different nuances but often used interchangeably are avant-garde, experimental and independent film. The term experimental film has perhaps the advantage of being able to encompass a greater variety of films – those which are clearly avant-garde in terms of ideas or subject matter and those which are innovative in the sense that they present new technical developments or experiment with form and content. Two books that cover the avant-garde and experimental film are *Film Is...* by Stephen Dwoskin (London: Peter Owen, 1975) and *Experimental Cinema* by David Curtis (London: Studio Vista, 1971). The terminology of the avant-garde or experimental film is quite extensive. The following list of entries includes most varieties: **ABSTRACT FILM, AVANT-GARDE, CITY SYMPHONY, EXPANDED CINEMA, EXPRESSIVE-REALIST FILM, FILM POEM, FUTURIST FILM, IMPRESSIONIST FILM, INDEPENDENT PRODUCTION, NEW AMERICAN CINEMA, STRUCTURAL FILM, SURREALIST FILM, UNDERGROUND FILM.**

Explicit Film *see* **SEX EXPLOITATION FILM**

Explicit Sex Film *see* **HARD-CORE PORNO FILM**

EXPLOITATION FILM Exploitation films are those made with the intention of cashing in on some current trend, fashion, or exploitable element that has some sensational appeal attached to it. As such, they are as old as the motion film industry itself. They can be expensively or cheaply produced; it is nevertheless a fact that the majority of exploitation films strive for big returns in exchange for low investments. Quite a few are actually successful in making a profit, and some even become trend-setters, soon to be flanked by a swarm of cheap imitators. Since the fifties, exploitation pictures have sought to exploit such diverse subjects as outdoor sports (beach party movies, surf epics), youth rebellion and campus contestation, the hippie and drug cultures, anti–Vietnam protest films, black ghetto films (blaxploitation) and the occult revival trend. The exploitation filmmakers have even jumped onto the nostalgia bandwagon. However, two major fields remain the exclusive domain, so to speak, of the exploitation film. They are the sexploitation genre with its main variants usually centering on the soft- or hard-core element that determines what kind of audience will patronize a sex film; and the films whose focus of interest is gore or hard-core violence. These films engage in graphic, visceral portrayals of atrocities. These gore films are often considered the lowest point of the film industry and are attended by a very specialized audience. Outside these two main areas of exploitation, a recent tendency is to rush into production films that will cash in on some actual momentous happening while the news is still fresh in the minds of the viewers. Two examples that illustrate this trend are the Mexican production *Los supervivientes de los Andes / Survive!* (1975) that dwells on the fact that a few people had to resort to cannibalism to survive the rigors of being stranded in the Andes after an air crash, and *Guyana — El crimen del siglo / Guyana: Cult of the Damned* (1979), another Mexican product by the same director, René Cardona, Jr., which exploits the Jonestown mass suicide. All these different fields of action are the stuff which exploitation films are made of and on which they thrive. For exploitation films see under their particular category or genre, e.g. splatter **(GORE FILM, VIOLENCE FILM), BLAXPLOITATION (BLACK FILM),** sexploitation **(SEX EXPLOITATION FILM),** hard-core **(HARD-CORE PORNO FILM),** and so on.

> *Mom and Dad* (47) William Beaudine *aka A Family Story.*   *Blood Feast* (63) Herschell Gordon Lewis.   *The Trip* (67) Roger Corman.   *The Stewardesses* (70) Alf Silliman, Jr. (Allan Silliphant) *aka Airline Stewardesses* (69) [1st American 3-D feature shown in 70mm].   *Deep Throat* (72) Jerry Gerard (Gerard Damiano) *aka The Doctor Makes a Call.*   *The Exorcist* (73) William Friedkin.   *Scream, Blacula, Scream!* (73) Bob Kelljan *aka Blacula II / Blacula Is Beautiful / Blacula Lives Again / The Name Is Blacula.   The Texas Chainsaw Massacre* (74) Tobe Hooper [subtitled: "Who Will Be Left ... and What Will Be Left of Them?"].   *Los supervivientes de los Andes* (Mex 75) René Cardona *aka Survival / Survive!   Guyana — El crimen del siglo / Guyana: Cult of the Damned* (Mex / Sp / Pan 79) René Cardona, Jr. *aka Guyana — Crime of the Century.*

Exploration Film   *see*   **TRAVEL FILM**

Explosion Film   *see*   **SHORT: Multi-Shot Film**

EXPO MOVIE (Exhibition Film)   The unusual nature of some films prevents them from being shown in ordinary theaters; they usually are showpieces of experimentation or research which offer glimpses of possible things to come. This type of film (mostly in the fashion of documentaries or travelogues) requiring giant screens, multiple separate screens or special buildings in order to be projected and shown to an audience, is normally exhibited at world fairs or in some locale or pavilion forming part of a museum or permanent exhibition grounds. These films have been with us since Raoul Grimoin-Sanson introduced his Cinéorama to audiences visiting the Paris Exposition Universelle of 1900. Expo films come in diverse shapes and sizes and are mostly made for the purpose of demonstrating some new technological invention or device. *See also* **WIDE SCREEN.**

To Fly! (76) Greg MacGillivray, Jim Freeman [filmed in IMAX]. *Energy Creation Story* (82) Jack Boyd [70mm widescreen presentation]. *Impressions of France* (82) Rick Harper. *Magic Journeys* (82) Murray Lerner [1st American film in dual 70mm widescreen 3-D]. *O Canada!* (82) Bill Boshé, Randy Bright [*Circle-Vision* presentation]. *Symbiosis* (82) Paul Gerber [70mm widescreen presentation]. *Wonders of China* (82) Jeff Blyth [*Circle-Vision* presentation]. *Skyward* (Can / J 85) Stephen Low [filmed in IMAX]. *Captain EO* (86) Francis Coppola [3-D dual Super Panavision 70]. *The Seas* (86) Paul Gerber. *Ring of Fire* (91) George Casey [filmed in IMAX].

Exposé Documentary *see* **DOCUMENTARY: PERSUASIVE DOCU-MENTARY**

EXPOSÉ FILM (Muckraking Film) The exposé film is an old form. Filmmakers and film producers have often sought to expose crime, rackets, malpractice, vice, corruption, greed, inequity, injustice, and any other kind of evil that may infect society or endanger the country. As such, the exposé film performs a socially useful function as it brings to public awareness existing abusive conditions in different sectors of the community or government. *See also* **SOCIAL CONSCIOUSNESS FILM** and **GANGSTER FILM: Exposé Films**.

Traffic in Souls (13) George Loane Tucker. *The Match King* (32) Howard Bretherton. *The House of 92nd Street* (45) Henry Hathaway *aka House of 92nd Street / Now It Can Be Told*. *Force of Evil* (48) Abraham Polonsky *aka The Numbers Racket / The Story of Tucker's People / Tucker's People*. *The Sellout* (51) Gerald Mayer. *The Captive City* (52) Robert Wise. *The Phenix City Story* (55) Phil Karlson. *Slaughter on Tenth Avenue* (57) Arnold Laven. *Murder, Inc.* (60) Burt Balaban, Stuart Rosenberg.

Expressionism *see* **EXPRESSIONIST FILM**

EXPRESSIONIST FILM (Expressionism) Expressionism is a movement in the arts which gained impetus at the turn of the century as a reaction against the artistic currents of Impressionism, Naturalism and neo-Romanticism. In the film medium, it evolved in Germany after World War I and exerted a world-wide influence. Even though two or three early films exhibited some expressionist characteristics, it is *Das Cabinet des Dr. Caligari / The Cabinet of Dr. Caligari* (1919) which started a series of art films clearly marked by a cinematic style that came to be known as film expressionism (the term *caligarisme* is also used in France). Although the purely expressionist films were few, the period of German Expressionist cinema extended from 1913 to 1933 and was very influential in many subsequent films made in different countries. Many Hollywood-made films of the thirties and forties (e.g., *The Old Dark House*, 1932; *Citizen Kane*, 1940) show strong expressionist characteristics. This was obviously due to the assimilation of the techniques and devices employed by German filmmakers, technicians and actors who had left their country for Hollywood.

Expressionist filmmakers rejected the imitation of reality and relied instead on extreme stylization. Expressionist films were almost always shot in the studios with artificial, distorted sets, ample use of dramatic lighting, plays on shadows, stylized acting, and the symbolic use of objects and figures to create meaning and atmospheric tension. The films were somber, subjective expositions of an individual's inner troubled self in the grips of some persecuting emotional experience or other and confined to a hostile environment.

A semi-expressionist variant, the *Kammerspielfilm* (Chamber film), differed from the expressionist film proper in the use of psychological characterization (in expressionist films characterization was unidimensional) and was marked by a return to surface naturalism. It was a reaction against expressionism, but the *Kammerspiel* films kept most of its techniques. *Der letzte Mann / The Last Laugh* (1924) is considered the masterpiece of its kind. A few of these films centered their action on life in the streets of the big city; they were appropriately termed "street films" (q.v.) by the film critic Siegfried Kracauer.

An acknowledged first-class study of German Expressionism in film is Lotte H. Eisner, *The Haunted Screen* (Berkeley and Los Angeles: University of California Press, 1973). It includes a filmography of 98 titles. For a more recent work, *see* John D. Barlow, *German Expressionist Film* (Boston: Twayne, 1982). *See also* **KAMMERSPIELFILM**.

Das Cabinet des Dr. Caligari (G 19) Robert Wiene *aka The Cabinet of Dr. Caligari / Das Kabinett des Dr. Caligari.* **Genuine** (G 20) Robert Wiene. *Der Golem: Wie er in die Welt Kam* (G 20) Paul Wegener, Carl Boese *aka The Golem / The Golem: How He Came into the World.* **Von Morgens bis Mitternachts** (G 20) Karl Heinz Martin *aka From Morning to Midnight.* **Der Müde Tod** (G 21) Fritz Lang *aka Between Two Worlds / Between Worlds / Beyond the Wall / Destiny / The Light Within / The Three Lights / The Weary Death.* **Nosferatu — eine Symphonie des Grauens** (G 21) Friedrich Wilhelm Murnau *aka Die zwölfte Stunde — eine Nacht des Grauens* (G 30 sound v.) */ Dracula / Nosferatu / Nosferatu, the Vampire / Nosferatu — A Symphony of Horror [Terror] / The Terror of Dracula.* **Verlogene Moral** (G 21) Hanns Kobe *aka Torgus.* **Dr. Mabuse der Spieler / Dr. Mabuse der Grosse Spieler** (G 21-22) Fritz Lang [in 2 parts: *Der Spieler — ein Bild der Zeit; Inferno — ein spiel von Menschen unserer Zeit*] *aka Dr. Mabuse / Dr. Mabuse the Gambler — Part I: Dr. Mabuse, the Great Gambler / The Great Gambler — Image of a Generation; Part II: Dr. Mabuse, King of Crime / Inferno — People of a Generation aka The Fatal Passion* [parts I & II abridged into a single feature]. **Schatten, eine Nachtliche Halluzination** (G 22) Arthur Robinson *aka Warning Shadows.* **Raskolnikow** (G 23) Robert Wiene *aka Schuld und Sühne / Crime and Punishment.* **Der letzte Mann** (G 24) F. W. Murnau *aka The Last Laugh / The Last Man.* **Die Nibelungen — ein deutsches Heidenlied** (G 22-24) Fritz Lang [2 parts: I. *Siegfried / Siegfrieds Tod*; II. *Kriemhilds Rache*] *aka The Nibelunge Saga (Siegfried; The Vengeance of Kriemhild / Kriemhild's Revenge).* **Das Wachsfigurenkabinett** (G 24) Paul Leni *aka Three Wax Works / Three Wax Men / Waxworks.* **Die freudlose Gasse** (G 25) G. W. Pabst *aka Cheerless Lane / The Joyless Street / The Street of Sorrow / Streets of Sorrow* (37 sound version). **Metropolis — das Schicksas einer Menschheit im Jahre 2000** (G 26) Fritz Lang *aka Metropolis.*

Expressive Realism *see* **EXPRESSIVE-REALIST FILM**

EXPRESSIVE-REALIST FILM (Expressive Realism, Formalism, Formalist Film, Montage Film, Soviet Expressionism)   The term is used in connection with the Russian avant-garde cinema of the mid-twenties.[32] It was an antinaturalistic style of filmmaking whose main characteristics were the use of creative editing or montage (the juxtaposition of two different shots to create new meaning by means of analogy or symbolism, e.g., Kerensky standing by the entrance of the Czar's chambers in the Winter Palace followed by a shot of a peacock spreading its tail in the film *Oktyabr'* */October*, 1927), the use of types or representative characters rather than characterization, and the use of a mass or collective hero instead of an individual hero as protagonist in the people's struggle to impose Bolshevik rule and ideology, thus transforming the old order and society. Eisenstein, Pudovkin, Dvzhenko, and Vertov were its major exponents and the period of expressive realism runs from 1925 to 1930.[33] Expressive realism includes fiction films as well as documentaries, e.g., Vertov's *Chelovek s kinoapparatom* */Man with a Movie Camera* (1928). By 1930, the prevailing Stalinist policy in the Soviet government put an end to experimentation and avant-gardism in the arts in favor of an official state style known as socialist realism.

Stachka (USSR 24) Sergei M. Eisenstein *aka (The) Strike.* *Bronenosets "Potyomkin"* (USSR 25) Sergei M. Eisenstein, Grigori Alexandrov *aka The Armoured Cruiser Potemkin / Battleship Potemkin / Bronenosets Potemkin / Potemkin.* *Mat'* (USSR 26) Vsevolod I. Pudovkin *aka (The) Mother.* *Oktyabr* (USSR 27) Sergei M. Eisenstein, Grigori Alexandrov *aka October / Oktyabre / Ten Days That Shook the World.* *Chelovek s kinoapparatom* (USSR 28) Dziga Vertov; Mikhail Kaufman (photography) *aka (The) Man with a Movie Camera.* *Arsenal* (USSR 29) Alexander Dovzhenko. *Novyi Vavilon* (USSR 29) Grigori Kozintsev, Leonid Trauberg *aka (The) New Babylon.* *Staroe i novoye* (USSR 29) Sergei M. Eisenstein, Grigori Alexandrov *aka The General Line / Generalnaya linya / The Old and the New.* *Zemlya* (USSR 30) Alexander Dovzhenko *aka (The) Earth/Soil.*

Extrapolative Film *see* **SCIENCE FICTION FILM**

Eyewitness News *see* **TELEVISION NEWS: Action News**

Faction *see* **DOCUDRAMA;** *see also* **TELEVISION DRAMA: Documentary Drama**

FACTUAL FILM   A broad term for any film not generally meant for commercial showing but made for the presentation of a great variety of subjects and for conveying information in a clear, factual manner. Under this label are grouped many different types and categories of films. *See also* **DOCUMENTARY** and **NONFICTION FILM.**

——**Advertising Film (Sales Film)**   Advertising films, publicity films, promotional films, commercials (including television commercials), public relations films, and, to a certain extent, sponsoring films, all seek to predispose the viewer towards the firm, sponsoring body, or the product the films are promoting. In the case of commercials, the main object is obviously to sell or create a market for a certain product.

——**Background Film**   Usually an educational film which gives information on a particular topic or subject.

——**Concept Film**   A short 8mm loop or classroom film used as an aid for teachers in the presentation of specific scientific or technical points in easily understood visuals. As a teaching tool, the concept film had its day in the 1960s. *See also* **SINGLE-CONCEPT FILM**.

——**Educational Film**   A general term for a nontheatrical film meant for teaching skills and demonstrating concepts. These films are mostly used in educational centers like schools, colleges and universities. Educational films range from some kinds of documentaries to classroom films or school films. As such, they may be restricted to specific subjects, e.g., agricultural films, biology films, business films, ecology films, films on economics, geography films, popular science films, and many other subjects.

——**Government Film (Government-Sponsored Film)**   Many factual films are sponsored or produced by government agencies. They include films made by the military and the different ministry departments. These films encompass many different types and deal with diverse subjects.

——**How-to-Do-It Films (How To)**   A film which shows step-by-step how to do things—how to paint one's house, how to become a better tennis player, how to keep fit. How tos cover a vast range of activities. Their function extends from professional use in business, industry and commerce to private self-improvement. They can be excellent educational tools and, with the advent of videotapes, quite accessible to the public at large.

——**Industrial Film**   In many instances, a film that relays information on some industrial concern or shows some of the processes involved in manufacturing some commodity.

——**Informational Film (Information Film)**   Informational films cover the whole spectrum of man's knowledge and as the term indicates, their purpose is to inform about any subject the maker of the film chooses for elucidation.

——**Instructional Film (Instruction Film)**   Instructional films are meant to illustrate how things are put together, how they work, or why certain events take place; they are largely used for training and teaching and they cover a broad range of subjects.

——**Jeopardy Film (Industrial Jeopardy Film, Industrial Safety Film, Safety Film)**   They comprise a broad range of films illustrating different kinds of accidents and mishaps that may occur or to which we may be prone when handling tools, crossing the road, walking in the woods, engaging in sport or sex, or puttering at home. They have been called variously fear or shock films (films which instill fear, show the progress of some unspeakable disease or drug-taking habit or which present in gory detail the aftermath of some accident) and do's and don'ts films (films that demonstrate how to do things in the proper way or act in the correct manner). Jeopardy films present fictive social scenarios and reenact accident situations, although sometimes actual, graphic footage is used, for instance, in highway safety films.

————**Nuts-and-Bolts Film**   Either an informational, instructional or skill film which presents information in a simple way. It sometimes has a pejorative connotation.

————**Persuasive Film**   A film that tends or seeks to persuade the viewer to a certain way of thinking or kind of behavior. Propaganda films (q.v.), advertising films, and documentary films (q.v.) are different types of the persuasive film.

————**Programmed Film**   A film which gives information in a sequential fashion as is the usual practice in a learning program. These films are used for individual study.

————**Record Film (Film Record)**   A film made for the storage and preservation of data or to keep a permanent record of some function, event or happening—theatrical performances, sport encounters—which may be retrieved at any time for analysis and study. Home movies fall under the label of record films.

————**Research Film (Scientific-Research Film)**   Scientific and research films are used by scientists and technicians as aids to their work. They are tools of the trade, so to speak, and are employed to document their findings or to provide information which may not be discernible to the naked eye but that becomes clear on the subsequent viewing and study of the film. Research films may use special camera techniques such as time-lapse photography, high speed cinematography, cinemicroscopy, endoscopic cinematography, and any other highly advanced technique available.

————**Single-Concept Film**   A short film composed of one or a few shots and made to demonstrate a single idea, principle, or procedure.

————**Skill Film (Psychomotor Film)**   A short film designed for the purpose of stimulating the development of certain skills. It shows in detail how to perform a particular task by imitating the instructions, e.g., how to use a particular tool.

————**Sponsored Film**   A sponsored film may be any type of film—advertising film, travelogue, documentary. Sponsored means only that the film in question has been subsidized, budgeted or financed by some industry (e.g., Shell International), professional organization, local charity, or government. They are sometimes seen commercially.

——**Training Film (Teaching Film)**   A film made for the purpose of teaching the skills required to perform certain duties or functions. Training films are greatly used by the military and industry.

——**Trigger Film**   Trigger films are open-ended dramatic shorts meant to start a discussion by stimulating the viewers into finding a possible answer to some vital issue or problem of difficult solution. The concept of the trigger film was initiated in the 1960s at the University of Michigan.

Factual War Films   *see*   **WAR FILM**

Fairground Movie   *see*   **CIRCUS FILM: Funfair Movies**

Fairy Story   *see*   **FAIRY TALE**

FAIRY TALE (Fairy Story)   Fairy tales have a rich and long literary tradition. They address themselves to children and adults of all ages, and they are equally enjoyed by both age groups. The film industry has often adapted the best known amongst the literary classics of the genre into visual terms. Some well-known masterpieces (e.g., *Cinderella*) have been remade many times in different versions.[34] Fairy tales are basically fantasy films. In many cases, they involve a prince who is under some sort of evil spell and who relies on the good will of a sincere maiden to break the incantation in order that he may regain his original freedom and appearance; or, otherwise, it may be a princess or fair maiden who is the victim of some spell and, in turn, relies on the kindness of a genteel young man to deliver her from her predicament. Fairy tales are also full of mischievous supernatural spirits, fairies with magic wands, old hags, portentous happenings, dragons, and wizards. In the late sixties and seventies, the vast pool of fairy tales was examined by some erotic filmmakers, and soft-core and hard-core versions of fairy stories have been made of the better-known classics.

   The Blue Bird (18) Maurice Tourneur.   *Le Voyage imaginaire* (F 25) René Clair *aka L'Anneau des fées / Le Songe d'un jour d'été / The Imaginary Voyage.   Cenerentola e il Signor Bonaventura* (It 41) Sergio Tofano *aka Princess Cinderella.   La Belle et la bête* (F 46) Jean Cocteau, René Clément *aka Beauty and the Beast.   Fun and Fancy Free* (46) Jack Kinney, Bill Roberts, Hamilton Luske, William Horgan.   *Jack and the Beanstalk* (52) Jean Yarbrough.   *Die Prinzessin und der Schweinehirt* (G 53) Herbert B. Fredersdorf *aka The Princess and the Swineherd.   tom thumb* (GB 58) George Pal.   *Cinderfella* (60) Frank Tashlin.   *Snow White and the Three Stooges* (61) Walter Lang.   *The Daydreamer* (66) Jules Bass.   *Grimms Märchen von lüsternen Pärchen* (G 69) Rolf Thiele *aka The Erotic Adventures of Snow White / Grimms Fairy Tales for Adults / The New Adventures of Snow White.   Peau d'âne* (F 70) Jacques Demy *aka Donkey Skin / The Magic Donkey.   Whoever Slew Auntie Roo?* (GB / US 71) Curtis Harrington *aka Ginger Bread House / Who Slew Auntie Roo?* **Cinderella** (76) Michael Pataki *aka The Other Cinderella.* **Fairy Tales** (78) Harry Trampa *aka Adult Fairy Tales.* **Gevatter Tod** (G 80) Wolfgang Hubner *aka Godfather Death.* **Elle voit des nains partout** (F 81) Jean-Claude Sussfeld. **The Company of Wolves** (GB 84) Neil Jordan. **Maid to Order** (87) Amy Jones [subtitled "Once upon a time. . ."]. **The Princess Bride** (87) Rob Reiner. **Rumpelstiltskin** (87) David Irving. **Frog** (88) David Grossman.

Fallen Woman Film   *see*   **CONFESSION FILM**

Family Comedy   *see*   **DOMESTIC COMEDY**

FAMILY FILM (Family-Oriented Film)   A film intended for the whole family which may safely be viewed by its members; that is to say, the film will not contain any offending material of a sexual or violent nature that might upset the family or intrude into the family sanctum if shown on television at family viewing hours. Many films rated G in the United States (suggested for general audiences) and U in Britain (passed for general exhibition) are considered to be suitable for all ages and may be classed as family fare. Apparently, it is difficult to make a film that will please everybody, and many of these films come and go quickly, box-office failures because lack of attendance is the rule. Hence, the family movie label has acquired a certain derogatory sense for exhibitors and patrons alike. Nevertheless, a few family classics keep reappearing on the screen, and parents and their children flock to these screenings. Walt Disney studios are deservedly known for their successful family films.

Pollyanna (20) Paul Powell. *Little Miss Marker* (34) Alexander Hall. *The Adventures of Tom Sawyer* (38) Norman Taurog. *The Little Princess* (39) Walter Lang. *So Dear to My Heart* (48) Harold Schuster. *Never Take No for an Answer* (GB / It 51) Maurice Cloche, Ralph Smart. *The 5,000 Fingers of Dr. T* (53) Roy Rowland *aka Crazy Music.* *20,000 Leagues Under the Sea* (54) Richard Fleischer *aka Jules Verne's Twenty Thousand Leagues Under the Sea.* *Le Ballon rouge* (F 55) Albert Lamorisse *aka The Red Balloon.* *Johnny Tremain* (57) Robert Stevenson. *Old Yeller* (57) Robert Stevenson. *Darby O'Gill and the Little People* (58) Robert Stevenson. *Third Man on the Mountain* (59) Ken Annakin. *Swiss Family Robinson* (60) Ken Annakin. *Misty* (61) James B. Clark. *Moon Pilot* (62) James Neilson. *The Horse Without a Head* (63) Don Chaffey. *The Sound of Music* (65) Robert Wise. *Those Calloways* (65) Norman Tokar. *The Fighting Prince of Donegal* (66) Michael O'Herlihy. *The Railway Children* (GB 70) Lionel Jeffries. *Scandalous John* (71) Robert Butler. *Where the Red Fern Grows* (74) Norman Tokar. *The Adventures of the Wilderness Family* (75) Stewart Rafill. *Huckleberry Finn* (75 TV) Robert Totten. *The Further Adventures of the Wilderness Family* (77) Frank Zuniga *aka Wilderness Family, Part II.* *The Sea Gypsies* (78) Stewart Rafill. *Somewhere Tomorrow* (83) Robert Wiemer. *The Journey of Natty Gann* (85) Jeremy Kagan. *The Girl Who Spelled Freedom* (86 TV) Simon Wincer. *Honey, I Shrunk the Kids* (89) Joe Johnston. *Lantern Hill* (Can 90 MCTV) Kevin Sullivan. *Shipwrecked* (US / Nor 91) Nils Gaup. *Wild Hearts Can't Be Broken* (91) Steve Miner.

Family Genre Film   *see*   **GENRE FILM**

Family Melodrama   *see*   **MELODRAMA: Domestic Melodramas**

Family-Oriented Adventure Film   *see*   **ANIMAL PICTURE**

Family-Oriented Film   *see*   **FAMILY FILM**

Family Saga   *see*   **SAGA**

Fanny Film   *see*   **HARD-CORE PORNO FILM**

Fantastic Comedy   *see*   **FANTASY FILM: Fantasy-Comedy**

FANTASTIC FILM   Under this overall classification are grouped the horror, science fiction, and fantasy genres. These genres in turn split into different subgenres or groupings. The term fantasy has often been used to cover all films that do not deal with the normally accepted conception of reality – that is to say, it has been used for films that deal with nonplausible situations, future events, prehistoric tales, supernatural occurrences, and the like. The fantastic film, although it can be considered a genre, covers too vast a field to be discussed under this label. The three main divisions are treated separately. It is important as well to note that horror is very often mixed with science fiction and with fantasy, and science fiction with fantasy. These three genres intermix freely.[35]

There are various definitions of the fantastic as a genre. According to Tzvetan Todorov's definition, here briefly summarized, the fantastic is the hesitation we experience when faced with supposedly supernatural happenings. If we come out of this uncertainty, we are no longer dealing with the fantastic but with two adjacent genres – the uncanny and the marvelous. In the uncanny we find a perfectly logical explanation for the happenings; in the marvelous we accept the supernatural for what it is supposed to be. If the hesitation is sustained for a long period but is eventually resolved, we are dealing not with the fantastic proper but with its subgenres, either the fantastic-uncanny or the fantastic-marvelous.[36]

It is a clever and neat definition which would exclude most films from membership. Only those films that keep an open end (and so prevent us from comng out of our hesitation) would fit into the purely fantastic genre. Below are a few examples of films which would fulfill or almost fulfill Todorov's strict boundaries.

Cat People (42) Jacques Tourneur.   *I Walked with a Zombie* (42) Jacques Tourneur.   *Portrait of Jennie* (48) William Dieterle *aka Jennie / Tidal Wave*.   *The Innocents* (US / GB 61) Jack Clayton *aka Suspense*.   *L'Homme qui ment / Muz ktery Ize* (F / Cz 67) Allen Robbe-Grillet *aka The Man Who Lies*.   *Duel* (71 TV) Steven Spielberg.   *Picnic at Hanging Rock* (Aust 75) Peter Weir.   *Martin* (76) George A. Romero [rel. in 78] *aka Martin the Blood Lover*.   *Hombre mirando al sudeste* (Arg 86) Eliseo Subiela *aka Man Facing South East*.   *Apprentice to Murder* (US / Nor 87) R. L. Thomas.

Fantasy, Fantasy Comedy   *see*   **FANTASY FILM**

FANTASY FILM (Fantasy) In its broadest definition, fantasy film covers a vast spectrum – the portrayal of the supernatural, the representation of imaginary or recreated beasts, the working of fanciful or speculative science, the visualization of dreams. All these matters and others have, at one time or another, formed part of the fantasy film. However, certain manifestations of fantasy are better classed among other genres, e.g., the horror film and the science fiction film. (See, for instance, the definition for fantastic film.)

Films dealing with the wonders of magic and magicians, with the doings of gods, demigods, angels, elves, sprites, fairies, gnomes, and similar creatures are better and properly classified as fantasy films. This is equally true of films that present us with the fanciful worlds of fairy tales or imaginary lands. Other films that warrant inclusion as fantasy films are those that use trick photography to create fantastic or illusionistic effects – earlier examples are the films of Georges Méliès – or nonrealistic comedies, e.g., *Topper* (1937), *Here Comes Mr. Jordan* (1941).

A possible way to separate horror films and science fiction films from fantasy proper is to have in mind that the purpose of the horror film is to induce terror or horror and that the science fiction film has to present technology or future worlds from a scientific point of view with a plausible scientific basis at its core (e.g., a flying carpet is fantasy, a space vehicle powered by solar energy is science fiction). If a film mixes the scientific with the unscientific it is mere fantasy. Nevertheless, the borderlines are very indistinct indeed, and the genres encroach on one another, at times pollinating and fertilizing each other.

Paris qui dort (F 23) René Clair *aka At 3:25 / The Crazy Ray / Le Rayon diabolique (Paris qui dort) / Le Rayon invisible*. *A Connecticut Yankee* (31) David Butler. *Berkeley Square* (33) Frank Lloyd. *Gabriel Over the White House* (33) Gregory La Cava. *Les Visiteurs du soir* (F 42) Marcel Carné *aka The Devil's Envoys*. *The Enchanted Cottage* (45) John Cromwell. *A Matter of Life and Death* (GB 45) Michael Powell, Emeric Pressburger *aka Stairway to Heaven*. *La Belle et la bête* (F 46) Jean Cocteau, René Clément *aka Beauty and the Beast*. *Repeat Performance* (47) Alfred Werker. *A Connecticut Yankee in King Arthur's Court* (48) Tay Garnett *aka Mark Twain's A Connecticut Yankee in King Arthur's Court / A Yankee in King Arthur's Court*. *Pandora and the Flying Dutchman / Pandora* (GB / US / F 50) Albert Lewin. *L'Année dernière à Marienbad / L'anno scorso a Marienbad* (F / It 60) Alain Resnais *aka Last Year at Marienbad*. *The Magic Sword* (62) Bert I. Gordon *aka St. George and the Dragon / St. George and the 7 Curses*. *Fifi la Plume* (F 65) Albert Lamorisse *aka Circus Angel*. *The Gnome-Mobile* (67) Robert Stevenson. *The Vengeance of She* (GB 67) Cliff Owen. *Attack of the Killer Tomatoes!* (77) John De Bello. *The Car* (77) Elliot Silverstein *aka Wheels*. *The Two Worlds of Jennie Logan* (79 TV) Frank De Felitta. *Dreamscape* (84) Joseph Ruben. *Cocoon* (85) Ron Howard. *Biggles* (GB 86) John Hough *aka Biggles: Adventures in Time*. *Der Himmel über Berlin / Les Ailes du désir* (G / F 86-87) Wim Wenders *aka The Sky Above Berlin*. *The Navigator: A Mediaeval Odyssey* (Aust /

NZ 87) Vincent Ward. *The Adventures of Baron Munchausen* (GB / G 88) Terry Gilliam. *Field of Dreams* (89) Phil Alden Robinson. *Def by Temptation* (90) James Bond III. *Teenage Mutant Ninja Turtles* (90) Steve Barron *aka Teenage Mutant Ninja Turtles — the Movie.*

———**Arabian Nights Fantasy Films**   A very distinct category of fantasy films are those that find inspiration for their adventures in the classic collection of tales which go as far back as the tenth century. They are known as *The Arabian Nights* or *The Thousand and One Nights* and were introduced to the West by their translator, the Frenchman Antoine Galland in the early 18th century.

The Thief of Bagdad (24) Raoul Walsh. *The Thief of Bagdad* (GB / US 40) Ludwig Berger, Michael Powell, Tim Whelan (uncredited: Zoltan Korda, William Cameron Menzies, Alexander Korda). *The Seventh Voyage of Sinbad* (58) Nathan Juran. *Jack the Giant Killer* (61) Nathan Juran. *Il Fiore delle mille e una notte / Les Mille et une nuits* (It / F 73) Pier Paolo Pasolini *aka Arabian Nights.* *The Golden Voyage of Sinbad* (US / GB 73) Gordon Hessler *aka Sinbad's Golden Voyage.* *Sinbad and the Eye of the Tiger* (GB / US / Sp 77) Sam Wanamaker *aka Sinbad at the World's End.* *Arabian Adventure* (GB 79) Kevin Connor.

———**Cartoons**   Fantasy is ingrained in the art of animation, and from their beginnings cartoons have made ample use of fantasy material. *See also* **CARTOON FILM**.

Gulliver's Travels (39) Dave Fleischer. *Pinocchio* (39) Ben Sharpsteen, Hamilton Luske. *Alice in Wonderland* (51) Clyde Geronimi, Hamilton Luske, Wilfred Jackson. *Peter Pan* (53) Hamilton Luske, Clyde Geronimi, Wilfred Jackson. *Lady and the Tramp* (55) Hamilton Luske, Clyde Geronimi, Wilfred Jackson. *One Hundred and One Dalmatians* (60) Wolfgang Reitherman, Hamilton Luske, Clyde Geronimi. *Saiyu-ki* (J 60) Taiji Yabushita, Osamu Tezuka *aka Alkazam the Great / The Enchanted Monkey.* *Wizards* (77) Ralph Bakshi *aka War Wizards.* *The Lord of the Rings* (78) Ralph Bakshi. *Les Maîtres du temps / Herrscher der Zeit* (F / G / Swiz / GB / Hung 80) René Laloux *aka The Masters of Time / Time Masters.* *The Plague Dogs* (82) Martin Rosen.

———**Children's Classic Fantasies (Children's Fantasy Films)**   Whether adapted from famous children's stories or created for the screen, these films are very enjoyable and are intended for both children and adults. Recently, some children's fantasy films have emphasized the quandaries of pubescent girls and boys, making ample use of animation and live action, and relying heavily on special effects. *See also* **MUSICAL: Children's Fantasy Musicals**.

Alice in Wonderland (33) Norman Z. McLeod. *Jack and the Beanstalk* (52) Jean Yarbrough. *The Wonderful World of the Brothers Grimm* (60) Henry Levin. *Alice Through the Looking Glass* (66 TV) Alan Handley. *The Phantom Tollbooth* (68) Chuck Jones. *Time Bandits* (GB 81) Terry Gillian. *The Dark Crystal* (US / GB 82) Jim Henson, Frank Oz *aka The Crystal.* *The Company of Wolves* (GB 84) Neil Jordan. *Die unendliche Geschichte / The NeverEnding Story* (G / GB 84) Wolfgang Petersen.

Legend (GB 85) Ridley Scott. *Labyrinth* (GB / US 86) Jim Henson. *Crystalstone* (87) Antonio Pelaez. *Paperhouse* (GB 88) Bernard Rose. *The NeverEnding Story II: The Next Chapter* (US / G 90) George Miller.

——**Comic Strip Superheroes Films (Superhero Films)** From Buck Rogers to Flash Gordon (*see* **SCIENCE FICTION FILM: Space Operas**), Superman, and a host of others, these comic strip or comic book superheroes (better known as "long-underwear heroes" by their creators) have invaded the worlds of science fiction and fantasy alike. With a fluctuating degree of success, fantasy films have frequently sought to transpose to the screen their adventures. These films already form a sizeable group.

Batman (66) Leslie H. Martinson. *Diabolik / Signé Diabolik* (It / F 67) Mario Bava *aka Danger: Diabolik*. *Wonder Woman* (74 TV) Vincent Mc-Eveety. *Doc Savage: The Man of Bronze* (75) Michael Anderson. *The New, Original Wonder Woman* (75 TV) Leonard Horn. *The Incredible Hulk* (77 TV) Kenneth Johnson, Sigmund Neufeld, Jr. [followed by *The Return of the Hulk / The Return of the Hulk: Death in the Family / The Return of the Incredible Hulk* (77 TV) Alan J. Levi]. *Spider-Man* (77 TV) E. W. Swackhamer *aka The Amazing Spiderman*. *Dr. Strange* (78 TV) Philip DeGuere. *Superman* (GB / US 78) Richard Donner *aka Superman the Movie* [4 films in the series up to 1986]. *Captain America* (79 TV) Rod Holcomb. *Mandrake* (79 TV) Harry Falk. *Condorman* (GB / US 80) Charles Jarrott. *The Return of Captain Invincible* (Aust / US 81) Philippe Mora *aka Captain Invincible / Legend in Leotards*. *Supergirl* (GB 84) Jeannot Szwarc. *The Incredible Hulk Returns* (88 TV) Nicholas Corea [followed by *The Trial of the Incredible Hulk* (89 TV) Bill Bixby and *The Death of the Incredible Hulk* (90 TV) Bill Bixby]. *Batman* (89) Tim Burton. *The Rocketeer* (91) Joe Johnston.

——**Fantasy-Comedy (Comedy Fantasy, Fantastic Comedy)** Fantasy has often used mythological or supernatural beings for comic purpose. These films usually show playful devils, ghosts (*see* **Ghost Comedies**), angels, or God interfering with the absurd lives of mortals. Another branch of fantasy-comedy deals with incredible inventions or with machines having a mind of their own.

The Ghost Goes West (GB 35) René Clair. *Here Comes Mr. Jordan* (41) Alexander Hall. *Heaven Can Wait* (43) Ernst Lubitsch. *It Happened Tomorrow* (43) René Clair. *Harvey* (50) Henry Koster. *Un ángel pasó por Brooklyn / Un angelo è sceso a Brooklyn* (Sp / It 57) Ladislao Vajda *aka The Man Who Wagged His Tail*. *The Shaggy Dog* (59) Charles Barton [followed by *The Shaggy D. A.* (76) Robert Stevenson and *The Return of the Shaggy Dog* (87 TV) Stuart Gillard]. *The Absent-Minded Professor* (60) Robert Stevenson. *7 Faces of Dr. Lao* (63) George Pal *aka The Circus of Dr. Lao*. *The Love Bug* (68) Robert Stevenson *aka Boy-Car-Girl* [4 films (1969-80) in the series]. *Brewster McCloud* (70) Robert Altman *aka Brewster McCloud's Flying Machine*. *Poor Devil* (73 TV) Robert Scheerer. *Oh God!* (76) Carl Reiner [sequels: *Oh God! Book II* (80) Gilbert Cates and *Oh, God! You Devil* (84) Paul Bogart]. *All of Me* (84) Carl Reiner. *The Purple Rose of Cairo* (84) Woody Allen. *Second Time Lucky* (GB / NZ 84) Michael Anderson. *Splash* (84) Ron Howard. *Shadey* (GB 85) Philip Saville. *Peggy Sue Got Married* (86) Francis Coppola.

——**Ghost Comedies**   Real or fake ghosts, mostly inhabiting haunted castles, mansions and lesser dwellings, have appeared often enough in fantasy comedies to form a subgenre of their own. Featuring apparitions, spectres, spirits, spooks, and other ethereal denizens of the netherworld, the ghost comedy is a well-established type dating back at least to the slapstick days of the early silent comedies. *See also* **HAUNTED HOUSE FILM** and **FILM BLANC**.

Haunted Spooks (20) Harold Lloyd, Alf Goulding.   *Topper* (37) Norman Z. McLeod [followed by *Topper Takes a Trip* (39) McLeod and *Topper Returns* (41) Roy Del Ruth].   *Hold That Ghost* (41) Arthur Lupin.   *The Canterville Ghost* (44) Jules Dassin.   *The Ghost Catchers* (44) Edward F. Cline.   *Blithe Spirit* (GB 45) David Lean.   *The Time of Their Lives* (46) Charles Barton *aka The Ghost Steps Out*.   *Scared Stiff* (52) George Marshall.   *The Spirit Is Willing* (66) William Castle.   *Questi fantasmi / Fantôme à l'Italienne* (F / It 67) Renato Castellani *aka Ghosts—Italian Style*.   *Blackbeard's Ghost* (68) Robert Stevenson.   *Dona Flor e seus dois maridos* (Braz 76) Bruno Barreto *aka Dona Flor and Her Two Husbands*.   *Kiss Me Goodbye* (82) Robert Mulligan.   *Ghostbusters* (84) and *Ghostbusters II* (89) Ivan Reitman.

Musical Fantasy (Fantasy Musical)   *see*   **MUSICAL: Musical Fantasy**

——**Mythological-Fantasy Films**   Closely allied to the Arabian Nights fantasy films, the mythological fantasy pictures borrow from the vast pool provided by mythology. *See* **EPIC** and **PEPLUM**.

I giganti della Tessaglia (Gli Argonauti) / Le Géant de Thesalie (It / F 60) Riccardo Freda *aka The Giants of Thessaly / Jason and the Golden Fleece*.   *Teseo contro il minotauro* (It 60) Silvio Amadio *aka The Minotaur / The Wild Beast of Crete / The Warlord of Crete*.   *Jason and the Argonauts* (GB 63) Don Chaffey *aka Jason and the Golden Fleece*.   *Clash of the Titans* (GB 79-81) Desmond Davis.   *Hercules* (It / US 83) Lewis Coates (Luigi Cozzi).   *Hercules II* (It / US 84) Lewis Coates (Luigi Cozzi) *aka The Adventures of Hercules [II] / Le avventure dell'incredibile Ercole*.

——**Sword-and-Sorcery Films**   They form an important branch of fantasy, previously known as science fantasy. Other terms that have been used are weird fantasy, fantastic romance, and heroic fantasy. These films deal with magic, wizards, and super-heroes, with tribal and feudal societies in exotic settings, either earthbound or in the domain of outer space. It is a fantasy-action genre including the legendary, the primitive, and the supernatural. **See SWORD-AND-SORCERY FILM**.

The Beastmaster (80) Don Coscarelli *aka The Beast Master*.   *Dragonslayer* (US / GB 81) Matthew Robbins.   *Excalibur* (GB / Ir 81) John Boorman *aka Knights / Knights Film / Merlin Lives*.   *The Warrior and the Sorceress / Kain del planeta oscuro* (US / Arg 82) John Broderick, Hill Stout [rel. in 84] *aka Kain of the Dark Planet*.   *Krull* (GB 83) Peter Yates *aka Dragons of Krull / Dungeons and Dragons / The Dungeons of Krull / Krull: Invaders of the Black Forest*.   *Ladyhawke* (US / It 85) Richard Donner.

Fantasy Musical   *see*   **MUSICAL: Musical Fantasy**

FARCE (Farcical Film, Film Farce)   Farce is not easy to define. It is a comedy form which has often been referred to as low comedy and a pejorative sense has been attributed to it.[37] But, in truth, the range of farce is quite wide, and it may go from low, to broad, to high comedy. Recently, it has even taken new directions to include tragic undertones as in the absurd comedies called tragic farces, although this latter tendency has not translated too well from theater to screen (e.g., *Rhinoceros* [1973]). Farce seeks to disconcert and produce laughter by auditory, visual, and physical means. It thrives on insults and humiliations, engages in outrageous behavior, and its characters frequently find themselves in ludicrous situations. It is often illogical, and does not respect social conventions. Slapstick, sex comedy, anarchic comedy, and parody fall under the banner of farce.

   Tillie's Punctured Romance (14) Mack Sennett *aka Dressler No. 1 / For the Love of Tillie / Marie's Millions / Tillie's Big Romance / Tillie's Nightmare.* *The Housekeeper's Daughter* (39) Hal Roach. *Road Show* (41) Hal Roach. *The Miracle of Morgan's Creek* (42) Preston Sturges [rel. in 44]. *Family Honeymoon* (48) Claude Binyon. *Carlton-Browne of the F.O.* (GB 58) Jeffrey Dell, Roy Boulting *aka Man in a Cocked Hat.* *The Magic Christian* (GB 69) Joseph McGrath. *Rhinoceros* (US / Can 73) Tom O'Horgan. *Entre tinieblas* (Sp 83) Pedro Almodóvar *aka Dark Habits.* *Finders Keepers* (US / Can 84) Richard Lester. *La corte del Faraón* (Sp 86) José Luis Sánchez *aka Pharaoh's Court.* *La ley del deseo* (Sp 86) Pedro Almodóvar *aka The Law of Desire.* *Ruthless People* (86) Jim Abrahams, David Zucker, Jerry Zucker. *A Fish Called Wanda* (GB 88) Charles Crichton. *Nuns on the Run* (GB 90) Jonathan Lynn.

Farcical Film   *see*   **FARCE**

Farm Comedy   *see*   **RURAL COMEDY**

Farmer Film, Farm Movie   *see*   **RUSTIC DRAMA**

Fear Film   *see*   **FACTUAL FILM: Jeopardy Film**

Feature   *see*   **FEATURE FILM**

FEATURE FILM (Feature, Feature-Length Film, Full-Length Motion Picture, Multiple-Reeler, Multiple-Reel Film)   Various meanings have been attached to the word feature or feature film. In the first instance, a feature film refers in common usage to a fictional narrative or entertainment picture as opposed to a documentary; nevertheless, a documentary or a nonfiction film may equally be designated a feature or feature-length film if it meets the necessary length requirements. Secondly, a feature film, as opposed to a short or short film, means, broadly speaking, any film which runs for 60 minutes or more; this ruling is flexible, however, as different countries and film organizations tend to vary the minimum length required to qualify the film as a feature. For example, in the United Kingdom the minimum length for a feature film was officially set at three reels (3000 ft.) or 33.5 minutes of screen time. Many silent films and low-budget Hollywood films run for under 60 minutes. A feature has also been defined as a moving picture which runs for at least 5 reels, or 50 minutes of running time; still others set the running time at a minimum of 40 minutes. And thirdly, the feature film means the main feature, usually a high-budget picture, in a program featuring several films or in a double feature or double bill program. The world's first feature intended for commercial release was the 4000 ft. long Australian film *The Story of the Kelly Gang* (1906) made by Charles Tait. It was premièred at the Athenaeum Hall, Melbourne, on December 26, 1906. France followed with Michel Carré's *L'Enfant prodigue* (1907). In the United States and Great Britain, feature films began to be produced in 1912. Sometimes, the word featurette is used for a short or medium-length motion picture. Theatrical feature is a term sometimes used for categorizing films meant for general distribution as distinct from telefeatures or miniseries meant to be shown on television.

On television, the word feature is interpreted as meaning a nonfiction item or documentary. *See also* **CO-FEATURE.**

Feature-Length Film *see* **FEATURE FILM;** *see also* **FICTIONAL FILM**

Featurette *see* **FEATURE FILM;** *see also* **SHORT**

Federal Agent Films *see* **POLICE FILM;** *see also* **GANGSTER FILM: G-Man Films**

Feminist Documentary *see* **DOCUMENTARY**

FEMINIST FILM (Women's Lib Picture)   With the upsurge of feminist activity in the seventies, feminist filmmakers came to the fore, and a noticeable body of feminist film emerged. A feminist movie is that which seeks to validate a feminist philosophy and point of view. It seeks to further the fight of women for complete emancipation from the tethers of past and present convention. It reevaluates the position of women in the so-called bourgeois, patriarchal-oriented society and, judging them culturally, economically, and politically oppressed, seeks to redress, or at least bring to attention, this fact. In the women's movement or feminist credo, a film which maintains feminine and masculine stereotyping is labelled a sexist film; on the other hand, films which refute or denounce male and female roles are known as anti-sexist films. Feminist filmmaking means almost exclusively films made by women for women; men, if not excluded altogether, are relegated to the peripheral areas of women's spheres of concern.[38]
Ålskande par (Sw 65) Mai Zetterling *aka Loving Couples. La Vie rêvée / Dream Life* (Can 71) Mireille Dansereau *aka The Dreamed Life. Nathalie Granger* (F 72) Marguerite Duras. *Film about a Woman Who...* (74) Yvonne Rainer. *India Song* (F 74) Marguerite Duras. *Je, tu, il, elle* (Belg / F 74) Chantal Akerman *aka I... You... He... She.... Superdyke* (75) Barbara Hammer. *Erikas Leidenschaften* (G 76 TV) Ula Stöckl *aka Erica's Passion. Néa* (F / G 76) Nelly Kaplan *aka Néa ou la lettre à Emmanuelle / A Young Emmanuelle. Das zweite Erwachen der Crista Klages* (G 77) Margarethe von Trotta *aka The Second Awakening of Crista Klages. Getting Ready* (77) Janet Meyers. *Io sono mia* (It 77) Sofia Scandurra. *Madame X—Eine*

absolute Herrscherin (G 77) Ulrike Ottinger *aka Madame X—An Absolute Ruler.* *Riddles of the Sphinx* (GB 77) Laura Mulvey, Peter Wollen. *Rapunzel Let Down Your Hair* (GB 78) Asa Sjöström, Susan Shapiro, Esther Ronay, Francine Winham. *Thriller* (GB 79) Sally Potter. *Maeve* (GB 81) Pat Murphy, John Davies. *Coup de foudre* (F 83) Diane Kurys *aka At First Sight / Entre Nous / Between Us.* *De Stilte Rond Christine M.* (Hol 82) Marleen Gorris *aka A Question of Silence.* *Anita, Tänzerin des Lasters* (G 87) Rosa von Praunheim *aka Anita—Dances of Vice.*

——**Women's Suffrage Films (Suffrage Films)**   A short-lived, early manifestation of feminist-oriented pictures apparently ignored by historians and critics which appeared in the 1900s.[39] These films reflected the aim of the suffrage movement which fought for women's right to vote in the years preceding World War I and contrasted with suffrage/antisuffrage films which, mostly as comedies and satires, poked fun at women activists and suffragettes.

Votes for Women (12) Hal Reid *aka Independent Votes for Women.* *Eighty Million Women Want—?* (13) Produced by the Women's Political Union; Florence Maule Cooley (scenarist) *aka What Eighty Million Women Want.* *Your Girl and Mine: A Woman Suffrage Play* (14) Giles Warren *aka Your Girl and Mine.*

Feminist-Oriented Film   *see*   **FEMINIST FILM**

Fiction Film   *see*   **FICTIONAL FILM**

FICTIONAL FILM (Dramatic-Narrative Film, Fiction Film, Fictive Film)   The fictional film—film drama, film play, screen drama, screenplay, or story film, as it has at times been called—is a film in which actors perform in front of a camera to create fictitious situations or tell an invented story with the purpose of showing it to an audience; hence the terms entertainment film, theatrical film, and feature film have also been used with analogous meaning. Entertainment film and theatrical film also imply the kind of film made for commercial screening at a film theater or cinema, although eventually it may be transferred to videocassette or shown elsewhere, e.g., television, film societies. Fictional film or fiction film stands in opposition to factual or documentary film.

Fictionalized Documentary   *see*   **DOCUMENTARY: Documentary-Style Film**

Fictive Film   *see*   **FICTIONAL FILM**

Fight Film   *see*   **BOXING PICTURE;**   *see also*   **GANGSTER FILM: Boxing Gangster Films**

FILLER   A film, usually a short, meant to fill or round off a program.

FILM (Cinematograph Film, Flick, Flicker, Motion Picture, Movie, Moving Picture, Pic / Pix, Picture)   Regardless of the different nuances and context in which they are used, the above words are accepted terminology in today's speech for a series of continuous images which are usually projected on a screen, telecast, or shown on a viewer. Earlier expressions in older publications include shadow-play, photo-drama, photo-play, and picture play. More specialized terms for a motion picture are "road show" and "hard ticket" for films which are exhibited in major cinemas. Admission to these films is more expensive than normal, and seats are usually booked in advance.

FILM A CLEF (Cinéma à Clef, Movie à Clef)   A *roman à clef* ("key novel") is a novel in which the main characters are based on real people, but whose identities, although easily recognized by well-informed readers, are nevertheless veiled to avoid any printing interdiction or legal prosecution. The same applies to movies which use similar techniques for concealing the character's (or characters') real-life identity. Most of these films are concealed biographies and deal with Hollywood personalities. They have been referred to as films *à clef.*

> *Citizen Kane* (40) Orson Welles *aka The American. Caught* (48) Max Ophüls. *Sunset Boulevard* (49) Billy Wilder. *The Goddess* (58) John Cromwell. *Imitation of Life* (59) Douglas Sirk. *The Carpetbaggers* (63) Edward Dmytryk. *The Last Tycoon* (76) Elia Kazan. *Network* (76) Sidney Lumet. *Washington Behind Closed Doors* (77 TV) Gary Nelson [in 6 parts]. *The Greek Tycoon* (US / GB 78) J. Lee Thompson. *Ein Mann wie Eva* (G 83) Radu Gabrea *aka A Man Like Eve.*

Film About Aging   *see*   **FILM ABOUT OLD AGE**

Film About Antiquity   *see*   **ANCIENT FILM**

FILM ABOUT ART (Art Film)   The film medium is ideally suited to the understanding and appreciation of art. The camera can focus on a work of art and show in detail aspects of its composition thus enabling the viewer to become much more aware of its artistic value. Films about art or art films draw attention to a particular painting or paintings, sculpture, the work of an artist, a group of artists or a particular school of art or movement. They are a well-established form of cinematic expression. The term art film (q.v.) is also used for a film shown in an art house or specialized cinema devoted to the showing of quality films or acknowledged film classics.

> *Le Monde de Paul Delvaux* (Belg 46) Henri Storck *aka The World of Paul Delvaux. Van Gogh* (F 48) Alain Resnais. *Le Mystère Picasso* (F 55) Henri-George Clouzot *aka The Picasso Mystery. Painter's Painting* (73) Emile De Antonio. *Rodin, 1840–1917 / Changes Rodin 1840–1917* (F / GB G 74 TV) Leslie Megahey. *Géricault* (GB 82 TV) Leslie Megahey *aka Théodore Géricault 1791–1824. Paul Delvaux* (Belg 87) Adrian Maben *aka The Sleepwalker of Saint-Idesbald Paul Delvaux.*

Film About Children   *see*   **CHILDREN'S FILM**

FILM ABOUT FILMS (Film on Filmmaking, Hollywood Film on Hollywood, Hollywood-on-Hollywood Film)   Films about films or films on filmmaking are an ever-growing group of films with many characteristics in common. They are films which portray the life of a film personality (star, scriptwriter, director) or the career of a movie mogul (producer, studio head) who has greatly influenced the industry. They may also focus on a particular period of film history or show the intricacies of the film business and the secrets of putting together a film. If such is the case, the film-within-a-film is a recurrent device. In the American context, a film about films usually means a film about Hollywood.[40] But, films on film stars, film genres, film history and filmmaking range far and wide and are not just the prerogative of Hollywood — they are made by many nations. These films include biographies, musicals, comedies, parodies, even horror movies, but overriding the conventions of a particular genre, the overall theme of a film about films must be firmly based on the art and craft of making movies or on the movie world if the film is about a film personality. *See also* **BIOGRAPHICAL FILM: Show Business Biographical Films.**

The Last Command (28) Josef von Sternberg *aka The General. Show People* (28) King Vidor. *Movie Crazy* (32) Clyde Bruckman. *What Price Hollywood?* (32) George Cukor *aka The Truth About Hollywood. Bombshell* (33) Victor Fleming *aka Blonde Bombshell. A Star Is Born* (37) William Wellman. *Sullivan's Travels* (40) Preston Sturges. *Crazy House* (43) Edward F. Cline. *In a Lonely Place* (49) Nicholas Ray *aka Behind This Mask / Late at Night. Sunset Boulevard* (49) Billy Wilder. *The Bad and the Beautiful* (52) Vincente Minnelli *aka Tribute to a Bad Man. The Star* (52) Stuart Heisler. *The Big Knife* (55) Robert Aldrich. *8½ / Huit et demi* (It / F 62) Federico Fellini *aka La bella confusione / 8½ (Otto e mezzo) / Federico Fellini's 8½. What Ever Happened to Baby Jane?* (62) Robert Aldrich. *Warnung vor einer heiligen Nutte / Attenzione alla putana santa* (G / It 70) Rainer Werner Fassbinder *aka Attenzione alla sacra putana / Beware of a Holy Whore / Pride Goes Before the Fall. Heat* (71) Paul Morrissey. *La Nuit américaine / Effetto notte* (F / It 72) François Truffaut *aka Day for Night. Blazing Saddles* (73) Mel Brooks *aka Black Bart. The Day of the Locust* (75) John Schlesinger. *Hearts of the West* (75) Howard Zieff *aka Hollywood Cowboy. Hollywood on Trial* (76) David Helpern, Jr. *The Stunt Man* (78) Richard Rush. *Hollywood* (GB 79 TV) Kevin Brownlow, David Gill [in 13 parts]. *Pociag do Hollywood* (Pol 87) Radoslaw Piwowarski *aka Train to Hollywood.*

Film About Marriage *see* **SEX COMEDY: Marital Comedies**

FILM ABOUT MIDDLE AGE (Middle-Age Film, Midlife-Crisis Film) Films about the middle-aged focus on people from about the age of 40 to 60 undergoing what is commonly termed a middle-age crisis. Sudden loss of employment, disillusionment with one's profession, dissatisfaction with oneself, marital problems, the death of a loved one are some of the causes that trigger a crisis characterized by acute frustration of one kind or another. Middle-age films may be presented as drama or comedy showing people in conflict or in humorous situations.

Middle of the Night (59) Delbert Mann. *Inadmissible Evidence* (GB 68) Anthony Page. *The Arrangement* (69) Elia Kazan. *Les Choses de la vie / L'amante* (F / It / Swiz 69) Claude Sautet *aka The Things of Life. Lovers and Other Strangers* (69) Cy Howard. *Loving* (69) Irving Kershner *aka*

Brooks Wilson Ltd. *Husbands* (70) John Cassavetes. *Save the Tiger* (72) John G. Avildsen. *Steppenwolf / Le Loup des steppes* (US / Swiz 74) Fred Haines. *Vincent, François, Paul et les autres / Tre amici, le mogli e (affettuosamente) le altre* (F / It 74) Claude Sautet *aka Vincent, François, Paul and the Others.* *The Turning Point* (77) Herbert Ross. *House Calls* (78) Howard Zieff. *Middle Age Crazy / Deux Fois vingt ans ... faut en profiter* (Can / US 79) John Trent [rel. in 82]. *"10"* (79) Blake Edwards. *The Tempest* (82) Paul Mazursky. *Polioty vo sne naiavou* (USSR 83) Roman Balayan *aka Dream Flights.* *Twice in a Lifetime* (85) Bud Yorkin. *Walls of Glass* (85) Scott Goldstein *aka Flanagan.* *Le Déclin de l'empire américain / The Decline of the American Empire* (Can 86) Denys Arcand. *O Melissokomos / L'Apiculteur* (Gr / F 86) Theodore Angelopoulos *aka The Bee Keeper.* *That's Life!* (86) Blake Edwards. *Another Woman* (88) Woody Allen.

FILM ABOUT OLD AGE (Film About Aging, Geriatric Film, Gerontological Film) A small, ever-increasing percentage of films may be grouped together because they deal with the lives of old people or the problems of growing old. These films approach their subject matter with great sensitivity and feeling. They portray the life of the old, their solitude, forlornness and at times describe the hardships of being destitute or show the slow process of sinking into senility. These films, for the most part, bypass the trappings of melodrama, and are fine drama material with a high degree of humanity in them.

Make Way for Tomorrow (37) Leo McCarey. *Umberto D* (It 51) Vittorio De Sica. *La Vieille Dame indigne* (F 64) René Allio *aka The Shameless Old Lady.* *Smesny pán* (Cz 69) Karel Kachyna *aka The Funny Old Man / The Funny Man.* *Harry and Tonto* (74) Paul Mazursky. *La Vie devant soi* (F 77) Moshe Mizrahi *aka Madame Rose.* *A Family Upside Down* (78 TV) David Lowell Rich. *Comme chien et chat* (F 79 TV) Roland-Bernard. *Going in Style* (79) Martin Brest. *On Golden Pond* (81) Mark Rydell. *Right of Way* (83 CTV) George Schaefer. *The Trip to Bountiful* (85) Peter Masterson. *Travelling North* (Aust 86) Carl Schultz. *Des amis pour la vie / Friends for Life* (Can 88) Alain Chartrand.

FILM ABOUT SEXUAL RELATIONSHIPS Since the late sixties when censorship barriers started to break down, sexuality on the screen has been expressed more and more openly. As distinct from movies which are meant only to be erotic or pornographic, a few filmmakers attempt to depict the workings of the mind when involved in sexual relationships. These psychological dramas deal with human sexuality to the fullest. They present in a totally uninhibited manner the byways of sex between man and woman in a labyrinth of often unspoken sexual needs and desires. The sex content in these films is always very high in terms of nudity and physical action, but totally in accord with its chosen theme.

Stille Dage in Clichy (Den 69) Jeus Jørgen Thorsen Enna *aka Not So Quiet Days / Quiet Days in Clichy.* *Tropic of Cancer* (69) Joseph Strick. *Ultimo Tango a Parigi / Le Dernier Tango à Paris* (It / F 72) Bernardo Bertolucci *aka Last Tango in Paris.* *Malizia* (It 73) Salvatore Samperi *aka Malicious.*

Il Portiere di notte / The Night Porter (It / US 73) Liliana Cavani. *Turks Fruit* (Hol 73) Paul Verhoeven *aka The Sensualist / Turkish Delight.* *Grandeur nature / Tamaño natural / Life Size-Grandezza naturale* (F / Sp / It 73) Luis García Berlanga *aka Life Doll / Life Size.* *La Bête* (F 75) Walerian Borowczyk *aka The Beast / The Beast in Heat.* *La Dernière Femme / L'Ultima donna* (F / It 75) Marco Ferreri *aka The Last Woman.* *Histoire d'O / Die Geschichte der O* (F / G 75) Just Jaeckin *aka The Story of O.* *Ai no koriida / L'Empire des sens* (J / F 76) Nagisa Oshima *aka Ai no Corrida / (The) Empire of the Senses / In the Realm of the Senses / The Realm of the Senses.* *Bilitis* (F 76) David Hamilton, Henry Colpi. *Maîtresse* (F 76) Barber Schroeder, Paul Voujargol. *La Marge* (F 76) Walerian Borowczyk *aka The Margin / The Streetwalker.* *The Sailor Who Fell from Grace with the Sea* (GB 76) Lewis John Carlino. *Bilbao* (Sp 77) Josep Bigas Luna *aka Bilbao, una historia de amor.* *Ai no borei / L'Empire de la passion* (J / F 78) Nagisa Oshima *aka Empire of Love / (The) Phantom of Love.* *Eu te amo* (Braz 80) Arnaldo Jabor *aka I Love You.* *Shina Ningyo / Les Fruits de la passion* (F / J 80) Shuji Terayama *aka The Fruits of Passion.* *La Chiave / The Key* (It / US 83) Tinto Brass. *Crimes of Passion* (GB / US 84) Ken Russell. *La Gabbia* (It / Sp 86) Giuseppe Patroni Griffi *aka The Cage / Collector's Item / The Trap.* *Matador* (Sp 86) Pedro Almodóvar. *¡Atame!* (Sp 89) Pedro Almodóvar *aka Tie Me Up! Tie Me Down!* *Henry & June* (90) Philip Kaufman.

Film About the Holocaust   *see*   **HOLOCAUST FILM**

FILM ABOUT THE TELEVISION MEDIUM   Television, at its beginnings at odds with the film industry, is nowadays coexisting happily with the film medium in a mutually beneficial alliance of sorts. A number of films have focussed on the TV medium or its personnel. At times they just describe the workings and problems encountered in the normal running of a television network; at other times they expose or satirize their shortcomings. *See also* **PARODY: Television Parodies.**

Meet Mr. Lucifer (GB 53) Anthony Pelissier. *The Great Man* (56) Jose Ferrer. *A Face in the Crowd* (57) Elia Kazan. *Will Success Spoil Rock Hunter?* (57) Frank Tashlin *aka Oh, for a Man!* *The Thrill of It All* (63) Norman Jewison. *Medium Cool* (69) Haskell Wexler *aka Concrete Wilderness.* *The Barefoot Executive* (71) Robert Butler. *The Love Machine* (71) Jack Haley, Jr. *Network* (76) Sidney Lumet. *Pray TV* (80) Rick Friedberg *aka K-GOD.* *Pray TV* (82 TV) Robert Markowitz. *Videodrome* (Can / US 81) David Cronenberg [rel. in 83]. *My Favorite Year* (82) Richard Benjamin. *Special Bulletin* (83 TV) Edward Zwick. *The Ratings Game* (84 TV) Danny DeVito. *Ginger e Fred / Ginger et Fred* (It / F / G 85) Federico Fellini *aka Ginger and Fred.* *TerrorVision* (US / It 85) Ted Nicolaou. *Broadcast News* (87) James L. Brooks. *Komikku zasshi nanka iranai!* (J 87) Yojiro Takita *aka Comic Magazine.* *Switching Channels* (88) Ted Kotcheff.

FILM ABOUT THE THEATER   Films about films (q.v.) or filmmaking are plentiful. Films about the theater, vaudeville or burlesque, although not very numerous, form an interesting grouping of their own. Such films deal with stage actors and actresses, comedians, entertainers and performers of all sorts who all share a complete dedication to their art, love of the lime-light and an unmitigated eagerness for success and the audience's applause. *Applause* (29) Rouben Mamoulian. *The Royal Family of Broadway* (30) George Cukor. *Morning Glory* (33) Lowell Sherman. *Dangerous* (35) Alfred E. Green. *The Great Garrick* (37) James Whale. *It's Love I'm After* (37) Archie Mayo. *Stage Door* (37) Gregory La Cava. *Entrée des Artistes* (F 38) Marc Allégret *aka The Curtain Rises. Les Enfants du Paradis* (F 43-45) Marcel Carné [2 parts: *Le Boulevard du Crime* and *L'Homme blanc*]. *A Double Life* (47) George Cukor *aka The Art of Murder / Inspiration. All About Eve* (50) Joseph L. Mankiewicz. *The Country Girl* (54) George Seaton. *The Entertainer* (GB 60) Tony Richardson. *Shakespeare Wallah* (Ind 65) James Ivory. *The Night They Raided Minsky's* (68) William Friedkin *aka The Night They Invented Striptease. Riten / Ritorna* (Sw 68 TV) Ingmar Bergman *aka The Rite / The Ritual. Mephisto* (Hung / G / Aus 80-81) István Szabó. *The Dresser* (GB 83) Peter Yates.

Film Adaptation   *see*   **ADAPTATION**

Film Adaptation of Stage Musicals   *see*   **MUSICAL: Adaptations of Broadway Musicals**

Film Allegory   *see*   **ALLEGORY**

Film as Film   *see*   **STRUCTURAL FILM**

Film Biography   *see*   **BIOGRAPHICAL FILM**

FILM BLANC (Afterlife Film, Heavenly Comedy, Life-After-Death Fantasy)   A category or variety of fantasy film singled out by Peter L. Valenti from the vast pool of fantasy films and named film *blanc* (in contrast to film *noir*).[41] The films belonging to this category present an array of traditional supernatural beings and personifications (for the most part benevolent) — God, the Devil, angels, messengers of Heaven, mischievous ghosts — which either interfere with mortals or help them mend their crooked ways and raise up their morale if they falter in the face of adversity. At the end every one is integrated in a paradisiacal community of good will. In other words, the film *blanc* makes Earth look a better place to live than it actually is. This type of fantasy has been popular in many countries, and it was most evident in the Hollywood of the 30s and 40s. It strives towards light rather than darkness, and it represents the victory of good over evil. It is mainly presented in the mode of comedy, although it may appear in different genres, e.g., the Western, the war film. Afterlife film is a more restrictive term. *See* **FANTASY FILM.**

The Return of Peter Grimm (35) George Nicholls, Jr. *The Scoundrel* (35) Ben Hecht, Charles MacArthur. *Here Comes Mr. Jordan* (41) Alexander Hall. *A Guy Named Joe* (43) Victor Fleming. *A Matter of Life and Death* (GB 45) Michael Powell, Emeric Pressburger *aka Stairway to Heaven. It's a Wonderful Life* (46) Frank Capra. *The Bishop's Wife* (47) Henry Koster. *Heaven Only Knows* (47) Albert S. Rogell *aka Montana Mike. The Angel Who Pawned Her Harp* (GB 54) Alan Bromly. *Oh, God!* (77) Carl Reiner.

Heaven Can Wait (78) Warren Beatty, Buck Henry. *Always* (89) Steven Spielberg.

Film Classic *see* **CLASSIC**

Film Clip *see* **CLIP**

Film Comedy *see* **COMEDY**

Film d'actualité *see* **ACTUALITY**

FILM D'ART (Theatrical Film) *Le Film d'Art* was a French film company founded in 1907 in order to produce quality films which were basically adaptations of literary works and stage plays performed by well-known (e.g., Réjane, Sarah Bernhardt) and lesser-known contemporary thespians. The end-product were stagy films (*films d'art*), no more nor less than static, filmed stage productions. The company ceased to exist in 1929. Besides stage plays, the company also produced films directed by Abel Gance (1889–1981), soon to become well-known for *J'accuse* (1918-19), *La Roue* (1920-22), and *Napoléon* (1925-27). Some of the more successful among the films produced by the Film d'Art studios are *L'Assassinat du Duc de Guise* (1908), *Les Amours de la reine Elisabeth / Queen Elizabeth* (1912) with Sarah Bernhardt, and *Madame Sans-Gêne* (1911) with the actress Réjane. The *films d'art* influenced other countries greatly, in particular Italy, which in 1909 saw the formation of its own *Film d'Arte Italiana*. The Famous Players Film Company, founded in 1912 by Adolph Zukor and the distributors of *Queen Elizabeth*, was the American counterpart to the French *Film d'Art*. It produced a few films under the banner "Famous Players in Famous Plays."

> *L'Assassinat du Duc de Guise* (F 08) Charles Le Bargy, André Calmettes *aka The Assassination of the Duke de Guise.* *Madame Sans-Gêne* (F 11) André Calmettes. *Les Amours de la reine Elisabeth / Queen Beth* (F / GB 12) Louis Mercanton, Henri Desfontaines *aka Elisabeth, reine d'Angleterre / Queen Bess / Queen Elizabeth / La Reine Elisabeth.*

Film d'Auteur *see* **AUTEUR FILM**

Film Diary *see* **UNDERGROUND FILM**

Film Drama *see* **FICTIONAL FILM**

Film Epic *see* **EPIC**

Film Essay *see* **DOCUMENTARY: Analytical Documentary**

Film Eye *see* **KINO-GLAZ**

Film Farce *see* **FARCE**

Film for Children *see* **CHILDREN'S FILM**

Film Kitsch *see* **KITSCH**

Film Made Entirely of Stills   *see*   **ANIMATED FILM: Animated Stills**

Film Maudit   *see*   **TURKEY**

Film Melodrama   *see*   **MELODRAMA**

Film Musical   *see*   **MUSICAL**

FILM NOIR (Black Cinema, Cinema Noir)   Film noir is a well-documented body of films mostly produced between 1940 and 1958.[42] The term *film noir* originated in France and it was an extension applied to film by French film critics of the French *roman noir* or *série noire*, a category of popular novels dealing with the underworld. Although *film noir* has also been produced in France and England, it came to group together those American films which, in many cases, were adaptations or were based on the work of writers that specialized in detective fiction and that dealt with the twilight world of petty criminals and down-and-out characters. Many of these films took place in dimly lit surroundings and at night in dark, wet streets. The term crossed the Atlantic and is now generally accepted as designating an important, original, American cinematic manifestation.

Films classified as *noir* were stylistically influenced by German Expressionism, French Poetic Realism and, to a certain extent, by Italian Neorealism after the war. The *film noir* portrays a world populated by bleak characters usually alienated from society. They are returned war veterans seeking to redress some wrong inflicted on them, psychotic individuals, corrupt cops, private eyes down on their luck, femmes fatales, and other assorted misfits. These protagonists, if they are men, show strong misogynistic tendencies and, if they are women, they tend to be misandrous. Dramatically, they are tainted by Existentialism or Freudianism. Violence or sexual obsession is their most common characteristic. Films which belong to different genres have also been attached to *film noir* and this has made it difficult to decide if *film noir* is itself a genre or not. Some critics regard it as a genre; others regard it as a movement or a style of filmmaking; still other critics contend it is a mixture of both, genre and style. Taking into account all these claims, one strong point is that *film noir* achieves true homogeneity through its remarkable visual style. Genres in which *films noirs* have been found include the gangster film, the police film, the private detective film, the prison film, the boxing film, the period film, and even the Western, not to mention different kinds of melodramas and thrillers.[43] *See* Spencer Selby's filmography, *Dark City: The Film Noir* (Jefferson, NC: McFarland, 1984). *See also* **GANGSTER FILM: Film Noir.**

The Letter (40) William Wyler.   *The Maltese Falcon* (41) John Huston *aka The Gent from Frisco.*   *The Glass Key* (42) Stuart Heisler.   *Double Indemnity* (43) Billy Wilder.   *Phantom Lady* (43) Robert Siodmak.   *Christmas Holiday* (44) Robert Siodmak.   *The Woman in the Window* (44) Fritz Lang. *The Blue Dahlia* (45) George Marshall.   *Deception* (46) Irving Rapper. *Gilda* (46) Charles Vidor.   *Humoresque* (46) Jean Negulesco.   *The Killers* (46)

Robert Siodmak *aka A Man Afraid*. *They Won't Believe Me* (46) Irving Pichel. *Three Strangers* (46) Jean Negulesco. *The Big Clock* (47) John Farrow. *Body and Soul* (47) Robert Rossen *aka An Affair of the Heart*. *Brute Force* (47) Jules Dassin. *The Macomber Affair* (47) Zoltan Korda. *Out of the Past* (47) Jacques Tourneur *aka Build My Gallows High*. *Ride the Pink Horse* (47) Robert Montgomery. *Key Largo* (48) John Huston. *All the King's Men* (49) Robert Rossen. *The Asphalt Jungle* (49) John Huston. *Caged* (49) John Cromwell *aka Locked In*. *D.O.A.* (49) Rudolph Maté. *In a Lonely Place* (49) Nicholas Ray *aka Behind the Mask*. *The Reckless Moment* (49) Max Opuls (Ophuls). *The Big Carnival* (50) Billy Wilder *aka Ace in the Hole / The Human Interest Story*. *The Breaking Point* (50) Michael Curtiz. *Panic in the Streets* (50) Elia Kazan *aka Outbreak*. *The Narrow Margin* (51) Richard Fleischer *aka The Target*. *Strangers on a Train* (51) Alfred Hitchcock. *Pickup on South Street* (52) Samuel Fuller. *The Big Heat* (53) Fritz Lang. *Kiss Me Deadly* (54) Robert Aldrich. *Suddenly* (54) Lewis Allen. *Tight Spot* (55) Phil Karlson. *Sweet Smell of Success* (56) Alexander Mackendrick. *Touch of Evil* (58) Orson Welles. *Der amerikanische Freund / L'Ami américain / The American Friend* (G / F / US 77) Wim Wenders.

————**Postnoir Films**   The term may be used to distinguish films made from the late 1950s on which, consciously or unconsciously, convey the *film noir* mood or style of the 1940s and 1950s.

The Third Voice (59) Hubert Cornfield. *Cape Fear* (61) J. Lee Thompson *aka The Executioners*. *Experiment in Terror* (61) Blake Edwards *aka The Grip of Fear*. *Hoodlum Priest* (61) Irvin Kershner. *The Manchurian Candidate* (62) John Frankenheimer. *The Naked Kiss* (64) Samuel Fuller *aka The Iron Kiss*. *Mickey One* (65) Arthur Penn. *Mirage* (65) Edward Dmytryk. *The Incident* (67) Larry Peerce. *In Cold Blood* (67) Richard Brooks. *Point Blank* (67) John Boorman. *The Friends of Eddie Coyle* (72) Peter Yates. *Chinatown* (74) Roman Polansky. *Farewell My Lovely* (GB 74) Dick Richards. *Hustle* (75) Robert Aldrich *aka City of the Angels / Home Free*. *Taxi Driver* (76) Martin Scorsese. *Body Heat* (81) Lawrence Kasdan. *Vortex* (81) Scott and Beth B. *Blood Simple* (83) Joel Coen. *Tchao Pantin* (F 83) Claude Berri. *Stormy Monday* (GB 87) Mike Figgis. *Gotham* (88 MCTV) Lloyd Fonvielle.

Film-Novel   *see*   **CINE-ROMAN**

Film of Empire   *see*   **BRITISH EMPIRE FILM**

Filmograph   *see*   **ANIMATED FILM: Animated Stills**

Film on Economics   *see*   **FACTUAL FILM: Educational Film**

Film on Filmmaking   *see*   **FILM ABOUT FILMS**

Film Opera   *see*   **OPERA FILM**

Film Play   *see*   **FICTIONAL FILM**

FILM POEM (Cinepoem, Cine Poem, Poetry-Film)   A term sometimes used for an avant-garde film whose imagery develops a metaphor. It is a very broad term which includes almost any film with poetic undertones, e.g., avant-garde documentaries (*Manhatta* [1921]), surrealist and trance films (*Le Sang d'un poète* [1930]; *Meshes of the Afternoon* [1943]), underground films (*Desistfilm* [1954]; *Cosmic Ray* [1961]; *Oh Dem Watermelons* [1965]; *Relativity* [1963-66]).

> *Manhatta* (21) Charles Sheeler, Paul Strand (photographers) *aka Mannahatta*. *Le Sang d'un poète* (F 30) Jean Cocteau *aka The Blood of a Poet / La Vie du poète*. *Meshes of the Afternoon* (43) Maya Deren, Alexander Hammid [sound added in 58]. *Desistfilm* (54) Stan Brakhage. *Cosmic Ray* (61) Bruce Conner. *Oh Dem Watermelons* (65) Robert Nelson. *Relativity* (63-66) Ed Emshwiller.

Film Portrait   *see*   UNDERGROUND FILM

Film Record   *see*   FACTUAL FILM: Record Film

Film Revues   *see*   MUSICAL

Film Serial   *see*   SERIAL

Film Series   *see*   SERIES

Film with a Medieval Setting   *see*   SWASHBUCKLER: Chivalric Films

Filmed Opera   *see*   OPERA FILM

Films About the Devil   *see*   RELIGIOUS FILM

First Avant-Garde   *see*   IMPRESSIONIST FILM

First Cinema   *see*   THIRD WORLD FILM

First Feature   *see*   A-PICTURE

Firstrun Program, Firstrun Syndication   *see*   TELEVISION PROGRAM

Five-Handkerchief Film   *see*   WEEPIE

Flatties   *see*   3-D FILM

Fleshfeast, Flesh-Flick   *see*   SKIN FLICK

Flick, Flicker   *see*   FILM

Flicker Film   *see*   STRUCTURAL FILM

Flop   *see*   TURKEY

Flying Film   *see*   AVIATION FILM

Follow-Up   *see*   SEQUEL

FOOTBALL FILM (Gridiron Film)   Football films have come mostly in the form of college campus comedies or college campus musicals with few inroads into the field of drama. Colleges are the breeding ground for future pro football players, and they provide a ready-made scenario for these football comedies. However, American football has produced some fine films which do capture the essence and spirit of the game. More recently, the trend has been to demythologize the sport and stress the violence and aggressiveness inherent in it.

The Freshman (25) Sam Taylor, Fred Newmeyer *aka College Days. College Coach* (33) William Wellman. *College Humor* (33) Wesley Ruggles. *Pigskin Parade* (36) David Butler. *Knute Rockne—All-American* (40) Lloyd Bacon *aka A Modern Hero. Saturday's Hero* (51) David Miller *aka Idols in the Dust. The Fortune Cookie* (66) Billy Wilder *aka Meet Whiplash Willie. Paper Lion* (68) Alex March. *Footsteps* (72 TV) Paul Wendkos *aka Nice Guys Finish Last. Blood Sport* (73 TV) Jerrold Freedman. *The Longest Yard* (74) Robert Aldrich *aka The Mean Machine. Semi-Tough* (77) Michael Ritchie. *North Dallas Forty* (79) Ted Kotcheff. *Coach of the Year* (80 TV) Don Medford. *All the Right Moves* (83) Michael Chapman. *Quarterback Princess* (83 TV) Noel Black. *Wildcats* (86) Michael Ritchie. *Everybody's All-American* (88) Taylor Hackford.

Foreign Legion Film   *see*   LEGION FILM

Foreign Release   *see*   RELEASE

FOREIGN VERSION   A film version meant for a country other than that in which it originates. Foreign versions simply consisted of prints with foreign language intertitles (in silent movies), or were a matching film shot in the language of the intended foreign market. This meant that some of the major roles were entrusted to native-speaking actors, and possibly supervised by a different director.[44] This was common practice in the introductory years of sound to motion pictures. At present, a foreign version mainly means a dubbed or subtitled version and, in some cases, a version with more or less controversial matter according to the country of destination.

Formal Film   *see*   STRUCTURAL FILM

Formalism, Formalist Film   *see*   EXPRESSIVE-REALIST FILM

FORMULA FILM   When the audience can predict what is going to happen next, it is an indication that the audience is watching a film which follows a formula that has been tried before with success. It does not ensure that the formula will succeed once more, but this possibility does not prevent film producers from backing films which try again what has worked previously. A formula film does not necessarily entail a remake. James Bond's films, or television film series, e.g., *Columbo* (1971-77), are formula films.

Found-Footage Film   *see*   UNDERGROUND FILM: College Films

Four Handkerchief Picture, Four-Hankie Pic   *see*   WEEPIE

Frankenstein Films   *see*   HORROR FILM

FREE CINEMA (Free Cinema Film)   A British documentary movement which materialized in a series of six programs of films shown at the London National Film Theatre between 1956 and 1959. The programs included films by Lindsay Anderson, Karel Reisz, Tony Richardson and others, as well as some by foreign filmmakers. It was short-lived and mainly sustained by the ideas expressed by Anderson and Reisz through articles published mostly in *Sequence* and *Sight and Sound*. Briefly summarized, these ideas stood for freedom on the part of the filmmaker to express himself through his film, the need to comment on contemporary society, and the necessity for "commitment" in the sense of doing something to accomplish his aims. Most filmmakers connected with Free Cinema went on to make feature films. Some of the influences of Free Cinema are obvious in films like Richardson's *Look Back in Anger* (1958), Reisz's *Saturday Night and Sunday Morning* (1960) and Anderson's *This Sporting Life* (1963). *See* "Free Cinema," in *Studies in Documentary* by Alan Lovell and Jim Hillier (London: Secker and Warburg, 1972), 133–72.

O Dreamland (GB 53) Lindsay Anderson. *Momma Don't Allow* (GB 56) Karel Reisz, Tony Richardson. *Every Day Except Christmas* (GB 57) Lindsay Anderson [1st film in the series "Look at Britain"]. *We Are the Lambeth Boys* (GB 59) Karel Reisz.

Free Cinema Film   *see*   **FREE CINEMA**

French Impressionism   *see*   **IMPRESSIONIST FILM**

French Movie   *see*   **STAG FILM**

French New Wave   *see*   **NOUVELLE VAGUE**

Fringe Musical   *see*   **MUSICAL: Borderline Musicals**

Fuck and Die Film   *see*   **SLASHER FILM**

Fuck Movie, Full-Action Film   *see*   **HARD-CORE PORNO FILM**

Full-Length Motion Picture   *see*   **FEATURE FILM**

Funfair Movies   *see*   **CIRCUS FILM**

Funny Film   *see*   **COMEDY**

Future Barbarian Movies, Future Film   *see*   **SCIENCE FICTION FILM**

Futurism   *see*   **FUTURIST FILM**

FUTURIST FILM (Futurism)   Futurism, a term coined in 1909 by the poet Filippo Tommaso Marinetti (1876–1944), emerged in Italy in 1910 as an art movement strongly opposed to tradition and devoted to change. It looked towards the future for renewal and extolled the importance of modern life, the machine and technological development. It issued several manifestos and was very influential in Russia and England. One of the manifestos entitled *La Cinematografia Futurista*, published in 1916 by F. T. Marinetti, Bruno Corra, Emilio Settimelli, Arnaldo Ginna, Giacomo Balla and Remo Chiti, gave an outline for a Futurist cinema in which objects were to be animated and humanized in a filmed dream context rather than in a realistic setting. It produced only a few films, for the most part no longer extant.

Mondo baldoria (It 14) Aldo Molinari. *Il perfido incanto* (It 16) Anton Giulio Bragaglia *aka The Perfidious Enchantment*. *Thais* (It 16) Antonio Giulio Bragaglia. *Vita futurista* (It 16) Arnaldo Ginna *aka Futurist Life*. *Vita Futurista: Italian Futurism 1909–44* (GB 87) Lutz Becker.

Futuristic Film *see* SCIENCE FICTION FILM

GADGET COMEDY   A term that has been used for comedies that create their humor by using mechanical devices or gadgets to do common, simple chores. *Mon Oncle* (1958) by Jacques Tati is an amusing satire which could also be described as a gadget comedy.

The Scare Crow (20) Buster Keaton, Eddie Cline. *It's a Gift* (23) Hugh Fay. *Modern Times* (36) Charlie Chaplin. *Mon Oncle / Mio Zio* (F / It 58) Jacques Tati *aka My Uncle / My Uncle, Mr. Hulot*.

Gag Comedy *see* ANARCHIC COMEDY

Gallows Humor *see* BLACK COMEDY

Game Show *see* TELEVISION SHOW

GAMBLING PICTURE (Gambling Drama)   Films on gambling may take place in any setting or location; whether they deal with professional gamblers or not, they all have in common a great deal of suspense which hinges on the outcome of a bet or the gambler's reaction to his good or bad fortune. Gambling is very often addictive, and this fact alone provides motivation for good drama as the viewer follows a gambler's struggle to shake the habit. Some gambling pictures are Westerns, others are period pieces or the setting may be contemporary. They often feature poker games, baccarat, billiards, dice, or roulette, but any game of chance fits properly into the gambler's agenda.

Gambling Lady (34) Archie Mayo. *The Man Who Broke the Bank at Monte Carlo* (35) Stephen Roberts. *Lady Luck* (46) Edwin L. Marin. *The Queen of Spades* (GB 48) Thorold Dickinson. *The Great Sinner* (49) Robert Siodmak. *The Lady Gambles* (49) Michael Gordon. *Mississippi Gambler* (53) Rudolph Maté *aka Danger on the River*. *Bob le Flambeur* (F 55) Jean-Pierre Melville *aka Bob the Gambler*. *The Hustler* (61) Robert Rossen. *La Baie des Anges* (F 62) Jacques Demy *aka Bay of Angels*. *The Cincinnati Kid* (65) Norman Jewison. *La Dame de pique* (F 65) Léonard Keigel *aka The Queen of Spades*. *A Big Hand for the Little Lady* (66) Fielder Cook *aka Big Deal at Dodge City*. *The Gamblers* (69) Ron Winston. *Thursday's Game* (71 TV) Robert Moore [rel. in 74]. *California Split* (74) Robert Altman. *La città gioca d'azzardo* (It 74) Sergio Martino *aka The Cheaters / Gambling City*. *Cockfighter* (74) Monte Hellman *aka Born to Kill / Gamblin' Man /*

Wild Drifter. *The Gambler* (74) Karel Reisz. *Atlantic City / Atlantic City U.S.A.* (Can / F 79-80) Louis Malle *aka Bamboozle / The Neighbor. Stacy's Knights* (83) Jim Wilson. *The Color of Money* (86) Martin Scorsese. *House of Games* (87) David Mamet.

Gang Film   *see*   **GANGSTER FILM;**   *see also*   **TEEN MOVIE: Teen-Violence Films**

Gangland Film   *see*   **GANGSTER FILM: Syndicate Films**

Gangster Biographies, Gangster Comedies   *see*   **GANGSTER FILM**

GANGSTER FILM (Gang Film)   A violent, well-documented American genre, the gangster film sprang onto the screen in 1912 with the showing in New York of *The Musketeers of Pig Alley*, a one-reeler shot on location with actual gangsters by D. W. Griffith. By the early thirties the conventions of the gangster movie were already well-established and, as with other genres, it could be subdivided into categories or subgenres. The gangster movie is rich in iconography and populated by well-defined gangster variants, e.g., the bootlegger, the racketeer, the hitman, or complementary characters—the moll, the shyster, the G-man, the hoodlum. Besides the United States, France, Italy, and Japan also possess a rich tradition in gangster films. Eugene Rosow, in *Born to Lose* (New York: Oxford University Press, 1978), pp. 395–400, includes a "Filmography" listing 581 gangster films; his "Annotated Filmography," pp. 355–93, describes 83 of the most important gangster films. James Robert Parish and Michael R. Pitts include a selection of 386 gangster films in *The Great Gangster Pictures* (Metuchen, NJ: Scarecrow, 1976) and an additional 412 titles are in *The Great Gangster Pictures II* (Metuchen, NJ: Scarecrow, 1987).

The Musketeers of Pig Alley (12) D. W. Griffith. *The Gangsters and the Girl* (14) Thomas Ince. *Dock of New York* (28) Josef von Sternberg. *The Racket* (28) Lewis Milestone. *City Streets* (31) Rouben Mamoulian. *The Public Enemy* (31) William Wellman *aka Enemies of the Public. Star Witness* (31) William Wellman. *Night World* (32) Hobart Henley. *Lady Killer* (33) Roy Del Ruth. *The Last Gangster* (37) Edward Ludwig *aka Another Public Enemy. Marked Woman* (37) Lloyd Bacon. *The Amazing Dr. Clitterhouse* (38) Anatole Litvak. *The Roaring Twenties* (39) Raoul Walsh. *The Gangster* (47) Gordon Wiles. *The Threat* (49) Felix Feist. *Panic in the Streets* (50) Elia Kazan. *Tight Spot* (55) Phil Karlson. *Party Girl* (58) Nicholas Ray. *Borsalino* (F / It 69) Jacques Deray. *Città violenta / La Cité de la violence* (It / F 69) Sergio Sollima *aka The Family / The Final Shot / Ultimo colpo / Violent City. Get Carter* (GB 70) Mike Hodges. *La Course du lièvre à travers les champs / La corsa della lepre attraverso i campi / And Hope to Die* (F / It / US 72) René Clément. *Prime Cut* (72) Michael Ritchie. *Charley Varrick* (73) Don Siegel. *Mean Streets* (73) Martin Scorsese.

——**Black Gangster Films**   In the late sixties and early seventies with the black-oriented feature films that flooded the American market, an obvious and popular genre for exploitation was the gangster film. *See also* **BLACK FILM.**

Slaughter (72) Jack Starrett.   *Super Fly* (72) Gordon Parks Jr. *aka Superfly.*
Black Caesar (73) Larry Cohen *aka The Godfather of Harlem.*   *Black Samson* (73) Charles Bail *aka Black Samson, White Delilah.*   *Hell Up in Harlem* (73) Larry Cohen.   *Slaughter's Big Rip Off* (73) Gordon Douglas.   *Willie Dynamite* (74) Gilbert Moses.   *The Human Tornado* (76) Cliff Roquemore *aka Dolemite II.*

———**Boxing Gangster Films**   The world of boxing has been permeated from time to time by gangster elements trying to influence and cash in on the lucrative sport. The fight movies that focus on the gangster aspect form a clear-cut subdivision of the genre. *See* **BOXING PICTURE.**
Kid Galahad (37) Michael Curtiz.   *City for Conquest* (40) Anatole Litvak.   *Body and Soul* (47) Robert Rosen *aka An Affair of the Heart.*   *Champion* (49) Mark Robson.   *The Set-Up* (49) Robert Wise.   *The Harder They Fall* (56) Mark Robson.   *Body and Soul* (81) George Bowers.

———**Cop Movies**   In these films, a cop becomes the gangster's nemesis. In some of the early cop movies, the policeman has to pretend to be a hoodlum in order to infiltrate the gangster's environment and bring him to justice. *See* **POLICE FILM.**
The Beast of the City (32) Charles Brabin.   *Bullets or Ballots* (36) William Keighley.   *The Big Heat* (53) Fritz Lang.   *Dragnet* (54) Jack Webb.   *Madigan* (67) Don Siegel.   *Bullitt* (68) Peter Yates.   *Coogan's Bluff* (68) Don Siegel.   *Dirty Harry* (71) Don Siegel *aka Dead Right* [5 "Inspector Callahan" films up to 1988].   *The French Connection* (71) William Friedkin.   *French Connection II* (US / F 74) John Frankenheimer *aka French Connection Number 2.*   *Contract on Cherry Street* (77 TV) William A. Graham.

———**Exposé Films**   The exposure of rackets and citywide crime conditions was the subject matter of these films, mostly shot in a documentary style. There was a cycle of them in the fifties. *See* **EXPOSÉ FILM.**
Hoodlum Empire (52) Joseph Kane.   *Kansas City Confidential* (52) Phil Karlson *aka The Secret Four.*   *Inside Detroit* (55) Fred F. Sears.   *New York Confidential* (55) Russell Rouse.   *The Phenix City Story* (55) Phil Karlson.   *The Houston Story* (56) William Castle.   *Chicago Confidential* (57) Sidney Salkow.

———**Film Noir**   Among the many shadows of the night that populated these pictures, the tragic figure of the gangster, a clear outsider, is one of the major components of the *film noir* (q.v.).
High Sierra (40) Raoul Walsh.   *The Dark Corner* (46) Henry Hathaway.   *Kiss of Death* (47) Henry Hathaway.   *Out of the Past* (47) Jacques Tourneur *aka Build My Gallows High.*   *Force of Evil* (48) Abraham Polonsky *aka The Numbers Racket / The Story of Tucker's People / Tucker's People.*   *The Naked City* (48) Jules Dassin *aka Homicide.*   *Thieves' Highway* (49) Jules Dassin.   *White Heat* (49) Raoul Walsh *aka Sin Street Confidential.*   *His Kind of Woman* (50) John Farrow *aka Smiler with a Gun.*   *The Racket* (51) John Cromwell.   *The Big Combo* (54) Joseph Lewis.

———**Gangster Biographies**   They are usually period biographies set in the thirties about historical gangsters, but similar to the majority of Hollywood biographies, the fictional elements in most of these films outweigh the real ones.

Dillinger (45) Max Nosseck. *Baby Face Nelson* (57) Don Siegel. *Machine Gun Kelly* (58) Roger Corman. *Al Capone* (59) Richard Wilson. *The Rise and Fall of Legs Diamond* (60) Budd Boetticher. *Crazy Joe* (It / US 73) Carlo Lizzani. *Dillinger* (73) John Milius. *Lepke* (74) Menahem Golan. *The Story of Pretty Boy Floyd* (74 TV) Clyde Ware *aka Pretty Boy Floyd. The Lady in Red* (79) Lewis Teague *aka Guns, Sin and Bathtub Gin. Nitti* (88 TV) Michael Switzer. *The Revenge of Al Capone* (89 TV) Michael Pressman.

———**Gangster Comedies** Some very good gangster comedies, ranging from the hilarious to the comical, have been made since the thirties.

Welcome Danger (29) Mal St. Clair (silent version); Clyde Bruckman (sound version). *High Pressure* (32) Mervyn LeRoy. *Jewel Robbery* (32) William Dieterle. *The Little Giant* (33) Roy Del Ruth. *Penthouse* (33) W. S. Van Dyke *aka Crooks in Clover. A Slight Case of Murder* (37) Lloyd Bacon. *Brother Orchid* (40) Lloyd Bacon. *Larceny, Inc.* (42) Lloyd Bacon. *Some Like It Hot* (59) Billy Wilder. *Little Cigars* (73) Chris Christenaberry. *Wise Guys* (86) Brian DePalma.

———**Gangster Musicals** The musical blends well with the gangster genre and this combination has existed since the beginnings of the musical and gangster genres alike. Some musicals have a gangster background.

Lights of New York (28) Bryan Foy [1st all-talking feature]. *Broadway* (29) Paul Fejos. *Stolen Harmony* (35) Alfred Werker. *Broadway* (42) William A. Seiter. *Casbah* (48) John Berry. *Guys and Dolls* (55) Joseph Mankiewicz. *Love Me or Leave Me* (55) Charles Vidor. *Robin and the 7 Hoods* (64) Gordon Douglas *aka Robbo. Bugsy Malone* (GB 76) Alan Parker.

———**G-Man Films** These films shifted their focus of attention from the gangster to the law-enforcement special agent working for the F.B.I. or some other government agency. The gangster was no longer the protagonist or idealized hero of the film; instead, the protagonist's role went to the dedicated government man relentlessly pursuing the criminals, intent on reinstating order by apprehending or killing the gangsters. *See also* **POLICE FILM: Federal Agent Films.**

G-Men (35) William Keighley. *Show Them No Mercy!* (35) George Marshall *aka Tainted Money. Special Agent* (35) William Keighley. *Street with No Name* (48) William Keighley. *Down Three Dark Streets* (54) Arnold Laven. *Underworld U.S.A.* (60) Samuel Fuller. *The F.B.I. Story—The F.B.I. Versus Alvin Karpis, Public Enemy Number One* (74 TV) Marvin Chomsky *aka Alvin Karpis / Alvin Karpis Versus the F.B.I. / The F.B.I. Story—Alvin Karpis / The F.B.I. Versus Alvin Karpis. Melvin Pervis—G-Man* (74 TV) Dan Curtis *aka The Legend of Machine Gun Kelly. The Kansas City Massacre* (75 TV) Dan Curtis. *The Untouchables* (87) Brian DePalma.

———**Heist Films (Caper Films)** Whether considered a subgenre of the adventure film or of the crime film, the robbery or caper film becomes a category of the gangster film when gangsters are involved in the heist. *See* **CAPER FILM.**

The Asphalt Jungle (49) John Huston. *The Big Steal* (49) Don Siegel. *Criss Cross* (49) Robert Siodmak. *The Killing* (56) Stanley Kubrick. *Seven Thieves* (60) Henry Hathaway. *Las Vegas, 500 Millones / Les hommes de*

Las Végas / An einem Freitag in Las Vegas / Radiografia d'un colpo d'oro (Sp / F / G / It 67) Antonio Isasi *aka They Came to Rob Las Vegas*. *Cops and Robbers* (73) Aram Avakian. *The Brink's Job* (78) William Friedkin.

———**Hostage-Holding Gangster Movies**   The invasion by criminals of private homes to be used as a hideout with the gangsters terrorizing the family until their demands are fulfilled or until they see fit to leave (although as a rule they end up dead or captured) is a recurrent theme in many gangster movies. A variant involves holding hostages in a roadside restaurant or in a bank when the robbery has gone awry, with the bank robbers offering the hostages in exchange for their own safety and freedom. All these films form a neat category. Films in which a by-stander is taken by the gangsters to ensure their getaway, or in which the kidnapping of individuals is effected for ransom purposes are not included in the "hostage-holding" category.

Heat Lightning (34) Mervyn LeRoy.   *The Petrified Forest* (36) Archie Mayo. *Key Largo* (48) John Huston.   *The Small Voice* (GB 48) Fergus McDonnell *aka Hideout*.   *The Dark Past* (48) Rudolph Mate.   *He Ran All the Way* (51) John Berry.   *The Desperate Hours* (55) William Wyler.   *Le Mâle du siècle* (F 74) Claude Berri *aka Male of the Century*.   *Dog Day Afternoon* (75) Sidney Lumet.   *Die Katze* (G 88) Dominik Graf *aka Lives of a Cat*.   *Desperate Hours* (89) Michael Cimino.

———**Outlaw Gangster Films (Bandit Gangster Films, Outlaw-Couple Films)** This subgenre shares with the urban gangster movie the gunplay, the car chases and general defiance of the law characteristic of the genre. The films are set in a rural environment as the outlaws move from town to town in their search for banks to rob or small business to pillage. Romance is a strong element in some of them.

You Only Live Once (37) Fritz Lang.   *They Live by Night* (47) Nicholas Ray *aka (The) Twisted Road / Your Red Wagon*.   *Gun Crazy* (49) Joseph H. Lewis *aka Deadly Is the Female*.   *The Bonnie Parker Story* (58) William Witney.   *Bonnie and Clyde* (67) Arthur Penn.   *Boxcar Bertha* (72) Martin Scorsese.   *The Getaway* (72) Sam Peckinpah.   *Big Bad Mama* (74) Steve Carver.

———**Prison Films**   Prison settings have always featured in crime movies; when these films involve gangsters, they can be classed as a category of the gangster film. *See* **PRISON FILM**.

The Big House (30) George W. Hill.   *The Last Mile* (32) Sam Bischoff. *20,000 Years in Sing Sing* (33) Michael Curtiz.   *Brute Force* (47) Jules Dassin.   *My Six Convicts* (52) Hugo Fregonese.   *Riot in Cell Block II* (54) Don Siegel. *The Penitentiary* (79) Jamaa Fanaka [followed by *The Penitentiary II* (82) and *The Penitentiary III* (87) also by Fanaka].

———**Syndicate Films (Gangland Films, Organized-Crime Films, Syndicate-Oriented Films)**   Films dealing with organized crime form an important category of the gangster movie. Whether organized crime is referred to as the Syndicate, the Mafia, the mob, or simply the outfit in the film in question, it supposedly presents the grim reality of a corrupt society, in part controlled by underworld gangsters. *See also* **MAFIA FILM**.

Inside the Mafia (59) Edward L. Cahn. *Murder, Inc.* (60) Burt Balaban, Stuart Rosenberg. *Hail Mafia* (65) Raul Levy. *Le Samurai / Frank Costello faccia d'angelo* (F / It 67) Jean-Pierre Melville *aka The Godson / The Samurai.* *The Brotherhood* (68) Martin Ritt. *The Godfather* (71) Francis Ford Coppola. *Honor Thy Father* (71 TV) Paul Wendkos. *The Family Rico* (72 TV) Paul Wendkos. *The Valachi Papers / Cosa Nostra; Dossier Valachi* (It / F 72) Terence Young *aka L'Affaire Valachi / Cosa Nostra / Joe Valachi: I segreti di Cosa Nostra.* *The Outfit* (73) John Flynn. *The Godfather, Part II* (74) Francis Ford Coppola. *The Godfather, Part III* (90) Francis Ford Coppola.

——**Vigilante Films** In these films, the private citizen or a group of citizens, a cop or a group of cops bound by secrecy and without the knowledge of their superiors, take the administering of the law into their own hands. See **VIGILANTE FILM.**

The Secret Six (31) George W. Hill. *This Day and Age* (33) Cecil B. DeMille. *Death Squad* (73 TV) Harry Falk. *Magnum Force* (73) Ted Post. *Vigilante Force* (76) George Armitage. *Vigilante* (82) William Lusting *aka Street Cop / Street Gang.*

GAY FILM (Homosexual Film)   The image of the homosexual in film has been examined in several books.[45] Homosexuality, however, has been a taboo subject for many years, and although homosexuality has been acknowledged in some films and both male and female homosexuals have appeared sporadically in movies, it was only in the sixties that homosexuality started to emerge as an overall, central theme. These films seek to explore, present and illustrate the way of life of the homosexual. The picture of the gay community that these films project is not always accurate, and obviously some films reflect the ignorance of the filmmakers on the subject, giving us stereotyped characters and situations, if not an altogether distorted image. Homosexual films may be categorized into two general groups—those made by homosexual filmmakers personally familiar with the subject and those made by nonhomosexuals. Gay films may also deal exclusively with male homosexuality or with lesbianism only. For a filmography of 272 gay and lesbian films *see* James Robert Parish, *Gays and Lesbians in Mainstream Cinema* (Jefferson, NC: McFarland, 1993). *See* **LESBIAN FILM.**

Anders als die Andern (G 19) Richard Oswald *aka Different from the Others.* *Un Chant d'amour* (F 50) Jean Genêt. *Victim* (GB 61) Basil Dearden. *The Fox* (66) Mark Rydell. *Reflections in a Golden Eye* (67) John Huston. *The Killing of Sister George* (68) Robert Aldrich. *The Boys in the Band* (70) William Friedkin. *Happy Birthday Davy* (70) Richard Fontaine. *Nicht der Homosexuelle ist pervers, sondern die Situation, in der er lebt* (G 70) Rosa von Praunheim *aka It Is Not the Homosexual Who Is Perverse, but the Situation in Which He Finds Himself.* *Something for Everyone* (70) Harold Prince *aka Black Flowers for the Bride / The Cook / The Rock.* *Sunday Bloody Sunday* (GB 71) John Schlesinger. *A Very Natural Thing* (73) Christopher Larkin *aka For as Long as Possible.* *Je, tu, il, elle* (Belg / F 74) Chantal Akerman *aka I... You... He... She.* *Saturday Night at the Baths* (74) David Buckley. *Du er ikke alene* (Den 77) Lasse

Nielsen, Ernst Johansen *aka You Are Not Alone. I'm Not from Here* (77) Harvey Marks. *Die Konsequenz* (G 77) Wolfgang Petersen *aka The Consequence. Outrageous!* (Can 77) Richard Benner. *Word Is Out* (77) by the Mariposa Film Group: Peter Adair, Nancy Adair, Andrew Brown, Robert Epstein, Lucie Massie Phenix, Veronica Selver *aka Who Are We? La Cage aux folles / Il vizietto* (F / It 78) Edouard Molinaro *aka Birds of a Feather* [followed by *La Cage aux folles II* (F / It 80) also by Molinaro and *La Cage aux folles 3* (F / It 85) Georges Lautner]. *Cruising* (80) William Friedkin. *Liv og død* (Nor 80) Svend Wam, Petter Vennerød *aka Life & Death / Life or Death. Taxi zum Klo* (G 81) Frank Ripploh *aka Taxi to the Toilet (Loo). Querelle—ein Pakt mit dem Teufel / Querelle* (G / F 82) Rainer Werner Fassbinder. *My Beautiful Laundrette* (GB 85 TV) Stephen Frears. *Parting Glances* (86) Bill Sherwood. *Maurice* (GB 87) James Ivory. *Prick Up Your Ears* (GB 87) Stephen Frears. *Taxi nach Kairo* (G 87) Frank Ripploh *aka Taxi to Cairo. The Fruit Machine* (GB 88) Philip Saville *aka Wonderland. Torch Song Trilogy* (88) Paul Bogard.

General Release   *see*   **RELEASE**

Generic Title   *see*   **TELEVISION SERIES**

GENRE FILM   A film which clearly shares similar features and iconography with other films and which is easily recognizable as belonging to a particular group of films or genre, e.g., a Western, a gangster film, a war film. It is not always easy to define a genre and often there is disagreement among critics as to what constitutes its delimitations or which films should be included within its boundaries. A film's genre is sometimes difficult to determine because many films share some of the attributes of two or more genres or they are hybrids belonging to no specific genre. Besides genre films, it is also possible to speak of megagenre or family genre films for films belonging to genres which are broad enough to be subdivided into several other genres or subgenres (e.g., crime films, horror films).

Formula and convention are the bases of genre films which are myth-making and purveyors of ritual. The antigenre film seeks to undermine these bases and demythologize genre. *See* **FORMULA FILM**.

Geography Film   *see*   **FACTUAL FILM: Educational Film**

Geriatric Film, Gerontological Film   *see*   **FILM ABOUT OLD AGE**

Ghost Comedies   *see*   **FANTASY FILM**

GHOST FILM   Apparitions (spirits, poltergeists, wraiths, revenants) take many configurations and manifest themselves in a variety of different ways. They may be friendly or unfriendly, horrible or cute. They may inspire laughter or fear. Ghosts are not limited to human form alone and, besides beast ghosts and other ghostly beings, there have been ghost towns, ghost trains, phantom coaches, and phantom ships. The cinema started the trend in ghost films early, but they were mostly ghost romances and comedies with more or less spooky situations often set in haunted houses or old castles. Most film ghosts, if not engaged in haunting a place, are busy making amends for some wrong doings done while alive, trying to uncover who committed a crime, discover who murdered them, or visiting the living as guardian spirits in order to protect them. The serious ghost story and the ghost horror film have not been plentiful; however, there has been a recent resurgence of the ghost film, especially in the horror field. *See also* **HAUNTED HOUSE FILM** and **FANTASY FILM: Ghost Comedies.**

The Scoundrel (35) Ben Hecht, Charles MacArthur. *The Return of Peter Grimm* (35) George Nicholls, Jr. *The Remarkable Andrew* (41) Stuart Heisler. *Thunder Rock* (GB 42) Roy Boulting. *Don't Take It to Heart* (GB 44) Jeffrey Dell. *Sylvie et le fantôme* (F 45) Claude Autant-Lara *aka Sylvie and the Ghost / Sylvia and the Phantom.* *Ghost Ship* (GB 52) Vernon Sewell. *The Bespoke Overcoat* (GB 55) Jack Clayton. *Yotsuda kaidan* (J 59) Kenji Misumi *aka The Ghost of Yotsuda.* *13 Ghosts* (60) William Castle [filmed in Illusion-O]. *Sole Survivor* (69 TV) Paul Stanley. *Gli orrori del castello di Norimberga / Baron Blood* (It / G / US 71) Mario Bava *aka The Blood Baron / Chamber of Tortures / Gli orrori del castello nero di Norimberga / The Thirst of Baron Blood / The Torture Chamber of Baron Blood.* *The Amazing Mr. Blunden* (72) Lionel Jeffries. *Sand Castles* (72 TV) Ted Post. *Reflections of Murder* (74 TV) John Badham. *The Turn of the Screw* (74) Dan Curtis. *Yin-yang chieh* (HK 74) Ting Shan-Hsi *aka Blood Reincarnation.* *Ai no borei / L'Empire de la passion* (J / F 78) Nagisa Oshima *aka Empire of Passion / Phantom Love / The Phantom of Love.* *Dominique* (GB / US 78) Michael Anderson *aka Avenging Spirit / Dominique Is Dead.* *The Fog* (79) John Carpenter. *The Ghost of Flight 401* (78 TV) Steven Hillard Stern. *Sir Henry at Rawlinson End* (GB 80) Steve Roberts. *Don't Go to Sleep* (82 TV) Richard Lang. *O'Hara's Wife* (82) William S. Bartman. *The Entity* (83) Sidney J. Furie. *Somewhere Tomorrow* (83) Robert Wiemer. *Quian nu youhun* (HK 87) Chin Siu-Tung (Chen Xiaodong) *aka A Chinese Ghost Story.* *Ghost Town* (88) Richard Governor. *Lady in White* (88) Frank LaLoggia.

Ghoulies   *see*   **SEX AND VIOLENCE PICTURE**

GIALLO (Italian Thriller, Thriller all'Italiana)   The *giallo* (yellow) is a term used in Italy for a genre of gory and violent thrillers which antedate the American slasher movies of the 1980s. It takes its name from the yellow cover of a popular series of Italian tough police detection novels of the 40s and 50s. Its origins are found in Mario Bava, whose *La ragazza che sapeva troppo* (1962) and *Sei donne per l'assassino* (1964) paved the way. Besides Mario Bava, Dario Argento is the other outstanding filmmaker of Italian thrillers, a genre that reached its zenith in the 70s. The *giallo* usually falls into two major categories: the *giallo-poliziesco* dealing with crime and criminals and the *giallo-fantastico*, imbued with touches of horror and the supernatural, filmed in a stylish manner and replete with dazzling effects. Its best examples are found in the films of Dario Argento. This genre of Italian thrillers often includes masked, black leather-clad assassins with sadistic tendencies who enjoy disposing of their victims by stabbing, slashing or cutting; for this purpose, they use knives, razors, axes, meat cleavers, pieces of glass, or any sharp implements at their disposal. Realistic and baroque at the same time, these thrillers are fast-paced and character-ized by a brilliant visual style. *La ragazza che sapeva troppo* (It 62) Mario Bava *aka The Evil Eye.* *Sei donne per l'assassino / Six Femmes pour l'assassin / Blutige Seide* (It / F / G 64) Mario Bava *aka Blood and Black Lace / Fashion House of Death.* *La lama nel corpo / Les Nuits de l'épouvante* (It / F 65) Elio Scardamaglia (Michael Hamilton) *aka Murder Clinic / Murder Society / The Night of Terrors / Revenge of the Living Dead.* *Orgasmo* (It / F 68) Umberto Lenzi *aka Paranoia / A Quiet Place to Kill.* *Il rosso segno delle follia / Una hacha para la luna de miel* (It / Sp 69) Mario Bava *aka Un'acceta per la luna di miele / Blood Brides / Hatchet for the Honeymoon.* *L'uccello dalle piume di cristallo / Das Geheimnis der Schwarzen Handschuhe* (It / G 69) Dario Argento *aka The Bird with the Crystal Plumage / The Bird with the Glass Feathers / The Gallery Murders / Phantom of Terror.* *Cinque bambole per la luna d'agosto* (It 70) Mario Bava *aka 5 Dolls / Five Dolls for an (the) August Moon.* *Il gatto a nove code / Le Martinet / Die neunschwänzige Katze* (It / F / G 70) Dario Argento *aka The Cat O'Nine Tails / Le chat à neuf queues.* *La bestia uccide a sangue freddo* (It 71) Fernando Di Leo *aka Asylum Erotica / Cold Blooded Beast / Slaughter Hotel.* *Una lucertola con la pelle di donna / Le Venin de la peur / Una lagartija con piel de mujer* (It / F / Sp 71) Lucio Fulci *aka A Lizard in a Woman's Skin / Schizoid.* *Quattro mosche di velluto grigio / Quatre Mouches de velours gris* (It / F 71) Dario Argento *aka Four Flies on Grey Velvet.* *Reazione a catena* (It 71) Mario Bava *aka Antefatto / Antefatto ecologia del delitto / A Bay of Blood / Before the Fact — Ecology of a Crime / Bloodbath / Carnage / Ecologia del delitto / Last House on the Left Part II / Twitch of the Death Nerve.* *Lo strano vizio della signora Ward / La perversa Señora Ward* (It / Sp 71) Sergio Martino *aka Next! / Uno strano fiore con cinque gocce di sangue.* *La Tarantola dal ventre nero / La Tarantule au ventre noir* (It / F 71) Paolo Cavara *aka The Black Belly of the Tarantula.* *Cosa avete fatto a Solange? / Das Geheimnis des Grauen Stecknadeln* (It / G 72) Massimo Dallamano *aka What Have You Done to Solange?* *Perché quelle strane gocce di sangue sul corpo di Jennifer?* (It 72) Anthony Ascott (Giuliano Carmineo) *aka Erotic Blue.* *I corpi presentano tracce di violenza carnale* (It 73) Sergio Martino *aka Torso.* *Nude per l'assassino* (It 75) Andrea Bianchi *aka Strip Nude for Your Killer.* *Profondo rosso* (It 75) Dario Argento *aka Deep Red / Dripping Deep Red / The Hatchet Murders / The Sabre Tooth Tiger.* *Shock* (It 77) Mario Bava *aka Al 33 di Via Orologio fa sempre freddo / Beyond the Door 2 / Shock transfert-suspence-hypnos / Suspense.* *Suor omicidi* (It 78) Giulio Berruti *aka (The) Killer Nun.* *Macabro* (It 80) Lamberto Bava *aka Macabre.* *Lo squartatore di New York* (It 82) Lucio Fulci *aka The New York Ripper.* *Tenebre* (It 82) Dario Argento *aka Darkness / Sotto gli occhi dell'assassino / Unsane / Tenebrae.* *La casa con la scala nel (al) buio* (It 83) Lamberto Bava *aka A Blade in the Dark / House of (with) the Dark Staircase.*

Giant Insect Film, Giant-Monster Genre *see* **HORROR FILM: Other Denizens of Horror Movies**

Gig Film *see* **GIRL GANG FILM**

GIRL GANG FILM (Gig Film, Girls-in-Gangs Film) Girls-in-gangs films are discussed by Mike Wilkins in "Jail Birds Among Others," *Film Comment* 22.4 (1986): 62–69. These movies deal with women in groups or gangs sharing some common concern or goal in a kind of amiable sisterhood. The women are a variegated lot and include cheerleaders, nurses, biker girls, stewardesses, high school kids, college students, prison inmates, and assorted women in uniform. The films are primarily geared to the exploitation market and are mostly R-rated as they may include some nudity or violence or both. *See also* **Women's Prison Films, Nurse Films** and **Softcore Teenpix** in the respective entries for **PRISON FILM** and the **SOFTCORE SEX-EXPLOITATION FILM.**

The Violent Years (56) William M. Morgan (Franz Eichorn) *aka Female. High School Hellcats* (58) Edward Bernds. *She-Devils on Wheels* (68) Herschell Gordon Lewis. *Five Loose Women* (74) A. C. Stephen *aka Five on the Loose / Fugitive Girls. Truck Stop Women* (74) Mark L. Lester. *Switchblade Sisters* (75) Jack Hill *aka The Jezebelles / Playgirl Gang. The Great Texas Dynamite Chase* (76) Michael Pressman *aka Dynamite Women. The Young Cycle Girls* (77) Peter Perry, John Arnoldy. *H.O.T.S.* (79) Gerald Seth Sindell. *Chained Heat / Das Frauenlager* (US / G 82) Paul Nicholas. *Hell Squad* (84) Kenneth Hartford. *The Naked Cage* (85) Paul Nicholas. *Reform School Girls* (86) Tom DeSimone.

Gladiator Epic   *see*   **PEPLUM**

G-Man Films   *see*   **GANGSTER FILM;**   *see also*   **POLICE FILM: Federal Agent Films**

Gorefest   *see*   **HORROR FILM**

GORE FILM (Blood-and-Gore Thriller, Blood Film, Blood 'n' Gore Movie, Gore-Fest, Meat Movie, Splatter Movie, Ultra-Violent Movie) The most explicit of all the genres that thrive on violence, the gore film presents graphic scenes of mayhem or what is known as hard-core violence. The violence is extremely explicit and of a horrifying or shocking nature with heads and limbs chopped off, tongues torn out, eyes gouged out, disembowelments and guts galore spilled. The beginning of the gore film can be traced to one man, Herschell Gordon Lewis, director of low-budget films meant for the exploitation market, who, in association with producer David Friedman, started the new fad.[46] The film *Blood Feast* (1963) demonstrated that there was an eager audience ready to patronize this sort of movie, and other filmmakers soon followed the same path. Now gore movies are well-established and although most of them have not been able to break into the major motion-picture theaters, they are shown in neighborhood cinemas and drive-ins. Many countries still ban this type of picture.

As happens with any genre, some gore films are better made than others. The degree of explicitness also varies. An alarming new development seemed to emerge with the so-called "snuff" movies (a movie in which an unsuspecting actor, or actors, are butchered while the cameras are rolling), but even if people persist in believing that these films are circulating, to date there is no evidence of the existence of such films. *See* John McCarty, *Splatter Movies* (New York: St. Martin's, 1984), *The Official Splatter Movie Guide* (New York: St. Martin's, 1989) for a descripton of 447 splatter movies, and *John McCarty's Official Splatter Movie Guide Volume 2* (New York: St. Martin's, 1992) for additional films.

Blood Feast (63) Herschell Gordon Lewis.   *Two Thousand Maniacs!* (64) Herschell Gordon Lewis.   *The Gruesome Twosome* (66) Herschell Gordon Lewis.   *The Ghastly Ones* (67) Andy Milligan *aka Blood Rites.   Reazione a catena* (It 71) Mario Bava *aka Antefatto / Antefatto ecologia del delitto / A Bay of Blood / Before the Fact — The Ecology of a Crime / Bloodbath / Carnage / Ecologia del delitto / Last House on the Left Part II / Twitch of the Death Nerve.   The Last House on the Left* (72) Wes Craven *aka Krug and Company / Sex Crime of the Century.   Snuff* (Arg / US 71) no credits; released in 1974 by Allan Shackerton; Michael Findley, Roberta Findlay (additional gore scenes) *aka The Slaughter.   The Texas Chainsaw Massacre* (74) Tobe Hooper [subtitled: "Who Will Be Left . . . And What Will Be Left of Them?"].   *The Hills Have Eyes* (76) Wes Craven.   *Dawn of the Dead / Zombie* (US / It 77-78) George A. Romero *aka Dawn of the Living Dead / Zombie Dawn of the Dead / Zombies.   Suor omicidi* (It 78) Giulio Berruti *aka (The) Killer Nun.   Antropophagus* (It 79) Joe D'Amato *aka The Anthropophagous Beast.   The Driller Killer* (79) Abel Ferrara.   *Giallo a Venezia* (It 79) Mario Landi.   *Antropophagus 2* (It 80) Peter Newton (Joe D'Amato) *aka Absurd / Anthropophagous 2.   Maniac* (80) William Lustig.   *Bad Taste* (NZ 87) Peter Jackson.   *Nekromantik* (G 89) Jörg Buttgereit.

Gothic Cinema   *see*   **GOTHIC FILM**

GOTHIC FILM (Gothic Cinema)   The term Gothic is often applied to horror films which deal with the supernatural; films which draw their source of inspiration from, or are influenced by, Gothic literature, that is, the branch of literature that originated in England in the 18th century with Horace Walpole's *The Castle of Otranto* (1764), the first Gothic novel, and continued into the 19th century.[47] Most Gothic cinema comes from Great Britain, yet other countries have successfully recreated a Gothic atmosphere in their horror films. American Gothic films have a source of inspiration of their own in the works of Edgar Allan Poe, and European Gothic also has ample traditional sources from which to draw. Germany, for instance, has a rich Gothic-Romantic tradition, and one must not forget that the main myths of horror originated in Europe. Constant or frequently recurring motifs in Gothic cinema are solitary abbeys, haunted castles, dark old houses with hidden rooms or passages, ghosts, witchcraft, vampires and werewolves, and ladies in distress. The atmosphere in period Gothic films, or in films with contemporary settings, is brooding and foreboding of unspeakable things. It is a cinema of dark happenings in which quite often good confronts evil and is not always victorious. *See* **HORROR FILM**.

House of Darkness (GB 47) Oswald Mitchell.   *The Curse of Frankenstein*

(GB 56) Terence Fisher *aka Birth of Frankenstein.* **Dracula** (GB 57) Terence Fisher *aka The Horror of Dracula.* **Night of the Demon** (GB 57) Jacques Tourneur *aka Curse of the Demon / Haunted.* **House of Usher** (60) Roger Corman *aka The Fall of the House of Usher.* **La maschera del demonio** (It 60) Mario Bava *aka Black Sunday / House of Fright / Mask of the Demon / Revenge of the Vampire.* **Psycho** (60) Alfred Hitchcock [followed by 3 sequels: (1983–90)]. **The Pit and the Pendulum** (61) Roger Corman. **Tales of Terror** (61) Roger Corman *aka Poe's Tales of Terror / Tales of Horror.* **The Masque of the Red Death** (US / GB 64) Roger Corman. **Tomb of Ligeia / The Tomb of Ligeia** (US / GB 64) Roger Corman *aka House at the End of the World / The Last Tomb of Ligeia / Ligeia / Lygeia / Tomb of Lygeia / Tomb of the Cat.* **Histoires extraordinaires / Tre passi nel delirio** (F / It 67) Roger Vadim, Louis Malle, Federico Fellini *aka Powers of Evil / Spirits of the Dead / Storie Straordinarie / Trois Histoires extraordinaires d'Edgar Poe / Tales of Mystery / Tales of Mystery and Imagination.* **Dear Dead Delilah** (72) John Farris. **Gothic** (GB 86) Ken Russell. **American Gothic** (GB / Can 87) John Hough. **Sister Sister** (87) Bill Condon.

Gothic Melodrama   *see*   **PERIOD FILM: Period Thrillers**

Gothic Romance Films   *see*   **ROMANCE**

Government Film, Government-Sponsored Film   *see*   **FACTUAL FILM**

Grade-B Picture   *see*   **B-MOVIE**

Grade-Z Picture   *see*   **Z PICTURE**

GRAND GUIGNOL   The term is derived from the Parisian Théâtre du Grand Guignol, founded by Oscar Métenier in 1897, which was mostly dedicated to the presentation of horror melodramas. This kind of theater sought to shock its audience with scenes dealing with the supernatural, murder, and violence: rapes, stabbings, decapitations, maimings, the flow of blood, and the like were its stock-in-trade. It sought to awaken pleasurable terror by the sensational nature of the situations and horrors portrayed. Its influence may be seen today in the horror subgenre of gore or splatter films. Grand Guignol shows are seen in the British film *Theatre of Death* (1966), and in the more recent *The Incredible Torture Show* (1976), also known as *Blood Sucking Freaks*. The French film *Grand Guignol* (1986) also gives a good idea of what the original theater presentations were about. *See* **GORE FILM**.
Theatre of Death (GB 66) Samuel Gallu *aka Blood Fiend / Female Fiend.* **The Flesh and Blood Show** (GB 72) Pete Walker *aka Asylum of the Insane.* **The Incredible Torture Show** (76) Joel M. Reed *aka Blood Sucking Freaks / Sardu / T.I.T.S.* **Grand Guignol** (F 86) Jean Marboeuf.

Graphic Animation   *see*   **ANIMATED FILM: Cameraless Animated Film**

Graphic Films   *see*   **ABSTRACT FILM**

Graphics Film   *see*   **ANIMATED FILM: Animation of Still Paintings and Drawings**

Greed Show   *see*   **TELEVISION SHOW: Game Show**

Gridiron Film   *see*   **FOOTBALL FILM**

Grind, Grind Policy   *see*   **RELEASE**

Groin Grinder   *see*   **HARD-CORE PORNO FILM**

Guerrilla Cinema   *see*   **REVOLUTIONARY FILM: Guerrilla Films**

Gunfighter Film   *see*   **WESTERN: Outlaw Films**

Hack-and-Slash Film, Hack-'Em-Up Film   *see*   **SLASHER FILM**

Hack Film   *see*   **SLEAZY FILM**

Hagiographies   *see*   **RELIGIOUS FILM**

Hand-Colored Film   *see*   **COLOR FILM**

Hand-Drawn Film   *see*   **ANIMATED FILM: Cameraless Animated Films**

Handicap Movie   *see*   **DISABILITY PICTURE**

Hand Made Film   *see*   **ABSTRACT FILM: Synthetic Films**

Hankie Pic   *see*   **WEEPIE**

"Happy Talk" Show   *see*   **TELEVISION NEWS**

Hard-Action Film   *see*   **HARD-CORE PORNO FILM**

Hard-Boiled Detective Film   *see*   **PRIVATE DETECTIVE FILM**

Hardcore, Hardcore Erotic Movie   *see*   **HARD-CORE PORNO FILM**

Hard-Core Gay Film   *see*   **HARD-CORE PORNO FILM: Homosexual Porno Movie**

Hard-Core Loop, Hard-Core Movie   *see*   **HARD-CORE PORNO FILM**

HARD-CORE PORNO FILM (Adult Film, Blue Film, Dirty Movie, Explicit Sex Film, Fuck Movie, Full-Action Film, Hard-Action Film, Hardcore, Hardcore Erotic Movie, Hard-Core Movie, Porno Film, Sexplicit Film, Sexually Explicit Film, Sexvid, Stag Film, Triple-X Feature, X-Rated Film)   Before hard-core movies or explicit sex films hit the open market, exhibitors tried for a while to please their patrons with short films called "beavers" in which the female pubic area was shown (later on, male beavers appeared). These early beavers were on the whole devoid of sexual action; they involved women undressing to end up nude, writhing on top of a bed to show their nakedness from the best vantage point. Later variations were known as the "split beaver" in which the camera focussed almost exclusively on the woman's vagina for a revealing close-up look; the "spread beaver" in which women are photographed masturbating; and the "action beaver" which showed sexual activity, mostly lesbian, of a simulated nature. By 1969 hard-core loops were already being shown in San Francisco.[48] At the beginning, hard-core material made its way into features meant for wide commercial release under the umbrella of the sex information film and "how-to-do-it" documentaries, otherwise known in the trade as "white coaters" for the standard laboratory garments worn in them. *Censorship in Denmark: A New Approach* (1969), for instance, showed footage taken from Danish hard-core movies. Other documentaries with hard-core content were the compilation films tracing the history of the stag film. (*See* **SEX DOCUMENTARY**.) Closely following these pseudodocumentaries, there appeared the theatrical, hard-core 16mm feature-length film. There is a lack of information as to which film may rightly claim to be the first hard-core porno feature ever made, but the first to be widely known and acclaimed as a successful hard-core movie was *Mona: The Virgin Nymph* (1970), directed by Bill Osco.[49] The film contains many of the standard sex thrills that an addicted porno audience expects: incest, lesbianism, masturbation, bondage, oral sex. It was a fairly well-made movie which proved that hard-core sex worked well in a dramatic context. After *Mona,* hard-core 16mm features were produced at an ever-increasing rate. Then in 1972 came *Deep Throat*, perhaps the most famous or infamous porno movie ever made, whose title became a household word. It made porno fashionable and catapulted its director, Gerard Damiano, and its stars, Linda Lovelace and Harry Reems, to instant fame. Targeted by morality enforcers and subjected to repeated court battles, *Deep Throat*, an opus on the art of penilinctus, has continued to play in the country ever since its premiere in New York at the New World Theatre on 49th Street in June 1972, and it has been exported on film and videotape all over the world.

The same categories and subgenres of the soft-core porno feature apply to the hard-core porno movie.

Hard-core movies are made at the present time in several countries (most frequently in the United States, France, Scandinavia, Germany, Holland and Italy). Besides explicit sexual intercourse, fellatio, cunnilingus, analingus, and buggery, they may feature anything within the realm of the possible and the permissible. Sexual deviations may be reckoned by the hundreds: they form a vast pool from which porno filmmakers may draw at will for inspiration. Only the very extreme deviations (necrophilia, sex murder) have not been played for real in films, although they are featured in simulated soft-core situations. Borderline subject matter includes bestiality and coprophilia which, involving willing adults, have been allowed in some instances. Child pornography dealing with the underaged has been condemned everywhere, including Denmark, the most permissive country in sexual matters.

The same categories and subgenres of the soft-core porno feature apply to the hard-core porno movie.

The best work so far to deal with the pornographic movie is Kenneth

Turan and Stephen F. Zito, *Sinema* (New York: Signet Books, 1975). *See also* **STAG MOVIE, PORNO CHIC.**
As with the soft-core porno movie, hard-core adapts itself to any genre. Besides movies with a homosexual leaning which are a different species altogether, the following categories have recently had priority in the filmmaker's agenda: adaptations from classics, rip-offs or parodies of recent hits, comic pornographic features or comedy spoofs. For a survey of trends in hard-core films, *see* Joseph W. Slade, "The Porn Market and Porn Formulas: The Feature Film of the Seventies," *The Journal of Popular Film 6* (1977): 168–86, and "Recent Trends in Pornographic Film," in *Film in Society*, ed. Arthur Asa Berger (New Brunswick, NJ: Transaction Books, 1980): 121–35. *See also* Robert H. Rimmer, *The X-Rated Videotape Guide* (New York: Harmony Books, 1984).

———**Adaptations from Classics**   Quite a few porno films seek their inspiration in literary sources. The films, for the most part, are loose adaptations of well-known classic or contemporary authors.
   The Passions of Carol (74) Amanda Barton.   *Alice in Wonderland* (75) Bud Townsend [subtitled: "An X-Rated Musical Fantasy"].   *Bel Ami* (Sw 75) Mac Ahlberg.   *The Naughty Victorians* (75) Robert Kinger.   *The Opening of Misty Beethoven* (75) Henry Paris (Radley H. Metzger).   *Autobiography of a Flea* (76) Jim and Artie Mitchell.   *Expose Me, Lovely* (76) Armand Weston.   *Through the Looking Glass* (76) Jonas Middleton.   *The Erotic Adventures of Candy* (77) Gail Palmer.   *Seven into Snowy* (77) Antonio Shepher.   *Beauty* (82) Warren Evans.   *A Thousand and One Erotic Nights* (82) Stephen Lucas.

———**Comic Pornographic Feature (Spoof Comedy)**   The comic, spoof, or satirical film is a staple of the hard-core genre. *See also* **Rip-Offs.**
   It Happened in Hollywood (72) Peter Locke.   *Baby Face* (77) Alex De Renzy. *Babylon Pink* (77) Henri Pachard.   *Blonde Velvet* (77) Dexter Eagle.   *Pretty Peaches* (77) Alex De Renzy *aka Alex De Renzy's Pretty Peaches*.   *Debbie Does Dallas* (78) Jim Clark.   *Captain Lust and the Pirate Women* (79) Beau Buchanan.   *Blonde Ambition* (80) John and Lem Amero.   *Garage Girls* (80) Robert McCallum.   *Dracula Exotica* (80) Warren Evans *aka Dracula Erotica / Love at First Gulp*.   *The Blonde Next Door* (82) Joe Sherman. *Puss 'n Boots* (82) Chuck Vincent.   *Titillation* (82) Damon Christian.

———**Homosexual Porno Movie (Hard-Core Gay Film)**   As is the case with the heterosexual component of society, some sectors of the gay community have felt the need for hard-core porno films geared to their sexual proclivities. The gay hard-core porno film fulfills this need. Male audiences in gay circles are better catered for than female. Lesbian films made for women are rare. Early homosexual porno movies were known in trade circles as "beefcake" or "meat-rack" films.
   Boys in the Sand (71) Wakefield Poole.   *Sex Garage* (71) Fred Halsted.   *Bijou* (72) Wakefield Poole.   *L. A. Plays Itself* (72) Fred Halsted.   *Adam and Yves* (73) Peter De Rome.   *The Back Row* (73) Doug Richards.   *The Experiment* (73) Gordon Hall.   *The Light from the Second Story Window* (73)

David L. Allen. *Passing Strangers* (74) Arthur Bressan. *Catching Up* (75) Tom DeSimone. *Cruisin' 57* (75) Toby Ross. *The Destroying Angel* (75) Peter De Rome. *More More More* (76) Wallace Potts. *Nights in Black Leather* (76) Ignation Rutkowski. *La Chambre des phantasmes* (F 79) Jean-Michel Sénécal. *Ixe* (F 80) Lionel Soukaz.

———**Rip-Offs (Take-Offs)** An ongoing trend in the hard-core business is the ripping-off of film hits. Porno filmmakers copy plot situations from successful pictures and come up with a sort of hard-core version.

Eruption (76) Stanley Kurlan. *A Coming of Angels* (77) Joel Scott. *Sex World* (77) Anthony Spinelli. *The Violation of Claudia* (77) Billy Bagg (William B. Lustig). *Chorus Call* (78) Antonio Sheperd. *Take Off* (78) Armand Weston. *The Budding of Brie* (79) Henri Packard. *Downstairs / Upstairs* (80) Lisa Barr. *11* (80) Louis Lewis. *Sex Boat* (80) Svetlana. *8 to 4* (81) Louis Lewis. *The N*U*R*S*E*S of the 407th* (82) Tony Kendrick. *Lust on the Orient Xpress* (84) Tim MacDonald. *Driller* (85) Joyce James.

———**Terminology** The terminology of the pornographic film is very abundant. Some of the better-known terms are: *Black Sox Movie* Old porno short in which the male lead always kept his socks on. *Cableporn* Porno movies shown on cable television to home subscribers. *Cold Print* A hardcore porno film in which the explicit sex scenes have been shortened, cut, masked, or modified for censorship reasons or to accommodate wider audiences. *Eroduction* A film production with erotic subject matter. *Fanny Film* A term used to describe films which depict anal intercourse. *Groin Grinder* A colorful colloquialism for a sex film. *Hot Print* The reverse of a "cold print." A sex film with the hard-action sequences left in. *Jiggle Film* A movie with women sporting large breasts that bounce when they move. *Kiddie Porn* Pornographic material involving the underaged. Although some kiddie porn films circulate sub rosa, they are prohibited by law in most countries. *One-Hander* An erotic film which is supposedly hot enough to induce the male viewer to masturbate. *Single-O* A film showing one person masturbating in front of the camera. *Smoker* Another term for a stag film. *Tease Film* A film which raises one's expectations of screen sex, but which does not fulfill them. *White Sox Movie* A movie, mostly with erotic content, starring athletes.

Mona: The Virgin Nymph (70) Bill Osco *aka Mona. Deep Throat* (72) Jerry Gerard (Gerard Damiano) *aka The Doctor Makes a Call. The Private Afternoons of Pamela Mann* (74) Henry Paris (Radley Metzger). *Baby Rosemary* (75) Howard Perkins. *A Dirty Western* (75) David Fleetwood. *Mary! Mary!* (75) Bernard Morris. *Naked Came the Stranger* (75) Henry Paris (Radley Metzger). *Sodom and Gomorrah — The Last Seven Days* (75) Jim Mitchel and Artie Mitchel. *Anna Obsessed* (77) Martin and Martin. *"V" The Hot One* (77) Robert McCallum. *Fairy Tales* (78) Harry Trampa *aka Adult Fairy Tales. Tangerine* (78) Robert McCallum. *Champagne for Breakfast* (79) Billy Thornberg. *Exposed* (79) Jeffrey Fairbanks. *"F"* (79) Svetlana. *Hot Legs* (79) Bob Chinn. *Amanda by Night* (80) Robert McCallum. *Talk Dirty to Me* (80) Anthony Spinelli. *Ultra Flesh* (80) Svetlana. *Bad Girls* (81) David I. Frazer, Svetlana. *Nothing to Hide* (81)

Anthony Spinelli. *Wanda Whips Wall Street* (81) Larry Ravene *aka Stocks and Blondes.* *Wicked Sensations* (81) Ron Chrones. *Peaches & Cream* (82) Robert McCallum. *Talk Dirty to Me Part 2* (82) Tim McDonald. *Coffee, Tea or Me* (83) Bob Vossé. *Naughty Girls* (83) Edwin Brown *aka Naughty Girls Need Love Too.* *Suzie Superstar* (83) Robert McCallum. *Surrender in Paradise* (84) David J. Frazer, Svetlana.

Hardhat Film   *see*   **MALE-ORIENTED PICTURE**

Hard News   *see*   **TELEVISION NEWS**

Hard Quiz Show   *see*   **TELEVISION SHOW: Game Show**

Hard Ticket   *see*   **FILM**

HAUNTED HOUSE FILM (Old Dark House Mystery, Old-House Thriller) Films with haunted houses or old dark mansions are basically mystery films — a mystery has to be solved. These dwellings are usually isolated, perhaps in a ruinous state, and sometimes uninhabited, the previous owner having just come to an untimely end. A visitor, a couple (with or without children), or a party of people arrive to collect an inheritance, carry out a bet, or just as a dare spend a night in the place, and the inexplicable occurrences or hauntings begin immediately. Often, they are meant only to drive away the unwelcome visitors, but equally prevalent is the situation in which a murder or murders occur.

These haunted house films belong to the crime or horror genres; many are comedy-thrillers and frequently fall under two general categories: the supernatural and the nonsupernatural.

In the supernatural category, the mischievous, often evil, spooks have limited or unlimited control over their surroundings. Three species of houses are common: a) *Haunted Houses* (a ghost, ghosts or other supernatural beings do the haunting; b) *Possessed Houses* (the supernatural beings and their kin have taken possession of the house and control it); c) *Malevolent Houses* (the house itself is evil, or has been taken over by evil).

In the nonsupernatural type of old-house film, the haunting is happily resolved as being a series of pranks, the incidents or murders are the doings of a human (at times psychopathic) agent. These are d) *Mystery Houses* (not really "haunted" but roamed through by a prankster or a killer). *The Cat and the Canary* (27) Paul Leni. *The Old Dark House* (32) James Whale. *Thark* (GB 32) Tom Walls. *The Ghost Breakers* (40) George Marshall. *The Uninvited* (43) Lewis Allen. *A Place of One's Own* (GB 45) Bernard Knowles. *The Ghost and Mrs. Muir* (47) Joseph L. Mankiewicz. *The House in Marsh Road* (GB 60) Montgomery Tully *aka The Invisible Creature / The House on Marsh Road.* *The Haunting* (US / GB 63) Robert Wise. *The Haunted House of Horror* (GB 68) Michael Armstrong *aka The Dark / The Dark Horror House / Horror House.* *Un tranquillo posto di campagna / Un Coin tranquille à la campagne* (It / F 68) Elio Petri *aka A Quiet Place in the Country.* *The House in Nightmare Park / Night of the Laughing Dead* (GB / US 72) Peter Sykes *aka Crazy House / Nightmare Park.* *The Legend of Hell House* (GB / US 72) John Hough. *Something*

Evil (70 TV) Steven Spielberg. *Céline et Julie vont en bateau* (F 74) Jacques Rivette *aka Celine and Julie Go Boating.* *Ghost Story* (GB 74) Stephen Weeks *aka Asylum of Blood / Madhouse Mansion.* *Full Circle / Le Cercle infernal* (GB / Can 76) Richard Loncraine *aka The Haunting of Julia.* *The Evil* (77) Gus Trikonis *aka Cry Demon / The Force Beyond.* *The Amityville Horror* (79) Stuart Rosenberg [5 "Amityville" films up to 1989]. *The Changeling / L'Enfant du diable* (Can / US 78-79) Peter Medak. *The Shining* (GB / US 79) Stanley Kubrick. *Beyond Evil* (80) Herb Freed. *Ghost Story* (81) John Irving. *The House Where Evil Dwells* (US / J 82) Kevin Conner. *Poltergeist* (82) Tobe Hooper [followed by *Poltergeist II: The Other Side* (86) Brian Gibson and *Poltergeist III* (88) Gary Sherman]. *The Haunting Passion* (83 TV) John Korty. *Beetle Juice* (88) Tim Burton.

"Heart Comedy" *see* **SITUATION COMEDY**

Heavenly Comedy *see* **FILM BLANC**

HEIMATFILM (Homeland Film)   A perennial favorite among some German audiences, the *Heimatfilm*, or "homeland" film, is a true German genre that idealizes the countryside and country folk. The films are mostly set in southern Germany or Bavaria and present an idyllic, sentimental, and highly romanticized portrait of rural Germany in which nothing ever goes terribly wrong. They are a kind of pastoral cinematic exercise into pure escapism, intent on avoiding the reality and real issues of peasant life and life in general. During the reemergence of German cinema in the late sixties and early seventies, some of the New German Cinema (q.v.) directors used the format of the *Heimatfilm* to criticize the genre, expose false ideas of the mythical, idyllic countryside, and tackle current issues.

Schwarzwaldmädel (G 50) Hans Deppe *aka Black Forest Girl.* *Grün ist die Heide* (G 51) Hans Deppe *aka Green Is the Heath.* *Schloss Hubertus* (G 54) Helmut Weiss *aka Hubertus Castle.* *Sissi* (Aus 55) Ernst Marischka [followed by *Sissi—die junge Kaiserin* (56) and *Sissi—Schicksalsjahre einer Kaiserin* (57)]. *Nachtschatten* (G 71) Niklaus Schilling *aka Night Shade.* *Schloss Hubertus* (G 73) Harald Reinl *aka Hubertus Castle.* *Herz aus Glas* (G 76) Werner Herzog *aka Heart of Glass.* *Der Mond is nur a nackerte Kugel* (G 81) Jörg Graser *aka The Moon Is a Naked Ball / The Moon Is but a Naked Globe.* *Heimat* (G 80-84) Edgar Reitz *aka Homeland* [also as an 11-part TV series: *Heimat—eine Chronik in elf Teilen von Edgar Reitz*]. *Herbstmilch* (G 89) Joseph Vilsmaier *aka Autumn Milk.*

————**Critical Heimat Films (Anti-Heimat Films)** *Jagdszenen aus Niderbayern* (G 68) Peter Fleischmann *aka The Hunters Are the Hunted / Hunting Scenes from Bavaria / Hunting Scenes from Lower Bavaria.* *Der plötzliche Reichtum der armen Leute von Kombach* (G 70) Volker Schlöndorff *aka The Sudden Fortune (Wealth) of the Poor People of Kombach.* *Ich liebe dich, ich töte dich* (G 71) Uwe Brandner *aka I Love You, I Kill You.* *Jaider—der einsame Jäger* (G 71) Volker Vogler *aka Jaider—The Lonely Huntsman.*

Heist Film *see* **CAPER FILM;** *see also* **GANGSTER FILM: Heist Films**

He-Man Picture *see* MALE-ORIENTED PICTURE

Heroic-Fantasy Film *see* SWORD-AND-SORCERY FILM

Heroic Film *see* EPIC

High-Budget Film *see* A-PICTURE

High Comedy *see* COMEDY OF MANNERS; *see also* SOPHIS-TICATED COMEDY, SCREWBALL COMEDY

Highjacking Film *see* CRIME FILM: Hijacking Films

High School Films *see* TEEN MOVIE; *see also* HIGH SCHOOL PICTURE

HIGH SCHOOL PICTURE   High school pictures fit properly into the broader teen movie (q.v.) genre. This notwithstanding, their proliferation in the seventies and eighties plus some clearly distinguishable characteristics make them a genre of their own. Naturally, at the center of these pictures there is the high school which plays a prominent role as most of the teenagers' activities revolve around it. The high school is usually the place where first they meet each other, intermingle, assert their burgeoning values and, more often than not, rebel against authority. The genre may be traced back to some family pictures in which teenagers attend high school or to the juvenile delinquency films (q.v.) of the fifties. Nevertheless, as different from the above genres, high school movies are directed at their young audiences rather than the family as a whole or adults. As such, high school films address the youngsters' concerns which may vary from the need to validate one's views, a desire for revenge for having been misunderstood or mistreated, a deep interest in rock or punk music to sex and how to go about getting it.[50]

High School Caesar (60) O'Dale Ireland. *Lord Love a Duck* (66) George Axelrod. *Cooley High* (75) Michael Schultz. *Carrie* (76) Brian DePalma. *Jennifer* (77) Brice Mark *aka Jennifer (The Snake Goddess).* *Rock 'n' Roll High School* (79) Allan Arkush. *Grad Night* (80) John Tenorio. *The Class of 1984 / La Classe de 1984* (Can 81) Mark L. Lester *aka Battle Zone — Adams High / Classe 1984.* *Fast Times at Ridgemont High* (82) Amy Heckerling *aka Fast Times.* *All the Right Moves* (83) Michael Chapman. *Baby, It's You* (83) John Sayles. *High School U.S.A.* (83 TV) Rod Amateau. *Sixteen Candles* (84) John Hughes. *Terror Squad* (84) Peter Maris. *Ferris Bueller's Day Off* (86) John Hughes. *Pretty in Pink* (86) Howard Deutch. *Some Kind of Wonderful* (87) Howard Deutch. *Summer School* (87) Carl Reiner. *Three O'Clock High* (87) Phil Joanou. *Class of 1999* (90) Mark L. Lester.

Highway Safety Film *see* FACTUAL FILM: Jeopardy Film

HILLBILLY FILM   A film set in the rural area of America — the open roads, the backwoods, the swamps; especially one dealing with Southern themes and mainly addressed to the working man. Hillbilly films may be traced back to the silents but were very popular in the mid-sixties. They mostly played in drive-ins. They are exploitation films ranging from road movies and moonshine epics to country music films and steamy melodramas.[51] *See also* **REDNECK MOVIE**.

Child Bride (37) Harry Revier *aka Child Bride of the Ozarks*. *Mountain Music* (37) Robert Florey. *The Arkansas Traveler* (38) Alfred Santell. *Dreaming Out Loud* (40) Harold Young. *Sis Hopkins* (41) Joseph Santley. *Joan of Ozark* (42) Joseph Santley. *Ma and Pa Kettle* (49) Charles Lamont [9 films (1949-57) in the "Ma and Pa Kettle" series]. *Feudin', Fussin' and a-Fightin'* (48) George Sherman. *Bayou* (57) Harold Daniels *aka Poor White Trash* (61). *The Shotgun Wedding* (63) Boris L. Petroff. *The Girl from Tobacco Road* (66) Ron Ormond. *Girl on a Chain Gang* (66) Jerry Gross. *Las Vegas Hillbillys* (66) Arthur C. Pierce *aka Country Music U.S.A.* *Road to Nashville* (66) Will Zens. *The Exotic Ones* (68) Ron Ormond *aka The Monster and the Stripper*. *Moonshiner's Woman* (68) D. E. Davison. *Preacherman* (71) Albert T. Viola. *God's Bloody Acre* (75) Harry E. Kerwin. *Poor White Trash II!* (75) S. F. Brownrigg *aka Scum of the Earth*. *Bad Georgia Road* (77) John C. Broderick. *Baseball Bimbos in Hillbilly Hell* (89) Tanya Rosenberg.

Historical, Historical Drama   *see*   **HISTORICAL FILM**

Historical Epics   *see*   **EPIC**

HISTORICAL FILM (Historical, Historical Drama, History Film)   In terms of the fictional film, an historical film is a restaging of historical events or happenings which are mostly presented in a compressed or abridged form. It follows as a matter of course that historical films are a filmmaker's interpretation of such events and accuracy of fact, or detail, is dependent on his own personal vision.

Two broad approaches to the historical film are current: a) the filmmaker reproduces the historical material as truthfully and as well as he can, and b) the historical element is just an excuse for spectacle, romance, and entertainment. These two major divisions of historical films comprise, on one hand, a minority of films which honestly try to recreate history; and on the other, a vast majority of historical or pseudohistorical films which transmute history or use it as a mere background. Historical films naturally encompass all other genres whose films have as their frame of reference an historical period, happening, or personality, e.g., Westerns, sports films, biographical movies, war films, political films.

The Birth of a Nation (14) D. W. Griffith *aka The Birth of the Nation;* or *The Clansman / The Clansman*. *Konets Sankt-Peterburga* (USSR 27) Vsevolod Pudovkin *aka The End of St. Petersburg*. *Oktyabr'* (USSR 27) Sergei M. Eisenstein, Grigori Alexandrov *aka October / Ten Days That Shook the World*. *Catherine the Great* (GB 34) Paul Czinner, Alexander Korda (uncredited) *aka The Rise of Catherine the Great*. *1860* (It 34) Alessandro Blasetti *aka Gesuzza la sposa Garibaldina*. *The Scarlet Empress* (34) Josef von Sternberg *aka Catherine the Great / Her Regiment of Lovers [Cf. Catherine the Great* (GB 34)]. *Campo di maggio / Hundert Tage* (It / G 35) Gioacchino

Forzano, Franz Wenzler. *Mary of Scotland* (36) John Ford. *Tudor Rose* (GB 34) Robert Stevenson *aka Lady Jane Grey / Nine Days a Queen.* *La Marseillaise* (F 37) Jean Renoir *aka The Marseillaise.* *Gone with the Wind* (39) Victor Fleming (uncredited: George Cukor, Sidney Franklin, Sam Wood) *aka GWTW / Tomorrow Is Another Day / The Wind.* *Wilson* (44) Henry King. *Christopher Columbus* (GB 48) David Macdonald. *Prince of Foxes* (49) Henry King. *Senso* (It 54) Luchino Visconti *aka Cuztoza / Uragano d'estate / The Wanton Countess.* *Viva l'Italia* (It / F 60) Roberto Rossellini *aka Long Live Italy.* *Il Gattopardo / Le Guépard / The Leopard* (It / F / US 63) Luchino Visconti. *Kings of the Sun* (63) J. Lee Thompson. *Becket* (US / GB 64) Peter Glenville. *A Man for All Seasons* (GB 66) Fred Zinnemann. *La Prise de pouvoir par Louis XIV* (F 66 TV) Roberto Rossellini *aka The Rise of Louis XIV / The Rise to Power of Louis XIV.* *Anne of the Thousand Days* (GB 69) Charles Jarrott. *Cromwell* (GB 70) Ken Hughes. *Nicholas and Alexandra* (GB 71) Franklin Schaffner. *Bronte: cronaca di un massacro che i libri di storia non hanno raccontato* (It 72) Florestano Vancini. *Que la fête commence...* (F 74) Bertrand Tavernier *aka La Grande Dame du royaume / Let Joy Reign Supreme / Let the Festivities Begin.* *Babatou ou les trois conseils* (F 76) Jean Rouch, Boubou Hama *aka Babatou or Three Pieces of Advice.* *In nome del Papa Re* (It 76) Luigi Magni *aka In the Name of the Pope-King.* *Masada* (US / Isr 80 TV) Boris Sagal [in 4 parts; also as a feature: *The Antagonists*]. *Danton* (F / Pol 82) Andrzej Wajda *aka L'Affaire Danton.* *La Nuit de Varennes / Il mondo nuovo* (F / It 82) Ettore Scola *aka Lontananze e prospettive / Revolution.* *Lady Jane* (GB 85) Trevor Nunn.

————**Popular History Films**   These films look at the role of the working class in an historical context. They study the importance of the individual in society, or focus on the different attempts by a group of individuals to modify their position on the social scale.

Souvenirs d'un France (F 74) André Téchiné *aka French Provincial.* *Cecilia / La Cécilia* (It / F 75) Jean-Louis Comolli. *Moi Pierre Rivière, ayant égorgé ma mère, ma soeur et mon frère* (F 75) René Allio [*Cf. Je suis Pierre Rivière* (F 75) Christine Lipinska]. *Winstanley* (GB 75) Kevin Brownlow, Andrew Mollo. *Guerres civiles en France* (F 76) Vincent Nordon, François Barat, Joël Fargas. *In the Forest* (GB 78) Phil Mulloy. *The Wobblies* (79) Stewart Bird, Deborah Shaffer. *Le Retour de Martin Guerre* (F 81) Daniel Vigne *aka The Return of Martin Guerre.*

Historical Play   *see*   **TELEVISION DRAMA: Documentary Drama**

Historical Romances   *see*   **ROMANCE**

Historical War Films   *see*   **WAR FILM**

History Film   *see*   **HISTORICAL FILM**

Hollywood Film on Hollywood, Hollywood-on-Hollywood Film   *see* **FILM ABOUT FILMS**

HOLOCAUST FILM (Film About the Holocaust)   Especially after the American NBC television network broadcast of the miniseries *Holocaust* in 1978, the term has become even more widely used and accepted as an apt designation for the German massacre or genocide of Jews that took place during World War II in German occupied territories, concentration camps and extermination camps. The aftermath has been recorded in documentaries and the actual events recreated in an ever-growing number of fiction films. Hence, the need to group together the films that describe or allude to the Holocaust has prompted to date several articles and book publications specifically treating these films, e.g., Annette Insdorf's *Indelible Shadows: Film and the Holocaust* (New York: Vintage Books, 1983; 2nd ed., New York: Cambridge UP, 1989) and Ilan Avisar's *Screening the Holocaust* (Bloomington: Indiana University Press, 1988). Films about the Holocaust, besides offering historical fact, serve as a reminder of the horror and enormity of the events that took place under Nazi rule.

Ostatni etap (Pol 47) Wanda Jakubowska *aka The Last Stop / The Last Stage*. *Daleká cesta* (Cz 48) Alfréd Radok *aka Distant Journey / Ghetto Terezin / The Long Journey*. *Nuit et brouillard* (F 55) Alain Resnais *aka Night and Fog*. *Kapo / Kapò* (F / It / Yug 59) Gillo Pontecorvo. *Transport z ráje* (Cz 63) Zbynek Brynych *aka Transport from Paradise*. *Il giardino dei Finzi-Contini / Der Garten der Finzi Contini* (It / G 70) Vittorio De Sica *aka The Garden of the Finzi-Continis*. *The Final Solution* (GB 75 TV) Michael Darlow. *Mr. Klein* (F / It 76) Joseph Losey *aka Mister Klein / Monsieur Klein*. *Jakob der Lügner* (EG 77) Frank Beyer *aka Jacob the Liar*. *Holocaust* (78 TV) Marvin J. Chomsky [in 3 parts] *aka Holocaust: The Story of the Family Weiss*. *Kitty: Return to Auschwitz* (GB 79 TV) Peter Morley, Kevin Sim. *Charlotte* (Hol / G 80) Frans Weisz. *Playing for Time* (80 TV) Daniel Mann. *Regentropfen* (G 81) Michael Hoffmann, Harry Raymon *aka Raindrops*. *Shoah* (F 74-84) Claude Lanzmann [in 2 parts] *aka Immolation*. *Wannseekonferenz* (G / Aus 84 TV) Heinz Scheik *aka The Wannsee Conference*. *Au revoir les enfants* (F / G 87) Louis Malle *aka Goodbye Children*. *Escape from Sobibor* (US / Yug 87 TV) Jack Gold. *Murderers Among Us: The Simon Wiesenthal Story* (US / GB / Hung 89 MCTV) Brian Gibson.

HOMAGE FILM Homage films, as distinct from parodies which mainly seek to poke fun at the object of their parody, are films which pay tribute to a genre's clichés and peculiarities, to a particular film, or to a studio or actor's output, and they look lovingly through their recreated sequences at those images that made the genre or style of filmmaking particularly well-known to its audience.

À bout de souffle (F 59) Jean-Luc Godard *aka Breathless*. *El Topo* (Mex 70) Alexandro Jodorowsky *aka The Mole*. *The Boy Friend* (GB 71) Ken Russell *aka The Boyfriend*. *Play It Again Sam* (72) Herbert Ross. *Sisters* (72) Brian DePalma *aka Blood Sisters*. *The Man with Bogart's Face* (79) Robert Day *aka Sam Marlowe, Private Eye*. *Stardust Memories* (80) Woody Allen. *Raiders of the Lost Ark* (81) Steven Spielberg. *Creepshow* (81-82) George A. Romero. *C'era una volta in America / Once Upon a Time in America* (It / US / Can 83) Sergio Leone. *Blood Simple* (84) Joel Coen. *The Cotton Club* (84) Francis Coppola. *The Bedroom Window* (86) Curtis Hanson. *Autour de minuit / 'Round Midnight* (US / F 86) Bertrand Tavernier.

Home Front Film   *see*   **WAR FILM: Civilian War Films**

Homeland Film   *see*   **HEIMATFILM**

Home Movie   *see*   **AMATEUR FILM**

Homosexual Film   *see*   **GAY FILM**

Homosexual Porno Film   *see*   **HARD-CORE PORNO FILM**

HOOKER FILM (Working Girl Film)   It is debatable which is the oldest profession, soldiering or whoring. Prostitution, like war, goes back to the dawn of civilization. Prostitutes in minor and major roles have figured in many films since the beginning of motion pictures. Part-time or full-time, streetwalkers and call girls all have in common the selling of their bodies for profit. Hooker films fall under two major categories—those in which whores operate independently or under the surveillance of a pimp, and bordello films in which the whores are employees of a brothel. Hooker movies form an interesting group of films sharing many characteristics. For a filmography including 389 films *see* James Robert Parish, *Prostitution in Hollywood Films* (Jefferson, NC: McFarland, 1992).

> *Butterfield 8* (60) Daniel Mann.   *Vivre sa vie* (F 62) Jean-Luc Godard *aka It's My Life / My Life to Live.*   *Irma La Douce* (63) Billy Wilder.   *Klute* (71) Alan J. Pakula.   *The Happy Hooker* (75) Nicholas Sgarro.   *Die Ehe der Maria Braun* (G 78) Rainer Werner Fassbinder *aka The Marriage of Maria Braun.*   *Prostitute* (GB 80) Tony Garnett.   *Angel* (83) Robert Vincent O'Neil.   *Risky Business* (83) Paul Brickman.   *Crimes of Passion* (GB / US 84) Ken Russell.   *Streetwalkin'* (84) Joan Freeman.   *Rosa la rosa, fille publique* (F 85) Paul Vecchiali.   *Half Moon Street* (GB 86) Bob Swaim.   *Mona Lisa* (GB 86) Neil Jordan.   *Personal Services* (GB 86) Terry Jones.   *Warm Nights on a Slow Moving Train* (Aust 86) Bob Ellis.   *Pretty Woman* (90) Garry Marshall.   *Whore* (91) Ken Russell.
>
> *Bordello Films (Brothel Films:)* *Walk on the Wild Side* (62) Edward Dmytryk.   *Belle de jour / Bella di giorno* (F / It 66) Luis Buñuel.   *Film d'amore e d'anarchia, ovvero stamattina alle 10 in via dei Fiori, nella nota casa di tolleranza...* (It 72) Lina Wertmüller *aka Love and Anarchy.*   *Bordellet—En glaedespiges erindringer* (Den 72) Ole Ege *aka Bordello / The Bordello—Memoir of a Pleasure Girl.*   *Sandakan hachiban shokan: bokyo* (J 75) Kei Kumai *aka Sandakan-8.*   *Madame Claude* (F 76-77) Just Jaeckin *aka The French Woman / The Girls of Madame Claude.*   *Pretty Baby* (77) Louis Malle.   *The Best Little Whorehouse in Texas* (82) Colin Higgins.   *Chicken Ranch* (83) Nick Broomfield, Sandi Sissel.   *Gebroken Spiegele* (Hol 84) Marleen Gorris *aka Broken Mirrors.*   *Candy Regentag* (Aust 86) James Ricketson *aka Kiss the Night.*   *Working Girls* (86) Lizzie Borden.

Horror Comedies   *see*   **HORROR FILM**

HORROR FILM (Gorefest, Monster Movie, Terror Film)   Horror films cover a vast field in which all sorts of monsters and creatures lurk in the dark, spring up from murky waters and steamy swamps, are summoned from beyond the grave, or arrive from outer space. The genre is very diversified, having multiple subgenres and revitalizing new cycles throughout its development. Major cycles in the horror film genre are distinguished by one or two seminal, outstanding films, with a host of lesser ones following in their wake. The earliest cycle started in Germany in the silent era with such films as *Das Cabinet des Dr. Caligari* (1919), *Der Golem* (1920), and *Nosferatu* (1921); the second major cycle took place in Hollywood with *Dracula* (1930) and *Frankenstein* (1931), and lasted until the mid-forties. In the fifties, the filmmakers' imagination found expression in a cycle of science-fiction horror movies based on the fear of atomic radiation unleashing untold horrors, e.g., *Them!* (1953), with giant mutant ants menacing mankind, and in a Teenage Monster cycle, e.g., *I Was a Teen-age Werewolf* (1957), *Blood of Dracula* (1957). Another momentous cycle came from Britain's Hammer studios: *Dracula* (1957), or *The Horror of Dracula* as it was known in America, brought on a renaissance of the horror film in the form of several remakes of the perennial horror classics and a string of sequels in full Technicolor. In the seventies, *The Exorcist* (1973), preceded by *Rosemary's Baby* (1968), reawakened a keen interest in demonology and the occult—an interest which has not yet abated. In the interim, and as a result of this continuous interest in horror movies, all the major and minor producing countries have made horror films at one time or another.

Horror movies are better classified thematically, by content, or by the nature of the monster appearing in them. Some monsters are so recurrent that they form genres of their own, e.g., the vampire. Horror mixes well with science fiction and sometimes it is difficult to decide to which genre a film belongs[52]; for instance, both genres have a claim on *Frankenstein*. However, in many cases, when there is enough advanced technology or science involved, or the setting is futuristic, the film in question clearly belongs to science fiction or to the science-fiction horror genre.

At times, a horror movie is referred to as a "chiller," a "chiller-diller," or a "spinechiller," terms which are also used to describe a thriller. "Shocker" is a word applied to that which causes a sensational effect; that is, to what is horrifying, offensive, or repulsive. As such, it applies to a horror film as well as to a sex film. *See also* **GORE FILM, HAUNTED HOUSE FILM, KAIJU EIGA, PSYCHOPATHIC THRILLER, SEX AND VIOLENCE FILM, VAMPIRE FILM, WITCH FILM, ZOMBIE MOVIE.**

Das Cabinet des Dr. Caligari (G 19) Robert Wiene *aka Das Kabinett des Dr. Caligari / The Cabinet of Dr. Caligari.*   *Der Golem* (G 20) Paul Wegener, Carl Boese *aka Der Golem: Wie er in die Welt kam / The Golem.*   *Nosferatu—eine Symphonie des Grauens* (G 21) Friedrich Wilhelm Murnau *aka Dracula / Nosferatu / Nosferatu—A Symphony of Horror (Terror) / Nosferatu, the Vampire / The Terror of Dracula / Die zwölfte Stunde—eine Nacht des Grauens* [*The Twelve Hour* (bowdlerized sound version); rel. in 30]. *Dracula* (30) Tod Browning [Spanish version: *Drácula* (30) George Melford]. *Frankenstein* (31) James Whale.   *Dr. Jekyll and Mr. Hyde* (31) Rouben Mamoulian.   *The Mummy* (32) Karl Freund.   *White Zombie* (32) Victor Halperin.   *Bride of Frankenstein* (35) James Whale *aka Frankenstein Lives Again / The Return of Frankenstein.*   *Werewolf of London* (35) Stuart

Walker *aka Unholy Hour.* *The Wolf Man* (41) George Waggener *aka Destiny.* *I Walked with a Zombie* (42) Jacques Tourneur. *The Creature from the Black Lagoon* (53) Jack Arnold *aka Black Lagoon* [followed by *Revenge of the Creature* (54) also by Arnold, and *The Creature Walks Among Us* (56) John Sherwood]. *Them!* (53) Gordon Douglas. *Blood of Dracula* (57) Herbert L. Strock *aka Blood Is My Heritage / Blood of the Demon / I Was a Teenage Dracula.* *Dracula* (57) Terence Fisher *aka The Horror of Dracula.* *I Was a Teen-age Werewolf* (57) Gene Fowler, Jr. *aka Blood of the Werewolf.* *Night of the Living Dead* (67-68) George A. Romero *aka Flesh Eaters / Night of Anubis / Night of the Flesh Eaters.* *Rosemary's Baby* (68) Roman Polansky. *Willard* (70) Daniel Mann. *The Exorcist* (73) William Friedkin. *It's Alive* (73) Larry Cohen *aka The Monster* [followed by *It's Alive II / It Lives Again* (78) and *It's Alive III: Island of the Alive* (87) also by Cohen]. *Carrie* (76) Brian DePalma. *Halloween* (78) John Carpenter [5 films in the series up to 1988]. *Phantasm* (78) Don Coscarelli *aka The Never Dead* [followed by *Phantasm II* (88) Don Coscarelli].

——**Body Horror (Body-Horror Films)**   A trend in contemporary horror and science fiction horror films which relies on the destruction of the body for shock effect. In this kind of horror, bodies or parts of the body explode, ooze, are crushed, or melt away on-screen. Otherwise, the body may be made to burst open so as to allow some supernatural form or an alien's offspring to shoot out or crawl nauseatingly into view, or the body may be subjected to some vile and gory surgical experiment.

Carne per Frankenstein / De la chair pour Frankenstein / Flesh for Frankenstein (It / F / G / US 73) Paul Morrissey, Anthony M. Dawson (Antonio Margheriti) *aka Andy Warhol's Flesh for Frankenstein / Andy Warhol's Frankenstein / The Devil and Dr. Frankenstein / Frankenstein / The Frankenstein Experiment / Il mostro è in tavola... Barone Frankenstein / Up Frankenstein.* *The Manitou* (77) William Girdler. *Scanners* (Can 79) David Cronenberg [rel. in 81] *aka The Sensitives.* *The Evil Dead* (80) Sam Raimi *aka Book of the Dead.* *The Beast Within* (81) Philippe Mora. *Re-Animator* (85) Stuart Gordon *aka H. P. Lovecraft's Re-Animator.* *The Fly* (86) David Cronenber. *The Fly II* (89) Chris Walas.

——**Demonic Films (Black Magic Films, Demon Movies, Devil Movies, Satanic Films, Witchcraft Movies)**   This subgenre touches the subjects of satanism, possession by demons in accord with the Christian canon (e.g., *The Exorcist*), witchcraft, reincarnation, and other aspects of the occult. *See also* **Possession Movies** in this genre and **WITCH FILM**.

The Seventh Victim (43) Mark Robson. *La Chambre ardente / I peccatori della foresta nera* (F / It 61) Julien Duvivier *aka The Burning Court.* *Night of the Eagle* (GB 61) Sidney Hayers *aka Burn, Witch, Burn / Conjure Wife.* *The Sorcerers* (GB / US 66) Michael Reeves. *Satan's Skin* (GB 70) Piers Haggard *aka (The) Blood on Satan's Claw / The Devil's Touch / Satan's Claw.* *The Mephisto Waltz* (71) Paul Wendkos. *Necromancy* (71) Bert I. Gordon *aka A Life for a Life / The Toy Factory / The Witching.* *Night of Dark Shadows* (71) Dan Curtis *aka Curse of the Dark Shadows.* *Simon, King of the Witches* (71) Bruce Kessler *aka Simon, King of the Warlocks.*

Don't Look Now / *A Venezia un dicembre rosso shocking* (GB / It 73) Nicolas Roeg. *The Exorcist* (73) William Friedkin. *The Reincarnation of Peter Proud* (74) J. Lee Thompson. *To the Devil a Daughter* / *Die Baut des Satans* (GB / G 74) Peter Sykes. *The Omen* (US / GB 76) Richard Donner *aka The Anti-Christ* [1st in a trilogy which includes *Damien-Omen II* (78) Don Taylor, and *The Final Conflict* (US / GB 81) Graham Baker; followed by *Omen IV: The Awakening* (Can 91) Jorge Montesi, Dominique Othenin-Gerard]. *Ghost Story* (81) John Irvin.

——**Frankenstein Films**   The saga of Dr. Victor Frankenstein who made a monster out of human parts gathered from corpses is well-known. Baron Frankenstein and his monster were the creation of Mary Wollstonecraft Shelley (1797–1851) who in 1818 saw the publication of *Frankenstein; or, The Modern Prometheus*. It was brought to the stage in 1823 and to the screen in 1910 in what was the Frankenstein monster's first film appearance, played by actor Charles Ogle. The monster's most celebrated appearance was, however, that of Boris Karloff in *Frankenstein* (1931) which, in conjunction with *Dracula* (1930), launched Universal's famous series of horror-monster films. Since Karloff's first appearance with astounding, specially designed makeup, the monster has figured in over a hundred films. Although various actors have taken up the part, most were not as adept in the role as Karloff. The Frankenstein monster remains one of the most famous horror creations in film history.[53]

Frankenstein (10) J. Searle Dawley.   *Frankenstein* (31) James Whale.   *The Ghost of Frankenstein* (42) Erle C. Kenton.   *La Figlia di Frankenstein* / *Lady Frankenstein* (It / G 71) Mel Welles (Ernst von Thaumer) *aka Madame Frankenstein*.   *The Curse of Frankenstein* (GB 56) Terence Fisher *aka Birth of Frankenstein* [1st in a Hammer series of 7 films].   *Frankenstein and the Monster from Hell* (GB 72) Terence Fisher [7th and last film in the Hammer series (1956-72)].   *Frankenstein: The True Story* (GB 73 TV) Jack Smight *aka Frankenstein*.   *Doctor Franken* (79 TV) Marvin J. Chomsky *aka The Franken Report*.   *Frankenstein 90* (F 84) Alain Jessua.   *The Vindicator* (Can / US 84) Jean-Claude Lord [rel. in 86] *aka Frankenstein '88* / *The Frankenstein Factor*.   *The Bride* (GB / US 85) Franc Roddam.   *Frankenhooker* (90) Frank Henenlotter.   *Frankenstein Unbound* (US / It 90) Roger Corman.

——**Horror Comedies**   They are numerous and varied. It seems that the next best thing to a monster movie is to make fun of one once it has lost its shock value by frequent exposure and imitation. As a result, horror comedies and spoofs are plentiful.

Abbott and Costello Meet Frankenstein (47) Charles T. Barton *aka Abbott and Costello Meet the Ghosts* / *Bud Abbott and Lou Costello Meet Frankenstein* / *The Brain of Frankenstein*.   *Abbott and Costello Meet the Mummy* (55) Charles Lamont.   *The Raven* (62) Roger Corman.   *The Incredibly Strange Creatures Who Stopped Living and Became Mixed-Up Zombies* (63) Ray Dennis Steckler *aka Face of Evil* / *The Incredible Strange Creatures or Why I Stopped Living and Became a Mixed-Up Zombie* / *The Incredibly Strange Creatures* / *Teenage Psycho Meets Bloody Mary*.   *The Folks at Red Wolf Inn* (72) Bud Townsend *aka Terror at Red Wolf Inn* / *Terror House* / *Terror on the Menu. Microwave Massacre* (78) Wayne Berwick. *An American Werewolf in London* (GB / US 81) John Landis. *O segredo da Múmia* (Braz 82) Ivan Cardoso *aka Lago maldito. The Return of the Living Dead* (84) Dan O'Bannon. *Psychos in Love* (85) Gormand Bechard. *The Stuff* (85) Larry Cohen. *The Toxic Avenger* (85) Michael Herz, Samuel Weil [followed by *The Toxic Avenger, Part II* (89) Michael Herz, Lloyd Kaufman *The Toxic Avenger Part III — The Last Temptation of Toxie* (89) also by Herz and Kaufman]. *Vamp* (86) Richard Wenk. *Brain Damage* (88) Frank Henenlotter.

——**Malevolent Children Horror Films**   A very distinctive brand of horror focuses on the wrongdoings of perverse children getting their comeuppance on adults by murdering them. This is frequently a subject of horror films and some science fiction films, e.g., *The Damned* (1961), *Demain . . . les mômes* (1975).

The Bad Seed (55) Mervyn LeRoy. *The Damned* (GB 61) Joseph Losey *aka On the Brink / These Are the Damned. Our Mother's House* (GB / US 67) Jack Clayton. *The Nightcomers* (GB 71) Michael Winner. *Night Hair Child* (GB 71) James Kelly *aka What the Peeper Saw. The Other* (72) Robert Mulligan. *The Killing Kind* (73) Curtis Harrington. *Devil Times Five* (74) Sean McGregor *aka The Horrible House on the Hill / Peopletoys. Demain . . . les mômes* (F 75) Jean Pourtalé. *The Little Girl Who Lives Down the Lane / La Petite Fille au bout du chemin* (Can / F / Swiz 75) Nicholas Gessner [rel. in 77]. *¿Quién puede matar a un niño? / Would You Kill a Child?* (Sp / GB 75) Narciso Ibáñez Serrador *aka Death Is a Child / Island of the Damned / Los Niños / ¿Puede Usted matar a un niño? Alice, Sweet Alice* (76) Alfred Sole *aka Communion / Holy Terror. The Godsend* (GB / US 79) Gabriel Beaumont. *Bloody Birthday* (80) Ed Hunt *aka Blood Birthday. Children of the Corn* (84) Fritz Kiersch.

——**Movie Monsters**   A facet of the horror film is movie monsters. These could be sorted into a choice pantheon of 16 or so different species. They involve creation, reanimation, metamorphosis, and duplication.[54]

Creation: 1. *Frankenstein monster.* This popular monster has appeared in well over one hundred films. *See* **Frankenstein Films.** 2. *The Golem* (man of clay brought to life) e.g., *It!* (1966). 3. *The Homunculus* (an artificially created being in the likeness of man) e.g., *Homunculus* (1916). 4. *The Computer.* Usually becoming sentient and, as a result, trying to take over from man, it appears mostly in science fiction films. This category, besides computers, may include automatons, robots, androids, and cyborgs. An interesting film in the computer category is *The Demon Seed* (1977); a more recent example is *Tron* (1982).

Reanimation: 5. *The Mummy. See* **Mummy Films.** 6. *The Zombie* (the walking dead: corpses reanimated by witchcraft). *See* **Zombie Movie.** 7. *The Ghoul.* An oriental spirit or demon that mostly feeds on human hearts. In films, a reanimated corpse that eats human flesh, e.g., *The Mad Ghoul* (1943); *Children Shouldn't Play with Dead Things* (1973). Ghouls are usually grouped among the zombies. *See* **Zombie Movie.**

Metamorphosis: 8. *The Vampire.* Carmilla, Dracula, Nosferatu and his victims, the Undead. *See* **Vampire Film.** 9. *The Werewolf* (or lycanthrope).

See **Werewolf Movie.** 10. *The Cat* (tigers, black panthers). The metamorphoses of a human being into werebeast or vice versa, e.g., *Cat People* (1982). 11. *The Ape* (man transformed or retrogressed into a simian) e.g., *The Ape Man* (1943). 12. *The Beast.* Man or woman metamorphosed into a whole menagerie of monstrous animals, including snakes, flies, alligators, spiders, etc. The films mostly combine horror and science fiction, e.g., *The Alligator People* (1959), *The Blood Beast Terror* (1967), *Sssssss* (1973). 13. *The Brute.* A classical example is R. L. Stevenson's *The Strange Case of Dr. Jekyll and Mr. Hyde* (1886), adapted into an ever-recurring series of remakes and reworkings of the story, e.g., *Dr. Jekyll and Mr. Hyde* (1908), *Edge of Sanity* (1987). 14. *The Mutant* (either man or beast, usually the result of atomic radiation, fallout or toxic waste) e.g., *Mutant* (1983), *Impulse* (1984). 15. *The Mask.* Or people who have become—usually by accident—freaks of one sort or another. People with scarred or burned faces who try to hide their ugliness and thus avoid the repulsion they inspire, e.g., *The Phantom of the Opera* (1925).

Duplication: 16. *The Double* (one's own reflection or shadow). This is basically a German preoccupation: The *Doppelgänger,* e.g., *Der Student von Prag* (1926). 17. *The Clone* (a replica of a human being) e.g., *The Cloning of Clifford Swimmer* (1974 TV).

Dr. Jekyll and Mr. Hyde (08) Prod. William N. Selig *aka The Modern Dr. Jekyll.* *Homunculus* (G 16) Otto Rippert [a serial in 6 chapters]. *The Phantom of the Opera* (25) Rupert Julian. *Der Student von Prag* (G 26) Henrik Galeen *aka The Man Who Cheated Life / The Student of Prague.* *Were Wolf of London* (35) Stuart Walker *aka Unholy Hour.* *The Ape Man* (43) William Beaudine *aka Lock Your Doors.* *The Mad Ghoul* (43) James P. Hogan. *The Alligator People* (59) Roy Del Ruth. *It!* (GB / US 66) Herbert J. Leger *aka Anger of the Golem / The Curse of the Golem.* *The Blood Beast Terror* (GB 67) Vernon Sewell *aka Blood Beast from Hell / The Deathshead Vampire / The Vampire-Beast Craves Blood.* *Children Shouldn't Play with Dead Things* (72) Benjamin Clark *aka Zreaks.* *Sssssss* (73) Bernard L. Kowalski *aka Sssnake.* *The Cloning of Clifford Swimmer* (74 TV) Lela Swift. *The Demon Seed* (77) Donald Cammell. *Cat People* (82) Paul Schrader. *Tron* (82) Steven Lisberger *aka Tron: The Electronic Gladiator* [1st feature-length film using computer animation]. *Mutant* (83) John "Bud" Cardos *aka Dark Shadows / Night Shadows.* *Impulse* (84) Graham Baker. *Edge of Sanity* (GB / Hung 87) Guérard Kikoine.

——**Mummy Films** The lineage of the mummy goes back into millennia since its origins are found in ancient Egypt. In cinema, it appeared early if sporadically in short nonhorror fantasy tales, as for instance in Georges Méliès' *Cléopâtre* (1899). It was, however, the striking appearance by Boris Karloff in *The Mummy* (1932) that catapulted to fame this early cinematic monster. In spite of its early success, the output of mummy films has been relatively small and, with the exceptions of the Universal "Kharis" series of mummy films in the 40s, a Mexican series, and some films produced by the British Hammer Studios, its manifestation in film has not been prolific. The mummy, awakened from its lethargy and let loose from its sarcophagus into the present-day world to begin its depredations, is not as spectacular, awe-inspiring, or fearsome as other personalities in the realm of the undead and walking dead like vampires, zombies and ghouls.

Cléopâtre (F 1899) Georges Méliès *aka Robbing Cleopatra's Tomb. Die Augen der Mumie Ma* (G 18) Ernst Lubitsch *aka The Eyes of the Mummy. The Mummy* (32) Karl Freund. *The Mummy's Hand* (40) Christy Cabanne [1st of the "Kharis" series (1940-44)]. *The Mummy's Tomb* (42) Harold Young. *The Mummy's Ghost* (43) Reginald LeBorg. *The Mummy's Curse* (44) Leslie Goodwins. *La Maldición de la Momia Azteca* (Mex 57) Rafael Portillo *aka The Curse of the Aztec Mummy. La Momia Azteca* (Mex 57) Rafael Portillo *aka Attack of the Mayan Mummy / La Momia / The Mummy / The Mummy Strikes. La Momia Azteca vs el Robot Humano* (Mex 57) Rafael Portillo *aka El Robot Humano / The Robot vs the Aztec Mummy. The Mummy* (GB 59) Terence Fisher *aka Terror of the Mummy. Curse of the Mummy's Tomb* (GB 64) Michael Carreras. *Las Luchadoras contra la Momia* (Mex 64) René Cardona *aka The Wrestling Women vs the Aztec Mummy. The Mummy's Shroud* (GB 66) John Gillian. *Blood from the Mummy's Tomb* (GB 71) Seth Holt, Michael Carreras (uncredited). *Les Chemins de la violence / El secreto de la momia* (F / Sp 72) 85m Ken Rudder (Alejandro Parti, Gelabert and Pierre Chevalier) *aka Lips of Blood / Love Brides of the Blood Mummy / Le Sang des autres / Perversions sexuelles. Las momias de Guanajuato* (Mex 72) Tito Novarro *aka The Mummies of Guana-juato. La venganza de la momia* (Sp 73) Carlos Aured *aka The Mummy's Revenge / The Mummy's Vengeance / The Vengeance of the Mummy.*

Other Denizens of Horror Movies   *Aliens.* They are mostly presented as humanoids or as bizarre animal or vegetal, organic or inorganic sentient life (especially in science fiction horror movies), e.g., *Alien* (1979), *Xtro* (1982).

Animals (animals-on-the-rampage movies, revolt-of-nature films, insect films). Attack by normal animals in great numbers threatening human life—frogs, bees, dogs, ants, worms, rats—is a recurrent trend in horror films. *The Birds* (1963), directed by Alfred Hitchcock, brought the menace of the familiar close to home by burning previously inoffensive vertebrates into nasties.

Bigfoot. A kind of prehistoric man or a cousin ape called by various names and perhaps related to the Abominable Snowman or Yeti, e.g., *Big Foot* (1969), *Creature from Black Lake* (1975), *The Abominable Snowman* (1957), *Snowbeast* (1977).

Creatures. Usually half-man, half-fish emerging from lagoons, swamps, or the deep, e.g., *Revenge of the Creature* (1954), *Swamp Thing* (1981).

Death (in its many representations), e.g., *The Masque of the Red Death* (1964), *Soultaker* (1990).

Disembodied Parts. Mostly in the form of crawling hands and heads kept alive in some substance, e.g., *The Hand* (1981), *Re-Animator* (1985).

Freaks (by birth). Freaks are not widely used in horror films, except for hunchbacks and dwarfish creatures. A Hollywood horror classic is *Freaks* (1932).

Giant Forms (gigantism, big bug movies, giant insect films, giant-monster genre). Giant apes (*King Kong*, 1933; 1976), etc.; but mostly all sorts of insects or arachnids, including giant ants, grubs, spiders, crabs, e.g., *The Black Scorpion* (1957). The Japanese made a specialty of this category, e.g., *Gojira / Godzilla* (1954) and company (*see* **KAIJU EIGA**).

The Mad Doctor / Mad Scientist. He either creates monsters or performs horrifying surgery and transplants (the transplants often becoming monsters themselves), e.g., *Island of Lost Souls* (1933), *Captive Wild Women* (1943), *L'Homme au cerveau greffé* (1972), *The Kindred* (1986).

Mythological Creatures (Medusas, Harpies, Pandoras, The Devil), e.g., *The Gorgon* (1963), *Fear No Evil* (1981).

Prehistoric Monsters. They are usually brought to life from permafrost by some upheaval, or they are found inhabiting inaccessible areas or regions hitherto hidden or undiscovered, e.g., *The Beast from 20,000 Fathoms* (1953). *See* **SCIENCE FICTION FILM**.

Psychopaths. See **PSYCHOPATHIC THRILLER**.

Supernatural Beings. This section includes ghosts, spirits, revenants, ghouls, transmigrating souls, e.g., *La noche del terror ciego / Night of the Blind Dead* (1971), *Poltergeist* (1982). *See* **GHOST FILM**.

The Witch. The witch is found mainly in fantasy films and in witchcraft movies, e.g., *I Married a Witch* (1942), *La Maschera del demonio / Black Sunday* (1960). *See* **WITCH FILM**.

Freaks (32) Tod Browning *aka Barnum / Forbidden Love / The Monster Show / Nature's Mistakes.* *Island of Lost Souls* (33) Erle C. Kenton *aka The Island of Dr. Moreau.* *King Kong* (33) Merian C. Cooper, Ernest B. Schoedsack *aka The Beast / The Eighth Wonder / The Eighth Wonder of the World / King Ape / King Kong (The Eighth Wonder of the World) / Kong* [1st feature sound film to use model animation]. *I Married a Witch* (42) René Clair. *Captive Wild Women* (43) Edward Dmytryk [followed by *Jungle Woman* (44) Reginald LeBorg, and *Jungle Captive aka Wild Jungle Captive* (45) Harold Young]. *The Beast from 20,000 Fathoms* (53) Eugene Lourié. *Gojira* (J 54) Inoshiro Honda; Terry Morse (U.S. version) *aka Godzilla / Godzilla, King of the Monsters.* *Revenge of the Creature* (54) Jack Arnold. *The Abominable Snowman / The Abominable Snowman of the Himalayas* (GB / US 57) Val Guest. *The Black Scorpion* (57) Edward Ludwig. *La maschera del demonio* (It 60) Mario Bava *aka Black Sunday / House of Fright / Mask of the Demon / Revenge of the Vampire.* *The Birds* (63) Alfred Hitchcock. *The Gorgon* (GB 63) Terence Fisher. *The Masque of the Red Death* (US / GB 64) Roger Corman. *Big Foot* (69) Robert F. Slatzer [rel. in 71]. *La noche del terror ciego* (Sp / Port 71) Amando de Ossorio *aka The Blind Dead / Crypt of the Blind Dead / Night of the Blind Dead / La noche de la muerte ciega / Those Cruel and Bloody Vampires / Tombs of the Blind Dead* [4 films in the Blind Dead (1971-75) series; all directed by Ossorio]. *L'Homme au cerveau greffé / L'uomo dal cervello trapiantato* / *Der Mann mit dem zweiten Gehirn* (F / It / G 72) Jacques Doniol-Valcroze *aka The Man with the Transplanted Brain.* *Creature from Black Lake* (75) Joy Houck, Jr. *King Kong* (76) John Guillermin *aka King Kong: A (The) Legend Reborn.* *Snowbeast* (77 TV) Herbert Wallerstein. *Alien* (GB / US 79) Ridley Scott *aka Starbeast* [followed by *Aliens* (GB 86) James Cameron and *Alien 3* (GB / US 92) Dand Finder]. *Fear No Evil* (80) Frank Laloggia *aka Mark of the Beast.* *The Hand* (81) Oliver Stone. *Swamp Thing* (81) Wes Craven [followed by *Return of the Swamp Thing* (89) Jim Wynorski]. *Poltergeist* (82) Tobe Hooper [followed by *Poltergeist II* (86) Brian Gibson and *Poltergeist III* (87) Gary Sherman; *Cf. Something Evil* (72 TV) Steven Spielberg]. *Xtro* (GB 82) Harry B. Davenport *aka Judas Goat.* *Re-Animator* (85) Stuart Gordon *aka H.P. Lovecraft's Re-Animator* [followed by *Bride of Re-Animator* (90) Brian Yuzna]. *The Kindred* (86) Jeffrey Obrow, Stephen Carpenter. *Soultaker* (90) Michael Rissi.

Any of the movie monsters and other apparitions of the horror film could be the subject of a horror subgenre of its own, and most of them boast an ample output of films to fit into it. Besides the horror created by monsters and by psychopaths, another great source of horror is the occult. This kind of horror deals with demonology and witchcraft, with reincarnation and the world beyond, with Edgar Allan Poe and H. P. Lovecraft, with the supernatural in general.

——**Possession Movies**   Possession may be defined as the taking control of an organism by a supernatural entity, a demon, or the spirit of a deceased person. Movies have also depicted possessed dwellings, machines and assorted objects. Although a few early films have featured possession, e.g., *Orlacs Hände / The Hands of Orlac* (1924) in which the transplanted hands of a murderer have a will of their own, it was with *The Exorcist* (1973) that demonic possession became popular. Its release brought about a host of imitations. Most possession films are horror movies. The comedy variety, e.g. *All of Me* (1984) is not included here. *See also* **HAUNTED HOUSE FILM.**

Orlacs Hände (Aus 24) Robert Wiene *aka The Hands of Orlac / The Sinister Hands of Orlac / Die unheimlichen Hände des Dr. Orlak.* *Supernatural* (33) Victor Halperin. *Mad Love* (35) Karl Freund *aka The Hands of Orlac.* *Les Mains d'Orlac / The Hands of Orlac* (F / GB 60) Edmond T. Gréville *aka Hands of a Strangler.* *Hands of a Stranger* (62) Newt Arnold *aka The Answer! / Hands of Terror.* *The Possession of Joel Delaney* (71) Waris Hussein. *The Exorcist* (73) William Friedkin. *Chi sei? / Beyond the Door* (It / US 74) Oliver Hellman (Ovidio Assonitis), Richard Barretti *aka Behind the Door / Devil Within Her / Who?* *L'Ossessa* (It 74) Mario Gariazzo *aka The Eerie Midnight Horror Show / The Obsessed / The Sexorcist / Tormented.* *I Don't Want to Be Born* (GB 75) Peter Sasdy *aka The Baby / The Devil Within Her / It's Growing Inside Her / The Monster / Sharon's Baby.* *Cathy's Curse / Une si gentille petite fille* (Can / F 76) Eddy Matalon *aka Cauchemares / The Evil Lives On / It Lives On / Le Maléfice / Une étrange petite fille.* *Ruby* (76) Curtis Harrington, Stephanie Rothman *aka Blood Ruby.* *Shock* (It 77) Mario Bava *aka Al 33 di Via Orologio fa sempre freddo / Beyond the Door 2 / Shock Transfer-Suspence-Hypnos / Suspense.*

The Awakening (GB / US 80) Mike Newell. *Mausoleum* (81) Michael Dugan. *Christine* (82) John Carpenter. *Killer Party* (Can 84) William Fruet. *Retribution* (86) Guy Magar. *Hello Mary Lou: Prom Night II* (Can 87) Bruce Pittman. *Child's Play* (88) Tom Holland.

——**Sex Horror Films**   A certain degree of eroticism has been present in most horror movies. However, in the sixties horror films started to include sex openly as a major element in the movie. Heroines began to appear naked or seminaked, ravished and killed by villains and monsters. In the process, the films proved that sex mixes well with horror.

La Rose écorchée (F 69) Claude Mulot *aka The Blood Rose / Ravaged. Las amantes del diablo / I diavolici convegni* (Sp / It 70) Joe Lacy (José María Elorrieta) *aka The Devil's Lovers / The Diabolical Meeting. The Virgin Witch* (GB 70) Ray Austin *aka Lesbian Twins. La notte dei dannati* (It 71) Peter Rush (Filippo Maria Ratti) *aka The Night of the Damned. Carne per Frankenstein / De la chair pour Frankenstein / Flesh for Frankenstein* (It / F / G / US 73) Paul Morrissey, Anthony M. Dawson (Antonio Margheriti) *aka Andy Warhol's Flesh for Frankenstein / Andy Warhol's Frankenstein / The Devil and Dr. Frankenstein / Frankenstein / The Frankenstein Experiment / Il mostro é in tavola . . . Barone Frankenstein / Up Frankenstein. Les Démoniaques* (F / Belg 73) Jean Rollin *aka Demoniacs / Les Demoniaques (Revenge of the Virgins) / Deux Vierges pour Satan / Les Diablesses / Tina, la Naufrageuse perverse. Les Expériences érotiques de Frankenstein / La maldición de Frankenstein* (F / Sp / Port 73) Jesús Franco *aka The Curse of Frankenstein / The Erotic Adventures of Frankenstein / Les Exploits érotiques de Frankenstein / La Malédiction de Frankenstein. Prey* (GB 77) Norman J. Warren. *Notti erotiche dei morti viventi* (It 79) Joe D'Amato *aka Erotic Nights of the Living Dead / Island of the Zombies. Malabimba* (It 79) Andrew White (Andrea Bianchi). *Los ritos sexuales del diablo* (Sp 81) José Ramón Larraz.

Horror of Personality Film *see* **PSYCHOPATHIC THRILLER**

Horse Loving Films *see* **HORSE PIC**

Horse Opera *see* **HORSE PIC;** *see also* **WESTERN**

Horse Opry *see* **WESTERN**

HORSE PIC (Equine Picture, Horse Opera)   The horse has enjoyed a major role in an impressive number of pictures. Movies in which horses play an important part may be divided into a few categories. Foremost among them are the horse racing movies. Other categories are horse loving films, films on polo players, stories about jockeys, horsebreeding, and films which fit no specific horse picture group except that the horse is an important or essential element in them, e.g., *Equus* (1977). On the subject of horse movies, *see* H. F. Hintz, *Horses in the Movies* (South Brunswick: A. S. Barnes; London: Thomas Yoseloff, 1979).

Polo Joe (36) William McGann. *Three Men on a Horse* (36) Mervyn LeRoy. *Kentucky* (38) David Butler. *The Rocking Horse Winner* (GB 49) Anthony Pelissier. *The Lemon Drop Kid* (51) Sidney Lanfield. *Gypsy*

Colt (54) Andrew Marton.   *The Misfits* (61) John Huston.   *The Horse Without a Head* (63) Don Chaffey.   *The Horse in the Gray Flannel Suit* (68) Norman Tokar.   *Running Wild* (73) Robert McCahon.   *Mustang Country* (76) John Champion.   *Equus* (GB 77) Sidney Lumet.   *Black Beauty* (78 TV) Daniel Haller.   *The Man from Snowy River* (Aust 81) George Miller.

———**Horse Loving Films**   This category includes films in which well-meaning folks try to save horses from some impending menace (confinement, exploitation, cruelty, destruction), or the films describe the relationship between a child and a horse. Usually a child or youngster falls in love with the animal and they go through countless adventures together or the child is in conflict with his/her family which does not understand his/her attachment to a horse. This latter species of film is an ever-increasing variety of the horse opera. It is a type of kiddie-weepie that often develops into a sentimental story.

Smoky (33) Eugene Forbes.   *My Friend Flicka* (43) Harold Schuster.   *Thunderhead—Son of Flicka* (45) Louis King.   *Smoky* (46) Louis King.   *The Red Pony* (49) Lewis Milestone.   *The Littlest Outlaw / El pequeño proscrito* (US / Mex 53) Roberto Gavaldon [rel. in 55].   *The Sad Horse* (59) James B. Clark.   *Misty* (61) James B. Clark.   *The Red Pony* (73 TV) Robert Totten.   *Escape from the Dark* (77) Charles Jarrott *aka The Littlest Horse Thieves.   Run for the Roses* (77) Henry Levin *aka Thoroughbred.   The Black Stallion* (US / Can 79) Carroll Ballard.   *The Electric Horseman* (79) Sydney Pollack.   *The Black Stallion Returns* (US / Can 83) Robert Dalva.

———**Horse Racing Movies (Racehorse Operas, Turf Stories)**   Here are grouped films about racing: race-track films; quarter-horse racing, steeplechase riding, harness racing (trotting racing), horse jumping competitions. This category falls under the sports genre.

Broadway Bill (34) Frank Capra *aka Strictly Confidential.   A Day at the Races* (37) Sam Wood.   *It Ain't Hay* (43) Earl C. Kenton *aka Money for Jam.   Home in Indiana* (44) Henry Hathaway.   *National Velvet* (44) Clarence Brown.   *Black Gold* (47) Phil Karlson.   *The Story of Seabiscuit* (49) David Butler *aka Pride of Kentucky.   Boots Malone* (52) William Dieterle.   *Derby Day* (GB 52) Herbert Wilcox *aka Four Against Fate.   For the Love of Mike* (60) George Sherman.   *Bite the Bullet* (75) Richard Brooks.   *Casey's Shadows* (78) Martin Ritt.   *International Velvet* (GB / US 78) Bryan Forbes.   *Phar Lap* (Aust 82) Simon Wencer *aka Phar Lap—Heart of a Nation.   Champions* (GB 83) John Irving.

Hospital Drama   *see*   **HOSPITAL FILM**

HOSPITAL FILM (Doctor Drama, Hospital Drama, Medical Drama)   Films set in hospitals, peopled by doctors, interns, nurses, orderlies, and patients are fertile ground for dramatic situations, melodramatic soap operas, suspenseful mysteries, and comedy. Most of the action in these films takes place in general hospitals (whose size alone makes them ideally suited for pandemonium) and in hospital wards or in private clinics. The movies themselves may be categorized as dramas, melodramas, thrillers, farces and occasionally satires. The nature of the hospital setting makes it fitting for a wide range of cinematic approaches. Most hospital films extol the dedication of the medical corps, but a few also stress the corruption, malpractice, and general incompetence prevailing among the staff.

On television, hospital soap opera serials are long-standing and a category unto themselves.[55]

Life Begins (32) James Flood *aka The Dawn of Life*. *Young Doctor Kildare* (38) Harold S. Bucquet [16 films (1937-47) in the "Dr. Kildare" series]. *Green for Danger* (GB 46) Sidney Gilliat. *The Sleeping City* (50) George Sherman. *People Will Talk* (51) Joseph L. Mankiewicz. *White Corridors* (GB 51) Pat Jackson. *Behind the Mask* (GB 58) Brian Desmond Hurst. *Carry On Nurse* (GB 58) Gerald Thomas. *The Young Doctors* (61) Phil Karlson. *The Interns* (62) David Swift. *The New Interns* (64) John Rich. *The Hospital* (71) Arthur Hiller. *The Carey Treatment* (72) Blake Edwards *aka A Case of Need / Emergency Ward*. *Bisturi: la Mafia bianca* (It 73) Luigi Zampa. *Coma* (78) Michael Crichton. *House Calls* (78) Howard Zieff. *Opname* (Hol 79) Erik van Zuylen, Maria Kok *aka Hospitalized / In for Treatment*. *X-Ray* (80) Boaz Davidson *aka Be My Valentine or Else... / Hospital Massacre / Ward 13*. *Whose Life Is It Anyway?* (81) John Badham. *Britania Hospital* (GB 82) Lindsay Anderson. *Terminal Choice* (Can 82) Sheldon Larry [rel. in 85] *aka Critical List / Death Bed / Death List / Trauma*. *Variola vera* (Yug 82) Goran Markovic *aka True Small-Pox*. *Young Doctors in Love* (82) Garry Marshall. *Gross Anatomy* (89) Thom Eberhardt. *Paper Mask* (GB 90 TV) Christopher Morahan.

Hostage-Holding Gangster Movies   *see*   **GANGSTER FILM**

Hot Car Film   *see*   **ROAD MOVIE**

Hot Print   *see*   **HARD-CORE PORNO FILM**

Hot-Rod Movie   *see*   **TEEN MOVIE**

Howdunit   *see*   **WHODUNIT**

How To   *see*   **FACTUAL FILM: How-to-Do-It Film**

How-to-Do-It Documentary   *see*   **HARD-CORE PORNO FILM;**   *see also*   **SEX DOCUMENTARY: Sex Explanation Films**

Humorous Film   *see*   **COMEDY**

HYBRID (Cross-Genre Movie, Mixed-Genre Film)   In film terms, a picture which partakes of or mixes different genres or which includes characteristics of diverse genres and subgenres. This is a tendency which some recent films seem to embrace. For instance, *The Witches of Eastwick* (1987) may be classified as a fantasy, a horror film, a comedy, a romance, a small-town movie, or it may be subclassified as a witch or devil movie; indeed, its ramifications are many (*see* Raymond Dugnat's article "Up Jumped the Devil or, The Jack-in-Pandora's Box: The Genres of Eastwick." *Monthly Film Bulletin,* September 1987: 265–68).

The Hurricane (37) John Ford. *All Through the Night* (42) Vincent Sherman. *South Sea Woman* (53) Arthur Lubin. *Hex* (72) Leo Garen *aka The Shrieking*. *Angel Heart* (87) Alan Parker. *Dudes* (87) Penelope Spheeris. *Fatal Attraction* (87) Adrian Lyne. *Off Limits* (87) Christopher Crowe *aka Saigon*. *Wall Street* (87) Oliver Stone. *The Witches of Eastwick* (87) George Miller. *Lady in White* (88) Frank LaLoggia. *Ghost* (90) Jerry Zucker.

Hybrid Westerns *see* **WESTERN**

Ice-Skating Musicals *see* **MUSICAL**

Imperial Film *see* **BRITISH EMPIRE FILM**

Impressionism *see* **IMPRESSIONIST FILM**

IMPRESSIONIST FILM (French Impressionism, Impressionism) Impressionism, as it applies to cinema, dates from the silent twenties when Louis Delluc (1890–1924) gathered around him a group of intellectuals who were called by critics (Delluc himself used the term) "Film Impressionists." Besides Delluc, they included Germain Dulac (1882–1942), Marcel L'Herbier (1890–1979), Abel Gance (1889–1981) and Jean Epstein (1897–1953). They formed what was to be known as *L'École impressioniste* (1920–1927), a film movement also referred to as the "First Avant-Garde" (*première avant-garde*).

The movement was related to the French Impressionist painters (Manet, Monet, Degas, Renoir) in so far as they shared similar views as to the importance of light and composition in their work and the belief that subjective matter is more important than the objective fixing of realistic images. Also in common with the impressionist painters, the impressionist filmmakers sought to capture glimpses of life, fleeting moments of thought and mood. To this end, they used all kinds of cinematic techniques like soft-focus photography, distortion of images, superimpositions, and diverse, odd camera angles.

The impressionist leaning is not restricted to the French Impressionist School of the twenties. It is observed in some contemporary films from various countries, e.g., Bo Widerberg's *Elvira Madigan* (1967), Robert Altman's *Images* (1972), Louis Malle's *Pretty Baby* (1977). On the subject of impressionist film, *see* David Bordwell's *French Impressionist Cinema* (New York: Arno Press, 1980).

La Dixième Symphonie (F 18) Abel Gance. *La Fête espagnole* (F 19) Germaine Dulac. *Le Carnaval des vérités* (F 20) Marcel L'Herbier. *Eldorado* (F 21) Marcel L'Herbier. *La Roue* (F 20-22) Abel Gance. *La Souriante Madame Beudet* (F 22) Germaine Dulac *aka The Smiling Mme Beudet*. *Coeur fidèle* (F 23) Jean Epstein. *En rade* (F 27) Alberto Cavalcanti *aka Sea Fever*. *La Glace à trois faces* (F 27) Jean Epstein. *Charleston* (F 27) Jean Renoir *aka Sur un Air de Charleston / Charleston-on-Parade*. *L'Argent* (F 28) Marcel L'Herbier. *La Chute de la maison Usher* (F 28) Jean Epstein *aka The Fall of the House of Usher*. *La Petite Marchante d'allumettes* (F 28)

Jean Renoir *aka The Little Match Girl.* *Finis Terrae* (F 29) Jean Epstein. *Nogent Eldorado du dimanche* (F 29) Marcel Carné, Michel Sanvoisin. *Elvira Madigan* (Sw 67) Bo Widerberg. *Images* (Ire / US / GB 72) Robert Altman. *Pretty Baby* (77) Louis Malle.

Incentive Film *see* **DOCUMENTARY: War Documentary**

Independent Film *see* **INDEPENDENT PRODUCTION;** *see also* **UNDERGROUND FILM**

INDEPENDENT PRODUCTION (Alternative Cinema, Art Film, Concrete Film, Independent Film, Indie, Oppositional Film, Radical Film) Films which are not produced or financially backed by an established film production company are referred to as indies or independent productions. The films thus produced may be privately funded or financed by some organization or group of backers. In the United States John Cassavetes's films *Shadows* (1960) and *Faces* (1968), Stanley Kubrick's *Fear and Desire* (1953) and Jonas Mekas's *Guns of the Trees* (1961), for instance, fall under the designation of independent productions or independent films. The term independent film is also used as quasi-synonymous with that of avant-garde and underground film, both older appellations for experimental films or films of personal artistic expression made outside the mainstream of commercially produced films. *See* **AVANT-GARDE, UNDERGROUND FILM.**

Fear and Desire (53) Stanley Kubrick. *The Little Fugitive* (53) Ray Ashley. *Lovers and Lollipops* (55) Morris Engel, Ruth Orkin. *Come Back, Africa* (58) Lionel Rogosin. *Weddings and Babies* (58) Morris Engel. *Shadows* (60) John Cassavetes. *Guns of the Trees* (61) Jonas Mekas *aka Guns in the Trees.* *Faces* (68) John Cassavetes. *Skinflicker* (GB 72) Tony Bicat. *Justine* (GB 76) Stewart Mackinnon. *Billy in the Lowlands* (77) Jan Egelson. *The Kirlian Witness* (77) Jonathan Sarno *aka The Plants Are Watching.* *Telling Tales* (GB 78) Richard Woolley. *The Haunting of M* (79) Anna Thomas. *Heartland* (79) Richard Pearce. *Imposters* (G / US 79) Mark Rappaport. *Return of the Secaucus 7* (79) John Sayles. *Union City* (79) Mark Reichert. *Get Rollin'* (80) J. Terrence Mitchell. *The Weavers: Wasn't That a Time!* (81) Jim Brown. *Vernon, Florida* (81) Errol Morris. *Wild Style* (82) Charlie Ahearn. *Stranger Than Paradise* (84) Jim Jarmusch. *Parting Glances* (86) Bill Sherwood. *Stand and Deliver* (87) Ramon Menendez *aka Walking on Water.*

——**No Wave Filmmakers**   A group of independent filmmakers, mostly based in New York and variously referred to as no wave, punk or new wave, who in the 1970s disagreed with commercial, Hollywood cinema and avant-garde, formalist product. They wanted to make imexpensive films which would be accessible to the local community. The new wave filmmakers were noted for their use of Super-8 equipment as well as for their critical stance with regard to current practices of production and distribution. Outstanding representatives of the group are Vivienne Dick who is from Ireland but worked in New York at the time, and Beth B and Scott B during their collaborative period.

Black Box (78) Beth B, Scott B.   *G-Man* (78) Beth B, Scott B.   *She Had Her Gun All Ready* (78) Vivienne Dick.   *Beauty Becomes the Beast* (79) Vivienne Dick.

India's New Cinema   *see*   **NEW INDIAN CINEMA**

Indian Western   *see*   **WESTERN: Indian Films**

Indie   *see*   **INDEPENDENT PRODUCTION**

Industrial Film   *see*   **FACTUAL FILM**

Industrial Jeopardy Film, Industrial Safety Film   *see*   **FACTUAL FILM: Jeopardy Film**

Informational Film, Information Film   *see*   **FACTUAL FILM**

Injun Picture   *see*   **WESTERN: Indian Films**

Insect Film   *see*   **HORROR FILM: Other Denizens of Horror Movies**

Instant Analysis   *see*   **TELEVISION NEWS**

Instructional Film, Instruction Film   *see*   **FACTUAL FILM**

Interest Film   *see*   **ACTUALITY**

Invasion Films   *see*   **SCIENCE FICTION FILM**

Investigative Film   *see*   **POLICE FILM;**   *see also*   **PRIVATE DETECTIVE FILM**

Italian Thriller   *see*   **GIALLO**

Italian Western, Italo-Western   *see*   **SPAGHETTI WESTERN**

Jail Movie   *see*   **PRISON FILM**

James Bond Films   *see*   **SPY FILM**

Japanese Monster Picture   *see*   **KAIJU EIGA**

JAPANESE NEW WAVE CINEMA (Nuberu Bagu)   The label applies to the work of a group of film directors who in the 1960s made films which differed considerably in content and form from the films of established directors like Yasujiru Ozu, Kenji Mizoguchi, or Akira Kurosawa, to mention just three of the best-known and esteemed Japanese filmmakers. These new film directors—Shohei Imamura, Nagisa Oshima, Masahiro Shinoda, Koji Wakamatsu, Yoshishinge Yoshida and several others—sought to renew Japanese cinema by introducing into their films untouched themes of a social, political and sexual nature. They represent a reaction against the old, traditional school of Japanese filmmaking as well as being critical of contemporary Japanese society. The Japanese New Wave cinema of the 1960s has been described in David Desser's *Eros Plus Massacre* (Bloomington: Indiana University Press, 1988). *Nihon no yoru to kiri* (J 60) Nagisa Oshima *aka Night and Fog in Japan.* *Seishun zankoku monogatari* (J 60) Nagisa Oshima *aka Cruel Story of Youth.* *Buta to gunkan* (J 61) Shoei Imamura *aka Hogs and Warships / Pigs and Battleships.* *Kawaita hana* (J 63) Masahiro Shinoda *aka Pale Flower.* *Nippon konchuki* (J 63) Shohei Imamura *aka The Insect Woman.* *Onibaba* (J 64) Kaneto Shindo *aka The Demon / Devil Woman / The Hole.* *Kabe no naka no nimegoto* (J 65) Koji Wakamatsu *Affairs Within Walls / Secret Act Inside Walls.* *Andes no hanayome* (J 66) Susumo Hani *aka Bride of the Andes.* *Jinruigaku nyumon* (J 66) Shohei Imamura *aka The Amorist / The Pornographer(s) / The Pornographers: Introduction to Anthropology.* *Tanin no kao* (J 66) Hiroshi Teshigahara *aka The Face of Another.* *Okasareta byakui* (J 67) Koji Wakamatsu *aka Violated Angels / Violated Women in White.* *Hatsukoi jigokuhen* (J 68) Susumu Hani *aka The Inferno of First Love / Nanami.* *Koshikei* (J 68) Nagisa Oshima *aka Death by Hanging.* *Moetsukita chizu* (J 68) Hiroshi Teshigahara *aka Man Without a Map / The Ruined Map.* *Seiyugi* (J 68) Masao Adachi *aka Sexual Play.* *Eros purasu gyakusatsu* (J 69) Yoshishinge Yoshida *aka Eros plus Massacre / Eros + Massacre.* *Shinjuku dorobo nikki* (J 69) Nagisa Oshima *aka Diary of a Shinjuku Burglar / Diary of a Shinjuku Thief.* *Tokyo senso sengo hiwa* (J 70) Nagisa Oshima *aka He Died After the War / The Man Who Left His Will on Film / Secret Story of the 'Post Tokyo' War Period* [subtitled: *Eiga de isho o nokoshite shinda otoko no monogatari*]. *Himiko* (J 74) Masahiro Shinoda. *Yashagaike* (J 79) Masahiro Shinoda *aka Demond Pond.* *Eihanaika* (J 80) Shohei Imamura *aka Why Not.* *Narayama bushi-ko* (J 82) Shohei Imamura *aka The Ballad of Narayama.*

J. D. Film   *see*   **JUVENILE DELINQUENCY FILM**

Jeopardy Film   *see*   **FACTUAL FILM**

Jidai-Geki   *see*   **SAMURAI FILM**

Jiggle Film   *see*   **HARD-CORE PORNO FILM**

John Wayne War Films   *see*   **WAR FILM**

John Wayne Westerns   *see*   **WESTERN**

Journalism Drama   *see*   **NEWSPAPER FILM**

der junge deutsche Film   *see*   **NEW GERMAN CINEMA**

JUNGLE FILM   With the opening up and colonization of Africa by European powers in the 19th century came a liking for stories set in the Dark Continent. Mass media writers like H. Rider Haggard (1856–1925) and Edgar Rice Burroughs (1875–1950), creator of Tarzan, set the pace for adventure stories with a jungle background. Hollywood quickly seized on the idea of transmuting these stories into celluloid, and the jungle film was born. Serials also contributed to the popularity of this type of film which is essentially a branch of the adventure film. From the start, jungle movies have been replete with such ingredients as safaris, white hunters, preserve wardens, warring tribes, hidden treasures, white witches, Amazons, goddesses, lost cities, and of course, Tarzan. It goes without saying that jungle movies, including the Tarzan ones, are not restricted to Africa, and other jungle settings or semi-desert locations (for safari films) do equally well.

Trader Horn (30) W. S. Van Dyke II. *King of the Jungle* (33) H. Bruce Humberstone. *The Jungle Princess* (36) William Thiele. *Elephant Boy* (GB 37) Robert Flaherty, Zoltan Korda. *Five Came Back* (39) John Farrow. *The Jungle Book* (42) Zoltan Korda *aka Rudyard Kipling's Jungle Book*. *Jungle Jim* (48) William Berke [16 films (1948-55) in the "Jungle Jim" series]. *Africa Screams* (49) Charles Barton. *Bomba, the Jungle Boy* (49) Ford Beebe [12 films (1949-55) in the "Bomba the Jungle Boy" series]. *The Naked Jungle* (53) Byron Haskin. *Back from Eternity* (56) John Farrow. *Fitzcarraldo* (G / Peru 81) Werner Herzog. *The Emerald Forest* (GB / US 85) John Boorman. *The Mosquito Coast* (86) Peter Weir.

——**Ape Movies**   Apes figure prominently in horror movies (q.v.) but most of the time they are under the control of mad scientists or go rampant in the city. However, their natural habitat is the jungle. An ape film that combines both settings is the legendary *King Kong* (1933).

King Kong (33) Merian C. Cooper, Ernest B. Schoedsack *aka The Beast / The Eighth Wonder / The Eighth Wonder of the World / King Ape / King Kong (The Eighth Wonder of the World) / Kong* [1st feature sound film to use model animation]. *The Son of Kong* (33) Ernest B. Schoedsack *aka Jamboree*. *Nabonga* (43) Sam Newfield *aka The Girl and the Gorilla / Gorilla / The Jungle Woman*. *White Pongo* (45) Sam Newfield *aka Adventure Unlimited*. *The White Gorilla* (47) Harry L. Fraser. *Mighty Joe Young* (49) Ernest B. Schoedsack *aka The Great Joe Young / Mr. Joseph Young of Africa*. *Zamba* (49) William Berke *aka The Girl and the Gorilla / Zamba the Gorilla*. *Bride of the Gorilla* (51) Curt Siodmak. *Bela Lugosi Meets a Brooklyn Gorilla* (52) William Beaudine *aka The Boys from Brooklyn / The Monster Meets the Gorilla*. *The Bride of the Beast* (57) Adrian Weiss. *The Mighty Gorga* (70) David Hewitt. *Queen Kong* (GB / It 76) Frank Agrama *aka Queen Gorilla*. *Tanya's Island / La Bête d'amour* (Can 79) Alfred Sole *aka Horrors of Sorts: Tanya's Island*. *In the Shadow of Kilimanjaro* (US / GB / Ken 86) Raju Patel. *Gorillas in the Mist* (88) Michael Apted.

——**Cannibal Films**   An Italian subgenre of jungle movies that apparently started with Umberto Lenzi's *Il paese del sesso selvaggio* (1972). This type of film thrives on scenes of wild animals devouring each other, horrific acts of violence and, of course, anthropophagous primitives engaged in consuming the day's spoils.

Emanuelle e gli ultimi cannibali (72) Joe D'Amato. *Il paese del sesso selvaggio* (72) Umberto Lenzi *aka Cannibalis sexe story / Deep River Savages / Man from Deep River / Mondo cannibale / Sacrifice!* *Ultimo mondo cannibale* (It 76) Ruggero Deodato *aka Cannibal / Cannibal Holocaust / Carnivorous / Last Cannibal World / The Last Survivor*. *La montagna del dio cannibale* (It 78) Sergio Martino *aka The Mountain of the Cannibal God / Prisoner of the Cannibal God / Slave of the Cannibal God*. *Antropophagus*

(It 79) Joe D'Amato *aka The Anthropophagus Beast / The Green Reaper.*
Cannibal holocaust (It 79) Ruggero Deodato. *Antropophagus 2* (It 80)
Peter Newton (Joe D'Amato) *aka Absurd. Il cacciatore di uomini* (It / Sp
/ G 80) Jesus Franco *aka Devil Hunter. Cannibal ferox* (It 80) Umberto
Lenzi *aka Make Them Die Slowly / Woman from Deep River. Mangiati vivi*
(It / Sri Lanka 80) Umberto Lenzi *aka Doomed to Die / Eaten Alive / Eaten
Alive by [the] Cannibals / Emerald Jungle / Mangiati vivi dai cannibali.*

——**Safari Movies**   White man going after trophies, ivory, or treasure or
a white hunter protecting or destroying (if his is corrupt) the natural, indigenous habitat are the backbone of these movies which often are laced
with strong doses of romance.

> *The Macomber Affair* (47) Zoltan Korda *aka The Short Happy Life of Fran-
> cis Macomber. King Solomon's Mines* (50) Compton Bennett, Andrew
> Marton. *The Snows of Kilimanjaro* (52) Henry King. *Mogambo* (53)
> John Ford. *Safari* (GB 56) Terence Young. *Hatari!* (62) Howard
> Hawks. *White Hunter, Black Heart* (90) Clint Eastwood.

——**Tarzan Pictures**   A prominent place among the jungle films is held by
the Tarzan movies. As early as 1917, the immortal creation of Edgar Rice
Burroughs was brought to the screen by Scott Sidney under the title of *Tarzan of the Apes.* Credited with being one of the longest film series, a landmark in the Tarzan pictures was *Tarzan the Ape Man* (1932), which
introduced Johnny Weissmuller (1904–1984) in the leading role and fixed his
image as the prototypal Tarzan of the screen. As recently as 1984, the series
was enriched by the inclusion of the British film *Greystoke: The Legend of
Tarzan, Lord of the Apes*, a prestigious production which indicates that interest in the legendary hero is still very much alive. The character of Tarzan
has also inspired a host of imitations and spurious incarnations, including
female counterparts.[56]

> *Tarzan of the Apes* (17) Scott Sidney [Tarzan's 1st screen appearance]. *Tar-
> zan the Ape Man* (32) W. S. Van Dyke II [1st of 14 films (1932-48) in the "Tar-
> zan" film series with Johnny Weissmuller]. *Tarzan and His Mate* (34)
> Cedric Gibbons, Jack Conway. *Tarzan Escapes* (36) James McKay, John
> Farrow, Richard Thorpe *aka The Capture of Tarzan. Tarzan Finds a Son!*
> (39) Richard Thorpe *aka Tarzan in Exile. Tarzan's New York Adventure*
> (42) Richard Thorpe *aka Tarzan Against the World. Tarzan Triumphs!* (42)
> William Thiele. *Tarzan's Greatest Adventure* (GB 59) John Guiller-
> min. *Tarzan the Magnificent* (GB 60) Ray Day. *Tarzan Goes to India* (GB
> / US 62) John Guillermin. *Tarzoon la honte de la jungle* (F / Belg 74) Picha
> (Jean-Paul Walravens), Boris Szulzinger *aka Jungle Burger / Shame of the
> Jungle / Tarzoon, Shame of the Jungle* [animated feature-length
> film]. *Greystoke: The Legend of Tarzan, Lord of the Apes* (GB / US 84)
> Hugh Hudson *aka Greystoke* [1st film in Super Techniscope].

> *Female Counterparts: The Savage Girl* (33) Harry Frazer. *Jungle Girl*
> (41) William Witney, John English [15-part serial]. *Liane – das Mädchen aus
> dem Urwald* (G 56) Edward von Borsoy *aka Liane, Girl of the Jungle. Liane –
> die weiße Sklavin / Liana, la schiava bianca* (G / It 57) Herman Leitner *aka*

Liane, The White Slave. Liane, die Tochter des Dschungels (G 57) Herman Leitner *aka Liane, Daughter of the Jungle. Luana, la figlia della foresta vergine* (It 68) Bob Raymond (Roberto Infascelli) *aka Luana / Luana Virgin of the Jungle. Tarzana sesso selvaggio* (It 69) James Reed. *Mistress of the Apes* (79) Larry Buchanan. *Sheena* (US / GB 84) John Guillermin *aka Sheena — Queen of the Jungle.*

Junk Film *see* **SLEAZY FILM**

Junk Sports *see* **TELEVISION SHOW:** Trash-Sport Show

"Juve" Movie *see* **TEEN MOVIE**

JUVENILE DELINQUENCY FILM (Delinquent Movie, Hoodlum Drama, J. D. Film) A substantial number of youth films (q.v.) deal with delinquency among teenagers. These films form a group by themselves, and have been referred to as a distinct genre.[57] Delinquency among the young is prevalent in modern society, and the movies have broached the subject repeatedly. Rebellious youths have figured mainly in exposé or exploitation films, in films dealing with delinquency in high schools or reform schools, in films dealing with youngsters' misdeeds or with the rivalries prevailing among street gangs competing for power or territorial rights (*The Warriors* [1979] started a short-lived trend in this variant of the J. D. film). Delinquency amongst the young has also been shown in a variety of different settings. At times, it has formed part of other genres, e.g., the motorcycle film (q.v.), or it has been mixed freely with other genres resulting in hybrid products, e.g., gangster/delinquency, musical/delinquency films. *See also* **CRIME FILM: Juvenile Delinquent Films; TEEN MOVIE** and **SOCIAL CONSCIOUSNESS FILM** .

The Mayor of Hell (33) Archie Mayo. *Wild Boys of the Road* (33) William A. Wellman *aka Dangerous Age. Dead End* (37) William Wyler. *Angels with Dirty Faces* (38) Michael Curtiz. *The Angels Wash Their Faces* (39) Ray Enright. *City Across the River* (49) Maxwell Shane. *So Young, So Bad* (50) Bernard Vorhaus. *The Wild One* (54) Laslo Benedek. *Blackboard Jungle* (55) Richard Brooks. *Rebel Without a Cause* (55) Nicholas Ray. *Die Halberstarken* (G 56) Georg Tressker *aka Teenage Wolfpack. The Delicate Delinquent* (57) Don McGuire. *Jailhouse Rock* (57) Richard Thorpe. *The Young Stranger* (57) John Frankenheimer. *High School Confidential!* (58) Jack Arnold *aka Young Hellions. Beat Girl* (GB 60) Edmond T. Greville *aka Wild for Kicks. Furyo shonen* (J 60) Susumu Hani *aka Bad Boys. The Boys* (GB 61) Sidney J. Furie. *The Hoodlum Priest* (61) Irvin Kershner. *The Young Savages* (61) John Frankenheimer. *The Wild Angels* (66) Roger Corman *aka All the Fallen Angels. The Incident* (67) Larry Peerce. *To Sir with Love* (GB 67) James Clavell. *Halls of Anger* (70) Paul Bogart. *Badlands* (73) Terrence Malick. *The Lords of Flatbush* (74) Stephen F. Verona. *The Warriors* (79) Walter Hill. *Bad Boys* (83) Rick Rosenthal.

Juvenile Delinquent Films *see* **CRIME FILM;** *see also* **SOCIAL CONSCIOUSNESS FILM**

KAIJU EIGA (Japanese Monster Picture) In the American film *The*

Beast from 20,000 Fathoms (1953), a rhedosaurus from the Arctic is un-frozen by an atomic explosion and makes its way to New York to wreak havoc on the city. The Japanese were quick to seize upon the idea and in 1954 made *Gojira* about a giant, prehistoric, fire-breathing lizard intent on wrecking Tokyo. An instant success in Japan, it proved equally successful in America when released as *Godzilla, King of the Monsters* in 1956, a modified, shorter version with added scenes featuring Raymond Burr in the role of a reporter chronicling the plunderings of the reptile. Since then, Go-jira has appeared in more than 15 pictures and is responsible for the upsurge in popularity of the Japanese monster genre known as *Kaiju eiga.*

Soon after the release of *Gojira*, the Japanese screens were flooded with a vast zoo of giant monsters of terrestrial and extraterrestrial origin battling over Japan and destroying a few cities in the process. A strictly codified genre, Japanese monster movies are essentially very different from their Western counterparts. They do not horrify, and they proved to be very ap-pealing to Japanese children to whom they are mostly addressed. The monsters have become household pet toys. Besides superstar Gojira/God-zilla, other well-known monsters are: Radon/Rodan (a giant pterodactyl), Baran/Varan (a scaly, giant lizard), Mosura/Mothra (a giant moth), Baragon (a reptile patterned on Godzilla), Ghidorah/Ghidrah (a three-headed flying dragon from outer space), Gamera/Gammera (a friendly, giant prehistoric turtle), Barugon (a copy of Toho's Baragon by the Daiei studios), and a host of other monsters. Most Japanese monster movies fit into the science fiction mold.

Gojira (J 54) Inoshiro Honda, Terry Morse (U.S. version) *aka Godzilla / Godzilla, King of the Monsters* [15 "Godzilla" films up to 1975]. *Radon* (J 56) Inoshiro Honda *aka Radon the Flying Monster / Rodan.* *Daikaiju Baran / Varan the Unbelievable* (J /US 58) Inoshiro Honda, Jerry A. Baer-witz (U.S. version) *aka The Monster Baran.* *Mosura* (J 61) Inoshiro Honda *aka Mothra.* *Kingu Kongu tai Gojira / King Kong vs. Godzilla* (J / US 62) Inoshiro Honda, Thomas Montgomery. *Furankenshutain tai Baragon / Frankenstein Conquers the World* (J / US 64) Inoshiro Honda *aka Franken-stein vs. the Giant Devilfish.* *Ghidorah sandai kaiju chikyu saidai no kessan* (J 65) Inoshiro Honda *aka The Biggest Battle (Fight) on Earth / Chikyu saidai no kessan / Ghidora the Three Headed Monster / Ghidrah / Ghidrah, the Three-Headed Monster / Monster of Monsters / Sandai kaiju chikyu saidai no kessan.* *Daikaiju Gamera* (J 65) Noriaki Yuasa, Sandy Howard (U.S. version) *aka Gammera, the Invincible.* *Kaiju daisenso* (J 65) Inoshiro Honda *aka Battle of the Astros / Godzilla Randon King-Gidorah / Godzilla vs. Monster Zero / Invasion of Astro-Monsters / Invasion of Planet X / In-vasion of the Astros / Monster Zero.* *Gamera tai Barugon* (J 66) Shigeo Tanaka *aka Gamera Versus Barugon / Gambara Versus Barugon / War of the Monsters.* *Daikyaju Gappa* (J 67) Haruyasu Noguchi *aka Gappa the Trifibian Monster / Monster from a Prehistoric Planet.* *Kaiju soshingeki* (J 68) Inoshiro Honda *aka Destroy All Monsters / The March of the Monsters / Operation Monsterland.* *Gojira tai Hedora* (J 71) Yoshimitsu Banno *aka Godzilla Versus Hedora / Godzilla vs. the Smog Monster.* *Meka-Gojira no*

Gyakusyu (J 75) Inoshiro Honda *aka The Escape of Megagodzilla / Monsters from the Unknown Planet / Terror of Mechagodzilla / Terror of Godzilla.* *Gojira* (J 84) Koji Hashimoto, R. J. Kizer *aka Godzilla 1985.*

KAMMERSPIELFILM (Chamber Film)   The Kammerspiele was a small Berlin theater in which Max Reinhardt (1873–1943) directed intimate "chamber plays." Its influence on German cinema resulted in the *Kammerspiel* films of the 1920s, a film style which was a reaction against expressionist film (q.v.), the other concurrent German cinematic style of the epoch. The *Kammerspiel* films deal with the lives and worries of the humble people and present a psychological analysis of their character. The films are set in a simplified, sparse décor with just a few characters, and the overall impression is naturalistic. As in theater, the films kept the three unities of action, time and place. *See also* **EXPRESSIONIST FILM.**
   Hintertreppe (G 21) Leopold Jessner, Willy Hameister *aka Backstairs.* *Scherben* (G 21) Lupu-Pick *aka Fragments / Shattered / Shattered Fragments.* *Sylvester* (G 23) Lupu-Pick *aka New Year's Eve.* *Der letzte Mann* (G 24) F. W. Murnau *aka The Last Laugh / The Last Man.* *Nju* (G 24) Paul Czinner. *Variété* (G 25) E. A. Dupont *aka Variety / Vaudeville.*

Keystone Comedy   *see* **SLAPSTICK**

Kiddie-Movie   *see* **CHILDREN'S FILM**

Kiddie Porn   *see* **HARD-CORE PORNO FILM**

Kiddie-Weepie   *see* **HORSE PIC**

KIDNAP DRAMA   Films involving kidnapping may range from war and spy melodramas to political and crime thrillers to psychological drama, e.g. *The Collector* (1964) and even to offbeat comedy, e.g. *Raising Arizona* (1987). Kidnappings are usually staged to extract ransom from the victim's relatives, firm or professional organization, or they are politically motivated. Quite often the victims of kidnappings are children seized for monetary gain or for family reasons. Less often the victims are young women abducted by sexual deviants and psychotic characters who want to use them for their own purposes, or by disgruntled suitors and frustrated lovers who are seen unfavorably by the young woman's family if not by the young woman herself. In any case, the plight under which the kidnapped victims find themselves offers ample ground for dramatic situations. The kidnap drama fits into the crime, political, or war film genres; however, here they are treated collectively.
   The Man Who Knew Too Much (GB 34) Alfred Hitchcock. *My Name Is Julia Ross* (45) Joseph H. Lewis *aka The Woman in Red.* *No Orchids for Miss Blandish* (GB 48) John L. Clowes. *The Sound of Fury* (51) Cyril Endfield *aka Try and Get Me.* *The Man Who Knew Too Much* (55) Alfred Hitchcock. *Ill Met by Moonlight* (GB 56) Michael Powell, Emeric Pressburger *aka Night Ambush.* *Tengoku to jigoku* (J 62) Akira Kurosawa *aka Heaven and Earth / Heaven and Hell / High and Low / The Ransom.* *The Collector* (US / GB 64) William Wyler. *The Night of the Following Day*

(68) Hubert Cornfield. *The Grissom Gang* (70) Robert Aldrich. *Papa, les petits bateaux* (F 71) Nelly Kaplan. *Etat de siège / L'Amerikano / Der unsichtbare Aufstand* (F / It / G 72) Costa-Gravas *aka State of Siege*. *Nada / Sterminate "Gruppo Zero"* (F / It 73) Claude Chabrol *aka The Nada Gang*. *The Black Windmill* (GB 74) Don Siegel. *Abduction* (75) Joseph Zito. *La Cage* (F 75) Pierre Granier-Deferre. *La città sconvolta: caccia spietata ai rapitori* (It 75) Fernando Di Leo *aka Dirty Deal*. *Katherine* (75 TV) Jeremy Kagan. *L'Orca* (It 75) Eriprando Visconti *aka Oedipus Orca / Prisoners of Passion*. *Rosebud* (75) Otto Preminger. *Snatched* (75) Robert Mitrotti. *The Lindbergh Kidnapping Case* (76 TV) Buzz Kulik. *Sky Riders* (US / Gr 76) Douglas Hickox. *The Squeeze* (GB 77) Michael Apted. *The Kidnapping of the President* (US / Can 79) George Mendeluk. *The Ordeal of Patty Hearst* (79 TV) Paul Wendkos. *Tattoo* (80) Bob Brooks. *The King of Comedy* (82) Martin Scorsese. *Parker* (GB 84) Jim Goddard *aka Bones*. *Streets of Fire* (84) Walter Hill [subtitled: "A Rock & Roll Fable. Another Time, Another Place"]. *Captive* (GB / F 87) Paul Mayersberg. *Man on Fire* (It / F 87) Elie Chouraqui. *Raising Arizona* (87) Joel Coen. *Patty Hearst* (88) Paul Schrader.

Kids' Film   *see*   **CHILDREN'S FILM**

Kinaesthetic Film   *see*   **EXPANDED CINEMA**

Kine, Kinescope   *see*   **KINESCOPE RECORDING**

KINESCOPE RECORDING (Kine, Kinescope, Kinnie, Telerecording) A film record of a live television show or television program before videotape became operational. Kinescope films are made by photographing from the TV tube the images shot by television cameras, thus preserving them for storage or later use. In Britain, kinescope recordings are known as telerecordings. Kinescopes are still in use.

Kinetograph, Kinetophone, Kinetophone Film, Kinetophonograph   *see*   **SHORT**

Kinetoscope Film   *see*   **SHORT: Kinetograph**

Kinkies   *see*   **SEX-AND-VIOLENCE PICTURE**

Kinnie   *see*   **KINESCOPE RECORDING**

Kino-Eye   *see*   **KINO-GLAZ;**   *see also*   **CINEMA VERITE**

KINO-GLAZ (Cine-Eye, Film Eye, Kino-Eye, Kino-Oki) *Kino-Glaz* is the name Dziga Vertov (1896–1954) gave to his theory of objective film reportage in which the camera's goal was to perform better than the human eye in capturing scenes from life. Between 1922 and 1925, he made 23 versions of a newsreel called *Kino-Pravda* (cinema truth) to which he applied his theories. He wanted to capture reality on the spot, but he was not averse to mixing filmed events with stock shots, animation, and montage to achieve the desired effect. His theories are well-illustrated in the deservedly famous *Chelovek s kinoapparatom / The Man with a Movie Camera*

(1928). One of his documentaries shared the name, *Kinoglaz / Cinema Eye* (1924), with his theory that was formulated in a 1922 magazine article. He was very influential among Russian filmmakers and abroad, and he is the acknowledged father of the French *cinéma vérité* movement.

Kinoglaz (USSR 24) Dziga Vertov *aka Cinema Eye*. *Kinopravda* (USSR 22-25) Dziga Vertov [a series of 23 newsreels, no. 1 to no. 23]. *Chelovek s kinoapparatom* (USSR 28) Dziga Vertov; Mikhail Kaufman (photography) *aka (The) Man with a Movie Camera*.

Kino-Oki, Kino-Pravda *see* **KINO-GLAZ;** *see also* **CINEMA VERITE**

Kitchen-Sink Drama *see* **KITCHEN SINK FILM;** *see also* **WOMAN'S PICTURE**

KITCHEN SINK FILM (British Social Realism, Social Realist Film)   Kitchen sink drama was a term much used in the mid-fifties for the kind of British drama which realistically portrayed working-class characters living in squalor or whose lives revolved, literally speaking, around the kitchen sink. It was a slightly derogatory term. The label kitchen sink applies likewise to films, more precisely to a cycle of realistic British films, roughly covering the period between 1957 and 1963, which focussed on the drabness of the daily life of the contemporary working-man.

Woman in a Dressing Gown (GB 57) J. Lee Thompson. *Look Back in Anger* (GB 58) Tony Richardson. *Room at the Top* (GB 58) Jack Clayton. *A Kind of Loving* (GB 61) John Schlesinger. *A Taste of Honey* (GB 61) Tony Richardson. *This Sporting Life* (GB 63) Lindsay Anderson. *That'll Be the Day* (GB 73) Claude Whatham.

KITSCH (Film Kitsch, Kitsch Movie)   Kitsch is a German word that has been widely used to refer to bad taste in artistic and popular cultural manifestations of the arts. Kitsch pervades all aspects of modern life, and it is obviously present in motion pictures. Some biblical epics—*The Prodigal* (1955) and *The Ten Commandments* (1956) for instance—are full of kitsch. Kitsch is related to camp (q.v.), but without the positive connotations associated with the latter which make it an amusing and entertaining experience. Kitsch appeals mainly to unsophisticated and undemanding viewers.

Fighting Youth (35) Hamilton MacFadden. *The Garden of Allah* (36) Richard Boleslawski. *Heidi* (37) Allan Dwan. *The Prodigal* (55) Richard Thorpe. *The Ten Commandments* (56) Cecil B. DeMille. *Attack of the 50 Foot Woman* (57) Nathan Hertz *aka The Astounding Giant Woman / The Giant Woman*. *Blood of Dracula's Castle* (67) Al Adamson *aka Dracula's Castle*.

Kitsch Movie *see* **KITSCH**

Knife-Kill Movie *see* **VIOLENCE FILM**

Knockabout Comedy *see* **SLAPSTICK**

KUNG FU FILM (Chop-chop Film, Chop-'em-Sock-'em Flick, Chopsocky Picture)   An extremely popular genre in the early to mid-seventies, the kung fu films, originating in Hong Kong and later imitated in other countries, came and went as the repetitive and familiar plots of this type of martial arts film saturated the market. Their success in the West may be attributed in part to the extraordinary performances of Bruce Lee, who starred in several films and developed his own style of kung fu (*jeet kune do* or "The Way of the Intercepting Fist") before his untimely death in Hong Kong in July 1973. Another reason for the films' success is their fast-paced action, violent tone, and novelty of approach to the old plot device of an unassuming hero confronting a powerful villain. The essence of the kung fu film resides in the beautifully choreographed combats in which a single hero or heroine faces untold odds and great numbers of adversaries armed with all sorts of unusual weapons — hooks, claws, chains, darts, sticks, clubs, or blades.[58] The plots of the kung fu films frequently center on the theme of revenge, the hero often having to accept reluctantly the task of avenging some injustice or the death of his/her mentor, teacher, family or friends. The way in which he/she undertakes this honorable act of revenge provides the substance for many kung fu films. Kung fu has also been blended with other genres, e.g., Western and horror films. *See* **MARTIAL ARTS FILM.**

Big Boss / T'ang shanta-hsiung (HK 71) Lo Wei *aka The Big Boss / Fists of Fury.*   *Fist of Fury / Ching-v'u men* (HK 71) Lo Wei *aka Chinese Connection.*   *Invincible Boxer / T'ien-hsia ti-yi ch'üan* (HK 72) Cheng Chang Ho *aka Five Fingers of Death / King Boxer.*   *Enter the Dragon / Lung cheng hu tou* (HK / US 72) Robert Clouse.   *The Way of the Dragon* (HK 72) Bruce Lee *aka Return of the Dragon.*   *One Armed Boxer / Dop bey kuan wan* (HK 72) Wang Yu.   *Black Belt Jones* (73) Robert Clouse.   *Cleopatra Jones* (73) Jack Starrett.   *Blood Money / The Stranger and the Gunfighter* (HK / It / Sp / US 74) Anthony M. Dawson (Antonio Margheriti).   *The Legend of the Seven Golden Vampires* (GB / HK 74) Roy Ward Baker *aka Dracula and the 7 Golden Vampires / The 7 Brothers Meet Dracula / Sherlock Holmes and the Seven Golden Vampires.*   *Shao Lin Martial Arts / Hung Ch'uan yu Yung-Ch'un* (HK 74) Chang Cheh *aka Five Fingers of Death.*   *Circle of Iron* (US / Isr 78) Richard Moore *aka The Silent Flute.*   *Game of Death / Siwang yu hsi* (HK / US 78) Robert Clouse, Bruce Lee *aka Bruce Lee's Game of Death.*   *The Big Brawl* (80) Robert Clouse *aka Battle Creek Brawl.*   *The Retrievers* (81) Elliot Hong *aka Hot and Deadly.*   *They Call Me Bruce* (82) Elliot Hong *aka A Fistful of Chopsticks.*   *Police Story / Jingcha gushi* (HK 85) Jackie Chan *aka Jackie Chan's Police Story / Police Force.*   *The Last Dragon* (85) Michael Schultz *aka Berry Gordy's The Last Dragon.*   *Kung Fu: The Movie* (86 TV) / Richard Lang *aka Kung Fu.*   *Best of the Best* (89) Bob Radler.

LABOR FILM (Blue-Collar Film, Proletariat Film, Worker Film) Labor films are mostly nonfiction; however, some films have presented in dramatic form workers' issues and concerns. Worker films focus on worker-management relations, on the fight for better working conditions, on union problems, grievances, strikes and illegal workers. These films may also be included amongst the social consciousness film or the social issue film (qq.v).

Our Daily Bread (34) King Vidor *aka The Miracle of Life. The Angry Silence* (GB 59) Guy Green. *Adalen 31* (Sw 69) Bo Widerberg *aka Ådalen 31 / The Adalen Riots. The Molly Maguires* (69) Martin Ritt. *Joe Hill* (Sw / US 71) Bo Widerberg *aka The Ballad of Joe Hill. Harlan County, U.S.A.* (72-76) Barbara Kopple, Nancy Baker, Anne Lewis. *Alambrista!* (77) Robert M. Young *aka Illegal. Over-Under, Sideways-Down* (77) Eugene Corr, Steve Wax, Peter Gessner. *Baara* (Mali 78) Souleymane Cissé. *Blue Collar* (78) Paul Schrader. *F.I.S.T.* (78) Norman Jewison. *Northern Lights* (78) John Hanson, Rob Nilsson. *Norma Rae* (79) Martin Ritt. *Eles não usam black-tie* (Braz 81) Leon Hirszman, Carlos A. Diniz *aka They Don't Wear Black Tie. Bayan ko-kapit sa Patalim* (Phil / F 84) Lino Brocka *aka Bayan Ko: My Own Country. Comrades* (GB 86) Bill Douglas. *Strike* (GB 88) Peter Richardson.

Lampoon   *see*   SATIRE

Landmark Film   *see*   SEMINAL FILM

Late-Night Movie   *see*   MIDNIGHT MOVIE

Law Enforcement Drama   *see*   POLICE FILM

LAWYER FILM (Courtroom Drama, Courtroom Picture, Legal Drama, Trial Melodrama)   The lawyer, along with the newspaperman, at times leaves his office to carry out investigations and detective work in order to solve a case or to clear his clients of false accusations. More often, however, he is seen in court in his professional capacity as attorney for the prosecution or as a defense lawyer. Courtroom dramas have always held the interest of the spectator; television's *Perry Mason* with Raymond Burr in the leading role is probably the most famous fictional attorney.

The Mouthpiece (32) James Flood, Elliott Nugent. *State's Attorney* (32) George Archainbaud *aka Cardigan's Last Case. Counsellor-at-Law* (33) William Wyler. *Crime Without Passion* (34) Ben Hecht, Charles MacArthur. *The Case of the Curious Bride* (35) Michael Curtiz. *Boomerang* (47) Elia Kazan. *The Enforcer* (50) Bretaigne Windust *aka Murder, Inc. 12 Angry Men* (57) Sidney Lumet. *Witness for the Prosecution* (57) Billy Wilder. *Anatomy of a Murder* (59) Otto Preminger. *Compulsion* (59) Richard Fleischer. *The Story on Page One* (59) Clifford Odets. *Inherit the Wind* (60) Stanley Kramer. *Judgement at Nuremberg* (61) Stanley Kramer. *The Dock Brief* (GB 62) James Hill *aka Trial and Error. The Lawyer* (69) Sidney J. Furie. *Garde à vue* (F 81) Claude Miller *aka The Inquisitor. The Verdict* (82) Sidney Lumet. *Jagged Edge* (85) Richard Marquand. *Suspect* (87) Peter Yates. *The Accused* (88) Jonathan Kaplan. *True Believer* (89) Joseph Ruben.

Legal Drama   *see*   LAWYER FILM

LEGION FILM (Foreign Legion Film)   The French Foreign Legion (*Légion étrangère*) was formed in 1831 in Algeria. It is composed mainly of foreigners because it accepts volunteers of any nationality although the officers are French. (A Spanish Foreign Legion [*Legión española* or *Tercio*] was founded in 1920.) The Foreign Legion has inspired a fair number of films which have used it as background or the main setting for their plots. The Legion has offered refuge to countless adventurers, heroes and villains alike who wanted to bury their past and be forgotten. Above all, they were men of action and hence were well-suited to the requirements of the adventure picture. However, the Legion film is a very distinctive category and is easily singled out from other types of action and adventure films. Besides the United States, France obviously has also contributed significantly to the production of Foreign Legion films.

>　　*Beau Geste* (26) Herbert Brenon. *Beau Sabreur* (28) John Waters. *Morocco* (30) Josef von Sternberg *aka Amy Jolly.* *Renegades* (30) Victor Fleming. *Beau Hunks* (31) James Horne *aka Beau Chumps.* *Beau Idéal* (31) Herbert Brenon. *Le Grand Jeu / La donna dai due volti* (F / It 33) Jacques Feyder *aka Card of Fate / The Great Game / The Full Deck.* *La Bandera* (F 35) Julien Duvivier *aka Escape from Yesterday / La Grand Relève.* *Un de la Légion* (F 36) Christian-Jaque. *Under Two Flags* (36) Frank Lloyd. *Beau Geste* (39) William Wellman. *The Flying Deuces* (39) A. Edward Sutherland *aka Flying Aces.* *¡A mí la legión!* (Sp 42) Juan de Orduña. *Ten Tall Men* (51) Willis Goldbeck. *Le Grand Jeu / Il grande giuoco* (F / It 53) Robert Siodmak *aka The Big Game / Card of Fate / Flesh and the Woman.* *Legion of the Doomed* (58) Thor Brooks. *Marcia o crepa / Héros sans retour / Marcha o muere / Marschier oder krepier* (Belg / It / Sp / G 62) Frank Wisbar *aka Commando / Legion's Last Patrol / March or Die.* *Follow That Camel* (GB 66) Gerald Thomas *aka Carry On . . . Follow That Camel / Carry On in the Legion.* *Il sergente Klems* (It / Sp 71) Sergio Grieco *aka Man of Legend.* *The Last Remake of Beau Geste* (77) Marty Feldman. *March or Die* (GB 77) Dick Richards. *La Légion saute sur Kolwezi* (F 79) Raoul Coutard.

LEGITIMATE FILM (Straight Film)　A term often used to distinguish between films approved by the Screen Actors Guild and those films which are exploitation or independent productions. In the field of sexploitation, straight differentiates between porno and nonporno films, gay and nongay.

Lemon　*see*　**TURKEY**

LESBIAN FILM　Fewer in number than their male gay counterparts, lesbian movies have become more prevalent in recent years. This is due mainly to the relaxation of sexual mores and the work of gay activists and feminists campaigning for women's rights. Past films dealing with lesbian love are scarce and surveys of lesbian films frequently mention *Mädchen in Uniform / Girls in Uniform* (1931) and *The Children's Hour* (1961) as the two main landmarks on the theme of lesbianism. Indeed, except for graphic female couplings in pornographic films where the sex scene amongst women is almost de rigueur, lesbian films were almost nonexistent until the seventies. At present, they have joined mainstream cinema and may portray platonic or physical love and may be implicit or explicit in their depiction of lesbianism. *See* **GAY FILM**.

Mädchen in Uniform (G 31) Leontine Sagan *aka Children in Uniform / Girls in Uniform / Maidens in Uniform.* *Olivia* (F 50) Jacqueline Audry *aka The Pit of Loneliness.* *The Children's Hour* (61) William Wyler *aka Infamous / The Loudest Whisper.* *Kattorna* (Sw 65) Henning Carlson *aka The Cats.* *Les Biches / Les biches-le cerbiatte* (F / It 67) Claude Chabrol *aka The Does / The Girlfriends.* *Therese and Isabelle / Therese und Isabell* (US / G 68) Radley H. Metzger. *Anne und Edith* (G 73) Gerrit Neuhaus (directed by Cristina Perincioli). *Comedy in Six Unnatural Acts* (75) Jan Oxenburg. *Apartments* (Aust 77) Megan McMurcky. *Madame X -eine absolute Herrscherin* (G 77) Ulrike Sander, Sarah Schumann *aka Madame X (an Absolute Ruler).* *Io sono mia* (It 77) Sofia Scandurra. *Maidens* (Aust 78) Jenni Thornley. *A Question of Love* (78 TV) Jerry Thorpe. *Immacolata e Concetta, l'altra gelosia* (It 79) Salvatore Piscicelli *aka The Other Side of Jealousy.* *After the Game* (80) Donna Gray. *Ella une vraie famille* (F 80) Micka Gorki. *Weggehen um anzukommen* (G 81) Alexandra v. Grote *aka Depart to Arrive.* *Bond / Weld* (82) Cathy Joritz. *Egymásra nézve* (Hung 82) Károlky Makk *aka Another Way.* *Home-Made Melodrama* (GB 80-82) Jacqui Duckworth. *Personal Best* (82) Robert Towne. *Lianna* (83) John Sayles. *On Guard* (Aust 83) Susan Lambert. *Dorian Gray im Spiegel der Boulevardpresse* (G 84) Ulrike Ottinger *aka Dorian Gray in the Mirror of the Popular Press.* *Verführung: die grausame Frau* (G 84) Monika Treut, Elfi Mikesch *aka Seduction: the Cruel Woman.* *Desert Hearts* (85) Donna Deitch. *Seventeen Rooms, or What Do Lesbians Do in Bed?* (GB 85) Caroline Sheldon. *Echoes of Past Lives* (GB 86) Cind Oestreicher. *The Mark of Lillith* (GB 86) Bruna Fionda, Polly Gladwin, Isiling Mack-Nataf. *The Passion of Remembrance* (GB 86) Maureen Blackwood, Isaac Julien.

Life-After-Death Fantasy   *see*   **FILM BLANC**

Life of Christ Film   *see*   **RELIGIOUS FILM: Christ Films**

Light Film   *see*   **COMEDY;**   *see also*   **STRUCTURAL FILM: Flicker Film**

Limited Series   *see*   **TV SERIES: Mini-Series**

LIVE-ACTION FILM   The term is used sometimes in contrast to animation. For instance, the Walt Disney Studios have used the appellation to distinguish between animation films and their other productions made with real people or animals and also in conjunction with animation to indicate a combination of both.

Living Cinema   *see*   **DIRECT CINEMA**

LOCAL COMEDY (Native Comedy, Provincial Comedy)   Some types of comedy are too localized to be funny or understood beyond their provincial confines. They do not translate well. Every country has specimens of broad or low comedy for local consumption. These comedies do not require feats of mental introspection to grasp their meaning and appreciate their coarse humor (if you are a local), and they appeal to the great majority who enjoy a guffaw or two. Examples of such comedies are the British *Carry On* series, the Luis de Funès *Gendarme*, or Les Charlots French series, the

Italian films of Totò, or the films of the sometimes duet Bud Spencer and Terence Hill. Comedies of a provincial nature can be cited country by country. They rarely go beyond their national borders, except to those countries which share a common language. French low comedy does well in Quebec, although Quebec native comedy is not equally appreciated in France.

Totò a Parigi / Parisien malgré lui (It / F 58) Camillo Mastrocinque. *Le Gendarme en ballade / Sei gendarmi in fuga* (F / It 70) Jean Girault [6 films (1964-82) in the "Gendarme" series]. *Les Bidasses s'en vont en guerre / Die Trottel von der 3 Kompanie* (F / G 74) Claude Zizi. *Carry On England* (GB 76) Gerald Thomas [29 films (1958-78) in the "Carry On" series]. *Due superpiedi quasi platti / Crime Busters* (It / US 76) E. B. Clucher (Enzo Barboni) *aka Two Super-Cops. Olsen-Banden over alle bjerge* (Den 81) Erik Balling *aka The Olsen Gang over the Hill* [13 films (1970-81) in the "Olsen Gang" series].

Logo *see* **TELEVISION COMMERCIAL**

Long Form *see* **TELEVISION PROGRAM**

Long Play *see* **SHORT: Short Play**

Loop *see* **HARD-CORE PORNO FILM**

Loop Film *see* **STRUCTURAL FILM**

LOST FILM   A term used for a film thought to be no longer in existence. Many lost films have been recovered following searches of garrets and odd places. However, the great majority of old films are irretrievable as their film stock made from a cellulose nitrate base (films made before 1950) is highly flammable and disintegrates with the passing of time.

Lost-World Film *see* **SCIENCE FICTION FILM: Prehistoric Fantasies**

LOVE STORY   Love is the most ubiquitous of themes in literature and motion pictures alike. When it appears openly as the main subject of a film it is called a love story. A love story may be presented with any kind of background or under the guise of any genre. It shows the gradual falling in love, willingly or unwillingly, of its two protagonists, who in spite of themselves are overwhelmed by a sentiment they cannot control and which binds them to each other while it lasts. It very often involves a couple of lonely people who see each other and themselves in a new light. It encompasses the young, the middle-aged and the old because love is not restricted to any age group. If the feeling that drives the main characters in a love story is to move the spectators, it requires an extremely delicate handling on the part of the actors and director of the film; otherwise, the performance may easily sink into mediocrity and wet sentimentality and miss the point of the love story—the presentation of a lofty abstraction in visual, human terms. *See also* **ROMANCE** and **ROMANTIC FILM.**

Broken Blossoms, or The Yellow Man and the Girl (19) D. W. Griffith *aka Broken Blossoms / The Chink and the Child. Seventh Heaven* (27) Frank

Borzage. *A Farewell to Arms* (32) Frank Borzage. *Liebelei* (G 32) Max Ophüls *aka Love Affair / Une histoire d'amour* (F.v.). *A Man's Castle* (33) Frank Borzage. *Peter Ibbetson* (35) Henry Hathaway. *Beloved Enemy* (36) H. C. Potter. *Camille* (36) George Cukor. *Zangiku monogatari* (J 39) Kenji Mizoguchi *aka The Story of the Late (Last) Chrysanthemums. Waterloo Bridge* (40) Mervyn LeRoy. *Le Diable au corps* (F 47) Claude Autant-Lara *aka (The) Devil in the Flesh. Les Amants de Vérone* (F 48) André Cayatte. *Viaggio in Italia / L'Amour est le plus fort* (It / F 52) Roberto Rossellini *aka La divorcée de Naples / Journey to Italy / The Lonely Woman / Voyage in Italy. A Time to Love and a Time to Die* (58) Douglas Sirk. *Dama o sobachkoy* (USSR 59) Iosif Kheyfitz *aka The Lady with the Dog. Un homme et une femme* (F 66) Claude Lelouch *aka A Man and a Woman. Made for Each Other* (71) Robert B. Bean. *Neither the Sea nor the Sand* (GB 72) Fred Burnley. *Una breve vacanza* (It 73) Vittorio De Sica *aka A Brief Vacation. Queen of the Stardust Ballroom* (75 TV) Sam O'Steen. *Griffin and Phoenix: A Love Story* (76 TV) Daryl Duke *aka Today Is Forever. Once in Paris...* (78) Frank D. Gilroy. *The Black Marble* (80) Harold Becker. *Lonely Hearts* (Aust 81) Paul Cox *aka Close to the Heart. Rok spokojnego slonca / Year of the Quiet Sun* (Pol / US / G 84) Krzysztof Zanussi. *Stealing Heaven* (GB / Yug 88) Clive Donner.

Low Comedy *see* **SLAPSTICK**

LOW-BUDGET FILM (Cheap Film) A term used very often to indicate a film made cheaply with a modicum of investment. *See* **B-MOVIE** and **CHEAPIE**.

Low-Budget Production *see* **B-MOVIE**

Lyrical Cinema *see* **UNDERGROUND FILM: Lyrical Film**

Macaroni Western *see* **SPAGHETTI WESTERN**

Machismo Film, Machodrama *see* **MALE-ORIENTED PICTURE**

Mad Doctor / Mad Scientist Film *see* **SCIENCE FICTION FILM: SF Horror Films**

Mad Slasher Film *see* **PSYCHOPATHIC THRILLER**

Madcap Comedy *see* **SCREWBALL COMEDY**

Made-For *see* **VIDEO**

Made-for-Cable TV Movie *see* **TELEVISION MOVIE: Made-for-Pay-TV Movies**

Made-for-TV Movie *see* **TELEVISION MOVIE**

MAFIA FILM The origins of the Mafia date to 15th century Sicily where it started as a secret organization intent on administering its own kind of law and justice. It soon diversified its criminal activities and branched off to America where it was named *Cosa Nostra* ("Our Thing") and was organized into families, each governed by a *capo*. A board of 12 *capos* was to administer it nationally. The Mafia is a very active criminal organization which, besides the United States, Canada and Italy, has manifested itself in other countries where the Italian migrant population is substantial, e.g. Australia and Argentina.

Mafia films are usually included in the gangster genre and perhaps its *magnum opus* to date is Francis Ford Coppola's *The Godfather* (1972) and *The Godfather, Part II* (1974). Hollywood films deal mainly with the American activities of the Mafia, which are sometimes shown as being connected with its place of origin. On the other hand, Italy, where Mafia films are also being produced in significant numbers, mainly deals with the Mafia activities in Sicily and on the Italian mainland. *See* **GANGSTER FILM: Syndicate Films.**

In nome della legge (It 48) Pietro Germi *aka In the Name of the Law.   The Black Hand* (50) Richard Thorpe.   *Pay or Die* (60) Richard Wilson.   *Mafioso* (It 62) Alberto Lattuada.   *Johnny Cool* (63) William Asher.   *Confessione di un commissario di polizia al procuratore della Repubblica* (It 71) Damiano Damiani *aka Confessions of a Police Captain.   Il Boss / Le boss / Der Mafia- Boß-sie töten wie Schakale* (It / F / G 72) Fernando Di Leo *aka The Mafia Boss / Murder Inferno / Il polizotto è marcio / Wipeout!   The Godfather* (72) Francis Ford Coppola.   *La mala ordina / The Italian Connection* (US / It / G 72) Fernando Di Leo *aka Hired to Kill / Manhunt / Manhunt in Milan.   The Don Is Dead* (73) Richard Fleischer *aka Beautiful but Deadly.   The Godfather, Part II* (74) Francis Ford Coppola.   *Perchè si uccide un magistrato?* (It 74) Damiano Damiani *aka The Murder of a Magistrate / Why Does One Kill a Magistrate?   Gente di rispetto* (It 75) Luigi Zampa *aka Carte di rispetto / The Flower in His Mouth / The Masters / Respectable People.   The Executioner* (78) Duke Mitchell.   *Gloria* (80) John Cassavetes.   *Sitting Ducks* (80) Henry Jaglom.   *The Godfather: The Complete Epic, 1902-1958* (81) Francis Ford Coppola [combines *The Godfather* (72) and *The Godfather, Part II* (74) plus additional footage; the television version is titled *The Godfather Saga* (77)].   *Cento giorni a Palermo / Cent Jours à Palerme* (It / F 83) Giuseppe Ferrara *aka A Hundred Days in Palermo / Kill Dalla Chiesa.   Final Justice* (US / Malta 84) Greydon Clark.   *Agent on Ice* (85) Clark Worswick *aka Silent Partners.   Il cugino americano / Blood Ties* (It / US 85) Giacomo Battiato [originally a 4-hour TV miniseries].   *La piovra* (It 84 TV) Damiano Damiani [in 6 parts; followed by 4 sequels (1984-90)] *aka The Octopus.   Things Change* (88) David Mamet.   *High Stakes* (89) Amos Kollek *aka Melanie Rose.   The Freshman* (90) Andrew Bergman.   *The Godfather, Part III* (90) Francis Ford Coppola.   *Goodfellas* (90) Martin Scorsese.

Magazine Film   *see*   **NEWSREEL**

Magazine Format   *see*   **TELEVISION PROGRAM**

Main Feature   *see*   **DOUBLE FEATURE**

Male-Action Pictures   *see*   **MALE-ORIENTED PICTURE**

Male Beaver   *see*   **HARD-CORE PORNO FILM**

Male-Initiation Films   *see*   **MALE-ORIENTED PICTURE**

MALE-ORIENTED PICTURE (He-Man Picture, Man's Picture, Men's Picture) A frequent source of irritation to women feminist film critics, male-oriented pictures are well-entrenched in a variety of genres. They range from male-action films to buddy films, machodramas, and sex exploitation films. Men's pictures, as purveyors of fiction, cater to men's escapist needs in the same way that women's pictures supposedly fulfill women's fantasies and please female audiences. In the field of comedy, a recently ubiquitous subgenre of the male-oriented film is the male-initiation film or sexual-initiation film. These comedies are obviously addressed to adolescent crowds, a powerful box-office constant.

Hellfighters (68) Andrew V. McLaglen. *Chino / Valdez il mezzo sangue / Caballos salvajes* (F / It / Sp 73) John Sturges, Duilio Coletti *aka Valdez Horses / Valdez, the Halfbreed / The Wild Horses*. *Billy Jack* (71) T. C. Frank (Tom Laughlin). *The Last Detail* (73) Hal Ashby. *Brannigan* (GB 75) Douglas Hickox. *Convoy* (78) Sam Peckinpah. *Hooper* (78) Hal Needham. *Steel* (79) Steve Carver *aka Look Down and Die / Men of Steel*. *Murphy's Law* (86) J. Lee Thompson. *Messenger of Death* (88) J. Lee Thompson.

———Male-Action Pictures Male-action pictures, "hardhat" or machismo films make inroads in all sorts of traditional genres: melodrama, science fiction, gangster film and war film.

Too Late the Hero (70) Robert Aldrich *aka Suicide Run*. *A Clockwork Orange* (GB 71) Stanley Kubrick. *Straw Dogs* (GB 71) Sam Peckinpah. *The Godfather* (72) Francis Ford Coppola. *Busting* (73) Peter Hyams. *The Super Cops* (74) Gordon Parks. *The Dogs of War* (GB / US 80) John Irvin. *Bullies* (Can 85) Paul Lynch. *Commando* (85) Mark L. Lester. *Rambo* (85) George P. Cosmatos *aka Rambo: First Blood Part II*. *Die Hard* (88) John McTiernan. *Tango & Cash* (89) Andrei Konchalovsky.

———Male-Initiation Films Sexual-initiation films are very numerous; they encompass both drama and comedy. The theme of these films is usually to get sex at all costs. When the initiation is in the guise of comedy (sometimes these films are referred to as "tits and ass" movies), the humor varies according to individual films from high to very low, but the goal of the youngsters is straightforward and sex-oriented.

The Graduate (67) Mike Nichols. *Goodbye, Columbus* (69) Larry Peerce. *The Last Picture Show* (71) Peter Bogdanovich. *The Summer of '42* (71) Robert Mulligan. *American Graffiti* (73) George Lucas. *Saturday Night Fever* (77) John Badham. *Breaking Away* (79) Peter Yates. *Porky's / Chez Porky* (US / Can 81) Bob Clark [followed by *Porky's II: The Next Day* (Can 83) also by Clark and *Porky's Revenge* (85) James Komack]. *Hot Chili* (US / Mex 85) William Sachs. *Private Resort* (85) George Bowers.

Malevolent Children Horror Films *see* **HORROR FILM**

Man-Made Disaster Films *see* **DISASTER FILM**

Man's Picture *see* **MALE-ORIENTED PICTURE**

Marijuana Film *see* **DRUG FILM: Marijuana Drug Films**

Marital Comedy *see* **SEX COMEDY: Marriage Comedies**

MARITAL DRAMA Films on the unhappily married, dealing with unfaithfulness, marital triangles, adultery, divorce and even murder have been made by the hundreds. Some are just melodramas, women's pictures or soap operas; others are fine drama and may even border on tragedy. Whether centering on the couple's infidelities, on straying wives or murderous husbands, or just on the couple's bickering, these films may all be classed as marital dramas.

> *Cynara* (32) King Vidor *aka I Was Faithful. Strange Interlude* (32) Robert Z. Leonard *aka Strange Interval. L'Atalante* (F 34) Jean Vigo *aka Le chaland qui passe. Dodsworth* (36) William Wyler. *In Name Only* (39) John Cromwell. *Intermezzo: A Love Story* (39) Gregory Ratoff *aka Escape to Happiness / Intermezzo. We Are Not Alone* (39) Edmund Goulding. *All This and Heaven Too* (40) Anatole Litvak. *Easy Living* (49) Jacques Tourneur. *Harriet Craig* (50) Vincent Sherman *aka The Lady of the House. Bachelor Party* (57) Delbert Mann. *Gertrud* (Den 64) Carl Th Dreyer. *Who's Afraid of Virginia Woolf?* (66) Mike Nichols. *Scener ur ett äktenskap* (Sw 73 TV) Ingmar Bergman [in 6 parts; also in feature-length version] *aka Scenes from a Marriage. L'innocente / L'Innocent* (It / F 76) Luchino Visconti *aka The Innocent / The Intruder. A Good Thing Going* (Aust 77 TV) Arch Nicholson. *Mogliamante* (It 77) Marco Vicario *aka Wifemistress. Kramer vs. Kramer* (79) Robert Benton. *Smash Palace* (NZ 81) Roger Donaldson. *The Burning Bed* (84 TV) Robert Greenwald. *My First Wife* (Aust 84) Paul Cox. *The Dead* (GB / US / G 87) John Huston. *A Handful of Dust* (GB 87) Charles Sturridge. *Phobia* (Aust 88) John Dingwall. *True Love* (89) Nancy Savoca.

Marriage Comedies *see* **SEX COMEDY**

MARTIAL ARTS FILM Martial arts films are a very specialized kind of action movie. They expound a philosophy of mental and physical interaction and alertness without which a martial arts expert could not function. The practitioner of the martial arts needs to attain a state of oneness in mind and body to be a successful fighter; and, indeed, training and preparation for the forthcoming fight is a recurrent ingredient of many martial arts films. Although combat between two opponents, or a single man facing several aggressors, features in many film genres, the term martial arts film is better applied to oriental styles, forms and techniques of hand-to-hand fighting, with or without weapons. The forms and techniques used in the art of aggression and self-defense number several hundred; the most readily identifiable to the non-expert is different forms of jiujitsu like judo and aikido, karate, sword-fighting, kung fu, Thai boxing, hapkido, stick fighting, and sumo. The kung fu pictures, the Japanese samurai films and the Chinese swordplay movies best exemplify the genre. Western-made films with fighters employing the techniques of their oriental counterparts also qualify as martial arts films. Very often, recent action-adventure films include some form or other of martial arts expertise; for instance, sumo

wrestling, judo, stick fighting, and hapkido have appeared in James Bond spy films. *See* **CHINESE SWORDPLAY MOVIE, KUNG FU PICTURE, SAMURAI FILM,** and **NINJA FILM.**
Sugata Sanshiro (J 43) Akira Kurosawa *aka Judo Saga / Sanshiro Sugata. Bad Day at Black Rock* (54) John Sturges. *Billy Jack* (71) T. C. Frank (Tom Laughlin). *Kung-Fu* (71 TV) Jerry Thorpe. *Cleopatra Jones and the Casino of Gold* (US / HK 74) Chuck Bail *aka Cleopatra Jones Meets the Dragon Lady / Cleopatra Jones vs. the Dragon Lady. Men of the Dragon* (74 TV) Harry Falk. *Kill or Be Killed* (SA / US 77) Ivan Hall. *Circle of Iron* (US / Isr 78) Richard Moore *aka The Silent Flute. A Force of One* (73) Paul Aaron. *Jaguar Lives!* (79) Ernest Pintoff. *Kill and Kill Again* (US / SA 81) Ivan Hall. *Kill Squad* (81) Patrick G. Donahue *aka Attack Squad. Raw Force* (81) Edward Murphy *aka Shogun Island. Alley Cat* (82) Edward Victor *aka Dragonfly. Forced Vengeance* (82) James Fargo *aka The Jade Jungle. The Karate Kid* (84) John G. Avildsen. *The Protector* (GB / HK / US 84) James Glickenhaus. *Rage of Honor* (US / Arg 86) Gordon Hessler. *Bloodsport* (US / HK 87) Newt Arnold. *Black Eagle* (US / GB 88) Eric Karson. *Angel Town* (89) Eric Karson. *Blind Fury* (89) Phillip Noyce. *Kickboxer* (89) Mark DiSalle.

Massacre Movie   *see*   **SLASHER FILM**

Master Criminal Film   *see*   **CRIME FILM**

Materialist Film   *see*   **STRUCTURAL FILM**

Maternal Melodramas   *see*   **MELODRAMA**

MCTV Film   *see*   **TELEVISION MOVIE: Made-for-Pay-TV Movies**

Meat Movie   *see*   **SKIN FLICK;**   *see also*   **GORE FILM**

Meat-Rack Film   *see*   **HARD-CORE PORNO FILM**

Medical Drama   *see*   **HOSPITAL FILM**

Medium-Length Film   *see*   **CARTOON FILM**

Mega-Genre Film   *see*   **GENRE FILM**

Meller, Melo   *see*   **MELODRAMA**

MELODRAMA (Film Melodrama, Meller, Melo, Melodramatic Film)
Due to the pejorative undertones attached to such terms as "melodrama" and "melodramatic," films are not usually labelled as melodramas. However, several studies have demonstrated the genre's relevance to the film medium.[61] Melodrama, either as a mode or as a full-fledged genre, is well embedded in the film production of most countries. By and large, the great majority of films are melodramas of one type or another, and although at times such films are not readily recognized as melodramas due to the modernization and increasing sophistication of the form, they belong, nevertheless, to this most popular of genres.
The starting point of melodrama as a popular dramatic genre occurred in

the late 18th century as a development from plays that used music to underscore dramatic or emotional moments. Although melodrama has always existed as a dramatic form, it especially blossomed in 19th century France and quickly spread the world over.[60] Since that time, the examples of the genre have been many and have extended from the stage to fiction narrative, to radio serials, film and television (where daytime soap operas continue to be popular).

Acknowledged characteristics of traditional melodrama are a clear-out division between good and evil as well as a clear distinction between hero / heroes and villain / villains, and the notion that good must prevail in the end, even if this is not always a strictly kept rule. There is also a great deal of simplification in the portrayal of human psychological motivation, and story plots are often contrived and artificial. In other words, traditional melodrama emphasized plot and action at the expense of characterization. It may be said, then, that the main object of melodrama is to arouse one's emotions in the most direct way possible. Traditional film melodrama as an extension of stage melodrama is best represented by the films of the silent period, and especially by the films of D. W. Griffith — *The Birth of a Nation* (1914), *Broken Blossoms* (1919), *Way Down East* (1920), *Orphans of the Storm* (1921).

Melodrama, in theatrical or cinematic terms, often conjures up in our minds the kind of acting which was visually expressive in the silent era of filmmaking; that is, acting in which the emotions of the actors were strongly emphasized and stressed by way of facial reactions and gesticulation. This type of melodramatization tended to disappear with the coming of sound to the screen. However, the techniques of traditional melodrama are still the basic components of most film production in third world countries — Arab, Asian, and some Latin American cinema thrive on their implementation.

Besides the obvious division between traditional and modern (contemporary, current) melodrama, the genre may also be sectioned into melodrama of action and melodrama of passion.

Action melodramas, as the title suggests, are found in other genres dependent mainly upon action such as adventure films, crime thrillers, swashbucklers, war films, Westerns and the like. On the other hand, passion melodramas rely not on dynamic action but on a display of emotions, personal relationships and affairs of the heart; they will be found amongst women's pictures (although not all women's films are women's melodramas), in romance or romantic films, in domestic melodrama, in the Gothic film, the *film noir*, and among psychological melodramas.

The Birth of a Nation (14) D. W. Griffith *aka The Birth of the Nation; or The Clansman / The Clansman*. *Rebecca of Sunnybrook Farm* (17) Marshall Neilan. *Blind Husbands* (18) Eric von Stroheim. *Broken Blossoms, or The Yellow Man and the Girl* (19) D. W. Griffith *aka Broken Blossoms / The Chink and the Child*. *Way Down East* (20) D. W. Griffith. *Orphans of the*

Storm (21) D. W. Griffith *aka Two Orphans*. *Chortovo koleso* (USSR 26) Grigori Kozintsev, Leonid Trauberg *aka The Devil's Wheel*. *Sparrows* (26) William Beaudine. *Sous les toits de Paris* (F 30) René Clair *aka Under the Roofs of Paris*. *La Chienne* (F 31) Jean Renoir. *Marked Woman* (37) Lloyd Bacon. *La Bête humaine* (F 38) Jean Renoir *aka The Human Beast / Judas Was a Woman*. *Five Came Back* (39) John Farrow. *Only Angels Have Wings* (39) Howard Hawks. *The Spy in Black* (GB 39) Michael Powell *aka U-Boat 29*. *Crimes at the Dark House* (GB 40) George King, David Mac-Donald (uncredited). *Mr. Skeffington* (44) Vincent Sherman. *The Purple Heart* (44) Lewis Milestone. *The Red House* (47) Delmer Daves. *Easy Living* (49) Jacques Tourneur. *Bonjour Tristesse* (57) Otto Preminger. *La Signora senza Camelie / Corps sans âmes ou La Dame sans camélias* (It / F 53) Michelangelo Antonioni *aka The Lady Without Camellias / Woman Without Camellias*. *Mannequins für Rio* (G 54) Kurt Neumann *aka Models for Rio / They Were So Young*. *Muhomatsu no Issho* (J 58) Hiroshi Inagaki *aka Rickshaw Man / Rikisha-Man*. *Imitation of Life* (59) Douglas Sirk.

——**Domestic Melodramas (Family Melodramas, Small Town Melodramas)**   They deal with emotional situations involving several inviduals, members of the same family, or groups of people interacting with other members of the same community.

Kings Row (41) Sam Wood. *In This Our Life* (42) John Huston. *Cass Timberlane* (47) George Sidney. *Banshun* (J 49) Yasujiro Ozu *aka Late Spring*. *Madame Bovary* (49) Vincente Minnelli. *Clash by Night* (52) Fritz Lang. *All I Desire* (53) Douglas Sirk. *Magnificent Obsession* (54) Douglas Sirk. *Bigger Than Life* (56) Nicholas Ray. *The Man in the Gray Flannel Suit* (56) Nunnally Johnson. *Written on the Wind* (56) Douglas Sirk. *The Tarnished Angels* (57) Douglas Sirk. *The Long Hot Summer* (58) Martin Ritt. *Home from the Hill* (60) Vincente Minnelli. *Splendor in the Grass* (61) Elia Kazan.

——**Maternal Melodramas**   A subgenre of the woman's picture, the maternal melodrama appeared early in cinema history and is found in most film producing countries. It focuses on self-sacrificing mothers who undergo any kind of hardship for the sake of their offspring. *See also* **CONFESSION FILM.**

Way Down East (20) D. W. Griffith. *Stella Dallas* (25) Henry King. *Madame X* (29) Lionel Barrymore. *The Sin of Madelon Claudel* (31) Edgar Selwyn *aka The Lullaby*. *Blonde Venus* (32) Josef von Sternberg. *Pension Mimosas* (F 34) Jacques Feyder. *Stella Dallas* (37) King Vidor. *The Old Maid* (39) Edmund Goulding. *The Great Lie* (41) Edmund Goulding. *To Each His Own* (46) Mitchell Leisen. *Okasan* (J 52) Mikio Naruse *aka Mother*. *Madame X* (65) David Lowell Rich.

——**Modern Melodramas**   No longer relying on melodramatics to reach their audience, current melodramas are sleek and sophisticated; they include glossy productions, biographies mainly of performing artists, stories of terminal illness, and melodramas geared to a young audience.

Love Story (70) Arthur Hiller. *Jacqueline Susann's Once Is Not Enough* (75) Guy Green *aka Once Is Not Enough*. *The Other Side of the Mountain*

(75) Larry Peerce *aka A Window to the Sky*. *Griffin and Phoenix: A Love Story* (76 TV) Daryl Duke *aka Today Is Forever*. *W. C. Fields and Me* (76) Arthur Hiller. *The Gathering* (77 TV) Randal Kleiser. *The Other Side of Midnight* (77) Charles Jarrott. *The Other Side of the Mountain, Part II* (77) Larry Peerce. *Valentino* (GB 77) Ken Russell. *Absolution* (GB 78) Anthony Page. *The Greek Tycoon* (US / GB 78) J. Lee Thompson. *Ice Castles* (78) Donald Wrye. *International Velvet* (GB / US 78) Bryan Forbes. *Chère inconnue* (F 79) Moshe Misrahi *aka I Sent a Letter to My Love*. *A Shining Season* (79 TV) Stuart Margolin. *Voices* (79) Robert Markowitz. *Oltre la porta* (It / Mor 82) Liliana Cavani *aka Behind the Door / Beyond the Door / Beyond Obsession*. *Agnes of God / Agnès de Dieu* (US / Can 84-85) Norman Jewison. *Five Corners* (88) Tony Bill. *Punchline* (88) David Seltzer. *The Kissing Place* (90 MCTV) Tony Wharmby.

————**Murder Melodramas** Under this label fit many suspense thrillers, crime of passion films, period thrillers, films about murderous psychopaths, *films noirs* in which individuals are involved in murder as a result of adultery, blackmail, hatred, or because they are bent on revenge; or they may be driven by cupidity, jealousy, evil, or by a desire to protect their kin and friends.

The Unholy Three (30) Jack Conway. *Payment Deferred* (32) Lothar Mendes. *Thirteen Women* (32) George Archainbaud. *The Kiss Before the Mirror* (33) James Whale. *Crime Without Passion* (34) Ben Hecht, Charles MacArthur. *Bordertown* (35) Archie Mayo. *Kind Lady* (35) George B. Seitz. *Night Must Fall* (37) Richard Thorpe. *Ladies in Retirement* (41) Charles Vidor. *Gaslight* (44) George Cukor *aka Angel Street / The Murder in Thornton Square*. *The Lodger* (44) John Brahm. *Mildred Pierce* (45) Michael Curtiz. *They Won't Believe Me* (46) Irving Pichel. *The Reckless Moment* (49) Max Opuls (Ophuls).

————**Psychological Melodramas** Psychological problems and hang-ups are at the center of the intrigue. Hitchcock's films illustrate perfectly this type of melodrama.

Rebecca (40) Alfred Hitchcock *aka Alfred Hitchcock's Rebecca*. *Random Harvest* (42) Mervyn LeRoy. *Madonna of the Seven Moons* (GB 44) Arthur Crabtree. *The Seventh Veil* (GB 45) Compton Bennett. *Spellbound* (45) Alfred Hitchcock *aka Alfred Hitchcock's Spellbound*. *The Dark Mirror* (46) Robert Siodmak. *Mine Own Executioner* (GB 47) Anthony Kimmins. *Possessed* (47) Curtis Bernhardt. *Caught* (49) Max Ophuls.

————**Romantic Melodramas** They are based on love stories. *See also* ROMANCE, WOMAN'S PICTURE.

Break of Hearts (35) Philip Moeller. *Peter Ibbetson* (35) Henry Hathaway. *Wuthering Heights* (39) William Wyler. *Kitty Foyle* (40) Sam Wood. *Waterloo Bridge* (40) Mervyn LeRoy. *Casablanca* (42) Michael Curtiz. *Now, Voyager* (42) Irving Rapper. *The Constant Nymph* (43) Edmund Goulding. *Leave Her to Heaven* (45) John M. Stahl. *Letter from an Unknown Woman* (48) Max Ophuls. *Abismos de passión* (Mex 53) Luis Buñuel *aka Cumbres borrascosas / The Depths of Passions / Wuthering Heights*. *Love Is a Many Splendored Thing* (55) Henry King. *By Love*

Possessed (61) John Sturges.   *Wuthering Heights* (GB / US 70) Robert Fuest.

——**Tropical Melodramas**   These films present torrid stories of alcoholics, bored wives, trollops, exiles, those fleeing their past, dropouts of all sorts beached in some forsaken place in the tropics—often a steamy hellhole in Africa, Asia, the South Pacific, or Latin America, in puportedly sinful cities like Singapore, Hong Kong, Shanghai, Havana, or Panama which often harbor assorted misfits hoping for a last chance at rehabilitation. Tropic melodramas were popular in the thirties.

Dangerous Paradise (30) William Wellman *aka Flesh of Eve.   Safe in Hell* (31) William A. Wellman *aka The Lost Lady.   Susan Lenox: Her Fall and Rise* (31) Robert Z. Leonard *aka The Rise of Helga.   Kongo* (32) William Cowen.   *Rain* (32) Lewis Milestone.   *Red Dust* (32) Victor Fleming.   *The Narrow Corner* (33) Alfred E. Green.   *When Strangers Marry* (33) Clarence Badger.   *Mandalay* (34) Michael Curtiz.   *The Letter* (40) William Wyler.

——**Woman's Melodramas**   A woman's concern and expectations are the core of the narrative. They include films like *Stella Dallas* (1925, 1937) and *Stage Door* (1937). *See* **Maternal Melodramas** in this genre and the separate entry **WOMAN'S PICTURE**.

Stella Dallas (25) Henry King.   *Back Street* (32) John M. Stahl.   *Stage Door* (37) Gregory La Cava.   *Stella Dallas* (37) King Vidor.   *Dark Victory* (39) Edmund Goulding.   *Back Street* (41) Robert Stevenson.   *Suspicion* (41) Alfred Hitchcock.   *Love Story* (GB 44) Leslie Arliss *aka A Lady Surrenders.   They Were Sisters* (GB 45) Arthur Crabtree.   *All That Heaven Allows* (55) Douglas Sirk.

Melodramatic Film   *see*   **MELODRAMA**

Men's Picture   *see*   **MALE-ORIENTED PICTURE**

Mental Institution Films   *see*   **PSYCHIATRIC FILM**

Message Film   *see*   **SOCIAL CONSCIOUSNESS FILM**

Middle-Age Film, Midlife-Crisis Film   *see*   **FILM ABOUT MIDDLE AGE**

MIDNIGHT MOVIE (Late-Night Movie)   A movie, usually bizarre, controversial, offbeat, or low-budget, shown in a theater which specializes in late-night picture shows. Most midnight movie shows have a cult following and are breeding grounds for cult movies. J. Hoberman and Jonathan Rosenbaum in *Midnight Movies* (New York: Harper & Row, 1983) highlight these unusual films. *See also* **CULT FILM**.

Glenn or Glenda? (52) Edward D. Wood, Jr. *aka Glen or Glenda? / He or She / I Changed My Sex / I Led Two Lives / Transvestite.   Night of the Living Dead* (67-68) George A. Romero *aka Flesh Eaters / Night of Anubis / Night of the Flesh Eaters.   Performance* (GB 68) Donald Cammell, Nicolas Roeg [rel. in 70] *aka The Performers.   Multiple Maniacs* (69) John Waters.   *El Topo* (Mex 70) Alexandro Jodorowsky *aka The Mole.   The Harder They Come*

(Jam 72) Perry Henzell. *Pink Flamingos* (72) John Waters. *The Rocky Horror Picture Show* (GB 75) Jim Sharman. *Eraserhead* (76) David Lynch. *Martin* (76) George A. Romero [rel. in 78] *aka Martin the Blood Lover.*

Milestone Film   *see*   **SEMINAL FILM**

Militant Film   *see*   **REVOLUTIONARY FILM**

Military Comedy   *see*   **WAR FILM: Comedy War Films**

Military Film, Military School Films   *see*   **WAR FILM**

Military Training Films   *see*   **WAR FILM: Training Camp Films**

Minimal Cinema   *see*   **MINIMAL FILM;**   *see also*   **STRUCTURAL FILM**

MINIMAL FILM (Minimal Cinema)   A film made by reducing to a minimum the use of artistic and technical devices. Thus a minimal film tends to avoid or minimize camera movement (e.g., Andy Warhol's *Sleep* [1963] and *Empire* [1963]), editing and, in general, the filmmakers's intervention. It is a form of extreme, plain realism which is primarily found in experimental cinema. *See* **STRUCTURAL FILM.**

Empire (63) Andy Warhol, John Palmer [an 8-hour opus]. *Sleep* (63) Andy Warhol [in 10-minute segments, each shown twice]. *Naissant* (GB 64) Stephan Dwoskin. *Soft Rain* (68) Ken Jacobs. *Un film* (F 69) Sylvina Boissonas *aka A Film.* *1 to 60 Seconds* (73) Taka Iimura.

Mini-Series   *see*   **TELEVISION NOVELIZATION;**   *see also*   **TELEVISION SERIES**

Mixed-Genre Film   *see*   **HYBRID**

Mixed-Media Films   *see*   **ANIMATED FILM**

Modernist Cinema   *see*   **MODERNIST FILM**

MODERNIST FILM (Modernist Cinema)   In the late 1950s and 1960s, new forms of film narrative (e.g., *Hiroshima mon amour* [1959]) which differed from most Hollywood-style films became more frequent on the commercial screens. Roy Armes contrasts these two kinds of cinema — the modern (or modernist) and the traditional.[61] Instead of presenting a linear development of the story following the canons of realism characteristic of traditional cinema, the modernist film combines the power of the image with the increasing sophistication of the modern narrative found, for instance, in the films of Ingmar Bergman, Michelangelo Antonioni, Alain Resnais, Jean-Pierre Melville, Jean-Luc Godard, Alain Robbe-Grillet, Miklós Jancsó, Pier Paolo Pasolini, Walerian Borowczyk, Jean-Marie Straub, and Dusan Makavejev. It is a cinema in which the filmmakers' hints to comprehension are ambiguous — indeed, ambiguity seems to be its most marked feature — and difficult for the viewer to interpret. The later work of some of these filmmakers and others has also been called postmodernist. *See also* **CINÉ-ROMAN** and **NON-LINEAR FILM.**

Hiroshima mon amour / Nijúyokikan no jóji (F / J 59) Alain Resnais *aka Hiroshima, My Love / Twenty-Four Hour Affair.* *L'Année dernière à Marienbad / L'anno scorso a Marienbad* (F / It 60) Alain Resnais *aka Last Year at Marienbad.* *Pierrot-le-fou / Il bandito delle 11* (F / It 65) Jean-Luc Godard *aka Il bandito delle ore undici / Le démon de 11 heures / Pierrot le fou (Crazy Pete).* *Blow-Up / Blow-up* (GB / It 66) Michelangelo Antonioni *aka Blowup.* *Persona* (SW 66) Ingmar Bergman. *Trans-Europe-Express* (F / Belg 66) Alain Robbe-Grillet. *Chronik der Anna Magdalena Bach / Cronaca di Anna Magdalena Bach* (G / It 67) Joan-Marie Straub, Danièle Huillet *aka Chronicle of Anna Magdalena Bach.* *Je t'aime, je t'aime* (F 67) Alain Resnais. *Ljubavni slucaj ili tragedija sluzbenice P.T.T.* (Yug 67) Dusan Makavejev *aka An Affair of the Heart / The Case of the Switchboard Operator/ Love Affair / Love Affair; or the Case of the Missing Switchboard Operator / A Love Dossier / Love Dossier, or the Tragedy of a Switchboard Operator / A Love Story / The Switchboard Operator / The Tragedy of a Switchboard Operator.* *Le Samourai / Frank Costello faccia d'angelo* (F / It 67) Jean-Pierre Melville *aka The Godson / The Samurai.* *Goto, l'île d'amour* (F 68) Walerian Borowczyk. *Teorema / Théorème* (It / F 68) Pier Paolo Pasolini *aka Theorema.* *Égi bárány* (Hung 70) Miklós Jancsó *,aka* Agnus Dei. *Tokyo senso sengo hiwa* (J 70) Nagisa Oshima *aka He Died After the War / The Man Who Left His Will on Film / Secret Story of the 'Post Tokyo' War Period* [subtitled: *Eiga de isho o nokoshite shinda otoko no monogatari*].

Modern Melodrama *see* **MELODRAMA**

Modern Westerns *see* **WESTERNS**

MONDO FILM (Shockumentary)   Well within the definition of exploitation and sexploitation, the "mondo" film is a type of documentary that takes its name from *Mondo Cane* (1961), directed by Gualtiero Jacopetti. It differs from previous documentaries on travel, exotica and primitive peoples by its crude presentation of oddities around the world for the sake of sensationalism. Designed to cash in on a morbid appetite for the bizarre and the unusual, the genre was inaugurated by Alessandro Blassetti's *Europa di notte / Europe by Night* (1958-59) which showed a series of nightclub acts in several European cities. But it was Jacopetti's film and its sequels exploiting sexual attitudes worldwide, tribal customs and erotica, which gave rise to a flood of similar documentaries. They were mostly Italian-made, but other countries also hurried to jump onto the bandwagon and produce their own mondos. Some of the filmmakers of these pseudo-documentaries were not beyond faking some of the sensational sequences, reconstructing incidents or violating privacy in order to secure the footage they required for their films. The trend of producing mondos has continued in Italy to this day where the genre has taken a more extreme form, emphasizing the erotic and violence. *Ultime grida dalla savana* (1975), for instance, contains amateur footage of an unsuspecting tourist leaving the safety of his car to photograph wild beasts and then being mauled and killed by a lion in an African wildlife preserve.

Europa di notte / Nuits d'Europe (F / It 58-59) Alessandro Blasetti *aka European Nights*. *Mondo cane* (It 61) Gualtiero Jacopetti *aka A Dog's Life / Mondo Cane No. 1*. *La donna nel mondo* (It 62) Gualtiero Jacopetti, Paolo Cavara, Franco Prosperi *aka Eva sconosciuta*. *La Femme-Spectacle* (F 63) Claude Lelouch *aka Night Women / Paris in the Raw*. *Mondo cane . . . n.2* (It 63) Gualtiero Jacopetti, Franco Prosperi *aka Crazy World / Insane World / Mondo Cane No. 2 / Mondo Insanity / Mondo Pazzo*. *Le schiave esistono ancora / Les Esclaves existent toujours* (It / F 64) Roberto Malenotti (started by Folco Quilici) *aka Slave Trade in the World Today*. *Africa addio!* (It 66) Gualtiero Jacopetti, Franco Prosperi *aka Africa, Blood and Guts*. *Svezia, inferno e paradiso* (It 68) Luigi Scattini *aka Sweden—Heaven and Hell / Sweden—Heaven or Hell*. *Australia After Dark* (Aust 75) John Lamond. *Ultime grida dalla savana* (It 75) Antonio Climati, Mario Morra *aka Savage Man, Savage Beast*. *Sex O-clock U.S.A.* (F 76) François Reichbach. *This Is America* (76) Romano Vanderbes *aka Crazy Ridiculous American People / Jabberwalk*. *Addio ultimo uomo* (It 77) Angelo Castiglioni, Alfredo Castiglioni. *The Killing of America* (81) Sheldon Renan. *Shocking Asia* (G / HK 81) Emerson Fox. *Africa dolce e selvaggia* (It 82) Angelo Castiglioni and Alfredo Castiglioni. *Dolce e selvaggio* (It 83) Antonio Climati, Mario Morra *aka Sweet and Savage*. *Faces of Death* (84) Rosilyn T. Scott. *Shocking Asia 2* (G / HK 84) Emerson Fox. *Faces of Death Part II* (85) Rosilyn T. Scott. *Mondo New York* (87) Harvey Keith.

Monochrome Film　*see*　**BLACK-AND-WHITE FILM**

Monster Film　*see*　**SCIENCE FICTION FILM: SF Horror Films**

MONSTER MOVIE (Creature Feature)　The term is interchangeable with that of horror film (see the section on movie monsters). However, in a stricter sense, monster movies, as the name indicates, deal exclusively with monsters which have in most cases malevolent intentions and prey on human life and property. Besides, not all horror movies include monsters. There are all sorts of monsters: supernatural, extraterrestrial, man-made, nature-made and god-made. *See also* **SCIENCE FICTION FILM** and **KAIJU EIGA**.

The Mad Monster (42) Sam Newfield. *The Monster Maker* (44) Sam Newfield. *The Fiend Without a Face* (GB 58) Arthur Crabtree. *Gorgo* (GB 59) Eugène Lourié *aka The Night the World Shook*. *The Hideous Sun Demon* (59) Robert Clarke *aka Blood on His Lips / Terror from the Sun*. *El Barón del terror* (Mex 61) Chano Urueta *aka The Brainiac*. *Squirm* (74) Jeff Lieberman. *The Super Inframan* (HK 75) Hua Shan *aka Infra-Man / The Infra Superman*. *The Island of Dr. Moreau* (77) Don Taylor. *Spawn of the Slithis* (77) Stephen Traxier *aka Slithis*. *Alien* (GB / US 79) Ridley Scott *aka Starbeast*. *Alligator* (80) Lewis Teague. *Humanoids from the Deep* (80) Barbara Peters *aka Monster*. *The Evil Dead* (80) Sam Raimi *aka Book of the Dead*. *Basket Case* (81) Frank Henenlotter. *The Slayer* (81) J. S. Cardone. *Of Unknown Origin* (Can / US 82) George Pan Cosmatos *aka The Visitor*. *Q* (82) Larry Cohen *aka Q—The Winged Serpent / Q: Quetzalcoatl / Serpent / The Winged Serpent*. *The Thing* (82) John Carpenter. *Boggy Creek II* (83) Charles B. Pierce [rel. in 85] *aka The Barbaric Beast of Boggy*

Creek, Part II [third in the series, following *The Legend of Boggy Creek* (72) by Pierce and *Return to Boggy Creek* (77) Tom Moore]. *C.H.U.D.* (84) Douglas Cheek [the acronym means "Cannibalistic Humanoid Underground Dwellers"]. *Creature* (84) William Malone *aka Titan Find.* *Demoni* (It / G 85) Lamberto Bava *aka Demons.* *TerrorVision* (US / It 85) Ted Nicolaou. *Cameron's Closet* (87) Armand Mastroianni. *Shadowzone* (89) J. S. Cardone. *Nightbreed* (Can / GB 90) Clive Barker.

Montage Film   *see*   EXPRESSIVE-REALIST FILM

Monumental Film   *see*   EPIC

Moonshine Films   *see*   CRIME FILM

Moral Epics   *see*   EPIC

MORALITY PLAY (Morality Tale)   Some films have been referred to as morality plays (a theatrical term) or morality tales. They are basically allegories focusing on man's eternal dilemma when confronted with good and evil, or they illustrate his struggle in trying to conquer some moral problem or temptation besieging him. Morality tales always warn us about some personified, abstract peril which may endanger our soul or our integrity. Their purpose is frequently religious, doctrinal, didactic, or political, and they present a moral or ethical lesson. *See* ALLEGORY.
The Road to Ruin (28) Norton S. Parker. *Freaks* (32) Tod Browning *aka Barnum / Forbidden Love / The Monster Show / Nature's Mistakes.* *The Treasure of the Sierra Madre* (47) John Huston. *All the King's Men* (49) Robert Rossen. *O Pagador de promesas* (Braz 61) Anselmo Duarte *aka The Given Word.* *Carnal Knowledge* (71) Mike Nichols. *The Devil in Miss Jones* (72) Gerard Damiano. *Des Teufels Advokat / L'avvocato del Diavolo* (G / It 76) Guy Green *aka The Devil's Advocate.* *Wall Street* (87) Oliver Stone.

Morality Tale   *see*   MORALITY PLAY

Motion Picture   *see*   FILM

Motor Racing Film   *see*   MOTORCAR RACING FILM

MOTORCAR RACING FILM (Automobile Racing Film, Auto-Racing Film, Car Race Movie, Car Racing Drama, Motor Racing Film)   Motor racing as a sport comes in many forms: Grand Prix or Formula 1 racing, sports-car racing, cross-country road racing, vintage auto racing, karting, demolition derby, dirt-track racing, stock car racing, off-road racing, hot rod racing and drag racing. They all have in common a race as the basis for a challenge to man and machine. Auto-racing films stress the tension that builds up during the race, and all other happenings such as romance, comic relief, musical interlude, or grief are secondary to the real business of the racers, to compete and win the race. Many car race movies are boring and repetitive, but occasionally an above-average film surfaces and validates the genre.

The Crowd Roars (32) Howard Hawks.   *The Big Wheel* (49) Edward Ludwig. *Genevieve* (GB 53) Henry Cornelius.   *Drive a Crooked Road* (54) Richard Quine.   *Johnny Dark* (54) George Sherman.   *Mask of Dust* (GB 54) Terence Fisher *aka Race for Life*.   *The Racers* (55) Henry Hathaway *aka Such Men Are Dangerous*.   *The Devil's Hairpin* (57) Cornel Wilde.   *Viva Las Vegas* (63) George Sidney *aka Love in Las Vegas*.   *The Lively Set* (64) Jack Arnold.   *The Great Race* (65) Blake Edwards.   *Red Line 7000* (65) Howard Hawks.   *Spinout* (66) Norman Taurog *aka California Holiday*. *Monte Carlo or Bust / Gonflés à bloc / Quei temerari sulle loro pazze, scatenate scalcinate carriole* (GB / F / It 68) Ken Annakin *aka Those Daring Young Men in Their Jaunty Jalopies*.   *Winning* (69) James Goldstone.   *Le Mans* (71) Lee H. Katzin.   *Corky* (72) Leonard Horn *aka Lookin' Good*. *The Last American Hero* (73) Lamont Johnson *aka Hard Driver*.   *Bobby Deerfield* (77) Sydney Pollack.   *Fast Company* (Can 78) David Cronenberg. *Heart Like a Wheel* (83) Jonathan Kaplan.

Motorcycle Gang Films   *see*   **MOTORCYCLE MOVIE**

MOTORCYCLE MOVIE (Bike Movie, Biker Film, Cycle Film, Wheeler Picture)   Subcultures operating on the fringes of society have always aroused a degree of curiosity and a certain fascination. With a few exceptions (e.g., the hippie culture), they have not been portrayed in a consistent body of films. Another of the exceptions comprises the motorcycle gang riders who form part of bike clubs with defiant names like Hell's Angels or Satan's Sadists. Movies have frequently appeared in which the deeds and misdeeds of these "outlaws" have been depicted. Obviously, this type of film is geared to specialized audiences and is mostly played in drive-ins and suburban cinemas; but they form a coherent body of films with a well-defined formula, recurring visual patterns and well-established rituals. In short, they form a distinct genre. The motorcycle gang movie had a precursor of sorts with the excellent portrayal of a rebel youth by Marlon Brando and the equally gripping characterization by Lee Marvin in Laslo Benedek's *The Wild One* in 1954. Then in 1966, the cycle began in earnest with the American International Pictures launching of *The Wild Angels* with Peter Fonda.[62]

There are basically two types of motorcycle movies: the motorcycle gang film and movies just featuring motorcyclists. In this latter category, a variant is lone riders (*Easy Rider* [1969], *Girl on a Motorcycle* [1967]). In these films, the biker (or bikers) is a solitary rider not belonging to a gang, crisscrossing the nation in search of thrills or adventure.

Movies featuring motorcycle racers are of a different order altogether and are better categorized as sports films.

The Leather Boys (GB 63) Sidney J. Furie.   *Girl on a Motorcycle / La Motocyclette* (GB / F 67) Jack Cardiff *aka Naked Under Leather*.   *Easy Rider* (69) Dennis Hopper.   *Evel Knievel* (71) Marvin Chomsky.   *On Any Sunday* (71) Bruce Brown.   *Hex* (73) Leo Garen.   *L'Agression / Appuntamento con l'assassino* (F / It 74) Gérard Pirés *aka Sombre vacances / Act of Aggression*.   *Pray for the Wildcats* (74 TV) Robert Michael Lewis.   *Knightriders*

(80-81) George A. Romero *aka Knights. The Dirt Bike Kid* (86) Hoite C. Caston. *Eat the Peach* (Ire 86) Peter Ormrod. *Cyclone* (87) Fred Olen Ray.

——**Motorcycle Gang Films (Outlaw Bike Gang Films)** These are an important branch of the exploitation film as they thrive on the portrayal of violence and sex and on defiance of the well-established canons of society. In these films, the bikers are usually considered outlaws.

The Wild One (54) Laslo Benedek. *Motorcycle Gang* (57) Edward L. Cahn. *Motorpsycho!* (65) Russ Meyer *aka Motor Mods and Rockers / Rio Vengeance. The Wild Angels* (66) Roger Corman *aka All the Fallen Angels. The Born Losers* (67) T. C. Frank (Tom Laughlin). *Hell's Angels on Wheels* (67) Richard Rush. *The Rebel Rousers* (67) Martin B. Cohen *aka Limbo. The Savage Seven* (68) Richard Rush. *She-Devils on Wheels* (68) Herschell Gordon Lewis. *Hell's Belles* (69) Maury Dexter *aka Girl in a Mini Skirt / Girl in the Leather Suit. Naked Angels* (69) Bruce Clark. *Angels Die Hard!* (70) Richard Compton *aka The Violent Angels. Black Angels* (70) Laurence Merrick *aka Black Bikers from Hell. Chrome and Hot Leather* (71) Lee Frost. *The Jesus Trip* (71) Russ Mayberry. *Psychomania* (GB 71) Don Sharp *aka The Death Wheelers / The Frog / The Living Dead / Psycho Maniacs. Werewolves on Wheels* (71) Michael Levesque *aka Angel Warriors / Frankenstein Meets the Hell's Angels. Stone* (Aust 73) Sandy Harbutt. *Darktown Strutters* (74) William Witney *aka Get Down and Boogie. The Northville Cemetery Massacre* (76) William Dear, Thomas L. Dyke. *The Loveless* (81) Kathryn Bigelow, Monty Montgomery. *Hell's Angels Forever* (83) Richard Chase, Kevin Keating, Leon Gast. *Savage Dawn* (85) Simon Nuchtern.

——**Motorcycle Racing Films** Movies on the subject of motorbike racing have become more prevalent since the 1950s, and some have also included the motorcycle gang motif. Movies featuring motorcycle racing are a subdivision of the sports movie.

Once a Jolly Swagman (GB 48) Jack Lee *aka Maniacs on Wheels. C. C. and Company* (70) Seymour Robbie. *Little Fauss and Big Halsy* (70) Sidney J. Furie. *Sidecar Racers* (US / Aust 74) Earl Bellamy *aka Sidecar Boys. Sidewinder I* (77) Earl Bellamy. *Deathsport* (78) Henry Suso, Allan Arkush. *Silver Dream Racer* (GB 80) David Wickes. *Spetters* (Hol 80) Paul Verhoeven *aka Spatters. Space Riders* (GB 83) Joe Maggot. *Winners Take All* (86) Fritz Kiersch. *Race for Glory* (89) Rocky Lang.

MOUNTAIN FILM (Mountaineering Film) The mountain film revealed itself as a genre in the early twenties; it was especially popular in Germany where, in the late twenties and early thirties, the mountain film (*Bergfilm*) fit in with that country's cult of youth and nature. The mountain film focussed on the outdoors and the pristine landscape. It dramatized the raw, awesome essence of the mountain and its monumental grandeur against which man or a party of men pitted themselves. The mountain had to be conquered by reaching its peak, and the climbers either succeeded or perished in the enterprise. Besides Germany, good examples of mountain films are also found in Scandinavia, France, Italy and other countries.

Das Wunder des Schneeschuhs (G 20) Arnold Fanck *aka Marvels of Ski.* *Die weisse Hölle vom Piz Palü* (G 29) Arnold Fanck, G. W. Pabst *aka The White Hell of Piz Palü.* *Stürme über dem Montblanc* (G 30) Arnold Fanck *aka Avalanche / Storm Over Mont Blanc.* *Das blaue Licht / La bella maledotta* (G / It 32) Leni Riefenstahl *aka The Blue Light.* *The Challenge* (GB 37) Milton Rosmer. *Premier de Cordée* (F 43) Louis Daquin. *The White Tower* (50) Ted Tetzlaff. *The Conquest of the Everest* (GB 53) no director credited. *Victoire sur l'Annapurna* (F 53) Marcel Ichac *aka Conquest of Annapurna.* *The Mountain* (56) Edward Dmytryk. *Third Man on the Mountain* (59) Ken Annakin. *Climb an Angry Mountain* (72 TV) Leonard Horn. *Constans* (Pol 80) Krzysztof Zanussi *aka Constant / The Constant Factor.* *High Ice* (80 TV) Eugene S. Jones. *Five Days One Summer* (82) Fred Zinnemann. *A Breed Apart* (84) Philippe Mora. *The Climb* (Can 86) Donald Shebib. *K2* (91) Franc Roddam.

Mounted Movie   *see*   **MOUNTIE PICTURE**

MOUNTIE PICTURE (Canadian Western)   The Mountie or Royal Canadian Mounted Policeman, that dashing, red-coated, familiar figure, has often graced the screen (mostly in Hollywood-made movies). He has scouted the forests in search of wanted criminals, canoed across many lakes and down rivers, dogsledded through the frozen lands of the Canadian winter, and always got his man. His image appeared early in American films: a one-reeler, *The Cattle Thieves* made by the Kalem Company in 1909, was the first Mountie movie.[63] The American film studios were quick in importing and romanticizing this picturesque character. The end product was a highly glamorized cinematic version in a series of melodramas and romances that were a transposition of the American West to Canada with half-baked ideas of what the Northern neighbor and its Mounted Police were supposed to be. These Canadian Westerns or Mounted movies, although not very numerous in terms of the parent genre, and rather uninspired in their conception, are sufficiently different from most traditional Westerns to form a distinct category.

The Cattle Thieves (09) Prod. Kalem Company. *Men of the North* (Can / US 30) Hal Roach [in 5 versions: English, French, German, Spanish and Italian]. *Rose Marie* (36) W. S. Van Dyke II *aka Indian Love Call.* *Renfrew of the Royal Mounted* (37) Al Herman [first in a series of 8 "Renfrew" films (1937-40)]. *Susannah of the Mounties* (39) William A. Seiter. *North West Mounted Police* (40) Cecil B. DeMille. *The Royal Mounted Patrol* (41) Joseph H. Lewis *aka Giants A 'Fire.* *Northern Pursuit* (43) Raoul Walsh. *Mrs. Mike* (49) Louis King. *The Wild North* (51) Andrew Marton *aka The Big North.* *Pony Soldier* (52) Joseph M. Newman *aka MacDonald of the Canadian Mounties.* *Fort Vengeance* (53) Lesley Selander. *The Wild North* (53) Andrew Marton. *Saskatchewan* (54) Raoul Walsh *aka O'Rourke of the Royal Mounted.* *The Canadians* (US / GB 61) Burt Kennedy. *Alien Thunder / La Tonnerre rouge* (Can 72) Claude Fournier [rel. in 74] *aka Dan Candy's Law.* *Mad Trapper of the Yukon* (72) Tay Garnett *aka The Mad Trapper / Challenge to Be Free.* *Death Hunt* (81) Peter Hunt. *The Dawson Patrol* (85) Peter Kelly. *Cold Front* (Can 89) Paul Bnarbic (Allan S. Goldstein).

Movie *see* **FILM**

Movie à clef *see* **FILM A CLEF**

Movie-for-TV, Movie Made-for-Television *see* **TELEVISION MOVIE**

Movie Monsters *see* **HORROR FILM**

Moving Picture *see* **FILM**

Moyen métrage *see* **SHORT**

Muckraking Film *see* **EXPOSÉ FILM**

Multiple Grind *see* **RELEASE**

Multiple-Murder Film *see* **SLASHER FILM**

Multiple-Reeler, Multiple-Reel Film *see* **FEATURE**

Multiple-Scene Film *see* **SHORT: Multi-Shot Film**

Multiple-Screen Projection Films *see* **EXAPANDED CINEMA**

Multiple Story Film *see* **EPISODE FILM**

Multiseries *see* **TELEVISION SERIES**

Multi-Shot Film *see* **SHORT**

Multi-Star War Musical *see* **WAR FILM: War Musicals**

Mummy Films *see* **HORROR FILM**

Murder Comedy *see* **BLACK COMEDY**

Murder Melodramas *see* **MELODRAMA**

Murder Movie *see* **VIOLENCE FILM**

Murder Mystery *see* **MYSTERY FILM;** *see also* **WHODUNIT**

Muscle / Muscleman Epic *see* **PEPLUM**

Music Clip *see* **MUSIC VIDEO**

Music Film *see* **MUSICAL**

Music Short *see* **SOUNDIES**

MUSIC VIDEO (Clip, Music Clip, Vidclip, Video Clip, Video Music Clip) A comparatively new form, music videos or video clips may be dated from the mid-seventies and their broad popularity dated from 1981 when MTV (Music Television), the first 24-hour music channel, was made available through cable television in the United States.[64]
  Very successful among young audiences, video clips began as promotional devices meant to stimulate the sale of rock music. They soon evolved

into a new art form which offered a training ground for aspiring filmmakers and a new field of creative possibilities to well-established film directors. From an initial length of about three minutes, just about the duration of a song, video clips may now run for over thirty minutes and may include a combination of songs or an extended performance by an artist or group.

Performance videos, the earliest and now less popular type of music video, is more or less a straight performance piece featuring the artist or band in actual or simulated concert conditions. These were followed by conceptual videos (or "concept" clips) in which the song and visuals bear little relation to each other. A third type, the "story" video, integrates closely the plot and music. Obviously, "concept" and "story" videos offer greater possibilities for expression and experimentation than performance videos, and filmmakers frequently use visual images of a fantastic, surrealist, or dreamlike nature to accompany the performer's song. Besides performance and conceptual music videos may be short form, lasting for anything up to ten minutes or long form which may include just one long clip, a compilation or extracts from various clips, or they may consist of a video album made up of a selection of the artist's work.[65] On the subject of music videos and MTV, *see* E. Ann Kaplan's *Rocking Around the Clock* (London: Methuen, 1987).

> *Elephant Parts* (81) Michael Nesmith. *Olivia Newton-John: Physical* (GB 81) Brian Grant. *Duran Duran* (GB 82) Russell Mulcahy; Kevin Godley, Lol Creme, Ian Emes, et al. *Grace Jones: A One Man Show* (GB 82) Jean-Paul Goude. *David Bowie* (83) David Mallet. *Eurythmics: Sweet Dreams— The Video Album* (GB 83) Derek Burbidge *aka Eurythmics: Sweet Dreams.* *Thriller* (83) John Landis *aka Michael Jackson's Thriller.* *Heartbeat City* (84) Andy Warhol, Don Munroe, Timothy Hutton, et al. *aka Heartbeat City: The Cars / The Cars: Heartbeat City.* *Jazzin' for Blue Jean* (84) *aka David Bowie: Jazzin' for Blue Jean.* *Madonna* (84) Steve Barron, Mary Lambert, et al. *Video Rewind— The Rolling Stones Great Video Hits* (84) Julien Temple. *Duran Duran: Arena* (85) Russell Mulcahy. *Iron Maiden — Live After Death* (GB 85) Jim Yukich, David Mallett. *Madonna: Ciao Italia* (88) Egbert Van Hees.

MUSICAL (Film Musical, Musical Comedy Film, Musical Film, Music Film, Song-and-Dance Film, Songfest Film) Clive Hirschhorn in his monumental *The Hollywood Musical,* 2nd rev. ed. (London: Pyramid Books, 1991) describes 1,399 musicals; John Russell Taylor and Arthur Jackson in the reference section of *The Hollywood Musical* (London: Secker & Warburg, 1971) list 1,437 "Hollywood musicals"; both works omit the many low-budget musicals of the forties, the voluminous output of such singing cowboys as Roy Rogers, Gene Autry, Dick Foran, and Tex Ritter, and the occasional sexploitation musical (soft or hard-core) of the late sixties and seventies; this attests to the importance of the genre, if only numerically, as compared to other lesser genres.

The musical emerged in America with the coming of sound to the screen. Its earlier manifestation was in *The Jazz Singer* in 1927, a part-talkie where

Al Jolson sang the famous song "Mammy." It represented a breakthrough and was the beginning of a new genre, indebted obviously to operetta, musical revue and stage musical comedy, but which was soon to become a new art form in its own right. Naturally, what distinguishes the genre is the use of music, song and dance, but these elements are not the prerogative of the musical alone as they may also appear in films of other genres. However, music and song, music and dance, or music, song and dance fuse in this type of film to form a whole rather than simply a lapse or impromptu in a movie's action, and it is this pervasiveness that distinguishes the musical from the picture having occasional songs, musical numbers or dance.

The stages of the musical's evolution can be simplified thus: first there were musical acts in revue form; then there was song in operettas; later on, abstract dance or musical patterns appeared in Busby Berkeley's musicals, followed by dance Fred Astaire-style. Finally, as exemplified in the work of Vincente Minnelli, music, song and dance sought to integrate themselves dramatically in order to propel the story forward and create atmosphere.

The first possible divisions musicals fall into are those of singing only (singing musicals) or dancing only (dancing musicals) or a combination of both skills (singing and dancing musicals). The Jeanette MacDonald–Nelson Eddy or the Astaire-Rogers musicals of the thirties are typical examples corresponding to the first two divisions. The Gene Kelly musicals offer a good example of the mixed singing and dancing category.

Other possible and important distinctive divisions are those of films adapted from a stage musical comedy (a great majority of musicals fall under this category) and original musicals created for the screen.

Trends soon developed into subgenres or well-defined forms: the film revue, the operetta, the backstage musical, the campus musical and the biographical musical.[66]

The Jazz Singer (27) Alan Crosland [1st feature-length part-talkie]. *Die Dreigroschenoper / The Threepenny Opera* (G / US 30) G. W. Pabst *aka L'Opéra de quat'sous* (F.v. 31). *Der Kongress tanzt* (G 31) Erik Charell *aka The Congress Dances / Congrès s'amuse* [German, English and French versions]. *Le Million* (F 30-31) René Clair. *International House* (33) A. Edward Sutherland. *Evergreen* (GB 34) Victor Saville. *Zou-Zou* (F 34) Marc Allégret. *Princesse Tam-Tam* (F 35) Edmond T. Gréville. *Born to Dance* (36) Roy Del Ruth. *It's Love Again* (GB 36) Victor Saville. *San Francisco* (36) W. S. Van Dyke II. *Girl Crazy* (43) Norman Taurog. *Cover Girl* (44) Charles Vidor. *Two Girls and a Sailor* (44) Richard Thorpe. *State Fair* (45) Walter Lang *aka It Happened One Summer*. *Tonight and Everynight* (45) Victor Saville. *Wonder Man* (45) H. Bruce Humberstone. *Easter Parade* (48) Charles Walters. *The Pirate* (48) Vincente Minnelli. *The Barkleys of Broadway* (49) Charles Walters. *Summer Stock* (50) Charles Walters *aka If You Feel Like Singing*. *It's Always Fair Weather* (55) Gene Kelly, Stanley Donen. *Les Girls* (57) George Cukor. *Gigi* (58) Vincente Minnelli. *Expresso Bongo* (GB 59) Val Guest. *It Happened at the World's Fair* (63) Norman Taurog. *Les Parapluies de Cherbourg / Die Regenschirme von Cherbourg* (F / G 64) Jacques Demy *aka The Umbrellas of Cherbourg.* *Let It Be* (GB 70) Michael Lindsay-Hogg. *All That Jazz* (79) Bob Fosse. *Pennies from Heaven* (81) Herbert Ross.

———**Adaptations of Broadway Musical Comedies (Broadway-to-Hollywood Musicals)** Film adaptations of stage musicals form a great majority of Hollywood musicals and are based on Broadway hits. They have been prevalent since the 1950s.

Whoopee! (30) Thornton Freeland. *Show Boat* (36) James Whale. *Too Many Girls* (40) George Abbott. *Best Foot Forward* (43) Edward Buzzell. *Girl Crazy* (43) Norman Taurog. *On the Town* (49) Gene Kelly. *Guys and Dolls* (55) Joseph L. Mankiewicz. *Oklahoma!* (55) Fred Zinnemann. *Carousel* (56) Henry King [1st film in CinemaScope 55 but released in 35mm]. *The King and I* (56) Walter Lang. *Pal Joey* (57) George Sidney. *Damn Yankees* (58) George Abbott, Stanley Donen *aka What Lola Wants.* *South Pacific* (58) Joshua Logan. *The Bells Are Ringing* (60) Vincente Minnelli. *West Side Story* (61) Robert Wise, Jerome Robbins. *Gypsy* (62) Mervyn LeRoy. *My Fair Lady* (64) George Cukor. *The Sound of Music* (65) Robert Wise. *Camelot* (67) Joshua Logan. *Hello, Dolly!* (69) Gene Kelly. *Sweet Charity* (69) Bob Fosse. *Fiddler on the Roof* (71) Norman Jewison. *Cabaret* (72) Bob Fosse.

———**Adaptations from Comedies** The reworking of film comedies into film musicals is not uncommon and some musicals are remakes of comedies and farces.

Comedies	Musicals
The Marriage Circle (28) Ernst Lubitsch.	= *One Hour with You* (32) Ernst Lubitsch, George Cukor.
Three Blind Mice (38) William A. Seiter.	= *Moon Over Miami* (41) Walter Lang.
Room Service (38) William A. Seiter.	= *Step Lively* (44) Tim Whelan.
It Happened One Night (34) Frank Capra.	= *Eve Knew Her Apples* (45) Will Jason.
Ball of Fire (41) Howard Hawks.	= *A Song Is Born* (48) Howard Hawks.
The Shop Around the Corner (40) Ernst Lubitsch.	= *In the Good Old Summertime* (49) Robert Z. Leonard.
Nothing Sacred (37) William A. Wellman.	= *Living It Up* (54) Norman Taurog.
My Sister Eileen (42) Alexander Hall.	= *My Sister Eileen* (55) Richard Quine.
The Philadelphia Story (40) George Cukor.	= *High Society* (56) Charles Walters.
It Happened One Night (34) Frank Capra.	= *You Can't Run Away from It* (56) Dick Powell.
Tom, Dick and Harry (41) Garson Kanin.	= *The Girl Most Likely* (57) Mitchell Leisen.
Ninotchka (39) Ernst Lubitsch.	= *Silk Stockings* (57) Rouben Mamoulian.

——**All-Star War Effort Musicals**   In the early forties wartime musicals were meant to build up morale at home and overseas. These musicals were star-studded extravagances.

Star Spangled Rhythm (42) George Marshall.   *Thank Your Lucky Stars* (43) David Butler.   *This Is the Army* (43) Michael Curtiz.   *Thousands Cheer* (43) George Sidney.   *Hollywood Canteen* (44) Delmer Daves.

——**Animated Film Musicals**   The first American full-length animated film was a cartoon musical: *Snow White and the Seven Dwarfs* (1937). Many of the best animated musicals were produced by the Walt Disney organization.

Snow White and the Seven Dwarfs (37) David Hand (supervising director). *Pinocchio* (39) Ben Sharpstein, Hamilton Luske.   *Fantasia* (40) Ben Sharpstein (production supervisor) *aka Concert Feature* [1st U.S. film in stereophonic sound: Fantasound].   *Bambi* (42) David Hand (supervising director).   *Peter Pan* (53) Hamilton Luske, Clyde Geronimi, Wilfred Jackson.   *Lady and the Tramp* (55) Hamilton Luske, Clyde Geronimi, Wilfred Jackson.   *A Boy Named Charlie Brown* (69) Bill Melendez.   *Charlotte's Web* (73) Charles A. Nichols, Iwao Takamoto.   *The Rescuers* (77) Wolfgang Reitherman, John Lounsbery, Art Stevens.   *The Little Mermaid* (89) John Musker, Ron Clements.

——**Aqua-Musicals (Aquacade-Type Films)**   Esther Williams's swimming spectaculars offer a good example of the type. "By the Waterfall" in *Footlight Parade* (1933), staged by Busby Berkeley, was one of the earliest examples of an aquacade that ran for almost fifteen minutes.

Footlight Parade (33) Lloyd Bacon.   *Bathing Beauty* (44) George Sidney.   *Neptune's Daughter* (49) Edward Buzell.   *Million Dollar Mermaid* (52) Mervyn LeRoy *aka The One-Piece Bathing Suit*.   *Easy to Love* (53) Charles Walters.

——**Backstage Musicals**   One of the earliest manifestations of the musical, they were very prolific and very American. The plot consists in "putting-on-the-show." *See also* **Busby Berkeley Musical Extravagances**.

The Broadway Melody (29) Harry Beaumont.   *42nd Street* (33) Lloyd Bacon *aka Forty-Second Street*.   *On the Avenue* (37) Roy Del Ruth.   *You Can't Have Everything* (37) Norman Taurog.   *Dance, Girl Dance* (40) Dorothy Arzner.   *Footlight Serenade* (42) Gregory Ratoff.   *The Band Wagon* (53) Vincente Minnelli *aka I Love Louise*.   *Kiss Me Kate* (53) George Sidney.

——**Ballet Films**   Films that are connected with ballet or in which ballet is the subject but which are not outright filmed ballet fall under the category of musicals. Ballet sequences have featured in many Hollywood musicals, e.g., *The Goldwyn Follies* (1938), *An American in Paris* (1951) and *Hans Christian Andersen* (1952). *See also* **BALLET FILM**.

The Goldwyn Follies (38) George Marshall.   *The Red Shoes* (GB 48) Michael Powell, Emeric Pressburger.   *An American in Paris* (51) Vincente Minnelli.   *Hans Christian Andersen* (52) Charles Vidor.   *Invitation to the Dance* (52) Gene Kelly, Stanley Donen [rel. in 57].   *The Tales of Beatrix Potter* (GB 71) Reginald Mills *aka Peter Rabbit and Tales of Beatrix Potter* [1st original feature-length ballet film]. *Don Quixote* (Aust 72) Rudolph Nureyev, Robert Helpmann.

——**Black Musicals**   Musicals with an all-black or predominantly black cast. *Hallelujah!* (29) King Vidor [1st all-black feature-length talking picture]. *Hearts in Dixie* (29) Paul Sloane. *Song of Freedom* (GB 36) J. Elder Wills. *Paradise in Harlem* (39) Joseph Seiden. *Way Down South* (39) Bernard Vorhaus. *Cabin in the Sky* (42) Vincente Minnelli. *Stormy Weather* (43) Andrew L. Stone. *Reet, Petite, and Gone* (47) William Forest Crouch. *Carmen Jones* (54) Otto Preminger. *Porgy and Bess* (59) Otto Preminger. *Lost in the Stars* (73) Daniel Mann.

——**Borderline Musicals**   Films with some musical content but in which other ingredients predominate and thus they cannot be thought of as full-fledged musicals. Clive Hirschhorn names them "fringe" musicals and lists 198 of them (Hirschhorn's *The Hollywood Musical*, pp. 440–46).
Blonde Venus (32) Josef von Sternberg. *The Devil's Brother* (32) Hal Roach, Charles R. Rogers *aka Fra Diavolo*. *Night World* (32) Hobart Henley. *Cavalcade* (33) Frank Lloyd. *Lady of Burlesque* (43) William Wellman *aka Striptease Lady*. *A Foreign Affair* (48) Billy Wilder. *The Paleface* (48) Norman Z. McLeod. *The Country Girl* (54) George Seaton. *I'll Cry Tomorrow* (55) Daniel Mann. *Some Like It Hot* (59) Billy Wilder. *The Ladies' Man* (61) Jerry Lewis. *Bound for Glory* (76) Hal Ashby.

——**Busby Berkeley Musical Extravagances**   The trademark of these musicals was the big song and dance production numbers with dozens of chorus-girls forming abstract patterns of beautiful groupings, all of which take place in huge settings (although the plot-line pretended that it took place on a limited theater stage). The Busby Berkeley (1895–1976) musicals revitalized the genre and rescued it from the doldrums.
Whoopee! (30) Thornton Freeland. *Footlight Parade* (33) Lloyd Bacon. *42nd Street* (33) Lloyd Bacon *aka Forty-Second Street*. *Gold Diggers of 1933* (33) Mervyn LeRoy *aka High Life*. *Roman Scandals* (33) Frank Tuttle. *Dames* (34) Ray Enright. *Fashions of 1934* (34) William Dieterle *aka Fashions / Fashion Follies of 1934*. *Gold Diggers of 1935* (35) Busby Berkeley. *Take Me Out to the Ball Game* (49) Busby Berkeley *aka Everybody's Cheering*.

——**Campus Musicals (College Campus Musicals, College Musicals)**   With the film revue, the backstage musical, and the operetta, this is one of the earliest forms of the musical. It concentrated on the activities of youngters in and around colleges.
So This Is College (29) Sam Wood. *College Humor* (33) Wesley Ruggles. *Pigskin Parade* (36) David Butler. *Varsity Show* (37) William Keighley. *College Swing* (38) Raoul Walsh *aka Swing, Teacher, Swing*. *Hold That Co-ed* (38) George Marshall *aka Hold That Girl*. *Start Cheering* (38) Albert S. Rogell. *Too Many Girls* (40) George Abbott. *Good News* (47) Charles Walters. *The Affairs of Dobie Gillis* (53) Don Weis.

——**Children's Fantasy Musicals**   Made for the delight of children and adults alike, these films, in which children always have a prominent role in fairyland adventures, plunge us into a world of fantasy.

The Wizard of Oz (39) Victor Fleming, King Vidor, Richard Thorpe, George Cukor. *The Pied Piper of Hamelin* (57 TV) Bretaigne Windust. *tom thumb* (GB 58) George Pal. *Mary Poppins* (64) Robert Stevenson. *Bedknobs and Broomsticks* (71) Robert Stevenson. *Tom Sawyer* (73) Don Taylor. *The Little Prince* (GB 74) Stanley Donen. *The Muppet Movie* (GB / US 79) James Frawley.

———**Child-Star Musicals**   The child performer, whether a tot or a teenager, has always formed part of show business. These pictures were ideally suited for family entertainment.

Shirley Temple: Little Miss Marker (34) Alexander Hall *aka Girl in Pawn*. *Curly Top* (35) Irving Cummings. *Captain January* (36) David Butler. *Deanna Durbin: Three Smart Girls* (36) Henry Koster. *One Hundred Men and a Girl* (37) Henry Koster. *Mad About Music* (38) Norman Taurog. *Judy Garland: Pigskin Parade* (36) David Butler. *Broadway Melody of 1938* (37) Roy Del Ruth. *The Wizard of Oz* (39) Victor Fleming. *Judy Garland, Mickey Rooney: Thoroughbreds Don't Cry* (37) Alfred E. Green. *Love Finds Andy Hardy* (38) George B. Seitz. *Babes in Arms* (39) Busby Berkeley. *Gloria Jean: The Underpup* (39) Richard Wallace. *If I Had My Way* (40) David Butler. *A Little Bit of Heaven* (40) Andrew Marston.

———**Comedy Musicals**   The comedy element is present in many musicals. Comedy musicals include all types of comedies, oddball, romps, farces. *See also* **Musical Comedy.**

I'm No Angel (33) Wesley Ruggles. *She Done Him Wrong* (33) Lowell Sherman *aka Diamond Lili / Ruby Red*. *The Bohemian Girl* (36) James W. Horne, Charles R. Rogers. *At the Circus* (39) Edward Buzzell *aka Marx Brothers at the Circus*. *Hellzapoppin'* (41) H. C. Potter. *Road to Utopia* (44) Hal Walker [rel. in 46]. *The Perils of Pauline* (47) George Marshall. *The Inspector General* (49) Henry Koster. *The Girl Can't Help It* (57) Frank Tashlin. *A Funny Thing Happened on the Way to the Forum* (66) Richard Lester. *The Blues Brothers* (80) John Landis. *Victor / Victoria* (GB / US 82) Blake Edwards.

———**Courtship-Romance Musicals (Dance Musicals, Musical Romances)** Dance as a primary element of courtship characterizes these film musicals. The best examples are found in the 1930s films of the duo Fred Astaire (1899–1987) and Ginger Rogers.

Flying Down to Rio (33) Thornton Freeland. *The Gay Divorcée* (34) Mark Sandrich *aka The Gay Divorce*. *Top Hat* (35) Mark Sandrich. *Follow the Fleet* (36) Mark Sandrich. *Swing Time* (36) George Stevens. *A Damsel in Distress* (37) George Stevens. *Shall We Dance?* (37) Mark Sandrich. *Carefree* (38) Mark Sandrich. *You Were Never Lovelier* (42) William A. Seiter. *Neptune's Daughter* (49) Edward Buzzell. *Royal Wedding* (51) Stanley Donen *aka Wedding Bells*. *Funny Face* (57) Stanley Donen.

———**Exotic Locale Musicals**   A trend prevalent at the Fox studios in the forties of placing the action of musicals in exotic locations.

Argentine Nights (40) Albert S. Rogell. *Down Argentine Way* (40) Irving Cummings. *That Night in Rio* (41) Irving Cummings. *Week-End in Havana* (41) Walter Lang. *Springtime in the Rockies* (42) Irving Cummings.

———**Film Revues (All-Star Movie Revues, Musical Revues)** One of the earliest forms the musical took. They consisted mostly of filmed musical shows made up of sketches or numbers and in which the stars abounded. *Glorifying the American Girl* (29) Millard Webb, John Harkrider. *The Hollywood Revue of 1929* (29) Charles F. Riesner. *The Show of Shows* (29) John G. Adolfi. *The King of Jazz* (30) John Murray Anderson. *Paramount on Parade* (30) Dorothy Arzner, Otto Brower, Edmund Goulding, Victor Heerman, Edwin Knopf, Rowland V. Lee, Ernst Lubitsch, Lothar Mendes, Victor Schertzinger, A. Edward Sutherland, Frank Tuttle. *Ziegfeld Follies* (44-45) Vincente Minnelli.

———**Ice-Skating Musicals** Obviously the forte in these musicals were the ballet-on-ice sequences or ice-shows. Sonja Henie (1912–69) starred in several of these minor musicals. *One in a Million* (36) Sidney Lanfield. *Thin Ice* (37) Sidney Lanfield. *Happy Landing* (38) Roy Del Ruth. *Ice Follies of 1939* (39) Reinhold Schunzel. *Sun Valley Serenade* (41) H. Bruce Humberstone. *Ice-Capades Revue* (42) Bernard Vorhaus *aka Rhythm Hits the Ice*. *Silver Skates* (43) Leslie Goodwins. *Hans Brinker* (79) Robert Scheerer *aka Hans Brinker and [of] the Silver Skates / The Silver Skates*.

———**Musical Biography (Biopics)** Another popular form of the musical is the biography, mostly of composers, musicians, singers, or impresarios. The fictional element is so strong in some of these biographical musicals that they bear no reality to the actual facts of the musician's life. *The Great Ziegfeld* (36) Robert Z. Leonard. *The Great Waltz* (38) Julien Duvivier. *The Story of Vernon & Irene Castle* (39) H. C. Potter. *My Gal Sal* (42) Irving Cummings. *Yankee Doodle Dandy* (42) Michael Curtiz. *Dixie* (43) A. Edward Sutherland. *Rhapsody in Blue* (45) Irving Rapper. *The Jolson Story* (46) Alfred E. Green. *Mother Wore Tights* (47) Walter Lang. *The Perils of Pauline* (47) George Marshall. *Three Little Words* (50) Richard Thorpe. *With a Song in My Heart* (52) Walter Lang. *Interrupted Melody* (55) Curtis Bernhardt. *Love Me or Leave Me* (55) Charles Vidor. *The Seven Little Foys* (55) Melville Shavelson. *The Joker Is Wild* (57) Charles Vidor *aka All the Way*. *Gypsy* (62) Mervyn LeRoy. *Funny Girl* (68) William Wyler. *Leadbelly* (76) Gordon Parks. *American Hot Wax* (78) Floyd Mutrux. *The Buddy Holly Story* (78) Steve Rash. *Elvis!* (79 TV) John Carpenter *aka Elvis, the Movie*. *Coal Miner's Daughter* (80) Michael Apted.

———**Musical Comedy (Musicomedy)** Musical comedy is a theatrical term for a show that includes songs, dance, dramatic content and usually spoken dialogue. Here the term is used to group together films that tend to be light-hearted, different from musical dramas which emphasize the dramatic. A great many screen musical comedies have been adaptations from stage musicals. *Diplomaniacs* (33) William A. Seiter. *Hallelujah I'm a Bum* (33) Lewis Milestone *aka Hallelujah I'm a Tramp / The Heart of New York*. *Roman Scandals* (33) Frank Tuttle. *Kid Millions* (34) Roy Del Ruth. *Broadway Melody of 1936* (35) Roy Del Ruth. *Thanks a Million* (35) Roy Del Ruth. *You'll Never Get Rich* (41) Sidney Lanfield. *Holiday Inn* (42) Mark Sandrich.

DuBarry Was a Lady (43) Roy Del Ruth.   *Boy! What a Girl* (46) Arthur Leonard.   *Here Comes the Groom* (51) Frank Capra.   *Gentlemen Prefer Blondes* (53) Howard Hawks.   *The Court Jester* (56) Norman Panama.   *The Pajama Game* (57) George Abbott, Stanley Donen.   *Bye Bye Birdie* (63) George Sidney.   *The Unsinkable Molly Brown* (64) Charles Walters.   *How to Succeed in Business Without Really Trying* (67) David Swift.   *Head* (68) Bob Rafelson.   *1776* (72) Peter H. Hunt.   *Grease* (78) Randal Kleiser.   *Starstruck* (Aust 81) Gillian Armstrong *aka Starstruck – The Road to Fame*. *Little Shop of Horrors* (86) Frank Oz.   *Earth Girls Are Easy* (89) Julien Temple.   *Cry-Baby* (90) John Waters.   *House Party* (90) Reginald Hudlin.

——**Musical Drama**   Film musicals which include dramatic content as well as music, dance, song or a combination of any of these elements may be categorized as musical dramas.

They Shall Have Music (39) Archie Mayo *aka Melody of Youth*.   *New Moon* (40) Robert Z. Leonard.   *Orchestra Wives* (42) Archie Mayo.   *Jolson Sings Again* (49) Henry Levin.   *Young Man with a Horn* (50) Michael Curtiz *aka Young Man of Music*.   *The Jazz Singer* (53) Michael Curtiz.   *Young at Heart* (54) Gordon Douglas.   *Love Me or Leave Me* (55) Charles Vidor.   *The Kind and I* (56) Walter Lang.   *Jailhouse Rock* (57) Richard Thorpe.   *King Creole* (58) Michael Curtiz.   *Never Steal Anything Small* (59) Charles Lederer.   *Paris Blues* (61) Martin Ritt.   *The Sound of Music* (65) Robert Wise.   *Oliver!* (GB 68) Carol Reed.   *Cabaret* (72) Bob Fosse.   *The Harder They Come* (Jam 73) Perry Henzell.   *Mr. Quilp* (GB 75) Michael Tuchner *aka The Old Curiosity Shop*.   *Sparkle* (76) Sam O'Steen.   *Honeysuckle Rose* (80) Jerry Schatzberg *aka On the Road Again*.   *Flashdance* (83) Adrian Lyne.   *Footloose* (84) Herbert Ross.   *Songwriter* (84) Alan Rudolph.   *Streets of Fire* (84) Walter Hill.   *Sunday in the Park with George* (86) James Lapine.   *La Bamba* (87) Luis Valdez.

——**Musical Fantasy**   These musicals are permeated with fantasy situations or characters (ghost villages, leprechauns, psychic powers), and sometimes there is also a great deal of romance. *See also* **Children's Fantasy Musicals**.

Just Imagine (30) David Butler.   *Where Do We Go from Here?* (45) Gregory Ratoff.   *A Connecticut Yankee in King Arthur's Court* (48) Tay Garnett.   *The 5,000 Fingers of Dr. T* (53) Roy Rowland.   *Brigadoon* (54) Vincente Minnelli.   *Li'l Abner* (59) Melvin Frank.   *Finian's Rainbow* (68) Francis Ford Coppola.   *On a Clear Day You Can See Forever* (69) Vincente Minnelli.

——**Musical Westerns**   This heading includes all musicals with a Western setting, and thus it would also comprise the vast output of the various singing cowboys that is usually excluded or overlooked by compilers of musical and western filmographies. The musical Western also includes comedies, satires, and parodies with a western background. *See also* **WESTERN**.

The Gay Desperado (36) Rouben Mamoulian.   *The Harvey Girls* (45) George Sidney.   *Annie Get Your Gun* (49) George Sidney.   *Calamity Jane* (53) David Butler.   *Red Garters* (54) George Marshall.   *Paint Your Wagon* (69) Joshua Logan.   *Zachariah* (70) George Englund.

——**Opera Films**   Films in which opera (or an opera singer) is the subject matter, but which are not in themselves outright filmed operas. *See* **OPERA FILM**.

Die 3-Groschen-Oper / The Threepenny Opera (G / US 30) G. W. Pabst *aka L'Opéra de quat'sous* (F.v. 31) / *The Threepenny Opera*. *One Night of Love* (34) Victor Schertzinger. *The Great Caruso* (50) Richard Thorpe. *Tales of Hoffman* (GB 51) Michael Powell, Emeric Pressburger. *Carmen Jones* (54) Otto Preminger. *Yes, Giorgio* (82) Franklin J. Schaffner.

——**Operettas** Inspired by stage operetta, they vary in tone and mood; the two main kinds are light operettas (farcical or satirical) and romantic operettas or romances. Operettas are one of the earliest forms of the musical.

The Love Parade (29) Ernst Lubitsch *aka Parade d'amour* (F.v.). *Love Me Tonight* (32) Rouben Mamoulian. *One Hour with You* (32) Ernst Lubitsch. *Bitter Sweet* (GB 33) Herbert Wilcox. *The Merry Widow* (34) Ernst Lubitsch *aka The Lady Dances / La veuve joyeuse* (F.v.). *Naughty Marietta* (35) W. S. Van Dyke II. *The Bohemian Girl* (36) James Horne. *Rose Marie* (36) W. S. Van Dyke II *aka Indian Love Call*. *Maytime* (37) Robert Z. Leonard. *The Mikado* (GB 38) Victor Schertzinger. *Bitter Sweet* (40) W. S. Van Dyke II. *The Merry Widow* (52) Curtis Bernhardt. *Rose Marie* (54) Mervyn LeRoy. *The Pirates of Penzance* (GB 82) Willford Leach.

——**Original Hollywood Musicals** Originally written for the screen rather than an adaptation from the stage.

Sunny Side Up (29) David Butler. *Meet Me in St. Louis* (44) Vincente Minnelli. *An American in Paris* (51) Vincente Minnelli. *Singin' in the Rain* (52) Stanley Donen, Gene Kelly. *Lili* (53) Charles Walters. *Seven Brides for Seven Brothers* (54) Stanley Donen *aka Sobbin' Women*.

——**Parodies** *see* **PARODY** for a definition of the form.

Thoroughly Modern Millie (67) George Roy Hill. *The Boy Friend* (GB 71) Ken Russell *aka The Boyfriend*. *Phantom of the Paradise* (74) Brian DePalma *aka Phantom / Phantom of the Filmore*. *At Long Last Love* (75) Peter Bogdanovich. "Baxter's Beauties of 1933" in *Movie Movie* (78) Stanley Donen.

——**Pop Musicals** Starting in the fifties, a series of films concentrated on popular music – rock 'n' roll, the twist or calypso. This section also includes the "Beach Party" movie musicals. For the "Beach Party" movies, *see* **TEEN MOVIE**.

Don't Knock the Rock (56) Fred F. Sears. *The Big Beat* (57) Will Cowan. *Calypso Joe* (57) Edward Dein. *Jamboree* (57) Roy Lockwood *aka Disk Jockey Jamboree*. *Don't Knock the Twist* (62) Oscar Rudolph. *Beach Party* (63) William Asher. *Winter à Go-Go* (65) Richard Benedict. *That Tennessee Beat* (66) Richard Brill *aka The Tennessee Beat*. *Wild, Wild Winter* (66) Lennie Weinrib. *Payday* (72) Daryl Duke.

——**Rock Concert Films (Concert Film, Rock-Concert Documentary, Rock Doc)** They fall under the category of documentaries and are a permanent record of the actual performance or happening in which folk or rock music is played to its audience, either in the open air or in enclosed locales. *See also* **ROCK FILM**.

Monterey Pop (67) James Desmond, Barry Feinstein, D. A. Pennebaker, Albert Maysles, Roger Murphy, Richard Leacock, Nick Proferes.   *Gimme Shelter* (70) David Maysles, Albert Maysles, Charlotte Zwerin.   *Woodstock* (70) Michael Wadleigh.   *Joe Cocker: Mad Dogs and Englishmen* (GB 71) Pierre Adidge *aka Mad Dogs and Englishmen*.   *Les Pink Floyd à Pompeï* (F / Belg / G 71) Adrian Maben *aka Pink Floyd at Pompeii / Pink Floyd Live at Pompeii*.   *The Concert for Bangladesh* (72) Saul Swimmer.   *Divine Madness!* (80) Michael Ritchie.   *No Nukes* (80) Danny Goldberg, Anthony Potenza, Julian Schlossberg *aka The MUSE Concert: No Nukes*.   *Stop Making Sense* (84) Jonathan Demme.   *Chuck Berry Hail! Hail! Rock 'n' Roll* (87) Taylor Hackford.   *Sign O' the Times* (87) Prince.   *U2: Rattle and Hum* (88) Phil Joanou.

——**Rock Operas (Rock Opera Movies)**   Operatic style musicals set to rock with modern or controversial transpositions of religious figures, literary masterpieces, or pop-culture heroes.

Catch My Soul (73) Patrick McGoohan *aka Santa Fe Satan*.   *Jesus Christ Superstar* (73) Norman Jewison.   *The Rocky Horror Picture Show* (GB 75) Jim Sharman.   *Tommy* (GB 75) Ken Russell.

——**Star Vehicles**   These musicals are associated with the star that appears in them. The star is the main asset in the film's promotion as it is the star, not the film, that the audiences want and pay to see. Star vehicles are a very old trend, as Hollywood studios sought to promote and build up the star quality of the stars that they held under contract.

Bing Crosby: *Going My Way* (44) Leo McCarey.   Deanna Durbin: *100 Men and a Girl* (36) Henry Koster *aka One Hundred Men and a Girl*.   Betty Grable: *Down Argentina Way* (40) Irving Cummings.   Danny Kaye: *Wonder Man* (44) H. Bruce Humberstone.   Mario Lanza: *The Great Caruso* (50) Richard Thorpe.   Ethel Merman: *Call Me Madam* (53) Walter Lang.   Elvis Presley: *Viva Las Vegas* (63) George Sidney *aka Love in Las Vegas*.   Mickey Rooney and Judy Garland: *Babes on Broadway* (41) Busby Berkeley.   Shirley Temple: *Poor Little Rich Girl* (36) Irving Cummings.   Esther Williams: *On an Island with You* (48) Richard Thorpe.

Musical Biography, Musical Comedy, Musical Comedy Film, Musical Drama   *see*   **MUSICAL**

Musical Fantasy   *see*   **FANTASY FILM;**   *see also*   **MUSICAL**

Musical Film   *see*   **MUSICAL**

Musical Revue   *see*   **MUSICAL: Film Revues**

Musical Romance   *see*   **MUSICAL: Courtship-Romance Musicals**

Musical Westerns   *see*   **MUSICAL;**   *see also*   **WESTERN**

Musicomedy   *see*   **MUSICAL: Musical Comedy**

MYSTERY FILM   The mystery film, as the name implies, is about a mystery. Usually a murder has been committed, there are several suspects who could possibly have committed it, and the mystery engages the audience (and a character or characters in the film) in a game of deduction trying to guess who is the murderer or murderess. It is imperative, then, that the identity of the killer not be revealed until the end, at the climax of the film; if the identity of the murderer is known from the start, it is not a mystery proper but a different kind of crime film altogether. However, not all mysteries have to do with murder. The mystery could be a search for an object, the solving of a puzzle, or the explanation for a strange happening. Since murder mysteries always have an amateur or professional sleuth finally finding the culprit, most films that deal with solving a murder also fall under either the genres of police film or private detective film. Another type of mystery is a thriller that has a man or a woman on the run, either suspected of murder or of spying activities – *The 39 Steps* (1935) provides one of the best examples. Mystery film is also a label that has been extensively applied, especially on television, to any kind of crime movie that involves apprehending or trapping a criminal. For those mysteries that take place in old mansions, with secret passageways and corpses piling on corpses, *see* **HAUNTED HOUSE FILM;** *see also* **WHODUNIT.**

The Thirteenth Guest (32) Albert Ray. *The Kennel Murder Case* (33) Michael Curtiz. *The 39 Steps* (35) Alfred Hitchcock. *The Mad Miss Manton* (38) Leigh Jason. *The Arsenal Stadium Mystery* (GB 39) Thorold Dickinson. *Hot Spot* (41) H. Bruce Humberstone *aka I Wake Up Screaming*. *Castle in the Desert* (42) Harry Lachman. *The Crime Doctor* (43) Michael Gordon [1st in a series of 10 Crime Doctor films (1943-49)]. *Candles at Nine* (GB 44) Jessie Matthews. *And Then There Were None* (45) René Clair *aka Ten Little Indians / Ten Little Niggers*. *Deadline at Dawn* (45) Harold Clurman. *Lady on a Train* (45) Charles David. *So Long at the Fair* (GB 50) Terence Fisher, Anthony Darnborough. *The Ringer* (GB 52) Guy Hamilton. *Witness for the Prosecution* (57) Billy Wilder. *Charade* (63) Stanley Donen. *The List of Adrian Messenger* (63) John Huston. *The Twelve Chairs* (69) Mel Brooks. *Sleuth* (72) Joseph L. Mankiewicz. *Agatha* (G / US 79) Michael Apted. *Hammett* (82) Wim Wenders. *Rehearsal for Murder* (82 TV) David Greene. *Gorky Park* (83) Michael Apted. *Vivement dimanche* (F 83) François Truffaut *aka Confidentially Yours*. *Le Nom de la rose / Der Name der Rose / Il nome della rosa* (F / G / It 86) Jean-Jacques Annaud *aka The Name of the Rose*.

Mystery-Thriller *see* **WHODUNIT**

Mythographic Film *see* **UNDERGROUND FILM: Mythopoeic Film**

Mythological Epics *see* **EPIC**

Mythological-Fantasy Films *see* **FANTASY FILM**

Mythological Film *see* **UNDERGROUND FILM: Mythopoeic Film**

Narcotics Film *see* **DRUG FILM**

NARRATIVE FILM (Story Film)   A film that tells a story, as opposed to a nonnarrative film which does not. The nonnarrative film has also been called a poetic film, a term introduced by Jonas Mekas to differentiate non-narrative film from the commercial, narrative fictional film.

National Comedy *see* **COMEDY**

National Epics *see* **EPIC**

Native Comedy *see* **LOCAL COMEDY**

Natural Disaster Films *see* **DISASTER FILM**

Naturalism *see* **NATURALISTIC FILM**

Naturalist Documentary *see* **DOCUMENTARY: Romantic Documentary**

NATURALISTIC FILM (Naturalism, Slice-of-Life Film)   Naturalism, a literary and dramatic theory initiated by Emile Zola (1840–1902) in the late 19th century, was very influential in literary and theatrical circles. Filmmakers also underwent its influence and some films soon started showing naturalistic tendencies.

Naturalism attempts to record social reality by adopting an objective, scientific, almost clinical approach in its reflection of life; however, it places great emphasis on heredity and environment as the main factors in shaping human character and destiny. Naturalism tends to look at the individual in an environmental deterministic light. Human life is predestined by social forces over which the individual has no control. To illustrate this better, naturalism tends to focus on the lower strata of society, on the downtrodden, the weak and infirm. In dramatic terms it presents a "slice of life" (*tranche de vie*), as Zola expressed it. The end result is an extreme kind of stark realism. Naturalism had its counterpart in Italy in the form of *verismo* propounded mainly by the Italian novelist/playwright Giovanni Verga. Naturalistic influences are also seen in the neorealist films of post–World War II Italy.

L'Assommoir (F 09) Albert Capellani. *Afgrunden* (Den 10) Urban Gad *aka The Abyss / Woman Always Pays*. *Den hvide Slavehandel* (Den 10) Alfred Lind *aka The White Slave Trade*. *Les Victimes de l'alcool* (F 11) Gérard Bourgeois. *Evangeliemandens Liv* (Den 14) Holger-Madsen *aka The Evangelist's Life / John Redmond, the Evangelist*. *Sperduti nel buio* (It 14) Nino Martoglio. *The Cheat* (15) Cecil B. DeMille. *The Italian* (15) Reginald Barker. *Le Coupable* (F 16) André Antoine. *Fièvre* (F 20) Louis Delluc *aka La Boue*. *La Terre* (F 21) André Antoine. *Greed* (23-24) Eric von Stroheim. *Die freudlose Gasse* (G 25) G. W. Pabst *aka Cheerless Lane / The Joyless Street / The Street of Sorrow / Streets of Sorrow* (37): U.S. sound version. *Toni* (F 35) Jean Renoir *aka Les Amours de Toni*. *Dead End* (37) William Wyler. *Une si jolie petite plage* (F 48) Yves Allégret *aka Riptide / Such a Pretty Little Beach*. *Un Homme marche dans la ville* (F 49) Marcel Pagliero *aka Un Homme marche dans la nuit*. *Los Olvidados* (Mex 50) Luis Buñuel *aka La manzana podrida / The Forgotten / The Young and the Damned*.

Nature Film *see* **DOCUMENTARY: Ethnographic Film**

Nautical Film *see* **SEA FILM**

Naval Battle Film *see* **WAR FILM: Sea War Films**

Naval Comedy *see* **WAR FILM: Comedy War Films**

NAZI-RETRO FILM   The Nazi regime exerts a certain fascination on filmmakers and audiences alike. Since the end of World War II many films have touched on the subject of Nazism and its effects in the countries occupied by or at war with Germany. It is a major output of films which seek to document, analyze, or simply to exploit (as in the case of the Italian Nazi-sadist pictures of the mid–1970s) the depredations of Hitler's National Socialism and its enforcers.

In terms of German film production, the Nazi-retro films form a substantial body. These films reexamine the Nazi era in order to explain or put into perspective the nation's involvement with Nazism. Robert C. Reimer has labelled them Nazi-retro and has recently investigated the genre and compiled (with Carol Reimer) a useful annotated filmography of Nazi-retro films.[67]

> *Die Mörder sind unter uns* (EG 46) Wolfgang Staudte *aka The Murderers Are Among Us. Der Verlorene* (G 51) Peter Lorre *aka The Lost One. Die letzte Brücke* (Aus / Yug 53) Helmut Käutner *aka The Last Bridge. Der letzte Akt* (Aust 55) G. W. Pabst *aka The Last Ten Days / The Last Ten Days of Adolf Hitler / Ten Days to Die. Hitler — ein Film aus Deutschland / Our Hitler / Hitler, un film d'Allemagne* (G / GB / F 77) Hans Jürgen Syberberg. *Die Blechtrommel / Le tambour* (G / F / Yug / Pol 78) Voker Schlöndorff *aka Le Crabe-tambour / The Tin Drum. Die Ehe der Maria Braun* (G 78) Rainer Werner Fassbinder *aka The Marriage of Maria Braun. Deutschland bleiche Mutter* (G 79) Helma Sanders-Brahms *aka Germany, Pale Mother. Das Boot ist voll* (Swiz 80) Markus Imhoof *aka The Boat Is Full. Mephisto* (Hung / G / Aus 80-81) István Szabó. *Bockerer* (Aus / G 81) Franz Antel, Karl Merkatz. *Jokehnen / Jokehnen oder Wie lange fährt man von Ostpreußen nach Deutsland?* (G 87 TV) Michael Lähn *aka Jokehnen, or How Far from East Prussia to Germany?*

Nazi-Sadist Pictures *see* **SOFT-CORE SEX-EXPLOITATION FILM**

Neo-Brechtian Cinema *see* **BRECHTIAN CINEMA**

Neorealism *see* **NEOREALIST FILM**

NEOREALIST FILM (Neorealism)   Neorealism as a style of filmmaking emerged in Italy after World War II with Roberto Rossellini's *Roma città aperta / Open City* (1945), generally acknowledged as the first neorealist film, and the movement apparently died with Vittorio De Sica's *Il tetto / The Roof* (1955).[68] That is, Italian neorealism spanned a period of ten years between 1945 and 1955, and its demise was due to government opposition and public apathy—both parties were averse to the drabness and unhappy endings of the films. However, neorealism continued to influence Italian filmmakers, and it had great sway in developing countries which adopted its style and credo.

Neorealism is simply a new approach to filmmaking. It rejects the old practice of shooting in the studio and takes to the streets where the major part of the film is shot; it also tends to use non-professional actors in major roles, and the films are shot without sound, being post-synchronized later on. Thematically, the films show the plight of the impoverished workers, the old, and the destitute in postwar Italy. Indeed, unemployment, poverty, social injustice and government indifference towards the ills of society are its main themes. Thus, neorealist films are films of social conflict and protest presenting to the viewer social problems. On the political side, neorealism was a cinema of the Left, and as such, not encouraged or approved of by a government that feared to be made responsible for the social imbalance it portrayed. For an account of Italian neorealism, *see* Roy Armes, *Patterns of Realism* (South Brunswick and New York: A. S. Barnes, 1971).

Roma città aperta (It 45) Roberto Rossellini *aka Città aperta / Open City / Rome, Open City.* *Il bandito* (It 46) Alberto Lattuada *aka The Bandit.* *Caccia tragica* (It 46) Giuseppe De Santis *aka Tragic Hunt.* *Un giorno nella vita* (It 46) Alessandro Blasetti. *Paisà / Paisan* (It / US 46) Roberto Rossellini *aka Ordinary People / Sette americani.* *Sciuscià* (It 46) Vittorio De Sica *aka Shoeshine.* *Il sole sorge ancora* (It 46) Aldo Vergano *aka Outcry / The Sun Rises Again.* *Vivere in pace* (It 46) Luigi Zampa *aka To Live in Peace.* *Anni difficili* (It 47) Luigi Zampa *aka Difficult Years / The Little Man.* *Germania, anno zero / Allemagne année zéro / Deutschland, im Jahre Null* (It / F / G 47) Roberto Rossellini *aka Germany Year Zero.* *La Terra trema* (It 47) Luchino Visconti *aka Episodio del mare / The Earth Trembles / Land in Crisis.* *In nome della legge* (It 48) Pietro Germi *aka In the Name of the Law.* *Ladri di biciclette* (It 48) Vittorio De Sica *aka The Bicycle Thief / Bicycle Thieves.* *Il mulino del Po* (It 48) Alberto Lattuada *aka The Mill on the Po.* *Riso amaro* (It 48) Giuseppe De Santis *aka Bitter Rise.* *Senza pietà* (It 48) Alberto Lattuada *aka Without Pity.* *Una domenica d'agosto* (It 49) Luciano Emmer *aka Sunday in August.* *E primavera!* (It 49) Renato Castellani *aka Springtime in Italy.* *Non c'è pace tra gli ulivi* (It 49) Giuseppe De Santis *aka Blood on Easter Sunday / No Peace Among the Olives.* *Achtung! banditi!* (It 50) Carlo Lizzani *aka Achtung Bandits!* *Il cammino della speranza* (It 50) Pietro Germi *aka The Road to Hope.* *Il Cristo proibito* (It 50) Curzio Malaparte *aka Forbidden Christ / Strange Deception.* *Roma ore 11* (It 52) Giuseppe De Santis, Michelangelo Antonioni, Federico Fellini, Carlo Lizzani, Dino Risi, Francesco Maselli *aka Rome, Eleven O'Clock.* *Umberto D* (It 51) Vittorio De Sica. *Processo alla città* (It 52) Luigi Zampa *aka A Town on Trial.* *I vinti* (It 52) Michelangelo Antonioni *aka Youth and Perversion.* *Amore in città* (It 53) Michelangelo Antonioni, Federico Fellini, Dino Risi, Cesare Zavatini, Francesco Maselli, Alberto Lattuada, Carlo Lizzani *aka Love in the City.* *Cronaca dei poverini amanti* (It 54) Carlo Lizzani *aka Chronicle*

of Poor Lovers / Stories of Poor Lovers / A Tale of Poor Lovers. *Gli sban-
dati* (55) Francesco Maselli *aka Fine d'estate*. *Il tetto* (It 55) Vittorio De Sica
aka The Roof.

Neo-Western *see* WESTERN: Anti-Westerns

Neo-Woman's Film *see* WOMAN'S PICTURE

Der Neue deutsche Film, das neue deutsche Kino *see* NEW GER-
MAN CINEMA

NEW AMERICAN CINEMA The term originated with the New
American Cinema Group, an organization created in 1960 in New York by
several filmmakers and film producers to promote the work of independent
filmmakers. It thus included the variously named avant-garde, experimental and underground film. However, the New American Cinema comprised
not only noncommercial films but independently made commercial films as
well. The New American Cinema Group and the Film-Makers' Coopera-
tive, founded in 1962, offered an alternative avenue to independent
filmmakers for their films other than the Hollywood-dominated distribution outlets. Nowadays, the term has lost its currency. *See* UNDER-
GROUND FILM and INDEPENDENT FILM.

NEW AUSTRALIAN CINEMA   It is not a film movement or a school.
The New Australian Cinema represents a sudden burst of cinematic activity
in the seventies, mostly due to government financial support and the creation of a national Film and Television School.[69] Between 1970 and 1979,
the Australian film industry produced about 150 feature films, and it succeeded in creating for itself a reputation for quality and originality. This
is a remarkable feat if it is taken into account that in the preceding decade
only 18 features were made. After forty years of lethargy, the industry
experienced a veritable renaissance with a film output that covers most film
genres in the fields of drama, comedy, action and adventure, fantasy, horror, and history. In spite of the broad spectrum in the industry's output of
genres, a noticeable trend is the production of period films through which
a sense of national identity is meant to be reaffirmed. *See also* OCKER
FILM.

Libido (Aust 72) John B. Murray, Tim Burstall, Fred Schepisi, David Baker.
Petersen (Aust 74) Tim Burstall *aka Campus / "Jock" Petersen*. *Sunday
Too Far Away* (Aust 74) Ken Hannan *aka The Shearers*. *The Devil's
Playground* (Aust 75) Fred Schepisi. *Picnic at Hanging Rock* (Aust 75)
Peter Weir. *Don's Party* (Aust 76) Bruce Beresford. *Eliza Frazer* (Aust
76) Tim Burstall *aka A Faithful Narrative of the Capture, Sufferings and
Miraculous Escape of Liza Frazer / Mrs. Eliza Frazer*. *Journey Among
Women* (Aust 76) Ton Cowan. *The Picture Show Man* (Aust 76) John
Power. *Blue Fire Lady* (Aust 77) Ross Dimsey. *The Chant of Jimmie
Blacksmith* (Aust 77) Fred Schepisi. *The Getting of Wisdom* (Aust 77)
Bruce Beresford. *The Last Wave* (Aust 77) Peter Weir. *Long Weekend*
(Aust 77) Colin Eggleston. *Mad Max* (Aust 77) George Miller. *Mouth to*

Mouth (Aust 77) John Duigan. *The Night Nurse* (Aust 77 TV) Igo
Auzins. *Patrick* (Aust 77) Richard Franklin. *Kostas* (Aust / Gr 78) Paul
Cox *aka Costas*. *The Last of the Knucklemen* (Aust 78) Tim Burstall. *My
Brilliant Career* (Aust 78) Gillian Armstrong. *Cathy's Child* (Aust / Gr 78)
Donald Crombie. *The Plumber* (Aust 78 TV) Peter Weir. *Alison's Birth-
day* (Aust 79) Ian Coughlan. *Blood Money* (Aust 79) Chris Fitchett *aka
Snatch / Softly Fall the Rain*. *'Breaker' Morant* (Aust 79) Bruce Beresford.
Final Cut (Aust 79) Ross Dimsey. *Harlequin* (Aust 79) Simon Wincer *aka
Dark Forces / The Minister's Magician*. *Gallipoli* (Aust 80) Peter Weir *aka
There and Back*.

NEW CHINESE CINEMA (Chinese New Wave)   The Cultural Revolution (1966–76) resulted in a setback for the arts in general in mainland
China and film production almost came to a standstill.

In 1978, the Beijing Film Institute (which had closed during the Cultural
Revolution) started training students again and by 1982 a group of young
filmmakers graduated from the fifth class of the school's Directing Department (hence they were named the "5th Generation," although the term has
broadened to include other young filmmakers).[70] It is mainly to these innovative directors, cinematographers and filmmakers that the impetus for
a "new cinema" is due. It is a cinema that departs from the old, traditional
Chinese style of filmmaking which was mostly melodramatic and heavily
indebted to the tenets of Socialist Realism (q.v.) which was readily accepted
in China by its Communist government.

Differing from the old style, the "new" filmmakers offer a more personal
approach, are somewhat critical of society (to the extent that this is permitted), and seek to apply new techniques of filmmaking more in keeping
with contemporary world tendencies than with traditional, insular style.
Although Zhang Junzhao's *Yige he bage / The One and the Eight* (1983)[71]
paved the way for the emergence of the "new cinema," Chen Kaige's *Huang
tudi / Yellow Earth* (1984) is the film usually credited with having brought
about this renewal and rejection of past cinematic conventions in Chinese
cinema. Even though the "new cinema" has encountered opposition at
home and the "5th Generation" has been subjected to criticism, their films
have been critically acclaimed abroad.

Yige he bage (Chn 83) Zhang Junzhao *aka One and Eight / The One and the
Eight*. *Huang tu di* (Chn 84) Chen Kaige *aka Yellow Earth*. *Ren sheng*
(Chn 84) Wu Tianming *aka Life*. *Dao ma zhei* (Chn 85) Tian
Zhuangzhuang *aka (The) Horse Thief*. *Da yue bing* (Chn 85) Cheng Kaige
[rel. in 87] *aka (The) Big Parade / Troop Review*. *Die xue hei gu* (Chn 85)
Wu Ziniu, Li Jingmin *aka Secret Decree*. *Gezi shu* (Chn 85) Wu Ziniu *aka
Dove Tree*. *Hai tan* (Chn 85) Teng Wenji *aka At the Beach*. *Hei pao shi
jian* (Chn 85) Huang Jianxin *aka The Black Cannon Affair / (The) Black
Cannon Incident*. *Jue xiang* (Chn 85) Zhang Zeming *aka Swan
Song*. *Liangjia funu* (Chn 85) Huang Jianzhong *aka Girl of Good Family*.
Lie chang zha sa (Chn 85) Tian Zuangzhuang *aka On the Hunting Ground*.
Nuer lov (Chn 85) Hu Mei *aka Army Nurse*. *Yie shan* (Chn 85) Yan Xueshu
aka In the Wild Mountains / Wild Mountains. *Qing chun ji* (Chn 86) Zhang

Nuanxin *aka Sacrificed Youth / Sacrifice of Youth.* *Yige sizhe dui shengzhe de fangwen* (Chn 86) Huang Jianzhong *aka Questions for the Living.* *Zhui hou de tai yang* (Chn 86) Jiang Haiyang *aka The Last Sun.* *Zuihou yi ge dongri* (Chn 86) Wu Ziniu *aka The Last Day of Winter.* *Hai zi wang* (Chn 87) Chen Kaige *aka (The) King of the Children.* *Hong gao liang* (Chn 87) Zhang Yimou *aka Red Sorghum.* *Lao jing* (Chn 87) Wu Tianming *aka Old Well.* *Wan zhong* (Chn 87) Wu Ziniu *aka Evening Bell* [rel. in 89].

NEW GERMAN CINEMA (der junge deutsche Film, das neue deutsche Kino / der neue deutsche Film, New German Film, Young German Cinema / Film) The term is used to bring together the films of a group of directors, Germanborn or foreigners, who work in West Germany, and whose films are in direct opposition to the commercial and popular entertainment genres of mainstream German cinema.[72]

The starting point of the New German Cinema is usually said to be 1962 when, during the eighth Oberhausen Short Film Festival, twenty-six young directors proclaimed their ideas on the kind of cinema they wanted to be able to make in a document later known as the Oberhausen Manifesto.

It has been pointed out repeatedly that the New German Cinema is not a film movement or a film school, but an assemblage of vastly divergent, individual filmmakers — film *auteurs* each having a clear, recognizable style. They have in common their rejection of the old, conservative, establishment cinema which they often refer to as *Opas Kino* (Grandpa's Cinema), and instead they choose to be engaged in the making of socially relevant cinema. Their films usually have a message and are critical of present-day society. The films attack the old popular film genres, the ruling classes, and illustrate the problems of old people, women, immigrant workers, maladjusted individuals, and the difficulties of fitting into the "ordered" German status quo. The better-known filmmakers of the New German Cinema are Rainer Werner Fassbinder, Werner Herzog, Wim Wenders, Volker Schlöndorff, Jean-Marie Straub, Alexander Kluge, and Hans Jürgen Syberberg.

Playgirl (G 65) Will Tremper *aka Berlin ist eine sünde Welt / That Woman.* *Der junge Törless / Les Désarrois de l'élève Törless* (G / F 65-66) Volker Schlöndorff *aka Young Torless.* *Mord und Totschlag* (G 66) Volker Schlöndorff *aka A Degree of Murder / Murder Homicide.* *Wilder Reiter GmbH* (G 66) Franz-Josef Spieker *aka Wild Rider Ltd.* *Jagdszenen aus Niederbayern* (G 68) Peter Fleishmann *aka The Hunters Are Hunted / Hunting Scenes from Bavaria / Hunting Scenes from Lower Bavaria.* *Warum läuft Herr R. Amok?* (G 69 TV) Michael Fengler, Rainer Werner Fassbinder *aka Why Did Herr R. Run amok? / Why Does Herr R. Run Amok?* *Der plötzliche Reichtum der armen Leute von Kombach* (G 70) Volker Schlöndorff *aka The Sudden Fortune (Wealth) of the Poor People of Kombach.* *Warnung vor einer heiligen Nutte / Attenzione alla sacra putana* (G / It 70) Rainer Werner Fassbinder *aka Attenzione alla putana santa / Beware of a Holy Whore / Pride Goes Before the Fall.* *Der Händler der vier Jahreszeiten* (Swiss / G 71) Rainer Werner Fassbinder *aka The Merchant of Four Seasons.* *Harlis* (G 72) Robert van Ackeren *aka Comédie larmoyante Harlis / Love Me Gently / Red Hot in Bed.* *Alice in den Städen* (G 73) Wim Wenders *aka Alice in the Cities. Angst essen Seele auf* (G 73) Rainer Werner Fassbinder *aka Ali: Fear Eats the Soul / Fear Eats the Heart (Soul). Supermarkt* (G 73) Roland Klick *aka Supermarket. Faustrecht der Freiheit* (G 74) Rainer Werner Fassbinder *aka First-Right of Freedom / Fox / Fox and His Friends. MitGift* (G 75) Michael Verhöven *aka Dangerous Dowry / Poisonous Inheritance. Aus einem deutschen Leben* (G 76) Theodor Kotulla *aka Death Is My Trade / From a German Life. Die Wildente* (G / Aus 76) Hans W. Geissendörfer *aka The Wild Duck. Der amerikanische Freund / L'Ami américain / The American Friend* (G / F / US 77) Wim Wenders. *Eine Reise ins Licht-Despair / Despair* (G / F 77) Rainer Werner Fassbinder. *Die Konsequenz* (G 77) Wolfgang Petersen *aka The Consequence. Die Blechtrommel / Le tambour* (G / F / Yug / Pol 78) Volker Schlöndorff *aka Le Crabe-tambour / The Tin Drum. Deutschland im Herbst* (G 78) Volker Schlöndorff, Alf Brustellin, Rainer Werner Fassbinder, Alexander Kluge, Maximiliane Mainka, Edgar Reitz, Katja Rupé, Hans Peter Cloos, Berhard Sinkel *aka Germany in Autumn. Messer im Kopf* (G 78) Reinhard Hauff *aka Knife in the Head. Die Reinheit des Herzens* (G 79) Robert van Ackeren *aka Pure of Heart. Christiane F. – Wir Kinder von Bahnhof Zoo* (G 81) Ulrich Edel *aka Christine F / Christiane F. – We Children of Zoo Station. Morgen in Alabama* (G 83-84) Norbert Kückelmann *aka A German Lawyer / Tomorrow in Alabama.*

New German Film *see* **NEW GERMAN CINEMA**

NEW INDIAN CINEMA (India's New Cinema)   With over 700 full-length films produced yearly since 1979, India has the largest production of feature films in the world. However, this massive production consists mostly of family-oriented, escapist films made strictly for entertainment. The genres favored are the mythological epic, the historical and devotional film (the latter on the life of preachers and saints) and the contemporary romance or film set in the present. As diversified as the films belonging to the above genres may be, they all virtually have an allotted quota of songs, music and dance as an expected and common denominator of Indian commercial cinema.

With the advent of the internationally known Satyajit Ray and the contribution of a few other equally remarkable filmmakers, an alternative cinema was to emerge; a cinema concerned with social issues and imbued with humanist views, intent on showing the reality of life in the context of modern India rather than visions of fantasy in a make-believe, fairy-tale world. The diverse filmmakers of this alternative or parallel cinema are grouped into what is known as the New Indian Cinema or India's New Cinema. Films like Bismal Roy's *Do Bigha Zameen / Two Acres of Land* (1953) and Satyajit Ray's *Pather Panchali / Song of the Road* (1955), a film which won the special jury prize in 1956 in the Cannes Film Festival, indicated that showing the plight of the poor could be made a valid concern of Indian cinema. The New Indian Cinema gathered momentum from the sixties on, and although its filmmakers have used different approaches — clearly discernible are the tendencies towards neorealism, political melodrama, Brechtian cinema, and films with multiple perspectives — and all try to show a reality which presents the Indian ethos and complexity of life at national and regional levels.[73] *See Film India: The New Generation 1960–1980* (New Delhi: Directorate of Film Festivals, 1981). *Do Bigha Zameen* (53) Bismal Roy *aka Two Acres of Land* [in Hindi]. *Pather Panchali* (55) Satyajit Ray *aka Song of the Road* [in Bengali]. *Charulata* (Ind 64) Satyajit Ray *aka The Lonely Wife* [in Bengali]. *Aranyer Din Raatri* (Ind 69) Satyajit Ray *aka Days and Nights in the Forest* [in Bengali]. *Samskara* (Ind 70) Pattabhi Rama Reddy *aka Funeral Rites* [in Kannada].*Chomana Dudi* (Ind 74) B. V. Karanth *aka Choma's Drum* [in Kannada]. *Garam Hava* (Ind 75) M. S. Sathyu *aka Hot Winds / Scorching Wind* [in Urdu]. *Kanchana Sita* (Ind 77) G. Aravindan *aka Golden Sita* [in Malayalam]. *Ek Din Pratidin* (Ind 79) Mrinal Sen *aka And Quiet Rolls the [Day] Dawn (One Day, Every Day) / And Still Breaks the Dawn / One Day Like Another* [in Bengali]. *22 June 1897* (Ind 79) Nachiket & Jayoo Patwardhan [in Marathi]. *Aakrosh* (Ind 80) Govind Nihalani *aka Cry of the Wounded* [in Hindi]. *Akaler Sandhaney* (Ind 80) Mrinal Sen *aka In Search of Famine* [in Bengali]. *Albert Pinto ko Gussa Kyon ata Hai* (Ind 80) Saeed Mirza *aka What Makes Albert Pinto Angry* [in Hindi]. *Bhavani Bhavai* (Ind 80) Ketan Mehta *aka A Folk Tale* [in Gujarati]. *Adaminte Variyellu* (Ind 83) K. G. George *aka Adam's Rib* [in Malayalam]. *Adi Shankaracharya* (Ind 83) G. V. Iyer [in Sanskrit]. *Jaane bhi do Yaaro* (Ind 83) Kundan Shah *aka Who Pays the Piper...* [in Hindi]. *Trikal* (Ind 83) Shyam Benegal *aka Past, Present and Future* [in Hindi]. *Damul* (Ind 84) Prakash Jha *aka Bonded Until Death* [in Hindi]. *Holi* (Ind 84) Ketan Mehta *aka The Festival of Fire* [in Hindi]. *Mohan Joshi Haazir Ho!* (Ind 84) Saeed Akhtar Mirza *aka A Summons for Mohan Joshi* [in Hindi]. *Paar* (Ind 84) Goutam Ghose *aka The Crossing* [in Hindi]. *Tarang* (Ind 84) Kumar Shahani *aka Wages and Profit* [in Hindi]. *Agnisnaan* (Ind 85) Dr. Bhabendra Nath Saikia *aka Ordeal* [in Assamese]. *Amma Ariyan* (Ind 86) John Abraham *aka Report to Mother* [in Malayalam]. *Oridath* (Ind 86) G. Aravindan *aka Somewhere* [in Malayalam].

News Film *see* **ACTUALITY;** *see also* **NEWSREEL**

News Item *see* **ACTUALITY**

News Magazine *see* **NEWSREEL**

News Magazine Series *see* **TV NEWS: News Serial**

NEWSFILM   Newsfilms are informational films whose object is to inform the viewer of noteworthy events which take place locally or worldwide. As newsreels (q.v.) and magazine films (previously shown in film theaters) have become obsolete in most countries, present-day newsfilms are relayed mostly through television. News is usually categorized as spot news for unexpected events which may be filmed as they are happening (accidents, calamities, crime), features which are longer items imparting more information on a particular subject, sports news items and public and current affairs programs which may include debates on political and social issues or news analysis. Coverage refers to the film made of a news event or to the filming of it.

NEWSPAPER FILM (Journalism Drama, Reporter Film) Popular with the coming of sound to the motion picture, the newspaperman steadily gained ground as an enduring American hero. Newspaper films form a sizeable body of pictures which mostly fall under the categories of melodramas, romances, comedies or crime movies. They cover all types of newspapermen, editors and publishers. These reporters in their capacity of amateur detectives, crusaders, gossip columnists or foreign correspondents seek to solve crimes, bust rackets, uncover smuggling or dope rings or nests of spies at home and abroad. To a man, they are single-minded in securing a scoop or in getting a story to their newspaper in time to break the news. If editors or publishers, they also seek to ensure that their newspaper continues to appear, increases its circulation (not always by honest means) and provides the kind of service its readership expects from it. Women also have their part in newspaper films. They are often relegated to the society news, the gossip columns or the woman's section of the newspaper. Hence, because of the sentiment attached to this kind of reportage, female reporters are also known as sob sisters. When not writing this sort of news, they are frequently busy trying to prove that they are equal, if not better, than any male reporter. Although they could be classed as a subcategory, some films dealing with television journalism and investigative reporting are also included under newspaper film. The genre, including films in which reporters play a significant role, has been documented with many titles (some by now forgotten) by Alex Barris in *Stop the Presses!* (South Brunswick and New York: A. S. Barnes, 1976).

Five Star Final (31) Mervyn LeRoy. *The Front Page* (31) Lewis Milestone. *Blessed Event* (32) Roy Del Ruth. *Libeled Lady* (36) Jack Conway. *Nothing Sacred* (37) William A. Wellman. *Tell No Tales* (38) Leslie Fenton. *Citizen Kane* (40) Orson Welles *aka The American. Foreign Correspondent* (40) Alfred Hitchcock *aka Personal History. His Girl Friday* (40) Howard Hawks. *Call Northside 777* (47) Henry Hathaway *aka Calling Northside 777. Chicago Deadline* (49) Lewis Allen. *Deadline U.S.A.* (52) Richard Brooks *aka Deadline. Front Page Story* (GB 53) Gordon Parry. *While the City Sleeps* (55) Fritz Lang *aka News Is Made at Night. Sweet Smell of Success* (57) Alexander Mackendrick. *Lonelyhearts* (58) Vincent J. Donehue. *Black Like Me* (64) Carl Lerner. *Der Fußgänger* (G / Swiz 73) Maximilian Schell *aka The Pedestrian. The Front Page* (74) Billy Wilder. *All the President's Men* (76) Alan J. Pakula. *Between the Lines* (77) Joan Micklin Silver. *Absence of Malice* (81) Sydney Pollack. *The Year of Living Dangerously* (Aust / US 82) Peter Weir. *Under Fire* (83) Roger Spottiswoode. *The Killing Fields* (GB 84) Roland Joffé. *The Mean Season* (84) Phillip Borsos. *Salvador* (US / Mex 85) Oliver Stone. *Street Smart* (87) Jerry Schatzberg.

NEWSREEL News films began with the enterprising Lumière brothers who sent cameramen all over the world to demonstrate their *cinématographe* and, at the same time, film on the spot any item of topical interest such as major sports events, royal functions, presidential inaugurations and the like. Some war correspondents equipped with a camera also made it to the fields of battle (Graeco-Turkish War of 1897, Boer War of 1899–1902) to film army deployments and troops engaged in combat. Anything newsworthy anywhere was quickly filmed and sent home, and if the makers of films were not able to be on the spot for the filming, news footage was quickly faked in reconstructed or simulated conditions at the studio or even in the home bathtub for naval battle scenes.[74] The public was unable to or disinterested enough not to see the fakery and accepted (at least for a while) as real what the screen showed them. Out of these news items emerged the newsreel, or the film solely devoted to the presentation of topical news and items of immediate relevance.

Day by Day claims to be the first newsreel. It was shown daily in 1906 at the London Empire Theatre situated at Leicester Square, provided that weather conditions had not impeded the filming of news. Its producer was Will G. Baker. The French had, starting in 1908, their *Pathé-Faits Divers* (soon rechristened *Pathé-Journal*), and other countries followed with their own newsreels. A parallel trend of the time was the issue of locally produced newsreels by enterprising cinema owners (e.g., *Paterson's Pictorial Review*, started in Aberdeen in 1907) which spread to big and small centers of population.[75]

In the 1930s, newsreels were fairly standardized, consisting of a string of independent news items or separate stories, each newsreel being issued once or twice a week and running for about fifteen minutes. Television eroded the usefulness of the newsreel and gradually took over its function starting in the late 1950s in country after country with few exceptions. Newsreels practically ceased to exist. Newsreels shot worldwide form a vast pool of material often used by makers of compilation films.

The news magazine (magazine film or cinemagazine) differs from newsreels in its selectiveness of material, preferring to concentrate on a minimum of items or on a single story; they were mostly issued on a weekly or monthly basis, e.g., *The March of Time* (1935–1951).

There have been "specialized newsreels" for specific audiences, mainly blacks (e.g., in the United States and South Africa), women and children. Sponsored and politically biased newsreels have also been issued from time to time.

For a history of the newsreel in America, *see* Raymond Fielding, *The American Newsreel 1911–1967* (Norman, OK: University of Oklahoma Press, 1972).

Day by Day (GB 06) Prod. Will G. Baker [1st newsreel]. *Paterson's Pictorial Review* (GB 07) [early local (Aberdeen) newsreel]. *Pathé-Faits Divers / Pathé Journal* (F 08) [early newsreel]. *The March of Time* (35-51) Prod. Louis de Rochemont [204 monthly issues plus 1 special issue].

Nighttime Soap Opera   *see*   **SOAP OPERA**

NINJA FILM   The Ninjas were families of spies and assassins in feudal

Japan, who hired themselves out to the Samurai to perform reprehensible acts that the Samurai code of behavior (or Bushido) would not allow them to do personally. Ninjas have, of course, figured in Japanese action films and in Hong Kong kung-fu movies. They also appeared in the James Bond adventure *You Only Live Twice* (1967). Their popularity in the West is due, however, to the film *Enter the Ninja* (1981), an exploitation item that hit the mark with lovers of action pictures. In these movies, there are good and evil Ninjas fighting each other. Costumed all in red, black, or white and masked, they look capable and threatening at the same time; they also have at their disposal a bizarre arsenal of weaponry, and being skilled in the martial art of Ninjutsu, they are powerful fighters and worthy opponents. A spate of Ninja movies has helped to make them a distinct class of the martial arts genre.

Enter the Ninja (US / J / Phil 81) Menahem Golan.   *The Last Ninja* (83 TV) William A. Graham.   *The Ninja Mission* (GB 83) Matt Helge.   *Revenge of the Ninja* (83) Sam Firstenberg.   *Ninja III—The Domination* (84) Sam Firstenberg.   *American Ninja* (US / Phil 85) Sam Firstenberg *aka American Warrior*.   *Pray for Death* (85) Gordon Hessler.   *White Phantom* (86) Dusty Nelson.   *American Ninja 2: The Confrontation* (87) Sam Firstenberg.   *American Ninja 3: Blood Hunt* (89) Cedric Sundstrom.   *Ninja Academy* (89) Nico Mastorakis.   *American Ninja 4: The Annihilation* (91) Cedric Sundstrom.

No Wave Filmmakers   *see*   **INDEPENDENT PRODUCTION**

Non-Arthurian Chivalric Film   *see*   **SWASHBUCKLER: CHIVALRIC FILMS**

Noncombat Film   *see*   **WAR FILM**

Noncommercial   Film *see*   **EXPERIMENTAL   FILM;**   *see also*   **STRUCTURAL FILM**

Nonexplicit Film   *see*   **SEX EXPLOITATION FILM**

Nonfeature Film   *see*   **SHORT**

NONFICTION FILM (Nonstory Film)   The term stands in opposition to fictional or fiction film and serves to group together all films which are meant to be educational or informational. It is used for films of a documentary nature and for films which have scientific, industrial or practical use. Another term is factual film, which in its most restrictive sense only deals with the presentation of facts. *See also* **DOCUMENTARY**.

NONLINEAR FILM (Disnarrative Film, Space-Time Movie)   In most narrative films, the plot unfolds in an uncomplicated, straightforward fashion. However, since Alain Resnais's *Hiroshima, mon amour* (1959) and *L'Année dernière à Marienbad* (1960), nonlinearity in film story structuring has become more prevalent. It is not a new technique in motion pictures: some interruption in the flow of the narrative had already been used in early films, e.g., D. W. Griffith's *Intolerance* (1914–16) intermingled four different stories taking place in different historical time periods and shifted the action back and forth from one to the other. Apart from similar early examples, it is since the Resnais' films, however, that nonlinearity in the cinema has become more ubiquitous and more sophisticated in its use of diverse devices (flash-backs, flash-forwards). A nonlinear film (or a space-time movie, as it has sometimes been called) simply means that the sequence of events represented on the screen does not follow a chronological order of cause-and-effect as in linear films. The temporal relationship of events has been interrupted; interior and exterior reality has blended; memory, dream and fact may have fused; and the action may move in time-lapses from past to present to future, back and forth, and not necessarily in any prearranged order. The nonlinear films may take the appearance of a series of discon-nected actions. It is merely an appearance, because the correlation exists, although it is left to the viewer to draw the sequences together and fathom the overall meaning. At times, this is only possible after having seen the film in its entirety or after having seen it more than once.

> *Hiroshima, mon amour / Nijúyokikan no jóji* (F / J 59) Alain Resnais *aka Hiroshima, My Love / Twenty-Four Hour Affair. L'Année dernière à Marienbad / L'anno scorso a Marienbad* (F / It 60) Alain Resnais *aka Last Year at Marienbad. Performance* (GB 68) Donald Cammell, Nicolas Roeg *aka The Performers* [rel. in 70]. *Petulia* (US / GB 68) Richard Lester. *Il Conformista / Le Conformiste* (It / F / G 69) Bernardo Bertolucci *aka The Conformist. Slaughterhouse-Five* (71) George Roy Hill. *200 Motels* (GB 71) Frank Zappa, Tony Palmer.

Nonnarrative Film   *see*   **NARRATIVE FILM**

Nonobjective Film   *see*   **ABSTRACT FILM**

Nonrealistic Comedy   *see*   **FANTASY FILM**

Nonrepresentational Film   *see*   **ABSTRACT FILM**

Nonsensical Comedy   *see*   **ANARCHIC COMEDY**

Nonstory Film   *see*   **NONFICTION FILM**

NONTHEATRICAL FILM   This term is used for a film made to be shown in some place (e.g., schools, universities, film societies, cultural organizations) other than cinema or film theater. It is also applied when referring to an educational or documentary-type film.

Nontheatrical Short   *see*   **SHORT**

NOSTALGIA FILM   Two films, Peter Bogdanovich's *The Last Picture Show* (1971) and Robert Mulligan's *Summer of '42* (1971) launched a string of nostalgia movies in America, reinforced by George Lucas's *American Graffiti* (1973). This movie in America and in other nations (France calls its nostalgia movies "films retro") romanticizes the past with affectionate longing. This kind of looking into the past has been shared by several art movements since the Italian Renaissance started to look at the legacy of Classical Antiquity. In contrast, current nostalgia films look at recent decades, mostly the forties and fifties, or the early sixties, a time the filmmakers tell us in which life was less complicated than today. The key element in nostalgia films is perhaps a kind of melancholy for the bygone era the films seek to recreate. In this, they differ from the mere historical or period movies which just present the past without subjective or emotional involvement. The nostalgia movie also differs from the "revisionist" film which seeks to debunk or to demythologize the past. Nostalgia films, besides looking at a bygone way of life, may also focus on cinema itself, on the way movies used to be made or on the characteristics of a particular genre, e.g., Dick Richard's *Farewell, My Lovely* (1974) evokes the atmospheric *film noir* films of the forties and fifties. *See also* **HOMAGE FILM**.

   The Happy Time (52) Richard Fleischer.   *Yoyo* (F 65) Pierre Etaix *aka Yo Yo*.   *Borsalino* (F / It 69) Jacques Deray.   *The Last Picture Show* (71) Peter Bogdanovich.   *Summer of '42* (71) Robert Mulligan.   *Save the Tiger* (72) John G. Avildsen.   *Amacord* (It / F 73) Federico Fellini *aka I Remember*.   *American Graffiti* (73) George Lucas.   *Class of '44* (73) Paul Bogart.   *Paper Moon* (73) Peter Bogdanovich.   *The Way We Were* (73) Sydney Pollack.   *Chinatown* (74) Roman Polanski.   *Farewell, My Lovely* (GB 74) Dick Richards.   *The Lords of Flatbush* (74) Stephen F. Verona, Martin Davidson.   *The Fortune* (75) Mike Nichols.   *Next Stop, Greenwich Village* (76) Paul Mazursky.   *Our Winning Season* (78) Joseph Ruben.   *Same Time, Next Year* (78) Robert Mulligan.   *Diner* (82) Barry Levinson.   *My Favorite Year* (82) Richard Benjamin.   *P'Tang, Yang, Kipperbang* (GB 82) Michael Apted.   *Racing with the Moon* (84) Richard Benjamin.   *Tro, Håb og Kærlighed* (Den 84) Bille August *aka Twist and Shout*.   *Hairspray* (88) John Waters.   *Shag* (88) Zelda Barron *aka Shag, the Movie*.

NOUVELLE VAGUE (French New Wave)   This was the first of such labels (see **CINEMA NOVO, CZECH NEW WAVE, NEW GERMAN CINEMA**) to be applied to a disparate group of filmmakers. In most cases, such groups form a loose movement held together by the initial impetus of a shared aim and the historical, recurrent fact of being on the spot when the conditions happen to be right for their emergence. The aim of such groups of filmmakers may be the desire to break with the old, traditional way of filming or just the desire to break into the film business. In the case of the *Nouvelle Vague*, a catch-phrase introduced in 1958 by François Giroud in the weekly *L'Express*, the term served to denote those French film directors who were making their first feature film. They were an assorted lot, but they had in common a deeply felt love for the film medium and strong motivation to make pictures. They had also a substantial body of theoretical work and film criticism upon which to base their own films: that is to say, the formulation of an *auteur* theory (*une politique des auteurs*). They wanted to establish a dialogue between themselves and their audiences rather than merely entertain them. They had something to communicate, a vision of their contemporary world to impart, and they wanted to express it through their own personal experiences and with their own style. They achieved it by shooting in the streets and real settings with lightweight equipment or hand-held cameras. They used actors, who often improvised their own acting and dialogue, rather than stars, and they produced their films with small budgets frequently paying homage or making reference to their own films or to films that had inspired them. They were strongly influenced by Hollywood genre films and by a selected group of film directors whom they considered *auteurs*. Agnès Varda's *La Pointe courte* (1954), Roger Vadim's *Et Dieu . . . créa la femme* (1956), and Claude Chabrol's *Le Beau Serge* (1957) have been regarded as forerunners of the *Nouvelle Vague*, but the New Wave really started in 1959 when twenty-four films were made by directors working on their first feature film, followed by 43 films made in 1960. It was a veritable cinematic boom which, as well as being very influential, created a reputation abroad and a new pantheon of French film directors. Some of these directors have become established figures of the commercial cinema, the same kind of cinema they once sought to renovate. The list of New Wave filmmakers is long and it includes the former *Cahiers du Cinéma* film critics François Truffaut, Jean-Luc Godard, Claude Chabrol, Eric Rohmer, Jacques Rivette, and Jacques Doniol-Valcroze, some "left-bank" filmmakers such as Alain Resnais, Agnès Varda, Jacques Demy, and others working independently like Louis Malle, Alexandre Astruc and Marcel Camus.

La Pointe courte (54) Agnès Varda. *Et Dieu . . . créa la femme* (56) Roger Vadim *aka . . . And God Created Woman / And Woman . . . Was Created.* *L'Ascenseur pour l'échafaut* (F 57) Louis Malle *aka Frantic / Lift [Elevator] to the Scaffold.* *Le Beau Serge* (57) Claude Chabrol *aka Bitter Reunion / Handsome Serge.* *Les Amants* (F 58) Louis Malle *aka The Lovers.* *Les Cousins* (F 58) Claude Chabrol *aka The Cousins.* *Orfeu Negro / Orfeo negro* (F / Braz / It 58) Marcel Camus *aka Black Orpheus.* *À bout de souffle* (F 59) Jean-Luc Godard *aka Breathless.* *A double tour / A doppia mandata* (F / It 59) Claude Chabrol *aka Léda / Web of Passion.* *Les Quatre Cents Coups* (F 59) François Truffaut *aka The 400 Blows.* *Tirez sur le pianiste* (F 59) François Truffaut *aka Shoot the Pianist / Shoot the Piano Player.* *L'Année dernière à Marienbad / L'anno scorso a Marienbad* (F / It 60) Alain Resnais *aka Last Year at Marienbad.* *Les Bonnes Femmes* (F 60) Claude Chabrol *aka The Girls.* *Chronique d'un été* (F 60) Jean Rouch, Edgar Morin *aka Chronicle of a Summer.* *Le Farceur* (F 60) Philippe De Broca *aka The Joker.* *Lola / Donna di vita* (F / It 60) Jacques Demy. *Paris nous appartient* (F 60) Jacques Rivette *aka Paris Belongs to Me / Paris Belongs to Us / Paris Is Ours.* *La Proie pour l'ombre* (F 60) Alexandre Astruc. *Zazie dans le Métro / Zazie nel metro* (F / It 60) Louis Malle *aka Zazie.* *Cléo de 5 à 7 / Cleo dalle 5 alle 7* (F / It 61) Agnès Varda *aka Cléo de 5 à 7 ou 90 minutes de la vie d'une femme / Cleo from 5 to 7.* *Jules et Jim* (F 61) François Truffaut *aka Jules and Jim.* *Les Snobs* (F 61) Jean-Pierre Mocky. *Une Femme est une femme / La donna è donna* (F / It 61) Jean-Luc Godard *aka A Woman Is a Woman.* *Adieu Philippine* (F 62) Jacques Rozier. *La Baie des anges* (F 62) Jacques Demy *aka Bay of Angels.* *La Dénonciation* (F 62) Jacques Doniol-Valcroze *aka The Immoral*

Moment.   *Les Dimanches de Ville d'Avray / L'uomo senza passato* (F / It
62) Serge Bourgignon *aka Cybèle / Sundays and Cybele*.   *L'Œil du malin* (F
62) Claude Chabrol *aka The Evil Eye / The Third Eye*.

Novel-for-Television   *see*   **TELEVISION NOVELIZATION**

Novel into Film   *see*   **ADAPTATION: Adaptations from Novels**

Novelization   *see*   **TELEVISION NOVELIZATION**

Now Film   *see*   **YOUTH FILM**

Nuberu Bagu   *see*   **JAPANESE NEW WAVE CINEMA**

NUCLEAR FILM   With the dropping of the atomic bomb on
Hiroshima and Nagasaki in 1945, the awesome reality of possible annihilation by the forces of nuclear fusion and the deadly after-effects of radiation
caused a paranoid syndrome that in cinematic terms resulted in a spate of
films exploiting the atomic fear. These films are labelled nuclear films by
some writers. The major wave of nuclear films came in the fifties and sixties
in America with Japan also contributing a large number of films. Films
centering on the fear of atomic holocaust continue to be made. Two noteworthy examples are *The China Syndrome* (1978) and the Australian *The
Chain Reaction* (1979). Joe Kane, in his article "Nuclear Films," *Take One*,
2.6 (1969–70): 9–11, divided the nuclear films of the fifties and sixties in four
basic subgenres: contamination-mutation films (radiation causes man to
mutate), bestial invocation films (atomic blast causes beast to be released
from confinement, or radiation causes it to mutate), post-holocaust films
(survival after atomic conflagration), and warning films (against the dangers
of atomic power). Mick Broderick's *Nuclear Movies: A Critical Analysis
and Filmography*... (Jefferson, N.C.: McFarland, 1991) includes an ample
selection of films. The nuclear films form part of the science fiction genre.
See **WAR FILM: Nuclear War Films**.

Seven Days to Noon (GB 50) John Boulting.   *Five* (51) Arch Oboler.   *Hiro-
shima* (J 53) Hideo Sekigawa.   *Them!* (53) Gordon Douglas.   *World
Without End* (56) Edward Bernds.   *The Amazing Colossal Man* (57) Bert I.
Gordon.   *The Deadly Mantis* (57) Nathan Juran *aka The Incredible Preying
Mantis*.   *The Incredible Shrinking Man* (57) Jack Arnold.   *Daigo fukuryu
maru* (J 58) Kaneto Shindo *aka Lucky Dragon No. 5*.   *The Last Woman on
Earth* (60) Roger Corman *aka World Without Women*.   *The Creation of the
Humanoids* (62) Wesley E. Barry.   *Dr. Strangelove* (GB / US 63) Stanley
Kubrick *aka Dr. Strange Love; or, How I Learned to Stop Worrying and
Love the Bomb*.   *Ladybug Ladybug* (63) Frank Perry.   *Lord of the Flies*
(GB 63) Peter Brook.   *The War Game* (GB 65 TV) Peter Watkins.   *Doom-
watch* (GB 72) Peter Sasdy *aka Island of the Ghouls / Something Like the
Truth*.   *Holocaust 2000* (It / GB 77) Alberto De Martino *aka The
Chosen*.   *Operation Ganymed* (G 77) Rainer Erler *aka Operation
Ganymede*.   *Red Alert* (77 TV) Billy Hale.   *Stronger Than the Sun* (GB 77
TV) Michael Apted.   *The China Syndrome* (78) James Bridges.   *The Chain
Reaction* (Aust 79) Ian Berry *aka The Man at the Edge of the Freeway*.   *The*

Plutonium Incident (80 TV) Richard Michaels.   *The Atomic Cafe* (82) Kevin Rafferty, Jayne Loader, Pierce Rafferty.   *Im Zeichen des Kreuzes* (G 82) Rainer Boldt *aka Due to an Act of God / The Sign of the Cross.   World War III* (82 TV) David Greene.   *The Day After* (83 TV) Nicholas Meyer.   *Kono no ko nokoshite* (J 83) Keisuke Kinoshita *aka Children of Nagasaki.   One Night Stand* (Aust 83) John Duigan.   *Silkwood* (83) Mike Nichols.   *Testament* (83) Lynne Littman.   *Theads* (GB 84 TV) Mick Jackson.   *Kuroi ame* (J 88) Shohei Imamura *aka Black Rain.   Hiroshima: Out of the Ashes* (90 TV) Peter Werner.

Nuclear War Films   *see*   **WAR FILM**

Nude Encounter Group Film   *see*   **DOCUMENTARY: Sex Encounter Group Documentaries**

NUDIE (Nudie-Cutie)   Films relying on the presentation of naked women for their box-office appeal were very popular in the sixties. One of the earliest types is the nudie-cutie. It was basically the result of one man's foresight in supplying the goods to a demanding male audience. That man was Russ Meyer who virtually created single-handedly a new genre of sexploitation movie. His *The Immoral Mr. Teas* (1959) was produced for about $24,000 and quickly reaped one million dollars profit, launching a flood of imitators. In time, it helped to proclaim Russ Meyer the King of Nudies or, as sometimes he was known, King Leer. The film only featured bare breasts and buttocks, but was filmed with gusto, and there was plenty of humor in its telling of a story concerning a man who, after having been given an anesthetic while at the dentist's, has the ability to see naked every woman that he encounters. In these films, there was no sexual touching involved; it was all wish-fulfillment fantasy. The nudie-cuties endured until the mid-sixties. By then, stronger fare was needed. T & A movie (or "tits and ass") applies also to a nudie movie. *See also* **SEX EXPLOITATION FILM**.

The Immoral Mr. Teas (59) Russ Meyer *aka Mr. Tease and His Playthings / Steam Heat.   Lucky Pierre* (59) Herschell G. Lewis *aka The Adventures of Lucky Pierre.   Eve and the Handy Man* (60) Russ Meyer.   *Not Tonight, Henry* (60) W. Merle Connell.   *Once Upon a Knight* (61) Bob Cresse, Fred Nyquist.   *The Ruined Bruin* (61) John K. McCarthy *aka The Bare and the Shapely / The Riotous Bruin.   Wild Gals of the Naked West!* (61) Russ Meyer *aka The Immoral West—and How It Was Lost / Immoral Girls of the Naked West / Naked Gals of the Golden West / The Naked West—and How It Was Lost.   The Bare Hunt; or My Gun Is Jammed* (63) *aka The Bear Hunt / My Gun Is Jammed.   Heavenly Bodies!* (63) Russ Meyer.   *Promises! Promises!* (63) King Donovan *aka Promise Her Anything.   Pardon My Brush* (64) John M. McCarthy.   *SINderella and the Golden Bra* (64) Loel Minardi *aka CINderella and the Golden— / Cinderella and the Golden Dress / Sinderella, Cindy and Her Golden Dress.   The Wonderful World of Girls* (65) Arthur P. Stootsberry.   *The Naked World of Harrison Marks* (GB 67) Harrison Marks *aka The Dream of Harrison Marks.   Uncle Tomcat's House of Kittens* (67) Gunther Purdue *aka Uncle Tomcat and His House of Kittens.*

Nudie-Cutie *see* **NUDIE**

NUDIST FILM (Nudist-Camp Film)   This species of sexploitation film was popular in the 1950s when censorship laws regarding nudity started to relax around the world. Nudist films were basically innocuous with little or no plot, presented as documentaries and featuring naked people cavorting in nudist camps, playing volleyball, watersports, sunbathing, or otherwise engaged in other innocent activities. Most nudist films only showed partial nudity avoiding full frontals and any activity that could be considered sexual. It was not until the mid-sixties that they started featuring unabashed nakedness; but, by then, the genre was already petering out. Nudist films can be traced back to Germany where they started to appear in the mid-1920s. Now and then, a nudist feature of a documentary nature is still made showing a Miss Nude Universe pageant or nudist spots around the world.

Wege zu Kraft und Schönheit (G 25) Wilhelm Prager *aka The Road to Strength and Beauty.   Garden of Eden* (54) Walter Ribo, Max Nosseck. *Naturisten-Ferien* (Swiz 58) Werner Kunz *aka Around the World with Nothing On / Insel der Sonnenfreude / Nacht um die Welt / Sonne auf der Haut / Vacances naturistes.   Nudist Paradise* (GB 59) Charles Saunders. *Nature Camp Confidential* (61) Doris Wishman *aka Diary of a Nudist / Nature Camp Diary / Nudist Camp / Nudist Confidential.   World without Shame* (GB 61) Donovan Winter.   *Sonne, Meer und nackte Menschen / Les filles du Dieu Soleil / Sole, mare e nudita* (Swiz 62) Alexander Swiagenin *aka The Nude Ones / Töchter der Sonne.   Goldilocks and the Three Bares* (63) Herschell Gordon Lewis *aka Singing in the Sun / (Goldilocks) Three Chicks. Nature's Sweethearts* (63) Larry Wolk *aka Nature's Beautiful Playmates.   The Raw Ones* (65) John Lamb *aka The Rare Ones.   She Did It His Way!* (68) John Lamb.   *The Naked Peacock* (Can 73-74) Denis Hargrave.   *The Miss Nude America Contest* (75) James P. Blake.

Nurse Films *see* **SOFT-CORE SEX-EXPLOITATION FILM**

Nudist-Camp Film *see* **NUDIST FILM;** *see also* **SEX EX-PLOITATION FILM**

Nuts-and-Bolts Film *see* **FACTUAL FILM**

Oater, Oats Opera *see* **WESTERN**

Oatuner *see* **WESTERN: Musical Westerns**

Object Animation Films *see* **ANIMATED FILM**

OCKER FILM (Ockerism)   The term "ocker," a recent Australian colloquialism, has been used to define a very basic characteristic of the Australian ethos. In motion pictures, it usually means the boisterous, rowdy, beer-drinking, uncultured Australian who, on homeground or abroad, makes his presence felt mainly with a series of vociferous expletives or through his boorish behavior. Most ocker films are comedies, but a few straight films also reflect the "ocker" attitude. *See* Tom O'Regan, "Cinema

Oz: The Ocker Films," in *The Australian Screen,* eds. Albert Moran and Tom O'Regan (Ringwood, Vic., Australia: Penguin, 1989): 75–98.
Stork (Aust 71) Tim Burstall *aka The Coming of Stork.* *The Adventures of Barry McKenzie* (Aust) Bruce Beresford. *The Office Picnic* (Aust 72) Tom Cowan. *Petersen* (Aust 74) Tim Burstall *aka Campus / "Jock" Petersen.* *Don's Party* (Aust 76) Bruce Beresford. *The F. J. Holden* (Aust 76) Michael Thornhill. *High Rolling* (Aust 77) Phillip Noyce *aka High Roll / High Roller / High Rolling in a Hot Corvette.* *Summer City* (Aust 76-77) Christopher Fraser.

Ockerism   *see*   **OCKER FILM**

Oddball Comedy   *see*   **SCREWBALL COMEDY**

Offnetwork Reruns   *see*   **TELEVISION PROGRAM**

Old Dark House Mystery, Old House Film, Old House-Thriller   *see*   **HAUNTED HOUSE FILM**

OLDIE   An often affectionate or nostalgic word for an old film. Usually, it is the viewer who decides which motion pictures he/she considers to be oldies.

Ombres chinoises   *see*   **ANIMATED FILM**

Omnibus Film   *see*   **EPISODE FILM**

Once-Only Show   *see*   **TELEVISION SPECIAL**

One-Hander   *see*   **HARD-CORE PORNO FILM**

One-Man Comedy Show   *see*   **STAND-UP COMEDY**

One-Off Play   *see*   **TELEVISION DRAMA: Single Play**

One-Off Special   *see*   **TELEVISION SPECIAL**

One-Reeler, One-Reel Film   *see*   **SHORT**

One-Shot Film   *see*   **SHORT: Multi-Shot Film**

One-Shot Program, One Time Only   *see*   **TELEVISION SPECIAL**

Opaskino   *see*   **NEW GERMAN CINEMA**

Open-End Series   *see*   **TELEVISION SERIES**

Open-Ended Show   *see*   **SOAP OPERA**

OPERA FILM (Film Opera)   Although there existed operatic films, filmed operas and dramatizations of operas during the silent years, the opera film proper belongs to the sound screen.[76] Fittingly, the first sound opera film was the Italian production *La serva padrona* (1932), directed by Giorgio Mannini. Yet most opera films have never been popular or commercially profitable, and their development has been slow. Biographies of opera singers and operettas have had more public appeal.

Opera films fall into three main types or forms: a) filmed records of staged operas; b) filmed interpretations of operas using techniques appropriate to the film medium; and c) operas specially created as opera films and television operas, or free adaptations of existing operas. *See* MUSICAL.
La serva padrona (It 32) Giorgio Mannini.   *Die verkaufte Braut* (G 32) Max Ophüls *aka The Bartered Bride.*   *Louise* (F 38) Abel Gance.   *Tosca* (It 41) Carlo Koch [begun by Jean Renoir] *aka La Tosca.*   *Rigoletto* (It 46) Carmine Gallone.   *The Medium* (51) Gian-Carlo Menotti.   *The Tales of Hoffman* (GB 51) Michel Powell, Emeric Pressburger.   *Aida* (It 53) Clemente Fracassi.   *Carmen Jones* (54) Otto Preminger.   *Don Giovanni* (GB 54) Paul Czinner, Alfred Travers.   *Giovanna d'Arco al rogo / Jean au Bûcher* (It / F 54) Roberto Rossellini *aka Joan of Arc at the Stake.*   *Madama Butterfly / Chocho Fujin* (It / J 54) Carmine Gallone.   *Der Rosenkavalier* (GB 60) Paul Czinner.   *Katerina Izmailova* (USSR 66) Mikhail Shapiro *aka Lady Macbeth of Mtsensk.*   *Owen Wingrave* (GB 70 TV) Vaclav Neumann (production manager).   *Moses und Aron / Moïse et Aaron / Mosè e Aronne* (G / F / It 74) Jean-Marie Straub, Danièle Huillet *aka Moses and Aaron. Trollflöjten / Die Zauberflöte* (Sw 74-75 TV) Ingmar Bergman *aka The Magic Flute.*   *Don Giovanni* (F / It / G / GB 79) Joseph Losey.   *Parsifal* (G 82) Hans Jürgen Syberberg.   *La Traviata* (It 82) Franco Zeffirelli *aka The Lady of Camellias. Otello* (It 86) Franco Zeffirelli.   *La Bohème* (F / It 87) Luigi Comencini.

Operatic Film   *see*   OPERA FILM

Operettas   *see*   MUSICAL

Oppositional Film   *see*   INDEPENDENT PRODUCTION

Organized-Crime Film   *see*   GANGSTER FILM: Syndicate Films

Oriental Swashbucklers   *see*   SWASHBUCKLER

Original Hollywood Musicals   *see*   MUSICAL

Oscar Show   *see*   TELEVISION SHOW: TV Award Show

Other Denizens of Horror Movies   *see*   HORROR FILM

OTO / One Time Only   *see*   TELEVISION SPECIAL

Outlaw Bike Gang Film   *see*   MOTORCYCLE MOVIE: Motorcycle Gang Films

Outlaw-Couple Film   *see*   GANGSTER FILM: Outlaw Gangster Films

Outlaw Films   *see*   WESTERN

Out-of-Camera Film   *see*   ANIMATION: Cameraless Animated Films

Pacifist Films   *see*   WAR FILM

Paella Western   *see*   SPAGHETTI WESTERN

Painted-On Film   *see*   ABSTRACT FILM: Synthetic Films

Panel Game   *see*   TELEVISION SHOW: Quiz Show

Panic Cinema   *see*   SURREALIST FILM

Panorama, Panoramic Film   *see*   EARLY FILM

Paranoid Thriller   *see*   CONSPIRACY FILM

Park Comedies, Park Films   *see*   SLAPSTICK

Parodies   *see*   MUSICAL

PARODY (Burlesque, Pastiche, Send-Up, Spoof, Takeoff, Travesty)
Movies started parodying other movies and the movie world early in the
silent era. All the major silent comedians of the time engaged in parody,
including Charlie Chaplin, Harold Lloyd and especially Buster Keaton.
Parody was then in its Golden Age. Parody is essentially a comic imitation
of something which already exists or has existed. It exaggerates and
ridicules. Films parody other films or a group of films, a theatrical work,
a film genre or several film genres, a filmmaker's style or a performer's acting and idiosyncrasies. In every case, parody presupposes a foreknowledge
or awareness of the object or person that is parodied on the part of the
reader, viewer or spectator of the parody.

A few spoofs of the sixties — *Cat Ballou* (1965), *Modesty Blaise* (1965) —
had their main characters address the audience, breaking the picture's continuity. For the most part, this technique has rarely been successful with
audiences and has only succeeded in alienating most spectators; the practice
has largely been discontinued. Parodies in the seventies had two major
practitioners — Mel Brooks and Woody Allen. They have continued to produce movies in their adopted fashion.

Burlesque (not in the sense of a striptease show) is used sometimes as a
synonymous term for parody. *Charlie Chaplin's Burlesque on Carmen*
(1915) is a famous example. The term travesty has a pejorative connotation
attached to it and thus it could also be applied to a movie. Pastiche is
another word for parody and may be used in a neutral or pejorative sense.
Very often parodies are branded as satires, but satire (q.v.) criticizes society
rather than art.

Charlie Chaplin's Burlesque on Carmen (15) Charles Chaplin *aka Carmen.*
The Three Must-Get-Theres (22) Max Linder.   *The Shriek of Araby* (23) F.
Richard Jones.   *The Three Ages* (23) Buster Keaton, Eddie Cline.   *Stand-In*
(37) Tay Garnett.   *Beat the Devil / Il tesoro dell'Africa* (US / It / GB 53)
John Huston.   *L'Homme de Rio / L'uomo di Rio* (F / It 63) Philippe De
Broca *aka That Man from Rio.   Casino Royal* (GB 65) John Huston, Ken
Hughes, Val Guest, Robert Parrish, Joe McGrath, Richard Talmadge, An-
thony Squire.   *Cat Ballou* (65) Elliot Silverstein.   *Modesty Blaise* (GB 65)
Joseph Losey.   *The Dove / De Duv* (68) George Coe, Anthony Lover. *Lone-
some Cowboys* (68) Andy Warhol.   *Support Your Local Sheriff!* (69) Burt

Kennedy *aka Latigo—Support Your Local Sheriff. Young Frankenstein* (74) Mel Brooks. *Love and Death* (75) Woody Allen. *The Cheap Detective* (78) Robert Moore. *Fairy Tales* (78) Harry Trampa *aka Adult Fairy Tales. Movie Movie* (78) Stanley Donen [in two parts: "Dynamite Hands" and "Baxter's Beauties of 1933"]. *Airplane!* (80) Jim Abrahams, David Zucker, Jerry Zucker *aka Flying High. Partners* (82) James Burrows. *Bullshot* (GB 83) Dick Clement. *The Man with Two Brains* (83) Carl Reiner. *Strange Invaders* (83) Michael Laughlin. *Zelig* (83) Woody Allen. *Transylvania 6-5000* (US / Yug 85) Rudy DeLuca. *I'm Going to Get You Sucka* (88) Keenen Ivory Wayans. *Ladri di saponette* (It 88) Maurizio Nichetti *aka The Icicle Thief / Icicle Thieves. The Naked Gun: From the Files of Police Squad* (88) David Zucker *aka The Naked Gun.*

————**Television Parodies**   An interesting form is the parody of the idiot box, as some would call the television set, although repetitive because it has to fall back continuously on its chosen subject. These films are made of a great number of sketches or brief vignettes spoofing anything that can be seen on television from beauty contests to commercials, including the six o'clock news.

The Groove Tube (74) Ken Shapiro. *Tunnel Vision* (75) Brad Swirnoff, Neil Israel *aka Tunnel Vision the no bullshit network. American Tickler* (76) Chuck Vincent *aka American Tickler or the Winner of 10 Academy Awards / Draws / The Winner of Ten Academy Awards. The Kentucky Fried Movie* (77) John Landis. *Video Vixens!* (79) Ronald Sullivan. *UHF* (89) Jay Levey.

Participatory Film *see* **STRUCTURAL FILM**

PARTISAN FILM ("Eastern")   Guerrillas fighting the Japanese in the Philippines, in China and other countries of South East Asia; the Maquis fighting the Germans in France; or partisans fighting the Germans and Italians in the Balkans during World War II: all have in common the mission to harass the enemy, rid the country of the occupying forces and gain ultimate victory. Films depicting the exploits of such resistance fighters have been made intermittently since the end of World War II. However, the partisan film is of particular importance in Eastern European countries where, besides providing entertainment by showing acts of heroism in the face of insurmountable odds, it also propounds Communist ideals.

Partisan films, or "Easterns" as they are sometimes labelled, have been made in different countries, but they are of major significance in the development of Yugoslav cinema where they evolved into a genre of their own, or rather, into a distinct subgenre of the war film.[77] *See also* **WAR FILM: Resistance Films.**

Sekretar raikom (USSR 42) Ivan Pyriev *aka Secretary of the District Committee. Ona zaschchishchayet rodinu* (USSR 43) Friedrich Ermler *aka She Defends Her Country. V gorakh Yugoslavii / U planinama Jugoslavije* (USSR / Yug 46) Abram Room, Viekoslav Afric *aka In the Mountains of Yugoslavia. Slavica* (Yug 47) Vjekoslav Afric. *Na svojoj zemli* (Yug 48) France Stiglic *aka On Their Own Ground. Partizani* (Bulg 58) Binka

Zhelyazkova *aka Life Flows Quietly By / Partisans / Zhivotat si teche tiho.*
Partizanske price (Yug 60) Stole Jankovic *aka Partisan Stories.* *Pleneno*
yato (Bulg 62) Ducho Mundrov *aka Captured Squadron.* *Tri* (Yug 65)
Aleksandar Petrovic *aka Three.* **Bitka na Neretvi / The Battle of Neretva**
/ La battaglia della Neretva / Die Schlacht an dei Neretva (Yug / US / It /
G 69) Veljko Bulajic *aka The Battle of the River Neretva.* **Osmiyat** (Bulg
69) Zako Heskia *aka The Eighth.*

Part-talkie *see* **SOUND FILM**

Passion Melodrama *see* **MELODRAMA**

Pastiche *see* **PARODY**

Pathfinder *see* **SEMINAL FILM**

PATRIOTIC MOVIE   In a way, patriotic movies are propaganda
movies praising the virtues of one's country, virtues which are found to be
righteous and better than those held by any other country. These films rally
to and advocate the defense of the cherished traditions, values and principles of the nation. Examples of patriotic films may be found in any mode
or genre.

An Officer and a Gentleman (81) Taylor Hackford. *The Right Stuff* (83)
Philip Kaufman. *Moscow on the Hudson* (84) Paul Mazursky. *The*
Natural (84) Barry Levinson. *Red Dawn* (84) John Milius. *Rambo* (85)
George P. Cosmatos *aka Rambo: First Blood Part II.* *Death Before*
Dishonor (US / Isr 86) Terry J. Leonard. *Top Gun* (86) Tony Scott.

Pattern Film *see* **ABSTRACT FILM**

Peep Show Film *see* **SEX EXPLOITATION FILM**

Penal Colony Films *see* **PRISON FILM**

People Show *see* **TELEVISION SHOW: Game Show**

PEPLUM (Sex-and-Sand Epic, S & S Movie)   Peplum is a term given
by French critics to an Italian-made or co-produced "epic" of the fifties and
sixties. In ancient times, the term meant either a kind of robe worn by
Greek women or an outer skirt. Peplums are minor epics featuring
mythological, biblical and Italian-created strongmen elevated to the
category of popular heroes: Hercules, Maciste, Ursus, Samson, Goliath,
Taur. These muscle men were known to overcome problems and difficulties
of any sort by sheer brawn rather than brain. They encountered all kinds
of enemies — Barbarians, Atlanteans, Amazons, Babylonians, Vikings,
Tartars, and supernatural beings like vampires, gorgons and other
monsters. These epics, produced in Cinecittà, experienced a Golden Age
and reached foreign markets. In the period 1953–1965 some 200 were made
before the cycle had run its course. The trend was not new on Italian
screens; the genre is Italian in its origins and goes back to the early 1900s.
Ursus and Maciste, two home-produced heroes, made their film debut

respectively in *Quo Vadis* (1912) and *Cabiria* (1913), the first directed by Enrico Guazzoni and the second by Giovanni Pastrone. The peplum has also been referred to as sword-and-sandal epic, sandal-and-spear/s epic, spear-and-sandal epic, cloak-and-sandal, gladiator, and muscle / muscle-man epic.[78] *See also* **EPIC.**

Quo Vadis (It 12) Enrico Guazzoni. *Cabiria* (It 13) Giovanni Pastrone. *Teodora, imperatrice di Bisanzio* (It 53) Riccardo Freda *aka Theodora / Theodora, Queen of Byzantium / Theodora, Slave Empress.* *Le Fatiche di Ercole* (It 57) Pietro Francisci *aka Hercules.* *Nel segno di Roma / Sous le signe de Rome / Im Zeichen Roms* (It / F / G 58) Guido Brignone, Riccardo Freda *aka La Regina del Deserto / The Sign of the Gladiator.* *La Battaglia di Maratona / La Bataille de Marathon* (It / F 59) Jacques Tourneur, Bruno Vailati *aka The Giant of Marathon.* *Cartagine in fiamme / Carthage en flammes* (It / F 59) Carmine Gallone *aka Carthage in Flames.* *Gli ultimi giorni di Pompeii / Los últimos días de Pompeya / Die letzten Tage von Pompeii* (It / Sp / Mon [G] 59) Mario Bonnard *aka The Last Days of Pompeii.* *I Colosso di Rodi / El coloso de Rodes / Le Colosse de Rhodes* (It / Sp / F 60) Sergio Leone *aka The Colossus of Rhodes.* *Saffo, venere di Lesbo / Sapho* (It / F 60) Pietro Francisci *aka Warrior Empress.* *Ursus* (It / Sp 60) Carlo Campogaliani *aka Mighty Ursus.* *Arrivano i Titani / Les Titans* (It / F 61) Duccio Tessari *aka I Titani / My Son the Hero / Sons of Thunder.* *Ercole al centro della terra* (It 61) Mario Bava *aka Hercules at the Centre of the Earth / Hercules in the Haunted World.* *Ercole alla conquista di Atlantide / Hercule à la conquête del'Atlantide* (It / F 61) Vittorio Cottafavi *aka Hercules and the Captive Women / Hercules Conquers Atlantis.* *Sodoma e Gomorrah / Sodome et Gomorrhe / Sodom and Gomorrah* (US / F / It 61) Robert Aldrich, Sergio Leone *aka The Last Days of Sodom.* *Maciste contro Ercole nella valle dei guai* (It / Sp 62) Mario Matou (Mario Mattoli) *aka Hercules in the Vale of Woe / Maciste Against Hercules in the Vale of Woe.* *Ercole contro i figli del Sole / Hércules contra los hijos del Sol / Hercule contre les fils du dieu soleil* (It / Sp / F 64) Osvaldo Civirani *aka Hercules Against the Sons of the Sun.* *Kampf um Rom I / La calata dei barbari* (G / It / Rum 68) Robert Siodmak *aka Battle for Rome / Fight for Rome / The Last Roman.* *Le calde notte di Caligula* (It 77) Roberto Montero *aka Caligula's Hot Nights.* *Caligola / Caligula* (It / US 77) Giovanni Tinto Brass. *Le Schiave di Caligola* (It 82) Lawrence Webber *aka Roma-l'antica chiave dei sensi / Caligula's Slaves / Roma—The Old Key of the Senses.*

Perceptual Film   *see*   **STRUCTURAL FILM: Flicker Film**

Performance Video   *see*   **MUSIC VIDEO**

Period Chiller   *see*   **PERIOD FILM: Period Thrillers**

PERIOD FILM   The term applies to a film set in an era other than the present. A handy defining line for what constitutes a period film is the late 19th century; films set in an earlier time are better designated costume or historical films. *See* **NOSTALGIA FILM.**

———**Period Thrillers (Gothic Melodramas)**   They are mostly Victorian melodramas, sometimes called atmospheric films or period chillers. They are an important branch of the period film.

The Lodger (44) John Brahm. *Hangover Square* (45) John Brahm. *The Suspect* (45) Robert Siodmak. *The Spiral Staircase* (45) Robert Siodmak aka *The Silence of Helen McCord / Some Must Watch*. *Ivy* (47) Sam Wood. *The Woman in White* (48) Peter Godfrey. *The Tall Target* (51) Anthony Mann.

Period SF Films   *see*   SCIENCE FICTION FILM

Period Thrillers   *see*   PERIOD FILM

Personal Film   *see*   UNDERGROUND FILM

Persuasive Documentary   *see*   DOCUMENTARY

Persuasive Film   *see*   FACTUAL FILM

Pesto Western   *see*   SPAGHETTI WESTERN

Phenomena Film   *see*   SPECULATIVE DOCUMENTARY

Photo-Drama, Photo-Play, Photoplay   *see*   FILM

Physical Comedy   *see*   SLAPSTICK

Physical Film   *see*   STRUCTURAL FILM

P. I. Film   *see*   PRIVATE DETECTIVE FILM

Pic / Pix   *see*   FILM

Picaresque   *see*   BLACK FILM: Black Genre Movies

Picaresque Comedy   *see*   SEX COMEDY: Stud Comedies

Picaresque Films   *see*   UNDERGROUND FILM

Picture, Picture Play   *see*   FILM

Pie-Throwing Film   *see*   SLAPSTICK

Piggyback   *see*   TELEVISON COMMERCIAL

Pill   *see*   CARTOON FILM

Pilot, Pilot Show   *see*   TELEVISION SERIES: Series Pilot

Pin-Board Animation, Pinhead Animation   *see*   ANIMATED FILM: Pin Screen Animation Films

Pirate Films   *see*   SWASHBUCKLER

Pixilated Films, Pixilation   *see*   ANIMATED FILM

Pocket Cartoon   *see*   CARTOON FILM

Pod   *see*   TELEVISION COMMERCIAL

Poetic Film   *see*   NARRATIVE FILM

Poetic Realism *see* **POETIC-REALIST FILM**

POETIC-REALIST FILM (Poetic Realism, Psychological Realism, Réalisme Poétique)   The term *réalisme poétique* is used to define a French film school and filmic style of the middle and and late 1930s which added a poetic element to its visualization of the prevalent social mood of the time. This school was greatly imbued with the leftist ideas of the Popular Front (*Front Populaire*), a coalition found at the inception of the Socialist and Communist political parties.

Typical of the films belonging to this school is the use of simple people as popular heroes, the interplay of love and destiny and the ever-present struggle between good and evil in a realistic, atmospheric milieu.

Le Grand Jeu / La donna dai due volti (F / It 33) Jacques Feyder *aka Card of Fate / The Full Deck / The Great Game*. *Pension Mimosas* (F 34) Jacques Feyder. *Le Crime de M. Lange* (F 35) Jean Renoir *aka L'Ascension de M. Lange / Dans la cour / Sur la cour / Un Homme se sauve / The Crime of Monsieur Lange*. *La Belle Équipe* (F 36) Julien Duvuvier *aka A Five Team / They Were Five*. *Pépé le Moko* (F 36) Julien Duvuvier *aka Les Nuits blanches*. *Une Partie de campagne* (F 36) Jean Renoir *aka Partie de Campagne / A Day in the Country*. *La Fin du jour* (F 38) Julien Duvivier *aka The End of the Day*. *Hôtel du Nord* (F 38) Marcel Carné. *Quai des brumes* (F 38) Marcel Carné *aka Le Quai des brumes / Port of Shadows*. *Le Jour se lève* (F 39) Marcel Carné *aka Daybreak*. *Remorques* (F 39) Jean Grémillon *aka Stormy Waters*. *Lumière d'été* (F 42) Jean Grémillon.

Poetry-Film *see* **FILM POEM**

Police Comedies, Police Department Films, Police Detective Films *see* **POLICE FILM**

POLICE FILM (Cop Movie, Investigative Film, Law Enforcement Drama, Police Procedural, Policier)   If the criminal's intention is to break the law, the law enforcement officer's job is to prevent the criminal from carrying out his intention or to apprehend the offender and make him pay his dues to society. This noble motivation does not ensure that the officer himself will not break the law, and the corrupt cop in the celluloid medium is as ubiquitous as the honest one. Cop movies emphasize, or focus on, the policeman rather than the criminal. These movies cover quite an extensive range, but as a rule they may be subdivided into three general sections: cops in uniform or policemen on the beat; the police commissioner, inspector, detective, or lieutenant in Homicide, the Drug Squad, or any other section of a Police Department; and the sheriff in townships or small rural communities carrying out the same duties as his counterparts in the cities. On the Federal level, the federal agent is able to pursue criminals interstate. The police film goes as far back as the crime film — whenever there was a crime there was a policeman ready to try to solve it. Naturally, some police films equally qualify as gangster pictures.

Kid Glove Killer (42) Fred Zinnemann. *He Walked by Night* (48) Alfred L.

Werker. *Where the Sidewalk Ends* (50) Otto Preminger. *On Dangerous Ground* (51) Nicholas Ray. *The Narrow Margin* (52) Alfred E. Green. *Rogue Cop* (54) Roy Rowland. *The French Connection* (71) William Friedkin. *Across 110th Street* (72) Barry Shear. *The Friends of Eddie Coyle* (72) Peter Yates. *The Offence* (GB 72) Sidney Lumet *aka Something Like the Truth*. *The Laughing Policeman* (73) Stuart Rosenberg *aka An Investigation of Murder*. *The French Connection II* (US / F 74) John Frankenheimer *aka French Connection Number 2*. *Law and Disorder* (74) Ivan Passer. *Demon* (76) Larry Cohen *aka God Told Me To*. *Law and Order* (76 TV) Marvin Chomsky. *The Onion Field* (79) Harold Becker. *Copkiller / Order of Death* (It / US 82) Roberto Faenza *aka L'assassino dei poliziotti / Cop Killers / Corrupt*. *Forbrydelsens Element* (Den 84) Lars von Trier *aka The Element of Crime*. *Tightrope* (84) Richard Tuggle. *Blackout* (85 MCTV) Douglas Hickox. *The Big Easy* (86) Jim McBride. *Above the Law* (88) Andrew Davis *aka Nico / Nico Above the Law*. *Action Jackson* (88) Craig R. Baxley. *Dead-Bang* (88) John Frankenheimer. *Deceptions* (89 MCTV) Ruben Preuss.

——**Buddy-Cop Films**   A police detective's life is often at risk when on duty and it helps to be able to trust one's partner. Buddy-cop movies in the 1980s had an abundance of combinations. Cops were paired off white and black, straight and gay, police officer and dog, American and Russian. Any acceptable combination was tried and filmed.

Future Cop (76 TV) Jud Taylor *aka Cleaver and Haven*. *Partners* (82) James Burrows. *The Hidden* (87) Jack Sholder. *Lethal Weapon* (87) Richard Donner. *Colors* (88) Dennis Hopper. *Red Heat* (88) Walter Hill. *K-9* (89) Rod Daniel. *Lethal Weapon 2* (89) Richard Donner. *Turner & Hooch* (89) Roger Spottiswoode. *Harbour Beat* (Aust 90) David Elfick.

——**Copper Films**   These films deal with the uniformed representatives of the law: men on the beat, rookie policemen or patrolmen carrying out their functions. It is, generally speaking, a less glamorized role than that of the police detective.

The Blue Lamp (GB 49) Basil Dearden. *The Prowler* (51) Joseph Losey. *The Strange Affair* (GB 68) David Greene. *The New Centurions* (72) Richard Fleischer *aka Precinct 45–Los Angeles Police*. *Electra Glide in Blue* (73) James William Guercio. *The Choirboys* (77) Robert Aldrich. *Fort Apache, the Bronx* (81) Daniel Petrie.

——**Federal Agent Films**   G-Men from the F.B.I., T-Men from the U.S. Treasury Department, and other types of federal agents came to the fore in the thirties when it was considered proper to deglamorize the gangster and instead enshrine the government man and other government enforcers. At present, films with special agents are not so popular, but they still keep reappearing. *See also* GANGSTER FILM: G-Man Films.

G-Men (35) William Keighley. *T-Men* (47) Anthony Mann. *The Street with No Name* (48) William Keighley. *The Undercover Man* (49) Joseph H. Lewis. *The FBI Story* (59) Mervyn LeRoy. *Hit!* (US / F 73) Sidney J. Furie.

——**Police Comedies**   The use of policemen as a butt for comedy goes back to the beginnings of the motion picture. One has only to think of the famous Keystone Kops brand of slapstick comedy of the silent era. The detective, usually in the guise of a blundering inspector, has also had his share of different incarnations. Among the many farces that have a foolish police officer, those of Peter Sellers as Inspector Clouseau and of Louis de Funès in the French *"gendarme"* series have been very popular in their respective countries of production.

Easy Street (17) Charlie Chaplin.   *Guardie e ladri* (It 51) Mario Monicelli, Steno *aka Cops and Robbers.   A Shot in the Dark* (US / GB 64) Blake Edwards.   *Le Gendarme à New York / Tre gendarmi a New York* (F / It 65) Jean Girault [6 films (1964-82) in the "Gendarme" series].   *Freebie and the Bean* (74) Richard Rush.   *Beverly Hills Cop* (84) Martin Brest.   *Police Academy* (Can 84) Hugh Wilson [6 films in the "Police Academy" series up to 1989].   *Les Ripoux* (F 84) Claude Zizi *aka My New Partner.   Beverly Hills Cop II* (85) Tony Scott.   *The Naked Gun: From the Files of Police Squad* (88) David Zucker.

——**Police Department Films**   A few police films do not place their emphasis on catching the criminal; instead, they try to show the working day or routine happenings inside a police precinct. They present the many problems encountered in the efficient running of the department, or the corruptible elements that may exist therein.

Detective Story (51) William Wyler.   *The Human Jungle* (54) Joseph M. Newman.   *Serpico* (73) Sidney Lumet.   *Report to the Commissioner* (74) Milton Katselas *aka Operation Undercover.   Assault on Precinct 13* (76) John Carpenter.   *A Question of Honor* (81 TV) Jud Taylor *aka Badge of Honor.   Prince of the City* (81) Sidney Lumet.   *Best Kept Secrets* (84 TV) Jerrold Freedman.   *Shakedown* (88) James Glickenhaus.   *Internal Affairs* (90) Mike Figgis.   *Q & A* (90) Sidney Lumet.

——**Police Detective Films**   In police investigation films, the detective may be a suave Sherlock Holmes–like fellow patiently unravelling the clues until he gets his man or woman; or a lieutenant or police inspector heading a battery of auxiliary detectives who, through massive detection or footwork, attain some results; or he may be a tough, rule-bending cop relentlessly pursuing his prey. He can also be a corrupt cop. The variations are endless.

Charlie Chan at the Opera (36) H. Bruce Humberstone [45 films (1929-49) in the "Charlie Chan" series].[79]   *Thank You, Mr. Moto* (37) Norman Foster [9 films (1937-65) in the "Mr. Moto" series].   *Laura* (44) Otto Preminger.   *The Naked City* (48) Jules Dassin *aka Homicide.   The Big Heat* (53) Fritz Lang. *The Long Arm* (GB 56) Charles Frend *aka The Third Key.   Madigan* (67) Don Siegel.   *Bullit* (68) Peter Yates.   *The Detective* (68) Gordon Douglas.   *Dirty Harry* (72) Don Siegel *aka Dead Right* [5 "Inspector Callahan" films up to 1988].   *Brannigan* (GB 75) Douglas Hickox.   *The Gauntlet* (77) Clint Eastwood.   *The First Deadly Sin* (80) Brian G. Hutton.   *48 HRS* (82) Walter Hill.   *Poulet au vinaigre* (F 84) Claude Chabrol *aka Cop au Vin.   Code of Silence* (85) Andrew Davis.   *Year of the Dragon* (85) Michael Cimino.   *Inspecteur Lavardin* (F 86) Claude Chabrol.

——**Sheriff Films**   The colorful sheriff of the traditional Western is still with us, although he now drives fast cars and his weaponry has become more sophisticated. The town sheriff oftentimes proves himself to be on a par with the city police detective.

Bobby Ware Is Missing (55) Thomas Carr. *The Chase* (65) Arthur Penn. *Coogan's Bluff* (68) Don Siegel. *Walking Tall* (72) Phil Karlson [followed by *Part 2, Walking Tall* (75) Earl Bellamy; *Final Chapter— Walking Tall* (77) Jack Starrett; *A Real American Hero* (78 TV) Lou Antonio]. *The Klansman* (74) Terence Young *aka The Burning Cross*. *The Killing Time* (87) Rick King. *Frame Up* (90) Paul Leder.

Police Procedural, Policier *see* **POLICE FILM**

Polite Comedy *see* **COMEDY OF MANNERS**

Political Allegory *see* **POLITICAL FILM**

Political Conspiracy Film *see* **CONSPIRACY FILM**

Political Extrapolation Films *see* **SCIENCE FICTION FILM**

Political Fiction Film *see* **POLITICAL THRILLER**

POLITICAL FILM   It has been stated that all films are political to a certain extent, since they convey at least the filmmaker's point of view and ideas, a point of view and ideas which in themselves may affect those of the viewers. This statement is too broad to be of any practical use in the categorizing of genres. Neither would it be practical to point out the political undercurrents in specific genres, e.g., horror, science fiction, Westerns. Here, we are concerned with films which are made with a political aim in mind, be it covert or overt. The desire to propound or disseminate a political ideology is very ancient, its goal being to reaffirm the political belief of its adherents and to gain further converts. Equally strong is the desire to uncover the motivations behind any political machinery that seeks to exploit the politically unaware citizen. With these goals, the political film has existed since the beginnings of the motion picture. There have been several waves of political films, mostly from totalitarian or rightist systems of government. It is, however, since the sixties that political films have proliferated. Indeed, there has been a definite resurgence of political films, especially on the part of the Left, films which contest most of the previously sacrosanct and firmly upheld values and principles of society and government. Hence, the political film extends itself not only to areas of political concern but of social concern as well. The political film has taken many diverse forms. Political films include, first of all, the propaganda film (q.v.). Then there is the political film that deals with a political topic, e.g., the rivalry among political parties, mismanagement, corruption or personal gain inside a political party, the run for the presidency, biographical films on the life of a political figure, or films which deal with sensitive international areas that may cause friction. There are also films which draw attention to a particular political issue, national or international.

This type of movie seeks to expose the injustice or corruption of politics, the practice of political expediency or the wrong in a prevailing political system of government (a seminal film in this vein is Costa-Garvas's *Z*, 1968). There is also the revolutionary film (q.v.) whose aim is to bring about changes by means of open revolution or by implanting revolutionary ideas. It should be noted as well that in totalitarian countries such as Spain during General Franco's dictatorship, France under German occupation, or in the Communist Eastern block countries, the political film, unable to express itself openly or clandestinely, has often taken the form of the political allegory (e.g., Jan Nemec's *O Slavnosti a hostech / A Report on the Party and the Guests*, 1965). *See also* **POLITICAL THRILLER**.

Camicia nera (It 33) Gioacchino Forzano.   *Morgenrot* (G 33) Grustav Ucicky *aka Dawn*.   *State of the Union* (48) Frank Capra.   *All the King's Men* (49) Robert Rossen.   *The Last Hurrah* (58) John Ford.   *Le Petit Soldat* (F 60) Jean-Luc Godard.   *No Love for Johnnie* (GB 61) Ralph Thomas.   *Salvatore Giuliano* (It 61) Francesco Rosi *aka Bandit's Revenge / Dreaded Mafia*. *Advice and Consent* (62) Otto Preminger.   *The Best Man* (64) Franklin J. Schaffner.   *O Slavnosti a hostech* (Cz 65) Jan Nemec *aka The Party and the Guests / A Report on the Party and the Guests*.   *La Chinoise* (F 67) Jean-Luc Godard *aka La Chinoise, ou plutôt a la Chinoise / La Chinoise, ou plutôt à la Chinoise, un film en train de se faire*.   *Jag är nyfiken—gul* (Sw 67) Vilgot Sjöman *aka I am Curious (Yellow)*.   *Memorias del sudesarrollo* (Cuba 68) Tomás Gutiérrez Alea *aka Memories of Underdevelopment*. *Quemada! / Queimada!* (F / It 68) Gillo Pontecorvo *aka Battle in the Antilles / Burn!*   *Sympathy for the Devil* (GB 68) Jean-Luc Godard *aka One Plus One / Sympathy for the Devil (1 + 1)*.   *Z* (F / Alg 68) Costa-Gavras [subtitled: "L'Anatomie d'un assassinat politique"].   *L'Aveu / La confession* (F / It 69) Costa-Gavras *aka The Confession*.   *Medium Cool* (69) Haskell Wexler *aka Concrete Wilderness*.   *Sanrizuka: Daini turide no hitobito* (J 71) Shinsuke Ogawa *aka Peasants of the Second Fortress*.   *The Candidate* (72) Michael Ritchie.   *Réjeanne Padovani* (Can 72) Denys Arcand.   *The Trial of the Catonsville Nine* (72) Gordon Davidson.   *L'Horloger de Saint-Paul* (F 73) Bertrand Tavernier *aka The Clockmaker / The Watchmaker of St. Paul*.   *Underground* (75) Emile De Antonio, Mary Lampson, Haskell Wexler.   *All the President's Men* (76) Alan J. Pakula.   *Eleanor and Franklin* (76 TV) Daniel Petrie.   *Uppdraget* (Nor / Sw 76-77) Mats Arehn *aka The Assignment*.   *Eleanor and Franklin: The White House Years* (77 TV) Daniel Petrie.   *Lady of the House* (78 TV) Ralph Nelson. *Kent State* (81 TV) James Goldstone.   *Eleanor, First Lady of the World* (82 TV) John Erman.   *Cal* (GB 84) Pat O'Connor.   *La Diagonale du fou* (F / Swiz 84) Richard Dembo *aka Dangerous Moves*.   *Secret Honor* (84) Robert Altman.   *Marie* (85) Roger Donaldson.   *Salvador* (US / Mex 85) Oliver Stone.   *Place of Weeping* (SA 86) Darrell Roodt.   *Unnatural Causes* (86 TV) Lamont Johnson.   *LBJ: The Early Years* (87 TV) Peter Werner.   *Scandal* (GB / US 88) Michael Caton-Jones.   *Romero* (89) John Duigan.

Political Paranoid Thriller   *see*   **CONSPIRACY FILM**

Political Prisoners Films   *see*   **PRISON FILM**

Political Spy Fims   *see*   **SPY FILM**

POLITICAL THRILLER (Political Fiction Film)   A genre (or sub-genre of the political film) usually traced back to Costa-Gavras's *Z* (1968) and his subsequent films. The political thriller mixes fiction with fact or, to some extent, fictionalizes or highly dramatizes recent political happenings. Besides beginning the genre, Gavras's films are a good example and serve to categorize this type of thriller which was quickly adopted by filmmakers in various countries. *See* **POLITICAL FILM** and **CONSPIRACY FILM**.

Z (F / Alg 68) Costa-Gavras [subtitled: "L'anatomie d'un assassinat politique"].   *The Chairman / The Most Dangerous Man in the World* (US / GB 69) J. Lee Thompson.   *Indagine su un cittadino al di sopra di ogni sospetto* (It 70) Elio Petri *aka Investigation of a Citizen above Suspicion.*   *L'Attentat / L'Attentato / Das Attentat* (F / It / G 72) Yves Boisset *aka The Assassination / The French Conspiracy / Plot.*   *État de siège / L'Amerikano / Der unsichtbare Aufstand* (F / It / G 72) Costa-Gavras *aka State of Siege.*   *Section spéciale / L'affare della sezione speciale* (F / It / G 74) Costa-Gavras *aka Special Section.*   *The Missiles of October* (74 TV) Anthony Page.   *Hennessy* (GB / US 75) Don Sharp *aka The 5th of November.*   *Black Sunday* (77) John Frankenheimer.   *Washington: Behind Closed Doors* (77 TV) Gary Nelson [in 6 parts].   *Capricorn One* (78) Peter Hyams.   *I . . . comme Icare* (F 79) Henri Verneuil.   *Missing* (81) Costa-Gavras.   *Under Fire* (83) Roger Spottiswoode. *Marie* (85) Roger Donaldson.   *Defence of the Realm* (GB 86) David Drury.   *The Whistle Blower* (GB 86) Simon Lagton.   *Assassination* (87) Peter Hunt *aka Assassin / The President's Wife.*

Pop Clip   *see*   **MUSIC VIDEO**

Pop Musicals   *see*   **MUSICAL**

Popular History Films   *see*   **HISTORICAL FILM**

Popular Science Film   *see*   **FACTUAL FILM: Educational Film**

POPULIST COMEDY   A type of comedy that sings the virtues of the common people, extols their values and reasserts their rights against rampant injustice and elitist pressures. The classical example of a populist comedy is Frank Capra's *Mr. Deed Goes to Town* (1936). On the subject of populist comedy, *see* Wes D. Gehring's "Populist Comedy" in *Handbook of American Film Genres*, edited by him (New York: Greenwood Press, 1988). *See* **SOCIAL CONSCIOUSNESS FILM: Social comedy** and **Populist Films.**

So This Is London (30) John Blystone.   *Mr. Deed Goes to Town* (36) Frank Capra.   *Mr. Smith Goes to Washington* (39) Frank Capra.   *The Talk of the Town* (42) George Stevens.   *Billy Jack Goes to Washington* (77) Tom Laughlin [last in a series of 4 "Billy Jack" films (1967-77)].   *Protocol* (84) Herbert Ross.

Populist Films   *see*   **SOCIAL CONSCIOUSNESS FILM**

Porn Film, Pornie   *see*   **SEX EXPLOITATION FILM**

PORNO CHIC   *Deep Throat*'s notoriety attracted well-known personalities, socialites and the news media to its screenings. Thus, it became fashionable and accepted for suburbia to go and see the hard-core movie (as well as other films like it) about which all the town was talking. A film critic (Stuart Klein) called the new filmgoing trend "porno chic" and the label stuck. Suddenly, a number of hard-core movies were not to be missed and people flocked to see them. Hard-core film production in the major American centers of New York, Los Angeles and San Francisco reached several hundred a year. Obviously, most of these pornos are just run-of-the-mill cheap productions, but a few would, with their competent craftsmanship, expensive sets, acting ability and glossy look, certainly uphold the expectations of a porno chic audience.

Adultery for Fun and Profit (71) Richard Robinson. *The Case of the Full Moon Murders* (71) Sean S. Cunningham, But Talbot *aka The Case of the Smiling Stiffs / Sex on the Groove Tube. Harlot* (71) Howard Ziehm, Mike Light. *Behind the Green Door* (72) Jim Mitchell, Artie Mitchell. *Deep Throat* (72) Jerry Gerard (Gerald Damiano) *aka The Doctor Makes a Call. The Devil in Miss Jones* (72) Gerard Damiano. *Little Sisters* (72) Alex de Renzy. *Bad Barbara* (73) Paul Gerber. *Deep Sleep* (73) Alfred Sole. *Devil's Due* (73) Ernest Danna. *Illusions of a Lady* (73) Jonas Middleton. *The Resurrection of Eve* (73) Artie Mitchell, Jon Fontana. *Teenage Cowgirls* (73) Ted Denver.

Porno Film, Pornographic Film   *see*   **HARD-CORE PORNO FILM;** *see also*   **SEX EXPLOITATION FILM**

Pornochanchada   *see*   **CHANCHADA**

Portmanteau Film   *see*   **EPISODE FILM**

Possession Movies   *see*   **HORROR FILM**

Post-Holocaust Film, Postnuclear Film   *see*   **SCIENCE FICTION FILM: SF Disaster Films**

Postnoir Films   *see*   **FILM NOIR**

POTBOILER   The term applies to an artistic or literary work of inferior or mediocre quality, produced merely to make money. When applied to movies, it has been used to categorize films of a lurid nature which exploit the baser instincts and unbridled passions to which humans are prone from time to time. It specifically applies to film adaptations of sensational best-sellers.

King's Row (41) Sam Wood. *The Bramble Bush* (60) Daniel Petrie. *L'ultimo avventuriero / The Adventurers* (It / US 70) Lewis Gilbert. *The Love Machine* (71) Jack Haley, Jr. *The Klansman* (74) Terence Young (started by Sam Fuller) *aka The Burning Cross. Mandingo* (75) Richard Fleischer. *Drum* (76) Steve Carver. *The Betsy* (78) Daniel Petrie.

P. O. W. Film   *see*   **WAR FILM: Prisoner-of-War Escape Films**

Preemptible Announcement   *see*   **TELEVISION COMMERCIAL**

Prehistoric Creature Drama, Prehistoric Film   *see*   **SCIENCE FIC-TION FILM: Prehistoric Fantasies**

Première avant-garde   *see*   **IMPRESSIONIST FILM**

Preparedness War Films   *see*   **WAR FILM**

Prequel   *see*   **SEQUEL**

Prerelease   *see*   **TELEVISION PROGRAM**

PRESTIGE FILM (Prestige Production)   Usually a big-budget film meant to enhance the reputation of a film studio. It may also happen that a film not conceived as a "prestige" production acquires such a label by critical acclaim or by winning awards.

Ealing Studios: *Scott of the Antarctic* (GB 48) Charles Frend.   Fox Film Corporation: *Sunrise – A Song of Two Humans* (27) F. W. Murnau *aka Sunrise*.   Paramount / Famous Players-Lasky: *The Covered Wagon* (23) James Cruze *aka Covered Wagon* [1st epic Western].   RKO: *Citizen Kane* (40) Orson Welles *aka American*.   Universal: *Foolish Wives* (20-21) Erich von Stroheim.   Warner Bros: *A Midsummer Night's Dream* (35) Max Reinhardt.

PRETEEN FILM   As with the teen movie (q.v.) which addresses itself mainly to teenagers, the preteen movie is geared to the likes and dislikes of children – especially to preteenagers in the nine- to twelve-year-old age group. In these movies, the youngsters are given a prominent role, and although the subject matter is intended to please young audiences, the films may also make good family viewing. The preteen movie has become more conspicuous in recent years.

Kidco (82) Ronald F. Maxwell.   *Clownhouse* (85) Victor Salva [rel. in 89].   *Frog Dreaming* (Aust 85) Brian Trenchard Smith *aka The Go-Kids / Spirit Chaser*.   *The Goonies* (85) Richard Donner.   *The Peanut Butter Solution / Opération beurre de pinottes* (Can 85) Michael Rubbo *aka Michael's Fright / La Vraie Histoire de la grande peur*.   *Flight of the Navigator* (86) Randal Kleiser.   *The Gate* (Can 86) Tibor Takacs.   *Invaders from Mars* (86) Tobe Hooper.   *The Outside Chance of Maximilian Glick* (Can 86) Allan A. Goldstein.   *Rad* (86) Hal Needham.   *Stand by Me* (86) Rob Reiner.   *Big Shots* (87) Robert Mandel.   *The Monster Squad* (87) Fred Dekker.

Preview, Prevue   *see*   **TRAILER**

Prime Time Serial   *see*   **SOAP OPERA**

Prison Camp Film   *see*   **WAR FILM: Concentration Camp War Films**

PRISON FILM (Jail Movie, Prisoner Film)   Prison films form a homogeneous group, and although they could be considered a branch of crime movies, it is preferable to treat them separately as a genre. Regardless of the country in which they are made, prison films all have one thing in common – they deal with inmates in close confinement, men and women imprisoned and having to adjust to life "inside" and to the conditions prevailing in jail.

Prison movies may deal with conditions as they exist in a particular jail, use that jail as a metaphor for jail conditions in general or point a finger at the judiciary system. They may show brutality, riots, attempts to escape (successful or not), or they may portray corrupt administrators or jail reformers trying to improve the prisoners' lot. They may show how the convicts wait on death row for the time of their execution, or how the inmates come to terms with their predicament and make the best of the circumstances. Homosexuality, both male and female, has also been a topic recently broached in prison movies. Whatever the type of subject chosen, these movies have a large dose of suspense injected into them and thus, if they are well-made, they are exciting and entertaining to watch. For a filmography of 219 titles, *see* Ronald B. Querry, "Prison Movies: An Annotated Filmography 1921–Present," *The Journal of Popular Film* 2.2 (Spring 1973): 181–97. James Robert Parish's *Prison Pictures from Hollywood* (Jefferson, NC: McFarland, 1991) includes 293 releases. *See also* Bruce Crowther's *Captured on Film: The Prison Movie* (London: B. T. Batsford, 1989).

The Prisoner of Shark Island (36) John Ford. *Castle on the Hudson* (40) Anatole Litvak *aka Years without Days.* *Two-Way Stretch* (GB 60) Robert Day *aka Nothing Barred.* *Convicts Four* (62) Millard Kaufman *aka Reprieve.* *Koshikei* (J 68) Nagisa Oshima *aka Death by Hanging.* *Breakout* (70 TV) Richard Irving. *Detenuto in attesa di giudizio* (It 71) Nanni Loy *aka Why?* *The Glass House* (72 TV) Tom Gries *aka Truman Capote's The Glass House.* *Ich war, ich bin, ich werde sein* (EG 74) Walter Heynowski, Gerhard Scheumann *aka I Was, I Am, I Shall Be.* *Breakout* (75) Tom Gries *aka The Second Jailbreak / The Ten-Second Jailbreak.* *Kill Me If You Can* (77 TV) Buzz Kulik. *Short Eyes* (77) Robert M. Young *aka Slammer.* *Midnight Express* (GB 78) Alan Parker. *Attica* (80 TV) Marvin J. Chomsky. *Brubaker* (80) Stuart Rosenberg. *Hoodwink* (Aust 80) Claude Whalham. *Stir Crazy* (80) Sidney Poitier. *The Executioner's Song* (82 TV) Lawrence Schiller. *Doing Life* (86 TV) Gene Reynolds. *Dead Man Out / Dead Man Walking* (GB / US / Can 88 MCTV) Richard Pearce. *Destroyer* (88) Robert Kirk. *Ghosts ... of the Civil Dead* (Aust 88) John Hillcoat.

——**Big House Movies**   Prisons have always been a favorite subject of gangster films and crime films in general. Films on life in penitentiaries for men keep reappearing, showing that the theme is far from exhausted. *See also* **GANGSTER: Prison Films**.

The Big House (30) George W. Hill. *The Criminal Code* (31) Howard Hawks. *Each Dawn I Die* (39) William Keighley. *Birdman of Alcatraz* (62) John Frankenheimer. *Riot* (68) Buzz Kulik. *The Traveling Executioner* (70) Jack Smight. *Fortune and Men's Eyes / Aux yeux du sort et des humains* (Can / US 70-71) Harvey Hart *aka Aux yeux des hommes / Des prisons et des hommes.* *Escape from Alcatraz* (79) Donald Siegel. *An Innocent Man* (88) Peter Yates.

——**Chain Gang Movies**   The action of most prison films takes place in the big house. However, a few films have sought to expose or portray the deplorable conditions that existed in chain gang outfits.

Hell's Highway (32) Rowland Brown.   *I Am a Fugitive from a Chain Gang* (32) Mervyn LeRoy *aka I Am a Fugitive.   Laughter in Hell* (33) Edward L. Cahn.   *Chain Gang* (50) Lew Landers.   *Cool Hand Luke* (67) Stuart Rosenberg.   *Sweet Sugar* (72) Michel Levesque *aka Chaingang Girls.   Leadbelly* (76) Gordon Parks Sr.

——**Penal Colony Films**   Some secluded spots have, from time to time, been selected to lodge criminals. Among these convict settlements, one of the most infamous was the penal colony named Devil's Island in the French Guiana which was operational until 1950. Several films have illustrated the plight of the prisoners on that island and in other similar penal colonies. Besides showing the appalling conditions in such places, one of the main focuses of these films is the repeated attempts of the inmates to escape from captivity.

Condemned (29) Wesley Ruggles.   *Escape from Devil's Island* (35) Albert S. Rogell.   *Devil's Island* (39) William Clemens.   *Terror of the Bloodhunters* (62) Jerry Warren.   *I Escaped from Devil's Island* (73) William Witney. *Papillon* (73) Franklin J. Schaffner.   *Terminal Island* (73) Stephanie Rothman.   *Turkey Shoot* (Aust 81) Brian Trenchard-Smith *aka Escape 2000.*

——**Political Prisoners Films**   A small body of films exists that focus on the plight of the political prisoner who is incarcerated, often without trial, for a long stretch or for an unspecified period of time. It does not matter if the prisoners are guilty or not; they always find themselves behind bars for political reasons, and the action always takes place in countries situated behind the iron curtain or in the totalitarian countries of South America and elsewhere.

Prisoners-of-war films and concentration camp war films are treated separately under the **WAR FILM** genre.

The Prisoner (GB 55) Peter Glenville.   *The Fixer* (68) John Frankenheimer. *L'Aveu / La confessione* (F / It 69) Costa-Gavras *aka The Confession.   One Day in the Life of Ivan Denisovich / En dag i Ivan Denisovitsj'liv* (GB / Nor 70) Caspar Wrede.   *The First Circle* (Den / G 72) Aleksander Ford. *The Tomorrow Man* (Can 78) Tibor Takacs [rel. in 82].   *Coming Out of the Ice* (82 TV) Waris Hussein.   *Les Yeux des oiseaux* (F 82) Gabriel Auer *aka The Eyes of the Birds.   Gulag* (GB 85 MCTV) Roger Young.   *O Beijo da mulher arahna / Kiss of the Spider Woman* (US / Braz 85) Hector Babenco.

——**Reform School Films (Reformatory Films)**   Juvenile delinquency has to be curtailed somehow and the usual method, if the youngsters are not released on parole after being severely reprimanded, is to send them to a reform school, an "open" or "closed" reformatory, or a juvenile detention home. The place they are sent to will vary according to the age and sex of the offender and the nature of the offense. These films form a sizeable part of the prison genre.

Boys Town (38) Norman Taurog.   *So Young, So Bad* (50) Bernard Vorhaus.   *The Loneliness of the Long Distance Runner* (GB 62) Tony Richards *aka Rebel with a Cause.   The Smashing Bird I Used to Know* (GB

69) Robert Hartford-Davis *aka House of Unclaimed Girls / School for Unclaimed Girls.* *Delinquent Schoolgirls* (73) Gregory Coralito *aka Carnal Madness / Sizzlers.* *Born Innocent* (74 TV) Donald Wrye. *Tattooed Tears* (78) Nick Broomfield, Joan Churchill. *Vasárnapi szülok* (Hung 79) János Rósza *aka Sunday Daughters.* *Bad Boys* (83) Rick Rosenthal. *Kingpin* (NZ 84) Mike Walter *aka Kingi's Story.* *Reform School Girls* (86) Tom DeSimone. *Prison for Children* (87 TV) Larry Peerce.

——**Women's Prison Films (Woman Prison Films, Women-in-Prison Films)** These films parallel men's prison movies or big house movies. One difference, as compared to the all-male prison films, is that they are easily prone to lurid sensationalism and sexploitation as seen by the frequency with which the producers of erotic films set their plots among women in prison. *Ladies of the Big House* (31) Marion Gering. *Caged* (49) John Cromwell *aka Locked In.* *Yield to the Night* (GB 56) J. Lee Thompson *aka Blonde Sinner.* *I Want to Live!* (58) Robert Wise *aka The Barbara Graham Story.* *99 mujeres / Der heisse Tod / 99 Women / 99 donne* (Sp / G / GB / It 68) Jesús Franco *aka Isle of Lost Women / Prostitutes in Prison.* *The Big Bird Cage* (72) Jack Hill *aka Women's Penitentiary II.* *Caged Heat* (74) Jonathan Demme *aka Renegade Girls.* *Chained Heat / Das Frauenlager* (US / G 82) Paul Nicholas (Lutz Schaarwächter). *Vendetta* (85) Bruce Logan *aka Angels Behind Bars.* *The Naked Cage* (86) Paul Nicholas.

Prisoner Film *see* **PRISON FILM**

Prisoners-of-War Film *see* **WAR FILM: Prisoner-of-War Escape Film**

PRIVATE DETECTIVE FILM (Detective Film, Investigative Film, P.I. Film, Private Eye Film, Shamus Movie)   The detective film falls neatly into two distinct varieties—the private detective film and the police detective film.[80] If we think in terms of crime investigation, the number of detective-like types increases and would include all sorts of investigators (e.g., district attorneys, lawyers, reporters). Here, only private detectives, whether professional or amateur, are included. Private detectives require a category of their own as they show marked differences from any other individual or agency set on uncovering the perpetrator or perpetrators of a crime. The private detective, private eye, sleuth or amateur detective is a highly individualistic operator who, most of the time, is at odds with the powerful forces against which he pits his superior mind and tenacity. He succeeds single-handedly in bringing to justice the culprits.

Private detectives come in many shapes and forms. There exist the classical, orthodox detectives and the unorthodox ones; those highly romantic and honorable individuals fighting crime and crooks according to the rules, and the violent, realistic, tough guys delving into the mire of the underworld, making up their own rules. They all have in common their incorruptibility and the single-mindedness with which they relentlessly pursue their targets. From Sherlock Holmes to Mike Hammer, from Father Brown to Miss Jane Marple, they are a legion.

——**Adventurer Detective Films**   A clear-cut category among the detectives is formed by the adventurer, be he a gentleman or not. They are usually men of means, ex–British Army officers, soldiers of fortune, or former crooks now gallantly fighting crime, but are not above flaunting the law if by doing so they can achieve their purpose. This group includes such luminaries as the Saint, the Falcon, the Lone Wolf, Boston Blackie and Bulldog Drummond.

Bulldog Drummond (29) F. Richard Jones [21 Bulldog Drummond films (1929-69)]. *Arsene Lupin* (32) Jack Conway.[81] *Lone Wolf Returns* (35) Roy William Neill [19 films (1926-49) in Columbia's Lone Wolf series]. *The Saint in New York* (38) Ben Holmes [8 films (1938-42) in RKO's the Saint series]. *Meet Boston Blackie* (41) Robert Florey [14 films (1941-49) in Columbia's Boston Blackie series]. *The Falcon Takes Over* (42) Irving Reis *aka The Gay Falcon* [16 films (1941-49) in the Falcon series]. *Deadlier Than the Male* (GB 66) Ralph Thomas [Bulldog Drummond film].

——**Amateur Detective Films**   This category includes anyone who through unforeseen circumstances is put into the position of having to try to solve a case or clear him/herself of a false accusation. It also includes those characters who take up detecting as a hobby or for sport. Sometimes these impromptu detectives team up with a cop or police detective who is usually a second-string or a foil to the amateur sleuth. These amateur detectives are a variegated lot. Lawyers, district attorneys, newspaper reporters and newspaper editors are excluded. Films in which these types engage in sleuthing belong to other genres.

The Penguin Pool Murder (32) George Archainbaud *aka The Penguin Pool Mystery* [6 films (1932-37) in RKO's Hildegarde Withers series]. *Fast Company* (38) Edward Buzzell *aka King of Sports / The Rare Book Murders* [followed by *Fast and Loose* (39) Edwin L. Marin and *Fast and Furious* (39) Busby Berkeley]. *Irish Luck* (39) Grant Withers. *Busman's Honeymoon* (GB 40) Arthur B. Woods *aka Haunted Honeymoon*. *Father Brown* (GB 54) Robert Hamer *aka The Detective*. *Murder at the Gallop* (GB 63) George Pollock [4 films (1962-65) in Margaret Rutherford's Miss Marple series]. *Gumshoe* (GB 71) Stephen Frears. *Missing Pieces* (83 TV) Mike Hodges.

——**Detective Comedy Films**   Almost any genre has its comic versions. Whether straight comedy, making the audience laugh with the gaucherie of its film detectives, or by spoofing the genre to please or displease the connoisseur, or by just being camp, the detective comedy film has achieved some very fine funny movies.

Sherlock, Jr. (24) Buster Keaton *aka Sherlock Junior*. *Bulldog Jack* (GB 34) Walter Frode *aka Alias Bulldog Drummond*. *The Mad Miss Manton* (38) Leigh Jason. *Whistling in the Dark* (41) S. Sylvan Simon. *Who Done It?* (42) Erle C. Kenton. *Beat the Devil / Il tesoro dell'Africa* (US / It / GB 53) John Huston. *Who Done It?* (GB 55) Basil Dearden. *Cry Uncle!* (71) John G. Avildsen *aka Super Dick*. *Murder by Death* (76) Robert Moore. *Dead Men Don't Wear Plaid* (81) Carl Reiner. *Bullshot* (GB 83) Dick Clement. *Who Framed Roger Rabbit?* (88) Robet Zemeckis.

——**Private-Eye Films**   The gamut of the private detective, private eye or shamus runs from the realistic (Michael Shayne), to the Oriental (Mr. Wong), to the debonair gentlemen (Philo Vance, Nick Charles), to the hard-boiled detectives (Sam Spade, Philip Marlowe, Mike Hammer), and many, many more.

The Maltese Falcon (31) Roy Del Ruth *aka Dangerous Female.* *The Kennel Murder Case* (33) Michael Curtiz [15 Philo Vance films (1929-47)]. *The Dragon Murder Case* (34) H. Bruce Humberstone [Philo Vance film]. *The Thin Man* (34) W. S. Van Dyke II [6 films (1934-47) in the series]. *After the Thin Man* (36) W. S. Van Dyke II. *Mr. Wong, Detective* (38) William Nigh [6 films (1938-40) in Monogram's Mr. Wong series]. *Sexton Blake and the Hooded Terror* (GB 38) George King. *Nick Carter – Master Detective* (39) Jacques Tourneur. *Michael Shayne, Private Detective* (40) Eugene Forde [12 films (1940-47) in the series]. *The Maltese Falcon* (41) John Huston *aka The Gent from Frisco.* *Eyes in the Night* (42) Fred Zinnemann. *The Big Sleep* (44) Howard Hawks [rel. in 46]. *Murder My Sweet* (44) Edward Dmytryk *aka Farewell, My Lovely* [8 Philip Marlowe films (1944-78)]. *Dick Tracy Meets Gruesome* (47) John Rawlins *aka Dick Tracy Meets Karloff / Dick Tracy's Amazing Adventure.* *I, the Jury* (53) Harry Essex [4 Mike Hammer films (1953-63)]. *Kiss Me Deadly* (54) Robert Aldrich [Mike Hammer film]. *Harper* (66) Jack Smight *aka The Moving Target.* *Tony Rome* (67) Gordon Douglas [followed by *Lady in Cement* (68) also by Douglas]. *Marlow* (69) Paul Bogart *aka The Little Sister.* *Cannon* (70 TV) George McCowan. *Klute* (71) Alan J. Pakula. *Shaft* (71) Gordon Parks. *Shamus* (73) Buzz Kulik. *Chinatown* (74) Roman Polansky. *Murder on the Orient Express* (GB 74) Sidney Lumet [Hercule Poirot film]. *Night Moves* (75) Arthur Penn. *The Late Show* (77) Robert Benton. *I, the Jury* (81) Richard T. Heffron. *The Empty Beach* (Aust 84) Chris Thompson. *Moonlighting* (85 TV) Robert Butler. *Dick Tracy* (90) Warren Beatty.

——**Sherlock Holmes Films**   The dean of all the famous movie detectives, Sherlock Holmes, came to be widely known when his creator, Sir Arthur Conan Doyle (1859–1930), committed him to print in 1887 with the publication of *A Study in Scarlet.* The earliest appearance on screen of the master detective dates from 1900. Up to 1984, 189 films (television series excluded) portraying Sherlock Holmes have been recorded. Of the many actors that have played Sherlock Holmes, only Basil Rathbone stands out in the public's imagination as the perfect representation of the British detective. Nigel Bruce is in turn the perfect recreation of Dr. Watson. For a list of titles of films in which Sherlock Holmes has appeared, *see* Patrick Robertson, *Guinness Movie Facts & Feats* (London: Guinness, 1991), pp. 45–47. An extensive but not exhaustive filmography (including television films and series up to 1974) is included in "Sherlock Holmes on Film," and "Sherlock Holmes on Television," in Michael Pointer, *The Public Life of Sherlock Holmes* (Newton Abbot: David & Charles, 1975), pp. 135–68; 190–92.

The Missing Rembrandt (GB 32) Leslie Hiscott. *The Adventures of Sherlock Holmes* (39) Alfred Werker *aka Sherlock Holmes.* *Hound of the Baskervilles* (39) Sidney Lanfield [14 films (1939-46) with Rathbone and Bruce]. *The Scarlet Claw* (44) Roy William Neill. *Dressed to Kill* (45) Roy William Neill *aka Sherlock Holmes and the Secret Code.* *The Hound of the*

Baskervilles (GB 59) Terence Fisher. *The Private Life of Sherlock Holmes* (US / GB 69) Billy Wilder. *They Might Be Giants* (71) Anthony Harvey. *Seven-Per-Cent Solution* (US / GB 76) Herbert Ross. *Sherlock Holmes in New York* (76 TV) Boris Sagal. *Murder by Decree / Meurtre par décret* (Can / GB 78) Bob Clark *aka Sherlock Holmes and Saucy Jack / Sherlock Holmes Meets Saucy Jack / Sherlock Holmes: Murder by Decree*. *The Hound of the Baskervilles* (GB 83 TV) Douglas Hickox. *The Sign of Four* (GB 83) Desmond Davis *aka Sir Arthur Conan Doyle's The Sign of Four*. *Masks of Death* (GB 84 TV) Roy Ward Baker.

Private-Eye Films   *see*   **PRIVATE DETECTIVE FILM**

Private Film   *see*   **STAG MOVIE**

Prize-Fight Film   *see*   **BOXING PICTURE**

Pro-Allies Film   *see*   **WAR FILM: Pro-Soviet War Films**

Problem Film   *see*   **SOCIAL CONSCIOUSNESS FILM**

Producer's Film   *see*   **AUTEUR FILM**

Product   *see*   **TELEVISION PROGRAM**

Program Filler   *see*   **PROGRAMMER**

Program Film   *see*   **FEATURE FILM;**   *see also*   **PROGRAMMER**

Programmed Film   *see*   **FACTUAL FILM**

PROGRAMMER (Program Filler, Program Film)   A trade term mainly used in the 1920s and 1930s for a low-budget, minor film which could be used as a support picture, a co-feature, or as required according to the needs of a theater to fill its program.

Between 1914 and 1920, program film meant a dramatic film of about 4 or 5 reels in length. At the time, longer films were called "specials."

Progressive Film   *see*   **REVOLUTIONARY FILM**

Pro-Indian Picture   *see*   **WESTERN: Indian Films**

Proletarian Film   *see*   **ARBEITERFILM**

Proletariat Film   *see*   **LABOR FILM**

Promo   *see*   **TELEVISION COMMERCIAL;**   *see also*   **MUSIC VIDEO**

Promo Clip, Promotional Clip   *see*   **MUSIC VIDEO**

Promotional Announcement   *see*   **TELEVISION COMMERCIAL**

Promotional Film   *see*   **FACTUAL FILM: Advertising Film**

Promotional Ident   *see*   **TELEVISION COMMERCIAL: Logo**

Promotional Video   *see*   **MUSIC VIDEO**

PROPAGANDA FILM   Propaganda is the use of statements or facts with the intention of persuading or predisposing the receiver to its content. As such, it is a weapon frequently used by political parties or by nations which want to spread their political ideologies and perhaps gain converts to their cause. The film medium is ideally suited for this purpose; hence the rise and continuous use of the propaganda film by different political factions either of the Right or Left, conservative or radical. Propaganda is a tool equally in use in totalitarian or democratic countries. Of course, in the case of totalitarian nations, it may safely be said that almost the entire film industry, being state controlled in most cases, uses propaganda (e.g., Soviet Russia, Nazi Germany). This is not the case with democracies where propaganda is used only in special cases (e.g., Hollywood's war propaganda films, British wartime films), or is an instrument of minority or militant groups.

There are examples of early propaganda films like *L'Affaire Dreyfus* (1899) by Georges Méliès, but it was during World War I that the propaganda film came into its own when governments began to commission films which would help the war effort and uplift their country's morale. Since then, propaganda films have continued to be made in time of war as well as in time of peace. Propaganda films range from shorts to feature-length, in both fiction and non-fiction form. Most propaganda films are political, but religious propaganda films are also made.

Agitprop, a term meaning agitation and propaganda, is at times used for politicaly oriented, highly propagandistic films. *See also* **POLITICAL FILM** and **WAR FILM**.[82]

L'Affaire Dreyfus (1899) Georges Méliès *aka The Dreyfus Affaire / The Dreyfus Case / Dreyfus Court Martial* [the film was shown as a serial in 11 episodes]. *The Battle Cry of Peace* (GB 15) J. Stuart Blackton.   *War Brides* (16) Walter Brenan.   *Neobychainye Prikluchniya mistera Vesta v stranye Bolshevikob* (USSR 24) Lev Kuleshov *aka The Extraordinary [Strange] Adventures of Mr. West in the Land of the Bolsheviks*.   *Triumph des Willens* (G 34-36) Leni Riefenstahl *aka The Triumph of the Will*.   *Friesennot* (G 35) Werner Kortwich, Peter Hagen *aka Dorf im roten Sturm / Frisians in Peril / German Destiny on Russian Soil / Village in the Red Attack*.   *Weisse Sklaven* (G 37) Karl Anton *aka Panzerkreuzer Sebastopol / White Slaves*.   *Aleksandr Nevskii* (USSR 38) Sergei Mikhailovitch Eisenstein, Dmitri Vasiliev *aka Alexander Newsky*.   *Der ewige Jude* (G 38) Fritz Hippler *aka The Eternal Jew / The Wandering Jew*.   *The Lion Has Wings* (GB 39) Michael Powell, Brian Desmond Hurst, Adrian Brunel.   *The Great Dictator* (40) Charles Chaplin. *Target for Tonight* (GB 40) Harry Watt.   *Jud Süß* (G 40) Veidt Harlan *aka Jew Süss*.   *The Next of Kin* (GB 41) Thorold Dickinson.   *G. P. U.* (G 42) Karl Ritter.   *Mrs. Miniver* (42) William Wyler.   *Mission to Moscow* (43) Michael Curtiz.   *Chelovek No. 217* (USSR 44) Mikhail Romm *aka (The) Man No. 217*. *Stalingradskaya Bitva* (USSR 49) Vladimir Petrov *aka The Battle of Stalingrad* [in 2 parts].   *Morir en España* (Sp 65) Mariano Ozores. *Hanoi, martes trece* (Cuba 67) Santiago Alvarez *aka Hanoi, Tuesday the 13th.   Loin du Vietnam* (F 67) Alain Resnais, Jean-Luc Godard, Joris Ivens, William Klein, Claude Lelouch, Chris Marker, Agnès Varda *aka Far from Vietnam*.

Propaganda War Films *see* **WAR FILM**

Propagandistic Film *see* **PROPAGANDA FILM**

Pro-Soviet War Film *see* **WAR FILM**

Provincial Comedy *see* **LOCAL COMEDY**

Pro-War Films *see* **WAR FILM**

Pseudodocumentary *see* **DOCUMENTARY: Documentary-Style Film**; *see also* **MONDO FILM**

Pseudoethnological Documentaries *see* **SEX DOCUMENTARY**

Pseudohistorical Film *see* **EPIC: DeMille Epics**; *see also* **HISTORICAL FILM**

Pseudoscientific Investigation Film *see* **SPECULATIVE DOCUMENTARY**

Psychedelic Films *see* **DRUG FILM**

PSYCHIATRIC FILM (Psychiatrically Oriented Film) Leaving aside films dealing with the excesses of homicidal maniacs and psychos, which are better integrated into the horror genre, psychiatric themes and the world of the mentally unbalanced have frequently figured in films. Psychiatric films depict the work of psychiatrists and psychoanalysts, [83] their patients' problems, their obsessions or state of mind, cures and remedies available and his or her eventual recovery if the treatment prescribed has been successful.

Not always sympathetic to the psychiatrist or psychoanalyst, a steady flow of productions makes the psychiatric film a distinct group of pictures. *See also* **HOSPITAL FILM.**

Le Système du Dr. Goudron et du Professeur Plume (F 09) Robert Saidreau *aka The Lunatics. Das Cabinet des Dr. Caligari* (G 19) Robert Wiene *aka The Cabinet of Dr. Caligari / Das Kabinett des Dr. Caligari. Geheimnisse einer Seele. Ein psychoanalytischer Film* (G 25) G. B. Pabst *aka Secrets of a Soul. Kurutta ippeiji* (J 26) Teinosuke Kinugasa *aka A Page of Madness. Private Worlds* (35) Gregory La Cava. *Blind Alley* (39) Charles Vidor. *Bedlam* (45) Mark Robson *aka Chamber of Horrors. Spellbound* (45) Alfred Hitchcock *aka Alfred Hitchcok's Spellbound / The House of Dr. Edwards. Mine Own Executioner* (GB 47) Anthony Kimmins. *The Dark Past* (48) Rudolph Mate. *La Tête contre les murs* (F 58) Georges Franju *aka The Keepers. Pressure Point* (62) Hubert Cornfield. *Captain Newman, M.D.* (63) David Miller. *Lilith* (64) Robert Rossen. *A Fine Madness* (66) Irvin Kershner. *Coming Apart* (69) Milton Moses Ginsberg. *The Psychiatrist: God Bless the Children* (70 TV) Daryl Duke *aka Children of the Lotus Eater. WR: Misterije Organizma / W.R. – Die Mysterien des Organismus* (Yug / G 71) Dusan Makavejev *aka Mysteries of the Organism. Blume in Love* (73) Paul Mazursky. *Diagnosis: Murder* (GB 74) Sidney Hayers. *A Woman Under the Influence* (74) John Cassavetes. *Equus* (GB / Can 77)

Sidney Lumet. *Bad Timing* (GB 79) Nicolas Roeg *aka Bad Timing: A Sensual Obsession / Illusions / A Sensual Obsession*. *Twinkle, Twinkle, "Killer" Kane* (79) William Peter Blatty *aka The Ninth Configuration*. *Birdy* (84) Alan Parker. *Committed* (83) Sheila McLaughlin, Lynne Tillman. *Lies* (83) Ken Wheat, Jim Wheat. *Palava enkeli / Brinnande ängel* (Fin 84) Lauri Törhönen *aka Burning Angel*. *House of Games* (87) David Mamet. *The Dream Team* (89) Howard Zieff.

——**Case Study Films**   A type of film found in the late forties and fifties mostly dealing with psychiatric cases. Usually, the films present the patient's illness, its treatment and recovery process.
The Snake Pit (48) Anatole Litvak. *The Three Faces of Eve* (57) Nunnally Johnson. *David and Lisa* (62) Frank Perry. *Diario di una schizofrenica* (It 68) Nelo Risi *aka Diary of a Schizophrenic*. *Sybil* (76 TV) Daniel Petrie [in 3 and in 2 parts]. *I Never Promised You a Rose Garden* (77) Anthony Page.

——**Mental Institution Films**   Some films are set in mental institutions where the insane and supposedly insane are confined for medical treatment and observation. These films present the care given to the patients or the abuse inflicted on the inmates by members of the medical staff. The mental institution film may be considered a subgenre of the prison film, but fits better into the psychiatric film group.
The Shrike (55) José Ferrer. *Shock Corridor* (63) Samuel Fuller *aka Long Corridor / Straightjacket*. *Shock Treatment* (64) Denis Sanders. *The Titicut Follies* (67) Frederick Wiseman. *One Flew Over the Cuckoo's Nest* (75) Milos Forman. *Matti da slegare* (It 75) Silvano Agosti, Marco Bellocchio, Sandro Petraglia, Stefano Rulli *aka Fit to Be Untied / Nessuno o tutti*. *Per le antiche scale / Vertiges* (It / F 75) Mauro Bolognini *aka Down the Ancient Stairs*. *The Other Side of Hell* (78 TV) Jan Kadar. *The Fifth Floor* (80) Howard Avedis.

Psychiatric Picture   *see*   **HOSPITAL FILM**

Psychiatrically Oriented Film   *see*   **PSYCHIATRIC FILM**

Psycho Movie   *see*   **PSYCHOPATHIC THRILLER**

Psychodrama   *see*   **UNDERGROUND FILM: Trance Film;**   *see also*   **PSYCHOPATHIC THRILLER**

Psychological Horror Film   *see*   **PSYCHOPATHIC THRILLER**

Psychological Melodramas   *see*   **MELODRAMA**

Psychological Realism   *see*   **POETIC-REALIST FILM**

Psychological Thriller   *see*   **PSYCHOPATHIC THRILLER**

Psychological Westerns   *see*   **WESTERN**

Psychomotor Film   *see*   **FACTUAL FILM: Skill Film**

PSYCHOPATHIC THRILLER (Mad Slasher Film, Psycho Movie, Psychodrama, Psychological Horror Film, Psychological Thriller, Psycho-

pathological Film, Psychopath Thriller, Psycho-Shocker, Psycho-Thriller, Shocker, Sick Film, Sickie)   Films with mentally disturbed characters have repeatedly been made through the years, one of the earliest being *Das Cabinet des Dr. Caligari* (1919), an early German Expressionist film, but it is only since the sixties that they have begun to appear in sufficient numbers to form an important genre. This category of films may be said to have had its beginnings with *Les Diaboliques*, a seminal French film of 1954. Although a mystery thriller rather than a psycho movie, it nevertheless had some of the essential ingredients that were to show up in later movies of the psychopathic type. It took a few years before the trend caught on. With the filming of *Psycho* in 1960 by Alfred Hitchcock, this subgenre of the horror film was fully launched. These films have to do with derangements of the mind, pathological states of the psyche and split personalities. The psychopathological movie deals with the homicidal proclivities of individuals prone to the effects of psychoses. These films present us with all kinds of psychopaths and psychotics—schizoids, schizophrenics, manic-depressives, paranoids—prowling about in search of unsuspecting or terrified victims. They provide the audience with thrills and chills in abundance. Charles Derry calls them "horror of personality films" and has examined them in "The Horror of Personality," *Cinefantastique 3* (1974): 14–27, and in *Dark Dreams* (Cranbury, NJ: A. S. Barnes, 1977). The horror in these films resides in the all-too-real and hardly understood world of the deranged. In the late seventies, *Halloween* (1978) rekindled interest in this sort of movie, and a new cycle began that continued into the eighties. *See* **SLASHER FILM.**

Das Cabinet des Dr. Caligari (G 19) Robert Wiene *aka The Cabinet of Dr. Caligari / Das Kabinett des Dr. Caligari.* *Les Diaboliques* (F 54) Henri-Georges Clouzot *aka Diabolique / The Fiends.* *Peeping Tom* (GB 59) Michael Powell *aka Face of Fear.* *Psycho* (60) Alfred Hitchcock [4 films in the series up to 1990]. *Homicidal* (61) William Castle. *Paranoiac* (GB 62) Freddie Francis. *Dementia 13* (US / Ir 63) Francis Ford Coppola *aka Dementia / The Haunted and the Hunted.* *Bunny Lake Is Missing* (GB 64) Otto Preminger. *The Collector* (US / GB 64) William Wyler. *Fanatic* (GB 64) Silvio Narizzano *aka Die! Die! My Darling! Hush ... Hush Sweet Charlotte* (64) Robert Aldrich *aka What Ever Happened to Cousin Charlotte? The Nanny* (GB 65) Seth Holt. *The Psychopath* (GB 65) Freddie Francis *aka Schizoid.* *Repulsion* (GB 65) Roman Polanski. *Games* (67) Curtis Harrington. *Paranoia* (Hol 67) Adriaan Ditvoorst. *Targets* (67) Peter Bogdanovich *aka Before I Die.* *Daddy's Gone A-Hunting* (69) Mark Robson. *Pretty Poison* (69) Noel Black *aka She Let Him Continue.* *Play Misty for Me* (71) Clint Eastwood. *What's the Matter with Helen?* (71) Curtis Harrington *aka Best of Friends?* *Blind Terror* (GB 74) Richard Fleischer *aka Buff / See No Evil.* *Frenzy* (GB / US 72) Alfred Hitchcock. *Sisters* (72) Brian De Palma *aka Blood Sisters.* *The Silent Partner / L'argent de la banque* (Can 77) Daryl Duke. *Halloween* (78) John Carpenter [5 films in the series up to 1989]. *Dressed to Kill* (80) Brian De Palma. *Eyes of a Stranger* (80) Ken Wiederhorn. *Friday the 13th* (80) Sean S. Cunningham [8 films in the series up to 1989]. *The Sender* (GB 82) Roger Christian. *The Fantasist* (GB / Ire 86) Robin Hardy. *A Judgement in Stone* (Can 86) Ousama Rawi *aka The Housekeeper*. *The Stepfather* (86) Joseph Ruben. *Der Kuss des Tigers / Voulez-vous mourir avec moi?* (G / F 87) Petra Haffter *aka The Kiss of the Tiger*.

Psychopathological Film, Psychopath Thriller, Psycho-Shocker, Psycho-Thriller *see* **PSYCHOPATHIC THRILLER**

Public Affairs Program *see* **TELEVISION NEWS**

Publicity Film, Public Relations Film *see* **FACTUAL FILM:** Advertising Film

Public School Films *see* **BRITISH EMPIRE FILM**

Punk Films *see* **INDEPENDENT PRODUCTION;** *see also* **ROCK FILM**

Puppet-Animation Film *see* **ANIMATED FILM:** Puppet Films

Pure Cinema *see* **ABSTRACT FILM:** Cinéma Pur

Pure Film *see* **STRUCTURAL FILM**

Quality Film *see* **ART FILM;** *see also* **FILM D'ART**

Quasi-Documentary *see* **DOCUMENTARY:** Documentary-Style Film

QUICKIE   A low-cost film, usually of poor quality, made in haste and with little expertise. *See also* **B-MOVIE.**

Quiz Program *see* **TELEVISION SHOW:** Quiz Show

QUOTA QUICKIE   This is a British designation for a very low-budget film made in the late 1920s and 1930s to comply with the regulations set by the Cinematograph Act of 1927 which stipulated that a certain percentage of the films shown every year in the country had to be British-made. As a result, a string of "quota quickies," films of poor quality and mostly boring, were produced. However, not all quota quickies were bad. A few were good and showed know-how; they were made mostly by directors who later moved on to do better films than quickies. Many quota quickies were made by American companies (MGM, Fox, Warner Bros.) who were also required by law to fill their quota of British films yearly.

Lazybones (GB 35) Michael Powell. *The Phantom Light* (GB 35) Michael Powell. *Crown v. Stevens* (GB 36) Michael Powell. *Twelve Good Men* (GB 36) Ralph Ince. *When the Poppies Bloom Again* (GB 37) David Macdonald. *They Drive by Night* (GB 38) Arthur Woods.

Race Film *see* **ETHNIC FILM;** *see also* **RACIST FILM**

Race-Horse Opera *see* **HORSE PIC:** Horse-Racing Movies

Race-Track Film *see* **HORSE PIC**

Racially Conscious Films *see* **SOCIAL CONSCIOUSNESS FILM**

Racing Movies *see* **ROAD MOVIE**

RACIST FILM (Race Film) As a basic credo, racism maintains that one race or ethnic group is superior to another, the other being good only for physical and economic exploitation. Racism, in its most extreme forms, has led to genocide and the extermination of the persecuted group. Quite a number of films have been singled out as tainted with racism (e.g., Griffith's *The Birth of a Nation* [1914] for its anti–Negro bias) at one time or another, but perhaps the most outstanding example of racist movies are the anti–Semitic films produced in Nazy Germany: most notably *Jud Süß, Die Rothschilds*, and *Der ewige Jude*, all made in 1940. On the positive side, an ever-growing number of antiracist films – G. W. Pabst's *Der Prozess* (1947); *I Accuse!* (1958); *Kapo* (1959); *Shadows* (1960); *La Permission* (1967) – have denounced racist practices. *See* **SOCIAL CONSCIOUSNESS FILM: Racially Conscious Films.**

The Birth of a Nation (14) D. W. Griffith *aka The Birth of the Nation; or The Clansman / The Clansman.* *Pettersson och Bendel* (Sw 33) Per-Axel Branner *aka Pettersson and Bendel.* *Robert und Bertram* (G 39) Hans Heinz Zerlett *aka Robert and Bertram.* *Der ewige Jude* (G 40) Fritz Hippler *aka The Eternal Jew / The Wandering Jew.* *Jud Süß* (G 40) Veidt Harlan *aka Jew Süss.* *Die Rothschilds* (G 40) Erich Waschneck *aka The Rothschilds / Die Rothschilds Aktien von Waterloo / The Rothschilds' Shares in Waterloo* (41, reedited version) [part of a trilogy which includes *Jud Süß* and *Der ewige Jude*]. *Amaya* (Sp 52) Luis Marquina. *Der Prozess* (Aus 47) G. W. Pabst *aka In Name der Menschlichkeit / The Trial.* *I Accuse!* (GB 58) José Ferrer. *Kapo / Kapò* (F / It / Yug 59) Gillo Pontecorvo. *Shadows* (60) John Cassavetes. *La Permission* (F 67) Melvin Van Peebles *aka The Story of a Three-Day Pass.* *Do the Right Thing* (89) Spike Lee.

Radical Documentary *see* **DOCUMENTARY: Committed Documentary**

Radical Film *see* **INDEPENDENT PRODUCTION;** *see also* **REVOLUTIONARY FILM, UNDERGROUND FILM**

RAILWAY FILM (Railroad Movie, Train Picture) Trains have figured in films since the beginning of motion pictures; arrivals and departures of trains were early favorite subjects filmed by the Lumière brothers, Thomas Edison and other film pioneers. Another early favorite subject was to make locomotives crash head-on, which resulted in a spate of crash films. The construction of the railway has also been the subject of some films. Trains have often provided a solid background for romance, intrigue, mystery and, at times, violent action in horror and war movies. Countless thrillers have been set in or around trains. Famous train runs include the Orient Express, the Trans-Siberian Railway and the transcontinental lines of Canada and the United States. One of the most famous early Westerns, *The Great Train Robbery* (1903), deals mostly with what the title indicates – a thrilling assault on a train, followed by the robbery of the mail car and passengers by masked bandits. In short, when most of the action takes place in a train or when trains figure prominently, the film may be designated a railway film. On the subject of railways in motion pictures, *see* John Huntley, *Railways in the Cinema* (London: Ian Allan, 1969); an "Index of Films" pp. 112–68 includes shorts and feature-length railway films, fiction and nonfiction films.

The Great Train Robbery (03) Edwin S. Porter. *La Roue* (F 20-22) Abel Gance. *The Iron Horse* (24) John Ford. *The General* (26) Buster Keaton, Clyde Bruckman. *Rome Express* (GB 32) Walter Forde. *Shanghai Express* (32) Josef von Sternberg. *The Last Train from Madrid* (37) James Hogan. *La Bête humaine* (F 38) Jean Renoir *aka The Human Beast / Judas Was a Woman*. *The Lady Vanishes* (GB 38) Alfred Hitchcock. *Union Pacific* (39) Cecil B. DeMille. *La Bataille du rail* (F 45) René Clément *aka Battle of the Rails*. *Berlin Express* (47) Jacques Tourneur. *Sleeping Car to Trieste* (GB 48) John Paddy Carstairs. *Train of Events* (GB 49) Sidney Cole, Charles Crichton, Basil Dearden. *The Narrow Margin* (51) Richard Fleischer *aka The Target*. *Time Bomb* (GB 52) Ted Tetzlaff *aka Terror on a Train*. *The Titfield Thunderbolt* (GB 52) Charles Crichton. *The Great Locomotive Chase* (56) Francis D. Lyon *aka Andrews' Raiders*. *North West Frontier* (GB 59) J. Lee Thompson *aka Flame Over India*. *Pociag* (Pol 59) Jerzy Kawalerowicz *aka Night Train*. *Compartiment tueurs / Vagone letto per assassini* (F / It 64) Costa-Gavras *aka The Sleeping Car Murders*. *The Train / Le Train / Il treno* (US / F / It 64) John Frankenheimer, Arthur Penn. *Von Ryan's Express* (65) Mark Robson. *Trans-Europe-Express* (F / Belg 66) Alain Robbe-Grillet. *Robbery* (GB 67) Peter Yates. *The Emperor of the North Pole* (72) Robert Aldrich *aka Emperor of the North*. *Pánico en el Transiberiano / Horror Express* (Sp / GB 72) Gene Martin *aka Panic in the Trans-Siberian Express*. *Silver Streak* (76) Arthur Hiller. *Il Treno per Istanbul / Isztambuli vonat* (It / Hung 79 TV) Gianfranco Mingozzi *aka Istanbul Train* [in 4 parts]. *Runaway Train* (85) Andrei Konchalovsky.

Realism *see* **REALIST FILM**

Réalisme poètique *see* **POETIC-REALIST FILM**

REALIST FILM (Realism, Realistic Film)   Definitions of what may be referred to as a realist film vary as realism is a polemical term which offers multiple interpretations. It is a broad label understood in various ways. Realism as a style of filmmaking appeared early in motion pictures. It is concurrent and often contrasted with fantasy, the other major area of filmmaking. Reality has frequently been associated with the work of Louis Lumière (1864–1948) and fantasy with the films of Georges Méliès (1861–1938). Both film pioneers have come to represent respectively these two major divergent tendencies in cinema; however, they were also active to a greater or lesser extent in both the realistic and fantasy fields.

Apart from the facts that reality is multifaceted (different people believe in and experience different realities) and that film can only give an illusion of reality, some films have been labelled realistic or nonrealistic according to different criteria. Also, the viewer's reaction to a particular film is dependent to some degree on the current state of the arts, social factors and on the technological innovations that cinematography has to offer to a contemporary audience. Today's audience acceptance and agreement about what may be considered a realistic film varies from that of previous decades; future audience estimation of what is realistic could again differ.

A criterion often used to assess if a movie is realistic takes into consideration the amount of discernible simulation. Thus, hard-core movies which do not fake sexual acts are realistic in this sense, as are documentaries and newsreels which film real occurrences as they are taking place and present them in an unadulterated form. Also, films which portray violence in a graphic manner are often judged realistic, at times *too* realistic for the community's prevailing set of standards.

Aside from documentary movements (e.g., *Cinéma vérité*, direct cinema) which embrace the realistic mode, fiction films also search for ways of creating reality or the appearance of reality through the filmed image. Thus a realist film seeks to recreate scenes that resemble reality without the use of unnecessary artifice and with as much objectivity as possible.

The tendency towards realism or a greater realism is a constant of motion pictures and a major preoccupation of some filmmakers. The 20s saw films that were clearly realistic like Erich von Stroheim's *Greed* (1923–24), Josef von Sternberg's *The Salvation Hunters* (1924), and King Vidor's *The Crowd* (1928); some of these films have also been labeled naturalistic as the differences between film realism and film naturalism (q.v.) are rather blurred and have never been clearly established.

Italian neorealism (*see* **NEOREALIST FILM**) is also an important affirmation of the realistc tendency in cinema which continues to be practiced in many contemporary films.

Realistic Film   *see*   **REALIST FILM**

Reconnaissance Film   *see*   **DOCUMENTARY: War Documentary**

RECONSTRUCTED FILM (Restructured Film)   Reconstructed, restructured, reduced or modified versions of a film and other such adjectival labels are euphemisms for what amounts to (often rigorous) censorship, a practice that rarely results from a genuine desire for improvement on the finished work. The cutting and recutting of films has become more and more frequent. As an indication or what may befall a completed film nowadays, the following points should be kept in mind: a) Recently, some films have been reissued in altered versions with new material incorporated and sections of the original version deleted, e.g., *The Special Edition* (1980) of *Close Encounters of the Third Kind* (1977) had 16 minutes removed from the released version and 13 minutes of new footage added with a new ending;

b) *Saturday Night Fever* (1977) was an R-rated picture, but an alternate, milder version had also been filmed which garnered a PG-rating; c) some foreign imports are "restructured" or "doctored" to suit the home audience, e.g., Luchino Visconti's *Gruppo di famiglia in un interno* (1974); d) some films undergo some cutting in order to have their ratings changed from X to R or PG (in America), or from X to AA or A (in Great Britain)[84]; e) when meant to be shown on television, recut films are common practice. The films are usually shortened (nudity, sex and violence excised), or altered by the addition of new footage, e.g., *The Godfather* and *The Godfather, Part II* (1971, 1974) were joined together with footage excised and new footage added, and issued on television as a mini-series; *The Deep* (1977) had 53 minutes of added material for the television version; and *Two Minute Warning* (1976) was shown on television in a totally different version from the original; f) there is also the parallel trend of shooting a version for theatrical release, and a longer version or mini-series for television, e.g., *A Man Called Intrepid* (1978) and *Shogun* (1980), or an original television pilot may be edited for theatrical release, e.g., *Battlestar Galactica* (1978). At times, made-for-television films may also go into theatrical release in an extended (longer) version, e.g., *Duel* (1971); g) another recent trend (in the case of films edited for an R-rated theatrical release) is the tendency to make two versions available on video—"uncut" and "theatrical," with the uncut version showing the bits originally excised in order to get the lower MPAA rating, e.g., *Crimes of Passion* (1984), *9½ Weeks* (1986); h) films are sometimes released on video in shorter versions, e.g., *Apartment Zero* (1988); j) there is also a tendency to restore movies to the original director's cut for video release, e.g., *Dr. Jekyll and Mr. Hyde* (1931), *Lost Horizon* (1936), *The Man Who Fell to Earth* (1976) and *New York, New York* (1977).

Recutting is a popular practice with producers shortening their films after initial release or preparing special prints for overseas. It is also done by distributors to suit different censorship codes. Then, naturally, there is the work of the censors themselves, snipping away offending segments in the films submitted to them in countries where censorship, rather than classification, prevails.

Finally, on a different level, projectionists-turned-collectors have been known to cut sections of a film for their own use at home. Television stations often cut films to fit a particular time slot or to introduce more advertising. Oftentimes, they show an abridged version at peak hours for convenience or to avoid offending viewers and a longer version later at night when they may have more time at their disposal or when it will not cause much of a stir.

Dr. Jekyll and Mr. Hyde (31) Rouben Mamoulian.   *Lost Horizon* (36) Frank Capra *aka Lost Horizon of Shangri-La / The Lost Horizon at Shangri-La.* *Duel* (71 TV) Steven Spielberg.   *The Godfather* (71) Francis Ford Coppola. *The Godfather, Part II* (74) Francis Ford Coppola.   *Gruppo di famiglia in un interno / Violence et Passion* (It / F 74) Luchino Visconti *aka Conversation*

Piece / *Family Groupe from Inside* / *Ritratto di famiglia* / *Ritratto di famiglia in una stanza.* **The Man Who Fell to Earth** (US / GB 76) Nicolas Roeg. **Two-Minute Warning** (76) Larry Peerce. **The Deep** (US / GB 77) Peter Yates. **New York, New York** (77) Martin Scorsese. **Saturday Night Fever** (77) John Badham. **The Special Edition: Close Encounters of the Third Kind** (77-80) Steven Spielberg. **Battlestar Galactica** (78) Richard A. Colla *aka Star Worlds.* **A Man Called Intrepid** / *Un homme s'appelle Intrépide* (GB / Can 78 TV) Peter Carter. **Shogun** (US / J 80 TV) Jerry London. **Crimes of Passion** (GB / US 84) Ken Russell. **9½ Weeks** (86) Adrian Lyne. **Apartment Zero** (GB 88) Martin Donovan.

Record Film   *see*   **FACTUAL FILM**

Red-Light Film   *see*   **VICE FILM**

REDNECK MOVIE (Country Movie)   Redneck movies are mostly action films set in the American rural South, whose protagonists are tough, no-nonsense, rugged, working-class types that reflect the redneck's lifestyle and mentality. Joe Don Baker, Peter Fonda, Harry Dean Stanton, Robert Mitchum, Paul Newman, Jack Nicholson, Warren Oates, Burt Reynolds and many others have embodied perfectly this type of Southern hero. Redneck movies form a sizeable group of films which have been singled out by Richard Thompson in his seminal article "What's Your 10-20?," *Film Comment* 16.4 (1980): 34–42. He classifies them into a few basic types.[85] It is a handy grouping for films usually included in various different genres. **Murder, He Says** (45) George Marshall. **Thunder Road** (58) Arthur Ripley. **The Intruder** (61) Roger Corman *aka I Hate Your Guts* / *Shame* / *The Stranger.* **Two Thousand Maniacs!** (64) Herschell Gordon Lewis. **The Chase** (65) Arthur Penn. **The Grissom Gang** (71) Robert Aldrich. **Walking Tall** (72) Phil Karlson [followed by *Part 2, Walking Tall* (75) Earl Bellamy, *Final Chapter— Walking Tall* (77) Jack Starrett and *A Real American Hero* (78 TV) Lou Antonio]. **Lolly Madonna XXX** (73) Richard C. Sarafian *aka The Lolly-Madonna War.* **Macon County Line** (73) Richard Compton. **White Lightning** (73) Joseph Sargent *aka Mcklusty.* **Cockfighter** (74) Monte Hellman *aka Born to Kill* / *Gamblin' Man* / *Wild Drifter.* **Thunderbolt and Lightfoot** (74) Michael Cimino. **Bobbie Joe and the Outlaw** (76) Mark L. Lester. **Fighting Mad** (76) Jonathan Demme. **Jackson County Jail** (76) Michael Miller. **High-Ballin'** / *Sacrée balade pour les gros bras* (Can 77) Peter Carter *aka Death Toll* / *The Fifth Wheel* / *P. F. Flyer.* **Urban Cowboy** (80) James Bridges. **Southern Comfort** (81) Walter Hill. **Hunter's Blood** (87) Robert Hughes.

Reflective Film   *see*   **REFLEXIVE FILM**

REFLEXIVE FILM (Reflective Film, Self-Consciously Made Film, Self-Referential Film, Self-Reflective Film, Self-Reflexive Film)   A critical term that groups together films that draw attention to themselves and tend to remind the viewer that he/she is watching a film. They clearly differ from those films which preserve an illusionist stance and which tend, for the most part, to plunge the spectator into the film's fictitious world. Reflexive films may examine the nature of film itself, the process of making a film, the response of the spectator to film, the film industry or they may try to demystify or deconstruct the notion of film as it is usually perceived by audiences. Thus reflexive films are to be found in the areas of modernist, postmodernist, structuralist or Brechtian film, in film parodies and even in films about film or Hollywood on Hollywood films. For a discussion of reflexive cinema, *see* Robert Stam, *Reflexivity in Film and Literature from Don Quixote to Jean-Luc Godard* (Ann Arbor: UMI, 1985).

Sherlock, Jr. (24) Buster Keaton *aka Sherlock Junior.   The Cameraman* (28) Edward Sedgwick.   *Chelovek s kinoapparatom* (USSR 28) Dziga Vertov, Mikhail Kaufman (photography) *aka (The) Man with a Movie Camera.   8 ½ / Huit et demi* (It / F 62) Federico Fellini *aka La bella confusione / 8 ½ (Otto e mezzo) / Federico Fellini 8 ½.   Les Carabiniers* (F / It 62-63) Jean-Luc Godard *aka The Riflemen / The Soldiers.   Le Mépris / Il disprezzo* (F / It 63) Jean-Luc Godard *aka Contempt / A Ghost at Noon.   Targets* (67) Peter Bogdanovich *aka Before I Die.   Macunaíma* (Braz 69) Joaquím Pedro de Andrade.   *La Nuit américaine / Effetto notte* (F / It 73) François Truffaut *aka Day for Night.   Jonas qui aura 25 ans en l'an 2000* (Swiz / F 75) Alain Tanner *aka Jonah Who Will Be 25 in the Year 2000 / Jonas.   Numéro Deux* (F 75) Jean-Luc Godard.   *Czlowiek z marmuru* (Pol 76) Andrzej Wajda *aka Man of Marble.   Ladrões de Cinema* (Braz 76) Fernando Coni Campos *aka Cinema Thieves / Sweet Thieves.   Amator* (Pol 79) Krzysztof Kieslowski *aka Amateur / Camera Buff.   Stardust Memories* (80) Woody Allen.   *Die Sehnsucht der Veronika Voss* (G 81) Rainer Werner Fassbinder *aka Veronika Voss.*

Reformatory Film   *see*   **PRISON FILM: Reform School Films**

REGIONAL FILM   A film that is set in a particular region and made outside main centers of film production like Los Angeles, London or Rome. In the United States, apart from the West (home of countless Westerns), the South and the Midwest have often provided a background for regional pictures which range far and wide and are not restricted to any specific locality. The term regional film also applies to regionally produced films. *See also* **REDNECK MOVIE** and **RUSTIC DRAMA**.

Cabin in the Cotton (32) Michael Curtiz.   *Come and Get It* (36) Howard Hawks *aka Roaring Timber.   Trail of the Lonesome Pine* (36) Henry Hathaway [first outdoor film in three-color Technicolor].   *Breaking Away* (79) Peter Yates.   *Gal Young 'Un* (79) Victor Nunez.   *The Return of the Secaucus Seven* (79) John Sayles.   *Tender Mercies* (82) Bruce Beresford.

Rehabilitation Films   *see*   **WAR FILM**

RELEASE   A film ready for distribution and public exhibition is called a release. The movie is a general release if it is made widely available for exhibition on a first-run basis. An exclusive is a film that plays only in one cinema in a determined distribution area. A foreign release is the film version meant to be shown outside the country of origin. It may be a version altered or modified to suit the country of export, and it may be dubbed or subtitled. A rerelease or rerun is when the film is made available once more after a certain period has elapsed from its original release. Some films like Disney's *Fantasia* (1939) are rereleased on a regular basis.

Saturation booking is applied to a movie which is released to many theaters for quick exploitation and a quick profit. In this context, grind, multiple grind and grind policy are also used. Grind also refers to a movie which is played continuously in an all-night cinema.

A sneak is a film shown at a sneak preview ahead of its general release to judge audience response. Sneaks are sometimes exhibited in a longer form and modifications by the producer or director may follow prior to its official opening.

Religious Comedy *see* **RELIGIOUS FILM: Clerical Comedies**

Religious Drama *see* **RELIGIOUS FILM: Clerical Melodramas**

Religious Epic *see* **EPIC: Biblical Epics**

RELIGIOUS FILM The label religious film has two broad acceptations. In the first instance, it is a motion picture which revolves around an easily recognizable religious subject, and it is most associated with the Christian religion; but the label obviously applies to any established religion. Thus a film about Islam or the life of Buddha would be a religious film. In the second instance, a religious film is also understood as being a film of religious inspiration and fervor, not necessarily on an obvious religious subject; hence the films of some well-known filmmakers — Ingmar Bergman, Federico Fellini, Ken Russell, Eric Rohmer — are considered to have a religious sensibility, and some of their movies are considered religious by some film scholars. Here, only categories of films with an obvious religious subject are included.

The Miracle Woman (31) Frank Capra. *Susan and God* (40) George Cukor. *Major Barbara* (GB 41) Gabriel Pascal (uncredited: Harold French, David Lean). *The Miracle of Our Lady of Fatima* (52) John Brahm *aka Miracle of Fatima.* *The Inn of Six Happiness* (US / GB 58) Mark Robson. *Elmer Gantry* (60) Richard Brooks. *Angel Baby* (61) Paul Wendkos. *Marjoe* (72) Howard Smith, Sarah Kernochan. *The Passover Plot* (US / Isr 75) Michael Campus. *Al-risala / The Message* (Libya / Kuwait / GB 76) Moustapha Akkad *aka Mohammad, Messenger of God.* *The Disappearance of Aimee* (76 TV) Anthony Harvey. *Wise Blood / Die Weisheit des Blutes* (US / G 79) John Huston. *KGOD* (80) Rick Friedberg *aka Pray TV.* *Resurrection* (80) Daniel Petrie. *Ticket to Heaven* (Can 81) R. L. Thomas (Ralph L. Thomas). *Pray TV* (82 TV) Robert Markowitz. *Split Image* (82) Ted Kotcheff. *Impure Thoughts* (85) Michael A. Simpson. *Witness* (85) Peter Weir. *The Mission* (GB 86) Roland Joffé. *Le Moine et la sorcière* (F 86) Suzanne Schiffman *aka The Sorceress.* *The Penitent* (86) Cliff Osmond [rel. in 88]. *The Believers* (US / Can 87) John Schlesinger.

——**Antireligious Films** Antireligious films obviously set out to attack and ridicule religion by showing its faults and weaknesses. It does not matter if it is done consciously or not; what emerges is an antireligious film. One film director, Luis Buñuel, is often cited as the "antireligious" filmmaker par excellence. Some of these films against religion are satires or make strong use of the satirical.

Prazdnik Svyatovo Iorgena (USSR 30) Yakov Protazanov *aka Festival at St. Jurgen.* **La Mort en ce jardin / La muerte en este jardín** (F / Mex 56) Luis Buñuel *aka Death in the Garden / Evil Garden / Gina.* *Nazarín* (Mex 58) Luis Buñuel. *Viridiana* (Sp / Mex 61) Luis Buñuel. *Heavens Above!* (GB 63) John Boulting, Roy Boulting. *Je vous salue Marie* (F / Swiz 83) Jean-Luc Godard *aka Hail Mary.*

————**Biblical Films (Bible Films)** Bible-inspired films go as far back as Ferdinand Zecca (1864–1947), a French film pioneer who in 1901 filmed *L'Enfant prodigue / The Prodigal Son* and in 1902 *Samson et Dalila.* Many of these biblical films are made in the grand manner of the epic film. The Bible epic genre owes much of its evolution to Enrico Guazzoni's *Quo Vadis* (1912).[86] *See also* **EPIC.**

L'Enfant prodigue (F 01) Ferdinand Zecca *aka The Prodigal Son.* *Samson et Dalila* (F 02) Ferdinand Zecca. *Quo Vadis* (It 12) Enrico Guazzoni. *Salome* (22) Charles Bryant. *The Ten Commandments* (22) Cecil B. DeMille. *The Wanderer* (25) Raoul Walsh. *Noah's Ark* (28) Michael Curtiz. *The Green Pastures* (36) William Keighley, Marc Connelly. *Samson and Delilah* (48) Cecil B. DeMille. *I grandi condottieri* (It 65) Marcello Baldi *aka The Great Leaders.* *La Bibbia / The Bible . . . In the Beginning* (It 64) John Huston *aka The Bible* [rel. in 66]. *Mosè / Moses* (It / GB 75 TV) Gianfranco De Bossio *aka Moses the Lawgiver.* *The Nativity* (US / GB 78 TV) Bernard L. Kowalski. *Peter and Paul* (81 TV) Robert Day. *Camminacammina* (It 83 TV) Ermanno Olmi *aka They Walked and Walked / Keep Walking.* *Samson and Delilah* (US / Mex 84 TV) Lee Philips. *The Fourth Wise Man* (85 TV) Michael Ray Rhodes. *King David* (85) Bruce Beresford. *L'inchiesta* (It / Tun 86) Damiano Damiani *aka The Inquiry.*

————**Christ Films (Life of Christ Films)** These films could be classed amongst the hagiographies or the biblical films, but it is useful to single them out as a distinctive category. They appear early in cinematic history as filmed records of Passion Plays as well as primitive renderings of Christ's life in a series of tableaux expositions. In 1897, Louis Lumière filmed *La Passion*, a one-reel short, and in 1912, Sidney Olcott filmed *From the Manger to the Cross*, a major production of its time.

La Passion (F 1897) Louis Lumière. *La Vie et la passion de Jésus-Christ* (F 02-04) Lucien Nonguet, Ferdinand Zecca *aka The Life and Passion of Jesus Christ.* *La Vie du Christ* (F 06) Alice Guy, Victor Jasset, Georges Hatot *aka The Life of Christ.* *From the Manger to the Cross; or Jesus of Nazareth* (12) Sidney Olcott *aka From the Manger to the Cross / The Life of Christ / The Life of Jesus Christ.* *Christus* (It 16) Giulio Cesare Antamoro. *I.N.R.I.* (G 23) Robert Wiene *aka Crown of Thorns.* *The King of Kings* (27) Cecil B. DeMille. *Ecce Homo* (F 35) Julien Duvivier *aka Behold the Man / Golgotha.* *Jesús de Nazareth* (Mex 42) José Díaz Morales. *King of Kings / Rey de Reyes* (US / Sp 61) Nicholas Ray *aka The Man from Nazareth.* *Il Vangelo Secondo Matteo / L'évangile selon saint-Matthieu* (It / F 64) Pier Paolo Passolini *aka The Gospel According to St. Matthew.* *Il Messia / Le Messie* (It / F 75) Roberto Rossellini *aka The Messiah.* *Jesus* (US / GB 79) Peter Sykes, John Krish *aka The Public Life of . . . Jesus.* *The Last Temptation of Christ* (US / Can 88) Martin Scorsese.

——**Christ-Figure Films**   This important group of films has as protagonist
a Christ-like figure who either behaves as the Savior would, performing acts
of kindness and miracles, or a protagonist who undergoes an empathic
identification with Jesus and often ends in a Christ-like martyrdom. In
other words, he has a cross to bear.[87]

Ordet (Sw 43) Gustaf Molander *aka The Word*. *Il Cristo proibito* (It 50)
Curzio Malaparte *aka Forbidden Christ / Strange Deception*. *Ordet* (Den
54) Carl Theodore Dreyer *aka The Word*. *Celui qui doit mourir / Colui che
deve morire* (F / It 56) Jules Dassin *aka Le Christ Recrucifié / He Who Must
Die*. *The Ruling Class* (GB 71) Peter Medak. *Auandar Anapu* (Mex 74)
Rafael Corkidi *aka El que cayó del cielo / The One Who Came from Heaven*.
Cercasi Gesù / L'Imposteur (It / F 81) Luigi Comencini *aka Looking for
Jesus*. *Jesus of Montreal / Jésus de Montréal* (Can / F 88) Denys Arcand.

——**Clerical Comedies (Religious Comedies)**   A popular European series
starred Fernandel as the droll Don Camillo, a country priest at odds with
disturbing elements in his parish. In fact, priests have always been very
reliable for providing most of the humor in religious film comedies.
Religious comedies, however, cover a vast field and include anything from
angels to devils.

The Pilgrim (23) Charlie Chaplin. *Miracolo a Milano* (It 50) Vittorio De
Sica *aka Miracle in Milan*. *Prima comunione* (It 50) Alessandro Blasetti *aka
Father's Dilemma / First Communion / His Majesty Mr. Jones*. *Il Piccolo
mondo di Don Camillo / Le Petit Monde de don Camillo* (It / F 51) Julien
Duvivier *aka Don Camillo / The Little World of Don Camillo* [5 films (1951-
65) with Fernandel]. *Djävulens öga* (Sw 60) Ingmar Bergman *aka The
Devil's Eye*. *Il prete sposato* (It / G / Sp 70) Marco Vicario *aka Intimacy
/ The Married Priest / Sexy Confessions / The Swinging Confessors*. *Poor
Devil* (72 TV) Robert Scheerer. *Nasty Habits* (GB 76) Michael Lindsay-
Hogg. *Heavenly Pursuits* (GB 86) Charles Gormly *aka The Gospel Accord-
ing to Vic*.

——**Clerical Melodramas (Religious Drama)**   Films about clerics, whether
they belong to the Catholic or the Protestant faith, are very abundant. For
the most part, these films stereotype religion, the priest, minister or nun as
the case may be. This is not so with serious religious drama. A celebrated
portrayal of a fictional priest is provided by Bing Crosby in *Going My Way*
(1944).

Gosta Berlings Saga (Sw 24) Mauritz Stiller *aka Gosta Berling's Saga / The
Legend of Gosta Berling / The Story of Gosta Berling*. *One Foot in Heaven*
(41) Irving Rapper. *Les Anges du péché* (F 43) Robert Bresson *aka Angels
of the Streets*. *Going My Way* (44) Leo McCarey. *The Keys of the
Kingdom* (44) John M. Stahl. *The Bells of St. Mary's* (45) Leo McCarey.
Come to the Stable (49) Henry Koster. *Le Journal d'un curé de campagne*
(F 50) Robert Bresson *aka (The) Diary of a Country Priest*. *Stars in My
Crown* (50) Jacques Tourneur. *The First Legion* (51) Douglas Sirk. *I Con-
fess* (53) Alfred Hitchcock. *The Nun's Story* (58) Fred Zinnemann. *Con-
spiracy of Hearts* (GB 60) Ralph Thomas. *Matka Joanna od Aniołów* (Pol
60) Jerzy Kawalerowicz *aka The Devil and the Nun / Joan of the Angels? /
Mother Joan of the Angels?* *Léon Morin, prête / Leon Morin prete* (F / It

61) Jean-Pierre Melville *aka The Forgiven Sinner / Leon Morin, Priest*. *Nattvardsgästerna* (Sw 62) Ingmar Bergman *aka The Communicants / Winter Light*. *La Religieuse* (F 65) Jacques Rivette *aka Suzanne Simonin, la religieuse de Diderot / The Nun*. *The Devils* (GB 71) Ken Russell. *Catholics* (73 TV) Jack Gold [subtitled "A Fable"]. *The Devil's Playground* (Aust 75) Fred Schepisi. *In This House of Brede* (75 TV) George Schaefer. *True Confessions* (80) Ulu Grosbard. *Mass Appeal* (84) Glenn Jordan. *Agnes of God / Agnès de Dieu* (US / Can 84-85) Norman Jewison. *Sous le soleil de Satan* (F 87) Maurice Pialat *aka Under Satan's Sun / Under the Sun of Satan*.

———**Films About the Devil**   While the darker satanic manifestations are best left to the horror genre, the Devil, the fallen angel in Christianity, has appeared in many films and has many names. Perhaps his most recurrent cinematic intervention is under the name of Mephistopheles in many remakes and screen versions of *Faust*.[88]

The Sorrows of Satan (GB 17) Alexander Butler. *Blade af Satanas Bog* (Den 19) Carl Theodore Dreyer *aka Leaves from Satan's Book*. *Faust — eine Deutsche Volkssager* (G 26) F. W. Murnau *aka Faust*. *The Sorrows of Satan* (26) D. W. Griffith. *The Devil and Daniel Webster* (40) William Dieterle *aka All That Money Can Buy / Daniel and the Devil / Daniel Webster and the Devil / Here Is a Man*. *Les Visiteurs du soir* (F 42) Marcel Carné *aka The Devil's Envoys*. *Angel on My Shoulder* (46) Archie Mayo. *Alias Nick Beal* (48) John Farrow *aka The Contact Man / Dark Circle*. *La Beauté du diable / La bellezza del diavolo* (F / It 49-50) René Clair *aka The Beauty of the Devil / The Beauty and the Devil / The Devil's Beauty*. *Meet Mr. Lucifer* (GB 53) Anthony Pelissier. *Bedazzled* (GB 67) Stanley Donen. *Doctor Faustus / Il dottor Faustus* (GB / It 67) Richard Burton, Nevill Coghill *aka Dr. Faustus*. *Invitation to Hell* (84 TV) Wes Craven. *Sous le soleil de satan* (F 87) Maurice Pialat *aka Under Satan's Sun*.

———**Hagiographies**   Hagiographies are works about the life of historical religious figures. They include films about Christ (see separate category), the Virgin Mary, saints and prophets. Amongst the saints, the story of Joan of Arc has frequently been filmed, as early as 1899 by Georges Hatot and by Georges Méliès in 1900.

Jeanne d'Arc (F 1898) Georges Hatot. *Jeanne d'Arc* (F 00) Georges Méliès *aka Joan of Arc*. *La Passion de Jeanne d'Arc* (F 27) Carl Theodore Dreyer *aka La Passion et la Mort de Jeanne d'Arc / The Passion of Joan of Arc*. *The Song of Bernadette* (43) Henry King. *La Virgen Morena* (Mex 43) Gabriel Soria, Alberto Santandar *aka The Virgin of Guadalupe*. *Monsieur Vincent* (F 47) Maurice Cloche. *Joan of Arc* (48) Victor Fleming. *Cielo sulla Palude* (It 49) Augusto Genina *aka The Sky Over the Marshes / Heaven Over the Marshes*. *Francesco, giullare di Dio* (It 50) Roberto Rossellini *aka I fioretti di San Francesco / St. Francis, Jester of God / The Flowers of St. Francis*. *Giovanna d'Arco al rogo* (It 54) Roberto Rossellini *aka Joan of Arc at the Stake*. *Il suffit d'aimer* (F / It 60) Roberto Darène *aka Bernadette of Lourdes*. *Le Procès de Jeanne d'Arc* (F 61) Robert Bresson *aka The Trial of Joan of Arc*. *Fratello Sole, sorella Luna / Brother Sun, Sister Moon* (It / GB 72) Franco Zeffirelli. *Agostino D'Ippona* (It 72 TV) Roberto Rossellini *aka Augustine of Hippo*. *Thérèse* (F 86) Alain Cavalier *aka Therese*. *Bernadette* (F 87) Jean Delannoy. *Romero* (89) John Duigan.

Religious Folk-Drama *see* **BLACK FILM: Black Genre Movies**

REMAKE   A remake is a film that takes a previously filmed story and films it again. Most remakes use the same title and are acknowledged or official remakes; some films are unofficial remakes, e.g., Luchino Visconti's *Ossessione* (1942) was an uncredited adaptation of James M. Cain's 1934 novel *The Postman Always Rings Twice*, already filmed in France in 1939 as *Le Dernier Tournant*, with new versions of the novel appearing again in 1945 and 1981. The story that has been filmed most often is *Cinderella*, followed by Shakespeare's *Hamlet*.[89]

   Le Dernier Tournant (F 39) Pierre Chenal *aka The Last Turning / The Postman Always Rings Twice. Ossessione* (It 42) Luchino Visconti. *The Postman Always Rings Twice* (45) Tay Garnett. *The Postman Always Rings Twice* (81) Bob Rafelson.

Renaissance Erotic Trend *see* **SOFT-CORE SEX-EXPLOITATION FILM**

Report Films *see* **SOFT-CORE SEX-EXPLOITATION FILM**

Reporter Film *see* **NEWSPAPER FILM**

REPRESENTATIONAL FILM   In terms of the experimental or independent film, the label representational film is commonly used in opposition to abstract film. Representational films deal with the real world, its people and its objects. Luis Buñuel's *Un chien andalou* (1928), for instance, is representational. Abstract or nonrepresentational films aim at providing sensory perceptions and eliciting intellectual responses by means of the film frame alone, and to this end they may use recognizable images, although the films themselves would not be considered representational. Michael Snow's structural film *Wavelength* (1966-67), for example, consists of a 45 minute zoom across a room and falls under the category of abstract film.

Rerelease *see* **RELEASE**

Rerun *see* **TELEVISION PROGRAM;** *see also* **RELEASE**

Research Film *see* **FACTUAL FILM**

Resistance Films *see* **WAR FILM**

"Rested" Film *see* **TELEVISION PROGRAM**

Restructured Film *see* **RECONSTRUCTED FILM**

Returning Vet Movie *see* **WAR FILM: Rehabilitation Films**

Retro *see* **NOSTALGIA FILM**

Revenge Films *see* **VIGILANTE FILM**

Revenge Westerns *see* **WESTERN**

Revisionist Epics *see* **EPIC**

REVISIONIST FILM   The term is applied to genre films which reexamine the traditional values and formulas of well-established genres (the Western, the epic, the horror film, the private-eye genre). Thus a revisionist film seeks to vary or change genre conventions, their treatment of subject matter, or it may query the way in which historical facts have been embellished or falsely presented. It subverts genre expectations.

  Rosemary's Baby (68) Roman Polansky. *Little Big Man* (70) Arthur Penn. *Cabaret* (72) Bob Fosse. *The Long Goodbye* (73) Robert Altman. *Night Moves* (75) Arthur Penn. *Buffalo Bill and the Indians or Sitting Bull's History Lesson* (76) Robert Altman.

Revisionist Western *see* **WESTERN: Anti-Western**

Revolt-of-Nature Films *see* **HORROR FILM: Other Denizens of Horror Movies**

REVOLUTIONARY FILM (Militant Film, Progressive Film, Radical Film, Subversive Film)   The revolutionary film aims at being a weapon of revolution, and as such, attempts to help to overthrow reactionary governments. It aims at the eradication of colonialism and of foreign intervention by major powers in the affairs of smaller nations. It is a radical cinema whose task is the dismantling of bourgeois values and the destruction of existing myths by propounding a frontal attack on state, church and wealth. To accomplish this, the revolutionary film may take the form of the documentary or of the fiction film, and the films may be government-sponsored or privately produced. They may be films made in exile or films clandestinely made by militant groups in their country of origin. At present, two currents seem to dominate the revolutionary film: the first uses the narrative approach of commercial cinema in order to reach a large audience, and its tone is highly didactic, e.g., *Histoires d'A* (1973), a French feminist film advocating abortion; the second, a more extreme current, is based on Brecht's principle of alienation and Vertov's montage theory. Their views greatly influenced this type of revolutionary film. The result is a nonnarrative cinema, a line of structural and analytical films that seek to demythologize almost anything, including cinema itself. They are revolutionary films in form as well as content. This tendency in filmmaking is best represented by the later products of Jean-Luc Godard, e.g., *Un film comme les autres* (1968), in which the face of the person who is speaking is never seen. For obvious reasons, these revolutionary film tracts are of limited appeal.

  Revolutionary films include the Soviet Expressive-Realist cinema of the 1920s, some of the films of Brazilian *Cinema Nôvo*, and many of the films of the New Cinema of Germany and the Eastern European countries as well as nations of the Third World. *See also* **POLITICAL FILM**.

  O.K. (EG 64) Walter Heynowski. *Troublemakers* (66) Robert Machover,

Norman Fruchter. *La Hora de los Hornos* (Arg 67) Fernando Solanas, Octavio Getino *aka The Hour of the Blast Furnaces / The Hour of the Furnaces. Le Peuple et ses fusils* (F / Laos 67) Joris Ivens *aka The People and Their Guns. Praise Mark and Pass the Ammunition* (GB 68) Maurice Hatton. *Un film comme les autres* (F 68) Jean-Luc Godard. *Charles mort ou vif—Petite fresque historique* (Swiz 69) Alain Tanner *aka Charles Dead or Alive. Pravda* (F 69) Jean-Luc Godard, Dziga Vertov group. *British Sounds* (GB 69 TV) Jean-Luc Godard, Jean-Henri Roger *aka See You at Mao. Vent d'est* (G / It / F 69) Jean-Luc Godard, Dziga Vertov group *aka East Wind. Yawar mallku / Blood of the Condor* (Bol 69) Jorge Sanjines. *Cream-Schwabing-Report / The Servicer* (G / US 70) Leon Capetanos. *Ice* (70) Robert Kramer. *Pioniere in Ingolstadt* (G 70) Rainer Werner Fassbinder *aka Pioneers in Ingolstadt / Recruits in Ingolstadt. Reed, México Insurgente* (Mex 70) Paul Leduc *aka Reed: Insurgent Mexico / Reed (Mexico Insurgent). The Revolutionary* (70) Paul Williams. *Uloga moje porodice u svetskoj revoluciji* (Yug 70) Bata Cengic *aka The Role of My Family in the Revolution. Vladimir et Rosa / Vladimir and Rosa* (G / US 70) Jean-Luc Godard, Dziga Vertov group. *WR: Misterije Organizma / W. R. — Die Mysterien des Organismus* (Yug / G 71) Dusan Makavejev *aka WR: Mysteries of the Organism. Skinflicker* (GB 72) Tony Bicat. *Themroc* (F 72) Claude Faraldo. *Histoires d'A* (F 73) Charles Belmont, Marielle Issartel. *La Tierra prometida* (Chile 73) Miguel Littín *aka The Promised Land. Numéro Deux* (F 75) Jean-Luc Godard. *Die dritte Generation* (G 79) Rainer Werner Fassbinder *aka The Third Generation.*

——Guerrilla Films (Guerrilla Cinema)   This term has been used to define the kind of militant films (mostly documentaries) that are made clandestinely with light equipment in order to expose a government's policies and attack the established order, thus contributing to its possible future overthrow.[90] Guerrilla films are prevalent in Third World countries where revolutionary movements and terrorist groups carry out their activities mostly underground.

El Coraje del pueblo / La notte di San Juan (Bol / It 71) Jorge Sanjines *aka The Courage of the People / The Night of San Juan. Last Grave at Dimbaza* (SA 73) Nana Mahomo. *El Salvador el pueblo vencerá* (El Salvador 80) Diego de la Texera *aka El Salvador the People Will Win.*

Revolutionary War Films   *see*   **WAR FILM**

Righter-of-Wrongs Films   *see*   **SWASHBUCKLER**

Rip-and-Read Newscast   *see*   **TELEVISION NEWS**

Rip-Off   *see*   **SEQUEL**

Rip-Offs   *see*   **HARD-CORE PORNO FILM**

ROAD MOVIE (Hot Car Film)   Road films qualify as action movies; however, in a road picture, the open road is the environment in which the central action takes place. The protagonists in this type of film are either rugged individualists who make the road their home and use it for some daredevil purpose or challenge, or they are solitary individuals who embrace the road as a way of life and whose simple goal is crisscrossing the vast expanses of open national highways, sometimes aimlessly. In a more restricted sense, a road movie is a film which has protagonists whose driving force is either to seek the freedom of the road as a refuge from a harrowing past, or to search for its exhilarating, liberating strength — the road is what makes them tick. Films in this genre fit into other categories or genres such as motorcycle films, cop movies and sports movies. Indeed, biker road movies are better treated separately (see motorcycle movie entry). Aside from the movies which obviously fit into other genres, the following categories or subgenres of road movies may be distinguished: racing movies, truck movies and the sci-fi road movies. On the subject of road movies, *see* Mark Williams, *Road Movies* (New York: Proteus, 1982).

Échappement libre / Scappamento aperto / Escape libre (F / It / Sp 64) Jean Becker *aka Backfire*. *Wanda* (70) Barbara Loden. *Two-Lane Blacktop* (71) Monte Hellman. *Vanishing Point* (GB / US 71) Richard C. Sarafian. *The Getaway* (72) Sam Peckinpah. *Payday* (72) Daryl Duke. *Your Three Minutes Are Up* (73) Douglas N. Schwartz. *Dirty Mary Crazy Harry* (74) John Hough. *Im Lauf der Zeit* (G 75) Wim Wenders *aka In the Course of Time / Kings of the Road*. *Backroads* (Aust 76) Phillip Noyce. *Joyride* (77) Joseph Ruben. *Corvette Summer* (78) Mathew Robbins *aka The Hot One / Stingray*. *Instant Pictures* (Hol 79) George Schouten. *The Cannonball Run* (80) Hal Needham. *Cannonball Run II* (84) Hal Needham. *Queen of the Road* (Aust 84 TV) Bruce Best. *Stranger Than Paradise* (84) Jim Jarmusch. *The Hitcher* (86) Robert Harmon. *Leningrad Cowboys Go America* (Fin / Sw 89) Aki Kaurismäki. *Wild at Heart* (90) David Lynch. *Thelma & Louise* (91) Ridley Scott.

——**Racing Movies**   Any movies which describe racing events of an official national or international nature, or movies focussing on some specific type of motor racing, e.g., drag racing, cross-country illegal car racing, stockcar racing. *See* **MOTORCAR RACING FILM**.

The Young Racers (63) Roger Corman. *Winning* (69) James Goldstone. *Little Fauss and Big Halsy* (70) Sidney J. Furie. *Le Mans* (71) Lee H. Katzin. *The Gumball Rally* (76) Chuck Ball. *Safari 3000* (82) Harry Hurwitz.

——**Sci-Fi Road Movies**   As in all science fiction pictures, these are set in the near or distant future and portray advanced technology or the remnants of old 20th century machinery adapted to function in a post-devastated world.

Death Race 2000 (75) Paul Bartel. *Mad Max* (Aust 77) George Miller. *The Last Chase* (Can / US 79) Martyn Burke [rel. in 82]. *Mad Max II / The Road Warrior* (Aust / US 81) George Miller *aka Mad Max 2*. *Wheels of Fire* (84) Cirio H. Santiago *aka Desert Warrior / Vindicator*. *Cherry 2000* (86) Steve De Jarnatt [rel. in 88]. *Circuitry Man* (89) Steven Lovy.

——**Truck Movies**   Truck or trucking movies have vehicles and their drivers, their fights, worries and hopes at the center of their action.

They Drive by Night (40) Raoul Walsh *aka Road to 'Frisco*. *Le Salaire de la peur / Vite perdute* (F / It 52) Henri-Georges Clouzot *aka Il salario della paura / Wages of Fear*. *Hell Drivers* (GB 57) Cy Endfield. *Duel* (71 TV)

Steven Spielberg. *Deadhead Miles* (72) Vernon Zimmerman. *Truck Stop Women* (74) Mark L. Lester. *White Line Fever / La Route de la violence* (Can 75) Jonathan Kaplan. *Road Games* (Aust 80) Richard Franklin.

Road Show *see* FILM

Robbery Film *see* CRIME FILM: Thievery Films; *see also* GANG-STER FILM: Heist Films

Robin Hood Film *see* SWASHBUCKLER: Chivalric Films

Rock and Jazz Documentary *see* BLACK FILM: Black Genre Movies

Rock and Roll Film, Rock and Roll Musical *see* ROCK FILM

Rock Clip *see* MUSIC VIDEO

Rock-Concert Documentary, Rock Concert Films, Rock Doc *see* MUSICAL

Rock Documentary *see* MUSICAL: Rock Concert Films; *see also* ROCK FILM

ROCK FILM (Rock and Roll Film, Rock and Roll Musical, Rock 'n' Roll Picture)   A subgenre of the musical, rock and roll movies came into being with *Rock Around the Clock*, produced in 1956 by Sam Katzman who rightly guessed that there was a young audience eager for this type of picture. However, not all rock films are musicals; some combine a rock soundtrack with strong dramatic content, e.g., *The Idolmaker* (1980), a fictionalized biography of rock producer Bob Marcucci. Rock films also include rock documentaries and rock concert films whose popularity began with *Monterey Pop* (1967), essentially a filmed record of the Monterey Pop and Jazz Festival in California in 1967, and gained impetus with *Woodstock* (1970). The rock concert film and rock documentary or rockumentary are a well-established genre in the rock scene. Besides presenting the evolution of the rock and roll movies, David Ehrenstein and Bill Reed, *Rock on Film* (New York: Delilah Books, 1982) give a listing (with credits) of 483 films in which rock music plays a major or important role. Linda J. Sandahl, *Encyclopedia of Rock Music on Film* (Poole, Dorset: Blandford Press, 1987) also lists over 400 films. *See also* MUSICAL: Rock Concert Films and Rock Operas.

The Girl Can't Help It (56) Frank Tashlin *aka Do Re Mi*. *Loving You* (56) Hal Kanter. *Rock Around the Clock* (56) Fred F. Sears. *A Hard Day's Night* (GB 64) Richard Lester *aka The Beatles*. *The T.A.M.I. Show* (64) Steve Binder, George Turpin, Charles LaForce *aka T.A.M.I. / Teenage Awards Music International / Teenage Music International*. *Monterey Pop* (67) James Desmond, Barry Feinstein, D.A. Pennebaker, Albert Maysles, Roger Murphy, Richard Leacock, Nick Proferes. *Elvis: That's the Way It Is* (70) Denis Sanders. *Woodstock* (70) Michael Wadleigh *aka Woodstock I & II* [first of the rockumentaries, filmed in Multi-Screen]. *Imagine* (GB 72)

John Lennon, Yoko Ono. *The Last Waltz* (78) Martin Scorsese. *Quadrophenia* (GB 79) Franc Roddam. *Rock 'n' Roll High School* (79) Allan Arkush. *The Idolmaker* (80) Taylor Hackford. *Rude Boy* (GB 80) Jack Hazan, David Mingay. *Pink Floyd – The Wall* (US / GB 82) Alan Parker *aka The Wall*. *Get Crazy* (83) Allan Arkush. *Give My Regards to Broad Street* (GB 84) Peter Webb. *This Is Spinal Tap* (84) Rob Riener *aka Spinal Tap*. *Purple Rain* (84) Albert Magnoli. *Dogs in Space* (Aust 86) Richard Lowenstein. *Imagine: John Lennon* (88) Andrew Solt. *Truth or Dare* (91) Alek Keshishian *aka In Bed with Madonna / Madonna Truth or Dare*.

——**Punk Films**   Punk defines a youth subculture which derives from and has as its core the world of rock music. Punk is also a strand of minimal rock music. Any film which deals with this type of music or its subculture is a punk film. *See* "Documenting Punk: A Subcultural Investigation" by Gina Marchetti in *Film Reader* No. 5 (1982): 269–84.

The Punk Rock Movie (GB 77) Don Letts. *Jubilee* (GB 78) Derek Jarman. *Asphaltnacht* (G 80) Peter Fratzscher *aka Asphalt Night*. *Breaking Glass* (GB 80) Brian Gibson. *Debt Begins at Twenty* (80) Stephanie Beroes. *D.O.A.: A Right of Passage* (80) Lech Kowalski. *Underground U.S.A.* (80) Eric Mitchell. *The Decline of Western Civilization* (81) Penelope Spheeris. *Liquid Sky* (82) Slava Tsukerman. *Rough Cut and Ready Dubbed* (GB 82) Hasan Shah, Dom Shaw. *Smithereens* (82) Susan Seidelman. *Suburbia* (83) Penelope Spheeris *aka The Wild Side*. *X: The Unheard Music* (85) W. T. Morgan. *Sid and Nancy* (GB / US 86) Alex Cox. *The Decline of Western Civilization Part II: The Metal Years* (88) Penelope Spheeris.

Rock 'n' Roll Picture   *see*   **ROCK FILM**

Rock Opera Movie, Rock Operas   *see*   **MUSICAL**

Rock Promo   *see*   **MUSIC VIDEO**

Rockumentary   *see*   **ROCK FILM**

Rockvid, Rock Video   *see*   **MUSIC VIDEO**

Rodeo Films   *see*   **WESTERN**

ROMANCE   Romance is associated with the women's picture and indeed forms one of its major branches along with the weepie, with which it shares common ground (some romances qualify as weepies as well). Romance is a broad category, and in a cinematic context it means a film whose emphasis is on sentimental relationships in romantic situations, that is to say, entanglements of the heart. Love, pain and emotion in general are at the core of romance; in fact, romance is synonymous with love story. Love is at the center of the film and its manifestations are many: unrequited love, forbidden love, forlorn love, undemanding love, self-sacrificing love – all these and many more facets of love serve to keep the romance going and the audience enraptured. Love at first sight, puppy love, the search for love, adulterous love relationships impeded by duty and convention are further examples of what these romances are about. They take place usually in domestic environments, in cities or small towns, or they flourish in exotic locations. In the latter surroundings, spirited, liberated, resolute or adventurous heroines are the norm, and their exciting adventures may occur in historical or contemporary settings. Romance is also an integral part of many genres; it is found in musicals, war movies, Westerns and comedy. Besides the above definition, romance is also broadly understood as romancing or wooing, an activity in which an interested party (usually male) sets out to impress the person of the other sex or win his/her affection. For an introductory article on the subject of romance and the women's picture, *see* Cynthia Rose, "Romance," in *Anatomy of the Movies,* ed. David Pirie (London: Windward, 1981), 232–41. *See also* **LOVE STORY, WOMAN'S PICTURE.**

7th Heaven (27) Frank Borzage. *Little Women* (33) George Cukor. *The Little Minister* (34) Richard Wallace. *Algiers* (38) John Cromwell. *Vessel of Wrath* (GB 38) Erich Pommer *aka The Beachcomber. Intermezzo: A Love Story* (39) Gregory Ratoff *aka Escape to Happiness / Intermezzo. Love Affair* (39) Leo McCarey. *Casablanca* (42) Michael Curtiz. *Brief Encounter* (GB 45) David Lean. *I Know Where I Am Going* (GB 45) Michael Powell, Emeric Pressburger. *Forever Amber* (47) Otto Preminger. *Saraband for Dead Lovers* (GB 48) Basil Dearden, Michael Relph *aka Saraband. Three Coins in the Fountain* (54) Jean Negulesco *aka We Believe in Love. Sayonara* (57) Joshua Logan. *The World of Suzie Wong* (60) Richard Quine. *Cousin, cousine* (F 75) Jean-Charles Tacchela. *Mayerling* (F / GB 68) Terence Young. *Ryan's Daughter* (GB / US 70) David Lean *aka Michael's Day. The Other Side of Midnight* (77) Charles Jarrott. *The Blue Lagoon* (US / Aust 79) Randal Kleiser. *Beau-père* (F 81) Bertrand Blier *aka Beau Pere. Racing with the Moon* (84) Richard Benjamin. *37°2 le matin* (F 86) Jean-Jacques Beineix *aka Betty Blue / Betty Blue 37°2 in the Morning / Betty Blue 37°2 le matin. Cousins* (89) Joel Schumacher.

——**Gothic Romance Films** They feature apprehensive heroines threatened by real or imaginary dangers, most often their husbands who may or may not harbor thoughts of killing them. The settings are mysterious or oppressive, usually gloomy abodes which recall the trappings of the Gothic novel. Often, Gothic romances are period films.

Gaslight (GB 39) Thorold Dickinson *aka Angel Street. Rebecca* (40) Alfred Hitchcock. *Suspicion* (41) Alfred Hitchcock *aka Before the Fact. Experiment Perilous* (44) Jacques Tourneur. *Jane Eyre* (44) Robert Stevenson. *Dragonwick* (46) Joseph L. Mankiewicz. *Secret Beyond the Door* (47) Fritz Lang. *Jane Eyre* (GB 70 TV) Delbert Mann.

——**Historical Romances** Romances in which the love-interest is set in an historical context with either real, historical, legendary or fictitious characters. They are costume pictures.

Madame Dubarry (G 19) Ernest Lubitsch *aka Passion. The Barretts of Wimpole Street* (34) Sidney Franklin *aka Forbidden Alliance. Catherine the Great* (GB 34) Paul Czinner *aka The Rise of Catherine the Great. Anna Karenina* (35) Clarence Brown. *Fire Over England* (GB 36) William K. Howard. *All This, and Heaven Too* (40) Anatole Litvak. *That Hamilton*

Woman (41) Alexander Korda *aka Lady Hamilton.*   *Kitty* (45) Mitchell Leisen.   *Desirée* (54) Henry Koster.   *Passione d'amore / Passion d'amour* (It / F 81) Ettore Scola *aka Passion d'Amore / Passion of Love.*

Roman-Ciné   *see*   **CINE-ROMAN**

ROMANTIC COMEDY   This is a blanket term that includes any comic film in which the protagonists, a man and a woman, engage in courtship, amorous dalliance and sexual games meant to seduce and entrap the member of the opposite sex. Whether the initiator of the games is the male or the female is irrelevant to the goal of the film which is, above all, to amuse and entertain by romancing. Romantic comedies are constructed around the ups and downs of a couple's relationship—the initial antagonism, the misunderstandings, the bouts of jealousy, the conflicts of interest, until all is well at the end of the film. The following types of comedy also qualify as romantic comedy: Marriage Comedy, Screwball Comedy, Sophisticated Comedy (qq.v.).

I Met Him in Paris (37) Wesley Ruggles.   *Tovarich* (37) Anatole Litvak.   *The Lady Eve* (40) Preston Sturges.   *Don't Take It to Heart* (GB 44) Jeffrey Dell.   *Sabrina* (54) Billy Wilder *aka Sabrina Fair.*   *Barefoot in the Park* (67) Gene Saks.   *Minnie and Moskowitz* (71) John Cassavetes.   *Love Among the Ruins* (75 TV) George Cukor.   *Annie Hall* (77) Woody Allen.   *The Goodbye Girl* (77) Herbert Ross.   *Heartaches / Coeurs à l'enver* (Can 80) Donald Shebib.   *All Night Long* (81) Jean-Claud Tramont.   *Lovesick* (83) Marshall Brickman.   *Romantic Comedy* (83) Arthur Hiller.   *The Buddy System* (84) Glen Jordan.   *The Woman in Red* (84) Gene Wilder.   *Moonstruck* (87) Norman Jewison.   *Roxanne* (87) Fred Schepisi.   *When Harry Met Sally...* (89 / Rob Reiner.

Romantic Documentary   *see*   **DOCUMENTARY**

Romantic Drama   *see*   **WOMAN'S PICTURE**

ROMANTIC FILM (Romanticism)   Films which capture, transpose or render into cinematic terms romantic ideals and credo may be said to be romantic films. Romanticism, as it arose in the 18th and 19th centuries, was a movement in the arts that sought to oppose the extreme rigidity of neoclassicism by breaking all the established, formal rules laid down by latter-day classicists. The romantics promoted individualism, encouraged revolutionary ideas, exalted feeling, spontaneity and passion and praised the working of the imagination. They adored living intensely, regardless of what it might cost them. Thus, when the romantic hero loved, his love was an all-consuming flame, an agony perhaps, which could easily end in death. This contrasts with romance. In romance, duty and convention come first, and if society would not approve of their relationship lovers are bound to part or, if there are no obstacles, they end in marriage. In films with romantic heroes or heroines, the lovers either flee together or die together; they certainly do not bow to convention or duty. It is an important distinction because terms become confused, and it is usual to call romantic (or "romantic drama") those films that would be better termed romances. In the strict sense of the romantic spirit, romantic films are characterized by a pervading sense of fatality. The protagonists are oftentimes doomed in their chosen paths. Good examples of romantic films are often found in adaptations from classic books of the Romantic period.

One Way Passage (32) Tay Garnett.   Queen Christina (33) Rouben Mamoulian.   Camille (36) George Cukor.   Mayerling (F 36) Anatole Litvak.   Romeo and Juliet (36) George Cukor.   L'Aigle à deux têtes (F 47) Jean Cocteau aka The Eagle Has Two Heads / Eagle with Two Heads.   Les Grandes Manoeuvres / Grandi manovre (F / It 55) René Clair aka The Grand Maneuver / Summer Maneuvers.   Elvira Madigan (Sw 67) Bo Widerberg.   Romeo and Juliet / Romeo e Giulietta (GB / It 67) Franco Zeffirelli.   Loulou (F 80) Maurice Pialat.

Romantic Melodramas see MELODRAMA

Romanticism see ROMANTIC FILM

Rotating Series see TELEVISION SERIES: Multiseries

Roughies see SEX-AND-VIOLENCE PICTURE

R-RATED FILM   R-rated film, in an American context, applies to any production that puts a certain emphasis on sex, nudity, violence or vulgar language. R-rated films contrast with X-rated films which portray sex in a graphic manner or make use of excessive violence. The great majority of R-rated films are exploitation movies made by "Independent" studios; that is, film companies not included in what are known as the Major and Minor production studios. R-rated films in the United States are restricted and persons under 17 years of age are not admitted unless they are accompanied by a parent or an adult guardian. Some films undergo some cutting in order to qualify for an R-rating or have their ratings changed from X to R by the Motion Picture Association of America. Even R-rated pictures may undergo some changes to receive a lesser rating grade. The nature of (or directives for) these changes are imprecise and in a permanent state of fluctuation as the moral standards of society change. For a selected filmography of the R-rated sexploitation variety, see Gregory A. Waller, "An Annotated Filmography of R-Rated Sexploitation Films Released During the 1970s," Journal of Popular Film and Television 9.2 (1981): 98–112.

R-Rated Sexploitation Film see SOFT-CORE SEX-EXPLOITATION FILM

RUNAWAY (Runaway Feature, Runaway Production)   Mainly, a film made abroad or in some location other than Hollywood in order to reduce its cost. The practice of making features abroad goes back to 1912 when the five-reel Kalem Company production From the Manger to the Cross was filmed in Palestine by Sidney Olcott.

Runaway Feature see RUNAWAY

Runaway Film *see* CHASE FILM

Runaway Production *see* RUNAWAY

Runover *see* TELEVISION PROGRAM

RURAL COMEDY (Farm Comedy) As with rural dramas (*see* **RUSTIC DRAMA**), rural comedies take place outside the big metropolitan centers and are in farmlands or small townships; indeed, they may be located anywhere in the countryside at large. They are often peopled with stock characters easily recognized by their attire, regional accents, mannerisms and also frequently by their raucous, jocular, rustic kind of humor. Rural comedies have been around since the early 1900s, although their popularity, at least in America, has waned considerably. Rural comedy at present takes place mostly on television. *See also* **HILLBILLY FILM** and **REDNECK MOVIE**.

Our Hospitality (23) Buster Keaton, Jack Blystone. *The Farmer's Wife* (GB 28) Alfred Hitchcock. *Kentucky Kernels* (34) George Stevens. *Kentucky Moonshine* (38) David Butler *aka Three Men and a Girl*. *Murder, He Says* (45) George Marshall. *The Egg and I* (47) Chester Erskine [followed by the "Ma and Pa Kettle" series (1949-57)]. *The Mating Game* (59) George Marshall. *Bootleggers* (74) Charles B. Pierce *aka The Bootleggers' Angel*. *Came a Hot Friday* (NZ 84) Ian Mune.

Rural Drama *see* RUSTIC DRAMA

RUSTIC DRAMA (Farm Movie, Farmer Film, Rural Drama) Rustic dramas, films depicting life on the farm and extolling the virtues of country as opposed to city life or focusing on the farmer's struggle to make a living and keep his farm, are perhaps less popular nowadays with American audiences. In other parts of the world, however, rustic dramas still have relevance. Many rural dramas are produced by Eastern European and Third World countries where village and peasant life plays an important role in the social strata of the nation.

The Canadian (26) William Beaudine. *Sunrise—A Song of Two Humans* (27) F. W. Murnau *aka Sunrise*. *State Fair* (33) Henry King. *The Stranger's Return* (33) King Vidor. *Come Next Spring* (56) R. G. Springsteen. *Codin / Codine* (Rum / F 63) Henri Colpi *aka La Brute et l'enfant*. *Holt vidék* (Hung 71) István Gaál *aka Dead Landscape*. *All Creatures Great and Small* (GB / US 74 TV) Claude Whatham. *Inutile Envoyer Photo* (F 77 TV) Alain Dhouailly. *L'albero degli zoccoli* (It 78 TV) Ermanno Olmi *aka The Tree of (the) Wooden Clogs*. *Heartland* (79) Richard Pearce. *Land og synir* (Icel 79) Agúst Gudmundsson *aka Land and Sons*. *Le Cheval d'orgueil* (F 80) Claude Chabrol *aka The Proud Ones*. *Cross Creek* (83) Martin Ritt. *Country* (84) Richard Pearce. *Places in the Heart* (84) Robert Benton. *The River* (84) Mark Rydell. *Los Santos inocentes* (Sp 84) Mario Camus *aka The Holy Innocents*. *Vigil* (NZ 84) Vincent Wart. *Jean de Florette* (F 85-86) Claude Berri [in 2 parts: *Jean de Florett & Manon des sources*]. *On the Black Hill* (GB 87) Andrew Grieve.

Sadean Film, Sadian Film *see* **SOFT-CORE SEX-EXPLOITATION FILM: De Sade**

Sadie-Massies, Sadomasochism, S and M Film *see* **SEX AND VIOLENCE PICTURE**

Safari Movies *see* **JUNGLE FILM**

Safety Film *see* **FACTUAL FILM: Jeopardy Film**

SAGA (Family Saga)   When the term is applied to a film production, it usually means a "family saga" — the fortunes and misfortunes of a household — or the rise of a hard-working individual of the lower classes forging his or her way to the top. It covers a whole life span from youth to old age and may entail the founding of a dynasty. It is an extended meaning of the original interpretation of the word saga, an epic-like account of some exploits of bygone times in a distinct Nordic or Scandinavian setting. The genre thrives today on television because television is able to provide more time to the full development of the story by dividing it in sections or episodes. At times, the term has a pejorative sense as it is applied to what otherwise would be classed as romance or melodrama. As with other genres, variations of the core elements are possible.

> *Sweepings* (33) John Cromwell. *The World Moves On* (34) John Ford. *This Happy Breed* (GB 44) David Lean. *The Forsyte Saga* (GB 67 TV) James Cellan Jones, David Giles [in 26 episodes]. *Louisiane / Louisiana* (Can / F 83 TV) Philippe de Broca (plus Jacques Demy) [in 3 parts; also as a feature version]. *A Woman of Substance* (GB 83 TV) Don Sharp [in 3 parts; also in 2 parts].

Sagebrusher *see* **WESTERN**

Sales Film *see* **FACTUAL FILM: Advertising Film**

SAMURAI FILM (Chambara Film, Samurai Swordplay Movie)   *Chambara* films (period films about samurai) are a violent Japanese film genre which gained popularity after World War II. They are well-known in the West, mainly through the films of Akira Kurosawa and the masterful characterizations of Toshiro Mifune. The *chambara* film is a genre within the *jidai-geki* which covers period or costume pictures set before 1868.

The samurai film, like the swashbuckler, relies on swordsmanship as the essential ingredient of the genre. Indeed, in order to be a successful samurai (a warrior attached to a clan) — or, for that matter, a *ronin* (a samurai without a master), a *kyokaku* (a commoner armed with a sword), or a *yojimbo* (a bodyguard) — the practitioner has to be well-versed in armed combat and the handling of the sword. Every self-respecting samurai ought to be able to take on several adversaries at the same time and come out victorious because of his skillful swordsmanship. The samurai film has often been compared with the Western, and for good reason, as the success of

John Sturges's *The Magnificent Seven* (1960), patterned on Kurosawa's *Shichinin no samurai / The Seven Samurai* (1954), and Sergio Leone's *Per un pugno di dollari / A Fistful of Dollars* (1964), based on *Yojimbo* (1961), demonstrate. In these films, the Japanese samurai plots are easily translated into Western terms. Some Westerns have also included samurai, e.g., Terence Young's *Soleil rouge / Red Sun* (1971), with Toshiro Mifune in the American West in search of a stolen Japanese sword. The samurai films, again in accord with Westerns, have little to do with the real samurai; they are a highly modified version of their historical counterparts. The samurai film is the traditional Japanese type of martial arts film.[91]

Rasho-mon (J 50) Akira Kurosawa *aka In the Woods / Rashomon*. *Miyamoto Musashi* (J 54) Hiroshi Inagaki *aka Master Swordsman / Samurai I: The Legend of Musashi*. *Shichinin no samurai* (J 54) Akira Kurosawa *aka The Magnificent Seven / The Seven Samurai*. *Ichijoji no ketto* (J 55) Hiroshi Inagaki *aka Samurai II: Duel at the Temple*. *Ketto Ganryujima* (J 55) Hiroshi Inagaki *aka Musashi and Kojiro / Samurai III: Duel on Ganryu Island* [third film in Inagaki's "Samurai" trilogy]. *Shin heike monogatari* (J 55) Kenji Mizoguchi *aka The Legend of the Taira Clan / New Tales / New Tales of the Taira Clan / The Sacrilegious Hero / Tales of the Taira Clan*. *Kumonoso-jo* (J 57) Akira Kurosawa *aka The Castle of the Spider's Web / Cobweb Castle / Kunonosu-Djo / Macbeth / (The) Throne of Blood*. *Kakushi toride no san-akunin* (J 58) Akira Kurosawa *aka The Bodyguard / The Hidden Fortress / Three Bad Men in a Hidden Fortress*. *Tsubaki Sanjuro* (J 61) Akira Kurosawa *aka Sanjuro*. *Yojimbo* (J 61) Akira Kurosawa *aka The Bodyguard*. *Seppuko* (J 62) Masaki Kobayashi *aka Harakiri*. *Sambiki no samurai* (J 64) Hideo Gosha *aka Three Outlaw Samurai*. *Zatoichi senryo-kubi* (J 64) Kazuo Ikehiro *aka Zatoichi and a Chest of Gold* [24 films (1962-72) in the "Zatoichi" series]. *Samurai* (J 65) Kihachi Okamoto *aka Samurai Assassin*. *Daibosatsu toge* (J 66) Kihachi Okamoto *aka The Sword of Doom*. *Joi-uchi* (J 67) Masaki Kobayashi *aka Rebellion / Samurai Rebellion*. *Sasaki Kojiro* (J 67) Hiroshi Inagaki *aka Kojiro*. *Bakumatsu* (J 70) Daisuke Ito *aka The Ambitious*. *Shura* (J 70) Toshio Matsumoto *aka Demons / Pandemonium*. *Kosure ookami-Sanzu no kawa no ubagurama* (J 72) Kenji Misumi *aka Baby Cart at the River Styx / Kosure ohkami n.2 / Shogun Assassin* (reedited version directed by Robert Houston) [*Kozure ohkami* (1972-73) *aka Lighting Swords of Death / Sword of Vengeance*: a series of 6 films; I-V by Kenji Misumi, VI by Yoshiyuki Kuroda]. *The Bushido Blade* (GB / J / US 78) Tom Kotani *aka The Bloody Bushido Blade*. *The Challenge* (US / J 82) John Frankenheimer.

Samurai Swordplay Movie *see* **SAMURAI FILM**

Sand-and-Surf Movie *see* **TEEN MOVIE: Beach Films**

Sandal-and-Spear/s Epic, S & S (Sandal and Spear/s, Sex and Sand) Movie *see* **PEPLUM**

Satanic Film *see* **HORROR FILM: Demonic Films**

SATIRE (Satirical Comedy, Satirical Film, Satiric Comedy) Satire seeks to make us aware of human faults and follies by ridiculing them. It casts an eye on society and its institutions and tries to expose wickedness, abuses of power and infringements of human rights and dignity. Its perennial targets are hypocrisy and vice. Straight satire is a continuous flow of scathing humor and caustic wit. It often uses exaggeration and fantastic occurrences to make its point. For instance, in *Modern Times* (1936), one of Charlie Chaplin's classic films, Chaplin is drawn into a huge machine by its conveyor belt with no physical ill-effects except to his pride. And in *Candy* (1968), the heroine undergoes frequent sexual assaults, but emerges none the worse for the experience. Other satirical films are more on the level of the probable, and they are gentler in their use of satire; nevertheless, they try equally to draw attention to society's wrongs. The most common types of satire are social satire, political satire and religious satire; they cover the three most important sections of society. The element of satire is itself present in many different types of films and comedies. Quite often, satire uses the vehicle of black comedy, science fiction or fable for its outer form of presentation. Parody and satire are sometimes confused. When the object of satire is a single individual rather than society, the term lampoon is often used.

À nous la liberté (F 31) René Clair *aka Liberté chérie / Freedom for Us / Give Us Freedom / Liberty for Us*. *Modern Times* (36) Charlie Chaplin. *The Demi-Paradise* (GB 43) Anthony Asquith *aka Adventure for Two*. *Animal Farm* (GB 51-54) John Halas, Joy Batchelor. *A King in New York* (GB 57) Charlie Chaplin. *Candy e il suo pazzo mondo / Candy* (It / F / US 68) Christian Marquand. *Hail* (70) Fred Levinson *aka Hail to the Chief / Washington, B.C.* *The Rise and Rise of Michael Rimmer* (GB 70) Kevin Billington. *Millhouse: A White Comedy* (71) Emile de Antonio. *Smile* (75) Michael Ritchie. *Chinesische Roulette* (G 76) Rainer Werner Fassbinder *aka Chinese Roulette*. *Welcome to L.A.* (77) Alan Rudolph. *Being There* (79) Hal Ashby. *Deal of the Century* (83) William Friedkin. *Entre tinieblas* (Sp 83) Pedro Almodóvar *aka Dark Habits*. *Kazoku gemu* (J 83) Yoshimitsu Morita *aka The Family Game*. *No habrá más penas ni olvido* (Arg 83) Hector Olivera *aka Funny Dirty Little War*. *The Act* (84) Sig Shore. *Repo Man* (84) Alex Cox. *Brazil* (GB / US 85) Terry Gilliam. *Männer* (G 85) Doris Dörrie *aka Men*. *Down and Out in Beverly Hills* (86) Paul Mazursky. *Salvation!* (86) Beth B. [subtitled "Have You Said Your Prayers Today?"]. *Glory! Glory!* (89 CTV) Lindsay Anderson.

Satirical Film, Satirical Comedy, Satiric Comedy   *see*   **SATIRE**

Saturation Booking   *see*   **RELEASE**

Sauerkraut Western   *see*   **SPAGHETTI WESTERN**

Scare Film   *see*   **DRUG FILM**

The Scene News   *see*   **TELEVISION NEWS**

Scenic   *see*   **TRAVEL FILM**

SCHLOCK MOVIE   Schlock is a common slang term of Yiddish origin often used in American parlance. When applied to movies, it means an inferior moving picture cheaply and quickly made and, in most cases, without redeeming social value. However, some schlock movies have become box-office hits. The schlock film variety thrives especially in the horror and science fiction genres. A legendary producer-director purveyor of schlock in the fifties, a decade in which schlock proliferated, was Roger Corman who made many creature movies for American International Pictures and Allied Artists Productions, two film companies that specialized in cheap and quick productions. Hollywood is not the only place to produce vast quantities of schlock; Italy, Spain and Japan are also well-known for their schlock movies. *See* **SLEAZY MOVIE** and **Z PICTURE**.

   Kongo (32) William Cowen. *Robot Monster* (53) Phil Tucker *aka Monster(s) from Mars / Monster(s) from the Moon / Robot Monster from Mars. Monster from the Ocean Floor* (54) Wyott Ordung *aka It Stalked the Ocean Floor / Monster Maker.* *King Dinosaur* (55) B. I. Gordon. *It Conquered the World* (56) Roger Corman *aka It Conquered the Earth.* *The Giant Claw* (57) Fred F. Sears *aka The Mark of the Claw.* *The Alligator People* (59) Roy Del Ruth. *Mr. Sardonicus* (61) William Castle *aka Sardonicus. Schlock!* (71) John Landis *aka The Banana Monster.* *Food of the Gods* (76) Bert I. Gordon.

Schlockbuster   *see*   **VIDEO**

School Exposé Flick   *see*   **TEEN MOVIE**

School Film   *see*   **FACTUAL FILM: Educational Film**

SCIENCE FICTION FILM (Extrapolative Film, Future Film, Sci-Fier, Sci-Fi Film, SF Film)   Science fiction films may be traced back to films like Georges Méliès' *Mésaventures d'un aéronaute* (1900) and *Le Voyage dans la lune* (1902), and Ferdinand Zecca's *À la conquête de l'air* (1901), which were actually more in line with fantasy then science fiction.[92] Nevertheless, these early films and the film pioneers that made them have a definite claim in what has become a well-established cinematic genre. Although many writers have tried their hand at an incisive definition of science fiction, such a definition continues to elude them. A clear-cut definition is not easy to formulate because science fiction encroaches on the adjacent genres of fantasy and horror, very often blending freely with them. For the sake of simplicity, science fiction is best defined as a genre that deals with imaginary journeys, imaginary worlds and societies from the standpoint of credible possibility presented in rational scientific terms. It speculates about what would happen, or what it could be like if a certain set of circumstances were to be applied. In this way, it can reshape or restructure history and legend relocating them in a new milieu, or it can extrapolate known facts in order to show hopefully the vagaries and follies of mankind. In this context, science fiction stories may take place in the near future, the far future or the remote past; in distant worlds, future worlds, alternate worlds or parallel worlds. Science fiction films are also made of aliens, bug-eyed monsters and creatures galore; robots, computers and other technological advances. As far as science is concerned, two general currents in science fiction are clearly discernible. Science fiction films are either pro- or anti-science, the latter trend being more common; this is attested to by the countless films warning us against the dangers of tampering with the natural order of things. It should also be noted that filmed science fiction falls into two main subgenres or branches. One limits itself to presenting science fiction in an extrapolative, serious way, and the other (by far the more common in terms of films produced) includes the horrific and the catastrophic. Its films are best defined as SF horror films.

Science fiction experienced a resurgence of interest and active production in America in the fifties that still continues today. This is due in part to some remarkable films that from time to time give renewed impetus to the genre. Some of these remarkable films have been: in the fifties, *Destination Moon* (1950) and *The Thing* (1951); in the sixties, *2001: A Space Odyssey* (1968); and in the seventies, *Star Wars* (1977) and *Close Encounters of the Third Kind* (1977).[93]

Mésaventures d'un aéronaute (F 00) Georges Méliès *aka The Balloonist's Mishap / Malheurs d'un aéronaute.   À la conquête de l'air* (F 01) Ferdinand Zecca *aka La Conquête de l'air / Conquest of the Air / The Flying Machine* [*Cf. Happy Hooligan in His Airship / The Twentieth Century Tramp* by Edwin S. Porter].   *Le Voyage dans la lune* (F 02) Georges Méliès *aka A Trip to the Moon / A Trip to Mars.   The Invisible Man* (33) James Whale [7 films (1933-51) in the Universal series].   *Gold* (G 34) Karl Hartl *aka L'Or* (F. v.).   *Destination Moon* (50) Irving Pichel.   *The Thing* (51) Christian Nyby, Howard Hawks (uncredited) *aka The Thing (from Another World) / Who Goes There?   Attack of the 50 Foot Woman* (57) Nathan Hertz.   *4D Man* (59) Irving Shortess Yeaworth, Jr. *aka The Evil Force / The Four Dimensional Man / Four-Dimensional Man / Master of Terror.   Charly* (68) Ralph Nelson.   *2001: A Space Odyssey* (US / GB 68) Stanley Kubrick *aka Journey Beyond the Stars / Space Odyssey.   The Andromeda Strain* (70) Robert Wise.   *Quest for Love* (GB 71) Ralph Thomas.   *The Crazies* (73) George A. Romero *aka Code Name Trixie / Cosmos 859.   Embryo* (75) Ralph Nelson *aka Created to Kill.   Close Encounters of the Third Kind* (77) Steven Spielberg *aka Experiences / Watch the Skies* [*Cf. The Special Edition: Close Encounters of the Third Kind* (80): reedited version].   *Star Wars* (77) George Lucas *aka Adventures of the Starkiller / The Star Wars / Star Wars Episode IV: A New Hope* [followed by *Star Wars Episode V: The Empire Strikes Back* (80) and *Star Wars Episode VI: Return of the Jedi* (83)].   *La Mort en direct / Death Watch-Der gekaufte Tod* (F / G 79) Bertrand Tavernier *aka Death in Full View / Deathwatch.   Altered States* (80) Ken Russell.   *Android* (82) Aaron Lipstadt.   *Creature* (84) William Malone *aka Titan Find.   Hands of Steel* (US / It 84) Martin Dolman.   *Enemy Mine* (US / G 85) Wolfgang Petersen.   *Cherry 2000* (86) Steve De Jarnatt.   *Deadly Friend* (86) Wes Craven.   *Eliminators* (US / Sp 86) Peter Manoogian.   *Innerspace* (87) Joe Dante.   *RoboCop* (87) Paul Verhoeven.   *High Desert Kill* (89 MCTV) Harry Falk.   *Circuitry Man* (90) Steven Lovy.   *Robocop 2* (90) Irvin Kershner.   *Total Recall* (90) Paul Verhoeven.

Recurrent themes in SF are very numerous and would require a long list. Here, only some of the main categories of science fiction are indicated. Obviously, some of these categories overlap. For some of the main components of SF horror movies, *see* **HORROR FILM** entry.[94]

——**Dystopian Films**   Future perfect societies (utopias) are highly improbable, and there are only a few examples of filmed utopias, e.g., *Just Imagine* (1930) and *Lost Horizon* (1936). It is more common among writers and filmmakers to portray the reverse of a utopia, a future world gone wrong, that is, a dystopia. These future societies are nightmare worlds where the inhabitants have been deprived of their freedom, individuality and even their self-esteem.

Metropolis – das Schicksas einer Menschheit im Jahre 2000 (G 26) Fritz Lang *aka Metropolis. Just Imagine* (30) David Butler. *Lost Horizon* (36) Frank Capra *aka Lost Horizon of Shangri-La. Things to Come* (GB 36) William Cameron Menzies *aka Whither Mankind / The Shape of Things to Come. 1984* (GB 55) Michael Anderson. *Sins of the Fleshapoids* (64) George Kuchar, Mike Kuchar. *Alphaville, une étrange aventure de Lemmy Caution / Agente Lemmy Caution: missione Alphaville* (F / It 65) Jean-Luc Godard *aka Alphaville / Tarzan versus I.B.M. Fahrenheit 451* (GB 66) François Truffaut. *Planet of the Apes* (67) Franklin J. Schaffner [5 films (1967-73) in the Apes series]. *THX 1138* (69) George Lucas. *A Clockwork Orange* (GB 71) Stanley Kubrick. *Soylent Green* (73) Richard Fleischer. *Rollerball* (75) Norman Jewison. *Futureworld* (76) Richard T. Heffron. *Logan's Run* (US / GB 76) Michael Anderson. *Brave New World* (78 TV) Burt Brinckerkoff. *Blade Runner* (82) Ridley Scott *aka The Android / Dangerous Days / Gotham City. Nineteen Eighty-Four* (GB 84) Michael Redford. *The Running Man* (87) Paul Michael Glaser. *Crime Zone* (US / Peru 88) Luis Llosa. *The Handmaid's Tale* (89) Volker Schlondorff. *Crash and Burn* (90) Charles Band.

——**Future Barbarian Movies**   Although John Carpenter's *Escape from New York* (1981) was clearly influential in the shaping of future barbarian films, George Miller's *Mad Max II* (1981) is the film which provided the blueprint for the influx, mostly from Italy, of the imitations and clones that followed. These films are set in a post-holocaust, futuristic landscape of wastelands and city ruins. As a rule, they have a leather-clad hero fighting single-handedly, Mad Max–style, against an assortment of motorized warring predators who wield all sorts of left-over weaponry and who drive reconditioned, armor-plated vehicles. The subgenre has also branched off into the future gladiatorial field in which the contestants fight each other for a prize. *See* section on **SF Disaster Films** and **ROAD MOVIE** entry.

Battletruck (US / NZ 81) Harley Cockliss *aka Warlords of the 21st Century. Escape from New York* (81) John Carpenter. *Mad Max II / The Road Warrior* (Aust / US 81) George Miller *aka Mad Max 2. Barbari 2000* (It / Sp 83) Jules Harrison *aka Sterminatore del anno 3000 / The Executor / The Exterminators of the Year 3000. Bronx lotta finale* (It 83) Steven Benson *aka Endgano / Endgame. Defcon-4* (Can 83) Paul Donovan *aka Dark Eyes / Ground Zero* [rel. in 85]. *I nuovi barbari* (It 83) Enzo G. Castellari *aka*

2019: I nuovi barbari / The New Barbarians / Warriors of the Wasteland.
Stryker (US / Phil 83) Cirio H. Santiago. ***L'ultimo guerriero*** (It 83) Romolo
Guerrieri *aka Gli Esecutori / The Final Executioner / Final Executor.* ***Rush***
(It 84) Anthony Richmond (Tonino Ricci) *aka Blood Rush / Rush the
Assassin.*

———**Invasion Films**   Aliens from beyond Earth fall into two groupings: invaders seeking to destroy and conquer or are scouts for a planned future invasion and visitors simply wanting to warn earthlings of some imminent danger, to communicate with them or to repair their ship and be on their way. These films were very popular through the 50s and 60s.

Invaders: ***The War of the Worlds*** (52) Byron Haskin *aka H. G. Wells' The
War of the Worlds.* ***Invaders from Mars*** (53) William Cameron Menzies.
Target Earth (54) Sherman Rose. ***Invasion of the Body Snatchers*** (55) Don
Siegel *aka The Body Stealers / I Am a Pod / Sleep No More / Thin Air.* ***Earth
vs. the Flying Saucers*** (56) Fred F. Sears *aka Invasion of the Flying
Saucers.* ***Kronos*** (57) Kurt Neumann *aka Kronos, Destroyer of the
Universe.* ***Quatermass II*** (GB 57) Val Guest *aka Enemy from Space* [second
in a trilogy which includes *The Quatermass Xperiment* (GB 55) also by Guest
and *Quatermass and the Pit* (GB 67) by Roy Ward Baker]. ***I Married a
Monster from Outer Space*** (58) Gene Fowler, Jr. *aka IMAMFOS.* ***Unearthly
Stranger*** (GB 63) John Krish. ***The Human Duplicators / Spaziale K1*** (US
/ It 64) Hugo Grimaldi. ***Invasion of the Bee Girls*** (73) Denis Sanders *aka
Graveyard Tramps.* ***Invasion of the Body Snatchers*** (78) Philip Kaufman.
Strange Invaders (83) Michael Laughlin. ***The Hidden*** (87) Jack Sholder.
Killer Klowns from Outer Space (87) Stephen Chiodo. ***Predator*** (87) John
McTiernan. ***High Desert Kill*** (89 MCTV) Harry Falk.

Visitors: ***The Day the Earth Stood Still*** (51) Robert Wise *aka Farewell to
the Master / Journey to the World.* ***It Came from Outer Space*** (53) Jack
Arnold *aka Atomic Monster / The Meteor / The Strangers from Outer
Space.* ***This Island Earth*** (54) Joseph M. Newman *aka War of the
Planets.* ***The 27th Day*** (57) William Asher. ***Not of this Earth*** (56) Roger
Corman. ***Invasion*** (GB 65) Alan Bridges. ***The Man Who Fell to Earth***
(GB / US 76) Nicolas Roeg. ***Close Encounters of the Third Kind*** (77) Steven
Spielberg *aka Experiences / The Special Edition: Close Encounters of the
Third Kind* (80; reedited version) */ Watch the Skies.* ***E.T. The Extra-
Terrestrial*** (82) Steven Spielberg *aka After School / Boy's Life / Close En-
counters II / E.T. and Me / E.T. The Extra-Terrestrial and His Adventure
on Earth / Growing Up / Night Skies.* ***Wavelength*** (82) Mike Gray. ***The
Brother from Another Planet*** (84) John Sayles. ***Starman*** (84) John Carpen-
ter. ***Morons from Outer Space*** (GB 85) Mike Hodges. ***Hyper Sapien: People from Another Star*** (US / Can 86) Peter Hunt. ***Alien Nation*** (88)
Graham Baker. ***My Step Mother Is an Alien*** (88) Richard Benjamin.

———**Period SF Films**   Works by some 19th-century writers who wrote speculative fiction have, at times, been adapted to the screen in period settings. This is very often the case with the works of Jules Verne (1828–1905) and H. G. Wells (1866–1946). The films have a marked Victorian flavor.

From the Earth to the Moon (58) Byron Haskin. ***Mysterious Island*** (GB /
US 60) Cy Endfield. ***Master of the World*** (61) William Witney. ***First Men***

in the Moon (GB / US 64) Nathan Juran. *The City Under the Sea / The War-Gods of the Deep* (GB / US 65) Jacques Tourneur *aka City in the Sea / Warlords of the Deep*. *Captain Nemo and the Underwater City* (GB 69) James Hill *aka Captain Nemo and the Floating City*. *Na komete* (Cz 70) Karel Zeman *aka Hector Servadac's Ark / On the Comet*.

————**Political Extrapolation Films** Science fiction set in the near future often has political implications. These films hypothesize about political assassinations, political takeovers, military coups, dictatorships, etc.

High Treason (GB 29) Maurice Elvey. *Rat* (Yug 60) Veljko Buljic *aka War*. *The Damned* (GB 61) Joseph Losey *aka On the Brink / These Are the Damned*. *The Manchurian Candidate* (62) John Frankenheimer. *Dr. Strangelove; or, How I Learned to Stop Worrying and Love the Bomb* (GB / US 63) Stanley Kubrick. *Seven Days in May* (64) John Frankenheimer. *The China Syndrome* (78) James Bridges.

————**Prehistoric Fantasies (Prehistoric Creature Drama)** Usually classed as SF rather than fantasy, these films, mostly based on pseudo-scientific premises, recreate or imagine prehistoric environments populated with early forms of man and all sorts of prehistoric reptiles, extinct long before the appearance of man on earth. A closely allied category, the lost-world film, has as its main theme the discovery by some travelers or explorers of lost pockets of ancient civilization or untrodden, primordial spots of vegetation where prehistoric conditions have continued to exist.

Lost-World Films: The Lost World (25) Harry Hoyt. *King Kong* (33) Merian C. Cooper, Ernest B. Schoedsack *aka The Beast / The Eighth Wonder / The Eighth Wonder of the World / King Ape / King Kong (The Eighth Wonder of the World) / Kong*. *Unknown Island* (48) Jack Bernhard. *The Lost Continent* (51) Samuel Newfield. *Journey to the Center of the Earth* (59) Henry Levin *aka Jules Verne's Journey to the Center of the Earth*. *The Land That Time Forgot* (GB 74) Kevin Connor. *At the Earth's Core* (GB 76) Kevin Connor. *Viaje al centro de la tierra* (Sp 76) Juan Piquer *aka Trip to the Center of the Earth / Where Time Began*. *The People That Time Forgot* (US / GB 77) Kevin Connor.

Prehistoric Films: One Million B.C. (40) Hal Roach, Sr., Hal Roach, Jr. (plus D. W. Griffith) *aka The Cave Dwellers / Cave Man / Man and His Mate*. *Prehistoric Women* (50) Greg Tallas. *One Million Years B.C.* (GB / US 65) Don Chaffey. *Slave Girls* (GB 66) Michael Carreras *aka Prehistoric Women*. *When Dinosaurs Ruled the Earth* (GB 69) Val Guest. *Caveman* (81) Carl Gottlieb. *Quest for Fire / La Guerre du feu* (Can / F 80-81) Jean-Jacques Annaud. *Baby ... Secret of the Lost Legend* (85) B. W. L. Norton *aka Baby / Dinosaur ... Secret of the Lost Legend*.

————**SF Comedies** As with other genres, science fiction is a fertile ground for satire and comedy.

Time Flies (GB 44) Walter Forde. *The Perfect Woman* (GB 49) Bernard Knowles. *Un Amour de poche* (F 57) Pierre Kast *aka Girl in His Pocket / Nude in His Pocket*. *Dinosauros* (60) Irvin S. Yeaworth, Jr. *Un Martien à Paris* (F 60) Jean-Daniel Daninos *aka A Martian in Paris*. *The Road to Hong Kong* (US / GB 61) Norman Panama *aka Road to the Moon*. *The*

Three Stooges in Orbit (62) Edward Bernds *aka The Three Stooges Meet the Martians*. *The Bed Sitting Room* (GB 69) Richard Lester. *Quando le donne avevano la coda* (It 70) Pasquale Festa Campanile *aka When Women Had Tails*. *Sleeper* (73) Woody Allen. *The Man with Two Brains* (83) Carl Reiner. *Short Circuit* (86) John Badham. *Hell Comes to Frogtown* (87) R. J. Kizer, Donald G. Jackson. *Dr. Alien* (88) Dave DeCoteau. *Short Circuit 2* (US / Can 88) Kenneth Johnson.

——**SF Disaster Films**   The two main species of SF disaster movies are the end-of-the-world films involving some catastrophic upheaval due to natural, man-made, or extraterrestrial causes and films dealing with post-holocaust situations in which remnants of Earth's population strive to make a go of it. *See also* **NUCLEAR FILM.**

End-of-the-World Films (Doomsday Films): La Fin du monde (F 30) Abel Gance *aka Das Ende der Welt* (G.v.) / *The End of the World*. *Deluge* (33) Felix E. Feist. *When Worlds Collide* (51) Rudolph Maté. *On the Beach* (59) Stanley Kramer. *The Time Machine* (60) George Pal *aka H. G. Wells' The Time Machine*. *The Day the Earth Caught Fire* (GB 61) Val Guest. *Dr. Strangelove; or, How I Learned to Stop Worrying and Love the Bomb* (GB / US 63) Stanley Kubrick. *Crack in the World* (64) Andrew Marton. *Beneath the Planet of the Apes* (69) Ted Post *aka Planet of the Apes Revisited / Planet of the Men*. *The Final Programme* (GB 73) Robert Fuest *aka The Last Days of Man on Earth*. *Where Have All the People Gone?* (74 TV) John Llewellyn Moxey. *End of the World* (GB / US 76) John Hayes. *World War III* (82 TV) David Greene [in 2 parts]. *Testament* (83) Lynne Littman. *Night of the Comet* (84) Thom Eberhardt. *The Quiet Earth* (NZ 84) Geoffrey Murphy.

Post-Holocaust Films (Postnuclear Films): Five (51) Arch Oboler. *Captive Women* (52) Stuart Gilmore *aka 3000 A.D. / 1000 Years from Now*. *The World, the Flesh and the Devil* (58) Ranald MacDougall *aka End of the World*. *Panic in the Year Zero!* (62) Ray Milland *aka The End of the World / Survive*. *Konec srpna v hotelu Ozón* (Cz 65) Jan Schmidt *aka The End of August in Hotel Ozone / Late August at the Hotel Ozone*. *Le Dernier homme* (F 67-69) Charles I. Bitsch *aka The Last Man*. *Gas-s-s-s ... or It May Become Necessary to Destroy the World in Order to Save It!* (69) Roger Corman *aka Arrowfeather / Gas! or It Became Necessary to Destroy the World in Order to Save It*. *Glen and Randa* (70) Jim McBride. *No Blade of Grass* (GB 70) Cornel Wilde. *The Omega Man* (71) Boris Sagal *aka I Am a Legend*. *Zardoz* (GB 73) John Boorman. *A Boy and His Dog* (74) L. Q. Jones. *The Ultimate Warrior* (75) Robert Clouse *aka The Barony*. *Damnation Alley* (77) Jack Smight *aka Survival Run*. *Le Dernier Combat* (F 82) Luc Besson *aka The Final Combat / The Last Battle*. *Forbrydelsens Element* (Den 84) Lars von Trier *aka The Element of Crime*. *Survivor* (86) Michael Shackleton. *Steel Dawn* (87) Lance Hool. *World Gone Wild* (87) Lee H. Katzin. *The Blood of Heroes / The Salute of the Jugger* (US / Aust 88) David Peoples.

——**SF Horror Films**   Two main subdivisions of the SF horror film come readily to mind: the mad doctor/mad scientist film and the SF monster film. In the first subdivision, the doctor's or scientist's experiments are ill-advised or go awry, the consequences being a series of deaths and general panic with the subsequent destruction of the doctor's creation. In the second sub-division, many different permutations are possible. The monsters are either alien "things" from outer space, creations of the mad doctors mentioned above, or they come from our own environment, having been reactivated by some cause (most frequently atomic radiation) and go on a rampage causing havoc until controlled by man's superior ingenuity.

Mad Doctor Category: ***Orlacs Hände*** (Aus 24) Robert Wiene *aka Die unheimlichen Hände des Dr. Orlak / The Hands of Orlac / The Sinister Hands of Dr. Orlak.* ***Frankenstein*** (31) James Whale. ***The Island of Lost Souls*** (33) Erle C. Kenton *aka The Island of Dr. Moreau.* ***Dr. Cyclops*** (39) Ernest B. Shoedsak. ***The Mad Monster*** (42) Sam Newfield. ***The Magnetic Monster*** (53) Curt Siodmak. ***The Fly*** (58) Kurt Neumann [followed by *The Return of the Fly* (59) Edward L. Bernds and *(The) Curse of the Fly* (GB 65) Don Sharp]. ***The Killer Shrews*** (59) Ray Kellogg. ***X — the Man with the X-Ray Eyes*** (63) Roger Corman *aka The Man with the X-Ray Eyes / X.* ***The Astro-Zombies*** (67) Ted V. Mikels *aka Space Vampires / Space Zombies.* ***The Terminal Man*** (73) Michael Hodges. ***The Island of Dr. Moreau*** (77) Don Taylor. ***Creator*** (85) Ivan Passer. ***Deadly Friend*** (86) Wes Craven. ***The Immortalizer*** (89) Joel Bender.

Monster Category: ***The Thing*** (51) Christian Nyby (uncredited: Howard Hawks) *aka The Thing (from Another World) / Whither Mankind.* ***The Beast from 20,000 Fathoms*** (53) Eugene Lourié. ***Them!*** (53) Gordon Douglas. ***Gojira*** (J 54) Inoshiro Honda (U.S. v. Terry Morse) *aka Godzilla / Godzilla, King of the Monsters.* ***The Quatermass Xperiment*** (GB 54) Val Guest *aka The Creeping Unknown / The Quatermass Experiment / Shock!* ***It Came from Beneath the Sea*** (55) Robert Gordon. ***Tarantula*** (55) Jack Arnold. ***20 Million Miles to Earth*** (57) Nathan Juran *aka The Giant Ymir.* ***The Blob*** (58) Irvin S. Yeaworth, Jr. *aka The Molden Meteor.* ***Alien*** (GB / US 79) Ridley Scott *aka Starbeast.* ***Inseminoid*** (GB 80) Norman J. Warren *aka Horror Planet.* ***Galaxy of Terror*** (81) B. D. Clark *aka Mindwarp: An Infinity of Terror / Planet of Horrors / Quest.* ***Mutant*** (82) Allan Holzman *aka Forbidden World.* ***The Thing*** (82) John Carpenter. ***The Blob*** (88) Chuck Russell. ***The Dark Side of the Moon*** (89) D. J. Webster. ***Shadowzone*** (89) J. S. Cardone.

——**SF Sex Films** Sex films, either soft-core or hard-core, have occasionally used a science fiction background for flesh exposure and lovemaking. ***Zeta One*** (GB 69) Michael Cort. ***Flesh Gordon*** (72) Michael Benveniste, Howard Ziehm. ***Stoßtrupp Venus — Fünf Mädchen blasen zum Angriff / Ach jodel mir noch einen (Stoßtrupp Venus bläst zum Angriff)*** (Aus / G 74) Hans G. Keil *aka 2069: A Sex Odyssey / 2069: A Space Odyssey / Sex Change.* ***The Sexplorer*** (GB 75) Derek Ford *aka Diary of a Space Virgin.* ***Sex World*** (78) Anthony Spinelli. ***Incontro mopto ravvicinato del quarto*** (It 79) Roy Garrett (Mario Garriazzo) *aka Incontri molto ravvicinati / Incontri molto ravvicinati di un certo tipo / Very Close Encounters of the Fourth Kind.* ***Ultra Flesh*** (80) Svetlana. ***Café Flesh*** (82) Rinse Dream.

——**Social Extrapolation Film** The social extrapolation film deals with the social consequences of political conditions or new inventions and the relationship between man and scientific and technological advances.

The Man in the White Suit (GB 51) Alexander Mackendrick. *It Happened Here* (GB 56-63) Keven Brownlow, Andrew Mollo. *Seconds* (66) John Frankenheimer. *Charly* (68) Ralph Nelson. *I Cannibali* (It 69) Liliana Cavani *aka The Cannibals / The Cannibals Among Us / The Year of the Cannibals*. *Colossus, the Forbin Project* (69) Joseph Sargent *aka Colossus 1980 / The Day the World Changed Hands / The Forbin Project*. *Dreamscape* (84) Joseph Ruben.

———**Space Operas**   The term is applied to space adventure stories with spaceships on some rescue mission or with intergalactic starships battling enemy forces, bug-eyed monsters and the like. It is the old conflict between good and evil played out once again. A famous recent example is *Star Wars* (1977).

Flash Gordon (36, serial) Frederick Stephani *aka Flash Gordon Space Soldiers*. *Buck Rogers* (39, serial) Ford Beebe, Saul A. Goodkind. *Barbarella* (It / F 67) Roger Vadim *aka Barbarella, Queen of the Galaxy*. *Star Wars* (77) George Lucas *aka Adventures of the Starkiller / The Star Wars / Star Wars Episode IV: A New Hope* [followed by *Star Wars Episode V: The Empire Strikes Back* (GB / US 79) Irwin Kershner and *Star Wars Episode VI: Return of the Jedi* (GB / US 83) Richard Marquand]. *Battlestar Galactica* (78) Richard A. Colla *aka Star Worlds*. *Buck Rogers in the 25th Century* (79 TV) Daniel Haller. *Battle Beyond the Stars* (80) Jimmy T. Murakami. *Flash Gordon* (GB 80) Michael Hodges. *Star Trek* (79) Robert Wise *aka Star Trek: The Motion Picture* [6 films in the series up to 1991]. *Star Trek II: The Wrath of Khan* (82) Nicholas Meyer. *Space Raiders* (83) Howard R. Cohen *aka Lost in Space / Star Child*. *The Last Starfighter* (84) Nick Castle.

———**Space Travel Films (Space Exploration Films, Space Films, Space Flight Films)**   Man's desire to lift off from planet Earth into outer space is realized in these films. Sometimes the flight ends in disaster, but this does not prevent man from reaching for the planets and occasionally the stars. Space operas fit into a different class of space flight films.

Die Frau im Mond (G 28) Fritz Lang *aka By Rocket to the Moon / The Girl in the Moon / Woman in the Moon*. *Things to Come* (GB 36) William Cameron Menzies *aka The Shape of Things to Come / Whither Mankind*. *Destination Moon* (50) Irving Pichel. *When Worlds Collide* (51) Rudolph Maté. *Riders to the Stars* (53) Richard Carlson. *Conquest of Space* (55) Byron Haskin. *Forbidden Planet* (56) Fred M. Wilcox. *Planeta Burg* (USSR 62) Pavel Klushantsev *aka Cosmonauts on Venus / Planet of Storms / Storm Planet*. *Mutiny in Outer Space / Ammutinamento nello spazio* (US / It 64) Hugo Grimaldi *aka Invasion from Mars / Space Station-X / Space Station X-14*. *Robinson Crusoe on Mars* (64) Byron Haskin. *Spaceflight IC-1* (GB 65) Bernard Knowles. *Countdown* (67) Robert Altman *aka Moonshot*. *Tumannosti Andromedi* (USSR 67) Eudgen Sherstobitov *aka [The] Andromeda Nebula*. *2001: A Space Odyssey* (US / GB 68) Stanley Kubrick *aka Journey Beyond the Stars / Space Odyssey*. *Doppelgänger* (GB 69) Robert Parrish *aka Journey to the Far Side of the Sun*. *Marooned* (69) John Sturges. *Moon Zero Two* (GB 69) Roy Ward Baker. *Silent Running* (71) Douglas Trumball *aka Running Silent*. *The Black Hole* (79) Gary Nelson *aka The Space Probe / Space Probe One / Space Station One*.

——**Time Travel Films**   One of the pet subjects of science fiction is to be able to displace oneself in time in order to observe the past or the future. The means by which the time travelers achieve this are various. They may fall asleep and awake in a different time and place; they may travel by way of their consciousness; they may awake in the future after having been frozen by a cryonic process; or, they may use a time machine.

World Without End (55) Edward Bernds.   *The Time Machine* (60) George Pal *aka H. G. Wells' The Time Machine.   The Time Travellers* (64) Ib Melchior *aka Time Trap.   Je t'aime, je t'aime* (F 67) Alain Resnais.   *Sleeper* (73) Woody Allen.   *Hu-man* (F 75) Jérôme Laperrousaz *aka Pleurs.   Time After Time* (79) Nicholas Meyer.   *The Final Countdown* (80) Don Taylor. *The Philadelphia Experiment* (84) Stewart Raffill.   *Terminator* (84) James Cameron.   *Trancers* (84) Charles Band *aka Future Cop.   Back to the Future* (85) Robert Zemeckis [a trilogy with *Back to the Future Part II* (89) and *Back to the Future Part III* (90) also by Zemeckis].   *Star Trek IV: The Voyage Home* (86) Leonard Nimoy.   *The Time Guardian* (Aust 86) Brian Hannant.   *Time Trackers* (88) Howard R. Cohen.

Science Fiction Horror Film *see* **SCIENCE FICTION FILM: SF Horror Films;** *see also* **HORROR FILM**

Scientific Film, Scientific-Research Film *see* **FACTUAL FILM: Research Film**

Sci-Fier, Sci-Fi Film *see* **SCIENCE FICTION FILM**

Sci-Fi Road Movies *see* **ROAD MOVIE**

Scratch Film *see* **ABSTRACT FILM**

Screen Biography *see* **BIOGRAPHICAL FILM**

Screen Classic *see* **CLASSIC**

Screen Comedy *see* **COMEDY**

Screen Drama, Screenplay *see* **FICTIONAL FILM**

SCREWBALL COMEDY (Crazy Comedy, Madcap Comedy, Oddball Comedy, Romantic Comedy, Wacky Comedy)   Howard Hawks's *Twentieth Century* and Frank Capra's *It Happened One Night*, both released in 1934, vie for recognition as the originators of screwball comedy. Both films are equally important in setting out the genre's main characteristics. This type of comedy which emerged in the thirties has been called by various names—oddball comedy, wacky comedy, crazy comedy—but the term screwball comedy is the one which has been most widely accepted.

The genre contains many elements already present in sophisticated comedy (q.v.) which antedates it. Screwball comedy differentiates itself from sophisticated comedy by broadening its scope to include among its protagonists not only the well-to-do, but members of the middle and working class. Screwball comedy is characterized by eccentric characters sparked by a fancy to do odd or whimsical things with total nonchalance. These characters are always charming because of their spontaneity and unconcern. Screwball comedies usually involve a couple in a battle-of-the-sexes tug-of-war that has to overcome an initial antagonism arising from their equally spirited dispositions, in order to finally fall in love. The revival of screwball comedy in modern productions is not quite the same, as this is essentially a genre of the thirties. Rather than capturing the flavor of the original screwball comedies, they are homages or nostalgic looks at the genre. At times, the term high comedy has been used to group together the sophisticated, screwball and populist comedy. For a study of screwball comedy *see* Duane Byrge and Robert Milton Miller, *The Screwball Comedy Films: A History and Filmography, 1934–1942* (Jefferson, NC: McFarland, 1991).

It Happened One Night (34) Frank Capra. *Twentieth Century* (34) Howard Hawks. *My Man Godfrey* (36) Gregory La Cava. *Theodore Goes Wild* (36) Richard Boleslawski. *The Awful Truth* (37) Leo McCarey. *Double Wedding* (37) Richard Thorpe. *It's Love I'm After* (37) Archie Mayo. *Stand-In* (37) Tay Garnett. *Boy Meets Girl* (38) Lloyd Bacon. *Bringing Up Baby* (38) Howard Hawks. *Holiday* (38) George Cukor *aka Free to Live / Unconventional Linda*. *The Bride Came C.O.D.* (41) William Keighley. *Mr. and Mrs. Smith* (41) Alfred Hitchcock. *Palm Beach Story* (42) Preston Sturges. *San Diego I Love You* (44) Reginald LeBorg. *A Millionaire for Christy* (51) George Marshall. *Man's Favorite Sport* (63) Howard Hawks. *For Pete's Sake* (74) Peter Yates. *Seems Like Old Times* (80) Jay Sandrich. *Arthur* (81) Steve Gordon. *Desperately Seeking Susan* (85) Susan Seidelman.

Sculptmation   *see*   **ANIMATION FILM: Object Animation Films**

SEA FILM (Nautical Film, Sea Drama)   Whether the setting is period or contemporary, sea film is a label used for films whose action, for the most part, takes place on the sea rather than on land. Their range is varied, but they are mostly adventure films. *See also* **DISASTER FILM, SWASH-BUCKLER: Pirate Films**, and **WAR FILM: Sea War Films**.

The Navigator (24) Donald Crisp, Buster Keaton. *The Windjammer* (GB 30) John Orton. *Tugboat Annie* (33) Mervyn LeRoy. *China Seas* (35) Tay Garnett. *Mutiny on the Bounty* (35) Frank Lloyd. *Captains Courageous* (37) Victor Fleming. *Windjammer* (37) Ewing Scott. *Saps at Sea* (39) Gordon Douglas. *The Long Voyage Home* (40) John Ford. *The Sea Wolf* (41) Michael Curtiz. *The Ghost Ship* (43) Mark Robson. *Lifeboat* (44) Alfred Hitchcock. *Western Approaches* (GB 44) Pat Jackson. *Captain Horatio Hornblower RN / Captain Horatio Hornblower* (GB / US 51) Raoul Walsh. *The Cruel Sea* (GB 53) Charles Frend. *Passage Home* (GB 55) Roy Baker. *A Night to Remember* (GB 58) Roy Baker. *The Old Man and the Sea* (58) John Sturges. *The Last Voyage* (60) Andrew L. Stone. *Damn the Defiant!* (GB 62) Lewis Gilbert. *Taiheiyo hitoribotchi* (J 63) Kon Ishikawa *aka Alone on the Pacific / My Enemy, the Sea / The Enemy, the Sea*. *Ship of Fools* (65) Stanley Kramer. *The Dove* (74) Charles Jarrott. *Golden Rendezvous* (77) Ashley Lazarus *aka Nuclear Terror*. *Les Trois Couronnes du matelot* (F 83) Raoul Ruiz *aka Three Crowns for the Sailor*.

——**Underwater Movies (Undersea Films)**   Obviously, in these movies the action takes place under the water. Jacques-Yves Cousteau's sea documentaries (e.g., *Le Monde du silence* [1955]; *Le Monde sans soleil* [1964]) fall under this category, as well as films involving divers and submarines. *See also* **WAR FILM: Submarine War Films.**

Hell Below (33) Jack Conway.   *Submarine D-1* (37) Lloyd Bacon.   *Destination Tokyo* (43) Delmer Daves.   *Morning Departure* (GB 49) Roy Baker *aka Operation Disaster*.   *The Frogmen* (51) Lloyd Bacon.   *20,000 Leagues Under the Sea* (54) Richard Fleischer.   *Le Monde du silence* (F 55) Jacques-Yves Cousteau, Louis Malle *aka The Silent World*.   *Operation Petticoat* (59) Blake Edwards.   *Voyage to the Bottom of the Sea* (61) Irwin Allen.   *Le Monde sans soleil / Il mondo senza sole* (F / It 64) Jacques-Yves Cousteau *aka Jacques-Yves Cousteau's World Without Sun / World Without Sun*.   *Around the World Under the Sea* (66) Andrew Marton.   *Ice Station Zebra* (68) John Sturges.   *Blue Water, White Death* (71) Peter Gimbel, James Lipscomb.   *Fer-de-Lance* (74 TV) Russ Mayberry *aka Death Dive*.   *The Deep* (US / GB 77) Peter Yates.   *The Abyss* (89) James Cameron.   *The Hunt for Red October* (90) John McTiernan.

Sea War Films   *see*   **WAR FILM**

Second Cinema   *see*   **THIRD WORLD CINEMA**

Second Feature   *see*   **B-MOVIE**

Secret-Agent Film, Secret Service Drama   *see*   **SPY FILM**

Self-Consciously Made Film, Self-Referential Film, Self-Reflective Film, Self-Reflexive Film   *see*   **REFLEXIVE FILM**

Semidocumentary   *see*   **DOCUMENTARY: Documentary-Style Film**

SEMINAL FILM (Breakthrough Film, Trend-Setting Film)   Seminal films are those rare motion pictures which are original and truly innovative, and which, as a rule, are followed by a host of imitations. Sometimes their influence is not immediately felt (e.g., *Les Diaboliques* [1954]), but they are often the starters or originators of movie genres or far-reaching cycles (e.g., *Dr. No* [1962]). Films which start new trends or which represent leading innovations in cinematic art and technical know-how have also been referred to as breakthrough films, cornerstone films, landmark films, milestone films, trailblazers, pathfinders and trendsetters. *See* **ARCHETYPE, SLEEPER.**

Frankenstein (31) James Whale.   *Les Diaboliques* (F 54) Henri-Georges Clouzot *aka Diabolique / The Fiends*.   *Psycho* (60) Alfred Hitchcock.   *Dr. No* (GB 62) Terence Young [18 "Bond" films up to 1989].   *Bonnie and Clyde* (67) Arthur Penn.   *2001: A Space Odyssey* (US / GB 68) Stanley Kubrick *aka Journey Beyond the Stars / Space Odyssey*.   *Easy Rider* (69) Dennis Hopper.   *Z* (F / Alg 68) Costa-Gavras [subtitled: *L'Anatomie d'un assassinat politique*].   *Le Chagrin et la pitié / Das Haus nebenan* (F / Swiz / G 69 TV) Marcel Ophüls *aka The Sorrow and the Pity*.   *Deep Throat* (72) Jerry Gerard (Gerard Damiano) *aka The Doctor Makes a Call*.   *The Exorcist* (73)

William Friedkin. *Star Wars* (77) George Lucas *aka Adventures of the Starkiller / The Star Wars / Star Wars Episode IV: A New Hope*. *Halloween* (78) John Carpenter *aka The Babysitter Murders* [5 films in the series up to 1989]. *National Lampoon's Animal House* (78) John Landis *aka Animal House* [6 films in the Lampoon series up to 1989]. *Alien* (GB / US 79) Ridley Scott *aka Starbeast*. *The Warriors* (79) Walter Hill.

Send-Up *see* **PARODY**

SENTIMENTAL COMEDY   When the emotions are stirred by mixing humor and pathos, the result is sentimental comedy of the kind that brings a lump to one's throat and wets the eyes. In other words, it involves laughter and tears. Some comedies with a religious mood fit the type.

Lady for a Day (33) Frank Capra. *Christmas in July* (40) Preston Sturges. *The Great McGinty* (40) Preston Sturges *aka Down Went McGinty*. *Going My Way* (44) Leo McCarey. *The Bells of St. Mary's* (45) Leo McCarey. *Pocketful of Miracles* (61) Frank Capra.

SEQUEL (Follow-Up, Spin-Off)   A sequel or follow-up is a film that is made in the wake of a successful initial picture. Sometimes, in anticipation of a hit, sequels are planned in advance. A sequel, often enough, proves to be less good than the original film, but there are many exceptions to this rule, e.g., *The Godfather, Part II* (1974). A sequel may continue the story of the previous picture or use the same characters in a different situation altogether. Prequels are sequels that trace the story further back than the events in the original films, e.g., *Butch and Sundance—The Early Days* (1979).

A spin-off is a word used to denote a film which is similar to or imitative of a successful hit, e.g., the Italian film *L'ultimo squalo / Great White* (1981), called in Great Britain *Shark*, follows very closely *Jaws* (1975). Finally, a rip-off is a term that has been applied to a sequel made exclusively for exploitation purposes and which does not add anything new to the original film. For a referential book on sequels and series, *see* Bernard A. Drew, *Motion Picture Series and Sequels: A Reference Guide* (New York: Garland, 1990). It includes 936 entries of movies which had sequels or were followed by a series.

The Godfather, Part II (74) Francis Ford Coppola. *L'ultimo squalo* (It 81) Enzo G. Castellari *aka Great White / Jaws 3 / The Last Jaws / Shark*. *Butch and Sundance—The Early Days* (79) Richard Lester.

SERIAL (Chapterplay, Cliffhanger, Episode Film)   Serials are action-adventure pictures or melodramas made strictly for their entertainment value with scarce dialogue and plenty of action. They were ideally suited for children and the Saturday matinée at the local movie house. They were meant to be shown in weekly installments or chapters. These chapters, parts or episodes were either self-contained units with the plot resumed in the next chapter, e.g., *The Perils of Pauline* (1914), or the chapter ended on a note of suspense. In such a case, the hero or heroine was placed in a situation of extreme danger that would not be resolved until the following week when the continuing chapter was shown; hence, the term cliffhanger (in the silent serials, heroines literally hung from cliffs) was applied to this latter type of serial.

The serial evolved from the film series which predated it by only a few years. The difference between a film series and a film serial is that in the former each film of the series is complete in itself without any narrative continuation, only the character or characters reappear in the next film of the series. On the other hand, in the serial there is continuity of story or narrative as well as of characters from episode to episode until its final resolution at the end of the serial. Most serials settled for two-reel chapters of under 20 minutes each, the first introductory chapter running a bit longer than the rest. The number of chapters was usually from 10 to 20, although the longest-running serial, *The Hazards of Helen,* released theatrically between 1914 and 1917, had 119 episodes of one reel each; its total runningtime was over 31 hours.

The first serial was a melodrama titled *What Happened to Mary* (1912), and even if it lacked the cliff-hanger element, its 12 episodes had story line continuity. *The Adventures of Kathlyn* (1913) was the first to include the suspense ingredient at the end of each chapter. *King of the Kongo* (1929) and *Ace of Scotland Yard* (1929) have both been cited as the first sound serials—they were made in silent and part-talkie versions.

A few countries have made serials, but the format was most popular in the United States, France and Spain. America has had by far the biggest output of serials. The number of silent serials made in the United States has been estimated at about 350, but only a handful are extant. Altogether, 231 talkies were made between 1929 and 1956 when they became obsolete, except for television which continued to make them. Today's television soap operas are modernized versions of the form. There is a kind of nostalgia attached to the serial, which has prompted several writers to illustrate its history and development—a substantial body of works on the serial exists. Some of the better serials were reedited into feature film versions, and some of these keep reappearing on television. The biggest number of serials were Westerns, but mysteries, science fiction fantasies, jungle adventures, aviation stories and other action genres were equally popular. The serial adapted many comic strip, radio and pulp magazine heroes, attracting in this way an already addicted audience. Ken Weiss and Ed Goodgold, *To Be Continued...* (New York: Bonanza Books, 1972) illustrate and give a synopsis of most of the 231 talkies made in America. *See also* Jim Harmon and Donald F. Glut, *The Great Movie Serials* (Garden City, NY: Doubleday, 1972).[95]

What Happened to Mary (12) [first serial, 12 chapters]. *The Adventures of Kathlyn* (13) F. J. Grandon [13 chapters]. *The Perils of Pauline* (14) Louis J. Gasnier, Donald Mackenzie [20 chapters]. *The Exploits of Elaine* (14-15) L. J. Gasnier, George B. Seitz [14 chapters]. *Les Vampires* (F 15) Louis Feuillade [10 chapters] *aka The Arch Criminals of Paris / The Vampires.*

The Hazards of Helen (14-17) J. P. McGowan, James Davis [119 Chapters]. *Judex* (F 16-17) Louis Feuillade [12 chapters]. *Ace of Scotland Yard* (29) Ray Taylor [10 chapters]. *King of the Kongo* (29) Richard Thorpe [10 chapters]. *The Three Musketeers* (33) Armand Schaefer, Colbert Clark [12 chapters] *aka* (feature version) *Desert Command*. *The Phantom Empire* (35) Otto Brower, Reeves Eason [12 chapters] *aka Gene Autry and the Phantom Empire*; (feature version) *Men with Still Faces / Radio Ranch*. *Flash Gordon* (36) Frederick Stephani [13 chapters] *aka Flash Gordon Space Soldiers;* (feature versions) *Atomic Rocketship / Rocketship / Spaceship to the Unknown / Space Soldiers*. *Undersea Kingdom* (36) B. Reeves Eason, Joseph Kane [12 chapters] *aka* (feature version) *Sharad of Atlantis*. *The Lone Ranger* (38) William Witney, John English [15 chapters] *aka* (feature version) *Hi-Yo Silver*. *Buck Rogers* (39) Ford Beebe, Saul Goodkind [12 chapters] *aka* (feature versions) *Destination Saturn / Planet Outlaws*. *Zorro's Fighting Legion* (39) William Witney, John English [12 chapters]. *Adventures of Captain Marvel* (41) William Witney, John English [12 chapters] *aka Return of Captain Marvel*. *Nyoka and the Tigermen* (42) William Witney [15 chapters] *aka* (feature version) *Nyoka and the Lost Secrets of Hippocrates*. *The Crimson Ghost* (46) William Witney, Fred C. Brannon [12 chapters] *aka* (feature version) *Cyclotrode "X"*. *Jesse James Rides Again* (47) Fred C. Brannon, Thomas Carr [13 chapters]. *Dangers of the Canadian Mounted* (48) Fred Brannon, Yakima Canutt [12 chapters] *aka* (feature versions) *R.C.M.P. / The Treasure of Genghis Khan*. *Superman* (48) Spencer Bennet, Thomas Carr [15 chapters]. *King of the Rocket Men* (49) Fred Brannon [12 chapters] *aka* (feature version) *Lost Planet Airmen*. *The Mysterious Dr. Satan* (49) William Witney, John English [15 chapters] *aka* (feature version) *Doctor Satan's Robot*. *The Invisible Monster* (51) Fred C. Brannon [12 chapters] *aka* (feature version) *Slaves of the Invisible Monster*. *Perils of the Darkest Jungle* (51) Wallace Grissell [12 chapters] *aka* (feature version) *Jungle Gold*. *Radar Men from the Moon* (51) Fred C. Brannon [12 chapters] *aka* (feature version) *Retik, the Moon Menace*. *Zombies of the Stratosphere* (52) Fred C. Brannon [12 chapters] *aka* (feature version) *Satan's Satellites*. *The Panther Girl of Kongo* (54) Franklin Adreon *aka* (feature version) *The Claw Monsters*.

Serial Drama   *see*   **TELEVISION DRAMA: Drama Series**

Serial-Killer Films   *see*   **CRIME FILM**

SERIES (Film Series, Series Film)   The film series (not to be confused with the *serial* which is made up of numerous episodes forming a continuing long story) comprises a number of films, shorts or features, which are independent stories. Each film of the series has the same character or characters and usually uses the same formula from film to film. They started simultaneously in Europe and the United States, with France contributing largely to the popularity of the form. In France, Victori Jasset's *Nick Carter* (1908) is the earliest example of the form; in the United States, D. W. Griffith's *Mr. Jones* (1908-09) qualifies as an early attempt. The series format became very popular in America in the 30s and following decades. Series films ran the whole gamut of Hollywood genres: Westerns, detective stories, different types of comedy, hospital films, jungle adventures and animal series. They thrived especially in the B-picture category as low-budget features intended for the bottom half of a double-bill program. Many of the film series originated as such, while others were the result of an initial successful film, e.g., *Frankenstein, Dracula, Lassie*; still other films became part of a series after a successful sequel led the way for other follow-ups, e.g., the James Bond and the *Planet of the Apes* series. The low-budget series were discontinued after World War II, and they gradually disappeared, with the exception of television programming which has always relied heavily on television series. Film series cover such an extensive field that to list them all would take several pages; as a guideline, only a few of the most successful series are listed below. *See also* **SEQUEL.**

Andy Hardy [16 films (1937-58)].   *Blondie* [28 films (1938-50)].   *Bomba* [11 films (1949-55)].   *Bowery Boys* [48 films (1946-58)].   *Carry On...* (GB) [29 films (1958-78)].   *Doctor Series* (GB) [7 films (1954-70)].   *Don Camillo* (It / F) [5 films (1951-55)].   *Dracula* [Universal: 6 films (1930-48); Hammer (GB): 9 films (1958-74)].   *Dr. Christian* [6 films (1939-41)].   *Dr. Kildare* [16 films (1937-47)].   *Francis (the Talking Mule)* [7 films (1949-56)].   *Frankenstein* [Universal: 8 films (1931-48); Hammer (GB): 7 films (1957-73)].   *Fu Manchu* [1st appeared in *The Mystery of Dr. Fu Manchu* (GB 23): a series of 25 films]. *Gidget* [6 films (1959-85)].   *Henry Aldrich* [11 films (1939-44)].   *Hopalong Cassidy* [66 films (1935-48)].   *James Bond* [18 films (1962-89)].   *Jungle Jim* [16 films (1948-55)].   *Ma and Pa Kettle* [10 films (1947-57)].   *Maisie* [10 films (1939-47)].   *Mr. Jones* [10 films (1908-09)].   *Nick Carter* (F) [3 film series: (1908), (1909), (1911)].   *Pink Panther / Inspector Clouseau* [7 films (1964-83)]. *Planet of the Apes* [5 films (1967-73)].   *"Road" pictures* [7 films (1940-61)]. *Tarzan* [first appeared in *Tarzan of the Apes* (17); 14 films (1932-48) with Johnny Weissmuller].   *The Three Mesquiteers* [52 films (1935-43)].

Series Drama, Serie-al   *see*   **TELEVISION DRAMA: Drama Series**

Series Film   *see*   **SERIES**

Series Pilot   *see*   **TELEVISION SERIES**

Series / Serial   *see*   **TELEVISION DRAMA: Drama Series**

Seriocomedy   *see*   **COMEDY-DRAMA**

Service Comedy   *see*   **WAR FILM: Comedy War Films**

Sex-and-Sand Epic   *see*   **PEPLUM**

SEX-AND-VIOLENCE PICTURE (Sadomasochism, S and M Film)
Following the wave of nudie-cuties, films in the sexploitation business were not "cute" any longer. In the sixties a new trend emerged. In trade circles and among connoisseurs, the films belonging to this new trend were labelled "sadie-massies" and featured plenty of sadism and masochism. These films laced sex with stronger emotions, and the subcategories were known as "roughies" for their violence, "ghoulies" for mixing horror elements with sex, and "kinkies" which exploited aberrant behavior. These movies owe their beginning to the collaboration of two men, the producer David Friedman

and the director Herschell Gordon Lewis who, in 1963, premiered the first of the blood and gore films, *Blood Feast*. They soon had imitators, and the trend continues to this day. At first, these films were not very explicit in matters of sex or nudity, but this was compensated for by the explicit nature of their violence. Besides rapes and bashings, the films featured frequent scenes of bondage, whippings, torture and killings. *See* **GORE FILM.**

Scum of the Earth! (61) Lewis H. Gordon *aka Devil's Camera*. *Blood Feast* (63) Herschell Gordon Lewis. *Lorna* (64) Russ Meyer. *Olga's Girls* (64) Joseph P. Mawra. *Olga's House of Shame* (64) Joseph P. Mawra *aka House of Shame / 36 Hours of Terror*. *White Slaves of Chinatown* (64) Joseph P. Mawra *aka Slaves of China Town / White Slaves*. *The Defilers* (65) R. Lee Frost. *Mud Honey* (65) Russ Meyer *aka Mudhoney! / Rope of Flesh*. *P.P.S. (Prostitutes' Protective Society)* (66) Barry Mahon *aka The Secret Society*. *The Sadistic Lover* (66) George Gunther. *A Smell of Honey, a Swallow of Brine!* (66) B. Ron Elliott *aka The Maneater / The Smell of Honey / A Taste of Honey, a Swallow of Brine*. *The Touch of Her Flesh* (67) Julian Marsh *aka The Touch of Her Life / Way Out Love*. *The Curse of Her Flesh* (68) Julian Marsh *aka The Curse of the Curious / The Curse of the Flesh*. *The Daughters of Lesbos* (68) *aka Dominique / Dominique in Daughters of Lesbos*. *Invitation to Ruin* (68) Kurt Richter. *The Kiss of Her Flesh* (68) Julian Marsh *aka The Love Hours / Wanting Hour*. *Love Camp 7* (68) R. L. Frost *aka Love Camp*. *Pleasure Plantation* (70) Jerry Denby.

SEX COMEDY (Comedy of Sexual Manners, Sexual Comedy)   The sex comedy has been around for a long time, and it ranges from the timid bedroom farce or boudoir comedy to the more explicit sex romp. Bedroom farce puts its emphasis on the sexual activities of its players; sex romps go for merriment and diversity in partners. However, it is only since the sixties that the theme of sex has become more acceptable and open to frank treatment on the screen. Sex comedies started to proliferate in that decade, and they showed what previously had been considered taboo subject matter. Former forbidden aspects of sexual relationships were increasingly portrayed on film. Quickly, two major types of sex comedy evolved — the marriage comedy and the stud comedy.

——Marriage Comedies (Films about Marriage, Marital Comedies)   The marriage comedy is not new to the screen. Already in the early twenties, Ernst Lubitsch had created a type (with *The Marriage Circle*, 1923) of sophisticated comedies (sophisticated marital farces) that dealt with marriage, divorce and extramarital affairs. The film began a popular cycle of similar comedies. More recently, the marriage comedy has been studied by I. C. Jarvie.[96]

At its most fundamental, the marriage comedy has a couple in different stages of courtship. As a rule, one of the partners (more often than not, the female) is intent on marrying and has to overcome the resistance and reluctance to marry on the part of the other person. Or, the marriage comedy reflects the disappointments, bickerings and incompatibility of the couple.

The marriage may end in divorce or, in certain cases, remarriage to the same partner after the friction has been cleared up. These comedies are a mirror of contemporary American and worldwide mores on the question of marriage and so-called wedded bliss (or lack of it).

The Marriage Circle (23) Ernst Lubitsch. *Two-Faced Woman* (41) George Cukor. *Woman of the Year* (42) George Stevens. *Every Girl Should Be Married* (48) Don Hartman. *Unfaithfully Yours* (48) Preston Sturges. *How to Marry a Millionaire* (53) Jean Negulesco. *Waltz of the Toreadors* (GB 62) John Guillermin *aka The Amorous General*. *How to Murder Your Wife* (65) Richard Quine. *A Fine Madness* (66) Irvin Kershner. *Any Wednesday* (66) Robert Ellis Miller *aka Bachelor Girl Apartment*. *Two for the Road* (GB / US 66) Stanley Donen. *A Guide for the Married Man* (67) Gene Kelly. *Bob & Carol & Ted & Alice* (69) Paul Mazursky. *Lovers and Other Strangers* (69) Cy Howard. *Diary of a Mad Housewife* (70) Frank Perry. *Carnal Knowledge* (71) Mike Nichols. *The Marriage of a Young Stockbroker* (71) Lawrence Turnan. *The Heartbreak Kid* (72) Elaine May. *The Last Married Couple in America* (79) Gilbert Cates *aka The Last Married Couple*. *The Four Seasons* (81) Alan Alda. *Le beau mariage* (F 82) Eric Rohmer. *Almost You* (84) Adam Brooks. *Always* (85) Henry Jaglom. *Car Trouble* (GB 85) David Green. *Heartburn* (86) Mike Nichols.

——**Stud Comedies** The breakthrough in stud comedy came with *Tom Jones* (1963) and the popular *Alfie* (1965), a film which catapulted to instant fame its young actor, Michael Caine, in the role of a callous Cockney seducer, and which consolidated this type of comedy. Stud comedies have for their protagonist a philandering young man always on the prowl for easy conquests. In a way, they are picaresque comedies based on the old Don Juan theme.

Knave of Hearts / Monsieur Ripois (GB / F 54) René Clément *aka Lover Boy / Lovers, Happy Lovers!* *Il sorpasso* (It 62) Dino Risi *aka The Easy Life / The Overtaking*. *Tom Jones* (GB 63) Tony Richardson. *Alfie* (GB 65) Lewis Gilbert. *What's New Pussy Cat? / Quoi de neuf, Pussycat* (US / F 65) Clive Donner. *Percy* (GB 71) Ralph Thomas. *Rektor på sengekanten* (Den 72) John Hilbard *aka Bedside Head / Bedside Headmaster / Danish Bed and Board*. *Alvin Purple* (Aust 73) Tim Burstall *aka The Sex Therapist*. *Alvin Rides Again* (Aust 74) David Bilcock, Robin Copping *aka Alvin Purple Rides Again*. *Percy's Progress* (GB 74) Ralph Thomas *aka It's NOT the Size That Counts! / Percy's Private Parts*. *Alfie Darling* (GB 75) Ken Hughes *aka Oh! Alfie*. *Shampoo* (75) Hal Ashby. *Adventures of a Plumber's Mate* (GB 78) Stanley Long.

SEX DOCUMENTARY The documentary form has often provided a bona fide excuse for the screen presentation of sex without incurring too much of the wrath of censorship boards. If the film can be termed informative, educational, mentally therapeutic or serve as a warning against the dangers of sex, then it is all right for it to be shown to the public at large. The sex documentary is an old form that has been around since the 1900s. One of its earliest manifestations is the sex education film; other types which have also used the cover of the documentary format to present sex on screen have included the pseudoethnological film, the "mondo" film (q.v.), the sex explanation film, the sex information film, the compilation film and the sex encounter group film.

——Compilation Films With the surfacing of the blue film into the commercial circuits, old stag movies were rescued from oblivion. They were inserted in compilation films that traced the history of the pornographic film. If nothing else, it proved that such films have always existed, and indeed, some were quite expertly made and possessed a fine sense of humor.

A History of the Blue Movie (70) Alex DeRenzy. *Hollywood Blue* (70) Bill Osco. *Making the Blue Movie* (71) J. Nehemara *aka Making the Blue Film. Porno Pop* (Den / US / Swiz 71) Phyllis Kronhausen, Eberhard Kronhausen *aka Love Me Darling. Room Service 75* (71) Fred Baker. *Erotikus* (73) Nicholas Grippo. *Linda Lovelace Meets Miss Jones* (75) Angelo Spaveni. *Old, Borrowed, Stag* (75) Al Di Lauro.

——Pseudoethnological Documentaries The pseudoethnological documentary is not a sex documentary proper. It is grouped here, however, because the filmmakers sought to spice these films with glimpses of native nudity and thus attract a larger audience to their films. They had learned from fictionalized documentaries like Robert Flaherty's *Moana* (1925), which deals with native life in Samoa, that nudity was acceptable if it was integral to the natural surroundings in which primitive peoples lived. Some producers quickly took advantage of this fact and the pseudoethnological documentary emerged as a viable exploitation product. These documentaries are a mixture of travel in exotic lands and a description of ethnological customs. A later development was the so-called "mondo" film (q.v.).

Moana of the South Seas (25) Robert J. Flaherty, Frances Hubbard Flaherty *aka Moana. L'Amazone nue* (F / Braz 54) Zygmunt Sulistrowski *aka Naked Amazon. Continente perduto* (It 54) Leonardo Bonzi, Mario Craveri, Enrico Gras, Giorgio Moser, Francesco Lavagnino *aka The Lost Continent. L'ultimo paradiso* (It 57) Folco Quilici *aka The Last Paradise. Le Ciel et la boue* (Belg / F / Hol 61) Pierre- Dominique Gaisseau *aka The Sky Above–The Mud Below.*

——Sex Encounter Group Documentaries (Nude Encounter Group Films) In today's society, psychosocial inhibitors prevent individuals from fulfilling their psychological and physical needs. To correct this imbalance, a host of psychotherapy groups have emerged. Some of these groups advocate freedom of sexual expression, and in their encounter sessions they encourage nudity and unrestricted love-making. The documentary has recorded some of these encounters. In these films, people usually sit around, bathe together, and work out their sexual problems in discussions with the help of trained psychologists or psychotherapists; they also engage in sexual activities and love-making.

Sexual Encounter Group (70) Alex DeRenzy *aka Group Encounter. Out of Touch* (Can 71) John Gaisford. *Touch Me* (71) Sam Weston. *Childhood II*

(72) Martin J. Spinelli.   *Here Comes Everybody* (GB / Swiz 72) John Whitmore.   *Sandstone* (76) Jonathan Dana, Bunny Peters Dana.

——**Sex Explanation Films (How-to-Do-It Films, Sex Instruction Films)** This term is a translation of the German since the genre originated in Germany. Differing mostly in scope and explicitness from previous sex education films, these sex explanation films of the late sixties and early seventies, besides illustrating the more conventional sexual matters of puberty, sex differences, pregnancy and child birth that featured in the earlier sex education documentaries, showed how-to-do-it with couples actually performing or faking coition on screen in any conceivable variation—some films included over fifty coital positions. Some of these documentaries were very matter-of-fact and static in their presentation of sex; others tried for a dramatized approach. A few had a panel of doctors and experts giving an introductory talk or intervening during the film with further comments or explanations. On the whole, the sex instruction film is a genre that came and went as the market reached saturation point.

Helga— Vom Werden des menschlichen Lebens (G 67) Erich F. Bender, Vers Terry Van Tell (English version) *aka Helga / Helga: From the Inception of Human Life.   Oswalt Kolle—deine Frau—das unbekannte Wesen* (G 68) Alexis Neve *aka Female Sexuality / Your Wife, the Unknown Creature.   Oswalt Kolle—dein Mann—das unbekannte Wesen* (G 69) Werner M. Lenz *aka The Naked Man / Your Husband, the Unknown Creature.   Kärlekens språk* (Sw 69) Torgny Wickman *aka Language of Love.   He and She* (70) Matt Cimber.   *Kärlekens XYZ* (Sw 70) Torgny Wickman *aka Mera ur kärlekens språk / More About (the) Language of Love / XYZ of Love.   Marital Fulfillment* (70) Ferdinand Sebastian.   *The Sexually Liberated Female* (70) narrator: Lindis Guiness *aka The Senxually Liberated Female / Woman and Lover.   The Zodiac Couples* (70) Bob Stein, A. Roberts.   *101 Acts of Love* (71) Eric Haims.   *Together* (71) Sean S. Cunningham.   *Sexual Customs in Scandinavia* (72) Sid Knigtsen.   *Sexual Liberty Now* (72) M. C. Von Hellen.

——**Sex Information Films**   Denmark abolished censorship laws for film on July 1, 1969. The gates were open to hard-core pornography; suddenly all kinds of sexual behavior could be photographed and presented to the viewer. This prompted the need to show what was happening in Scandinavia, and American filmmakers began making documentaries to inform the public about what the new freedom meant in terms of sex, sexuality and eroticism. The sex information film was born. These films showed uninhibited sex life styles, sex art exhibitions, live sex shows, how blue movies were being made and frequently interviewed people in the street to find out what their feelings were about pornography and the abolition of censorship laws.

Det kaere legetøj (Den 68) Gabriel Axel *aka Danish Blue.   Censorship in Denmark: A New Approach* (69) Alex DeRenzy *aka Denmark Report, 1970 / Pornography in Denmark: A New Approach.   Hven Ska' med Hvem?* (Den 70) Nils Vest *aka Who Does What to Whom.   Pornography: Copenhagen 1970* (70) Jorgen Lyhne *aka Wide-Open Copenhagen 70.   Sexual Freedom in Denmark* (70) M. C. Von Helled [filmed by Alex DeRenzy] *aka Dansk Sexualitet.   Welt-Sex-Report* (G 70) Richard R. Rimmel *aka World*

Sex Report. American Sexual Revolution (71) John William Abbot. *Censorship USA* (71) Alan Roberts. *Eroticon* (71) Richard Lacey *aka Erotikon. Hvorfor goer de det?* (Den / Swiss 71) Phyllis Kronhausen, Eberhard Kronhausen *aka Why? / Why Do They Do It? Inge og Sten spoer* (Den 71) Torgny Wickman *aka Inge and Sten Ask the Questions? Red, White and Blue* (71) Fred Sebastian, Beverly Sebastian. *Sub Rosa Rising* (71) Jerry Abrams [subtitled "Sex in San Francisco"] *aka Open City '72 / San Francisco Blue. Personals* (72) Armand Weston, Howard Winters. *Sex Freaks* (74) M. C. Von Hellen. *A Labor of Love* (77) Robert Flaxman, Daniel Goldman. *Not a Love Story: A Film about Pornography / C'est surtout pas de l'amour — Un film sur la pornographie* (Can 81) Bonnie Sherr Klein.

Sex Education Film, Sex Encounter Group Documentaries, Sex Explanation Films *see* **SEX DOCUMENTARY**

SEX EXPLOITATION FILM (Porn Film/Pornie/Porno Film, Pornographic Film, Skin Flick/Skinpic, Sexploitation Film/Sexploiter) The sex exploitation film is a type of exploitation movie that, as the name indicates, exploits the subject of sex for monetary gain. Throughout the history of the motion picture industry, there have always been films that are exploitation items; among exploitation films (q.v.), sexploitation pictures are a very important group. Some of the early peep show films exhibited at film arcades were already of a risqué nature, showing ladies in different stages of *déshabillé* or undress, and they certainly qualified as exploitation. Later, vice films on the perils of prostitution, white slavery, drugs and sex-related subjects also qualified as exploitation films. In the 50s, burlesque films (that is, those which filmed striptease shows straight from the stage and were devoid of any artistic merit whatsoever) and nudist films appeared. Nudie-cuties dominated the early sixties. Sexploitation films grew more sophisticated and daring. By the late 60s and early 70s, explicit pornographic films showing intercourse and other sexual acts had surfaced into the commercial cinemas. This made it necessary to differentiate between explicit and nonexplicit films, between films that showed it all and films that faked it. The explicit films were labelled hard-core and the ones that simulated sex were denominated soft-core. The following categories and genres are treated as separate entries: **HARD-CORE PORNO FILM, "MONDO" FILM, NUDIE, NUDIST FILM, SEX-AND-VIOLENCE PICTURE, SEX DOCUMENTARY, SOFT-CORE PORNO FILM, VICE FILM.**

SEX FILM (Sex-Oriented Film) A film whose main theme is the presentation of sex on the screen. Sex movies are classed under two general headings: Erotic film and Sex exploitation film.

Sex Film Series *see* **SOFT-CORE SEX-EXPLOITATION FILM**

Sex Horror Films *see* **HORROR FILM**

Sex Information Films *see* **SEX DOCUMENTARY**; *see also* **HARD-CORE PORNO FILM**

Sex Instruction Film   *see*   **SEX DOCUMENTARY: Sex Explanation Films**

Sex Romp, Sexual Comedy   *see*   **SEX COMEDY**

Sex Vampire Films   *see*   **VAMPIRE FILM**

Sexist Film   *see*   **FEMINIST FILM**

Sex-Oriented Film   *see*   **SEX FILM**

Sexplicit Film   *see*   **HARD-CORE PORNO FILM**

Sexploitation Film, Sexploiter   *see*   **SEX EXPLOITATION FILM**

Sexual-Initiation Film   *see*   **MALE-ORIENTED PICTURE**

Sexually Explicit Film   *see*   **HARD-CORE PORNO FILM**

SF Comedies, SF Disaster Films, SF Film, SF Horror Films, SF Sex Films   *see*   **SCIENCE FICTION FILM**

Shadow Play   *see*   **FILM**

SHAKESPEARE FILM (Shakespearean Film)   William Shakespeare (1564–1616) is for many the greatest playwright who ever lived; this is especially so in English-speaking countries. It is not surprising, then, that his plays should have often inspired film adaptations, screen transpositions or have been used as a source of inspiration in various film genres. Indeed, Shakespeare films have been made by filmmakers of different nationalities — British, American, Russian, Italian, Czech, German, Danish, Japanese. Many nations have attempted to interpret Shakespeare. Film adaptations of his works in the silent period alone number several hundred, but it was only with the coming of sound to the screen that the potential of Shakespeare on film has been fully realized. Besides the many film adaptations of Shakespeare's works, there are also a number of worthwhile films and video recordings of notable stagings of Shakespearean productions, and television has also contributed extensively to the corpus of Shakespearean films. Several filmographies of Shakespeare films have been compiled, e.g., Peter Morris, *Shakespeare on Film* (Ottawa: Canadian Film Institute, 1972); Barry M. Parker, *The Folger Shakespeare Filmography* (Washington, D.C.: The Folger Shakespeare Library, 1979); and Kenneth S. Rothwell and Annabelle Henkin Melzer, *Shakespeare on Screen: An International Filmography and Videography* (London: Mansell; New York: Neal-Schuman, 1990).

The Taming of the Shrew (29) Sam Taylor. *A Midsummer Night's Dream* (35) Max Reinhardt, William Dieterle. *As You Like It* (GB 36) Paul Czinner. *Henry V* (GB 45) Laurence Olivier. *Macbeth* (47) Orson Welles. *Hamlet* (GB 48) Laurence Olivier. *Othello* (US / F 51) Orson Welles. *Julius Caesar* (53) Joseph L. Mankiewicz. *Romeo and Juliet / Giulietta e Romeo*

(GB / It 54) Renato Castellani. *Richard III* (GB 55) Laurence Olivier. *Forbidden Planet* (56) Fred M. Wilcox. *Kumonosu-jo* (J 57) Akira Kurosawa *aka Castle of the Spider's Web / Cobweb Castle / Kunonosu-djo / Macbeth / Throne of Blood.* *Gamlet* (USSR 64) Grigori Kozintsev *aka Hamlet.* *Campanadas a medianoche* (Sp / Swiz 65) Orson Welles *aka Chimes at Midnight / Falstaff.* *Othello* (GB 65) Stuart Burge. *The Taming of the Shrew / La bisbetica domata* (US / It 66) Franco Zeffirelli. *Romeo and Juliet / Romeo e Giulietta* (GB / It 67) Franco Zeffirelli. *Korl' Lir* (USSR 70) Grigori Kozintsev *aka King Lear / Korol Lear.* *Macbeth* (GB 71) Roman Polanski. *Antony and Cleopatra* (Swiz / Sp / GB 72) Charlton Heston. *The Tempest* (GB 79) Derek Jarman. *Henry V* (GB 89) Kenneth Branagh. *Hamlet* (90) Franco Zeffirelli. *Prospero's Books* (GB / F / Hol / J 91) Peter Greenaway.

Shakespearean Film *see* **SHAKESPEARE FILM**

Shamus Movie *see* **PRIVATE DETECTIVE FILM**

Sheriff Films *see* **POLICE FILM**

Sherlock Holmes Films *see* **PRIVATE DETECTIVE FILM**

Shocker *see* **HORROR FILM;** *see also* **PSYCHOPATHIC THRILLER**

Shock Film *see* **FACTUAL FILM: Jeopardy Film**

Shockumentary *see* **MONDO FILM**

Shoot-'Em-Up *see* **WESTERN**

SHORT (Court-Métrage, Non-Feature Film, Short Film, Short-Footage Film, Short Subject)   At the inception of motion pictures, all films were of very short duration. Their length increased gradually between 1896 and 1906 from films that ran for one minute or less to ten-minute comedies and dramas; the ten-minute or one reel was the average length for a short subject until longer lengths also became acceptable.

A short film is mainly defined by its length, which has varied from time to time and from country to country, extending its footage from a maximum of 600 to 1800 or even 2000 meters for 35mm films intended for theatrical release. It is safer to consider any film of up to 30 minutes running time as a short; for films running longer than this, the term featurette (the French use *moyen métrage*) is sometimes applied. However, many countries and film organizations include anything under 60 minutes duration in the short or non-feature category.

The short film is easily divided into two main categories comprising theatrical and non-theatrical shorts. Further divisions, especially within the non-theatrical group, include independently made shorts (experimental, amateur films) and films financed by some industrial concern or governmental department. In the area of the factual film, shorts have become indispensable to illustrate a multitude of subjects and functions; they form several subcategories including sponsored films, government films, educational films, scientific films and research films.

Obviously, shorts are found in all areas of filmmaking, and they are a perfect training ground for future filmmakers. Many excellent shorts figure in the filmographies of prominent directors; films which they made as part of student projects or privately, with the help of friends, and for the sheer love of filmmaking.

———**Chaser**   In the late 1890s and early 1900s, short films were shown in America in vaudeville theaters; some placed at the beginning and end of each program were named "chasers."

———**Cut-Down Feature**   Offered for instructional or educational purposes, the cut-down feature consists of extracts of a particular film, often given a different title by the distribution company, e.g., *When Parents Grow Old*, culled from the theatrical feature *I Never Sang for My Father* (1969).

———**Kinetograph, Kinetoscope Film**   The film camera devised by Thomas Alva Edison (1847–1931) and W. K. L. Dickson (1860–1935) in 1888 and patented in 1891. The name was also applied to the half-minute films made with this camera and shown in the kinetoscopes or peep shows installed in the penny arcades of the 1890s. Kinetophonograph was the name used for a peep show with sound; the films used in this machine are referred to as kinetophones or kinetophone films.

———**Multishot Film (Multiscene Film)**   A designation for early silent films composed of several shots and that led to the development of the narrative film. They are a natural progression from the limitations of the one-shot film. Some of the better-known genres (excluding nonfiction films) which comprise these films of the early 1900s are the trick film (q.v.), the explosion film (a common trick film in which some object or artifact explodes), the close view genre (mostly one-shot films) showing people in closeups or semi-closeups, oftentimes the camera focussing on the facial expression of the performers, and the chase film (q.v.). The majority of these early fiction films were comedies, others were faked newsreels, or records of vaudeville acts, with serious dramas or melodramas increasing in output as motion pictures approached the end of the first decade of the 1900s. There was also an ongoing production of gentle erotic films to supply a growing demand for this type of film. A list of extant multishot films in American archives for the period of 1900 to 1906 is provided by Eileen Bowser in "The Brighton Project: An Introduction," *Quarterly Review of Film Studies* 4 (1979): 528–38.

———**One-Reeler (One-Reel Film)**   A silent film of ten or so minutes of running time (1000 feet of film). Many early films were just one-reelers. A split-reel refers to a film running for half-a-reel or less.

———**Short Play**   In the silent period, one-reelers were also known as short plays, and long plays were movies of more than one reel.

———**Two-Reeler**   The duration of a silent two-reeler was approximately 20 minutes. Many silent comedies are two-reelers (two-reel comedies). The short comedy film of two reels was a popular format until the 1940s and its running time could vary from 20 to 30 minutes.

Short Film, Short-Footage Film   *see*   **SHORT**

Short Form   *see*   **MUSIC VIDEO**

Short Play, Short Subject   *see*   **SHORT**

Showbiz Biography, Showbiz Biopic   *see*   **BIOGRAPHICAL FILM: Show Business Biographical Films**

SHYSTER FILM   In the thirties, a cycle of films dealt with corruption in the city, more often than not, New York City. As the name shyster implies, the city was populated with corrupt individuals who were mostly lawyers, politicians and newspapermen. These unscrupulous individuals, prone to graft, engaged in all kinds of dishonesty for their own gain. The shyster films deal with the schemes of these men. The shyster cycle is documented by Andrew Bergman, "The Shyster and the City," in *We're in the Money* (New York: New York UP, 1971) 18–29. *See also* **NEWSPAPER FILM, LAWYER FILM** and **SOCIAL CONSCIOUSNESS FILM.**
   Scandal Sheet (31) John Cromwell.   *Blessed Event* (32) Roy Del Ruth.   *The Dark Horse* (32) Alfred E. Green.   *Is My Face Red* (32) William A. Seiter. *Lawyer Man* (32) William Dieterle.   *Okay, America* (32) Tay Garnett *aka Penalty of Fame.   State's Attorney* (32) George Archainbaud aka *Cardigan's Last Case.   Washington Masquerade* (32) Charles Brabin *aka Mad Masquerade.*

Sicilian Comedy   *see*   **SOCIAL COMEDY**

Sick Comedy   *see*   **BLACK COMEDY**

Sick Film   *see*   **PSYCHOPATHIC THRILLER**

Sick Humor   *see*   **BLACK COMEDY**

Sickie   *see*   **PSYCHOPATHIC THRILLER**

Sight-Gag Comedy   *see*   **SLAPSTICK**

Silent   *see*   **SILENT FILM**

Silent Comedy   *see*   **COMEDY**

SILENT FILM (Silent)   The term is self-explanatory as it applies to a film without sound track or to a film of the "silent era," that is, up to 1928 when sound pictures became commercially viable. However, silent films were never strictly silent but were usually accompanied by music. Either an organist or a piano player would improvise atmospheric tunes to accompany the picture, or the picture itself would have its music recorded on a phonographic system. Silent pictures had practically ceased to exist by 1929, but a few sporadic films still appeared, e.g., George Medford's *The Poor Millionaire* (1930), the last commercial American picture without a sound track; Charlie Chaplin's *City Lights* (1931) and F. W. Murnau's *Tabu* (1931) both had synchronized music and sound effects. Although by 1931 most European countries had changed to sound, in other parts of the world the change was much slower. Now and then, films without dialogue or with only a few spoken words are still made, e.g., Kaneto Shindo's *Hadaka no shima / The Island* (1960) or Mel Brooks's *Silent Movie* (1976), in which the only word spoken during the 88 minutes of the film's duration is the French word *oui*. These, however, are just film oddities, forays into the silent film technique.

   The Poor Millionaire (30) George Medford.   *City Lights* (31) Charlie Chaplin.   *Tabu* (31) F. W. Murnau, Robert Flaherty.   *The Thief* (52) Russel Rouse.   *Dementia* (55) John Parker *aka Daughter of Horror*.   *Hadaka no shima* (J 60) Kaneto Shindo *aka The Island*.   *San Ferry Ann* (GB 65) Jeremy Summers.   *Gari zoshi* (J 72) Yoichi Takabayashi *aka The Water Was So Dear*.   *Night of Fear* (Aust 72) Terry Bourke.   *Vase de noces* (Belg 73) Theirry Zeno *aka Wedding Trough*.   *La Fille du garde barrière* (F 75) Jérôme Savary *aka The Gatekeeper's Daughter*.   *Robinson Columbus* (Den 75) Ib Steinaa. *Testament* (Yug 75) Milos Radivojevic.   *Coilin & Platonida* (GB 76) James Scott.   *Silent Movie* (76) Mel Brooks.   *Birjuk* (USSR 77) Roman Balaian *aka Lone Wolf*.   *Pentimento* (Hol 78) Fran Zartjes.   *Dirty Picture* (Hol 79) Pim de la Parra.   *Le Dernier Combat* (F 83) Luc Besson *aka The Final Combat / The Last Battle*.   *The Last of England* (GB 88) Derek Jarman.   *Sidewalk Stories* (89) Charles Lane.

Silhouette Films   *see*   **ANIMATION**

Simulated Film   *see*   **SOFT-CORE SEX-EXPLOITATION FILM**

Singing Cowboy Picture   *see*   **WESTERN: Musical Westerns**

Single Play   *see*   **TELEVISION DRAMA**

Single-Concept Film   *see*   **FACTUAL FILM**

Single-O   *see*   **HARD-CORE PORNO FILM**

Sitcom   *see*   **SITUATION COMEDY**

SITUATION COMEDY (Sitcom)   Essentially a television form, situation comedy or sitcom (usually designed to fill up a half-hour slot) has been a steady staple of television programming. It is usually a series with the same characters reappearing with each installment. Characteristic of this type of comedy is that the characters behave predictably in any given basic situation. Most situation comedies are located in the home, the setting for countless family situation comedies (*Till Death Us Do Part* [GB 1964-74];

All in the Family [1971-79]). Other sitcoms take place where the characters work — department store, hospital (*Are You Being Served?* [GB 1974]; *Doctor in the House* [GB 1970-73]), army or navy locations in the case of service sitcoms (*McHale's Navy* [1962-66]; *Hogan's Heroes* [1965-71]). The possibilities are varied — musical, fantasy, police sitcoms; situation comedies set in the past or the future. The situation comedy is an enduring form. Typical is the insertion of a laugh-track with canned laughter.

The term situation comedy is also applied to some films with just a few characters placed in a restricted environment or humorous situation.

Some television situation comedies have resulted in feature film spin-offs, and to a lesser extent some films (*M*A*S*H* [1969]; *The Odd Couple* [1968]) have also inspired television sitcoms. *See* David Grote, *The End of Comedy: The Sit-Com and the Comedic Tradition* (Hamden, Conn.: Archon Books, 1983).

Films: Brewster's Millions (45) Allan Dwan. *Adam's Rib* (49) George Cukor. *The Odd Couple* (68) Gene Saks. *M*A*S*H* (69) Robert Altman *aka MASH.* *Mr. Mom* (83) Stan Dragoti *aka Mr. Mum.* *Porridge* (GB 79) Dick Clement *aka Doing Time.* *High School U.S.A.* (83 TV) Rod Amateau.

TV: I Love Lucy (51-56 CBS) Marc Daniels, William Asher [179 episodes]. *McHale's Navy* (62-66 ABC) [138 episodes]. *The Beverly Hillbillies* (62-71 CBS) Joseph DePew, Robert Leeds [216 episodes]. *Steptoe and Son* (GB 64-73 BBC). *Till Death Us Do Part* (GB 64-74 BBC). *Hogan's Heroes* (65-71 CBS) [168 episodes]. *Father, Dear Father* (GB 68-73 ITV). *On the Buses* (GB 69-75 ITV). *Doctor in the House* (GB 70-73 ITV) [90 episodes]. *The Odd Couple* (70-75 ABC) [114 episodes]. *All in the Family* (71-79 CBS) Paul Bogart, John Rich, H. Wesley Kenney [207 episodes]. *M*A*S*H* (72-83 CBS) [250 episodes plus 1 long final episode: "Goodbye, Farewell and Amen"]. *Man About the House* (GB 73-76 ITV) [39 episodes]. *Are You Being Served?* (GB 74 BBC) [30 episodes]. *Fawlty Towers* (GB 75-79 BBC) [13 episodes: 6 (1975) and 7 (1979)]. *Three's Company* (77-84 ABC) Bill Hobin, Sam Gary, Michael Ross, Jack Shea, Dave Powers [164 episodes].

——"Heart" Comedy   A type of sentimental situation comedy which involves single parents and their children, a mixture of laughter and woe, e.g., *My Three Sons* (1960-72); *The Doris Day Show* (1968-73); *To Rome with Love* (1969-71). It is related to family situation comedy.

My Three Sons (60-65 ABC; 65-72 CBS) [369 episodes]. *The Doris Day Show* (68-73 CBS) [128 episodes]. *To Rome with Love* (69-71 CBS) Fred DeCordova, Earl Bellamy, James Sheldon [48 episodes].

Sketch Film   *see*   **EPISODE FILM**

Skill Film   *see*   **FACTUAL FILM**

SKIN FLICK (Fleshfeast, Flesh-Flick, Meat Movie)   A film in which emphasis is placed on the display of nudity. The showing of the naked body has been one of the main concerns of risqué cinema since its beginning.[97] At first the displays of nudity were rather coy but were immediately opposed by self-appointed moralists and regulatory censorship bodies. In spite of this, nakedness on the screen continued to progress gradually until it reached the present-day stage of no holds barred in countries where censorship laws against obscenity have been abolished. Skin flicks do not have to be necessarily pornographic. Pure examples of skin flicks are found in stag movies and in the nudist and nudie type films of the 1950s and 1960s. Besides **NUDIST FILM** and **NUDIE,** *see* **EROTIC FILM** and **SEX EXPLOITATION FILM.**

Skinpic   *see*   **SEX EXPLOITATION FILM**

Slapdash Film   *see*   **SLEAZY FILM**

SLAPSTICK (Classical Comedy, Clown Comedy, Custard-Pie Comedy, Knockabout Comedy, Low Comedy, Slapstick Comedy, Slapstick Farce). Film comedy began as low comedy or slapstick, as silent comedy is generally called. Although its beginnings are found in the films of the Lumière brothers (*see* **COMEDY**), its major development took place in America at the film studios of Mack Sennett (1880-1960), who specialized in parody combined with slapstick and in pure slapstick (Keystone Kops, bathing beauties and pies were slapstick's classic trademarks). Slapstick has a long theatrical tradition that goes back to the Italian *commedia dell'arte* of the 16th, 17th and 18th centuries. However, in cinematic terms, slapstick means the type of comedy characteristic of the silent era, practiced by almost all the screen comedians of the time. Among these silent comedians, it is generally agreed that four—Charlie Chaplin, Buster Keaton, Harold Lloyd and Harry Langdon—stand out as the true geniuses of the genre, to which Stan Laurel and Oliver Hardy could be added.

Slapstick is physical comedy with plenty of movement, made up mainly of falls, gags, pies generally landing on faces, and chases. Most silent slapstick comedies ended with a riotous chase in which all sorts of people and vehicles participated. Slapstick comedies thrived on bullying and violence, but they also relied on nonviolent pantomime for their comic bits, which has been named sight-gag comedy. Slapstick and sight gag were the main tools of the silent clowns. Pie-throwing was such a standard part of slapstick that custard-pie comedy, besides meaning a Mack Sennett film and a film in which pies or cakes are being thrown, has also been used as a synonym for slapstick comedy. Laurel and Hardy's *The Battle of the Century* (1927) is a good example of the pie-throwing film. Slapstick is still used in many modern comedies.

Keystone Comedies: In the Clutches of a Gang (14) Mack Sennett, George Nichols.   *The Plumber* (14) Dell Henderson, Mack Sennett (author).   *That Little Band of Gold* (15) Roscoe Arbuckle, Mack Sennett (author) *aka For Better or Worse*.   *Dirty Work in a Laundry* (15) Charles Parrott, Mack Sennett (author) *aka A Desperate Scoundrel*.

Charlie Chaplin: Easy Street (27) Charlie Chaplin.   *The Kid* (21) Charlie

Chaplin [subtitled: "A Picture with a Smile and Perhaps a Tear"].   *The Gold Rush* (25) Charlie Chaplin.   *City Lights* (31) Charlie Chaplin.

Buster Keaton: Sherlock, Jr. (24) Buster Keaton *aka Sherlock Junior. The Navigator* (24) Donald Crisp, Buster Keaton.   *The General* (26) Buster Keaton, Clyde Bruckman.   *The Railroader* (Can 65) Gerald Potterton.

Harry Langdon: The Strong Man (26) Frank Capra.   *Tramp, Tramp, Tramp* (26) Harry Edwards, Frank Capra.   *Long Pants* (27) Frank Capra.

Harold Lloyd: Grandma's Boy (22) Fred Newmeyer.   *Safety Last* (23) Fred Newmeyer, Sam Taylor.   *The Kid Brother* (27) Ted Wilde.

Laurel and Hardy: The Battle of the Century (27) Clyde Bruckman.   *Two Tars* (28) James Parrott.   *Big Business* (28) James Horne.   *Sons of the Desert* (33) William A. Seiter *aka Fraternally Yours.*

The Three Stooges: Have Rocket, Will Travel (59) David Lowell Rich *aka Race for the Moon.   The Three Stooges Go Around the World in a Daze* (63) Norman Maurer.   *The Outlaws Is Coming* (65) Norman Maurer.

Cockeyed Cavaliers (34) Mark Sandrich.   *Fit for a King* (37) Edward Sedgwick.   *The Mad Miss Manton* (38) Leigh Jason.   *Voyage-surprise* (F 46) Pierre Prévert.   *The Fuller Brush Man* (48) S. Sylvan Simon *aka That Mad Mr. Jones.   Smuggler's Cove* (48) William Beaudine.   *A Woman of Distinction* (50) Edward Buzzell.   *Casanova's Big Night* (54) Norman Z. McLeod.   *The Long, Long Trailer* (54) Vincente Minnelli.   *Two-Way Stretch* (GB 60) Robert Day *aka Nothing Barred.   It's a Mad, Mad, Mad, Mad World* (63) Stanley Kramer.   *The Man from the Diners' Club* (63) Frank Tashlin.   *The Disorderly Orderly* (64) Frank Tashlin.   *A Guide for the Married Man* (67) Gene Kelly.   *The Party* (68) Blake Edwards.   *National Lampoon's Animal House* (78) John Landis *aka Animal House* [6 "Lampoon" movies (1978-89)].   *The Gods Must Be Crazy* (Botswana / SA 80) Jamie Uys.   *Odio le bionde / Je hais les blondes / Ich hasse Blondinen* (It / F / G 80) Georgio Capitani *aka I Hate Blondes.   La Chèvre* (F / Mex 81) Francis Veber.   *The Gods Must Be Crazy II* (US / Botswana 85) Jamie Uys [rel. in 89].   *Assault on Matrimony* (87 TV) James Frawley.   *Outrageous Fortune* (87) Arthur Hiller.   *The Feud* (89) Bill D'Elia.

———**Park Films (Park Comedies)**   In many of Chaplin's early comedies— *Twenty Minutes of Love, Recreation* (1914), *Getting Acquainted, In the Park* (1915)—most of the action takes place in parks; hence, they are known as park films. Besides Chaplin, other slapstick comedians also made ample use of the park setting for their pranks.

Recreation (14) Charles Chaplin *aka In the Park 50 / Spring Fever.   Twenty Minutes of Love* (14) Joseph Madden *aka Cops and Watches / He Loved Her So / Love Friend / Passing Time.   Getting Acquainted* (15) Charles Chaplin *aka Exchange Is No Robbery / A Fair Exchange / The Flirts / Hullo Everybody.   In the Park* (15) Charles Chaplin *aka Charlie on the Spree.*

———**Thrill Comedies**   Thrill comedies were thus named because of the perilous situations in which the comics found themselves and the great deal of suspense which they contain. Many slapstick comedies are thrill comedies. *See* **THRILLER.**

High and Dizzy (20) Hal Roach. *Never Weaken* (21) Fred Newmeyer. *The Balloonatic* (23) Buster Keaton, Eddie Cline. *Safety Last* (23) Fred Newmeyer, Sam Taylor. *Sporting Youth* (23) Harry A. Pollard *aka The Spice of Life / There He Goes. The Flying Deuces* (39) A. Edward Sutherland *aka Flying Aces.*

Slapstick Comedy, Slapstick Farce *see* **SLAPSTICK**

Slash and Gash Film, Slash-and-Stab Film *see* **SLASHER FILM**

SLASHER FILM (Body-Count Movie, Dead-Teenagers Film, Fuck and Die Film, Hack-and-Slash Film, Hack-'em-Up Film, Massacre Movie, Multiple-Murder Film, Slash and Gash Film, Slash-and-Stab Film, Slaughter Movie, Slice and Dice Film, Slice 'n' Dice Film, Stalk-and-Slash Film, Stalk and Slice Film, Stalker Film, Teenie-Kill Movie, Teen Slash-'em-Up[s] Film, Woman-in-Danger Film)   The term slasher film gained currency with the success of *Halloween* (1978) and similar pictures. The object of these films is little more than to provide cheap thrills by presenting a murderous, deranged person slashing and stabbing random, innocent victims to assuage the urges of his or her warped mind. Many of these films are merely a succession of on-camera, gory killings — nine, ten or more slayings per picture are not unusual. The maniacs on the loose employ all sorts of cutting, stabbing or severing instruments ranging from swift and silent knives and axes to the more noisy chain saws and power drills. The trend, rather than abating after a few initial "Halloween"-type and *Friday the 13th* (1980) imitations, has continued to form a sizeable number of movies. The violence may be presented in a graphic or non-graphic manner according to the original intention and the audience sought by the filmmaker. *See* **GORE FILM** and **PSYCHOPATHIC THRILLER** entries.

Alice, Sweet Alice (76) Alfred Sole *aka Communion / Holy Terror. Upstate Murders* (76) David Paulsen *aka The Killer Behind the Mask / Savage Weekend. Halloween* (78) John Carpenter *aka The Babysitter Murders* [5 films in the series up to 1989]. *The Burning* (79) Tony Maylam *aka Don't Go in the House. Prom Night / Le Bal de l'horreur* (Can 79) Paul Lynch. *Silent Scream* (79) Denny Harris. *Friday the 13th* (80) Sean S. Cunningham [8 films in the series up to 1989]. *Maniac* (80) William Lustig. *Mother's Day* (80) Charles Kaufman. *My Bloody Valentine / Meurtres à la Saint-Valentin* (Can 80) George Mihalka *aka The Secret. Night School* (80) Kenneth Hughes *aka Terror Eyes. to all a good night* (80) David Hess. *Graduation Day* (81) Herb Freed. *Halloween II* (81) Rick Rosenthal. *Madman* (81) Joe Giannone *aka The Legend Lives / Madman Marz. Nightmare* (81) Romano Scavolini *aka Nightmares in a Damaged Brain / Schizo. Night Warning* (81) William Asher *aka Butcher Baker (Nightmare Maker) / Moma's Baby / Momma's Boy / Nightmare Maker / Thrilled to Death. Sweet Sixteen* (81) Jim Sotos *aka Sweet 16. The House on Sorority Row* (82) Mark Rosman *aka House of Evil / Seven Sisters. The Slumber Party Massacre* (82) Amy Jones *aka Sleepless Night / The Slumber Party Murders. Unhinged* (82) Don Gronquist. *Friday the 13th: The Final Chapter* (84) Joseph Zito *aka Friday the 13th Part IV — The Final Chapter. A Nightmare on Elm*

Street (84) Wes Craven [6 films in the series up to 1990]. *Silent Night, Deadly Night* (84) Charles E. Sellier, Jr. *Hello Mary Lou: Prom Night II* (Can 87) Bruce Pittman. *Sleepaway Camp 2: Unhappy Campers* (88) Michael A. Simpson.

Slaughter Movie   *see*   **SLASHER FILM**

Sleaze Film   *see*   **SLEAZY FILM**

SLEAZY FILM (Junk Film, Schlock Movie, Sleaze Film, Trash Film)   Trash, trashy, tacky, tawdry, slapdash, junk and hack film are appellations which have their own different nuances of meaning but all are terms usually reseved for films which make use of poor or bad taste, are very cheaply made, aspire to make a quick buck and are normally ignored by film critics. However, the most frequently used labels, when referring to films of this nature, are schlock movie (q.v.) and sleazy film.

Perhaps one of the best examples of sleazy filmmaking is the films of John Waters (*Multiple Maniacs* [1969]; *Pink Flamingos* [1972]; *Female Trouble* [1974]), who himself confessed in his memoirs that trashiness was his aim in making pictures[98]; in fact, his films stand out as truly sleazy creations in the full sense of the word and are films which have garnered him a solid reputation for bad taste as well as a cult following (e.g., *Pink Flamingos*). This seldom happens with trash films, but they help to enlarge the ranks of genre groupings; now and then, however, a real gem emerges. *See also* **KITSCH** and **Z PICTURE** entries.

> *The Brain That Wouldn't Die* (59) Joseph Green *aka The Black Door / The Head That Wouldn't Die*. *The Hypnotic Eye* (59) George Blair. *Who Killed Teddy Bear?* (65) Joseph Cates. *Multiple Maniacs* (69) John Waters. *Pink Flamingos* (72) John Waters. *A Scream in the Streets* (72) Carl Monson *aka Girls in the Streets*. *Female Trouble* (74) John Waters *aka Rotten Mind, Rotten Face*. *Maniac* (81) William Lustig. *Vice Squad* (81) Gary A. Sherman. *Courier of Death* (84) Tom Shaw. *Crawlspace* (US / It 86) David Schmoeller.

SLEEPER (Cinderella Film)   A film that somewhat unexpectedly becomes a popular success and a top grosser at the box-office. Such films are usually made at low production cost. They are not necessarily trendsetters although they stimulate quick imitations. The term is used also for a film which, although previously ignored by the critics, receives sudden acclaim by the cognoscenti or film enthusiasts.

> *Marty* (55) Delbert Mann. *Rocky* (76) John G. Avildsen. *Breaking Away* (79) Peter Yates. *I've Heard the Mermaids Singing* (Can 87) Patricia Rozena. *True Love* (89) Nancy Savoca. *House Party* (90) Reginald Hudlin. *Pretty Woman* (90) Garry Marshall.

Slice and Dice Film, Slice 'n' Dice Film   *see*   **SLASHER FILM;**   *see also*   **VIOLENCE FILM**

Slice-of-Life Film   *see*   **NATURALISTIC FILM**

Small-Town Melodrama   *see*   **MELODRAMA: Domestic Melodramas**

SMALL-TOWN MOVIE   In a recent study, Kenneth Mackinson has drawn attention to a film genre that focusses on life not in the big city and urban centers, but rather in small towns and on their inhabitants. Considering the quantity of extant films that revolve around the small town, it is unusual, to say the least, that the small-town movie should have remained until now a neglected genre. The small-town picture includes melodramas, comedies, musicals, science fiction movies, horror films, thrillers and films which clearly belong to other genres. However, the small-town film quite often presents the town community as the backbone of American society, the representative of its most traditional beliefs as it defends righteousness and morality as well as all else that is considered to be intrinsically American. For a definition of the genre and a selective list of small-town movies, *see* Kenneth Mackinson, *Hollywood's Small Towns* (Metuchen, NJ: Scarecrow, 1984), pp. 191–98.

Tol'able David (21) Henry King.   *Ah, Wilderness* (35) Clarence Brown. *Alice Adams* (35) George Stevens.   *Our Town* (40) Sam Wood.   *King's Row* (41) Sam Wood.   *Andy Hardy's Double Life* (42) George B. Seitz [16 films (1937-58) in the "Andy Hardy" series].   *Shadow of a Doubt* (42) Alfred Hitchcock. *The Human Comedy* (43) Clarence Brown.   *Invasion of the Body Snatchers* (55) Don Siegel *aka The Body Stealers / I Am a Pod / Sleep No More / Thin Air*.   *Picnic* (55) Joshua Logan.   *Peyton Place* (57) Mark Robson [4 "Peyton Place" movies (1957-85)].   *The Long Hot Summer* (58) Martin Ritt.   *Return to Peyton Place* (61) José Ferrer.   *The Music Man* (62) Morton Da Costa. *To Kill a Mockingbird* (62) Robert Mulligan.   *The Last Picture Show* (71) Peter Bogdanovich.   *Carrie* (76) Brian De Palma.   *Raggedy Man* (81) Jack Fisk.   *Promised Land* (88) Michael Hoffman *aka Young Hearts*. *Sweet Hearts Dance* (88) Robert Greenwald.   *Texasville* (90) Peter Bogdanovich.

Smell Movie   *see*   **SMELLIE;**   *see also*   **WIDE SCREEN**

SMELLIE (Smell Movie)   There have been a few short-lived attempts at presenting films accompanied by smells, that is, films which would give out scents for the audience to smell. By and large, they have been failed attempts. The first film which may be properly called a "smellie" was the Swiss feature *Mein Traum / My Dream* (1940). It used a process known as "Odorated Talking Pictures" (O.T.P.) which, it was claimed, could capture and reproduce 4,000 different smells. The film premiered on October 10, 1940, in the Swiss Pavilion at the New York World's Fair and disappeared from circulation after its first showing when the film and its O.T.P. system were seized by the police who alleged a similar process already existed in the United States. Other "smellies" include: an Italian documentary on China, *La muraglia cinese / Behind the Green Wall* (1957) which used a process called AromaRama; the whodunit *Scent of Mystery* (1960), made in Smell-O-Vision and shown with the animated short *The Tale of the Old Whiff* (1960); and *Polyester* (1981), a satirical comedy released in Odorama — a ten-aroma scratch-and-sniff card which the audience was supposed to activate after seeing a number flash on the screen.

Mein Traum (Swiz 40) Dr. Rudolf Eger, Valerian Schmidely (started by Kurt Früh) *aka Mon rêve / My Dream* [presented with O.T.P. (Odorated Talking Pictures), a smell process]. *La muraglia cinese* (It 57) Carlo Lizzani *aka Behind the Great Wall* [released in AromaRama in the United States only]. *Scent of Mystery* (60) Jack Cardiff [presented in Smell-O-Vision] *aka Holiday in Spain* (61) without the Smell-O-Vision process. *The Tale of the Old Whiff* (60) Alan Zaslove [animated short presented in Smell-O-Vision]. *Polyester* (81) John Waters [released in Odorama, a "scratch-and-sniff" card].

Smoker　*see*　**HARD-CORE PORNO FILM**

Sneak　*see*　**RELEASE**

Snuff Movie　*see*　**GORE FILM**

Soap, Soaper　*see*　**SOAP OPERA**

SOAP OPERA (Continuous Serial, Daytime Drama, Daytime Serial Drama, Soap, Soaper, Sudser)　The term soap opera was applied to daytime serials begun on the radio in the late 1920s and early 1930s. Since soap manufacturers mainly sponsored the programs, the label stuck. Television adopted its format in the 1950s, and ever since soap operas on the small screen have been highly successful and very profitable for the television networks. The term, in its primary sense, applies to daytime serials which are broadcast in the afternoon on a five-day-a-week basis for 52 weeks of the year. Soap operas are a kind of dramatic (or rather melodramatic) entertainment totally geared to a female audience, which supposedly relishes the intricacy of its multiple plot lines made of family and love tangles, marriages, divorces, deceptions and betrayals. When they are successful, soap operas are extremely long (individual segments have evolved from 15 minutes to half-an-hour to one hour in length, including commercials), open-ended shows that span decades in their running. *Search for Tomorrow*, the longest running soap opera to date, has been on the air since 1951. Purists of the form would exclude from the genre prime-time serials (*Dallas, Dynasty*), alleging they do not fit the format. Prime-time serials have a quicker pace, are broadcast on an average of only once a week, address themselves to a larger audience (not just to women) and, generally speaking, are more lavishly produced. The term has also been extended to include those evening serials which resemble the daytime soap operas.

Finally, the term soap opera or soaper has also been used to categorize films which clearly are of a sentimental nature or exhibit a penchant for romance, suffering and self-denial, have well-characterized female heroines and which are also geared towards female viewers: what in other terms has been labelled as a woman's picture (q.v.). On the subject of soap opera, *see* Muriel G. Cantor and Suzanne Pingree, *The Soap Opera* (Beverly Hills, CA: Sage Publications, 1983) and Charles Derry, "Television Soap Opera: 'Incest, Bigamy, and Fatal Disease,'" in *American Television Genres* by Stuart M. Kaminsky (Chicago: Nelson-Hall, 1985), 85–110. *See also* **WEEPIE**.

Daytime Serials (Soap Operas): Search for Tomorrow (51-82) CBS; 82-NBC) Charles Irving, Ned Stark, Bob Schwartz. *General Hospital* (63-ABC). *As the World Turns* (56- CBS). *The Edge of Night* (56-75 CBS; 75-84 ABC) Allen Fristoe, John Sedwick, Richard Pepperman, Andrew Weyman, Joanne Goodheart [7,420 episodes]. *Coronation Street* (GB 60- ITV) *aka Florizel Street* [biweekly daytime serial]. *Days of Our Lives* (65- NBC). *Dark Shadows* (66-71 ABC) [1,000 episodes]. *All My Children* (70- ABC). *The Young and the Restless* (73- CBS).

Prime-Time Serials (Nighttime Soap Operas): Peyton Place (64-69 ABC) Walter Doniger, Ted Post [514 episodes]. *Mary Hartman! Mary Hartman!* (76-77 Syndicated) [325 episodes]. *Dallas* (78-91 CBS) [356 episodes]. *Dynasty* (80-89 ABC).

Films: Stella Dallas (37) King Vidor. *Dark Victory* (39) Edmund Goulding. *Now Voyager* (42) Irving Rapper. *Mr. Skeffington* (44) Vincent Sherman. *To Each His Own* (46) Mitchell Leisen. *Love Is a Many Splendored Thing* (55) Henry King. *Peyton Place* (57) Mark Robson. *A Summer Place* (59) Delmer Daves. *The Bramble Bush* (60) Daniel Petrie. *Splendor in the Grass* (61) Elia Kazan. *Doctors' Wives* (70) George Schaefer.

———**Telenovela** The Spanish equivalent of the soap opera and Latin America's most popular television form. *Telenovelas* are also popular with Spanish-speaking audiences in the United States. A major difference between them and their English counterparts is that the Spanish *telenovela* rarely runs for more than four hundred segments while successful American soap operas may run into thousands of episodes.[99]

Sobby, Sob-Story *see* **WEEPIE**

SOCCER FILM Soccer or Association football is played in most countries of the world, and it is the favorite sport of countless spectators. Many countries have excellent soccer teams and have at one time or another produced soccer films. Indeed, the nationality of soccer films is quite varied, and besides Europe soccer movies have been made in the Americas and Asia. As with all sports movies, the playing or the players have to be central to the story rather than peripheral to it—the protagonists watching a match, for instance, would not make the movie a soccer film.[100]

The Great Game (GB 30) Jack Raymond. *The Great Game* (GB 52) Maurice Elvey. *Bloomfield* (GB 69) Richard Harris *aka The Hero. Die Angst des Tormanns beim Elfemter* (G / Aus 71) Wim Wenders *aka The Anxiety of the Goalie at the Penalty Kick / The Goalie's Anxiety at the Penalty Block (Kick) / The Goal-Keeper's Fear of the Penalty. L'Arbitro* (It 73) Luigi Filippo D'Amico *aka The Referee / The Umpire. Fimpen* (Sw 73-74) Bo Widerberg *aka The Butt / Stubby. Furia española* (Sp 74) Francisco Bertriu. *Coup de tête* (F 78) Jean-Jacques Annaud *aka Berserk / Hothead. Gregory's Girl* (GB 80) Bill Forsyth. *Victory* (80) John Huston *aka Escape to Victory. Those Glory Glory Days* (GB 83 TV) Philip Saville. *The Young Giants* (83) Terrell Tannen. *À mort l'arbitre* (F 84) Jean-Pierre Mocky. *Hotshot* (86) Rich King. *Ultimo minuto* (It 87) Pupi Avati.

SOCIAL COMEDY The term social comedy has been applied to a wide variety of comedies. It has been used for sophisticated comedies as some of them deal with the frolics of high society. It has been applied to Frank Capra's comedies of the thirties and to those of other directors that deal with populist themes (hence, populist comedy is another analogous term).[101] In broader film criticism, it means any comedy that reveals a preoccupation for pinpointing incongruity or outdated local customs in terms of today's world; for instance, Pietro Germi's Sicilian comedies (*Divorzio all'italiana / Divorce, Italian Style* [1961]; *Sedotta e abbandonata / Seduced and Abandoned* [1963]). Also, the label social comedy is used for comedies which are critical of some sector of society and its institutions.

Populist comedies (q.v.) began in the thirties and propounded a very American, middle class, idealistic attitude of equality and kinship among all; they were humanistic in tone, even if they did not reflect the reality of life at the time. *See also* SOCIAL CONSCIOUSNESS FILM and SOPHISTICATED COMEDY.

Ruggles of Red Cup (35) Leo McCarey. *You Can't Take It with You* (38) Frank Capra. *Mr. Smith Goes to Washington* (39) Frank Capra. *Meet John Doe* (40) Frank Capra *aka John Doe, Dynamite. The Devil in Miss Jones* (41) Sam Wood. *Let the People Sing* (GB 42) John Baxter. *Good Sam* (48) Leo McCarey. *The Mating Season* (51) Mitchell Leisen. *Divorzio all'italiana* (It 61) Pietro Germi *aka Divorce, Italian Style. Sedotta e abbandonata / Séduite et abandonée* (It / F 63) Pietro Germi *aka Seduced and Abandoned. Claudine* (74) John Berry. *Fun with Dick and Jane* (77) Ted Kotcheff. *Betsy's Wedding* (90) Alan Alda. *Metropolitan* (90) Whit Stillman.

Social-Conscience Film   *see*   SOCIAL CONSCIOUSNESS FILM;   *see also*   WAR FILM: Socially Conscious War Films

SOCIAL CONSCIOUSNESS FILM (Exposé Film, Problem Film, Social-Conscience Film, Social Problem Film, Sociological Drama, Timely Film, Topical Film)   The social consciousness film seeks to attract attention to some problem, evil or injustice existing in the community by denouncing or exposing corruption and malfeasance in business and in higher circles such as government and social institutions. Thus, it seeks to make possible their eradication from the social apparatus. The genre has been defined variously as the social consciousness (or socially conscious) film, the topical film, social problem film, social exposé film, social protest film, social crusading film, social oriented film or message film. It is a genre characterized by its highly didactic approach, delivering its message in a style of critical social realism. Although the social problem film already existed in the silent era, it was during the Depression that it came to full bloom. The genre has adjusted itself to already existing forms, altering its subject matter to suit its intended social purpose: to denounce and expose abuse of power and trust by institutions, as well as denouncing gain by exploitation. Peter Roffman and Jim Purdy include a filmography of 237 films in *The Hollywood Social Problem Film* (Bloomington: Indiana University Press, 1981), pp. 331–51.

Cabin in the Cotton (32) Vincente Minnelli.   *I Am a Fugitive from a Chain Gang* (32) Mervyn LeRoy *aka I Am a Fugitive.*   *Wild Boys of the Road* (33) William A. Wellman *aka Dangerous Age.*   *Fury* (36) Fritz Lang *aka The Mob / Mob Rule.*   *Modern Times* (36) Charlie Chaplin.   *You Only Live Once* (37) Fritz Lang.   *Citizen Kane* (40) Orson Welles *aka American.*   *The Grapes of Wrath* (40) John Ford.   *Meet John Doe* (40) Frank Capra *aka John Doe, Dynamite.*   *Sullivan's Travels* (40) Preston Sturges.   *The Southerner* (45) Jean Renoir.   *Monsieur Verdoux* (47) Charlie Chaplin *aka A Comedy of Murders.*   *The Next Voice You Hear* (50) William Wellman.   *On the Waterfront* (54) Elia Kazan.   *The China Syndrome* (78) James Bridges.   *Norma Rae* (79) Martin Ritt.

Some categories of the social problem film can easily be integrated into other genres, e.g., the rehabilitation films are mentioned in the War film entry. Here only a few categories of the social consciousness film are cited.

——**Confession Films (Confession Tale)**   In the early thirties, the gangster film, the prison film, the shyster film and the woman's picture were good vehicles for the social problem film. Among the woman's pictures, a group of films which dealt with fallen women were appropriately labelled confession films. They showed the plight of the unmarried mother having to raise her child alone, the mistress-heroine sacrificing herself for the sake of her married lover's family, or they presented the downfall of a woman forced into prostitution in order to feed her family. *See also* **CONFESSION FILM**.

Safe in Hell (31) William A. Wellman *aka The Lost Lady.*   *Susan Lennox: Her Fall and Rise* (31) Robert Z. Leonard *aka The Rise of Helga.*   *Back Street* (32) John M. Stahl.   *Blonde Venus* (32) Josef von Sternberg.

——**Juvenile Delinquent Films**   Juvenile delinquency has often been the subject of the social consciousness film. Juvenile delinquent films have mostly presented the problems of the young, the slum conditions where they grew up and the reform schools they were sent to. *See* **JUVENILE DELINQUENCY FILM**.

Dead End (37) William Wyler.   *They Made Me a Criminal* (39) Busby Berkeley.   *Knock on Any Door* (49) Nicholas Ray.   *Rebel without a Cause* (55) Nicholas Ray.

——**Populist Films**   Believing in the common people as the basis for a righteous society, these films attack individuals that abuse the system and erode institutions. They denounce the tycoons and the big capitalists that enrich their coffers at the expense of others. They extol country as opposed to city life. Frank Capra is one of the major exponents of the populist film.

The Crowd (28) King Vidor.   *American Madness* (32) Frank Capra.   *Heroes for Sale* (33) William A. Wellman.   *The Power and the Glory* (33) William K. Howard *aka Power and Glory.*   *The Working Man* (33) John G. Adolfi.   *A Modern Hero* (34) G. B. Pabst.   *Our Daily Bread* (34) King Vidor *aka The Miracle of Life.*   *Mr. Deed Goes to Town* (36) Frank Capra.   *One Hundred Men and a Girl* (37) Henry Koster.   *It's a Wonderful Life* (46) Frank Capra.

——**Racially Conscious Films**   They expose the discrimination directed at some minority ethnic groups — especially blacks, Jews, Native Americans and Chicanos — in the United States and in other countries as well.

Bordertown (35) Archie Mayo.   *Gentleman's Agreement* (47) Elia Kazan. *Intruder in the Dust* (49) Clarence Brown.   *Lost Boundaries* (49) Alfred L. Werker.   *Pinky* (49) Elia Kazan.   *The Jackie Robinson Story* (50) Alfred E. Green.   *The Well* (51) Leo Popkin.   *Salt of the Earth* (53) Herbert Biberman.   *Imitation of Life* (59) Douglas Sirk.

——**Shyster Films**   The shyster was a popular figure in films of the thirties, and he was frequently exposed as a corrupt individual in social consciousness films. *See also* separate entry for **SHYSTER FILM.**

Five Star Final (31) Mervyn LeRoy.   *The Dark Horse* (32) Alfred E. Green.   *Lawyer Man* (32) William Dieterle.   *The Mouthpiece* (32) James Flood, Elliott Nugent.

Social Crusading Film   *see*   **SOCIAL CONSCIOUSNESS FILM**

Social Disease Film   *see*   **VICE FILM**

SOCIAL DRAMA   A film whose content has general social import either by focussing on a particular question or theme or by dramatizing the lives of socially relevant individuals of the past or present.

The Life of Emile Zola (37) William Dieterle *aka Emile Zola*.   *Viva Zapata!* (52) Elia Kazan.   *One Potato, Two Potato* (64) Larry Peerce.   *Dog Day Afternoon* (75) Sidney Lumet.

Social Exposé Film   *see*   **SOCIAL CONSCIOUSNESS FILM**

Social Extrapolation Film   *see*   **SCIENCE FICTION FILM: Political Extrapolation Films**

SOCIAL ISSUE FILM   The term includes any film (short or feature length, factual or fictional) that focusses on some current social problem. By drawing attention to and informing of social matters, the films seek to arouse public awareness of the issues they illustrate. The social issue film covers a very broad range of topics. For a guide to such films, *see Reel Change,* ed. by Patricia Peyton (San Francisco, CA: The Film Fund, 1979).

Social Oriented Film, Social-Problem Film, Social Protest Film   *see*   **SOCIAL CONSCIOUSNESS FILM**

Social Realism   *see*   **SOCIAL REALIST FILM**

SOCIAL REALIST FILM (Social Realism)   A general term applied to films from diverse genres and film movements which examine, with a realistic approach, the imperfect social conditions having an effect on the common man in contemporary society. The broad categorization of social realism includes, for example, the social consciousness film (q.v.), the influential Italian neorealist film of the post–Second World War period (q.v.), the socialist-realist films of Communist countries (q.v.), and the British kitchen-sink films of the late 1950s and early 1960s (q.v.).

Socialist Film, Socialist Realism *see* **SOCIALIST-REALIST FILM**

SOCIALIST-REALIST FILM (Socialist Film, Socialist Realism)   With the consolidation of the Stalinist regime in the Soviet Union, all aesthetic, avant-garde, stylized trends in the arts were labelled "formalist" and, as such, at first totally discouraged and later proscribed and banned. In their place, a simplified, easily understood, mass-oriented style of filmmaking was officially endorsed. It became known as socialist realism. Socialist realism rejected a naturalistic approach to subject matter (naturalism, which tends to show the sordid side of life, is potentially subversive and thus contrary to party line) and propounded instead a Communist utopia. It favored the use of professional actors, the psychological portrayal of individuals, the cult of the personality hero and the use of editing continuity as opposed to montage. Socialist realism was to become an ossified, stereotyped cinema built to formula with abundant clichés and happy endings. It presented society and reality not as they truly were, but as they ought to be. It endured until Stalin's death in 1953 and its sphere of influence embraced the Eastern block and leftists the world over.
Putyovka v zhizn (USSR 31) Nikolai Ekk *aka A Pass to Life / Road to Life.* *Vstrechnyi* (USSR 32) Sergei Yutkevich, Friedrich Ermler *aka Counterplan.*   *Chapaev* (USSR 34) Georgi Vasiliev, Sergei Vasiliev, Yuri Muzykant (co-director) *aka Chapayev.*   *Yunost' Maksima* (USSR 34) Grigori Kozintsev, Leonid Trauberg *aka The Youth of Maxim* [first film in the "Maxim" trilogy]. *Krestyanye* (USSR 35) Friedrich Ermler *aka Peasants.*   *Deputat Baltik* (USSR 37) Josif Heifits, Alexander Zarkhi *aka Baltic Deputy.*   *Lenin v oktyabre* (USSR 37) Mickhail Romm, Dimitri Vasiliev *aka Lenin in October.* *Vozvrashchenie Maksima* (USSR 37) Grigori Kozintsev, Leonid Trauberg *aka The Return of Maxim* [second film in the "Maxim" trilogy].   *Chelovek s ruzholm* (USSR 38) Sergeii Yutkevich *aka The Man with a Gun.*   *Velikii grazhdanin* (USSR 38-39) Friedrich Ermler *aka A Great Citizen* [in 2 parts]. *Vyborgskaya storona* (USSR 39) Grigori Kozintsev, Leonid Trauberg *aka The Vyborg Side* [third film in the "Maxim" trilogy].   *Daleko ot Moskvi* (USSR 50) Alexander Stolper *aka Far from Moscow.*   *Kavalier Zolotoy Zvezdy* (USSR 50) Semion Babayevsky *aka The Dream of the Cossack.*

Socially Conscious Film *see* **SOCIAL CONSCIOUSNESS FILM**

Socially Conscious War Films *see* **WAR FILM**

Sociological Documentary *see* **DOCUMENTARY**

Sociological Drama *see* **SOCIAL CONSCIOUSNESS FILM**

Soft-Action Film, Softcore, Soft-Core Feature, Softcore Film, Soft-Core Porno Film *see* **SOFT-CORE SEX-EXPLOITATION FILM**

SOFT-CORE SEX-EXPLOITATION FILM (Dirty Movie, R-Rated Sexploitation Film, Simulated Film, Soft-Action Film, Softcore, Soft-Core Feature, Softcore Film, Soft-Core Porno Film, Softcore Sexploitation Movie, Soft-Porn Film, Soft Porno Film)   The story of the soft-core film in the sixties is one of a continuous testing ground between the makers of sex-exploitation films and the censors. Nudity and love-making were introduced into the pictures gradually. Indeed, the path of the soft-core movie is a curious one of slow progression as to the amount of nudity shown and how graphic the love-making that could be depicted. As a result of this long-term policy, at first only partial nudity was attempted and in love-making the man remained with his trousers or underwear on and the woman bare-breasted but with her panties on; appropriate panting sounds, sighs and words of encouragement accompanied the proceedings. In time, both partners were presented naked although it was still a while before the female pubic area and the male genitalia were shown. Foreplay grew more venturesome and from being limited initially to copious massaging, squeezing and sucking of breasts, progressed to hints of fellatio and cunnilingus. The sex action was strictly codified and most films included scenes of female masturbation, heterosexual love-making, a lesbian scene and an orgy sequence. Rape, wife swapping, promiscuity and nymphomania were favorite topics. The era of on-screen sex experimentation ended in the late sixties when a clear division was established between soft-core (simulated sex) and hard-core (explicit sex). Today, the soft-core porno film may include any sexual activity short of actual penetration (vaginal, oral or anal) and ejaculation which are the preserve of hard-core films. The soft-core film continues to fulfill the voyeuristic needs of its audience and in the United States this type of film is usually R-rated. If very obvious in its sexuality, it may garner an X-rating.

Fanny Hill (Sw 68) Mac Ahlberg *aka The Swedish Fanny Hill.   Vixen* (68) Russ Meyer *aka Russ Meyer's Vixen.   Cherry, Harry & Raquel* (69) Russ Meyer *aka Russ Meyer's Cherry, Harry & Raquel / Three Ways to Love. Christa / Swedish Fly Girls* (US / Den 69) Jack O'Connell.   *The Fabulous Bastard from Chicago* (69) Greg Corarito *aka The Bastard Wench from Chicago / The Chicago Kid / The Fabulous Kid from Chicago / The Man from Chicago.   Monique* (GB 69) John Brown.   *Threesome* (US / Den 69) Lee Beale (Brandon Chase) *aka Ursula.   Italian Stallion* (70) Morton Lewis *aka A Party at Kitty and Studs.   The Lickerish Quartet / Esotika Erotika Psicotika* (US / G / It 70) Radley Metzger *aka Hide and Seek / Stanza 315, ufficio sesso.   Love Me Like I Do* (70) J. Van Hearn.   *Love Thy Neighbor and His Wife* (70) B. Ron Elliott.   *Wild Honey* (70) Don Edmonds.   *The Orgy Box* (71) Ron Garcia *aka The Toy Box.   Adam & Nicole* (GB 73) Trevor Wren *aka Adam & Eve / Erotic Inferno / The Naked Key.   Liebesjagd durch 7 Betten* (G 73) Hans Billian *aka I Like Girls Who Do / Oh Lucky Boy!   A Man with a Maid* (Sw 73) Vernon P. Becker *aka The Groove Room / Tickled Pink / Teenage Tickle Girls / Vernon P. Becker's A Man with a Maid / What the Swedish Butler Saw.   Sex Play* (GB 74) Jack Arnold *aka Games Girls Play.   The Switch* (74) Joe Sarno.   *The Hardy Girls* (75) Allen Ruskin.   *Little Girl Big Tease* (75) Roberto Mitrotti.   *Vanessa* (G 75) Hubert Frank.   *Come Play with Me* (GB 77) George Harrison Marks.   *Let's Get Laid!* (GB 77) James Kenelm Clarke.   *Centrespread* (Aust 80) Tony Paterson *aka Behind the Centrespread.   Champagne for Breakfast* (80) Chris

Warfield *aka Boss Lady / Talk Naughty to Me*. **Erotica** (GB 80) Brian Smedley-Aston *aka Paul Raymond's Erotica*. **Nanà** (It / US 81) Dan Wolman. **R.S.V.P.** (84) Lem Amero.

Sex films may operate within the framework of any genre and have done so often enough. Keeping this in mind, it is not difficult to recognize the soft-core product in any guise in which it may appear. There have been soft-core private eye pictures, soft-core horror movies, soft-core Westerns, soft-core musicals. As a guideline, a few films are listed below with an indication of the category or subgenre into which they fall. The following categories, however, fit quite comfortably in the soft-core medium: nurse films, soft-core teenpix and costume pictures.

———**Costume Sexers**   They are either adaptations from literary classics and fairy tales or soft-core interpretations of the lives and loves of legendary heroes and cavaliers.

Fanny Hill Meets Lady Chatterly (67) Barry Mahon, George Matsui. **The Ribald Tales of Robin Hood** (69) Richard Kanter *aka The Affairs of Robin Hood / The Intimate Diary of Robin Hood and His Merry Maids / Robin Hood*. **The Secret Sex Lives of Romeo and Juliet** (69) A. P. Stootsberry *aka The Secret Love Lives of Romeo and Juliet / The Sex Life of Romeo and Juliet*. **The Joys of Jezabel** (70) A. P. Stootsberry *aka The Joy of Jesabelle / Jezebel*. **Pinocchio** (70) Corey Allen *aka The Erotic Adventures of Pinocchio*. **The Amorous Adventures of D. Quixote and Sancho Panza** (75) Raphael Nussbaum *aka The Amorous Adventures of Superknight / Sancho Panza / Sex Encounters of a Close Kind / Superknight / When She Was a Knightly Affair*. **The Notorious Cleopatra** (70) A. P. Stootsberry. **Siegfried und das sagenhafte Liebesleben der Nibelungen / The Long Swift Sword of Siegfried** (G / US 70) Adrian Hoven (US v.: David F. Friedman) *aka The Erotic Adventures of Siegfried / The Terrible Quick Sword of Siegfried*. **Cinderella** (76) Michael Pataki *aka The Other Cinderella*. **Fanny Hill** (GB 83) Gerry O'Hara *aka John Cleland's Fanny Hill "Memoirs of a Woman of Pleasure."*

———**De Sade (De Sade Adaptations, Sadean Films)**   Comte Donatien Alphonse François, Marquis de Sade (1740–1814), famous French philosopher and libertine, whose name gave us the term sadism and its derivatives, has inspired many films. His works have also inspired repeated loose film adaptations of a pornographic nature. The great 18th century sensualist exerts an enduring fascination on porno filmmakers and although no masterpiece based on his works has appeared so far, the Sadian film merits an entry of its own.

De Sade / Das ausschweifende Leben des Marquis de Sade (US / G 69) Cy Endfield, Roger Corman (uncredited) *aka Der Marquis de Sade*. **I, Marquis de Sade** (67) Richard Hilliard *aka I, the Marquis*. **Jag-en marki / Jag en markis — med uppdrag att älska** (Den / Sw 67) Mac Ahlberg *aka I, a Nobleman / The Reluctant Saint*. **Marquis de Sade, Justine / Justine: Le disavventure della virtù** (G / It 68) Jesús Franco *aka Justine / Justine and Juliet*. **Eugénie / Die Jungfrau und die Peitsche** (Lux / G 69) Jess Franco *aka De Sade 70 / Eugenie / Eugenie . . . The Story of Her Journey into Perversion / Philosophy* *in the Boudoir. La Philosophie dans le Boudoir* (F 69) Jacques Scandelari *aka Beyond Love and Evil. Justine de Sade / Justine* (Can / F / It 70) Claude Pierson [rel. in 72] *aka The Violation of Justine. Justine och Juliette* (Sw 74) Bert Torn (Mac Ahlberg) *aka Justine Virtuous. Justine* (GB 76) Stewart Mackinnon *aka Justine by the Marquis de Sade. Cruel Passion* (GB 77) Chris Boger *aka Justine / De Sade's Justine / Marquis De Sade's Justine.*

——**Emmanuelle**   After the initial commercial success of Just Jaeckin's *Emmanuelle* (1973), the name, sometimes spelled "Emanuelle," caught on and has been used in numerous films or spin-offs creating a kind of soft-core subgenre. The film starred Sylvia Kristel, a former Dutch porno actress with a lush figure and elegant demeanor, in exotic surroundings actively seeking a life of pleasure and dedicated to the discovery of new sex thrills. It was a slick production, excellently photographed; afterwards, the soft-core porno market was never the same—glamor had entered the sexploitation business. Sylvia Kristel starred in two follow-ups, and then dropped the series only to reappear in *Emmanuelle IV* (1984). Other actresses have taken up the role of Emmanuelle / Emanuelle; among them, the one who has played the character most consistently is the beautiful, dark-skinned Laura Gemser.

  Emmanuelle (F / Thai 73) Just Jaeckin. *Emanuelle e Françoise (le sorelline)* (It 75) Joe D'Amato *aka Blood Vengeance / Emanuelle and Francoise / Françoise and Emmanuelle / The Little Sisters. Emmanuelle 2 / Emmanuelle l'antivergine* (F / It 75) François Giacobetti *aka L'antivergine / Emmanuelle II L'antivierge / Emmanuelle seconde / Emmanuelle—The Joys of a Woman. Emanuelle gialla* (It 76) Albert Thomas *aka Il mondo dei sensi di Emy Wong—Yellow Emanuelle / Yellow Emanuelle. Emanuelle in America* (It 76) Joe D'Amato. *Emanuelle nera* (It 76) Albert Thomas *aka Black Emanuelle / Emanuelle's Holiday. Emanuelle: perchè violenza alle donne?* (It 77) Joe D'Amato *aka Confessions of Emanuelle. Goodbye Emmanuelle* (F 77) François Leterrier [third in the series]. *Carry On Emmanuelle* (GB 78) Gerald Thomas. *Emmanuelle IV* (F 84) Francis Giacobetti *aka Emmanuelle 4. Emmanuelle 5* (F 85) Walerian Borowczyk.

——**Nazi-Sadist Pictures**   A type of anti–Nazi films which emerged in Italy in the mid-1970s. They mix strong doses of sex with violence and their trademark is Nazi uniforms and the S.S. paraphernalia of the Third Reich. If Visconti's *La caduta degli dei / The Damned* (1969) and Cavani's *Il portiere di notte / The Night Porter* (1973) may be cited as forerunners, the cycle owes its inspiration to and was set in motion by Giovanni Tinto Brass's *Salon Kitty* (1975).

  La caduta degli dei / Götterdämmerung (Swiz / It / G 69) Luchino Visconti *aka The Damned / Die Verdammten. Ilsa: She Wolf of the SS* (US / Can 73) Don Edmonds. *Il portiere di notte / The Night Porter* (It / US 73) Liliana Cavani. *Salon Kitty* (It / G / F 75) Giovanni Tinto Brass *aka Madame Kitty. Casa privata per le SS.* (It / G 76) Jordan B. Matthews (Bruno Mattei) *aka Casa privata per le Schultz Staffen / S. S. Girls. Le lunghe notti della Gestapo* (It 76) Fabio De Agostini *aka The Red Nights of the Gestapo. L'ultima orgia del Terzo Reich* (It 76) Cesare Canevari *aka*

The Gestapo's Last Orgy. **SS lager 5 – l'inferno delle donne** (It / Sp 76) Sergio Garrone *aka Lager SS5 – L'inferno delle donne / Lager SSAdis Kastrat Kommandatur / S.S. Experiment Camp.* **Train spécial pour S.S.** (F / Sp 76) James Gartner (Alain Payet). **Bordel SS** (F 77) José Benazéraf. *Nathalie rescapée de l'enfer* (F 77) James Gartner.

——**Nurse Films**   Women in uniform have always had an erotic appeal. Boarding-school girls in school uniform, prison wardresses, nuns, stewardesses, teachers and, naturally, nurses have often caught the imagination of the porno filmmakers as suitable candidates for sex films. The nurse film is perhaps the most common among soft-core films exploiting the listed possibilities.

The Student Nurses (70) Stephanie Rothman [5 films (1970-74) in the "Nurses" series]. *Private Duty Nurses* (71) George Armitage [second "Nurses" film]. *Night Call Nurses* (72) Jonathan Kaplan [third "Nurses" film]. *The Young Nurses* (73) Clinton Kimbrough *aka Emergency Nurses / Games That Nurses Play* [fourth "Nurses" film]. *Tender Loving Care* (73) Don Edmonds. *Candy Stripe Nurses* (74) Allan Holleb [fifth "Nurses" film]. *L'infermiera* (It 75) Nello Rossati *aka The Sensuous Nurse / I Will If You Will.* *What's Up Nurse* (GB 77) Derek Ford.

——**Renaissance Erotic Trend**   Sex films set in the Renaissance originated in Italy with Pier Paolo Pasolini's *Il Decamerone* (1970). Soon there was a profusion of imitators, but the trend was short-lived. Porno filmmakers still sporadically use an historical setting for their soft-core porno movies.

Il Decamerone / Le Décameron / Decameron (It / F / G 70) Pier Paolo Pasolini *aka The Decameron.* *Addio, fratello crudele* (It 71) Giuseppe Patroni Griffi *aka 'Tis a Pity She's a Whore.* *I Racconti di Canterbury / Les Contes de Canterbury / The Canterbury Tales* (It / F / GB 71) Pier Paolo Pasolini. *La bella Antonia, prima monica e poi dimonia* (It 72) Mariano Laurenti *aka Naughty Nun.* *Il Decameron proibito* (It 72) Carlo Infascelli *aka Decamerone proibito – le altre novelle / Forbidden Decameron.* *Metti lo diavolo tuo ne lo mio inferno* (It 72) Bitto Albertini *aka Put Your Devil into My Hell.* *Racconti proibiti di nulla vestiti* (It 73) Brunello Rondi *aka Master of Love.* *Lucrezia giovane* (It 74) André Colbert (Luciano Ercoli).

——**Report Films**   An almost exclusively German brand of sex film which uses the reportage approach in an episode film format. The sketches or reports take the form of an inquest into the sexual mores of lifeguards, secretaries, newly-weds and the like. Some (like the housewives reports and the schoolgirls reports) go into series of their own.

Schulmädchen-Report (G 70) Ernst Hofbauer *aka Junior Kinsey* [13 films in the series up to 1980]. *Erotik im Beruf – was jeder Personalchef gern Verschweight* (G 71) Ernst Hofbauer *aka Sex in the Office.* *Hausfrauenreport – unglaublich, aber wahr!* (G 71) Eberhard Schröder *aka The Housewives Report / On the Side.* *Liebesspiele junger Mädchen-muntere Pärchen packen aus* (G 72) F. J. Gottlieb *aka After School Girls / Hungry for Sex.* *Die Stewardessen* (G 72) Michael Thomas *aka The Naked Stewardesses / The Stewardesses Report / The Swinging Stewardesses / The Swingin' Stewardesses / The Young Seducers.* *Bademeister-Report* (G 73) Guy (Sergio) Casstner *aka Hot and Sexy / Lifeguard's Report.*

——**Sex Film Series**   Soft-core sexploitation films have often inspired film series. These are usually centered around ribald or comic figures as in, for instance, the "Sexy Susan" German/Austrian series, the Danish Palladium Studio "Bedside" series or the "Confessions" series from Great Britain. Other sex film series concentrate on tough law-enforcement characters or sadistic types.

Susanne—die Wirtin von der Lahn (Aus / It / Hung 67) François Legrand (Franz Antel) *aka The Sweet Sins of Sexy Susan* [6 films (1967-73) in the "Frau Wirtin" series directed by Franz Antel]. *Ginger* (70) Don Schain [followed by *The Abductors* (72) and *Girls Are for Loving* (73) also by Don Schain]. *Mazurka på sengekanten* (Den 70) John Hilbard *aka Bedroom Magic / Bedroom Mazurka / Bedside Bedroom / Bedside Mazurka*. *Rektor på sengekanten* (Den 72) John Hilbard *aka Bedside Head / Bedside Headmaster / Danish Bed and Board*. *Confessions of a Window Cleaner* (GB 74) Val Guest [4 films (1974-77) in the series]. *Confessions of a Pop Performer* (GB 75) Norman Cohen [followed by *Confessions of a Driving Instructor* (GB 76) and *Confessions from a Holiday Camp* (GB 77) also by Cohen].

——**Soft-Core Teenpix**   These films are full of youngsters, coeds, college girls and teenagers having a good time on the beach, at college, riding their bikes and in cars or just generally playing around. The films offer, for the most part, harmless nudity and light-handed sex in a comedy setting.

The Cheerleaders (73) Paul Glicker. *Hollywood High* (76) Patrick Wright. *Slumber Party '57* (76) William A. Levey. *Hollywood High Part II* (81) Caruth C. Byrd, Lee Thomburg. *One Night Only* (Can 83-84) Timothy Bond [rel. on pay TV in 86] *aka For One Night . . . Only / New Year's Eve / Special Treatment*. *Preppies* (83) Chuck Vincent. *Thinkin' Big* (86) S. F. Browbrigg.

——**Variations and Permutations of the Soft-Core Porno Movie—Sub-genres**

Action-Adventure Picture: *Ilsa the Tigress of Siberia / Ilsa la tigresse de Sibéria* (Can 77) Jean-Lafleur *aka Ilsa, la tigresse du goulag / Ilsa III / The Tigress*. Blaxploitation: *Black Shampoo* (76) Greydon Clark. Boxing Picture: *Below the Belt* (71) Bethel Buckalew. Comedy: *How to Succeed with Sex* (69) Bert I. Gordon *aka How to Succeed with the Opposite Sex / Tom Cat*. Farce: *Not Now Darling* (GB 71) Ray Cooney, David Croft. Gangster Picture: *The Bang Bang Gang* (70) Van Guylder *aka The Bang Bang Girls / The Gun Girls / Kiss Kiss Bang Bang*. Horror Film: *The Velvet Vampire* (71) Stephanie Rothman *aka Blood Lover / Cemetery Girls / The Devil Is a Woman / Through the Looking Glass / The Walking Hour*. Horror Spoof: *Sorority Babes in the Slimeball Bowl-o-Rama* (87) David DeCocteau *aka The Imp*. Jungle Film: *Trader Hornee* (70) Tsanusdi. Musical: *The First Nude Musical* (75) Mark Haggard, Bruce Kimmel. Private Detective Film: *Adventures of a Private Eye* (GB 77) Stanley Long. Pseudodocumentary: *Is There Sex After Death* (71) Jean Abel, Alan Abel. Roman Epic: *The Arena* (US / It 73) Steve Carver *aka Naked Warriors*. Satire: *Loving and Laughing / Y'a plus de trous à percé* (Can 70) J. Johnsone (John Sone) *aka The Hippie Girls / The Importance of Being Sexy / You Know It Ain't Easy*. Science Fiction Fantasy: *Flesh Gordon* (72) Michael Benveniste,

Howard Ziehm.   Sex-Thriller: *Clinic Xclusive* (GB 71) Don Chaffey *aka Sex Clinic.*   Sports Picture: *Après ski* (Can 69-70) Roger Cardinal *aka Sex in the Snow / Sex on Skies / Snowballin' / Winter Games.*   Spy Spoof: *The Man from O.R.G.Y.* (70) James A. Hill *aka The Real Gone Girls.*   Western: *The Scavengers* (69) R. L. Frost *aka The Grabbers* (X-rated version).   Woman's Prison Movie: *Caged Heat* (74) Jonathan Demme *aka Renegade Girls.*

Soft-Core Teenpix, Soft-Porn Film, Soft Porno Film   *see*   SOFT-CORE SEX-EXPLOITATION FILM

Song-and-Dance Film, Songfest Film   *see*   MUSICAL

SOPHISTICATED COMEDY (High Comedy)   It deals with the quirks, manners and sometimes eccentric behavior of the very rich, the socialites and, generally speaking, with talented, debonair people. The dialogue in these comedies is urbane and witty; in short, the comedy tries to be worldly and sophisticated. They are, at times, referred to as social comedies and many deal with situations involving marriage and romance. The genre began early in the twenties and it is still popular with some audiences. *See also* **Marriage Comedies** under **SEX COMEDY.**
Trouble in Paradise (32) Ernst Lubitsch. *Design for Living* (33) Ernst Lubitsch. *Dinner at Eight* (33) George Cukor. *Holiday* (38) George Cukor *aka Free to Live / Unconventional Linda. The Talk of the Town* (42) George Stevens. *Indiscreet* (GB / US 58) Stanley Donen. *The Facts of Life* (60) Melvin Frank. *Breakfast at Tiffany's* (61) Blake Edwards.

Sophisticated Marital Farce   *see*   **SEX COMEDY: Marriage Comedies**

Sound Comedy   *see*   COMEDY

SOUND FILM (Talker, Talkie, Talking Picture)   The development of sound film was a slow process of experimentation. As far back as 1889, W. K. Laurie Dickson, Thomas Edison's assistant, demonstrated his Kinetophonograph (or Kinetophone) which consisted of a cylinder-gramophone linked to Edison's Kinetoscope viewing machine. (The Kinetophonograph demonstration is not authenticated.) It was the start of many attempts in different countries to develop a system that would integrate sound to film in a satisfactory manner. Berlin saw in September 1896 the first showing of sound films in front of a paying audience. In Paris, the first showing of talking pictures took place in June 1900. Sporadic presentations of sound and talking pictures, nonfictional and dramatic, continued to be made in different countries. In August 1926, the premiere of the silent film *Don Juan* took place in New York. A major dramatic work, it had synchronized musical score and sound effects. Popular acceptance of talking pictures, however, came only with the huge success of *The Jazz Singer*, a part-talkie; on October 6, 1927, at the Warner Theatre on Broadway, audiences cheered Al Jolson on hearing his first few, prophetic words, by now of historical interest: "Wait a minute, wait a minute. You ain't heard nothin' yet!..." The film has only two talking sequences. Afterwards came *Lights of New*

York, released in July 1928, which was the first all-talking feature. These two pictures use the Vitaphone synchronized sound system or sound-on-disc system perfected by Bell Telephone Laboratories and adopted by Warner Bros. This system proved to be less effective than the sound-on-film system (optical sound and later, magnetic sound) which eventually took over as the standard system used the world over in pictures. Silent films struggled along for a while, but they had to give way to the impact of the spoken and sung word. Talking pictures revolutionized the film industry, and by 1930 the talkies had virtually taken over in most countries. The sound era is usually dated from either 1927 or 1929. For historical information on the evolution of sound and talking pictures, *see* Harry M. Geduld, *The Birth of the Talkies* (Bloomington: Indiana University Press, 1975). The author includes an appendix (pp. 274–81) of sound feature films produced in Hollywood in 1929.

> *Don Juan* (26) Alan Crosland. *The Jazz Singer* (27) Alan Crosland [first feature-length part-talkie]. *Lights of New York* (28) Bryan Foy [first all-talking feature].

SOUNDIES   Soundies were musical shorts of three minutes' duration featuring jazz numbers or popular music with well- and lesser-known personalities that could be heard and viewed by putting a nickel in a jukebox equipped with a 24 by 18 inch plastic screen. They were first introduced to the public in Chicago in 1940 and spread to other cities. A reel-long program comprised eight soundies. Their popularity faded after World War II and the films ended up in the hands of collectors.

SOUTH SEAS PICTURE   The areas comprising the Indian and Pacific oceans have been favorite locales for the South Seas picture, especially the Polynesian islands of Hawaii and Tahiti, although most islands situated in the tropics (including the West Indies) have provided at one time or another the right setting for an exotic film.

Appealing mostly for their exoticism, the South Seas pictures have been shaped as adventure films, romances, musicals, interracial melodramas, disaster films and recently, as steamy sex films in the *Emmanuelle* mold. Films with a South Seas setting form a sizeable and variegated group.

> *Moana of the South Seas* (26) Robert J. Flaherty, Frances Hubbard Flaherty *aka Moana*. *White Shadows in the South Seas* (28) W. S. Van Dyke. *Tabu* (31) F. W. Murnau, Robert Flaherty. *The Bird of Paradise* (32) King Vidor. *We're Not Dressing* (34) Norman Taurog. *Mutiny on the Bounty* (35) Frank Lloyd. *Jungle Princess* (36) William Thiele. *Ebb Tide* (37) James Hogan. *The Hurricane* (37) John Ford. *Waikiki Wedding* (37) Frank Tuttle. *Her Jungle Love* (38) George Archainbaud. *Aloma of the South Seas* (41) Alfred Santell. *South Pacific* (58) Joshua Logan. *Mutiny on the Bounty* (62) Lewis Milestone, Carol Reed (plus George Seaton, Billy Wilder, Fred Zinneman). *Donovan's Reef* (63) John Ford. *Goodbye Emmanuelle* (F 77) François Leterrier. *The Bounty* (US / NZ / GB 83) Roger Donaldson *aka The Saga of HMS Bounty.*

Soviet Expressionism *see* **EXPRESSIVE-REALIST FILM**

Space Exploration Film, Space Film, Space Flight Film *see* **SCIENCE FICTION FILM: Space Travel Films**

Space Operas *see* **SCIENCE FICTION FILM**

Space-Time Movie *see* **NON-LINEAR FILM**

SPAGHETTI WESTERN (Continental Western, European Western, Italian Western, Italo-Western, Pesto Western) As early as 1907, European Westerns were being filmed in France, and there were also early Westerns made in Germany, but it was not until the early 1960s that the production of Westerns started in earnest in Europe. Italy, however, did not make its first feature-length Western until 1942; the film was called *Una signora dell'ouest* and was directed by Carlo Koch. In the early 1960s, a few German Westerns were very successful with German audiences. Quickly picking up the trend, Spain and Italy started producing Westerns. From 1963 on, Italian Westerns were made on a constant basis, and by 1969 the number of Spaghetti Westerns had reached several hundred, had conquered world markets, achieved genre status of their own as a new type of Western and influenced the future of Hollywood Westerns. Then it was all over; in the early 1970s, the wave of Italian Westerns started to wane.

The label Spaghetti Western, used first by American critics in a derogatory sense, is associated, naturally, with Italian-made Westerns; the fact is, though, that the majority of Italian Westerns are coproductions filmed in Spain with one or more countries as copartners in the production, sometimes with a non–Italian director. These coproducing countries are mainly Spain, Germany and France.[102]

At least twenty-five Westerns had been made by Italy before the appearance of Sergio Leone's *Per un pugno di dollari / A Fistful of Dollars* (1964), an unauthorized adaptation of Akira Kurosawa's *Yojimbo* (1961). The film, besides making its director famous and catapulting to instant renown a hitherto not very well-known American actor, Clint Eastwood, also made cinematic history and gave impetus to the Italian Western.

Among the many distinct features attributed to the Italian Western, the most remarkable is the strong individualization of the characters. This is seen in the way they dress (Clint Eastwood wearing a poncho and an almost permanent cigarillo in his mouth) or carry their guns, in themselves an interesting array of weaponry seldom seen in the Hollywood Westerns that predated the Spaghetti Western. These European Westerns are full of romantic characters, haggard and unkempt. Frequent use is made of bounty hunters, hired guns, Mexicans and individuals of assorted nationalities, all thrown together in a western landscape that frequently represents the Southwest or Mexico. Italian Westerns are also distinguished by the dramatic function given to their musical themes and for their portrayal of frontier brutality at its ugliest: a characteristic which later Italian filmmakers tried to rectify by injecting a humorous, playful note into the violence, e.g., *Lo chiamavano Trinità...* / *They Call Me Trinity* (1970) and *...Più forte, ragazzi* / *All the Way Boys* (1972). Massimo Moscati's *Western all'italiana. Il Timone*, no. 81-82 (Milano: Pan, 1978), includes a filmography of 407 Spaghetti Westerns. Thomas Weisser's *Spaghetti Westerns—the Good, the Bad and the Violent* (Jefferson, NC: McFarland, 1992) includes a filmography of 558 Spaghetti Westerns.

Una Signora dell'Ovest (It 42) Carlo Koch [first feature-length Italian Western]. *Minnesota Clay* / *L'homme du Minnesota* (It / Sp / F 64) Sergio Corbucci. *Per un pugno di dollari* / *Por un puñado de dólares* / *Für eine Handvoll Dollars* (It / Sp / G 64) Bob Robertson (Sergio Leone) *aka A Fistful of Dollars* / *Il magnifico straniero* / *Nur eine kam zurück*. *Django* / *Dyango* (It / Sp 65) Sergio Corbucci. *Per qualche dollaro in più* / *La muerte tenía un precio* / *Für ein paar Dollar mehr* (It / Sp / G 65) Sergio Leone *aka For a Few Dollars More* / *For Some Dollars More*. *7 Pistole per i MacGregor* / *Siete pistolas para los MacGregor* (It / Sp 65) Frank Garfield (Franco Giraldi) *aka Seven Guns for the MacGregors*. *Il buono, il brutto, il cattivo* / *El bueno, el feo y el malo* (It / Sp 66) Sergio Leone *aka The Good, the Bad and the Ugly* / *Two Magnificent Rogues*. *Pecos è qui: prega e muori* / *Jonny Madoc rechnet ab* (It / G 66) Maurice A. Bright (Maurizio Lucidi) *aka Due once di piombo*. *Quien sabe?* (It 66) Damiano Damiani *aka A Bullet for the General* / *El Chuncho*. *La resa dei conti* / *Colorado* (It / Sp 66) Sergio Sollima *aka The Big Gundown* / *El halcón y la presa*. *Al di là della legge* / *Die letzte Rechnung zahlst du selbst* (It / G 67) Giorgio Stegani *aka Beyond the Law* / *The Outsider*. *Da uomo a uomo* (It 67) Giulio Petroni *aka Death Rides a Horse*. *Dio perdona ... io no!* / *Tú perdonas ... yo no* (It / Sp 67) Giuseppe Colizzi *aka Blood River* / *God Forgives—I Don't*. *Il mercenario* / *Salario para matar* (It / Sp 68) Sergio Corbucci *aka The Mercenary* / *A Professional Gun*. *Once Upon a Time in the West* / *C'era una volta il West* (US / It 68) Sergio Leone *aka Una volta nel Far West*. *I quattro dell'Ave Maria* (It 68) Giuseppe Colizzi *aka Ace High* / *Asso piglia tutto* / *Four from Ave Maria* / *Revenge in El Paso*. *Joe ... cercati un posto per morire!* (It 68) Anthony Ascott (Giuliano Carmineo) *aka Find a Place to Die*. *Ognuno per sè* / *Das Gold von Sam Cooper* (It / G 68) Giorgio Capitani *aka Each Man for Himself* / *The Ruthless Four* / *Sam Cooper's Gold*. *Ciakmull—l'uomo della vendetta* (It 69) E. B. Clucher (Enzo Barboni) *aka The Unholy Four*. *Ehi, amico ... c'è Sabata, hai chiuso!* (It 69) Frank Kramer (Gianfranco Parolini) *aka Sabata* / *Sabata's Here ... Close Everything*. *Un Esercito di 5 uomini* / *The Five Men Army* (It / US 69) Don Taylor (Italo Zingarelli). *Giù la testa* / *Duck! You Sucker* (It / US 70) Sergio Leone *aka A Fistful of Dynamite* / *Once Upon a Time in the Revolution*. *Lo chiamavano Trinità...* (It 70) E. B. Clucher (Enzo Barboni) *aka They Call Me Trinity*. *Il mio nome è Shanghai Joe* (It 72) Mario Caiano *aka The Dragon Strikes Back* / *To Kill or to Die*. *...Più forte, ragazzi* (It / Col 72) Giuseppi Colizzi *aka ...All the Way Boys*. *Il mio nome è Nessuno* / *Mon nom est Personne* / *Mein Name Is Nobody* (It / F / G 73) Tonino Valerii *aka Mezzogiorno di fuoco per Han-Hao* / *My Name Is Nobody* / *A Time to Kill, a Time to Die*. *Un genio, due compari, un pollo* / *Un génie, deux associés, une cloche* / *Nobody ist der Grösste* (It / F / G 75) Damiano Damiani *aka A Genius / A Genius, Two Stooges and a Dupe.* *Una donna chiamata Apache* (It 77) George McRoots *aka Apache Woman.* *Amore, piombo e furore / China 9 Liberty 37* (It / Sp 78) Monte Hellman, Antonio Brandt *aka Clayton and Catherine.*

Spanish Civil War Films   *see*   **WAR FILM**

Spear-and-Sandal Epic   *see*   **PEPLUM**

Spec Film   *see*   **SPECULATION FILM**

Special   *see*   **PROGRAMMER;**   *see also*   **TELEVISION SPECIAL**

SPECIAL EFFECTS (Special-Effects Film)   Special effects of one sort or another are always present in motion pictures.[105] The range of special effects is quite large and extends from creating nonexistent creatures and objects to building life-size or small-scale replicas of real objects and events (storms, fires, earthquakes). The three main factors or principles on which special effects rest are first, that a film can be shot frame by frame and not necessarily continuously to obtain the illusion of motion when projected. Second, diverse objects like paintings, drawings, miniatures, models, stunt doubles and stunt artists can be filmed in such a way as to make them pass for the real thing. And third, different images can be combined to fuse into one complete whole. These principles create a wide variety of devices that go from the art of animation (q.v.), to the use of miniatures and glass shots, to rear and front projection, matte shots and traveling mattes; opticals (optical effects) such as fades, wipes, dissolves, freezes, masks, ghosts, multiple images and superimpositions may be used as well.[104] Special effects are of vital importance in film genres like horror films, disaster movies, fantasy, science fiction and animated films; in others like gangster pictures, Westerns and war movies, they enhance and add greater realism to the action. Of late, special effects have increased in importance, and in some cases they have eclipsed anything else in the movie: they have become the star. When this happens, we may speak of the special effects film *per se* (e.g., *2001: A Space Odyssey* [1968]; *Tron* [1982]). *See also* **TRICK FILM.**

King Kong (33) Merian C. Cooper, Ernest B. Schoedsack *aka The Beast / The Eighth Wonder / The Eighth Wonder of the World / King Ape / King Kong (The Eighth Wonder of the World) / Kong* [first feature sound film to use model animation]. *Dr. Cyclops* (39) Ernest B. Schoedsack. *Green Dolphin Street* (47) Victor Saville. *Destination Moon* (50) Irving Pichel. *The War of the Worlds* (52) Byron Haskin *aka H. G. Wells' The War of the Worlds.* *Forbidden Planet* (56) Fred M. Wilcox. *Jason and the Argonauts* (GB / US 63) Don Chaffey *aka Jason and the Golden Fleece.* *Fantastic Voyage* (66) Richard Fleischer *aka Microscopia / Strange Journey.* *2001: A Space Odyssey* (US / GB 68) Stanley Kubrick *aka Journey Beyond the Stars / Space Odyssey.* *The Poseidon Adventure* (72) Ronald Neame, Irwin Allen (uncredited). *Earthquake* (74) Mark Robson *aka Earthquake 1980* [first film in Sensurround]. *Superman* (GB / US 78) Richard Donner *aka Superman the Movie.* *Alien* (GB / US 79) Ridley Scott *aka Starbeast.* *The Black*

Hole (79) Gary Nelson *aka Probe One / The Space Probe / Space Probe One / Space Station One*. *1941* (79) Steven Spielberg. *The Thing* (82) John Carpenter. *Tron* (82) Steven Lisberger *aka Tron: The Electronic Gladiator* [first feature-length film using computer animation]. *Ghostbusters* (84) Ivan Reitman *aka Ghostmashers*. *The Last Starfighter* (84) Nick Castle. *Cocoon* (85) Ron Howard. *Aliens* (GB 86) James Cameron. *Terminator 2: Judgement Day* (91) James Cameron.

Special-Effects Film   *see*   SPECIAL EFFECTS

Special Mission War Film   *see*   WAR FILM: Adventure War Films

Specialized Newsreel   *see*   NEWSREEL

SPECTACLE (Spectacle Film, Spectacular)   The term applies to any film which tends to emphasize action on a grand scale and which features vast sets, imposing scenery, sumptuous interiors and an unlimited cast. The term is not restricted to a single genre but covers the epic, the adventure film, the war film and other genres.

> *The Four Horsemen of the Apocalypse* (20) Rex Ingram. *Gunga Din* (39) George Stevens. *The Rains Came* (39) Clarence Brown. *Red River* (48) Howard Hawks. *The Agony and the Ecstasy* (65) Carol Reed. *Doctor Zhivago* (GB / Sp 65) David Lean. *The Lion in Winter* (GB 68) Anthony Harvey. *Airport* (69) George Seaton, Henry Hathaway. *Nicholas and Alexandra* (GB 71) Franklin J. Schaffner. *The Hindenburg* (75) Robert Wise. *Revolution* (GB / Nor 85) Hugh Hudson. *L'ultimo imperatore / The Last Emperor* (It / GB / Chn 87) Bernardo Bertolucci.

Spectacle Film   *see*   SPECTACLE

Spectacular, Spectacular Film   *see*   EPIC;   *see also*   SPECTACLE and TELEVISION SPECIAL

SPECULATION FILM (Spec Film)   As opposed to a film made under contract, a speculation film has no investors or sponsors to cover its production costs. It is made in the hope of making a profit afterwards through rental or the selling of prints. *See* CONTRACT FILM.

SPECULATIVE DOCUMENTARY (Phenomena Film, Pseudoscientific Investigation Film)   A type of film which uses all sorts of materials and testimonies to advance theories and delve into matters of a speculative nature (like the existence of life after death, the Loch Ness monster, flying saucers, or the authenticity of the Savior's Holy Shroud) without furnishing concrete evidence or proof to substantiate its claims.

> *Erinnerungen an die Zukunft* (G 69-70) Harold Reinl *aka Back to the Stars / Chariots of the Gods*. *The Outer Space Connection* (74) Fred Warshofsky. *The Amazing World of Psychic Phenomena* (75) Robert Guenette. *The Mysterious Monsters* (75) Robert Guenette *aka Bigfoot, the Mysterious Monster*. *Death Is Not the End* (76) Richard Michaels. *In Search of Noah's Ark* (76) James L. Conway. *The Late Great Planet Earth* (76) Robert Amram. *Mysteries from Beyond Earth* (76) George Gale. *Secrets of the Bermuda Triangle* (77) Donald Brittain. *In Search of Historic Jesus* (79) Jenning G. Schellerup.

Spinechiller   *see*   HORROR FILM

Spin-Off   *see*   SEQUEL;   *see also*   TELEVISION SERIES

Splatter Movie   *see*   GORE FILM;   *see also*   VIOLENCE FILM

Split Beaver   *see*   HARD-CORE PORNO FILM

Split-Reel   *see*   SHORT: One-Reeler

Sponsored Film   *see*   FACTUAL FILM

Sponsoring Film   *see*   FACTUAL FILM: Advertising Film

Spoof   *see*   **PARODY**

Spoof Comedy   *see*   HARD-CORE PORNO FILM: Comic Pornographic Feature

Sporting Film   *see*   SPORTS PICTURE

SPORTS PICTURE (Sporting Film, Sports-Themed Film)   Sports and games are a favorite form of entertainment and relaxation for a large number of people. The list of sports, ancient and modern, is a long one, and each sport is theoretically suitable for dramatization and transposition to the screen. Indeed, a great number and variety of sports films have been made at one time or another.

Sports movies include the filming of Olympic Games, sports biographies and, naturally, films on any sport or match that may arouse the interest of the spectator. That most sports movies are dull viewing for many does not seem to prevent filmmakers from trying over and over again to make sports-themed movies. Now and then, expectations are fulfilled and an exciting, suspenseful sports movie is made. Obviously, some sports are more popular than others, and this is reflected in the number of movies made on those particular sports. Boxing, baseball, football and auto racing have figured prominently in films. In Europe and other parts of the world, soccer is the spectator sport par excellence. A few representative sports films are listed below. *Sports Films: A Complete Reference*, compiled by Harvey Marc Zucker and Lawrence J. Babich (Jefferson, NC: McFarland, 1987) has 1,827 entries describing all kinds of sports films.[105] *See* separate entries for: **BASEBALL FILM, BASKETBALL PICTURE, BOXING FILM, BULLFIGHTING FILM, FOOTBALL FILM, HORSE FILM, MOTOR-CAR RACING FILM, MOUNTAIN FILM, SOCCER FILM, SURF FILM** and **WRESTLING FILM.**

Athletics: *Pat and Mike* (52) George Cukor.   Auto Racing: *Winning* (69) James Goldstone.   Baseball: *Bang the Drum Slowly* (73) John Hancock.   Basketball: *Coach* (78) Bud Townsend.   Billiards / Pool: *The Hustler* (61) Robert Rossen.   Bowling: *Dreamer* (79) Noel Nosseck.   Boxing: *Rocky* (76) John G. Avildsen.   Cricket: *The Final Test* (GB 53) Anthony Asquith.   Cycle Racing: *Breaking Away* (79) Peter Yates.   Football: *The Longest Yard* (74) Robert Aldrich *aka The Mean Machine*.   Football — Aussi Rules: *The Club* (Aust 80) Bruce Beresford *aka David Williamson's The Club /*

Players. Golfing: *Follow the Sun* (51) Sidney Lanfield. Hammer-throwing: *Geordie* (GB 55) Frank Launder *aka Wee Geordie.* Hockey: *Slap Shot* (76) George Roy Hill. Horse Racing: *National Velvet* (44) Clarence Brown. Ice Skating: *Ice Castles* (78) Donald Wrye. Motorcycle Racing: *Fast Charlie . . . The Moonbeam Rider* (79) Steve Carver *aka Fast Charlie and the Moonbeam.* Olympics: *The First Olympics—Athens 1896* (84 TV) Alvin Rakoff. Roller Derby: *The Unholy Rollers* (72) Vernon Zimmerman. Rugby: *This Sporting Life* (GB 63) Lindsay Anderson. Running: *Running* (Can 78) Steven Hilliard *aka Le Vainqueur.* Skateboarding: *Freewheelin'* (76) Scott Dittrich. Skiing: *Last of the Ski Bums* (69) Dick Barrymore. Soccer: *Yesterday's Hero* (GB 79) Neil Leifer. Speedboat Racing: *Wild, Free and Hungry* (70) H. P. Edwards. Surfing: *Big Wednesday* (78) John Milius *aka Summer of Innocence.* Swimming: *The Swimmer* (68) Frank Perry. Tennis: *Racquet* (79) David Winters. Wrestling: *Vision Quest* (84) Harold Becker.

Sports-Themed Film *see* **SPORTS PICTURE**

Spot *see* **CARTOON FILM**

Spread Beaver *see* **HARD-CORE PORNO FILM**

Spy Adventure Films, Spy Comedies *see* **SPY FILM**

SPY FILM (Cloak and Dagger Drama, Espionage Film, Secret-Agent Film, Secret Service Drama, Spy Thriller) Espionage is an activity in which nations and individuals frequently engage. As such, it may be found in or form a subgenre of adventure stories, war movies, political thrillers, romance or crime films. Regardless of this, spy films have consistency in stereotypes, and similar patterns of behavior and situation keep recurring from film to film. It is best, then, to treat them as a unified, separate genre.

Spy films may deal with real spies in real situations or with fictional spies in fictitious and highly improbable circumstances. The spying may take place in time of war or in time of peace, and the film's treatment of the story may be highly romanticized and extremely glamorized, or it may be presented in sharp, realistic, down-to-earth terms. In fact, since the sixties, two general categories of spy movies have prevailed. The first type, patterned on the famous James Bond character created by Ian Fleming, features a superspy fighting supervillains who are very often megalomaniacs seeking to conquer or destroy the world for their own vainglory. The other category deals with the realistic portrayal of the unglamorized spy and his activities in an unfeeling world from which he is seldom able to opt out; this latter category of the realistic, down-trodden spy frequently fighting the system or its political machinations was inaugurated by Martin Ritt's *The Spy Who Came in from the Cold* (1965), based on a novel by John Le Carré. Other types of spying, e.g., industrial spying, are better included under the label of crime films.

James Robert Parish and Michael R. Pitts in *The Great Spy Pictures* include 463 entries (with full credits and précis) and 388 in *The Great Spy Pictures II* (Metuchen, NJ: Scarecrow, 1974; 1986).

——**James Bond Films (Bond Films)**   The notorious, licensed-to-kill super-spy is still going strong in spite of the fact that the craze for this type of film has abated. In their heyday, the James Bond films spawned a mass of imitators, from Matt Helm to Flint to Coplan to OSS117. Between 1964 and 1967, the Italians alone produced some 50 films dealing with all kinds of secret agents. The James Bond phenomenon has produced a solid body of critical research trying to explain its success. Sean Connery can be credited in part with this success, and he still remains the best impersonation of the suave, slightly cynical British Secret Service agent 007. The James Bond series and its imitators are also considered adventure or action-adventure films.

Dr. No (GB 62) Terence Young [18 "Bond" films up to 1989]. *Casino Royale* (GB 67) John Huston, Ken Hughes, Val Guest, Robert Parrish, Joe McGrath, Richard Talmadge, Anthony Squire [not part of the "official" series]. *On Her Majesty's Secret Service* (GB / US 69) Peter Hunt. *For Your Eyes Only* (GB / US 81) John Glen. *Never Say Never Again* (GB 83) Irving Kershner [not part of the "official" series]. *Licence to Kill* (GB / US / Mex 89) John Glen [the 16th official "Bond" film].

Imitations: A-001: operazione Giamaica / Scharfe Schüsse auf Jamaica / 011 Operación Caribe (It / G /Sp 65) Richard Jackson (Antonio del Amo) *aka A-001: Action in Jamaica / Our Man in Jamaica. A 077—Sfida ai killers / A 077 défie les tueurs* (It / F 65) Anthony Dawson (Antonio Margheriti) *aka Killers Are Challenged. The Liquidator* (GB 65) Jack Cardiff. *Modesty Blaise* (GB 65) Joseph Losey. *Our Man Flint* (65) Daniel Mann [followed by *In Like Flint* (67) Gordon Douglas and *Our Man Flint: Dead on Target* (76 TV) Joseph L. Scanlon]. *The Silencers* (65) Phil Karson [4 films (1965-68) in the "Matt Helm" series]. *Le spie uccidono a Beirut / Les Espions meurent à Beyrouth* (F / It 65) Martin Donan (Mario Donen) *aka Secret Agent Fireball / The Spy Killers. To Trap a Spy* (65) Don Medford [expanded from episode no. 1 "The Vulcan Affair" (63-64) of *The Man from U.N.C.L.E.* (64-67) TV series; followed by 7 additional films (1965-67)]. *A tout coeur à Tokyo pour OSS 117 / OSS 117 a Tokio si muore* (F / It 66) Michel Boisrond *aka Terror in Tokyo. Coplan sauve sa peau / Horror: L'assassino ha le ore contate* (F / It 67) Yves Boisset *aka Coplan Saves His Skin / Devil's Garden.*

Unglamorized Spy Film: The Spy Who Came In from the Cold (GB 65) Martin Ritt. *The Deadly Affair* (GB 66) Sidney Lumet. *Funeral in Berlin* (GB 66) Guy Hamilton [3 films (1965-67) in the "Harry Palmer" series]. *The Quiller Memorandum* (US / GB 66) Michael Anderson. *Vollmacht zum Mord / Permission to Kill* (Aus / US 74) Cyril Frankel. *Philby, Burgess and MacLean* (GB 77 TV) Gordon Flemyng *aka Philby, Burgess and MacLean: Spy Scandal of the Century. Tinker, Tailor, Soldier, Spy* (GB 80 TV) John Irvin [in 6 parts]. *The Whistle Blower* (GB 86) Simon Langton. *Yuri Nosenko, KGB* (US / GB 86 TV) Mick Jackson.

——**Political Spy Films**   The motivation behind the spies or the counteres-pionage organizations in these movies is mostly political rather than a show of bravado or a taste for adventure. The spies and counterspies are always defending democracy against the encroaching activities of foreign countries. The films warn against the dangers of Fascism, Communism and other extreme political credos.

Confessions of a Nazi Spy (39) Anatole Litvak.   *13 Rue Madeleine* (46) Henry Hathaway.   *Berlin Express* (47) Jacques Tourneur.   *The Iron Curtain* (48) William Wellman *aka Behind the Iron Curtain*.   *I Was a Communist for the FBI* (51) Gordon Douglas.   *Diplomatic Courier* (52) Henry Hathaway.   *La Guerre est finie / Kriget är slut* (F / Sw 65) Alain Resnais *aka The War Is Over*.   *Code Name: Heraclitus* (67) James Goldstone [original version shown as 2 segments of NBC's "Chrysler Theater"].   *Pueblo* (73 TV) Anthony Page *aka The Pueblo Affair*.   *The Osterman Weekend* (83) Sam Peckinpah.   *The Falcon and the Snowman* (85) John Schlesinger.

——**Spy Adventure Films**   Professional or amateur, the spies in this type of film are always involved in adventures and derring-do; they unerringly succeed in foiling their enemies and in carrying out the job expected of them. They quite often end up with the girl they have managed to rescue.

Spione (G 28) Fritz Lang *aka (The) Spies / The Spy*.   *The 39 Steps* (GB 35) Alfred Hitchcock.   *The Day Will Dawn* (GB 42) Harold French *aka The Avengers*.   *The Adventures of Tartu* (GB 43) Harold S. Bucquet *aka Tartu*.   *State Secret* (GB 50) Sidney Gilliat *aka The Great Manhunt*.   *Lisbon* (56) Ray Milland.   *The Two-Headed Spy* (GB 58) André de Toth.   *The Prize* (63) Mark Robson.   *The Ipcress File* (GB 65) Sidney J. Furie [first film on the Harry Palmer character; followed by *Funeral in Berlin* (GB 66) Guy Hamilton and *Billion Dollar Brain* (GB 67) Ken Russell].   *Arabesque* (US / GB 66) Stanley Donen.   *Fathom* (GB 67) Leslie H. Martinson.   *The Odessa File / Die Akte Odessa* (GB / G 74) Ronald Neame.   *The Next Man* (76) Richard C. Serafian *aka The Arab Conspiracy / Double Hit*.   *The Last Embrace* (79) Jonathan Demme.   *Reilly Ace of Spies* (GB 83 TV) Jim Goddard, Martin Campbell [in 12 episodes; also as a feature version] *aka Reilly: The Ace of Spies*.   *Agent on Ice* (85) Clark Worswick *aka Silent Partners*.   *The Fourth Protocol* (GB 87) John Mackenzie.   *Intrigue* (88 TV) David Drury.   *The Secret Life of Ian Fleming* (GB 90 TV) Ferdinand Fairfax.

——**Spy Comedies**   They are quite numerous and cover the whole spectrum from slapstick to sophisticated comedy.

Let George Do It (GB 40) Marcel Varnel.   *My Favorite Blonde* (42) Sidney Lanfield.   *To Be or Not to Be* (42) Ernst Lubitsch.   *A Night in Casablanca* (46) Archie Mayo.   *My Favorite Spy* (51) Norman Z. McLeod.   *Our Man in Havana* (GB 59) Carol Reed.   *A Touch of Larceny* (GB 59) Guy Hamilton.   *Hot Enough for June* (GB 63) Ralph Thomas *aka Agent 8¾ / Agent 008*.   *Where the Spies Are* (GB 65) Val Guest *aka One Spy Too Many / Passport to Oblivion*.   *Where the Bullets Fly* (GB 66) John Gilling.   *Darling Lili* (70) Blake Edwards.   *Le Grand Blond avec une chaussure noire* (F 72) Yves Robert *aka Follow That Guy with the One Black Shoe / The Tall Blond Man with the One Black Shoe / The Tall Blond Man with One Black Shoe*.   *Le Retour du grand blond / Il grande biondo* (F / It 74) Yves Robert *aka The Return of the Tall Blond Man with One Black Shoe*.   *Spies Like Us* (85) John Landis.

——**Spy Romances**   War and spying proved to be fertile ground for romance. Falling in love with the attractive agent and having to renounce one's great love upon discovery of his / her being an enemy spy meant the ultimate sacrifice, but it had to be done if only for the sake of those other great loves—the fatherland, honor and duty.

Mata-Hari (32) George Fitzmaurice.   *Dark Journey* (GB 37) Victor Saville.

The Spy in Black (GB 39) Michael Powell *aka U-Boat 29.*   *Casablanca* (42) Michael Curtiz.   *Notorious* (46) Alfred Hitchcock.   *The Young Lovers* (GB 54) Anthony Asquith *aka Chance Meeting.*   *Verboten!* (58) Samuel Fuller. *The Tamarind Seed* (Gb 74) Blake Edwards.   *Hopscotch* (80) Ronald Neame.

——**War Spy Films**   These films portray the activities of spies during time of war. They are either based on real or fictional wartime espionage operations. *See also* **WAR FILM: Spy War Films.**

Candlelight in Algeria (GB 43) George King.   *Five Graves to Cairo* (43) Billy Wilder.   *Watch on the Rhine* (43) Herman Shumlin.   *I See a Dark Stranger* (GB 46) Frank Launder *aka The Adventuress.*   *Odette* (GB 50) Herbert Wilcox.   *Decision Before Dawn* (51) Anatole Litvak *aka Legion of the Damned.*   *Carve Her Name with Pride* (GB 58) Lewis Gilbert.   *Five Fingers* (52) Joseph L. Mankiewicz.   *The Counterfeit Traitor* (61) George Seaton. *Fräulein Doktor / Gospodjica Doktor – Spijunka bez imena* (It / Yug 68) Alberto Lattuada *aka The Betrayal / Fraulein Doktor / Nameless.*   *Eye of the Needle* (GB 81) Richard Marquand.

Spy Romances, Spy Thriller   *see*   **SPY FILM**

Spy War Films   *see*   **WAR FILM**

Stag Film   *see*   **HARD-CORE PORNO FILM;** *see also*   **STAG MOVIE**

STAG MOVIE (Blue Movie, French Movie)   The term applies to any sex film of an explicit nature, but it is particularly suited to old pornographic or blue movies shown privately or at stag parties – hence the label stag film. The earliest known American stag movie is *A Free Ride,* alternatively known as *A Grass Sandwich,* which has been dated circa 1915. Thus, this type of film has been around for some time; the French *A l'Écu d'or ou la bonne auberge* dates from 1908. Lately, the history of these early porno shorts has een presented in several compilation films (*see* **SEX DOC-UMENTARY**). The article by Frank A. Hoffmann, "Prolegomena to a Study of Traditional Elements in the Erotic Film," *Journal of American Folklore* 78 (1965): 143–48, details the content of some of these formerly clandestine films. There has been a thriving mail order business for stag films, which were euphemistically termed "private films," or "eights" (as most films were 8mm or Super 8 shorts, soundless and of about 10 minutes' running time or 200 feet and shot in color). However, the videotape-cassette has gradually taken over the market for this kind of product. For a selected filmography of the stag movie, *see* Al Di Lauro and Gerard Rabkin, *Dirty Movies: An Illustrated History of the Stag Film, 1915–1970* (New York: Chelsea House, 1976).

Stage-to-Film Adaptation, Stage-to-Screen Adaptation   *see*   **ADAP-TATION: Adaptations from Plays**

Stagy Film   *see*   **FILM D'ART**

Stalk-and-Slash Film, Stalk and Slice Film, Stalker Film   *see*   **SLASHER FILM;**   *see also*   **VIOLENCE FILM**

STAND-UP COMEDY   Stand-up comics cracking jokes while facing the camera is a type of comedy that has proved successful on television, especially in Great Britain with programs such as *The Comedians* (1971).[106] Stand-up comedians sometimes combine jokes with short sketches, often complementary to their television stand-up appearances.

Feature-length stand-up comedy films are rare if filmed performances of comedians are excluded, e.g., *Richard Pryor Live on the Sunset Strip* (1982). *Comics* (1980), directed by Ron Clark, is a film which portrays sympathetically the world of the aspiring stand-up comedian.

The Lenny Bruce Performance Film (68) John Magnuson. *The Comedians* (GB 71 ITV) [106 episodes]. *Richard Pryor — Live in Concert* (79) Jeff Margolis. *Comics* (Can 80) Ron Clark [rel. in 83] *aka The Funny Farm*. *Bill Cosby, Himself* (81) William H. Cosby, Jr. *George Burns in Concert* (82) Jim Shaw. *Monty Python Live at the Hollywood Bowl* (GB 82) Terry Hughes. *Richard Pryor Live on the Sunset Strip* (82) Joe Layton. *Eddie Murphy — Delirious* (83) Bruce Gowers. *An Evening with Robin Williams* (83) Don Mischer. *Steve Martin Live* (86) Carl Gottlieb, Gary Weis. *Whoopi Goldberg Live* (86) Mike Nichols. *Bill Cosby: 49* (87) David Lewis, Camille Cosby.

STAR VEHICLE (Starrer, Vehicle)   A film designed to suit the particular talents of its principal performer, often elevated to the status of superstar. The star dominates the proceedings from start to finish. A starrer is expected to do well at the box office as it relies on the performer's drawing power for its success. *See also* **MUSICAL** and **WESTERN**.

Mae West: *Goin' to Town* (35) Alexander Hall *aka How Am I Doin'?* Shirley Temple: *Poor Little Rich Girl* (36) Irving Cummings. Errol Flynn: *Montana* (50) Ray Enright. Barbra Streisand: *Yentl* (GB / US / Cz 83) Barbra Streisand. Charles Bronson: *Murphy's Law* (86) J. Lee Thompson. Eddie Murphy: *Coming to America* (88) John Landis.

Static Film   *see*   **STRUCTURAL FILM**

Stereoscopic Film   *see*   **3-D FILM**

Still Animation   *see*   **ANIMATED FILM: Animated Stills**

Story Film   *see*   **FICTIONAL FILM;**   *see also*   **NARRATIVE FILM**

Story Video   *see*   **MUSIC VIDEO**

Straight Film   *see*   **LEGITIMATE FILM**

Strand   *see*   **TELEVISION SERIES**

STREET FILM   A term used by film critic Siegfried Kracauer to describe a type of psychological melodrama current in the German cinema of the 1920s and early 1930s. It was a popular genre having as its main motif the street to which the film's characters were fatalistically drawn. The genre emerged from the *Kammerspielfilm* (q.v.), a style of filmmaking to which some of the street films belong.

Phantom (G 22) F. W. Murnau. *Die Strasse* (G 23) Karl Grüne *aka The Street. Die freudlose Gasse* (G 25) G. W. Pabst *aka Cheerless Lane / The Joyless Street / The Street of Sorrow / Streets of Sorrow* (37) sound version. *Dirnentragödie* (G 27) Bruno Rahn *aka The Tragedy of a Street / Tragedy of the Street / Tragedy of the Whore. Überfall* (G 28) Ernö Metzner *aka Accident. Jenseits der Strasse* (G 29) Leo Mittler *aka Harbour Drift.*

Strip   *see*   **TELEVISION PROGRAM**

Stroboscopic Film   *see*   **STRUCTURAL FILM: Flicker Film**

STRUCTURAL FILM (Conceptual Film, Film as Film, Formal Film, Materialist Film, Minimal Film, Noncommercial Film, Perceptual Film, Physical Film, Pure Film, Structuralist Work)   The term structural film was used by P. Adams Sitney in *Film Culture* No. 47 (Summer 1969) to single out a group of independent or avant-garde films which showed similar characteristics. It is the most widely accepted term for a film which investigates the nature of film itself and explores the perception possibilities of the film medium. It does this by minimizing action and camera movement or by working on the film itself. It may make use of a continuous take by a fixed camera as in the static films of Andy Warhol, e.g., *Sleep* (1963), *Empire* (1963), *Kiss* (1963) and *Blow Job* (1963), or it may make use of repeated loops, extended zooms, flickering effects and other photographic techniques like filming images from a projected film. The aim of the structural filmmaker is to make film an aesthetic experience outside any symbolic association derived from more traditional forms of filmmaking. The structural film may be representational, abstract or semiabstract, and it usually avoids narrative or poetic content. The structure is the essence of the structural film. *See* Birgit Hein, "The Structural Film," in *Film as Film* (London: Arts Council of Great Britain, 1979), 93–105.

3/60 Bäume in Herbst (Aus 60) Kurt Kren *aka Trees in Autumn.   Blow Job* (63) Andy Warhol.   *Empire* (63) Andy Warhol, John Palmer.   *Kiss* (63) Andy Warhol [sequences with Naomi Levine shown also as *Andy Warhol Serial*].   *Sleep* (63) Andy Warhol [in 10-minute segments, each shown twice]. *Film in Which There Appear Edge Lettering, Dirt Particles, Sprocket Holes, etc.* (65) George Landow.   *Bolero* (Aust 67) Albie Thoms.   *Wavelength* (Can / US 66-67) Michael Snow.   *Documentary Footage* (68) Morgan Fisher.   *Tom, Tom, the Piper's Son* (69; revised 71) Ken Jacobs.   *History* (70) Ernie Gehr.   *Production Stills* (70) Morgan Fisher.   *La Région central / Central Region* (Can 70) Michael Snow *aka Earth.   Zorn's Lemma* (70) Hollis Frampton.   *Barn Rushes* (71) Larry Gottheim.   *Line Describing a Cone* (73) Anthony McCall.   *"Rameau's Nephew" by Diderot (Thanxs to Dennis Young) by Wilma Schoen* (Can 72-74) Michael Snow.   *31 / 75 Asyl* (Aus 75) Kurt Kren.   *After Manet, After Giorgione — Le Déjeuner sur l'Herbe ou Fête Champêtre* (GB 75) Malcolm Le Grice [4 screens].   *Presents* (Can 80-81) Michael Snow.

——**Flicker Film (Light-Film, Perceptual Film, Stroboscopic Film)**   In flicker films, images, light and dark or color frames alternate and appear briefly to blend together when projected, engaging the viewer in areas of new perceptual experience.

Arnulf Rainer (Aus 58-60) Peter Kubelka. *The Flicker* (66) Tony Conrad. *Piece Mandala / End War* (66) Paul Sharits. *Ray Gun Virus* (66) Paul Sharits. *Gammelion* (68) Gregory Markopoulos. *N:O:T:H:I:N:G* (68) Paul Sharits. *Shutter* (71) Taka Iimura.

——**Loop Film**   The loop film makes extensive use of loops which reappear at intervals during the film's spooling. The loops are composed of a loop-printed single image repeated in each frame.

15 / 67 TV (Aus 67) Kurt Kren. *Bardo Follies* (67) George Landow *aka Diploteratology. Yes, No, Maybe, Maybe Not* (GB 67) Malcolm Le Grice [2 screens]. *Loop* (GB 68) Peter Gidal. *Shower Proof* (68) Fred Drummond.

——**Participatory Film (Thematic Film)**   Evolving from the early structural films, the participatory film addresses itself directly to the viewers to awaken their ability to judge and make logical decisions for themselves.

Institutional Quality (69) George Landow. *Bleu Shut* (70) Robert Nelson. *Remedial Reading Comprehension* (70) George Landow. *Zorn's Lemma* (70) Hollis Frampton. *nostalgia* (71) Hollis Frampton [Part 1 of *Hapax Legomena;* 7 films (1971-72)].

——**Structural-Materialist Film**   This term has been used for the work of later structuralists, mostly for British and European films made in the late 1960s and early 1970s to differentiate them from earlier examples of structural film.[107]

Horror Film 2 (GB 72) Malcolm Le Grice [3-D shadow performance]. *Man with the Movie Camera* (GB 73) David Crosswaite. *Room Film 1973* (GB 73) Peter Gidal. *Film Print* (GB 74) Peter Gidal. *Condition of Illusion* (GB 75) Peter Gidal. *Portrait of Kurt Kren* (GB 76) Fred Drummond.

Structuralist Work, Structural-Materialist Film   *see*   **STRUCTURAL FILM**

Stud Comedies   *see*   **SEX COMEDY**

STUDENT FILM   A large body of films normally not available to the general public is composed of student films, usually made as part of a program of film studies, as a requirement for completing a university or college film course or as part of professional training at a film institute or film academy. It is not unusual to find some really outstanding pieces of work amongst student films. A student film may be of any length but most qualify as shorts and for the most part are shot in 8mm, 16mm or, more recently, in video tape. To make them more accessible for distribution, some student shorts have been strung together into a portmanteau feature (e.g., *Genesis 4* [1971]; a collection of 12 student films).

George Lucas, a graduate from the University of Southern California, is perhaps a prime example of a successful student whose student films demonstrated his future capability as a filmmaker. His 15-minute graduation film *THX-1138-4eb* (1967) formed the basis for his association with Francis Ford Coppola (himself a graduate from the University of California at Los Angeles) and was expanded into the feature-length version *THX 1138* (1969), a visually impressive film about a future computer-robot dominated society.[108]

Student films are found in most filmmakers' filmographies. Besides public screenings on campuses, student films are sometimes exhibited commercially or shown on local and international festivals. An early book on the subject of student films and film programs in the United States is Thomas Fensch, *Films on the Campus* (South Brunswick and New York: A. S. Barnes, 1970).

Dwaj ludzie z szafa (Pol 57) Roman Polanski *aka Two Men and a Wardrobe*. *Koncert* (Hung 61) István Szabó *aka Concert*. *Winter Kept Us Warm* (Can 64-65) David Sector. *THX-1138-4eb* (1967) George Lucas *aka The Electronic Labyrinth* [expanded into a feature-length version: *THX 1138* (69)]. *Erostratus II* (GB 69) Boaz Davidson. *Genesis 4* (71) [12 shorts: *Appointment Reminder* (Greg McCarty), *Ass* (Tom de Neve), *I Don't Know* (Penny Spheeris), *Intermission* (Marshall Harvey), *Forster's Release* (Terence Winkless, Milt Hubatka), *Last of the Schunue* (Mark Griffiths), *Marguerite* (Betty Yo-Jung Chen), *Mrs. Levant Graham* (Elliot Noyes), *Natural Habitat* (Ralph Arlych), *Number 1* (Richard Braverman), *Silent Majority* (Bruce Ward), *Star Spangled Banner* (Roger Flint)]. *Raw Nerves* (80) Manuel DeLanda. *Joe's Bed-Stuy Barbershop: We Cut Heads* (83) Spike Lee.

STUDIO FILM   A film mostly shot or completed in a film studio instead of on location. The filming of a motion picture in studio sets rather than on location was frequently done in the past.

STYLIZED FILM   A film whose most characteristic feature is the use of non-naturalistic or highly stylized sets as background, a practice which first manifested itself in the Italian film *Thais* (1916); it employed a fully stylized décor in its last scenes. A fairly recent example is *One from the Heart* (1982), a Francis Ford Coppola romantic comedy that uses an impressive stylized Las Vegas set. *See* **EXPRESSIONIST FILM**.

Thais (It 16) Anton Giulio Bragaglia. *Prunella* (18) Maurice Tourneur. *Die Puppe* (G 19) Ernst Lubitsch *aka The Doll*. *Salome* (22) Charles Bryant. *The Silver Chalice* (54) Victor Saville. *Perceval le gallois / Perceval* (F / It 78) Eric Rohmer. *Zoot Suit* (81) Luis Valdez. *One from the Heart* (82) Francis Coppola. *Trouble in Mind* (85) Alan Rudolph.

Subliminal Advertising   *see*   **TELEVISION COMMERCIAL**

SUBLIMINAL FILM   Back in the fifties, it was thought a novel idea to put a few seconds of flashing images into motion pictures. The images would be, it was believed, subliminally absorbed and subconsciously retained by the unsuspecting audience. Two films — *Terror in the Haunted House* (1958) and *A Date with Death* (1959), a horror movie and a crime melodrama respectively — were made using a process marketed as "Psychorama" which flashed for less than a second words and pictures onto the screen. The process was apparently of some use to advertisers who would thus induce people to buy their products. The practice was promptly banned.

Terror in the Haunted House (58) Harold Daniels *aka My World Dies Screaming.* *A Date with Death* (59) Harold Daniels.

Submarine War Films *see* **WAR FILM**

Subversive Film *see* **REVOLUTIONARY FILM**

Succès d'estime *see* **TURKEY**

Sudser *see* **SOAP OPERA**

Suffrage Film *see* **FEMINIST FILM: Women's Suffrage Films**

Sun-and-Sand Flick *see* **TEEN MOVIE: Beach Films**

Superhero Film *see* **FANTASY: Comic Strip Superheroes Films**

Superspectacular *see* **BLOCKBUSTER**

Supporting Feature *see* **DOUBLE FEATURE**

SURF MOVIE (Surfer Drama, Surfing Movie, Surf-Riding Film) Most surfing epics are of a semi-documentary nature; however, the fictional surfing movies, e.g., *Big Wednesday* (1978) and movies that use surfing as a background for youthful gambols and pranks, e.g., *Beach Party* (1963), are not lacking in the genre. Surf movies propound surfing as a way of life as much as biker movies propound that particular way of life. To ride the big waves, or the perennial trek from place to place searching for the elusive, mammoth swell becomes the be-all and end-all of a surfer's existence. Everything else revolves around this. Riding the waves, once an almost exclusively male activity, turns in these pictures into a rite of passage (or nonpassage) from adolescence into manhood. The surfing is often supplemented by partying at night and bouts of sentimentality as a surfer grows older and reminisces about the past or old friends.

Surfing movies originated in California, but Australia has produced a substantial number of such films.

Gidget Goes Hawaiian (61) Paul Wendkos. *Beach Party* (63) William Asher. *The Endless Summer* (66) Bruce Brown. *Pacific Vibrations* (70) John Severson. *Crystal Voyage* (US / Aust 73) Albert Falzon, George Greenough. *Shimmering Light* (Aust 77 TV) Don Chaffey. *Big Wednesday* (78) John Milius *aka Summer of Innocence.* *California Dreaming* (78) John Hancock. *A Personal History of the Australian Surf Being the Confessions of a Straight Poofter* (Aust 81) Michael Blakemore. *Puberty Blues* (Aust 81) Bruce Beresford. *Surf II* (83) Randall Badat. *North Shore* (87) William Phelps. *Aloha Summer* (88) Tommy Lee Wallace.

Surf-Riding Film *see* **SURF MOVIE**

Surrealism *see* **SURREALIST FILM**

SURREALIST FILM (Surrealism)   Surrealism is basically a movement that seeks to expand reality, to attain a supra-reality, so to speak, and thus free man from the constraints exerted by society and convention. It seeks to do this by exploring all possible avenues conducive to this end. In particular, it focuses its attention on the workings of the subconscious, the power of dreams, Freudian symbolism and the liberating forces of poetry, love and desire.

An offshoot of Dadaism, Surrealism was given life principally by its founder, André Breton (1896–1966), who laid down its doctrine in his First Manifesto (1924) and in his subsequent writings. Initially, it was a literary movement but it spread quickly to the other arts, especially painting and being highly suited for pictorial representation, to film. To its proponents, Surrealism was a way of life.

In its cinematic form, it is best illustrated by the early work of Luis Buñuel (1900–1983) in collaboration with Salvador Dalí (1904–1989): *Un Chien andalou / An Andalusian Dog* (1928) and *L'Age d'or / The Golden Age* (1930), the first of which its director proclaimed to be beyond interpretation, being a pure manifestation of random, automatic creation. It is obvious, however, that any viewer of a Surrealist film should feel free to draw his own conclusions as Surrealist films are laden with symbols. Foremost among the many techniques used by Surrealist filmmakers are the juxtaposition of different objects that one would not associate with each other and the lack of conscious logic in the imagery portrayed. Surrealism is a highly creative medium and its films reflect this tendency. It is a personal cinema and thus not too successful in reaching large audiences. The corpus of Surrealist films is very small, and it is mostly composed of shorts; full-length features are the exception rather than the norm. This fact has prompted many film critics and students of Surrealism to investigate instead, the influence exerted by Surrealism on many commercial films, or to label Surreal many films which show a marked Surrealist mood in their composition. However, films which are sometimes considered Surrealist in spirit are not properly Surrealist films. They include: Luis Buñuel's *Los olvidados / The Young and the Damned* (1950) and *Viridiana* (1961); films which show strong Surrealist tendencies like Victor Heerman's *Animal Crackers* (1930) and Leo McCarey's *Duck Soap* (1933), both rambunctious, zany Marx Brothers comedies; or, films which have *bona fide* surrealist dream sequences, e.g., Alfred Hitchcock's *Spellbound* (1945) with a dream sequence by Salvador Dalí. They fit better into some other type of classification.

La Coquille et le clergyman (F 28) Germaine Dulac *aka The Seashell and the Clergyman.*   *Un Chien andalou* (F 28) Luis Buñuel *aka An (The) Andalusian Dog / Es peligroso asomarse al exterior / El marista en la ballesta / Un perro andaluz.*   *L'Age d'or* (F 30) Luis Buñuel *aka ¡Abajo la Constitución! / Age of Gold / La bestia andaluza / Dans les eaux glacées du calcul égoïste / La edad de oro / En las aguas heladas del cálculo egoísta / The Golden Age.*

Malombra (It 42) Mario Soldati. *Dreams That Money Can Buy* (44-46) Hans Richter [episodes: *Desire* (Max Ernst), *The Girl with Prefabricated Heart* (Fernand Léger), *Ruth, Roses and Revolvers* (Man Ray), *Color Records and Nudes Descending a Staircase* (Marcel Duchamp), *A Ballet in the Universe* (Alexander Calder), *Circus* (Calder), *Narcissus* (Hans Richter)]. *The Potted Psalm* (46) Sidney Peterson, James Broughton. *El Angel exterminador* (Mex / Sp 62) Luis Buñuel *aka The Exterminating Angel / Los náufragos de la calle de Providencia*. *Le Voleur de rêves* (F 65) J. F. Arroyo. *Le Théâtre de Monsieur et Madame Kabal* (F 67) Walerian Borowczyk *aka The Theater of Mr. and Mrs. Kabal*. *Paris n'existe pas* (F 69) Robert Benayoun *aka Paris Does Not Exist*. *La Voie lactée / La via lattea* (F / It 69) Luis Buñuel *aka The Milky Way*. *Don Sajn* (Cz 70) Jan Svankmajer *aka Don Juan*. *Sérieux comme le plaisir* (F 74) Robert Benayoun *aka Je serai sérieux comme le plaisir*. *Europe After the Rain* (GB 78) Mick Gold. *Feverhouse* (GB 84) Howard Walmesley.

Animal Crackers (30) Victor Heerman. *Duck Soup* (33) Leo McCarey. *Spellbound* (45) Alfred Hitchcock *aka Alfred Hitchcock's Spellbound / The House of Dr. Edwards*. *Los olvidados* (Mex 50) Luis Buñuel *aka La manzana podrida / The Young and the Damned*. *Viridiana* (Sp / Mex 61) Luis Buñuel.

——**Dada (Dadaism)**   Dada was founded in 1916 in Zurich, Switzerland. It was an artistic and literary movement that rejected form and traditional art and instead endorsed new tendencies like Cubism, collage and abstract painting. It believed in "accidental" creation, automatic writing and drawing and the use of ready-mades for exhibition as works of art. It was a short-lived iconoclastic attitude to art, and although it was influential in the development of modern art, it produced few filmic manifestations, the movement being superseded by the more vigorous and optimistic surrealist venture.

Le Retour à la raison (F 23) Man Ray. *Entr'acte* (F 24) René Clair *aka Cinéma / Intermission*. *Emak Bakia* (F 26) Man Ray *aka Give Us a Rest / Leave Me Alone*.

——**Panic Cinema**   Fernando Arrabal, for many years a self-exiled Spanish playwright living in France, created the *théâtre de panique* ("theater of panic"). Besides writing for the theater, he has also directed a few films. The term "cinema of panic" fits Arrabal and those writer / directors who grouped themselves under the same banner. Panic cinema is strongly indebted to Surrealism and can be considered an extension of it.

Fando y Lis (Mex 68) Alexandro Jodorowsky *aka Fando and Lis / Tar Babies*. *Le Grand Cérémonial* (F 68) Pierre-Alain Joliver *aka Weird Weirdo*. *Viva la Muerte* (F / Tun 70-71) Fernando Arrabel.

SURVIVAL PICTURE   The survival film places man or woman in a harsh environment and challenges him / her to survive against nature and sometimes against their own kind. The individual has only at his / her disposal innate resourcefulness, ingenuity, courage and willpower to overcome the odds. The desert is a frequently used scenario for survival pictures, but the frozen wastes of the North, the jungle, the sea or any isolated location remote from civilization is equally suitable. These movies may be integrated into the adventure genre. Many science fiction post-nuclear films are survival pictures.

Five Came Back (39) John Farrow. *Inferno* (53) Roy Baker. *The Flight of the Phoenix* (65) Robert Aldrich. *The Naked Prey* (US / SA 65) Cornel Wilde. *Man in the Wilderness* (US / Sp 71) Richard C. Sarafian. *Deliverance* (72) John Boorman. *Jeremiah Johnson* (72) Sydney Pollack. *Hey, I'm Alive* (75 TV) Lawrence Schiller. *And I Alone Survived* (78 TV) William A. Graham. *Death Hunt* (81) Peter Hunt. *Killing at Hell's Gate* (81 TV) Jerry Jameson. *Fleshburn* (83) George Gage *aka Fear in a Handful of Dust*. *Lost!* (Can 86) Peter Rowe. *Damned River* (89) Michael Schroeder.

Suspense Film, Suspenser, Suspense Thriller   *see*   **THRILLER**

Sustaining Show   *see*   **TELEVISION PROGRAM**

SWASHBUCKLER (Swashbuckling Film, Sword-Fight Film)   Originating in the United States, the swashbuckler genre has had three main Hollywood cycles in the 1920s, 1930s and 1950s. Swashbuckling movies are perhaps best remembered by association with the stars that excelled in them — Douglas Fairbanks, Errol Flynn, Douglas Fairbanks, Jr., Tyrone Power and many others. Besides the United States, Great Britain, France and Italy have also produced swashbucklers of quality. In Japan and Hong Kong, there is also a market for swashbucklers, but their Samurai and Chinese Swordplay movies are in a different league altogether. Clearly, the main characteristic of the swashbuckler is its swordplay, performed by heroes and villains alike.[109] Whether using broadswords, sabres, rapiers or scimitars, the sword fights are at the center of the swashbuckler. However, swordplay is not restricted to swashbucklers alone as it also figures in many nonswashbuckling films (e.g., *Romeo and Juliet* [1936]; *Cyrano de Bergerac* [1950]; *The Mississippi Gambler* [1953]). Swashbucklers fall readily into five categories: chivalric films, cloak and sword film, righter-of-wrongs films, pirate films and Oriental swashbucklers. A good authoritative source on the swashbuckler genre and its variants is Jeffrey Richards, *Swordsmen of the Screen* (London: Routledge & Kegan Paul, 1977).

——**Chivalric Films (Chivalric Epics)**   In these swashbucklers, the chivalric world of the Middle Ages is recreated as knights and crusaders fight for honor and lofty ideals. These films are usually subdivided into : a) Arthurian films expanding the Arthurian myths; b) non–Arthurian chivalric films; c) Robin Hood filnms; and d) films with a medieval setting.

Robin Hood (22) Allan Dwan *aka Douglas Fairbanks in Robin Hood*. *The Crusades* (35) Cecil B. DeMille. *The Adventures of Robin Hood* (38) Michael Curtiz, William Keighley *aka Robin Hood*. *If I Were King* (38) Frank Lloyd. *The Black Arrow* (48) Gordon Douglas *aka The Black Arrow*

Strikes. The Flame and the Arrow (50) Jacques Tourneur *aka The Hawk and the Arrow. Ivanhoe* (52) Richard Thorpe. *The Story of Robin Hood and His Merrie Men* (GB 52) Ken Annakin *aka The Story of Robin Hood. Knights of the Round Table* (53) Richard Thorpe [first film in Perspecta Stereophonic Sound]. *The Dark Avenger* (GB 55) Henry Levin *aka The Warriors. El Cid* (US / Sp / It 61) Anthony Mann *aka Samuel Bronston's El Cid. The Warlord* (65) Franklin J. Schaffner *aka The War Lord. I Paladini. Storia d'armi e d'amori* (It 82) Giacomo Battiato *aka Le armi e gli amori / Hearts and Armour. Robin Hood: Prince of Thieves* (91) Kevin Reynolds.

———**Cloak and Sword Romances (Cape and Sword Films)**   Romance, heroism and adventure are their trademark. They range from the 16th to the 19th century as to their period setting and involve noblemen, roguish lovers (Don Juan, Casanova), conquistadores, mercenary soldiers and young blades defending King and country, or fighting for the lady of their heart. From Spain to Italy, from Ireland and Scotland to England, from France to the confines of Russia, from Mexico to old California, their exploits cover the continents.

The Iron Mask (29) Allan Dwan. *The Prisoner of Zenda* (37) John Cromwell. *The Man in the Iron Mask* (39) James Whale. *The Son of Monte Cristo* (40) Rowland V. Lee. *Captain from Castille* (47) Henry King. *The Exile* (47) Max Ophuls. *The Adventures of Don Juan* (48) Vincent Sherman *aka The New Adventures of Don Juan. The Three Musketeers* (48) George Sidney. *At Sword's Point* (49) Lewis Allen *aka Sons of the Musketeers. The Sword and the Rose* (53) Ken Annakin. *Captain Lightfoot* (55) Douglas Sirk. *The King's Thief* (55) Robert Z. Leonard. *The Moonraker* (GB 58) David Macdonald. *Les Trois Mousquetaires / I tre moschettieri* (F / It 60) Bernard Borderie [in 2 parts: *Les Ferrets de la reine / I tre moschettieri; La Vengeance de Milady / La vendetta dei moschettieri*]. *The Fighting Prince of Donegal* (66) Michael O'Herlihy. *The Three Musketeers* (Pan / Sp 73) Richard Lester *aka The Queen's Diamonds. Royal Flash* (GB 75) Richard Lester. *The Man in the Iron Mask* (GB / F 77 TV) Mike Newell.

———**Oriental Swashbucklers**   The cycle of Oriental swashbucklers started in the early forties with *Arabian Nights* (1942); they owe much to the fantasy genre, e.g., *The Thief of Bagdad* (1940) in particular. These films add Oriental settings and characters to the swashbuckling elements; they are a hybrid, and this species of desert melodramas used to be called in Hollywood "tits and sand" pictures.

Arabian Nights (42) John Rawlins. *Ali Baba and the Forty Thieves* (43) Arthur Lubin. *Sinbad the Sailor* (46) Richard Wallace. *The Flame of Araby* (51) Charles Lamont. *The Prince Who Was a Thief* (51) Rudolph Maté. *The Golden Blade* (53) Nathan Juran. *Veils of Bagdad* (53) George Sherman. *Siren of Bagdad* (53) Richard Quine. *The Adventures of Hajji Baba* (54) Don Weis.

———**Pirate Films**   These films center on the exploits of pirates, variously called corsairs, free-booters, buccaneers or privateers. Whether heroes or villains, they sailed the seven seas and in particular the Spanish Main.

The Black Pirate (26) Albert Parker.   *Captain Blood* (35) Michael Curtiz.
The Buccaneer (38) Cecil B. DeMille.   *The Sea Hawk* (40) Michael Curtiz
aka Beggars of the Sea. The Black Swan (42) Henry King.   *The Spanish
Main* (45) Frank Borzage.   *Anne of the Indies* (51) Jacques Tourneur.   *The
Crimson Pirate* (GB / US 52) Robert Siodmak.   *The Buccaneer* (58) Anthony
Quinn.   *La venere dei pirati* (It 60) Mario Costa *aka Queen of the Pirates.
Il dominatore dei sette mari / Seven Seas to Calais* (It / US 62) Primo Zeglio,
Rudolph Maté *aka I re dei sette mari.   La tigre dei sette mari* (It 62) Luigi
Capuano *aka Tiger of the Seven Seas.*

——**Righter-of-Wrongs Films**   Whether these films deal with 17th- or 18th-
century highwaymen (Claude Duval, Dick Turpin) who rob the rich to give
to the poor, or 19th-century masked avengers (Scarlet Pimpernel, Zorro,
Scaramouche) who engage in fighting despotism or any other kind of injustice caused by revolution, a tyrannic despot or a greedy government
official, the heroes of these films are all intent on righting wrongs.
   The Mark of Zorro (20) Fred Niblo *aka The Curse of Capistrano.   Dick Turpin* (24) John G. Blystone.   *Don Q. Son of Zorro* (25) Donald Crisp.   *Dick
Turpin* (GB 33) John Stafford, Victor Hanbury.   *The Scarlet Pimpernel* (GB
34) Harold Young; uncredited: Alexander Korda, Rowland V. Brown.   *The
Mark of Zorro* (40) Rouben Mamoulian *aka The Californian.   The Corsican
Brothers* (41) Gregory Ratoff.   *The Elusive Pimpernel* (GB 50) Michael
Powell, Emeric Pressburger.   *Scaramouche* (52) George Sidney.   *The Scarlet Pimpernel* (GB / Aust 82 TV) Clive Donner.   *The Corsican Brothers* (GB
84 TV) Ian Sharp.

Swashbuckling Film   *see*   **SWASHBUCKLER**

Sword-and-Sandal Epic   *see*   **PEPLUM**

SWORD-AND-SORCERY FILM (Heroic-Fantasy Film)   Sword and
sorcery is an important subgenre of fantasy. The form seems to have been
developed by Robert E. Howard (1906–36) in his "Conan" stories published
in the thirties. However, its present, well-established popularity among
readers is attributed to the enormous success of J. R. R. Tolkien's famous
trilogy, *The Lord of the Rings* (1954-55), rendered into an animated feature
by Ralph Bakshi in 1978, and to the work of other writers in the field such
as Fritz Leiber and Jack Vance. (The term sword and sorcery is said to have
been coined by Fritz Leiber in 1960.)
   Besides swordsmanship and magic, other essential components of heroic
fantasy are exotic backgrounds and the presence of a strong superhero
capable of performing extraordinary deeds and of being victorious in a confrontation between good and evil. The settings of his adventures will usually
be tribal or feudal societies located in the prehistoric past, the Dark Ages,
the future or in some science-fiction savage world.
   Although an occasional early film would fall readily under the category
of sword and sorcery, a cycle of such films really started in the late seventies
and early eighties. They are an appealing action-adventure type which seek

to reaffirm the old, cherished fable of the conquering legendary hero. *See also* **FANTASY FILM**.

Die Nibelungen — ein deutsches Heldenlied (G 22-24) Fritz Lang [2 parts: *I. Siegfried* and *II. Kriemhilds Rache*] *aka The Nibelunge Saga (Siegfried, The Vengeance of Kriemhild)*. *La Corona di Ferro* (It 41) Alessandro Blasetti *aka The Iron Crown*. *The Magic Sword* (62) Bert I. Gordon *aka St. George and the Dragon / St. George and the 7 Curses*. *The Lord of the Rings* (78) Ralph Bakshi. *Hawk the Slayer* (GB 80) Terry Marcel. *Conan, the Barbarian* (81) John Milius. *Heavy Metal / Métal hurlant* (Can / US 80-81) Gerald Potterton. *Conquest / La Conquista de la tierra perdida* (It / Sp / Mex 82) Lucio Fulci *aka Mace il fuorilegge*. *The Sorceress* (82) Brian Stuart *aka The Devil's Advocate (Traigon's Revenge)*. *Deathstalker / El cazador de la muerte* (US / Arg 83) John Watson. *Hundra l'ultima amazzone / Hundra* (It / Sp / US 83) Matt Cimber. *Il mondo di Yor* (It / Tur 83) Anthony M. Dawson *aka Yor, the Hunter from the Future / The World of Yor*. *The Sword and the Sorcerer* (83) Albert Pyun. *Conan the Destroyer* (84) Richard Fleischer. *Red Sonja* (85) Richard Fleischer. *Rock & Rule* (83) Clive A. Smith. *Amazons* (86) Alex Sessa. *Deathstalker II* (86) Jim Wynorski *aka Deathstalker II: Duel of the Titans*.

Sword-Fight Film   *see*   **SWASHBUCKLER**

Swordplay Film   *see*   **CHINESE SWORDPLAY MOVIE**

Synaesthetic Film   *see*   **UNDERGROUND FILM**

Syndicate Films, Syndicate-Oriented Film   *see*   **GANGSTER FILM**

Synthetic Films   *see*   **ABSTRACT FILM**

T & A (Tits and Ass) Movie   *see*   **NUDIE**

Tacky Film   *see*   **SLEAZY FILM**

Takeoff   *see*   **PARODY**;   *see also*   **HARD-CORE PORNO FILM: Rip-Offs**

Talent Show   *see*   **TELEVISION SHOW**

Talk Show   *see*   **TELEVISION SHOW**

Talker, Talkie, Talking Picture   *see*   **SOUND FILM**

Target Programming   *see*   **TELEVISION PROGRAM**

Tarzan Pictures   *see*   **JUNGLE FILM**

Tawdry Film   *see*   **SLEAZY FILM**

Teaching Film   *see*   **FACTUAL FILM: Training Film**

Tear-Jerker   *see*   **WEEPIE**

Tease Film   *see*   **HARD-CORE PORNO FILM**

Teaser   *see*   **TELEVISION COMMERCIAL**

Techtonic Film *see* **UNDERGROUND FILM: Mythopoeic Film**

TEEN MOVIE ("Juve" Movie, Teenage Movie, Teenpic, Youth Picture)
In the mid–1950s it was noticed that there was potential at the box-office for a previously untapped age-group. Thus, teenage pictures came into full bloom — that is, exploitation films addressed to youngsters in their teens. The field is a vast one in terms of what may possibly interest, or film producers think may interest, young audiences. Favorite subjects included rock 'n' roll and the perennial topic of juvenile delinquency, followed by beach party romps; minor subgenres included teenage monster movies, hotrod movies and school exposé films.[110]
Since the fifties, the teen movie has continued to expand its thematic range and has become most prolific in the high school variety and teenage-violence field. Although the exploitation label still hovers over most of the teen pix, some are genuine dramatic expositions of teen circles.
Other entries dealing with teen movies or with genres closely related to them are **EXPLOITATION FILM, JUVENILE DELINQUENCY FILM, MOTORCYCLE MOVIE, ROCK FILM,** and **YOUTH FILM.**

> *Rock Around the Clock* (56) Fred F. Sears. *Rock, Pretty Baby* (56) Richard Bartlett. *Hot Rod Rumble* (57) Leslie Martinson. *I Was a Teen-age Werewolf* (57) Gene Fowler, Jr. *aka Blood of the Werewolf. Jailhouse Rock* (57) Richard Thorpe. *Teenage Doll* (57) Roger Corman. *The Cool and the Crazy* (58) William Witney. *High School Confidential!* (58) Jack Arnold *aka Young Hellions. Date Bait* (60) O'Dale Ireland. *Wild Youth* (61) John Schreyer *aka Naked Youth. Last Summer* (69) Frank Perry. *The Van* (76) Sam Grossman *aka Chevy Van. A Little Romance / I Love You, je t'aime* (US / F 79) George Roy Hill *aka E = MC², mon amour. Van Nuys Blvd* (79) William Sachs. *Scarred* (83) Rose-Marie Turko *aka Street Love. Valley Girl* (83) Martha Coolidge. *River's Edge* (US / Can 86) Tim Hunter. *Pin...* (Can 87) Sandor Stern. *Stand and Deliver* (87) Ramon Menendez. *Shag* (88) Zelda Barron *aka Shag, the Movie. Say Anything* ... (89) Cameron Crowe.

———Beach Films (Beach-Blanket Films, Beach Blanket Party Pictures, Beach-Bunny Films, Beach Party Movies, Sand-and-Surf Movies, Sun-and-Sand Flicks) Most of the action in these movies takes place in or around the beach, and the films are peopled with beautiful teenagers who are mostly dedicated to gambolling with each other or eyeing the opposite sex. Beach films were a creation of American International Pictures who inaugurated the type with *Beach Party* in 1963, although *Gidget* (1959) and *Where the Boys Are* (1960) may be considered as having paved the way for this type of film. Beach party movies were at their apex during the sixties, but they continue to be made sporadically and are adjusted accordingly to the more permissible cinema of today.

> *Gidget* (59) Paul Wendkos [6 "Gidget" movies (1959-85) including 3 made for TV]. *Where the Boys Are* (60) Henry Levin. *Beach Party* (63) William Asher [7 films (1963-66) in the "Beach Party" series]. *Bikini Beach* (64) William Asher. *Ride the Wild Surf* (64) Don Taylor. *Beach Ball* (65)

Lennie Weinrib. *Beach Blanket Bingo* (65) William Asher. *It's a Bikini World* (67) Stephanie Rothman. *California Dreaming* (78) John Hancock. *Malibu Beach* (78) Robert J. Rosenthal *aka Sunset Cove*. *Hardbodies* (84 MCTV) Mark Griffths. *The Bikini Shop* (85) David Wechter *aka Malibu Bikini Shop*.

——**High School Films**   Films with high school kids are very abundant. The characters in these films are usually engaged in devising all sorts of pranks, in seducing pretty coeds, or in trying to lose their virginity in a hurry, something they ordinarily accomplish by the end of the picture. Some of these high school films may also be included in the teenage-violence movies. *See also* **HIGH SCHOOL PICTURE**.
Massacre at Central High (76) Renee Daader *aka Blackboard Massacre*. *Gregory's Girl* (GB 80) Bill Forsyth. *Porky's* (US / Can 81) Bob Clark [followed by *Porky's II: The Next Day* (Can 83) Bob Clark and *Porky's Revenge* (85) James Komack]. *Fast Times at Ridgemont High* (82) Amy Heckerling *aka Fast Times*. *Homework* (82) James Beshears. *Losin' It* (Can 82) Curtis Lee Hanson *aka Tijuana*. *Risky Business* (83) Paul Brickman. *Dangerously Close* (86) Albert Pyun. *Pretty in Pink* (86) Howard Deutch. *Hiding Out* (87) Bob Giraldi *aka Adult Education*. *Three O'Clock High* (87) Phil Joanou. *The Virgin Queen of St. Francis High* (87) Francesco Lucente. *Cutting Class* (88) Rospo Pallenberg.

——**Teen Comedies**   In the eighties, a very noticeable trend in teen comedies emerged; it ran a whole gamut of themes and genres including fantasy, high-tech, science fiction and horror.
I Wanna Hold Your Hand (78) Robert Zemeckis. *Hot T-Shirts* (79) Chuck Vincent. *Dreams Come True* (84) Max Kalmanowicz. *The Flamingo Kid* (84) Garry Marshall. *The Karate Kid* (84) John G. Avildsen [followed by *The Karate Kid, Part II* (86) and *The Karate Kid III* (89) also by Avildsen]. *Back to the Future* (85) Robert Zemeckis [followed by *Back to the Future Part II* (89) and *Back to the Future Part III* (90) also by Zemeckis]. *Better Off Dead. . .* (85) Savage Steve Holland. *Girls Just Want to Have Fun* (85) Alan Metter. *Once Bitten* (85) Howard Storm. *Real Genius* (85) Martha Coolidge. *Teen Wolf* (85) Rod Daniel *aka Wolfkill*. *Weird Science* (85) John Hughes. *Something Special* (86) Paul Schneider *aka I Was a Teenage Boy / Willy Milly*. *Vamp* (86) Richard Wenk. *Some Kind of Wonderful* (87) Howard Deutch. *Doin' Time on Planet Earth* (88) Charles Matthau.

——**Teen Sex Comedies (Youth Sexploitation Comedies)**   Amongst the teen comedies, a great many are, since the seventies, of the teen sex variety. They mostly feature inexperienced youths eager to make out with the opposite sex and ready to sow their wild oats. Some qualify also as high school films. *See also* **MALE-ORIENTED PICTURE**.
Hot Times (74) Jim McBride. *Hollywood High* (76) Patrick Wright. *Private Lessons* (80) Alan Myerson. *Shifshuf Naim / Eis am Stiel 3. Teil — Liebelein* (Isr / G 80) Boaz Davidson *aka Hot Bubblegum / Hot Bubblegum: Lemon Popsicle III / Lemon Popsicle III — Growing Up* [7 films (1977-87) in the "Lemon Popsicle" series]. *Hollywood High, Part II* (81) Caruth C. Bird, Lee Thomberg. *My Tutor* (82) George Bowers. *Screwballs* (Can 82) Rafal

Zielinski. *First Turn-On!!* (83) Michael Herz, Samuel Weil. *Hot Dog . . . The Movie* (83) Peter Markle. *Private School* (83) Noel Black. *Spring Break* (83) Sean S. Cunningham. *Hardbodies* (84 MCTV) Mark Griffiths. *Paradise Motel* (84) Cary Medoway. *Making the Grade* (84) Dorian Walker *aka The Last American Preppy.*

————**Teen-Violence Films (Teenage-Violence Movies)**   Violence in the teenager's world is mostly portrayed in teenage-horror pictures of the hack-'em-up or slasher film (q.v.) variety. Another type of film in which violence thrives is the youth gang film, which mostly forms part of the juvenile delinquency genre. In the category of teen-violence films, gore and, to a lesser extent, permissive sex are rampant. These films are frequently frowned upon by the conservative censorship boards of some countries which deplore their brutality and crudity.

Teenage-Horror Pictures: Black Christmas / Un Noël tragique (Can 74) Bob Clark *aka The Babysitter / Silent Night, Evil Night / Stop Me / Stranger in the House. Terror Train / Le Train de la terreur* (Can / US 79) Roger Spottiswoode *aka Le monstre du train / Train to Terror. Prom Night / Le Bal de l'horreur* (Can 80) Paul Lynch. *Graduation Day* (81) Herb Freed. *Sweet Sixteen* (81) Jim Sotos *aka Sweet 16. Friday the 13th Part V: A New Beginning* (85) Danny Stenmann *aka Friday the 13th—A New Beginning* [8 films in the series up to 1989]. *Bloody New Year* (86) Norman J. Warren *aka Time Warp Terror. Return to Horror High* (86) Bill Froehlich. *Deadly Obsession* (88) Jeno Hodi.

Youth Gang Films (Gang Films, Youth Street Films): Boulevard Nights (79) Michael Pressman. *Over the Edge* (79) Jonathan Kaplan. *The Wanderers* (US / Hol 79) Philip Kaufman. *Rumble Fish* (83) Francis Ford Coppola. *Suburbia* (83) Penelope Spheeris *aka The Wild Side. Streets of Fire* (84) Walter Hill [subtitled "A Rock & Roll Fable. Another Time, Another Place"]. *Tuff Turf* (84) Fritz Kiersch. *3:15* (84) Larry Gross [rel. in 86] *aka 3:15—The Moment of Truth. Angel Town* (89) Eric Karson. *Rooftops* (89) Robert Wise.

Teen Pic, Teen Sex Comedies *see* **TEEN MOVIE**

Teen Slash-'em-Up(s) Film *see* **SLASHER FILM**

Teen-Violence Films *see* **TEEN MOVIE**

Teenage-Horror Picture *see* **TEEN MOVIE: Teen-Violence Films**

Teenage Movie, Teenage-Violence Movie, Teen Comedies *see* **TEEN MOVIE**

Teenie-Kill Movie *see* **SLASHER FILM**

Telefeature, Telefilm *see* **TELEVISION MOVIE**

TELEFONI BIANCHI ("White Telephone" Films)   The designation *telefoni bianchi* ("White telephone" films) is often encountered in studies of Italian cinema surveying film production in Fascist Italy. It is simply a broad label used to group together innocuous and oft-termed escapist comedies made in Italy in the 1930s and early 1940s. The "white telephone" films were mostly romantic or sophisticated comedies dealing with the wealthy upper class or portraying characters inhabiting a kind of fantasy world in which hardships were not insurmountable and a "happy ending" could always be expected. They were patterned for the most part on Hollywood, German or Hungarian models. Although not completely devoid of social comment, these films usually presented an idealized view of reality. *Rubacuori* (It 31) Guido Brignone *aka Heartbreaker / Heart-Stealer. Gli uomini, che mascalzoni...* (It 32) Mario Camerini *aka Taxi / What Rascals Men Are! Al buio insieme* (It 33) Gennaro Righelli *aka Together in the Dark. O la borsa o la vita* (It 33) Carlo Ludovico Bragaglia *aka Money or Life. Paradiso* (It 33) Guido Brignone *aka Paradise. Darò un milione* (It 35) Mario Camerini *aka I'll Give a Million. La contessa di Parma* (It 37) Alessandro Blasetti *aka The Countess of Parma. Il signor Max* (It 37) Mario Camerini. *Grandi magazzini* (It 39) Mario Camerini *aka Department Stores. Mille lire al mese* (It 39) Massiliano Neufeld *aka A Thousand Lire a Month. L'amante segretta* (It 41) Mario Mattoli. *Teresa Venerdi* (It 41) Vittorio De Sice.

Telementary *see* **DOCUMENTARY**

Telenovela *see* **SOAP OPERA**

Telepic *see* **TELEVISION MOVIE**

Teleplay *see* **TELEVISION DRAMA: Single Play**

Telerecording *see* **KINESCOPE RECORDING**

Telethon *see* **TELEVISION SHOW**

Television Ad *see* **TELEVISION COMMERCIAL**

Television Award Show *see* **TELEVISION SHOW**

TELEVISION COMEDY (TV Comedy)   The most ubiquitous form of comedy on television is situation comedy (q.v.). Stand-up comedy (q.v.) also has its adherents, especially on British television. Styles and forms of comedy (excluding TV-movie comedies and TV-comedy plays) are very diversified, enjoying short or long runs as television series according to their demand and acceptability by television audiences. *The Muppet Show* (GB 1976-81), a puppet/marionette variety show which includes guest appearances by well-known show business celebrities, is the world's most popular television comedy series. It made such engaging characters as Miss Piggy and Kermit the Frog internationally known. *That Was the Week That Was* (GB 1962), familiarly known as *TW3*, was an influential and innovative satirical series of the sixties on British television; Rowan and Martin's *Laugh-In* (1968-72) was America's most influential comedy series of its decade and introduced an original format of fast sequences made up of skits, one-liners, stand-up comedy, dance, song, satire and irreverence; *Monty Python's Flying Circus* (GB 1969-74) was a cult variety show featuring a mélange of sketches and cartoons with John Cleese, Graham Chapman and other comedians; *Not the Nine O'Clock News* (GB 1979-82) was an innovative, satirical BBC series of the early eighties which also built up a cult following.

The Muppet Show (GB 76-81 ITV) Peter Harris, Philip Casson [120 episodes]. *That Was the Week That Was* (GB 62 BBC) A. Milne *aka TW3*. *Laugh In* (68-72 NBC) Mark Warreb, Gordon Wiles; hosts Dan Rowan, Dick Martin *aka Rowan and Martin's Laugh-In* [124 episodes]. *Monty Python's Flying Circus* (GB 69-74 BBC) Ian MacNaughton, John Davies [45 episodes]. *Not the Nine O'Clock News* (GB 79-82 BBC) [28 episodes].

——**Television Roast** A type of comedy that thrives on putting people down in the best of spirits and with the willing participation of the victim who knows that all is a happy joke. Its best example on television is found in the *Dean Martin's Celebrity Roast* (1974-79), in which a guest of honor was ritually insulted ("roasted") by his peers and friends who, it is understood, admire and love him.

Dean Martin's Celebrity Roast (74-79 NBC) Greg Garrison; host: Dean Martin [28 episodes; also *The Dean Martin Celebrity Roast* (84) 3 episodes].

TELEVISION COMMERCIAL (TV Commercial, TV Ad) Commercials are the main source of revenue (if not the only one) of commercial television stations. Advertisers either sponsor programs or buy time slots for their commercials which are inserted during breaks in the shows.[111] Commercials, except on public television or state-financed television, are ubiquitous in the medium and unwelcome to most viewers who, however, have acknowledged that they allow for free television. A commercial or promotional announcement is known in the trade as a "blurb." *See* **COMMERCIAL** entry.

——**Admag (Advertising Magazine)** A program of short duration inaugurated in Britain and operational until 1963, in which performers praised some product or other during the 15-minute run of the show. *Jim's Inn* (GB 1957-63 ITV) was the most popular and the best example of this type of advertising.

——**Advertising Pod** This is a term (meaning sequence) used by the industry. The duration of advertising pods varies according to the television channel's broadcasting policy. Two minutes and 30 seconds during prime time, or three-minute pods late at night are common.

——**Counter Commercial** Counter commercials are announcements which try to counteract the influence of regular commercials by denouncing or rebutting their claims; for example, a counter commercial about the dangers of smoking.

——**Logo (Promotion Ident, Television Logo, TV Network Logo)** An animated short of 10 to 15 seconds' duration which television stations broadcast every so often for self-identification and promotion. Logos are accompanied by the station's theme music. Most television logos are computer animated.

——**Preemptible Announcement** A reduced-cost commercial sold with the proviso that its broadcast time may be changed or even cancelled by the television station if another advertiser is willing to pay normal rates.

——**Promo** A promotional announcement by a television station to advertise future programs. It is sometimes accompanied by a sneak preview (of selected scenes) of its forthcoming shows.

——**Subliminal Advertising** Experimenting in subliminal advertising took place on American television in the fifties. It consisted of sending fast messages in single frames which were supposed to work subconsciously. Obviously, the practice was an attempt at devious persuasion and was quickly outlawed. *See* **SUBLIMINAL FILM.**

——**Teaser** A sort of introductory trailer composed of one or several interesting scenes from a program, played immediately before its commencement to motivate the viewer to stay tuned.

TELEVISION DRAMA (TV Drama) Television drama covers a vast array of formats and genres including television films (q.v.), television plays, series, serials, and adaptations. David Self, *Television Drama* (London: Macmillan, 1984) offers an overall introduction to the subject.

——**Documentary Drama** One of various interchangeable labels—drama documentary, dramatic reconstruction, historical play, faction (*see* **DOCU-DRAMA**)—between which it is difficult to differentiate. Generally speaking, the term documentary drama is applied to the dramatic reenactment of a real or factual event, or to a fictional story that looks as if it was real. In British television, the type is frequently traced back to some teleplays of the late 1960s, e.g., *Cathy Come Home* (1966), *The Lump* (1967) and *In Two Minds* (1967). A more recent example is *Invasion* (1980), a reconstruction of the take-over of Czechoslovakia by the Soviet military in the spring of 1968.
   Cathy Come Home (GB 66 TV) Ken Loach. *The Lump* (GB 67 TV) Jack Gold. *In Two Minds* (GB 67 TV) Kenneth Loach. *Invasion* (GB 80 TV) Leslie Woodhead.

——**Drama Serial (Serial Drama, Television Serial)** Drama serials mostly take the shape of television novelizations (q.v.), soap operas (q.v.), or children's adventure serials. Television soap operas have long been a regular feature of daytime television, and novelizations include all kinds of adaptations from novels, classic and modern. Their genres vary from family sagas to mini-series with an historical background, science fiction and thrillers.

——**Drama Series (Series Drama)** Usually shown on a weekly basis, drama series are comprised of independent episodes featuring the same main characters in a new (although repetitive and formulaic) set of adventures, each new adventure finishing that episode, a requirement that must be accomplished in about 50 minutes' time for a one-hour series. Television drama series cover a wide spectrum of genres: crime, Westerns, hospital stories, SF. Series number from three to thirteen, the required total to fill a television "season" or a thirteen-week quarter. Series are not continuing stories as are serials. A compromise between the two is known as a "series-al" or "series / serial" which includes self-contained stories within each episode as well as continuing stories for some of the characters.

————Single Play (One-Off Play, Teleplay, Television Play, TV Play)   Abundant in British television, television plays are complete dramatic works which do not form part of a series. Many television plays are shown under a generic or umbrella title such as *Armchair Theatre* (GB 1956-74 ITV) or *The Wednesday Play / Play for Today* (GB 1964- BBC). Single plays are regarded highly in terms of television drama since they allow their creators a great amount of artistic freedom. Their length may vary from 30 minutes to over two hours. *Up the Junction* (1965) and *Cathy Come Home* (1966) are two famous examples telecast under the *Wednesday Play* banner.
Up the Junction (GB 65 TV) Kenneth Loach.   *Cathy Come Home* (GB 66 TV) Ken Loach.

————Theatre Play (Theater Play)   Theater plays are mostly represented on television as direct recordings from the stage of classical plays, or as versions of stage plays more or less adapted to the television medium. An early television practice was to show portions of a stage play rather than the whole production. A recent example of classical plays made for showing on television is the BBC series "The Shakespeare Plays" (1978-84) which includes the dramatist's 37 plays.[112]

Television-Game Show   *see*   **TELEVISION SHOW: Game Show**

TVM   *see*   **TELEVISION MOVIE**

TELEVISION MOVIE (Made-for-TV Movie, Movie-for-TV, Movie Made-for-Television, Telefeature, Telefilm, TV Movie, TVM, Vidpic) Formerly, the designation television film used to mean a film of any length (including information and entertainment films) made for the purpose of being shown on television; in recent times, the term telefilm or TV film is generally used to mean a feature-length narrative film made exclusively for television, although some are released theatrically or made available on video-cassette.[113]
Made-for-television films are not a recent innovation. *High Tor* (1956), a ghost story starring Bing Crosby, is reportedly the first feature-length TV movie made specifically for television.[114] However, it was not until the late 1960s that production began in earnest, and it was only since 1972 that

telefeatures telecast on American networks outnumbered theatrical films shown on TV. Movies made-for-TV have replaced the ubiquitous Hollywood B-features used previously as regular fodder by the TV channels, and although a lot of TV-films are forgettable, their producers have strived for quality as the films' budgets have continued to rise, and some fine telefeatures have gained high critical praise.[115] Miniseries, novels for television and some docudramas are forms which differ from TV movies only by their greater length. *See* **DOCUDRAMA**.

High Tor (56 TV) CBS musical special.

———**Made-for-Pay-TV Movies (Made-for-Cable TV Movies, MCTV Films)** They differ from made-for-TV films only in that, since they are meant to be shown to pay TV subscribers, they are not as restricted as to content or duration. Made-for-pay-TV movies include material that most networks would censor, and they do not have to abide by the networks' running time limitations. *Pygmalion, A Case of Libel, Nobody Makes me Cry,* and *The Terry Fox Story*, all made in 1982 and 1983, are examples of this recent trend.

The Terry Fox Story / Terry Fox le coureur de l'espoir (Can 82 MCTV) Ralph Thomas *aka The Road to Thunder Bay / Terry / Terry Fox the Movie*. *A Case of Libel* (Can 83 MCTV) Eric Till. *Nobody Makes Me Cry* (Can 83 MCTV) Lou Antonio *aka Between Friends / Intimate Strangers*. *Pygmalion* (Can / US 83 MCTV) Alan Cooke.

Television Network Logo   *see*   **TELEVISION COMMERCIAL: Logo**

TELEVISION NEWS (TV News)   News, current affairs programs and weather reports may be grouped together as services meant to impart topical and factual information to millions of televiewers who, for the most part, have come to rely on them almost to the exclusion of any other source of news information. This is the case, for instance, in Britain and America where statistically more people rely on the news provided by television than by any other medium. In response to this public demand, networks and television stations have steadily increased the number and length of their news broadcasts which, besides short news bulletins, may include news programs of 15 minutes, half-hour, one hour, 90 minutes, or even of more than two hours' duration, minus commercials.

News programs usually include information on international, national and local levels, a weather rundown, sports news, entertainment, editorial and human interest items depending on available time.

Current affairs programs may be categorized as extensions of the news as they supply amplification and background information to what is topical and current at the time of broadcasting.

———**Action News**   A chummy, informal approach to the news which was prevalent in America in the late 60s and early 70s. It took different names (*Eyewitness News, The Scene News*) as it was adopted by many local television stations. The reporters themselves delivered the news rather than writing it down for newscasters to broadcast. It was characterized by a humorous style and a propensity for chatter in between news breaks. It was derogatorily named "happy talk" news.

——**Actualities**   The term refers to news programs, program segments or documentaries which present actual footage of events of historical interest.

——**Breakfast Television Show (Early Morning Program)**   A program, usually of two hours' duration, which combines morning news with music, talk, interviews, comedy and news summaries. It was first introduced in the United States by NBC in 1952 and named *Today / The Today Show*.

——**Hard News**   Hard news refers to the actual daily news as distinguished from other material such as features, stories, commentaries or human interest items which may be included in a newscast, but which are not connected with current events.

——**Instant Analysis**   In the United States, the practice of immediate analytical reporting by the networks of presidential addresses.

——**News Series (News-Magazine Series)**   Current affairs or public affairs programs aired daily or weekly consisting of panel discussions of topical issues (*Meet the Press*, 1947- NBC), interviews, matters of national interest or news analysis covering the world scene (*Panorama*, GB 1953- BBC; *60 Minutes*, 1968- CBS).

——**Public Affairs Program (Current Affairs Program)**   A topical, factual presentation of local, regional, national or international matters which in the United States of America, as defined by the FCC (Federal Communications Commission), may take the form of commentaries, round table discussions, speeches, editorials, documentaries, analysis, interview forums and political presentations.

——**Rip-and-Read Newscast**   The practice of reading news roundups straight or in edited form from the news copy provided by a Teletype machine.

TELEVISION NOVELIZATION (Classic Serial, Miniseries, Novel-for-Television, Novelization, Television Novel, TV Novelization)   Often labelled miniseries, TV novelizations are a good way of condensing classical and modern novels into a series of episodes for television. The serialization may consist of any number of segments shown in 30-minute, one hour, or two-hour slots. *The Forsyte Saga* (1967), a successful television adaptation of John Galsworthy's novels, comprises 26 episodes of about 50 minutes each.

Television novelizations have been very popular since the seventies, and most countries with television facilities have produced outstanding adaptations of national and foreign classics.

In the United States, the production of miniseries or adaptations of novels for television started in earnest after the success of various British series first shown on public television and later on commercial television. The success of *The Blue Knight* (1973), a 2-part, four-hour adaptation of Joseph Wambaugh's novel, and Leo Uris' *QBVII* (1974) established the form in the United States. *Roots* (1977), a 12-hour saga of a black family, and *Holocaust* (1978), a 9-hour story of a Jewish family during the Nazi persecution, are television landmarks and internationally successful.

The term television novel has been used to describe a serial written for television rather than adapted from a novel. *See* Paul Kerr, "Classic Serials—To Be Continued," *Screen* 23.1 (May-June 1982): 6–19.

The Forsyte Saga (GB 67 TV) James Cellan Jones, David Giles [26 episodes]. *Casanova* (GB 71 TV) John Glenister, Mark Cullingham [6 episodes]. *The Blue Knight* (73 TV) Robert Butler [originally shown in 4 parts; *Cf. The Blue Knight* (75 TV) J. Lee Thompson: TV pilot for CBS cop series (75-76)]. *QBVII* (74 TV) Tom Gries [originally shown in 2 parts]. *I, Claudius* (GB 76 TV) Herbert Wise [13 episodes]. *Roots* (77 TV) David Greene, John Erman, Gilbert Moses, Marvin Chomsky [twelve 60-minute episodes; 8-part miniseries; also syndicated as nine 90-minute episodes with Ben Vereen as host]. *Holocaust: The Story of the Family Weiss* (78 TV) Marvin J. Chomsky *aka Holocaust* [4 episodes]. *The Timeless Land* (Aust 79-80 TV) Michael Carson, Rob Stewart [8 episodes]. *Shogun* (US / J 80 TV) Jerry London [5 parts; narrated by Orson Welles]. *Brideshead Revisited* (GB / US 81 TV) Charles Sturridge, Michael Lindsay-Hogg [11-part TV novelization].

Television Play *see* **TELEVISION DRAMA: Single Play**

TELEVISION PROGRAM (Product, TV Program)   Any film, performance or show which is broadcast on television. Since its inception, television has adopted, developed and initiated different types of programs to fill its airtime. Some originated with other media and were adapted to the requirements of the new medium; others originated on television itself.

——**Firstrun Program**   A television program, series episode, television film or a motion picture which is broadcast for the first time.

——**Firstrun Syndication**   Programs made exclusively for syndication or imported programs not previously shown on American networks.

——**Long Form**   The term is used by the networks for programs longer than 60 minutes, especially when referring to 90-minute dramatic series.

——**Magazine Format**   A program composed of segments of various lengths and themes. Current affairs programs (e.g., *60 Minutes*) are a good example of the format.

——**Offnetwork Reruns**   Previously televised network programs that go into syndication.

——**Prerelease**   A term used to define the American practice of selling product (programs) to Canada for broadcasting on Canadian television before releasing it at home.

——**Rerun (Command Performance)**   A rerun is a reshowing of a television program. The plural reruns usually applies to entire series.

——**"Rested" Film**   A film or television series which has not been shown for several years and may be played again as a reissue.

——**Runover**   A program which runs beyond its expected duration time; this often happens with sporting events or on-the-spot political broadcasts.

——**Strip**   A program aired at the same time five or more consecutive days a week.

——**Sustaining Show**   A program shown by networks and stations without any advertisers' contribution or support.

——**Target Programming**   It consists of programs made for and addressed to minority audiences to serve their needs.
Television programming broadly covers the following areas: 1. News and Current Affairs (Public affairs) 2. TV Documentaries 3. Educational and Instructional Television — courses for schools, colleges and universities; instructional programs for adults including such diverse topics as art, astronomy, consumer programs, cookery, gardening and science 4. Children's Television — educational programs for different age-groups, stories and plays for children, cartoons and puppet shows 5. Politics and Political Programs — speeches, debates, party political broadcasts and televised elections 6. Music and the Arts 7. Religious Television (Pray TV) — religious services and various religious programs 8. Sports — televised sports and sports discussions 9. Drama 10. Light Entertainment — variety, comedy, game shows and talk shows 11. Publicity and Advertising — promotion of a channel's own programs, advance announcements and commercials.

Television Roast   *see*   **TELEVISION COMEDY**

Television Serial   *see*   **TELEVISION SERIES**

TELEVISION SERIES (TV Series)   Television series are either open-ended (continuing indefinitely) or closed-ended (made up of a determined number of spisodes). The word series and its compounds have taken diverse meanings in television parlance; some of these meanings and related words follow.

——**Anthology**   A series of independent stories with different characters in each story, but usually belonging to the same genre. Anthologies are sometimes introduced by a host, e.g., Rod Serling's *Twlight Zone* (1959-62; 1963-64), Boris Karloff's *Thriller* (1960-62) and *Alfred Hitchcock Presents* (1955-62).
Alfred Hitchcock Presents (55-60 CBS; 60-62 NBC) [268 episodes; host: Alfred Hitchcock].   *Twilight Zone* (59-62; 63-64 CBS) [134 thirty-minute

plus 17 sixty-minute episodes; host: Rod Serling]. *Thriller* (60-62 NBC) [67 episodes; host: Boris Karloff].

——**Miniseries (Limited Series, Mini-Series)** Since the mid-seventies, a loosely applied term which includes television films broadcast in two or more parts and serializations of novels running for as long as 26 hours, but less than 13 is the norm.[116] The term miniseries has also been applied to docudramas (q.v.) and to nonfiction in the form of episodic documentaries. Miniseries are programmed for limited runs on consecutive nights, or on a weekly basis for several weeks; they are a closed-end series as opposed to open-end series which run indefinitely according to audience interest. The miniseries is a distinctive television format. *See* **TELEVISION NOVELI-ZATION**.

——**Multiseries (Rotating Series)** Several series which alternate in the same broadcasting period. They are given a generic or umbrella title, e.g., *Mystery Movie* and *The Men*.[117] The generic or umbrella title is also used to group dissimilar films together under the same banner, e.g., *World Première*, *Movie of the Week* and *Million Dollar Movie*.

Million Dollar Movie Generic title used by WOR-TV (New York) for their nightly movie program. *Mystery Movie* Generic title for TV multiseries as in "NBC Mystery Movie" (71-72), "NBC Sunday Mystery Movie" (72-77), "NBC Tuesday Mystery Movie" (74) and "NBC Wednesday Mystery Movie" (72-74). *World Première* (71-72) Generic title for "NBC World Première Movie." *The Men* (72-73 TV) Generic title for three ABC alternating series: "Assignment Vienna," "The Delphi Bureau" and "Jigsaw" [altogether 24 episodes]. *Movie of the Week* Generic title for "The NBC Movie of the Week" (76-) and for ABC "Movie of the Week" (69-75) TV multiseries.

——**Series Pilot (Pilot, Pilot Show)** Pilots are television films which are meant to test public reaction to the proposed television series. They are made for the half-hour, one-hour or two-hour time airing periods. Many are television movies doubling as pilots; some are made as pilots which eventually turn up as television movies. Some series require several pilots (e.g., *The Love Boat* TV series had three experimental pilots) before they are fully launched.

The Love Boat (77-86 ABC) [preceded by the TV pilots *The Love Boat* (76 TV) Richard Kinon, Alan Meyerson, *The Love Boat II* (77 TV) Hy Averback and *The Love Boat III* (77 TV) Richard Kinon].

——**Spin-Off (Spinoff)** A new television series which has been inspired by and uses elements of an already-existing series. For instance, the comedy series *Maude* (1972-78), *The Jeffersons* (1975), *Good Times* (1974-79) and *Archie Bunker's Place* (1979-83) are spin-offs of *All in the Family* (1971-79), itself based on the BBC's *Till Death Us Do Part* (1964-74). The term is also used for an episode in a series, which introduces new situations and characters that, in turn, may form the basis for another series.

Till Death Us Do Part (GB 64-74 BBC). *All in the Family* (71-79 CBS) Paul Bogart, John Rich, H. Wesley Kenney [207 episodes]. *Maude* (72-78 CBS)

[142 episodes]. *Good Times* (74-79 CBS) [120 episodes]. *The Jeffersons* (75-85 CBS) Bob Lally, Jack Shea, Oz Scott, Tony Singletary. *Archie Bunker's Place* (79-83 CBS) [89 episodes].

——**Strand (Television Strand)** A number of units—several single plays, a series, a miniseries—usually supervised by a television producer.

——**Television Serial (Serial)** A television series consisting of episodes showing continuation of storyline from installment to installment. The open-end soap operas (q.v.) are the best-known form of television serial. Serials in the form of television novelizations have recently become very widespread as well.

TELEVISION SHOW (TV Show) A general term for a television program. In the field of what is termed light television entertainment (television comedy is treated separately), many different types of shows have emerged and gained popularity; they appear regularly as part of network or station programming. Some of these shows follow.

——**Game Show (Television Game Show)** A popular show in which the participants engage in games, spurred by some reward or other, and in the process provide spectator entertainment. Game shows are very varied and ingenious in devising new games to attract audience interest.[118] Examples of game shows:

Beat the Clock (50-58 CBS; 58-61 ABC) Leonard Valenta; host: Clayton "Bud" Collyer [*Beat the Clock* (79-80 CBS) Paul Alter; host: Monty Hall]. *It's a Knockout / Jeux Sans Frontières* (GB 66-82 BBC) Eurovision TV show. *The Dating Game* (68-73 ABC) John Dorsey; host: Jim Lange [*The New Dating Game* (73; 77-80 ABC)]. *The Generation Game* (GB 71- BBC). *Almost Anything Goes* (76- ABC).

——**Quiz Show (Quiz Program, Panel Game)** A television entertainment program in which a host or hostess addresses questions to selected contestants to determine who scores highest, wins more prizes or money. Panel games have several panelists provided with a set number of questions which help them to guess, for instance, the occupation of the contestants as in *What's My Line* (1950-67). There are different types of quiz shows. Some examples:

What's My Line (50-67 CBS) host: John Daly. *Name That Tune* (53-54 NBC; 54-59 CBS; 74-75 NBC; 77 NBC) Perry Laffery; host: Red Benson, Bill Cullen / John Dorsey, Terry Kyne; host: Tom Kennedy (74-75; 77) [also *The $100,000 Name That Tune* (74-81 Syndicated) John Dorsey, Richard Gottlieb; host: Tom Kennedy]. *$64,000 Question* (55-58 CBS) host: Hal March. *Hollywood Squares* (66-80 NBC) Jerome Shaw; host: Peter Marshall. *Mastermind* (GB 72 BBC). *Sale of the Century* (GB 72 ITV).

——**Talent Show** A show in which amateur participants demonstrate their skills and performing abilities. A talent show may include dancers, singers, musicians, comedians, clowns or any individual with talent and a desire for recognition in show business, e.g., the British *Opportunity Knocks* (1956-77 ITV) and *New Faces* (1973-78 ITV).

————**Talk Show (Chat Show)**   A talk or chat show is a television program in which a host or hostess chats with and interviews celebrity guests. In some talk shows, the conversation is interspersed with light variety, mostly provided by singers and comedians. Johnny Carson's *Tonight Show* (1954–1993, with Johnny as host from 1962) was the longest-running and most successful talk show in the United States. Dick Cavett, Mike Douglas, David Frost and Merv Griffin have been at one time or other well-known luminaries in the field.

   Tonight Show (53-54 WNBT [New York]); (54- NBC) hosts: Steve Allen (53-54; 54-57); Ernie Kovacs (56-57); Jack Paar (57-62); *The Tonight Show Starring Johnny Carson* (62-92) Bobby Quinn; host: Johnny Carson *aka Tonight's America After Dark* (57).

————**Telethon**   A very long television variety show telecast live and spanning several hours, usually meant to raise funds for charity or for a public-service organization. The show has several people answering telephones so televiewers may ring in to pledge donations.

————**Trash-Sport Show (Junk Sports)**   A gathering by the networks of celebrities or teams to compete with each other in a variety of sports, e.g., CBS's *Celebrity Challenge of the Sexes* (1978). This type of show garnered some popularity in the seventies. In a similar vein, celebrities appear in big top shows to perform circus acts of their choice, for which they have assiduously trained, e.g., CBS's *Circus of the Stars* (1977-84).

   Circus of the Stars (77-84 CBS) [9 TV variety specials]. *Celebrity Challenge of the Sexes* (78 CBS) Bernie Hoffman; host: Tom Brookshire [five 30-minute shows; also *Celebrity Challenge of the Sexes 1-5* (77-80) [five 120-minute CBS specials].

————**Television Award Show (Award Presentations)**   The granting of different types of awards is televised annually and attracts a considerable number of viewers. One of the top shows of the year is the *Academy Awards Telecast* (Oscar Show) instituted by the Academy of Motion Picture Arts and Sciences to reward excellence in motion pictures. They were first presented in 1929 and live telecasts started in 1953. They are watched globally by massive audiences. The television equivalent of the Oscars is the *TV Emmy Awards*, inaugurated in 1949 by the Academy of Television Arts and Sciences and telecast since 1955. Besides the United States, other nations have also instituted their own awards which are also televised in their respective countries.

————**Variety Show (Television Variety Show, Variety-Vaudeville, Vaudeo)** A variety show consists of different performing arts which include songs, dances, skits and various entertaining numbers, e.g. *The Ed Sullivan Show* (1948-71) and *The Good Old Days* (GB 1953). Vaudeo is a contraction of vaudeville and video, and it is applied to variety shows.

   The Ed Sullivan Show (55-71 CBS) John Wray, Jacques Andre, Tim Kiley; host: Ed Sullivan *aka Toast of the Town* (48-55). *The Good Old Days* (GB 53 BBC).

TELEVISION SPECIAL (Once-Only Show, One-Off Special, One-Shot Program, Oto / One Time Only, Special, Spectacular, TV Special) Specials made their appearance on American television as spectaculars in 1953, although as this type of program proliferated, this label was later dropped in favor of the more neutral "special." Specials are one-shot shows, sometimes telecast in two parts, which preempt normally scheduled programs. They are not part of a series or other continuous form. Specials began as variety shows, but at present the term applies to any kind of once-only presentation — news, light entertainment, drama, cultural items. Some television series originated as specials, e.g., *Laugh-In* (1968-72) and *The Untouchables* (1959-62).

   The Untouchables (59-62 ABC) Walter Winchell (narrator) [114 episodes].
   Laugh-In (68-73 NBC) Mark Warreb, Gordon Wiles; hosts: Dan Rowan, Dick Martin *aka Rowan and Martin's Laugh-In* [124 episodes].

Television Variety Show   *see*   **TELEVISION SHOW: Variety Show**

TELEVISION VERSION   It has become common practice in the United States to cut X-, R-, and even PG-rated features for television. These are usually aired with a barely noticeable "edited for television" warning. Nudity and coarse language are expurgated.

   Another recent practice has been to reconstruct a film by cutting the offending parts and adding unused footage, often resulting in longer running versions, usually duller than the original, released theatrically films. *The Godfather Saga* (1977, TV version), offers an example of a reedited and resequenced production (in this case altering *The Godfather*, 1971 and *The Godfather, Part II*, 1974) into a 4-part, 7½-hour television mini-series shown by NBC.

   Other countries, Australia for instance, may be more lenient in some of the material included in the original film (e.g., nudity) and use a different tag ("modified TV version"), but the premise of keeping television "clean" and "safer" for the homeviewer is the same. *See also* **RECONSTRUCTED FILM**.

   The Godfather Saga (77) Francis Ford Coppola *aka Mario Puzo's The Godfather: The Complete Novel for Television*.

Terror Film   *see*   **HORROR FILM**

Theatre Play   *see*   **TV DRAMA**

Theatrical Feature   *see*   **FEATURE FILM**

THEATRICAL FILM   The term theatrical film has three main acceptations: it is used to distinguish films which are shown in cinemas as distinct from nontheatrical films (q.v.) meant to be shown somewhere else; it is a term for films based on plays, that is, for films adapted from stage plays or musical shows; and finally, the term is also used to denote those films which closely imitate their theatrical source either by duplicating a stage play (filming it as it is being performed), or by using techniques which are more typical of the stage than of the film medium. To this last group of theatrical films belongs a sizeable percentage of the films (for the most part lost) produced between the inception of the moving picture and the advent of sound – more or less from 1896 to 1930. *See also* **ADAPTATION, FILM D'ART**, and **FICTIONAL FILM**.

> *The Count of Monte Cristo* (12) Edwin S. Porter. *Men and Women* (14) James Kirkwood, D. W. Griffith (supervisor). *The Warrens of Virginia* (14) Cecil B. DeMille. *The Ghost Talks* (28) Lewis Seiler. *Coquette* (29) Sam Taylor. *The Green Goddess* (29) Alfred Green. *The Letter* (29) Jean De Limur [F.v.:*La Lettre*; directed by Louis Mercaton]. *Taming of the Shrew* (29) Sam Taylor. *Anna Christie* (30) Clarence Brown [German and Swedish versions directed by Jacques Feyder].

Theatrical Short Film   *see*   **SHORT**

Thematic Film   *see*   **STRUCTURAL FILM: Participatory Film**

Thievery Films   *see*   **CRIME FILM**

Third Cinema, Third World Cinema   *see*   **THIRD WORLD FILM**

THIRD WORLD FILM (Third World Cinema)   A broad designation for a film originating in a third world country, that is, an underdeveloped nation from Africa, Asia or Latin America. The term has political implications since it has been associated with the work of activist and militant filmmakers. Teshome H. Gabriel's *Third Cinema in the Third World* (Ann Arbor, MI: UMI Research Press, 1982) focuses on this aspect of Third World Cinema; those films he calls "Third Cinema" diverge from the traditional cinema based on the Hollywood mold.[119] *See also* **REVOLUTIONARY FILM**.

> *Lucia* (Cuba 68) Humberto Solas. *El Chacal de Nahueltoro* (Chile 69) Miguel Littín *aka The Jackal of Nahueltoro*. *Gav* (Iran 69) Daryush Mehrjui *aka The Cow*. *Yawar Mallku / Blood of the Condor* (Bol 69) Jorge Sanjinés. *Les Mille et une mains* (Mor 72) Souhel Ben Barka *aka A Thousand and One Hands*. *Kaadu* (Ind 73) Girish Karnad *aka The Forest*. *Chronique des années de braise* (Alg 74) Mohammed Lakhdar-Hamina *aka Chronicle of the Years of Ashes*. *Dareyeh Mina* (Iran 74) Daryush Mehrjui *aka The Cycle / The Mina Cycle*. *Xala* (Sen 74) Ousmane Sembène *aka Impuissance temporaire*. *Actas de Marusia* (Mex 75) Miguel Littín *aka Letters from Marusia*. *El Chergui ou le silence violent* (Mor 75) Moumen Smihi *aka El Chergui / El Chergui* or *The Violent Silence*. *Manthan* (Ind 75) Shyam Benegal *aka The Churning* [with *Ankur / The Seedling* (Ind 74) and *Nishant / Night's End* (Ind 75) part of a trilogy on caste]. *Maynila sa mga kuko ng liwanag* (Phil 75) Lino Brocka *aka Manila in the Claws of Neon*. *El Otro Francisco* (Cuba 75) Santiago Llapur *aka The Other Francisco*. *Ceddo* (Sen 76) Ousmane Sembène. *Omar Gatlato* (Alg 76) Merzak Allouache. *La última cena* (Cuba 76) Tomás Gutiérrez Alea *aka The Last Supper*. *Insiang* (Phil 77) Lino Brocka. *Mababangong Bangungot* (Phil 77) Kidlaat Tahimik *aka The Perfumed Nightmare*. *El Rancheador* (Cuba 77) Sergio Giral *aka*

The Bounty Hunter. **Jaguar** (Phil 79) Lino Brocka. *Aiye* (Nig 80) Ola Balogun. **Love Brewed in the African Pot** (Ghana 80) Kwaw Paintsil Ansah. **Djeli, Conte d'aujourd'hui** (IvC 81) Kramo-Lanciné Fadika *aka Djelli.* **Sirab / La Ballade de mamlouk / Preludy pouste** (Tun / Cz 82) Abdel-Hafiz Bouasida. *Hasta cierto punto* (Cuba 83) Tomás Gutiérrez Alea *aka Up to a Certain Point.* **Khandar** (Ind 83) Mrinal Sen *aka The Ruins.*

3-D FILM (Stereoscopic Film, Three-Dimensional Film)   Three-dimensional films (or "depthies" and "deepies" as they sometimes have been called in opposition to "flatties" or two-dimensional pictures) have appeared on and off since *The Power of Love*, the world's first 3-D feature film, which opened in Los Angeles on September 27, 1922.[120]

Succinctly put, three-dimensional movies attempt to give the viewer not only a feeling of height and width, but of depth as well. This is achieved in motion pictures by filming simultaneously the same scene from slightly different angles which, when viewed by the spectator, will blend and create the illusion of depth perception which is not conveyed by the flat, two-dimensional images of film and television.[121]

The 1950s saw the first wave of 3-D films as Hollywood tried to recapture the audience being lured away by television in ever-increasing numbers. The film studios tried many gimmicks to solve the problem of diminishing audiences, and 3-D was one of them. Although 3-D films were a novelty for a while, the public soon lost interest and by 1954, 3-D productions had petered out. The success of *The Stewardesses* (1969), a soft-core porno film which, having cost less than $100,000, went on to gross over $26 million, spurred a smaller wave of 3-D films in the 1970s. In the 1980s, the film *Friday the 13th Part III* (1982) heralded a renewed interest in 3-D. A totally satisfactory 3-D system has still to be devised.[122] *See* R.M. Hayes, *3-D Movies: A History and Filmography of Stereoscopic Cinema* (Jefferson, NC: McFarland, 1989).

The Power of Love (22) Nat Deverich [first American 3-D feature]. *Bwana Devil* (52) Arch Oboler *aka The Lions of Gulu.* *House of Wax* (53) Andre de Toth *aka Waxworks.* *Kiss Me Kate* (53) George Sidney. *La marca del hombre lobo / Die toten Augen des Dr. Dracula* (Sp / G 67) Henry L. Egan (Enrique L. Equiluz) *aka Frankenstein's Bloody Terror / Hell's Creatures / El hombre lobo / The Mark of the Wolfman / Vampire of Dr. Dracula / The Wolfman of Count Dracula.* *The Stewardesses* (69) Alf Silliman, Jr. (Allan Silliphant) *aka Airline Stewardesses* [first American 3-D feature shown in 70mm]. *Il mostro è in tavola, Barone ... Frankenstein / De la chair pour Frankenstein / Flesh for Frankenstein* (It / F / US 73) Paul Morrissey, Anthony M. Dawson (Antonio Margheriti) *aka Andy Warhol's Flesh for Frankenstein / Andy Warhol's Frankenstein / Carne per Frankenstein / The Devil and Dr. Frankenstein / Frankenstein / The Frankenstein Experiment / Up Frankenstein.* *Friday the 13th—Part III* (82) Steve Miner *aka Friday the 13th Part 3-D.* *J'ai rencontré le père Noël* (F 84) Christian Gion *aka Here Comes Santa Claus / I Met Santa Claus.* *Starchaser: The Legend of Orin* (85) Steven Hahn.

Three-Handkerchief Film *see* **WEEPIE**

Thrill Comedies *see* **SLAPSTICK**

THRILLER (Suspense Film, Suspenser, Suspense Thriller) A very loose, much-used label that covers a broad range of films which may be included in many different genres. To qualify as a thriller, a film requires a substantial degree of suspense as its main ingredient. To many critics, thrillers do not constitute a genre *per se*, and the term itself does not tell us much as to what kind of picture is involved.[123] Further elucidation is needed; hence the many binary combinations with the word thriller: action thriller, comedy thriller, crime thriller, gangster thriller, heist thriller, horror thriller, mystery thriller, parody thriller, political thriller, psychological thriller, romantic thriller, science fiction thriller, sex thriller, spy thriller, suspense thriller and many more similar groupings.

Most thrillers are found in the subgenres of the crime movie, the horror movie and the adventure film, but not to the exclusion of other genres.

The type of film implied by the expression thriller is one in which the build-up of suspense progresses to a high point, keeping the viewers on tenterhooks as they wonder what is going to happen next. Such a film, if well made, is supposed to start the adrenaline flowing.

Besides a large amount of suspense, other components that help in categorizing a film as a thriller are intrigue, mystery and adventure. The right proportion of these elements makes a successful thriller or suspense film.[124]

This type of film has a worldwide, acknowledged master in Alfred Hitchcock (1899–1980), whose films have been mostly thrillers. Indeed, it would be unthinkable to talk about thrillers without paying homage to Hitchcock's genius in the art of creating suspense.

From cliff-hangers to movies made for television (a British series of features called *Thriller* may be recalled for their neatness and quality), the range of thrillers is vast, and they are perennially popular. *See also* **GIALLO, POLITICAL THRILLER.**

Safety Last (23) Fred Newmeyer, Sam Taylor. *Four Hours to Kill* (35) Mitchell Leisen. *Night Train to Munich* (GB 40) Carol Reed *aka Night Train.* *A Face Behind the Mask* (41) Robert Florey. *I See a Dark Stranger* (GB 46) Frank Launder *aka The Adventuress. Sorry, Wrong Number* (48) Anatole Litvak. *The Third Man* (GB 49) Carol Reed. *Cause for Alarm* (51) Tay Garnett. *Le Salaire de la peur / Vite perdute* (F / It 52) Henri-Georges Clouzot *aka Il salario della paura / Wages of Fear. Inferno* (53) Roy Baker. *Les Diaboliques* (F 54) Henri-Georges Clouzot *aka Diabolique / The Fiends. Du Rififi chez les hommes* (F 54) Jules Dassin *aka Rififi. Zero Hour!* (57) Hall Bartlett. *North by Northwest* (59) Alfred Hitchcock. *Psycho* (60) Alfred Hitchcock. *Cape Fear* (61) J. Lee Thompson *aka The Executioners. Mélodie en sous-sol / Colpo grosso al Casinò* (F / It 62) Henri Verneuil *aka Any Number Can Win / The Big Grab / The Big Snatch. Lady in a Cage* (63) Walter Grauman. *The Collector* (GB / US 64) William Wyler. *Blow-Up / Blow-up* (GB / It 66) Michelangelo Antonioni *aka Blowup. Wait until Dark* (67) Terence Young. *The Day of the Jackal / Chacal* (GB / F 73) Fred Zinnemann. *Charley Varrick* (73) Don Siegel. *Thriller* (GB

73-75 ITV) [TV anthology series of 42 episodes]. *Escape from Alcatraz* (79) Donald Siegel. *F/X* (85) Robert Mandel *aka F/X Murder by Illusion*. *Fatal Attraction* (87) Adrian Lyne. *Grievous Bodily Harm* (Aust 87) Mark Joffe. *No Way Out* (87) Roger Donaldson. *The Grasscutter* (NZ 88) Ian Mune.

Thriller *all'Italiana* *see* GIALLO

Time Travel Films *see* SCIENCE FICTION FILM

Timely Film *see* SOCIAL CONSCIOUSNESS FILM

Tits and Ass Movie *see* MALE-ORIENTED PICTURE; *see also* NUDIE

Tits and Sand Picture *see* SWASHBUCKLER: Oriental Swashbucklers

Topical *see* ACTUALITY

Topical Film *see* SOCIAL CONSCIOUSNESS FILM

Tourist Film *see* TRAVELOGUE

Traditional Melodrama *see* MELODRAMA

TRAGEDY   Tragedy has never been defined satisfactorily as it tends to change at different times. In dramatic terms, it usually describes the plight of a hero or heroine who has to face insurmountable obstacles and who is impelled, in spite of himself / herself, towards a tragic or disastrous fate which may end in death. Whether this is due to a personal shortcoming or some outside force, his / her final destiny is inevitable. Tragedy proper on the screen occurs infrequently. The films which may be called tragedies are mostly adaptations from classical plays, e.g., the works of Shakespeare (q.v.) and the Greek tragedians. Modern tragedy is also represented through adaptations of successful plays, e.g., Arthur Miller's *Death of a Salesman,* made into a film in 1951 and 1985.
Death of a Salesman (51) Laslo Benedeck. *Antigone* (US / Gr 61) George Tzavellas. *Elektra* (Gr 61) Michael Cacoyannis *aka Electra*. *Edipo re* (It / Mor 67) Pier Paolo Pasolini *aka Oedipus Rex*. *Oedipus the King* (GB 67) Philip Saville. *I cannibali* (It 69) Liliana Cavani *aka The Cannibals / The Cannibals Among Us / The Year of the Cannibals*. *Medea / Médée* (It / F / G 69) Pier Paolo Pasolini. *The Trojan Women* (Gr / US 71) Michael Cacoyannis. *Szerekmem, Elektra* (Hung 74) Miklól Jancsó *aka Elektreia / Electra*. *Death of a Salesman* (85 TV) Volker Schlondorff.

Tragic Farce *see* FARCE

Trailblazer *see* SEMINAL FILM

TRAILER (Coming Attraction Trailer, Preview, Prevue)   A short film made of excerpts from a movie advertised in cinemas as a forthcoming attraction.[125] A trailer or preview is basically a promotional device which sometimes includes original footage especially shot for it. Advertising for new films is also done on television in order to promote a particular film; it may take the form of very short clips accompanying a critic's appraisal. Old trailers have sometimes been made the subject of retrospective compilations, e.g., John Landis' *Coming Soon!* (1982), a film of about one hour, made mostly of Universal Pictures' previews of horror and science fiction movies. Specialized cinemas have also presented programs consisting only of trailers.

Train Film   *see*   **RAILWAY FILM**

Training Camp Films   *see*   **WAR FILM**

Training Film   *see*   **FACTUAL FILM;**   *see also*   **WAR FILM: Preparedness War Films**

Trance Film   *see*   **UNDERGROUND FILM**

Trash Film, Trashy Film   *see*   **SLEAZY FILM**

Trash-Sport Show   *see*   **TELEVISION SHOW**

TRAVEL FILM (Expedition Film, Exploration Film, Travelog, Travelogue)   Travel films began as "scenics" consisting usually of a panoramic view of a familiar site, or as filmed footage taken by the camera placed on a moving train or other fast means of transportation. Another early form of the travel film, the travel-interest film, described foreign customs, and its variant, the travel-industrial, focused on some special feature peculiar (like fishing in the North Sea or date harvesting in Egypt) to a region or country. A further development introduced expedition films about hunting big game in Africa, Asia and America, or exploring the polar regions.

At one time fashionable, travel films or travelogs were perfectly suited to armchair travelers and were shown as part of the regular program in many cinemas.[126] At their best, they capture the flavor of foreign lands and their people; at their worst, they are insipid and unimaginative. Early travelogs sought to portray the exotic appeal of distant countries by capturing the natural beauty of landscapes, magnificent monuments and local celebrations. Many travel agencies sponsor tourist films or travelogs to promote their package tours.

The Alaskan Eskimo (53) James Algar [first in a series of 14 Walt Disney's People and Places (1953-60) films]. *En Djungelsaga* (Sw 55) Arne Sucksdorff *aka The Flute and the Arrow / A Jungle Saga*. *The Ama Girls* (58) Ben Sharpsteen *aka Japan Harvests the Sea* [People and Places series]. *The Danube* (60) Ben Sharpsteen [last in the People and Places series]. *Iran* (Swiz 71) Claude Pinoteau, Claude Lelouch [no dialogue or narration]. *Winter with Dracula* (GB 71) John Dooley. *Alberta Adventure* (Can 74-75) Trevor Paige.

Travel-Industrial, Travel-Industrial Film, Travel-Interest Film, Travelog(ue) *see* **TRAVEL FILM**

Travesty *see* **PARODY**

Trendsetter, Trend-Setting Film *see* **SEMINAL FILM**

Trial Melodrama *see* **LAWYER FILM**

Tribute War Films *see* **WAR FILM**

TRICK FILM   The short *The Execution of Mary Queen of Scots* (1895), made to be shown in Edison's Kinetoscope peep machines, is reputed to be the world's first special-effects motion picture (q.v.). It showed, by the early use of stop-motion photography, the decapitation of the lady in question. However, the father of the trick film is Georges Méliès (1861–1938) who, having started in show business as a magician, carried over into moviemaking the magician's art of make-believe. He made many trick and fantasy films. Some of his most famous trick films include *Illusions fantasmagoriques / The Famous Box Trick* (1898), *L'Impressionist fin de siècle / An Up-to-Date Conjuror* (1899), *L'Homme à la tête de Caoutchouc / The Man with the Rubber Head* (1902), *Le Mélomane / The Melomaniac* (1903).

Trick films were popular during the early years of the silent screen, and Georges Méliès had many imitators. Trick films are essentially special-effects films, although the term trick film is usually restricted to films which make extensive use of trick photography or special optical effects such as stop motion, fast and slow motion, multiple exposure and the use of mattes. For an account of some early trick films and the special-effects movie, *see* Harold Schechter and David Everitt, *Film Tricks* (New York: Harlin Quist Book, 1980); the extant films of Méliès are described in John Frazer, *Artificially Arranged Scenes* (Boston: G. K. Hall, 1979).

The Execution of Mary Queen of Scots (1895) Alfred E. Clark. *Illusions fantasmagoriques* (F 1898) Georges Méliès *aka The Famous Box Trick*. *L'Impressioniste fin de sièle* (F 1899) Georges Méliès *aka Illusioniste fin de siècle / An Up-to-Date Conjuror*. *L'Homme à la tête de caoutchouc* (F 02) Georges Méliès *aka The Man with the Rubber Head / A Swelled Head*. *The Twentieth Century Tramp* (02) Edwin S. Porter *aka Happy Hooligan and His Airship*. *Animated Picture Studio* (GB 03) [English film bought by American Mutoscope and Biograph]. *Le Mélomane* (F 03) Georges Méliès *aka The Melomaniac*. *Saved!* (03) A. E. Weed (cameraman). *The Jonah Man; or, The Traveller Bewitched* (GB 04) Lewin Fitzhamon, Cecil Hepworth *aka The Bewitched Traveler*. *The "?" Motorist* (GB 05) Walter R. Booth. *A Pipe Dream* (05) Billy Bitzer. *The Dream of a Rarebit Fiend* (06) Edwin S. Porter. *Princess Nicotine; or, The Smoke Fairy* (09) Prod. J. Stuart Backton, Tony Gaudio (photographer). *La Folie du Docteur Tube* (F 14) Abel Gance *aka Story of a Madman*.

Trigger Film *see* **FACTUAL FILM**

Triple-X Feature *see* **HARD-CORE PORNO FILM**

Tropical Melodramas *see* MELODRAMA

Trucking Movie *see* ROAD MOVIE: Truck Movies

True-Life Adventure Film *see* DOCUMENTARY: Nature Film

Turf Story *see* HORSE PIC: Horse-Racing Movies

TURKEY (Badfilm, Bad Movie)   A turkey is a term commonly applied to a bad movie. Similar terms used when referring to bad movies are dog and dud. A bomb is a film that is badly received by both critics and audience and that fails at the box-office (in Great Britain, however, it means the opposite; a bomb is a big hit). Films which fail at the box-office are equally referred to as disasters, lemons and flops—films that do not recoup their production costs, although they are not necessarily bad movies. *Film maudit* refers to a film highly regarded by critics and film scholars but not successful commercially (e.g., *Citizen Kane*, 1940). Clinker, down the tube and down the toilet are other terms used for unsuccessful pictures. A *succès d'estime,* similar to a *film maudit,* is a film acclaimed by the critics but not by the public. It too, does not make money. Lately, some films considered awful have received a certain notoriety, and books have been published about them. If they are really bad, they are considered camp in certain circles and worth seeing. *See,* for instance, Harry and Michael Medved, *The Golden Turkey Awards* (London: Angus & Robertson, 1980).

Plan Nine from Outer Space (56) Edward D. Wood, Jr. [rel. in 59] *aka Grave Robbers from Outer Space.* **Attack of the 50 Ft. Woman** (57) Nathan Juran. **Wild Women of Wongo** (58) James L. Wolcott. **Revenge of the Dead** (59) Edward D. Wood, Jr. *aka Night of the Ghouls / Orgy of the Dead.* **Wild Guitar** (61) Ray Dennis Steckler. **The Madmen of Mandoras** (63) David Bradley *aka The Amazing Mr. H / The Return of Mr. H / They Saved Hitler's Brain.* **Creature of Destruction** (67) Larry Buchanan. **Attack of the Killer Tomatoes!** (77) John De Bello.

Flops: Intolerance (14-16) D. W. Griffith *aka Intolerance, Love's Struggle Through the Ages / Intolerance, a Sun-play of the Ages / Love's Struggle Through the Ages / The Mother and the Law* [in 1919, two 7-reel expanded versions of "The Babylonian Story" and "The Modern Story" episodes were released as *The Fall of Babylon* and *The Mother and the Law* respectively]. *Rosita* (23) Ernst Lubitsch. **Parnell** (37) Jan Stahl. **Ice Follies of 1939** (39) Reinhold Schunzel. **The Blue Bird** (40) Walter Lang. **Citizen Kane** (40) Orson Welles *aka American.* **Wilson** (44) Henry King. **That Hagen Girl** (47) Peter Godfrey. **Aaron Slick from Punkin Crick** (52) Claude Binyon. *A Countess from Hong Kong* (GB 67) Charlie Chaplin. **Star!** (68) Robert Wise *aka Gertie Was a Lady / Those Were the Happy Times.* **Lost Horizon** (72) Charles Jarrott. **Man of La Mancha** (72) Arthur Hiller. **Portnoy's Complaint** (72) Ernest Lehman. **At Long Last Love** (75) Peter Bogdanovich. **The Blue Bird / Sinyaya ptitsa** (US / GB / USSR 76) George Cukor. **New York, New York** (77) Martin Scorsese. **A Little Night Music** (78) Harold Prince. **Moment by Moment** (78) Jane Wagner. **Sextette** (US / GB 78) Ken Hughes. **The Swarm** (78) Irwin Allen. **1941** (79) Steven Spielberg.

Heaven's Gate (80) Michael Cimino. *Jinxed!* (82) Don Siegel. *Bolero* (84) John Derek. *Rhinestone* (84) Bob Clark. *A Chorus Line* (85) Richard Attenborough *aka A Chorus Line: The Movie. Howard the Duck* (85) Willard Huyck. *Revolution* (GB / Nor 85) Hugh Hudson. *Ishtar* (86) Elaine May. *Orphans* (87) Alan J. Pakula. *Great Balls of Fire!* (89) Jim McBride.

Two-Dimensional Film *see* **3-D FILM**

Two-Reel Comedy, Two-Reeler *see* **SHORT**

Ultra-Violent Movie *see* **GORE FILM**

Umbrella Title *see* **TELEVISION SERIES**

Uncontrolled Documentary *see* **DIRECT CINEMA**

UNDERGROUND FILM (Antiestablishment Film, Avant-Garde, Experimental Film, Independent Film, New American Cinema, Personal Film, Radical Film, Synaesthetic Film) Underground is the term applied in the 1960s to a body of films which may also be labelled avant-garde, experimental or independent films.[127] It was an apt label since at the time most underground movies circulated outside the main, commercial channels of distribution. In their heyday, the underground films of Jack Smith, George Kuchar, Mike Kuchar, Kenneth Anger, Andy Warhol and many others created a sensation, and as they surfaced into the open, attracted a great number of aficionados as well as the curious. The films of the underground often chose sex and taboo subjects, but not exclusively. The underground filmmakers included all kinds of different topics in their films. The films themselves are abstract or representational, adopt the narrative or the nonnarrative form and run for a few seconds or several hours. Since they are made by individuals rather than film companies, they include anything the amateur, student, artist or filmmaker thought worthwhile to express through the film medium. Underground films are mostly the personal statement of their creators and they are seldom made with the sole intention of making money. The American underground or new avant-garde inspired similar underground trends in other countries, principally in Western Europe, home of the first avant-garde and the place where there has always been a strong leaning towards experimental cinema. Outside Europe, Canada, Japan and Australia have also contributed to the output of underground films.[128] Many diverse types of underground movies, some originating in the avant-garde of the 1940s and 1950s, form sizeable groups of films or genres. A few of the more important are listed below. The earliest comprehensive study of underground movies is Sheldon Renan, *An Introduction to the American Underground Film* (New York: E. P. Dutton, 1967). *See also* Parker Tyler, *Underground Film: A Critical History* (New York: Grove Press, 1969), P. Adams Sitney, *Visionary Film: The American Avant-Garde*, 2nd ed. (New York: Oxford UP, 1979) and David E. James, *Allegories of Cinema: American Film in the Sixties* (Princeton, NJ: Princeton UP, 1989).

The Lead Shoes (49) Sidney Peterson. *Little Stabs at Happiness* (58-61) Ken Jacobs. *Science Friction* (59) Stan VanDerBeek. *A Town Called Tempest* (61) George Kuchar. *Blonde Cobra* (59-63) Ken Jacobs. *Flaming Creatures* (63) Jack Smith. *The Queen of Sheba Meets the Atom Man* (63) Ron Rice. *Chumlum* (64) Ron Rice. *Re-Entry* (64) Jordan Belson. *Sins of the Fleshapoids* (64) George Kuchar, Mike Kuchar. *Confessions of a Black Mother Succuba* (65) Robert Nelson. *Echoes of Silence* (62-65) Peter Emanuel Goldman. *My Hustler* (65) Andy Warhol, Chuck Wein *aka Temptations*. *Oh Dem Watermelons* (65) Robert Nelson. *The Chelsea Girls* (66) Andy Warhol [filmed in 16mm Dual Screen]. *Hold Me While I'm Naked* (66) George Kuchar. *Samadhi* (67) Jordan Belson. *The Bed* (68) James Broughton. *Blue Movie* (68) Paul Morrisey *aka Fuck / F**k / Viva and Louis*. *T,O,U,C,H,I,N,G* (68) Paul Sharits. *Invocation of My Demon Lover* (69) Kenneth Anger. *Moon 69* (69) Scott Bartlett. *Dreamwood* (72) James Broughton.

——**Collage Films**   Films made by intercutting the film with material from outside sources—stock shots, commercials, cartoons; or by affixing assorted materials onto the celluloid strip.[129]

A Movie (58) Bruce Conner. *Black and White Burlesque* (60) Richard Preston. *Cosmic Ray* (61) Bruce Conner. *The Soccer Game: The Forty and One Nights, or Jess's Didactic Nickelodeon* (60-61) Larry Jordan *aka Heavy Water*. *Mothlight* (63) Stan Brakhage *aka Dead Spring*. *Breath-Death* (63-64) Stan VanDerBeek. *Fist Fight* (64) Robert Breer. *Facescapes* (65) Stan VanDerBeek.

——**Dance Films**   Dance as subject matter has also interested the underground filmmakers, and excellent films exist on this subject.

A Study in Choreography for Camera (45) Maya Deren. *Horror Dream* (47) Sidney Peterson. *Introspection* (47) Sara Kathryn Arledge. *A Moment in Love* (57) Shirley Clarke. *Dance Chromatic* (59) Ed Emshwiller. *Thanatopsis* (60-62) Ed Emshwiller. *Totem* (62-63) Ed Emshwiller. *Tarantella* (66) Camen D'Avino.

——**Film Diary**   In the film diary, the filmmaker includes relevant moments of his life. Not chronologically but selectively, the filmmaker records on film what he considers important—impressions, recollections, notes on travel. See **AUTOBIOGRAPHICAL FILM** entry.

Notebook (62) Marie Menken [9 very short films]. *European Diaries* (65-66) Taylor Mead. *Late Superimpositions* (65-68) Harry Smith *aka Film #12*. *Kodak Ghost Poems—Part 1: The Adventures of the Exquisite Corpse* (68) Andrew Noren [followed by *Kodak Ghost Poems—Part II* (71)]. *Diaries, Notes and Sketches* (64-69) Jonas Mekas [in 4 parts]. *Reminiscences of a Journey to Lithuania* (71) Jonas Mekas. *Paradise Not Yet Lost (Oona's Third Year)* (80) Jonas Mekas.

——**Film Portrait**   As the name indicates, a film portrait is a description, however brief, of an individual's personality or character; it may be a portrait of a friend, a lover, a relative, a known personality or simply a striking person. In many instances, the image speaks for itself. The genre has been very popular among avant-garde and underground filmmakers.

Arabesque for Kenneth Anger (61) Marie Menken. *Bagatelle for Willard Maas* (61) Marie Menken. *Henry Geldzahler* (64) Andy Warhol. *The Thirteen Most Beautiful Women* (64) Andy Warhol. *15 Song Traits* (65) Stan Brakhage *aka XV Song Traits / Song XV. A Legend for Fountains (Fragments)* (76) Joseph Cornell. *Lisa and Joey in Connecticut, January '65: "You've Come Back!" "You're Still Here!* (65) Ken Jacobs. *The Thirteen Most Beautiful Boys* (64-65) Andy Warhol. *Breakaway* (66) Bruce Conner. *Galaxie* (66) Gregory Markopoulos. *Political Portraits* (69) Gregory Markopoulos.

————**Lyrical Film (Lyrical Cinema)** The lyrical form is a style of film composition developed by Stan Brakhage in which the filmmaker, behind the camera, makes his presence felt and portrays himself as the inspirational force behind the images that appear in his film.
Anticipation of the Night (57) Stan Brakhage. *Sirius Remembered* (59) Stan Brakhage. *The Dead* (60) Stan Brakhage. *Thigh Line Lyre Triangular* (61) Stan Brakhage. *Quixote* (65, revised 67) Bruce Baillie. *Castro Street* (66) Bruce Baillie.

————**Mythopoeic Film (Architectonic Film, Mythographic Film, Mythological Film, Techtonic Film)** Mythopoeic is a term used by P. Adams Sitney for a group of underground films which seek to create new myths or reinterpret old ones. At times, they may do this by comparing current myths or by remodelling traditional myths and mythological figures.
Inauguration of the Pleasure Dome (54, reedited 66) Kenneth Anger. *Narcissus* (58) Willard Maas, Ben Moore. *The Very Eye of Night* (58) Maya Deren. *Heaven & Earth Magic & Feature* (50-62) Harry Smith *aka The Magic Feature / No. 12. Twice a Man* (63) Gregory J. Markopoulos. *Dog Star Man* (61-64) Stan Brakhage [a "Prelude" and 4 parts; incorporated into *The Art of Vision* (65)]. *Kustom Kar Kommandos / KKK* (64, unfinished) Kenneth Anger. *Scorpio Rising* (62-64) Kenneth Anger. *The Art of Vision* (61-65) Stan Brakhage. *The Illiac Passion* (64-66) Gregory Markopoulos *aka The Markopoulos Passion.*

————**Picaresque Films** The picaresque film narrates the adventures, misadventures or vicissitudes of a picaresque hero, sometimes naive, intent on surviving in a frequently hostile environment.
The Flower Thief (59-60) Ron Rice. *Senseless* (62) Ron Rice. *The Queen of Sheba Meets the Atom Man* (63 and 68 version) Ron Rice. *The Great Blondino* (67) Robert Nelson.

————**Trance Film (Psychodrama)** A term devised by P. Adams Sitney for films in which a protagonist undergoes a search for self by way of a journey of discovery through unfamiliar places and landscapes. The films have a firm Freudian base, are dreamlike and often have a Surreal quality. If the self-search involves the filmmaker, it is called a psychodrama. The genre was common in the American avant-garde of the 1940s and 1950s.
Meshes of the Afternoon (43) Maya Deren, Alexander Hammid [sound added in 58]. *At Land* (44) Maya Deren. *Fragment of Seeking* (46) Curtis Harrington *aka Symbol of Decadence. Fireworks* (47) Kenneth Anger. *Images in the Snow* (43-48) Willard Maas. *Psyche* (47-48) Gregory Markopoulos.

Swain (Rain Black, My Love) (51) Gregory Markopoulos. *Reflections on Black* (55) Stan Brakhage. *The Way to Shadow Garden* (55) Stan Brahkage.

Undersea Film, Underwater Movies   *see*   **SEA FILM**

URBAN COMEDY (Big City Comedy)   If the countryside is the setting for rural comedy (q.v.), the big city is the natural habitat of urban comedy. A great number of comedies set in urban surroundings feature the foibles and eccentricities of city dwellers. The faster pace of life of the city offers a contrast with the more sedate way of life of the country, and the city has always attracted visitors and out-of-towners anxious to have a good time, catch a glimpse of the bright city lights, or, otherwise, settle and make it in the dynamic metropolis. The urbanites' shenanigans, the visitors' naiveté and success or lack of it in becoming city slickers have provided ample opportunity for comic situations and humor. Urban comedies are plentiful.
Speedy (28) Ted Wilde.   *City Lights* (31) Charlie Chaplin.   *Sidewalks of New York* (31) Jules White, Ziom Myers.   *The Magnificent Dope* (42) Walter Lang.   *So This Is New York* (48) Richard Fleischer.   *A Thousand Clowns* (65) Fred Coe.   *The Producers* (67) Mel Brooks.   *The Out of Towners* (69) Arthur Hiller.

VAMPIRE FILM   Several books have been devoted exclusively to the vampire film.[130] The ancestry of vampire films can be traced as far back as 1896, when *Le Manoir du diable* (known in the United States and Britain respectively as *The Haunted Castle* and *The Devil's Castle*) appeared. In it, its creator, the Frenchman Georges Méliès, transformed himself into a huge bat and later metamorphosed again into Mephistopheles. A few examples of similar, early films also exist, as well as a whole series in which the "vampire" is a *femme fatale* draining the vitality out of her male victims. The best extant forerunner of a true vampire is, however, Count Orlock as played by Max Schreck (surely the ugliest screen vampire ever) in *Nosferatu* (1921), an Expressionistic German film which was a slightly disguised adaptation of Bram Stoker's famous novel *Dracula* (1897). The vampire film is an important branch of the horror film and a genre in itself with a tradition and lore of its own. The conventions originate in literary sources and are well-established, and although many attempts have been made to parody them, they are firmly anchored as "serious" vampire films continue to be made.

Vampirism includes the belief in vampires, the vampire's activities (especially the practice of blood-sucking) and, in an extended context, any activity by a plant, animal, person or supernatural being which involves a general drawing of another's vital and psychic energies. It covers supernatural, sexual, psychological and pathological manifestations and exerts a powerful and alluring influence. It is not surprising, then, that filmmakers have repeatedly tried to mix the vampire myth with other genres, and we find vampires in Westerns, science fiction films and sex films. Indeed, the characteristics of the vampire film can be discerned in many different types of films.[131]

Le Manoir du diable (F 1896) Georges Méliès *aka The Devil's Castle / The Haunted Castle.* *Nosferatu — eine Symphonie des Grauens* (G 21) Friedrich Wilhelm Murnau *aka Die zwöfte Stunde — eine Nacht des Grauens* (G 30 sound version) */ Dracula / Nosferatu / Nosferatu, the Vampire / Nosferatu — A Symphony of Horror [Terror] / The Terror of Dracula.* *Mark of the Vampire* (35) Tod Browning *aka The Vampire of Prague / Werewolf of Paris.* *Kiss of the Vampire* (GB 62) Don Sharp *aka Kiss of Evil.* *The Last Man on Earth / L'ultimo uomo della terra* (US / It 63) Sidney Salkow, Ubaldo Ragona *aka Naked Terror / The Night Creatures / Night People / Vento di morte.* *Terrore nello spazio / Terror en el espacio / Planet of the Vampires* (It / Sp / US 65) Mario Bava *aka The Demon Planet / Haunted Planet / Haunted World / The Night of 21 Hours / Outlaw Planet / Planet of Blood / Planet of Terror / Planet of the Damned / Terror from Space.* *Track of the Vampire* (US / Yug 66) Jack Hill, Stephanie Rothman *aka Blood Bath.* *Doctors Wear Scarlet* (GB 69) Michael Burrowes (Robert Hartford-Davis) *aka Bloodsuckers / Incense for the Damned.* *Count Yorga, Vampire* (70) Bob Kelljan *aka Count Yorga, Vampire or Son of Dracula Meets the LA Volkswagen Bus Set / The Loves of Count Iorga — Vampire / Vampyre.* *House of Dark Shadows* (70) Dan Curtis *aka Dark Shadows.* *The Deathmaster* (71) Ray Danton *aka Khorda.* *Let's Scare Jessica to Death* (71) John Hancock *aka What Killed Sam Dorker?* *Night Stalker* (71 TV) John L. Moxey *aka Fee Fi Fo Fum, I Smell Blood / The Kolchak Papers.* *The Return of Count Yorga* (71) Bob Kelljan *aka The Abominable Count Yorga.* *Vampire Circus* (GB 71) Robert Young. *Captain Kronos [Kronus] — Vampire Hunter* (GB 72) Brian Clemens *aka Kronos / Vampire Castle.* *Grave of the Vampire* (72) John Hayes *aka Seed of Terror / Tomb of the Undead.* *The Night Walk / Dead of Night* (Can / GB / US 72) Bob Clark [rel. in 74] *aka The Chilling / Deathdream / Le mortvivant / The Night Andy Came Home / The Veteran.* *Mary, Mary, Bloody Mary* (US / Mex 74) Juan López Montezuma. *Salem's Lot* (79 TV) Tobe Hooper [in 2 parts] *aka Jerusalem's Lot / Salem's Lot: The Movie.* *Vampire* (79 TV) E. W. Swackhamer. *I, Desire* (82 TV) John Llewellyn Moxey. *The Hunger* (US GB 83) Tony Scott. *Fright Night* (85) Tom Holland. *Lifeforce* (GB / US 85) Tobe Hooper *aka Space Vampires.* *As sete vampiras* (Braz 86) Ivan Cardoso. *Graveyard Shift* (Can 86) Gerard Ciccoritti. *The Lost Boys* (87) Joel Schumacker. *Near Dark* (87) Kathryn Bigelow. *Vampire at Midnight* (87) Gregory McClatchy. *Dance of the Damned* (88) Katt Shea Rubin. *Fright Night Part 2* (88) Tommy Lee Wallace. *Pale Blood* (90) V. V. Dhubin Hsu, Michael W. Leighton. *Red Blooded American Girl* (Can 90) David Blyth.

——**Carmilla Films** Joseph Sheridan Le Fanu's short story "Carmilla" (1872) was first adapted to the screen by Carl Theodor Dreyer in *Vampyr* (1931). Since then, films based on the Karnstein family have been a good starting point for emphasizing the lesbian tendencies in female vampires. After Bram Stoker's *Dracula*, Carmilla is the vampire personality most frequently adapted to the screen.

Vampyr: L'Etrange Aventure de David Grey / Vampyr: Der Traum des Allay Gray (F / G 31) Carl Th. Dreyer *aka Castle of Doom / Not Against the Flesh / The Strange Adventure(s) of David Gray / Vampir / [The] Vampire.* *...Et mourir de plaisir / Il sangue e la rosa* (F / It 60) Roger Vadim *aka Blood and*

Roses / Le Sang et la rose.   La cripta e l'incubo / La maldición de los Karnstein (It / Sp 64) Camillo Mastrocinque *aka Carmilla / Crypt of Horror / The Crypt and the Nightmare / The Crypt of the Vampire / The Curse of the Karnsteins / Karnstein / The Karnstein Curse / Le maledizione dei Karnstein / Terror in the Crypt / The Vampire's Crypt.   Lust for a Vampire* (GB 70) Jimmy Sangster *aka Love for a Vampire / To Love a Vampire.   The Vampire Lovers* (GB 70) Roy Ward Baker.   *Twins of Evil* (GB 71) John Hough *aka The Gemini Twins / Twins of Dracula / Virgin Vampires.*

———**Countess Báthory Films**   The Hungarian Erzsébet Báthory, the Countess Nadshy, is another legendary figure frequently used in vampire films. She is said to have immolated some six hundred young girls in the 17th century for the sake of bathing in their blood because she attributed rejuvenating powers to the fluid. Although not herself a vampire, the connections with vampirism are obvious, and she has appeared as a supernatural vampire in some films.

Countess Dracula (GB 70) Peter Sasdy.   *Rouge aux lèvres / Les Lèvres rouges / Blut an den Lippen / La vestale di Satana* (Belg / F / G / It 70) Harry Kümel *aka Children of the Night / Daughters of Darkness / Erzebeth / The Promise of Red Lips / Red Lips.   Ceremonia sangrienta / Le vergini cavalcano la morte* (Sp / It 72) Jorge Grau *aka Blood[y] Ceremony / Countress Dracula / The Female Butcher / Lady Dracula / Legend of Blood Castle.   Il plenilunio delle vergine* (It 73) Paolo Solvay (Luigi Batzella) *aka Countess Dracula / The Devil's Wedding Night / Full Moon of the Virgins.   Contes immoraux* (F 74) Walerian Borowczyk *aka Immoral Tales.*

———**Dracula Films**   Between 1921 and 1991 Count Dracula appeared in 156 films.[132] Hence, it it the most important recurrent vampiric manifestation on film. Dracula in Walachia meant "son of Dracul" was applied to the historical Walachian ruler Vlad V, "The Impaler," son of Vlad III, called "Dracul" (Rumanian for the devil). Bram Stoker based his famous Gothic novel *Dracula* (1897) on the legendary Voivode (Prince) Dracula, the above mentioned 15th-century ruler of the Walachian principality of Muntenia, which bordered Transylvania.[133] Of the many actors who have portrayed the infamous vampire, two stand out as archetypal figures: Bela Lugosi and Christopher Lee. Christopher Lee's interpretation is to date the definitive screen representation of the malevolent Count. The archetypal image of Dracula's nemesis, the vampire hunter Van Helsing, belongs to Peter Cushing.

Dracula (30) Tod Browning [Sp. v.: *Drácula* (30) George Melford].   *Dracula* (GB 58) Terence Fisher *aka The Horror of Dracula* [7 Hammer films (1958-73) with Christopher Lee as Dracula].   *Dracula Has Risen from the Grave* (GB 68) Freddie Francis *aka Dracula's Revenge.   El conde Drácula / Nachts, wenn Dracula Erwacht / Il conte Dracula* (Sp / G / It 69) Jesús Franco *aka Bram Stoker's Count Dracula / Count Dracula / Dracula No. 1 / Dracula '71 / The Nights of Dracula.   Blacula* (72) William Crain.   *El gran amor del Conde Drácula* (Sp 72) Javier Aguirre *aka Cemetery Girls / Count Dracula's Great Love / Dracula's Great Love / Dracula's Virgin Lovers / El retorno de la duquesa Drácula / Vampire Playgirls.   Dracula cerca sangue di vergine ... e mori di sete!!! / Du sang pour Dracula* (It / F

73) Antonio Margheriti, Paul Morrissey *aka Andy Warhol's Blood for Dracula / Andy Warhol's Dracula / Andy Warhol's Young Dracula / Blood for Dracula / Dracula vuole vivere: cerca sangue di vergine! / Sangue per Dracula.* **Count Dracula** (GB / US 77 TV) Philip Saville. **McCloud: McCloud Meets Dracula** (77 TV) Bruce Kessler. **Dracula** (US / GB 78-79) John Badham. **Nocturna** (78) Harry Tampa *aka Dracula's Granddaughter / Granddaughter of Dracula.* **Nosferatu — Phantom des Nacht / Nosferatu, fantôme de la nuit** (G / F 78) Werner Herzog *aka Nosferatu, the Vampire [Vampyre] / Werner Herzog's Nosferatu.*

——**Sex Vampire Films**   The vampire's sexual connotations are obvious — the victims, hypnotically possessed, offer themselves languidly and expectantly to his depredations — and they have naturally proved to be fertile ground for sexploitation filmmakers.

Le Frisson des vampires (F 70) Jean Rollin *aka Sex and the Vampire / Terror of the Vampires.* **Le Sadique aux dents rouges** (Belg 70) Jean-Louis Van Belle *aka The Sadist with the Red Teeth.* **Vampyros Lesbos — Die Erbin des Dracula / El signo del vampiro** (G / Sp 71) Jess Franco *aka Dracula's Offspring / The Heiress of Dracula / The Heritage of Dracula / Las vampiras / Vampyros Lesbos (The Strange Adventures of Jonathan Harker).* **The Velvet Vampire** (71) Stephanie Rothman *aka Blood Lover / Cemetery Girls / The Devil Is a Woman / Through the Looking Glass / The Walking Hour.* **Vampyres** (GB 74) Joseph Larrath *aka Daughters of Dracula / Vampires / The Vampyre Orgy / Vampyres — Daughters of Darkness / Vampyres . . . Daughters of Dracula.* **Spermula** (F 75) Charles Matton. **Dracula Sucks . . . Blood** (79) Philip Marshak *aka Dracula's Bride / Dracula Sucks / Lust at First Bite.* **Dracula Exotica** (80) Warren Evans *aka Dracula Erotica.*

——**Vampire Parodies and Comedies**   They are very numerous, as if the filmmakers wanted to seal forever the coffins that shelter the vampires during daylight. The parodies range from catch-all Hollywood monster films to flimsy vampires played by Christopher Lee, David Niven, George Hamilton and others.

The House of Dracula (45) Erle C. Kenton. **Dance of the Vampires / The Fearless Vampire Killers; or, Pardon Me But Your Teeth Are in My Neck** (GB / US 67) Roman Polanski *aka Le Bal des vampires / The Fearless Vampire Killers / The Vampire Killers / Your Teeth in My Neck.* **Vampira** (GB 73) Clive Donner *aka Old Drac / Old Dracula / Vampir / Vampire / Vampirella.* **Nightmare in Blood** (75) John Stanley. **Dracula père et fils** (F 76) Edouard Molinaro *aka Dracula and Son / Voice of Blood.* **Love at First Bite** (78) Stan Dragoti *aka Dracula Sucks Again.* **Once Bitten** (85) Howard Storm. **A Polish Vampire in Burbank** (85) Mark Pirro. **Vamp** (86) Richard Wenk. **Beverly Hills Vamp** (88) Fred Olen Ray. **Nightlife** (89 MCTV) Daniel Taplitz. **Transylvania Twist** (89) Jim Wynorski. **Rockula** (90) Luca Bercovici.

Variations and Permutations of the Soft-Core Porno Movie Subgenres *see* **SOFT-CORE SEX-EXPLOITATION FILM**

Variety Show, Variety-Vaudeville, Vaudeo *see* **TELEVISION SHOW**

Vehicle *see* **STAR VEHICLE;** *see also* **MUSICAL** and **WESTERN: Star Vehicles**

Verismo *see* NATURALISTIC FILM

VICE FILM (Red-Light Film, Vice-Trust Movie) The success of a white slavery film made in Denmark, the two-reeler *Den hvide Slavehandel I / The White Slave Trade I* (1910), prompted a series of similar films.[134] The United States counteracted with the very successful *Traffic in Souls* (1913), directed by George Loane Tucher at Universal studios, and white slavery films became highly profitable. Other themes in vice films included drug addiction, alcoholism, prostitution and venereal disease. Vice films purported to warn against the dangers of sex, the abuse of drugs and other evils; they also claimed to expose rackets and circles of corruption. Some of these films were honest presentations of these social scourges, but most of them were just an excuse for a lurid glimpse into forbidden areas of sexuality and vice. For the early development of this type of exploitation films (the white slavery film, the drug film, the birth control film, the social disease film), *see* Kathleen Karr, "The Long Square-Up: Exploitation Trends in the Silent Film," *The Journal of Popular Film 3* (1974): 107–28. *See also* **SEX EXPLOITATION FILM.**

> *Den hvide Slavehandel I* (Den 10) August Blom *aka The White Slave Trade I.* *Traffic in Souls* (13) George Loane Tucker. *The Weaker Mind* (13) Romaine Fielding. *Damaged Goods* (14) Thomas Ricketts [divided in 3 acts]. *Where Are My Children?* (16) Lois Weber, Phillips Smalley *aka The Ill-born.* *Birth Control* (17) Margaret Sanger *aka The New World.* *Open Your Eyes* (19) Gilbert P. Hamilton. *The Street of Forgotten Men* (25) Herbert Brenon. *Damaged Lives* (33) Edgar G. Ulmer [rel. in 37]. *Reefer Madness* (36) Louis Gasnier *aka Assassin of Youth / The Burning Question / Dope Addict / Doped Youth / Love Madness / Tell Your Children.*

Vice-Trust Movie *see* **VICE FILM**

Victorian Melodrama *see* **PERIOD FILM: Period Thrillers**

Vidclip *see* **MUSIC VIDEO**

VIDEO (Videogram) The usual term for referring to a motion picture, television program or music performance which is recorded on videotape and packaged into a video-cassette for playing on a television set via a VCR (Videocassette Recorder) or VTR (Video Tape Recorder).[135] Since the introduction of videocassette recorders, a few new terms pertaining to the system and related to films released on videocassette have appeared.

——**A-Level Title** A big-budget film from a major distributor which goes into video release heralded by an advertising campaign.

——**B-Level Title** A lesser-known film, usually produced independently on a low budget, and which may not have gone into theatrical release.

——**Made-for** A film made specially for the home video market or for release through cable TV.

——**Schlockbuster**   An exploitation picture, usually a horror (q.v.) or splatter film (q.v.) which is theatrically successful and in the home video market.

Video, Video Album   *see*   **MUSIC VIDEO**

VIDEO ART (Artists' Video)   A term used to define the work of artists who choose to express their artistic leaning through the medium of videotape. Since the mid–1960s, when portable video recorders became readily available, videotape has increasingly been used by video artists and film-makers worldwide.

The Astrolabe of God (72) Jud Yalkut.   *Memoranda for a Dream of Magellan* (72) Hollis Frampton.   *The Santa Clara Tapes* (73) Douglas Davis. *Vertical Roll* (73) Joan Jonas.   *Pilobolus and Joan* (74) Ed Emshwiller.   *Internal Pornography* (Can 75) Lisa Steele [3-monitor format].   *Almost Out* (GB 84) Jayne Parker.   *Prisoners* (GB 84) Terry Flaxton.

Video Clip   *see*   **MUSIC VIDEO**

Video EP   *see*   **MUSIC VIDEO**

Video Music, Video Music Clip   *see*   **MUSIC VIDEO**

Video Nasty   *see*   **VIOLENCE FILM**

Video Rock Clip, Video Single, Video Wallpaper   *see*   **MUSIC VIDEO**

Videodisc   *see*   **VIDEO**

Videogram   *see*   **VIDEO**

Vidpic   *see*   **TELEVISON MOVIE**

Vietnam War Films   *see*   **WAR FILM**

VIGILANTE FILM   The vigilante concept is very old and in the past took the shape of the righter-of-wrongs, the masked avenger and, of course, avenging horsemen in Westerns and other tales of adventure. Vigilantes work in groups or alone, operating inside or outside the law. There also exist those who use their rank in the police force as a cover-up for their illegal vigilante activity. In whatever form, vigilantism is always motivated by a desire for revenge or by a feeling of frustration on the part of the citizen who takes up the role of vigilante in the face of widespread corruption, a slack law which frees criminals instead of jailing them, an inefficient police force and or a police force incapable of controlling crime and protecting the peaceful citizens. Films on the vigilante theme may be found as far back as the thirties. Recently, vigilantes are once more taking the law into their hands to protect their town and its citizens. They have resurfaced with renewed strength and violence. *See also* **GANGSTER FILM.**

The Secret Six (31) George W. Hill.   *The Four Just Men* (GB 39) Walter Forde *aka The Secret Four.* **Henker von London** (G 63) Edwin Zbonek *aka The Hangman of London / The Mad Executioners.* **Walking Tall** (72) Phil Karlson [followed by *Part 2, Walking Tall* (75) Earl Bellamy, *Final Chapter — Walking Tall* (77) Jack Starrett and *A Real American Hero* (78 TV) Lou Antonio]. *Death Squad* (73 TV) Harry Falk. *Gordon's War* (73) Ossie Davis. *Magnum Force* (73) Ted Post. *Outrage* (73 TV) Richard T. Heffron. *Death Wish* (74) Michael Winner [4 films in the series up to 1987]. *Law and Disorder* (74) Ivan Passer. *Vigilante Force* (76) George Armitage. *The One Man Jury* (78) Charles Martin *aka Dead on Arrival.* *The Exterminator* (80) James Glickenhouse. *Ms. 45* (81) Abel Ferrara *aka Angel of Vengeance.* *Fighting Back* (82) Lewis Teague *aka Death Vengeance.* *Vigilante* (82) William Lustig *aka Street Cop / Street Gang.* *The Star Chamber* (83) Peter Hyams. *Young Warriors* (83) Lawrence D. Foldes. *Exterminator 2* (84) Mark Buntzman, William Sachs. *Sudden Death* (85) Sig Shore.

——**Revenge Films** As a variant of the vigilante film, the revenge movie has in many cases a single-handed individual taking the law into his / her hands when the police fail to apprehend the culprits or the courts let the criminals off unpunished or with a light sentence. The motivation of the avengers in the revenge film is more the search for personal retribution or to avenge the death of a relative or friend than to protect society.

Lipstick (76) Lamont Johnson. *I Spit on Your Grave* (77) Meir Zarchi *aka Day of the Woman.* *Rolling Thunder* (77) John Flynn. *Class of 1984 / La Classe de 1984* (Can 81) Mark L. Lester *aka Battle Zone — Adams High / Classe 1984.* *An Eye for an Eye* (81) Steve Carter. *Alley Cat* (82) Edward Victor *aka Dragonfly.* *L'Été meurtrier* (F 82) Jean Becker *aka One Deadly Summer.* *Handgun* (GB / US 83) Tony Garnett *aka Deep in the Heart.* *Avenging Angel* (84) Robert Vincent O'Neil. *Vendetta* (85) Bruce Logan *aka Angels Behind Bars.* *Thou Shalt Not Kill ... Except* (87) Josh Becker. *Swift Justice* (88) Harry Hope.

VIOLENCE FILM (Violent Picture) A film which portrays violence in a realistic manner. Violence seems to be ingrained in human nature and in life itself. Societies past and present have furnished plentiful examples of violence in its most extreme forms. Films reflect this human proclivity for violence and have portrayed it in dramatic and exploitative films of all kinds. There are degrees of violence and this is also reflected in films. On the one hand, there are films which subdue their violence in a poetic ballet of slow-motion (films like *Bonnie and Clyde* [1967]; *A Clockwork Orange* [1971]; some kung-fu films). On the other hand, some films seek a more realistic approach (*Dirty Harry* [1971]; *Straw Dogs* [1972]; *Jaws* [1975]). All these films are, more or less, genuine manifestations of the capabilities of cinematic art. Another group of violent pictures thrives on violence for violence's sake. This latter category comprises films which have variously been referred to as murder movies, splatter films, slice-and-dice films, stalk-and-slash films and knife-kill movies; they are, to a greater or lesser degree, concerned with violence at the expense of plot, the body count and the bloodletting providing the thrills for an audience thirsty for this type of film. It is film violence expressed in its most graphic manner and nicknamed in Great Britain "video nasty" since its recent availability on video cassette. They are exploitation films. *See also* **GORE FILM** and **SLASHER FILM**. *Bonnie and Clyde* (67) Arthur Penn. *Night of the Living Dead* (67-68) George A. Romero *aka Flesh Eaters / Night of Anubis / Night of the Flesh Eaters. A Clockwork Orange* (GB 71) Stanley Kubrick. *Dirty Harry* (71) Don Siegel *aka Dead Right* [5 "Inspector Callahan" films up to 1988]. *The Last House on the Left* (72) Wes Craven *aka Krug and Company / Sex Crime of the Century. Straw Dogs* (GB 72) Sam Peckinpah. *The Texas Chainsaw Massacre* (74) Tobe Hooper [subtitled "Who Will Be Left . . . and What Will Be Left of Them?"]. *Jaws* (75) Steven Spielberg [4 "Jaws" films (1975-87)]. *Assault on Precinct 13* (76) John Carpenter. *Dawn of the Dead / Zombie* (US / It 77-78) George A. Romero *aka Dawn of the Living Dead / Zombie Dawn of the Dead / Zombies.*

Wacky Comedy   *see*   **SCREWBALL COMEDY**

War Biography   *see*   **WAR FILM: Biographical War Films**

War Comedies   *see*   **WAR FILM: Comedy War Films**

War Documentary   *see*   **DOCUMENTARY**

WAR FILM   One of the oldest cinematic genres, war films came into existence when reporting of war and armed hostilities was undertaken by cameraman reporters that traveled to the trouble spots of the world to record the conflict for posterity. Hence the factual war film predates the fictional war film in the evolution of the genre. Soon after, though, these early "documentaries" or news films showing scenes of the Graeco-Turkish War of 1897, the Spanish-American War of 1898, the second of the Boer Wars (1899–1902), or the Boxer Rising (1900) were being recreated in the studios, no doubt for lack of original, exciting material, and because it was cheaper; thus reconstructed and dramatized recreations of famous battles and war incidents appeared. From then on, the road was open to the fictional war story.

Although war spans the centuries, and is as old as mankind, the term war film is usually restricted to pictures describing modern warfare or dealing with situations closely allied to war or to the armed forces. A useful classification falls under the label of the particular war the film deals with; thus it is possible to classify films as Boer War films, World War I films,[136] World War II films, Cold War films and Vietnam War films. Under this first classification fall the subgenres: prisoner-of-war films, aviation films, spy films, biographical films of men dealing with the military and so on. Another possible classification corresponds to the different branches of the armed forces, e.g., the Army, the Navy, the Air Force, and their special units — commandos, paratroopers, marines, Navy intelligence.

A distinction has to be made as well between war films made during wartime and those made during peacetime. There are also those made by nations actually involved in war and those by neutral nations, sympathizing or not with the different warring factions.

War movies made during wartime may portray actual incidents of battle or be mere fantasies depicting actions that have not taken place, but that uplift the morale of the nation. Generally speaking, they will contain a message of a propagandistic nature, and will tend to be highly patriotic, or chauvinistic, denigrating or stereotyping the enemy.

War movies made during peacetime may again describe or recreate real battle incidents, or relate fictitious situations for the sake of entertainment; or they may be mere adventure-action pictures set in a war frame or with a war background and be of a heroic or melodramatic nature.

War movies are usually either prowar or antiwar. Antiwar movies are not usually popular with the military establishment, and obviously are only permitted to be made in peacetime, or they are made by nations not involved in war.

A further distinction may be made between war films which involve descriptions of warfare (battle films) and military films which involve or have as their background the armed forces but which actually deal with peacetime activities (recruiting, promotion) or in which actual warfare is not graphically portrayed. Thus ample criteria can be used when classifying the war movie genre. On the subject of war movies, *see* Ivan Butler's *The War Film* (Cranbury, NJ: A. S. Barnes, 1974) and Lawrence H. Suid's *Guts & Glory ... Great American War Movies* (Reading, MA.: Addison-Wesley, 1978). Jeanine Basinger's *The World War II Combat Film* (New York: Columbia University Press, 1986) examines World War II combat movies as a genre. For a description of some 2,000 American war and war-related films, *see* Larry Langman and Ed Borg's *Encyclopedia of American War Films* (New York: Garland, 1989).

——**Adventure War Films (Special Mission War Films)**   These films are mostly fictional exercises emphasizing the spectacular side of war, bearing little or no resemblance to actual war or war incidents. They concentrate on action, feats of heroism and brutality; they are fast-paced and, although some may be antimilitaristic, they actually glorify war.

A Walk in the Sun (45) Lewis Milestone.   *The Guns of Navarone* (US / GB 61) J. Lee Thompson, Alexander Mackendrick (replaced).   *Von Ryan's Express* (65) Mark Robson.   *The Dirty Dozen* (US / GB 67) Robert Aldrich [followed by 3 TV sequels (1985-88)].   *Where Eagles Dare* (GB 68) Brian G. Hutton, Yakima Canutt.   *Play Dirty* (GB 68) André de Toth *aka Written on the Sand*.   *The Eagle Has Landed* (GB / US 76) John Sturges.

——**Anti-Nazi War Films (Anti-Fascist Films)**   Obviously because of the threat that Nazism (or its counterpart, Fascism) represented to democracy, these films were highly propagandistic, endowing the Germans with evil purpose and casting them in the role of villains, the perpetrators of evil deeds, a practice that grew and continued all through World War II. It was only after the hostilities ceased that the stereotyped German villains have slowly changed and, in a way, been revindicated. The fact was stressed that it was their leaders who were to be blamed rather than the men who fought in the war. A parallel anti-Communistm theme can be seen in the Cold War movies of the fifties and early sixties, replacing the German villains with Russian or Chinese ones.

Desertir (USSR 33) Vsevolod I. Pudovkin *aka Deserter*. *Professor Mamlock* (38) Adolph Minkin, Herbert Rappoport. *Swamp Soldiers* (38) Alexander Macheret. *Escape* (40) Mervyn LeRoy. *Foreign Correspondent* (40) Alfred Hitchcock *aka Personal History*. *The Great Dictator* (40) Charlie Chaplin. *Hitler's Children* (42) Edward Dmytryk. *The Hitler Gang* (44) John Farrow. *None Shall Escape* (44) Andre de Toth.

———**Aviation War Films (Aerial War Movies, Air Combat Movies)**   From the dogfights of World War I aerial combat movies (in themselves a minor subgenre) to the bombing raids of World War II, to the development of a particular plane, e.g., the "Spitfire," the aviation war movie covers a wide range.

Wings (27) William A. Wellman. *The Dawn Patrol* (30) Howard Hawks *aka Flight Commander*. *The Dawn Patrol* (38) Edmund Goulding. *Moyuru ozora* (J 40) Abe Yutaka *aka The Great Burning Sky*. *Stukas* (G 41) Karl Ritter. *Air Force* (42) Howard Hawks. *The First of the Few* (GB 42) Leslie Howard *aka Spitfire*. *Hawai Maree oki kaisen* (J 42) Kajiro Yamamoto *aka The War at Sea from Hawaii to Malaya / The War at Sea Off Hawaii and Malaya*. *Besätzung Dora* (G 43) Karl Ritter *aka The Dora Crew*. *Kessen no ozora e* (J 43) Kunio Watanabe *aka Toward the Decisive Battle in the Sky*. *God Is My Co-Pilot* (45) Robert Florey. *The Way to the Stars* (GB 45) Anthony Asquith *aka Johnny in the Clouds*. *Fighter Squadron* (48) Raoul Walsh. *Twelve O'Clock High* (49) Henry King. *Der Stern von Afrika* (G 57) *aka The Star of Africa*. *633 Squadron* (GB 63) Walter Grauman. *The Blue Max* (GB 66) John Guillermin. *Battle of Britain* (GB 69) Guy Hamilton. *Von Richthofen and Brown* (70) Roger Corman *aka The Red Baron / Von Richthofen*. *Aces High / Le Tigre du ciel* (GB / F 76) Jack Gold.

———**Biographical War Films (War Biography)**   Biographies of soldiers, generals, nurses, politicians — anyone involved with the military of war — are an appropriate subject for the biographical war film.

Nurse Edith Cavell (39) Herbert Wilcox. *Sergeant York* (41) Howard Hawks. *The Iron Major* (43) Ray Enright. *The Story of Dr. Wassell* (44) Cecil B. DeMille. *The Eternal Sea* (55) John H. Auer. *To Hell and Back* (55) Jesse Hibbs. *Battle Hymn* (56) Douglas Sirk. *The Gallant Hours* (60) Robert Montgomery. *Hell to Eternity* (60) Phil Karlson. *The Outsider* (61) Delbert Mann. *Lawrence of Arabia* (GB / US 62; restored version 88) David Lean. *Patton* (69) Franklin J. Schaffner *aka Patton — Blood & Guts / Patton: Lust for Glory / Patton: Salute to a Rebel*. *The Big Red One* (80) Samuel Fuller.

———**Boer War Films**   Not many movies have the Boer Wars (1881, 1899–1902) for their subject. Although cinematographers were filming the Graeco-Turkish war of 1897, the Spanish-American War of 1898 and the Sudan War of the same year, the earliest surviving film documentation of armed conflict deals with the Second Boer War of 1899–1902. Thus, they are the first examples of war films.

Ohm Krüger (G 41) Hans Steinhoff *aka Uncle Krüger.* *Untamed* (55) Henry King. *Young Winston* (GB 72) Richard Attenborough. *Guns Aross the Veldt* ... *The Pursuit of General De Wet, South Africa 1897 / Spoor* (SA 75) Howard Rennie *aka De Wet's Spoor / Guns Across the Veldt.* *"Breaker" Morant* (Aust 79) Bruce Beresford.

——**Civil War Films (American Civil War Films)**　Films about the American Civil War (1861–65) date back to the early one reelers, and two of the most famous Hollywood films – *The Birth of a Nation* (1914) and *Gone with the Wind* (1939) – have for their subject matter this war. The War Between the States has produced a steady flow of films; however, films connected with the Civil War but whose political intrigue, skirmishes or combat action take place in the West rather than the South are better classed as Westerns (e.g. *Rocky Mountain* [1950], *Quantrill's Raiders* [1958]). *The Birth of a Nation* (14) D. W. Griffith *aka The Birth of the Nation; or The Clansman / The Clansman.* *The Crisis* (16) Colin Campbell. *So Red the Rose* (35) King Vidor. *Gone with the Wind* (39) Victor Fleming (uncredited: George Cukor, Sidney Franklin, Sam Wood) *aka GWTW / Tomorrow Is Another Day / The Wind.* *A Southern Yankee* (48) Edward Sedgwick *aka My Hero.* *The Red Badge of Courage* (51) John Huston. *A Time Out of War* (54) Denis Sanders, Terry Sanders. *Friendly Persuasion* (56) William Wyler. *The Great Locomotive Chase* (56) Francis D. Lyon *aka Andrews' Raiders.* *Raintree County* (57) Edward Dmytryk. *The Horse Soldiers* (59) John Ford. *La Rivière du Hibou* (F 62) Roberto Enrico *aka Incident at Owl Creek / An Occurrence at Owl Creek Bridge* [originally an episode in *Au coeur de la vie* (F 62)]. *Shenandoah* (65) Andrew V. McLaglen. *The Beguiled* (71) Don Siegel. *The Blue & The Gray* (82 TV) Andrew V. McLaglen [3-part miniseries]. *North and South* (85 TV) Richard T. Heffron [6-part miniseries]. *Glory* (89) Edward Zwick.

——**Civilian War Films (Home Front Films)**　How war or war conditions affect the civil population, how civilians react or cope with the state of war, how their lives are changed by what they are undergoing or have undergone as a result of war: all this and more is the domain of the Civilian War film drama. *Mrs. Miniver* (42) William Wyler. *Since You Went Away* (44) John Cromwell. *Roma città aperta* (It 45) Roberto Rossellini *aka Città aperta / Open City / Rome, Open City.* *Valahol Európában...* (Hung 46) Géza Radványi *aka Somewhere in Europe.* *Jeux interdits* (F 51) René Clément *aka Forbidden Games / The Secret Game.* *Hiroshima mon amour / Nijuyokikan no joji* (F / J 59) Alain Resnais *aka Hiroshima, My Love / Twenty-Four Hour Affair.* *The Diary of Anne Frank* (59) George Stevens. *De Aanslag* (Hol 86) Fons Rademakers *aka The Assault.* *Hope and Glory* (GB 87) John Boorman.

——**Cold War Films**　The term cold war applies to the state of tension existing between nations, especially between the United States and the Soviet Union which falls short of open war, but in which all the means at a nation's disposal (propaganda, espionage, economic pressures) are used to denigrate the adversary and impede any possibility of amicable exchange or communication. Hence movies in this category tend to be highly anti-Communist (or antidemocratic if from the other side), spreading the fear that Communism is the worst of all possible evils. The cycle started in 1948; a list of 107 films is provided by Russel E. Shain, "Cold War Films, 1948–1962: An Annotated Filmography," *Journal of Popular Film 3* (1974): 365–72.

The Iron Curtain (48) William Wellman *aka Behind the Iron Curtain. I Married a Communist* (49) Robert Stevenson *aka The Woman on Pier 13. Red Danube* (49) George Sidney. *I Was a Communist for the F.B.I.* (51) Gordon Douglas. *Big Jim McLain* (52) Edward Ludwig. *Diplomatic Courier* (52) Henry Hathaway. *Unos* (Cz 52) Ján Kadár, Elmar Klos *aka The Hijacking / Kidnapped. Walk East on Beacon!* (52) Alfred L. Werker. *The Commies Are Coming, the Commies Are Coming* (57) George Waggner. *North by Northwest* (59) Alfred Hitchcock. *Escape from East Berlin / Tunnel 28* (US / G 62) Robert Siodmak *aka Escape from Berlin. The Manchurian Candidate* (62) John Frankenheimer. *Born American* (US / Fin 86) Renny Harlin.

——Comedy War Films (Armed Forces Comedies, Army Comedies, Military Comedies, Naval Comedies, War Comedies)

A vast pool of war (combat) movies and military (noncombat) films dealing with any kind of comedy situation and style may be included in this category: wartime comedies, service comedies, slapstick, farces ridiculing the Nazi system, black comedies and satires.

Shoulder Arms (18) Charlie Chaplin. *Half Shot at Sunrise* (30) Paul Sloane. *Hail the Conquering Hero* (44) Preston Sturges. *I Was a Male War Bride* (49) Howard Hawks *aka You Can't Sleep Here. The Baby and the Battleship* (GB 56) Jay Lewis. *Don't Give Up the Ship* (59) Norman Taurog. *Very Important Person* (GB 62) Ken Annakin *aka A Coming Out Party. The Americanization of Emily* (64) Arthur Hiller *aka Emily. M*A*S*H* (69) Robert Altman *aka MASH. Private Benjamin* (80) Howard Zieff.

——Concentration Camp War Films (Prison Camp Films)

The term concentration camp is used to designate a camp where all kinds of prisoners-of-war, military prisoners, political prisoners or civilians are housed. Thus the category concentration camp war film is used to group movies that deal with concentration camps, internment camps, prison camps, extermination camps and the living conditions prevalent in them, excluding movies that deal mainly with escape plots during wartime; the term prisoner-of-war escape film is more apt to describe this latter type that, because of the numerous films dealing with a successful escape, forms a minor subgenre of its own.

Pastor Hall (GB 40) Roy Boulting. *The Cross of Lorraine* (43) Tay Garnett. *2,000 Women* (GB 44) Frank Launder. *The Captive Heart* (GB 46) Basil Dearden. *Act of Violence* (48) Fred Zinnemann. *Ostatni etap* (Pol 48) Wanda Jakubowska *aka The Last Stage. Three Came Home* (50) Jean Negulesco. *A Town Like Alice* (GB 56) Jack Lee *aka The Rape of Malaya. Eroica* (Pol 57) Andrzej Munk [2 parts: *Scherzo alla Polaca, Ostinatolugubre*] *aka Heroism. The Camp on Blood Island* (GB 58) Val Guest. *Kapò / Kapo* (It / F / Yug 59) Gillo Pontecorvo. *Pasazerka* (Pol 63) Andrzej Munk, Witold Lesiewicz *aka The Passenger. The Hill* (GB 65) Sidney Lumet. *King Rat* (65) Bryan Forbes. *When Hell Was in Session* (79 TV) Paul Krasny. *Playing for Time* (80 TV) Daniel Mann. *Merry Christmas, Mr. Lawrence / Senjo no Merii Kurisumasu* (GB / J 82) Nagisa Oshima. *Opposing Force* (Phil / US 86) Eric Karson *aka Hell Camp. Empire of the Sun* (US / Chn / Sp 87) Steven Spielberg. *Hanoi Hilton* (87) Lionel Chetwynd.

———**Court-Martial Dramas**   A minor subgenre that concentrates on the trial of military personnel accused of treason, insubordination, sedition, or any other crime punishable under military law. These films rely a lot on the skill of the prosecuting and defense attorneys and on the build-up of suspense.

The Winslow Boy (GB 48) Anthony Asquith. *The Caine Mutiny* (54) Edward Dmytryk. *Carrington, V.C.* (GB 54) Anthony Asquith *aka Court Martial. The Court-Martial of Billy Mitchell* (55) Otto Preminger *aka One Man Mutiny. The Rack* (56) Arnold Laven. *Paths of Glory* (57) Stanley Kubrick. *Time Limit* (57) Karl Malden. *Private Potter* (GB 62) Caspar Wrede. *King and Country* (GB 64) Joseph Losey *aka Hamp. Conduct Unbecoming* (GB 75) Michael Anderson. *Sergeant Matlovich vs. the U.S. Air Force* (78 TV) Paul Leaf. *"Breaker" Morant* (Aust 79) Bruce Beresford. *The Court-Martial of Jackie Robinson* (90 MCTV) Larry Peerce.

———**Desert War Films (Desert Warfare Movies, War in the Desert Films)**   The North African terrain is the natural setting for these war films, although other desert locations are sometimes used, e.g., *Destination Gobi* (1953), set in Mongolia.

The Lost Patrol (33) John Ford. *Sahara* (43) Zoltan Korda. *The Desert Fox* (51) Henry Hathaway *aka Rommel—Desert Fox. The Desert Rats* (53) Robert Wise. *Destination Gobi* (53) Robert Wise. *Amère Victoire / Bitter Victory* (F / GB 57) Nicholas Ray. *Ice Cold in Alex* (GB 58) J. Lee Thompson *aka Desert Attack. Sea of Sand* (GB 58) Guy Green *aka Desert Patrol.*

———**Factual War Films (Documentary War Films)**   During World War II, the war documentary reached full maturity. Those made in England were outstanding for their effectiveness in presenting the high spirits and morale of the different sectors that made up the country's population. The mixing of documentary and fictional techniques was an acknowledged asset in some of these war documentaries. The Americans contributed significantly, and their films were very influential. The Russians and Germans also amassed a great amount of material. From early reconstructions to documentaries, compilations and television film, the factual war film has taken many forms and has been put to many uses: newsreels, magazines, propaganda films, reports and training films.

Triumph des Willens (G 34-36) Leni Riefenstahl *aka The Triumph of the Will. Why We Fight* (42-45) Series of 7 films: *The Nazis Strike* (42) Frank Capra, Anatole Litvak; *Prelude to War* (42) Frank Capra; *The Battle of Britain* (43) Anthony Veiller; *The Battle of Russia / Battle for Russia* (43)

Anatole Litvak; *Divide and Conquer* (43) Frank Capra, Anatole Litvak; *The Battle of China* (44) Frank Capra, Anatole Litvak; *War Comes to America—I* (45) Anatole Litvak. *December 7th* (43) John Ford, Toland Gregg. *Desert Victory* (GB 43) Roy Boulting. *Tunisian Victory* (GB / US 43) Roy Boulting, Frank Capra. *Fires Were Started* (GB 43) Humphrey Jennings *aka I Was a Fireman*. *The Battle of San Pietro / San Pietro* (44) John Huston. *The Fighting Lady* (43-44) William Wyler. *Burma Victory* (GB 45) Roy Boulting. *Nuit et brouillard* (F 55) Alain Resnais *aka Night and Fog*. *Mourir à Madrid* (F 62) Frédéric Rossif *aka To Die in Madrid*. *Le 17ᵉ Parallèle: le Viêtnam en guerre* (F 67) Joris Ivens, Marceline Loridan *aka Dix-Septième Parallèle / Le 17ᵉ Parallèle / 17th Parallel: Vietnam in War*. *Le Chagrin et la pitié / Das Haus nebenan* (F / Swiz / G 69) Marcel Ophüls *aka The Sorrow and the Pity*.

———**Historical War Films**   If we exclude documentaries, the historical war films worthy of the name are few. Ideally, they should strive for historical accuracy and unbiased presentation of facts when recreating or reenacting battles of the past or present, or when retelling actual happenings in time of war or war conditions on the battlefield.

Thirty Seconds Over Tokyo (44) Mervyn LeRoy. *The Story of G. I. Joe* (45) William Wellman. *Battleground* (49) William Wellman. *Dunkirk* (GB 58) Leslie Norman.

———**John Wayne War Films**   John Wayne (1907–1979), the star of countless action-adventure movies, is the perfect Hollywood image of the American he-man war hero who always wins the war single-handedly at the end. Whether he plays a soldier, a commanding officer or an admiral, he remains John Wayne, an institution unto himself, turning a war movie (with few exceptions) into a star vehicle.

Flying Tigers (42) David Miller. *The Fighting Seabees* (44) Edward Ludwig. *Back to Bataan* (45) Edward Dmytryk. *They Were Expendable* (45) John Ford. *Sands of Iwo Jima* (49) Allan Dwan. *Flying Leathernecks* (51) Nicholas Ray. *Operation Pacific* (51) George Waggner. *The Longest Day* (62) Ken Annakin, Andrew Marton, Bernard Wicki, Gerd Oswald, Darryl F. Zanuck, Elmo Williams. *In Harm's Way* (65) Otto Preminger.

———**Military School Films**   As distinct from training camp films (q.v.) which specialize in turning civilians into GI's, military school films are set in military academies and show what it takes to become an officer. These films may also be listed as campus movies; *see* **COLLEGE FILM**.

West Point of the Air (35) Richard Rosson. *Brother Rat* (38) Bryan Forbes. *The Duke of West Point* (38) Alfred E. Green. *Brother Rat and a Baby* (40) Ray Enright *aka Baby Be Good*. *Ten Gentlemen from West Point* (42) Henry Hathaway. *The Spirit of West Point* (47) Ralph Murphy. *Beyond Glory* (48) John Farrow. *Francis Goes to West Point* (52) Arthur Lubin. *The Long Gray Line* (55) John Ford. *The Private War of Major Benson* (55) Jerry Hopper. *Dress Gray* (86 TV) Glenn Jordan.

———**Nuclear War Films**   They are mostly Cold War films, but because they deal with the hysteria and danger that the misuse of atomic power poses to humanity, they form a class of their own. The main themes are survival and the inability of man to control his technology; *see* Jack G. Shaheen, *Nuclear War Films* (Carbondale and Edwardsville: Southern Illinois University Press, 1978). *See* **NUCLEAR FILM.**

On the Beach (59) Stanley Kramer. *Dai sanji sekai taisen— Yonju-ichi jikan no kyofu* (J 60) Shigeaki Hidaka *aka The Final War / Jikan no kyofu / World War III Breaks Out. Rat* (Yug 60) Velko Bulajic *aka War. Sekai daisenso* (J 62) Shue Matsubayashi *aka The Final War / The Last War. Dr. Strangelove; or, How I Learned to Stop Worrying and Love the Bomb* (GB / US 63) Stanley Kubrick. *The Bedford Incident* (US / GB 65) James B. Harris. *Plutonium* (G 78 TV) Rainer Erler.

——**Pacifist Films (Antiwar Films)** Fewer in number than the pro-war films, they have nevertheless been around since the beginning of the war movie and, if they have not succeeded in eradicating war, at least they have played a role in educating a great many people about the foolhardiness of misplaced heroics and pro-war sentimentality.

All Quiet on the Western Front (30) Lewis Milestone. *Westfront 1918— Vier von Infanterie* (G 30) George W. Pabst *aka Comrades of 1918. Broken Lullaby* (32) Ernst Lubitsch *aka The Man I Killed. The Road to Glory* (36) Howard Hawks. *The Steel Helmet* (51) Samuel Fuller. *Attack!* (56) Robert Aldrich *aka The Fragile Fox. Biruma-no tategoto* (J 56) Kon Ichikawa *aka The Burmese Harp / The Harp of Burma. Paths of Glory* (57) Stanley Kubrick. *Hell Is for Heroes* (61) Don Siegel.

——**Preparedness War Films** Some films sought to foster the urgency for "being ready" for being prepared for war. These propreparedness, propaganda films encouraged recruitment by creating a positive image of the armed forces; some achieved this by showing the training methods (training films) used by the different branches of the military.

The Battle Cry of Peace (15) Wilfred North. *Wings of the Navy* (39) Lloyd Bacon. *Flight Command* (40) Frank Borzage. *Dive Bomber* (41) Michael Curtiz. *I Wanted Wings* (41) Mitchell Leisen, Theodore Reed (replaced).

——**Prisoner-of-War Escape Films (P.O.W. Films, Prisoners-of-War Films)** How the prisoners set into motion the planned escape is the gist of this type of movie; a variant, the concentration camp war film (q.v.), presents the plight or living conditions in which the captives find themselves. Sometimes both themes are found in the same film, e.g., *The Bridge on the River Kwai* (1957) which features life in a Japanese camp and the escape of one of its prisoners.

Everything Is Thunder (GB 36) Milton Rosmer. *La Grande Illusion* (F 37) Jean Renoir *aka Les Évasions du capitaine Maréchal / Grande Illusion / Grand Illusion. Who Goes Next?* (GB 38) Maurice Elvey. *The Wooden Horse* (GB 50) Jack Lee. *Albert, RN* (GB 53) Lewis Gilbert *aka Break to Freedom. Stalag 17* (53) Billy Wilder. *The Colditz Story* (GB 54) Guy Hamilton. *The Bridge on the River Kwai* (GB 57) David Lean. *The One That Got Away* (GB 57) Roy Baker. *Danger Within* (GB 58) Don Chaffey *aka Breakout. La Vache et le prisonnier / La vacca e il prigioniero / Ich und die Kuh* (F / It / G 59) Henri Verneuil *aka The Cow and I. A Very Important Person* (GB 61) Ken Annakin *aka A Coming Out Party. The*

Password Is Courage (GB 62) Andrew L. Stone. *The Great Escape* (63) John Sturges. *The McKenzie Break* (GB 70) Lamont Johnson *aka Wolfpack*. *The Birdmen* (71 TV) Philip Leacock *aka The Birdmen of Beckstadt / The Escape of the Birdmen*.

——**Propaganda War Films** Most war movies (documentary or fiction) have a high propaganda content infused into them; those films made during wartime are heavily propagandistic, be it for reasons of uplifting the morale of one's own people, for undermining the enemy's morale, or for trying to persuade other nations of the justness of the cause. Any film in any subgenre of the war movie can be at the same time a propaganda war film.
The Little American (17) C. B. DeMille. *The Kaiser, the Beast of Berlin* (18) Rupert Julian *aka The Beast of Berlin / The Kaiser*. *Hearts of the World* (18) D. W. Griffith *aka Love's Struggle*. *The Lion Has Wings* (GB 39) Michael Powell, Brian Desmond Hurst, Adrian Brunel. *The Mortal Storm* (40) Frank Borzage. *The Big Blockade* (GB 41) Charles Frend. *Air Force* (42) Howard Hawks. *Kak zakal yalav stal* (USSR 42) Mark Donskoi *aka How the Steel Was Tempered*. *Next of Kin* (GB 42) Thorold Dickinson. *Happy Land* (43) Irving Pichel. *Bataan* (43) Tay Garnett. *Sherlock Holmes in Washington* (43) Roy William Neill. *Chelovek No. 217* (USSR 44) Mikhail Romm *aka Man No. 217*. *The Purple Heart* (44) Lewis Milestone. *Raduga* (USSR 44) Mark Donskoi *aka Rainbow*. *Thirty Seconds Over Tokyo* (44) Mervyn LeRoy. *Objective Burma!* (45) Raoul Walsh.

——**Pro-Soviet War Films** As a result of the war effort a few films made in Hollywood dealt with the presentation of the Allies in a favorable light by depicting their gallant contribution towards winning the war. Besides pro–Allies films about England, France, China and other countries, there were those that were pro–Russia; they offer an interesting contrast with the Cold War films in the aftermath of World War II.
Mission to Moscow (43) Michael Curtiz. *The North Star* (43) Lewis Milestone *aka Armored Attack*. *Days of Glory* (44) Jacques Tourneur. *Counter-Attack* (45) Zoltan Korda *aka One Against Seven*.

——**Pro-War Films** Most movies that have been made on war matters are pro-war, some blatantly so, while others overplay the heroic side of war, exploiting violence and heroism for the sake of spectacle and or for propagandistic reasons.
The Road to Glory (36) Howard Hawks. *Sergeant York* (41) Howard Hawks. *A Yank in the R.A.F.* (41) Henry King. *Gung Ho!* (43) Ray Enright. *To Hell and Back* (55) Jesse Hibbs.

——**Rehabilitation Films (Returning Vet Movies)** Films on rehabilitation deal with the problems of readjusting to civilian life. The returning veterans have to learn how to come to terms with themselves and society, and in the case of the physically injured, how to cope with their disabilities. Not all returning soldiers succeed in reintegrating themselves into society. In such instances, the end result may be a final outburst of violence.
Pride of the Marines (45) Delmer Daves *aka Forever in Love*. *The Best Years of Our Lives* (46) William Wyler *aka Glory for Me*. *The Men* (50)

Fred Zinnemann *aka Battle Stripe.* *Tracks* (77) Henry Jaglom. *Coming Home* (78) Hal Ashby. *Who'll Stop the Rain* (78) Karel Reisz *aka Dog Soldiers.* *Some Kind of Hero* (81) Michael Pressman. *Ashes and Embers* (82) Hale Gerima. *Birdy* (84) Alan Parker. *Cease Fire* (84) David Nutter. *Distant Thunder* (US / Can 88) Rick Rosenthal. *Born on the Fourth of July* (89) Oliver Stone. *In Country* (89) Norman Jewison. *Jacknife* (89) David Jones.

————**Resistance Films**   Films that are about guerrilla activity, partisans, saboteurs and the French Maquis or Underground movements fall under the category of resistance films.

Det brinner en eld (Sw 43) Gustaf Molander *aka A Fire Is Burning.* *Edge of Darkness* (43) Lewis Milestone. *La Bataille du rail* (F 45) René Clément *aka Battle of the Rails.* *Pokolenie* (Pol 54) Andrzej Wajda *aka A Generation / Light in the Darkness* [first in the "Wajda" trilogy, followed by *Kanal* (56) and *Popiół i diament* (58)]. *Kanal* (Pol 56) Andrzej Wajda *aka Sewer / They Loved Life.* *Carve Her Name with Pride* (GB 58) Lewis Gilbert. *Popiół i diament* (Pol 58) Andrzej Wajda *aka Ashes and Diamonds.* *Il Generale Della Rovere / Le Générale della Rovere* (It / F 59) Roberto Rossellini *aka The General Della Rovere.* *Ivanovo detstvo* (USSR 62) Andrei Tarkovsky *aka Ivan's Childhood / My Name Is Ivan / The Youngest Spy.* *Le quattro giornale di Napoli / The Four Days of Naples* (US / It 62) Nanni Loy. *La Ligne de démarcation* (F 66) Claude Chabrol *aka The Line of Demarcation.*

————**Revolutionary War Films**   These films deal with revolutionary elements or revolutionary organizations intent on overthrowing the status quo of a nation by acts of war and terrorism, or they focus on freeing their country from colonial powers. They are distinct from films that deal with open, declared civil war.

Bronenosets "Potyomkin" (USSR 25) Sergei M. Eisenstein, Grigori Alexandrov *aka The Armoured Cruiser Potemkin / Battleship Potemkin / Bronenosets Potemkin / Potemkin.* *Viva Zapata!* (52) Elia Kazan. *La Battaglia di Algeri / Maarakat Alger* (It / Alg 65) Gillo Pontecorvo *aka [The] Battle of Algiers.* *La Insurrección / Der Aufstand* (G / CR 80) Peter Lienthal *aka The Uprising.*

————**Sea War Films (Naval Battle Films, War-at-Sea Films)**   Films in which the role of the Navy is highlighted, or the crew is engaged in action or enjoying shore leave, form an important section of the war film. *See also* **Submarine War Films.**

Convoy (GB 40) Pen Tennyson. *Stand By for Action* (42) Robert Z. Leonard. *Action in the North Atlantic* (43) Lloyd Bacon. *Lifeboat* (44) Alfred Hitchcock. *They Were Expendable* (45) John Ford. *Okinawa* (52) Leigh Jason. *The Silent Enemy* (GB 58) William Fairchild.

————**Socially Conscious War Films (Social Conscience Films)**   These films deal with ethnic or racial prejudice. They expose the deeply ingrained biases against Jews, blacks or any other persecuted minority, and they make a plea for understanding and tolerance.

Crossfire (47) Edward Dmytryk. *Home of the Brave* (49) Mark Robson.

Bright Victory (50) Mark Robson *aka Lights Out.   All the Young Men* (60) Hall Bartlett.   *A Soldier's Story* (84) Norman Jewison.

——**Spanish Civil War Films**   The Spanish Civil War (1936–39) was a testing ground for some of the weaponry and air bombing techniques that were later used in World War II. It was also a scenario where the political ideologies of the Left and Right fought for supremacy. It attracted intellectuals from all over the world, and many young men fought and died for their ideals. Many films have portrayed directly or indirectly the conflict.[137]
The Last Train from Madrid (37) James Hogan.   *Love Under Fire* (37) George Marshall.   *Blockade* (38) William Dieterle.   *L'Espoir / Sierra de Teruel* (F / Sp 38-39) André Malraux *aka Man's Hope.   L'Assedio dell'Alcazar / Sin novedad en el alcázar* (It / G / Sp 39) Augusto Genina *aka El Alcázar de Toledo.   Escuadrilla* (Sp 41) Antonio Román.   *Raza* (Sp 41) José Luis Sáenz de Heredia *aka Espíritu de una raza.   For Whom the Bell Tolls* (43) Sam Wood.   *Confidential Agent* (45) Herman Shumlin.   *The Angel Wore Red / La sposa bella* (US / It 60) Nunnally Johnson.   *La Fête espagnole* (F 61) Jean-Jacques Vierne.   *Le Mur* (F 66) Serge Roullet *aka The Wall.   Golpe de mano* (Sp 69) José Antonio de la Loma *aka ¡Explosión!   La orilla* (Sp 70) Luis Lucia.   *L'Arbre de Guernica / L'albero di Guernica* (F / It 73) Fernando Arrabal.   *Las largas vacaciones del 36* (Sp 75) Jaime Camino *aka The Long Vacations of '36.   The Good Fight* (83) Mary Dore, Sam Sills, Noel Buckner.   *La Vaquilla* (Sp 84) Luis García Berlanga *aka The Little Bull.   Requiem por un campesino español* (Sp 85) Francesc Bertriu *aka Requiem for a Spanish Peasant.*

——**Spy War Films (Espionage Films)**   Films about spies, during peacetime or wartime, are legion and they have always been popular with the audiences. In time of war or in pre-war conditions, they are a good vehicle for propaganda because the villainous enemy spy is a ready-made candidate for stereotyping, and if the spy is "ours," it is an opportunity to enhance the unselfishness, courage and heroism of the dedicated spy, ready to sacrifice his / her own life if need be. **See SPY FILM.**
Confessions of a Nazi Spy (39) Anatole Litvak.   *Paris Calling* (41) Edwin L. Marin.   *Secret Mission* (GB 42) Harold French.   *The Yellow Canary* (GB 43) Herbert Wilcox.   *The House on 92nd Street* (45) Henry Hathaway *aka House of 92nd Street / Now It Can Be Told.   Cloak and Dagger* (46) Fritz Lang.   *Five Fingers* (52) Joseph L. Mankiewicz.   *The Man Who Never Was* (GB 55) Ronald Neame.   *A Man Called Intrepid / Un Homme s'appelle Intrépide* (GB / Can 78 TV) Peter Carter [in 3 parts].

——**Submarine War Films**   Underwater warfare has always been a major topic of war films.
Submarine Patrol (38) John Ford.   *Escape to Glory* (40) John Brahm *aka Submarine Zone.   Action in the North Atlantic* (43) Lloyd Bacon.   *Crash Dive* (43) Archie Mayo.   *Destination Tokyo* (43) Delmer Daves.   *We Dive at Dawn* (GB 43) Anthony Asquith.   *Les Maudits* (F 47) René Clément *aka The Damned.   Morning Departure* (GB 49) Roy Baker *aka Operation Disaster.   Above Us the Waves* (GB 55) Ralph Thomas.   *The Enemy Below* (57) Dick Powell.   *Run Silent, Run Deep* (58) Robert Wise, Edward L. Beach.   *Das Boot* (G 79-81) Wolfgang Petersen *aka The Boat* [made in Vibrasound].

——**Training Camp Films (Military Training Films)**   These films show how recruits are turned into soldiers; they may or may not include battle scenes. In many war films the soldiers' training period is a prelude to being sent to the battlefront. Many training camp films are military comedies.

> *Bombardier* (43) Richard Wallace. *Marine Raiders* (44) Harold D. Schuster. *See Here, Private Hargrove* (44) Wesley Ruggles. *Take the High Ground* (53) Richard Brooks. *Soldier in the Rain* (63) Ralph Nelson.

——**Tribute War Films**   Some films pay tribute or homage to the men who fight, to women in uniform or to civilians on the home front.

> *Captains of the Clouds* (42) Michael Curtiz. *Action in the North Atlantic* (43) Lloyd Bacon. *So Proudly We Hail!* (43) Mark Sandrick. *They Were Expendable* (45) John Ford. *Go for Broke!* (51) Robert Pirosh.

——**Vietnam War Films**   The films for or against one of the most controversial wars (1956–1975) Americans have been involved in have often had a mixed reception. They usually fall into three categories: the effect of the war on those who stayed at home; the veteran adjusting to civilian life; and the films depicting actual combat. The Vietnam War films also include French and other countries' productions dealing with the conflict when the area was known as Indo-China. See Lawrence Thompson, Richard Welch and Philip Stephens, "A Vietnam Filmography," *The Journal of Popular Film and Television* 9 (1981): 61–67. For a comprehensive filmography of over 600 entries worldwide (including Vietnamese) *see* Jean-Jacques Malo and Tony Williams, *Vietnam War Films* (Jefferson, NC: McFarland, 1993); also of interest is Albert Auster and Leonard Quart, *How the War Was Remembered: Hollywood and Vietnam* (New York: Praeger, 1988).

> *Mort en Fraude* (F 56) Marcel Camus *aka Fugitive in Saigon*. *Patrouille de choc* (F 56) Claude Bernard-Aubert *aka Shock Patrol*. *A Yank in Vietnam* (63) Marshall Thompson *aka Commandos in Vietnam / The Year of the Tiger*. *Le Facteur s'en va-t-en guerre* (F 66) Claude Bernard-Aubert *aka Le Facteur de Diên Biên Fu / The Postman Goes to War*. *The Green Berets* (68) John Wayne, Ray Kellogg. *Go Tell the Spartans* (77) Ted Post. *Coming Home* (78) Hal Ashby. *The Deer Hunter* (78) Michael Cimino. *Apocalypse Now* (79) Francis Ford Coppola. *Karma* (US / Swiz / Vietnam 85) Ho Quang Minh. *Platoon* (US / Phil 86) Oliver Stone. *Full Metal Jacket* (87) Stanley Kubrick. *Gardens of Stone* (87) Francis Ford Coppola. *Good Morning, Vietnam* (87) Barry Levinson. *Hamburger Hill* (87) John Irving. *Off Limits* (87) Christopher Crowe *aka Saigon*. *Vietnam War Story* (87 TV) Kevin Hooks ("The Pass"), George Stanford Brown ("The Mine"), Ray Danton ("Home") [3 episodes]. *BAT 21* (88) Peter Markle *aka Bat*21*. *Dear America* (88) Bill Couturie *aka Dear America: Letters Home from Vietnam*. *Casualties of War* (89) Brian DePalma. *84 Charlie Mopic* (89) Patrick Duncan.

——**War Musicals**   They are musicals (some multistar) with a military background. *See* Allen L. Woll, *The Hollywood Musical Goes to War* (Chicago: Nelson-Hall, 1983). *See* **MUSICAL: All-star War Effort Musicals**.

The Gang's All Here (43) Busby Berkeley *aka The Girls He Left Behind*. *Stage Door Canteen* (43) Frank Borzage. *This Is the Army* (43) Michael Curtiz. *Follow the Boys* (44) A. Edward Sutherland.

——**War Romances** Romance has its place in war as it does in peace. Those romances with a military or war background fit into this category.
Today We Live (33) Howard Hawks. *The Clock* (45) Vincente Minnelli *aka Under the Clock*. *Tonight and Every Night* (45) Victor Saville. *My Foolish Heart* (49) Mark Robson. *A Time to Live and a Time to Die* (58) Douglas Sirk. *Ballada o soldatye* (USSR 58) Grigori Chukhrai *aka Ballad of a Soldier*. *Hanover Street* (GB / US 79) Peter Hyams. *Yanks* (GB / US 79) John Schlesinger.

——**War Spectaculars (Combat Spectaculars)** Although the term war spectacular includes many adventure war films, it is preferable to make a distinction between those movies that are sheer adventure-action pictures (the adventure war film) and those that recreate epic war exploits or battles in a grand manner.
Battleground (49) William Wellman. *The Longest Day* (62) Ken Annakin, Andrew Marton, Bernard Wicki, Gerd Oswald, Darryl F. Zanuck, Elmo Williams. *Battle of the Bulge* (65) Ken Annakin *aka The Battle of the Bulge*. *Osvobozhdyeniye* (USSR / Pol / Yug 69) Yuri Ozerov *aka The Great Battle*. *Tora! Tora! Tora!* (US / J 70) Richard Fleischer, Ray Kellogg, Toshio Masuda, Kinji Fukasaku *aka Tiger! Tiger! Tiger!* *A Bridge Too Far* (GB / US 76) Richard Attenborough. *Midway* (76) Jack Smight.

War in the Desert Film *see* **WAR FILM: Desert War Films**

War Musicals *see* **WAR FILM**

War Romances, War Spectaculars *see* **WAR FILM**

War Spy Films *see* **SPY FILM**

War-at-Sea Film *see* **WAR FILM: Sea War Films**

Warning Film *see* **NUCLEAR FILM**

Wartime Comedy *see* **WAR FILM: Comedy War Films**

Wartime Musical *see* **MUSICAL: All-Star War Effort Musicals**

Weather Reports *see* **TELEVISION NEWS**

Weeper *see* **WEEPIE**

WEEPIE (Five-Handkerchief Film, Four Handkerchief Picture, Four-Hankie Pic, Hankie Pic, Sobby, Sob-Story, Tear-Jerker, Three-Hanky Soap Opera, Weeper, Weepy) Most people think of the weepie in terms of the women's picture, but the fact is that weepies may also be effective with men, depending on the film's subject matter. The response to these movies is inevitably a highly subjective matter, and the strength of the personal reaction to the emotional stimuli determines whether the spectator has a good cry or not. Individual taste and the degree of sympathy for or identification with the characters or situations in the film influence one's reaction to them. The futility of death, the inexorability of an unexpected, terminal disease or simply forlornness are all effective in stimulating the tears. Women are said to respond readily to romance situations, men to self-sacrifice in wartime or to readiness to die for the sake of friendship. Many movies have poignant moments that make us cry, but whatever the subject matter employed, the main object of a tear-jerker is, of course, catharsis through tears. Other terms used synonymously with weepie are soap opera (q.v.), sobby and tear-jerker. *See also* **WOMAN'S PICTURE.**

Blossoms in the Dust (41) Mervyn LeRoy. *Random Harvest* (42) Mervyn LeRoy. *Letter from an Unknown Woman* (48) Max Ophuls. *Little Boy Lost* (53) George Seaton. *Magnificent Obsession* (54) Douglas Sirk. *Bigger Than Life* (56) Nicholas Ray. *An Affair to Remember* (57) Leo McCarey. *L'Arbre de Noël / L'albero di Natale* (F / It 69) Terence Young *aka The Christmas Tree / When Wolves Cry. Love Story* (70) Arthur Hiller. *Man, Woman and Child* (82) Dick Richards.

Weirdie *see* **HORROR FILM**

WEREWOLF MOVIE   The werewolf is another great in the pantheon of famous monsters. Along with the vampire, Frankenstein's monster and the zombie, the werewolf is the creature which most often keeps reappearing in horror films. *The Werewolf* (1913), directed by Henry McRae, featured the first apparition of a lycanthrope on film. In it, a Native American girl is transformed into a werewolf. Since then, screen werewolves have been plentiful, and thanks to the increasing sophistication of special effects, the transformations from man / woman to beast have become ever more remarkable and vivid. Although Universal made *The Werewolf of London* in 1935, it was with their *The Wolf Man* (1941) that the traditional lore of the werewolf was firmly established—those tainted with lycanthropy become werebeasts with a full moon; if bitten by a werewolf, the victim may become one also; only a silver bullet or a silver object can kill the beast, and so on. Successive werewolf pictures have introduced new trappings and detail variations into the legend.

The Werewolf (13) Henry McRae. *Werewolf of London* (35) Stuart Walker *aka Unholy Hour. The Wolf Man* (41) George Waggner *aka Destiny. The Mad Monster* (42) Sam Newfield. *The Undying Monster* (42) John Brahm *aka The Hammond Mystery. Frankenstein Meets the Wolf Man* (43) Roy William Neill. *Cry of the Werewolf* (44) Henry Levin *aka Daughter of the Werewolf. The Werewolf* (56) Fred F. Sears. *I Was a Teen-age Werewolf* (57) Gene Fowler, Jr. *aka Blood of the Werewolf. The Curse of the Werewolf* (GB 60) Terence Fisher *aka The Wolfman. Lycanthropus / Bei Vollmond Mord* (It / Aus 61) Richard Benson (Paolo Heusch) *aka Ghoul in a Girl's Dormitory / The Ghouls in School / I Married a Werewolf / Monster Among the Girls / Werewolf in a Girl's Dormitory. La Loba* (Mex 64) Rafael Baledon *aka Los Horrores del Bosque Negro / Los Misterios del Bosque*

Negro / The She Wolf. La marca del hombre lobo / Die toten Augen des Dr. Dracula (Sp / G 67) Enrique L. Equiluz *aka Frankenstein's Bloody Terror / Hell's Creatures / El Hombre Lobo / Mark of the Werewolf / The Mark of the Wolfman / Vampire of Dr. Dracula / The Werewolf's Mark / The Wolfman and Count Dracula / The Wolfman of Count Dracula* [first in the "Count Daninski" series: 10 films up to 1983]. *Las noches del hombre lobo* (Sp / F 68) René Govar *aka Nights of the Werewolf* [Daninski series]. *La furia del hombre lobo* (Sp 70) José María Zabalza *aka The Fury of the Wolfman* [Daninski series]. *La Noche de Walpurgis / Nacht der Vampire* (Sp / G 70) León Klimovsky *aka The Black Harvest of Countess Dracula / Shadow of the Werewolf / The Werewolf's Shadow / The Werewolf versus the Vampire Women* [Daninski series]. *The Boy Who Cried Werewolf* (73) Nathan H. Juran. *El retorno de Walpurgis* (Sp 73) Carlos Aured *aka The Black Harvest of Countess Dracula / Curse of the Devil / The Return of Walpurgis* [Daninsky series]. *The Beast Must Die* (GB 74) Paul Annett. *Legend of the Werewolf* (GB 74) Freddie Francis. *La Lupa Manara* (It 76) Rino Di Silvestro *aka Daughter of a Werewolf / Legend of the Wolfwoman / Werewolf Woman / The Wolf Man. Deathmoon* (78 TV) Bruce Kessler *aka Deathmoon-end. The Howling* (US / Can 80) Joe Dante [6 "Howling" films up to 1990]. *Wolfen* (80) Michael Wadleigh. *An American Werewolf in London* (GB / US 81) John Landis. *Full Moon High* (81) Larry Cohen *aka A Transylvanian Werewolf in America. The Company of Wolves* (GB 84) Neil Jordan. *Silver Bullet* (85) Daniel Attias *aka Stephen King's Silver Bullet. My Mom's a Werewolf* (88) Michael Fischa.

WESTERN (Cowboy Film, Western Film)   Influenced in its earlier stages by western fiction and western stage melodrama, the Western film was born in America and has remained a genuine American genre, even though many countries have made Westerns since they first appeared on the screen. Its origins can be traced back to *The Great Train Robbery* filmed by Edwin S. Porter in 1903, which, although it was not the first Western to be made, was very influential in the shaping of later Westerns.[138] The Western is a complex genre with an ever-growing amount of critical writing and interest in its development. As a genre, it boasts an impressive corpus of films which runs into several thousand.[139] Westerns are an amalgam of myth, history and legend — fantasy and reality intertwine. Set on the North American continent (movies set in Latin America, Australia, South Africa or other lands are not authentic Westerns), they are based on tradition and a solid historical heritage. Many western heroes existed in real life (Buffalo Bill, Billy the Kid, Jesse James, General Custer and Wyatt Earp for example) and some of the Western sagas describe real historical episodes of the conquest of the American West (the building of the railroads, the California gold rush, the Indian Wars). In short, the Western has a firm, historical foundation on which to draw and build its fantasies and to inspire countless tales of adventure and bravado.

Westerns are peopled by a profusion of colorful and familiar types — cowboys, Indians, cavalry men, gunfighters, outlaws, cattle rustlers, sheriffs, U.S. marshalls, rangers, bounty hunters, Mexicans, half-breeds, saloon girls, homesteaders, carpetbaggers and John Wayne who appeared in 153 movies (not all of them Westerns, naturally, but his western persona carries the weight). These characters form the basis for Western films which, as has become accepted by some, fall under seven basic plot types.[140]

The major discernible developments in the genre's checkered history have been a tendency towards psychological depth, the vindication of the Indian, an increase in realism together with a decrease in romanticism, and a general leaning towards the demythologization of the old West.

It is possible to subdivide the Western into many categories. A few examples are listed below. The terms oater, oats opera, horse opera or horse opry are synonymous with Western; they also have a derogatory meaning indicating a cheaply made film about cowboys—a B-Western.[141] A sagebrusher is another slang term for a Western. Shoot-'em-up is a broader term which applies to a film with a great deal of shooting and bloodshed. See **SPAGHETTI WESTERN.**

The Great Train Robbery (03) Edwin S. Porter. *Fighting Blood* (11) D. W. Griffith. *Hell's Hinges* (16) William S. Hart. *In Old Arizona* (29) Raoul Walsh. *Rider of Death Valley* (32) Albert Rogell. *The Texas Rangers* (36) King Vidor. *Drums Along the Mohawk* (39) John Ford. *Kit Carson* (40) George B. Seitz. *The Return of Frank James* (40) Fritz Lang. *The Ox-Bow Incident* (43) William Wellman *aka Strange Incident. My Darling Clementine* (46) John Ford. *The Wagonmaster* (50) John Ford. *Johnny Guitar* (54) Nicholas Ray. *Man Without a Star* (54) King Vidor. *The Fastest Gun Alive* (56) Russell Rouse. *The Last Wagon* (56) Delmer Daves. *Tribute to a Bad Man* (56) Robert Wise. *Gunfight at the O.K. Corral* (57) John Sturges. *Cowboy* (58) Delmer Daves. *Gunman's Walk* (58) Phil Karlson. *Man of the West* (58) Anthony Mann. *Saddle the Wind* (58) Robert Parrish. *The Hanging Tree* (59) Delmer Daves. *The Last Train from Gun Hill* (59) John Sturges *aka One Angry Day / Showdown at Gun Hill. The Magnificent Seven* (60) John Sturges [followed by 3 sequels (1966-72)]. *The Professionals* (66) Richard Brooks. *Welcome to Hard Times* (67) Burt Kennedy *aka Killer on a Horse. Will Penny* (67) Tom Gries. *The Ballad of Cable Hogue* (70) Sam Peckinpah. *Monte Walsh* (70) William A. Fraker. *Two Mules for Sister Sara* (70) Don Siegel. *The Hired Hand* (71) Peter Fonda. *Lawman* (71) Michael Winner. *The Bounty Man* (72 TV) John Llewellyn Moxey.*Wild Rovers* (71) Blake Edwards. *High Plains Drifter* (72) Clint Eastwood. *The Life and Times of Judge Roy Bean* (72) John Huston. *The Man Who Loved Cat Dancing* (73) Richard C. Serafian. *Breakheart Pass* (75) Tom Gries *aka Showdown at Breakheart Pass. The Last Day* (75 TV) Vincent McEveety. *Posse* (75) Kirk Douglas. *The Invasion of Johnson County* (76 TV) Jerry Jameson. *The Macahans* (76 TV) Bernard McEveety. *Mustang Country* (76) John Champion. *Pony Express Rider* (76) Robert Totten. *The New Maverick* (78 TV) Hy Averback. *Bronco Billy* (80) Clint Eastwood. *Cattle Annie and Little Britches* (80) Lamont Johnson. *Calamity Jane* (84 TV) James Goldstone. *Silverado* (85) Lawrence Kasdan.

——**Anti-Westerns (Neo-Westerns, Revisionist Westerns)** Robert Warshow called "anti-Westerns" those films that did not conform to the traditional pattern of the genre and instead introduced psychological motivation and social criticism into the Western cadre. He cites as prime examples *The Ox-Bow Incident* (1943) and *High Noon* (1952).[142] These movies were to be known as psychological or adult Westerns (q.v.). In the late 1960s and early 1970s a number of films sought to debunk the Western film myth by purportedly presenting the West as it really was or by making fun of its cinematic clichés; these revisionist Westerns and spoofs are the so-called anti–Westerns.

The Ox-Bow Incident (43) William Wellman *aka Strange Incident*. *High Noon* (52) Fred Zinnemann. *Ride the High Country* (62) Sam Peckinpah *aka Guns in the Afternoon*. *Cat Ballou* (65) Elliot Silverstein. *Hombre* (67) Martin Ritt. *Lonesome Cowboys* (68) Andy Warhol. *Little Big Man* (70) Arthur Penn. *Soldier Blue* (70) Ralph Nelson. *Doc* (71) Frank Perry. *The Great Northfield Minnesota Raid* (71) Philip Kaufman. *McCabe & Mrs. Miller* (71) Robert Altman. *Bad Company* (72) Robert Benton. *The Culpepper Cattle Company* (72) Dick Richards. *Dirty Little Billy* (72) Stan Dragoti. *Blazing Saddles* (74) Mel Brooks *aka Black Bart*. *Buffalo Bill and the Indians, or Sitting Bull's History Lesson* (76) Robert Altman. *The Missouri Breaks* (76) Arthur Penn. *Heaven's Gate* (80) Michael Cimino. *Lonesome Dove* (88 TV) Simon Wincer [in 4 parts].

———**B-Westerns** Hundreds of low-budget Westerns were made. They were especially popular in the 1930s and 1940s, and it was only with the influence of television in the fifties that the B-Western finally disappeared from the cinemas. Some B-Westerns starring Randolph Scott, Audie Murphy and Rory Calhoun were more expensively made, and some of them resulted in fine Westerns. *See also* **Star-Vehicles**.

To the Last Man (33) Henry Hathaway. *Hop-a-Long Cassidy* (35) Howard Bretherton *aka Hopalong Cassidy Enters* [first in a series of 66 "Hopalong Cassidy" films (1935-48)]. *Powdersmoke Range* (35) Wallace Fox (began the "official "Three Mesquiteers series; 52 films (1935-43)]. *The Durango Kid* (40) Lambert Hillyer [64 films (1940-52) in the Durango Kid series]. *The Gay Caballero* (40) Otto Brower [23 films (1929-50) in the Cisco Kid series]. *Arizona Bound* (41) Spencer G. Bennet [first of 8 films (1941-42) in the Rough Riders series]. *Arizona Cyclone* (41) Joseph H. Lewis. *West of the Law* (42) Howard Bretherton [last film in the Rough Riders series]. *Rider from Tucson* (50) Lesley Selander. *Santa Fe* (51) Irving Pichel. *Drums Across the River* (54) Nathan Juran. *Buchanan Rides Again* (58) Budd Boetticher.

———**Biographical Westerns** Westerns based on the life of historical characters have always been a staple subject of the genre; this is especially so with outlaw biographies. Some Western heroes form such an integral part of the Western tradition that, even if they are not the subject of a biographical sketch, they have repeatedly appeared as characters. William Frederick Cody (1846–1917), alias Buffalo Bill, holds the record so far with 53 appearances; William Bonney (1859–81), better known as Billy the Kid, has appeared in 49 films.[143]

Billy the Kid (30) King Vidor *aka The Highway Man Rides* [filmed also in

German and Spanish versions]. *Sutter's Gold* (36) James Cruze. *Jesse James* (39) Henry King. *When the Daltons Rode* (40) George Marshall. *Belle Starr* (41) Irving Cummings. *Bad Men of Missouri* (41) Ray Enright. *Buffalo Bill* (44) William Wellman. *Al Jennings of Oklahoma* (50) Ray Nazarro. *Kansas Raiders* (50) Ray Enright. *Davy Crockett, King of the Wild Frontier* (55) Norman Foster [originally a 5-episode TV chronicle]. *Custer of the West / Custer, l'homme de l'ouest* (US / GB / F / Sp 67) Robert Siodmak *aka Custer / A Good Day for Fighting*.

——**Cavalry Films**   The U.S. Cavalry pursuing or fighting Indians, defending a fort, coming to the rescue of besieged settlers or a wagon train is all too familiar and forms an important subgenre of the Western. John Ford specialized in this type of film.

They Died with Their Boots On (41) Raoul Walsh *aka To the Last Man*. *Fort Apache* (48) John Ford. *She Wore a Yellow Ribbon* (49) John Ford. *Rio Grande* (50) John Ford. *Last of the Comanches* (52) Andre de Toth *aka The Sabre and the Arrow*. *Escape from Fort Bravo* (53) John Sturges. *The Last Frontier* (55) Anthony Mann *aka Savage Wilderness*. *Sergeant Rutledge* (60) John Ford *aka Captain Buffalo*. *A Thunder of Drums* (61) Joseph M. Newman. *A Distant Trumpet* (64) Raoul Walsh. *Major Dundee* (65) Sam Peckinpah. *Duel at Diablo* (66) Ralph Nelson. *Ulzana's Raid* (72) Robert Aldrich.

——**Comedies and Parodies (Western Comedies)**   Westerns have frequently been the object of comedy since the genre readily lends itself to parody.

Out West – The Sheriff (18) Roscoe Arbuckle. *Go West* (25) Buster Keaton. *Way Out West* (36) James W. Horne. *Destry Rides Again* (39) George Marshall. *Buck Benny Rides Again* (40) Mark Sandrich. *Go West* (40) Edward Buzzell *aka Marx Brothers Go West*. *A Lady Takes a Chance* (43) William A. Seiter. *Along Came Jones* (45) Stuart Heisler. *The Paleface* (48) Norman Z. McLeod. *The Son of Paleface* (52) Frank Tashlin. *The Sheepman* (58) George Marshall. *The Sheriff of Fractured Jaw* (GB 58) Raoul Walsh. *Alias Jesse James* (59) Norman McLeod. *McLintock!* (63) Andrew V. McLaglen. *Carry On Cowboy* (GB 65) Gerald Thomas. *Cat Ballou* (65) Elliot Silverstein. *The Scalphunters* (68) Sydney Pollack. *The Shakiest Gun in the West* (68) Alan Rafkin. *Butch Cassidy and the Sundance Kid* (69) George Roy Hill. *Support Your Local Sheriff!* (69) Burt Kennedy *aka Latigo-Support Your Local Sheriff*. *Dirty Dingus Magee* (70) Burt Kennedy. *There Was a Crooked Man. . .* (70) Joseph L. Mankiewicz. *The Young Country* (70 TV) Roy Huggins. *Scandalous John* (71) Robert Butler. *Support Your Local Gunfighter* (71) Burt Kennedy. *Blazing Saddles* (73) Mel Brooks *aka Black Bart*. *Goin' South* (78) Jack Nicholson. *Hot Lead and Cold Feet* (78) Robert Butler. *Kate Bliss and the Ticker Tape Kid* (78 TV) Burt Kennedy. *Bronco Billy* (80) Clint Eastwood.

——**Epic Westerns**   These films are epic in the sense that they depict great feats of collective or personal endeavor as well as the fortitude and heroism that helped to settle the West and forge a nation.

(The) Covered Wagon (23) James Cruze [first epic Western]. *The Iron Horse* (24) John Ford. *The Vanishing American* (25) George B. Seitz. *The*

Virginian (29) Victor Fleming.   *The Big Trail* (30) Raoul Walsh [*Die grosse Fahrt* (G.v.) / *La Piste des géants* (F.v.)].   *Cimarron* (31) Wesley Ruggles. *The Plainsman* (36) Cecil B. DeMille.   *Union Pacific* (39) Cecil B. DeMille.   *Red River* (48) Howard Hawks.   *The Alamo* (60) John Wayne, John Ford (uncredited) [*Cf. The Last Command* (53) Frank Lloyd].   *How the West Was Won* (62) John Ford, George Marshall, Henry Hathaway. *Cheyenne Autumn* (64) John Ford *aka The Long Flight.*

——**Hybrid Westerns**   Filmmakers have at times sought to mix the western formula with other genres—the musical, the gangster film, the horror genre, the kung fu film. The resulting product is a hybrid and is very much abhorred by purists.

Aerial Western: *Cowboy in the Clouds* (43) Benjamin Kline.   Gangster Western: *Men of America* (32) Ralph Ince, *Broadway to Cheyenne* (32) Harry Fraser, *Crossfire* (33) Otto Brower.   Horror Western: *Curse of the Undead* (59) Edward Dein, *Billy the Kid vs. Dracula* (65) William Beaudine, *Jesse James Meets Frankenstein's Daughter* (65) William Beaudine, *Ghost Town* (88) Richard Governor.   Kung-Fu Western: *Kung Fu* (71 TV) Jerry Thorpe.   Mystery Western: *Tombstone Canyon* (32) Alan James, *Riders of the Whistling Skull* (37) Mack V. Wright [Three Mesquiteers series], *Hec Ramsey* (71 TV) Daniel Petrie *aka The Century Turns.*   SF Western: *The Phantom Empire* (35) Otto Brower, B. Reeves Eason [12-chapter serial; feature version: *Men with Steel Faces* (40)], *Ghost Patrol* (36) Sam Newfield, *Westworld* (73) Michael Crichton.

——**Indian Films (Indian Westerns, Injun Pictures)**   The Indian has figured in a great many Westerns.[144] Generally speaking, Indian films fall under two types: anti-Indian and pro-Indian pictures. Most films before *Broken Arrow* (1950) subscribed to the motto that "The only good Indian is a dead Indian," but with the appearance of that film there began a practice of redressing the injustice done by the screen representation of the Indian, and a more sympathetic portrayal became the norm in quite a number of films. *See also* **Cavalry Films.**

The Last of the Mohicans (36) George B. Seitz.   *Broken Arrow* (50) Delmer Daves.   *Devil's Doorway* (50) Anthony Mann.   *Tomahawk* (51) George Sherman.   *Escape from Fort Bravo* (53) John Sturges.   *The Indian Fighter* (55) Andre de Toth.   *Walk the Proud Land* (56) Jesse Hibbs.   *Comanche Station* (60) Budd Boetticher.   *Geronimo* (62) Arnold Laven.   *Cheyenne Autumn* (64) John Ford *aka The Long Fight.*   *Tell Them Willie Boy Is Here* (69) Abraham Polonsky.   *A Man Called Horse* (70) Elliot Silverstein [followed by *The Return of a Man Called Horse* (76) Irvin Kershner and *Triumphs of a Man Called Horse / El triunfo de un hombre llamado caballo* (US / Mex 82) John Hugh].   *Run, Simon, Run* (70 TV) George McCowan *aka Savage Run.*   *I Will Fight No More Forever* (75 TV) Richard T. Heffron. *Last of the Mohicans* (77 TV) James L. Conway.   *Ishi: The Last of His Tribe* (78 TV) Robert Ellis Miller.   *Dances with Wolves* (90) Kevin Costner.

——**John Wayne Westerns**   The Duke became an American institution unto himself. He is the traditional American hero par excellence. Whether in war epics (*see* **WAR FILM**) or Western films, his personality and charisma dominate the film.

Stagecoach (39) John Ford. *Allegheny Uprising* (39) William Seiter *aka Allegheny Frontier / The First Rebel.* *Dark Command* (40) Raoul Walsh. *Tall in the Saddle* (44) Edwin L. Marin. *Angel and the Badman* (47) James Edward Grant. *Fort Apache* (48) John Ford [first of Ford's cavalry trilogy followed by *She Wore a Yellow Ribbon* (49) and *Rio Grande* (50)]. *Red River* (48) Howard Hawks. *3 Godfathers* (48) John Ford. *Hondo* (53) John Farrow. *The Searchers* (56) John Ford. *Rio Bravo* (59) Howard Hawks [first of a Hawks loose trilogy with *El Dorado* (66) and *Rio Lobo* (70)]. *The Alamo* (60) John Wayne, John Ford (uncredited). *North to Alaska* (60) Henry Hathaway *aka The Alaskans / Go North.* *The Comancheros* (61) Michael Curtiz. *The Man Who Shot Liberty Valance* (62) John Ford. *The Sons of Katie Elder* (65) Henry Hathaway. *The War Wagon* (67) Burt Kennedy. *True Grit* (69) Henry Hathaway. *Rooster Cogburn* (75) Stuart Millar. *The Shootist* (76) Don Siegel [Wayne's last film].

——**Modern Westerns (Contemporary Westerns, Elegiac Westerns)** In contrast to the period setting of most Westerns, modern Westerns place their heroes amongst the artifacts of the 20th century, which they may either accept or reject. Many of these films present the West as a vanishing frontier and its individualistic heroes as a diminishing species alienated from today's world.

The Last Outlaw (36) Christy Cabanne. *Bad Day at Black Rock* (54) John Sturges. *Giant* (55) George Stevens. *The Misfits* (61) John Huston. *Hud* (62) Martin Ritt. *Lonely Are the Brave* (62) David Miller *aka The Last Hero.* *Ride the High Country* (62) Sam Peckinpah *aka Guns in the Afternoon.* *The Rounders* (64) Burt Kennedy. *Pocket Money* (72) Stuart Rosenberg. *Rancho Deluxe* (74) Frank Perry. *Comes a Horseman* (78) Alan J. Pakula. *The Grey Fox* (Can 80) Phillip Borsos [rel. in 82].

——**Musical Westerns (Singing Cowboy Pictures, Oatuners)** A Western setting has often featured in musicals (*see* **MUSICAL**), and the singing cowboy variety of musical, whose main stars were Gene Autry and Roy Rogers, was extremely popular in the thirties and forties. These singing cowboy pictures are frowned upon by Western devotees, but the fact is that they form part of Hollywood's and the Western's history.

Strawberry Roan (33) Alan James *aka Flying Fury.* *Tumbling Tumbleweeds* (35) Joseph Kane. *Song of the Gringo* (36) John P. McCarthy. *Under Western Stars* (38) Joseph Kane. *Colorado Sunset* (39) George Sherman. *South of the Border* (39) George Sherman. *Under Mexican Stars* (50) George Blair.

——**Outlaw Films (Gunfighter Films)** The outlaw has featured in dozens of films. Acting alone or in gangs, lawbreakers have terrorized whole communities, robbed banks, assaulted trains, rustled cattle, staged bloody gunfights and scourged the West from Canada to Mexico. *See also* **Biographical Westerns.**

Law and Order (32) Edward L. Cahn. *Jesse James* (39) Henry King. *The Outlaw* (41) Howard Hughes [rel. in 43]. *The Desperados* (43) Charles Vidor. *Badman's Territory* (46) Tim Whelan. *Bad Men of Tombstone* (49) Kurt Neumann. *Colorado Territory* (49) Raoul Walsh. *The Gunfighter*

(50) Henry King. *The Lawless Breed* (52) Raoul Walsh. *Shane* (53) George Stevens. *Vera Cruz* (54) Robert Aldrich. *The Halliday Brand* (57) Joseph H. Lewis. *The Bravados* (58) Henry King. *The Left-Handed Gun* (58) Arthur Penn. *The Wild Bunch* (69) Sam Peckinpah. *Bad Company* (72) Robert Benton. *The Outlaw Josey Wales* (76) Clint Eastwood. *The Long Riders* (79) Walter Hill. *Barbarosa* (82) Fred Schepisi. *Young Guns* (88) Christopher Cain. *Young Guns II* (90) Geoff Murphy.

——**Psychological Westerns (Adult Westerns)** A type of film which started in the forties and peaked in the fifties was the introduction into the Western of psychological notions, social problems and sex motivation.
The Outlaw (41) Howard Hawks [rel. in 43]. *Ox-Bow Incident* (43) William Wellman *aka Strange Incident*. *Duel in the Sun* (46) King Vidor. *Yellow Sky* (48) William Wellman. *The Furies* (50) Anthony Mann. *The Gun-fighter* (50) Henry King. *High Noon* (52) Fred Zinnemann. *Shane* (53) George Stevens. *Johnny Guitar* (54) Nicholas Ray. *Jubal* (56) Delmer Daves. *3:10 to Yuma* (57) Delmer Daves. *The Tin Star* (57) Anthony Mann. *The Big Country* (58) William Wyler. *The Left-Handed Gun* (58) Arthur Penn. *These Thousand Hills* (59) Richard Fleischer.

——**Revenge Westerns** One of the most common Western themes is avengers pursuing evil men to make them pay for the loss of spouse, family, sweetheart or friend.
Rustler's Paradise (35) Harry Fraser. *The Oklahoma Kid* (39) Lloyd Bacon. *Pursued* (47) Raoul Walsh. *Rancho Notorious* (52) Fritz Lang. *Gun Fury* (53) Raoul Walsh. *The Man from Laramie* (54) Anthony Mann. *Seven Men from Now* (56) Budd Boetticher. *The Bravados* (58) Henry King. *One-Eyed Jacks* (61) Marlon Brando. *An Eye for an Eye* (66) Michael Moore *aka Talion*. *The Shooting* (65) Monte Hellman [rel. to TV; theatrically in 71]. *Nevada Smith* (66) Henry Hathaway. *Hang 'em High* (67) Ted Post. *Return of the Gunfighter* (67 TV) James Neilson *aka Wyatt*. *Macho Callahan* (70) Bernard L. Kowalski. *The Trackers* (71 TV) Earl Bellamy *aka No Trumpets, No Drums*. *Kid Vengeance* (77) Joe Manduke.

——**Rodeo Films** Modern Westerns that focus on the cowboy's cherished activity, the rodeo, which is one of the few occupations that still gives the cowboy his freedom of movement in the face of an encroaching civilization.
Bronco Buster (52) Budd Boetticher. *The Lusty Men* (52) Nicholas Ray *aka This Man Is Mine*. *Arena* (53) Richard Fleischer. *Born Reckless* (59) Howard W. Koch. *The Honkers* (71) Steve Ihnat. *J. W. Coop* (71) Cliff Robertson. *When the Legends Die* (71) Stuart Miller. *Junior Bonner* (72) Sam Peckinpah. *Squares* (72) Patrick J. Murphy *aka Riding Tall*. *When the Legends Die* (72) Stuart Miller. *The Great American Cowboy* (74) Kieth Merrill. *Rodeo Girl* (80 TV) Jackie Cooper.

——**Star Vehicles** The heroes of numerous horse operas, William S. Hart, Tom Mix, Gene Autry and Roy Rogers were the Western stars that drew the audiences to their pictures every week. In a different league altogether, Gary Cooper, James Stewart, Henry Fonda, Clint Eastwood, John Wayne and many others, also had the kind of star quality that brought in the public.

Abbott and Costello: *Ride 'Em Cowboy* (42) Arthur Lubin.   Gene Autry: *Mule Train* (50) John English.   William Boyd: *Forty Thieves* (44) Lesley Selander [Hopalong Cassidy series].   Johnny Mack Brown: *Trail of Vengeance* (37) Sam Newfield.   Rod Cameron: *The Plunderers* (48) Joseph Kane. Larry "Buster" Crabbe: *Drift Fence* (36) Otto Lovering.   William S. Hart: *Tumbleweeds* (25) King Baggot.   Tim Holt: *Under the Tonto Rim* (47) Lew Landers.   Buck Jones: *The Texas Ranger* (31) Ross Lederman.   Tim McCoy: *The One Way Trail* (31) Ray Taylor.   Joel McCrea: *Wichita* (55) Jacques Tourneur.   Kermit Maynard: *Whistling Bullets* (37) John English.   Tom Mix: *The Great K & A Train Robbery* (26) Lewis Seiler.   Audie Murphy: *Ride Clear of Diablo* (54) Jesse Hibbs.   George O'Brien: *The Lone Star Ranger* (30) A. F. Erickson.   Elvis Presley: *Flaming Star* (60) Don Siegel. Roy Rogers: *Eyes of Texas* (48) William Witney.   Randolph Scott: *The Tall T* (57) Budd Boetticher.   Charles Starrett: *Trapped* (37) Leon Barsha.   Bob Steele: *Sunrise Trail* (31) J. P. McCarthy.   Tom Tyler: *Galloping Thru* (31) Lloyd Nosler.

Western Comedy   *see*   **WESTERN: Comedies and Parodies**

Wheeler Picture   *see*   **MOTORCYCLE MOVIE**

White Coater   *see*   **HARD-CORE PORNO FILM**

White Slavery Film   *see*   **VICE FILM**

White Sox Movie   *see*   **HARD-CORE PORNO FILM**

White Telephone Film   *see*   **TELEFONI BIANCHI**

WHODUNIT (Murder Mystery, Mystery-Thriller)   Whodunits, in cinema and literature alike, are usually concerned with solving a crime by identifying the criminal after a thorough investigation of all available clues and the clearing of any number of suspects have taken place (*see* **MYSTERY FILM**). Nowadays, variations on whodunits are also popular with whydunits and howdunits coexisting alongside the original type.
Secret of the Blue Room (33) Kurt Neumann.   *Murder at the Vanities* (34) Mitchell Leisen.   *Dinner at the Ritz* (GB 37) Harold Schuster.   *I Wake Up Screaming* (41) H. Bruce Humberstone *aka Hot Spot*.   *Black Angel* (46) Roy William Neill.   *Green for Danger* (GB 46) Sidney Gilliat.   *Ten Little Indians* (GB 65) George Pollock.   *The Last of Sheila* (73) Herbert Ross.   *Diez negritos / Dix Petits Nègres / ...E poi, non ne rimase nessuno / Ein Unbekannter rechnet ab* (Sp / It / F / G 74) Peter Collinson *aka And Then There Were None / Ten Little Indians*.   *Murder on the Orient Express* (GB 74) Sidney Lumet.   *Murder by Death / Neil Simon's Murder by Death* (76) Robert Moore.   *Stunts* (77) Mark L. Lester *aka Who Is Killing the Stuntmen?*   *Death on the Nile* (GB / Egy 78) John Guillermin.   *Who Is Killing the Great Chefs of Europe? / Die Schlemmer—Orgie* (US / G 78) Ted Kotcheff *aka Too Many Chefs*.   *Killjoy* (81 TV) John Llewellyn Moxey.

Whydunit   *see*   **WHODUNIT**

Wide Gauge Film   *see*   **WIDE SCREEN**

WIDE SCREEN (Wide-Screen Movie, Widescreen Picture)   During cinema's history, various film gauges and screens of different sizes and shapes have been in operation or the subject of experimentation. However, early in the history of cinematography, an aspect ratio (width and height of the printed or projected image) of 1.33:1 (4:3), known as standard, normal or academy ratio, was internationally accepted as the norm for 35mm film. Anything above the standard was considered wide screen. Although some attempts at wider formats were made at one time or another, the standard aspect ratio monopolized the film industry until the early 1950s when a variety of wide-screen systems were introduced in the hope of bringing back to film theaters the audiences that stayed at home watching television.[145] These wide-screen formats would vary from 1.66:1 to 2.76:1 (Ultra-Panavision 70) and beyond for more experimental processes. They were known by a profusion of trade names which, in most cases, covered similar systems and, for the most part, had a short life-span and were discontinued. The idea of films being projected onto big screens is an old one and demonstrations and experiments have been carried out throughout film's evolution. Louis Lumière gave one such demonstration at the Paris *Exposition Universelle* of 1900 by projecting a film onto a screen almost 70 feet wide and 53 feet high. In the same exhibition, the French inventor Raoul Grimoin-Sanson (1860–1941) introduced his Cinéorama which consisted of a cylindrical screen 330 feet in circumference lodged in a circular building equipped with 10 projectors for the demonstration. In 1927, Abel Gance projected part of his *Napoléon* (1925-27) onto three side-by-side screens in a wide-screen system known as Triptych; he also made use of Polyvision, a format which included several images in the same frame. Henry Chrétien (1879–1956) invented an anamorphic lens named Hypergonar, which Claude Autant-Lara used in the making of the film *Construire un feu* (1927). But apart from these and other sporadic attempts at widescreen films, it was not until 1952 with the advent of Cinerama, a process using three cameras and three projectors to project a single image onto a huge curved screen, and CinemaScope, an anamorphic system based on professor Chrétien's invention of 1927, that wide-screen processes caught on and became a viable commercial proposition.[146] Wide-screem systems comprise four main groupings: 1) the wide-screen effect is achieved by masking the top or bottom of standard 35mm film. However, this may result in cropping off heads or feet from the original image; 2) processes utilizing several cameras and projectors; 3) anamorphic films made with lenses that compress or "squeeze" the image when photographing it and "unsqueeze" it when projecting it onto the screen; 4) processes that use wide film — mostly any gauge over 35mm. Ideally, wide-screen systems should always be projected in their intended aspect ratios onto screen able to accommodate them; unfortunately, this is not always done. In the case of

CinemaScope films shown on television, as much as two thirds of the cinemascope image may be lost. At present, most wide-screen films are in the 1.66:1, 1.85:1 aspect ratios or made in Panavision. James L. Limbacher's *Four Aspects of the Film* (n.p. [New York: Brussel & Brussel], 1968) dedicates a section to wide-screen movies and includes a list of such films in one of his appendices. Besides surveying the development of wide-screen processes, he surveys as well the development of color, depth (3-D films), sound and some avant-garde innovations. A more recent and accurate work on the subject of wide screen is Robert E. Carr and R. M. Hayes's *Wide Screen Movies* (Jefferson, NC: McFarland, 1988). They include a vast filmography of important wide-screen and wide-gauge films with detailed credits and casts.

Filmed in Panoramic: *Il sacco di Roma* (It 20) Enrico Guazzoni, Giulio Aristide Sartorio *aka Clemente VII e il sacco di Roma.* Polyvision and Triptych: *Napoléon* (F 25-27) Abel Gance *aka Napoléon (vu par Abel Gance).* Hypergonar: *Construire un feu* (F 27) Claude Autant-Lara *aka Pour construire un feu.* 70mm Wide Film: *The Bat Whispers* (30) Roland West *aka Love in Chicago / Whispers.* Vitascope: *Kismet* (30) John Francis Dillon [G.v. William Dieterle]. Grandeur: *Song o' My Heart* (30) Frank Borzage. Realife: *The Great Meadow* (31) Charles Brabin. Cinerama: *This Is Cinerama* (52) Michael Todd, Walter Thompson, Fred Rickey, Merian C. Cooper (supervisors) *aka Cinerama.* Thrillarama: *Thrillarama Adventure* (56) Albert H. Reynolds, Dowlen Russell. Camera 65: *Raintree County* (57) Edward Dmytryk. Cinemiracle: *Windjammer* (58) Louis de Rochemont III, Bill Colleran. Superpanorama 70: *Shéhérazade / La schiava di Bagdad* (F / Sp / It 63) Pierre Gaspard-Huit, Jacques Bourdon *aka Scheherazade / Scorching Sands.* Kinopanorama 70: *Spyashchaya krasavitsa* (USSR 64) Apollinariy Dudko, Konstantin Sergeev *aka The Sleeping Beauty.* IMAX: *Circus World* (Can 74) Roman Kroitor. Sovscope 70: *Sibiriada* (USSR 77-79) Andrei Mikhalkov-Konchalovskiy *aka (The) Siberiad / Siberiade / Siberiade — A Siberian Saga.* OMNIMAX: *The Great Barrier Reef* (80) George Casey. Showscan: *New Magic* (84) Douglas Trumbull.

Wide-Screen Movie, Widescreen Picture *see* **WIDE SCREEN**

WITCH FILM (Witchcraft Film) The belief in witches and their magical powers, acquired through pacts with the devil, is very old. It dominated Europe from the 13th to the 17th century and has continued to the present day amongst the more credulous sectors of society. Walpurgis Night, witches' Sabbaths, brews and spells, all have an important role in the folklore of the witch. There are well-intentioned "white" witches who use their powers to help people and perform good deeds and there are malevolent "black" witches who employ their powers to foster evil for the pure pleasure of it or for self-gain. Whatever their leanings, witches have always been persecuted, and over the centuries, torture, burning at the stake and immolation have more often than not been their fate. Witches are good material for tale-spinning and fictitious narratives. Film has taken full advantage of this, and movies about witches, if not plentiful, are never-theless a very distinct group. The witch film includes both horror and non-horror films. Children's fantasy films and comedies in which witches appear are excluded from the witch film category. *See also* **HORROR FILM: Other Denizens of Horror Movies** and **Demonic Films**.

Häxan o Häxan / Heksen (Den / Sw 20-22) Benjamin Christensen *aka Witch-craft Through the Ages. Maid of Salem* (37) Frank Lloyd. *Vredens Dag* (Den 43) Carl Theodor Dreyer *aka Day of Wrath / Dies Irae. Noita Palaa Elämään* (Fin 52) Roland af Hällstrom *aka The Witch / The Witch Returns to Life. La bruja* (Mex 54) Chano Urueta *aka The Witch. Les Sorcières de Salem / Hexenjäger* (F / EG 56) Raymond Rouleau *aka The Crucible / The Witches of Salem. City of the Dead* (GB 60) John Moxey *aka Horror Hotel. El espejo de la bruja* (Mex 60) Chano Urueta *aka Cuentos de brujas / The Witch's Mirror. La maschera del demonio* (It 60) Mario Bava *aka Black Sunday / The Demon's Mask / House of Fright / Mask of the Demon / Revenge of the Vampire. Atacan las brujas* (Mex 64) José Diaz Morales *aka Santo ataca las brujas / Santo en la casa de las brujas / Santo Attacks the Witches. Witchcraft* (GB 64) Don Sharp *aka Witch and Warlock. La strega in amore* (It 66) Damiano Damiani *aka Aura / The Strange Obsession / The Witch / The Witch in Love. The Witches* (GB 66) Cyril Frankel *aka The Devil's Own. The Witchfinder General* (GB 67) Michael Reeves *aka The Conqueror Worm / Edgar Allan Poe's Conqueror Worm / Matthew Hopkins — Witchfinder General. Curse of the Crimson Altar* (GB 68) Ver-non Sewell *aka The Crimson Altar / The Crimson Cult / The Reincarnation / Spirit of the Dead. The Witchmaker* (68) William O. Brown *aka Legend of Witch Hollow. Angeli bianchi ... Angeli neri* (It 69) Luigi Scattini *aka The Satanists / Witchcraft '70. Hexen bis auf's Blut gequält / La tortura delle vergini* (G / It 69) Michael Armstrong *aka Austria 1700 / Brenn; Hexe, Brenn / Mark of the Devil / Satan / Tortur—Hexen aufs Blut gequält. El proceso de las brujas / Il trono di fuoco / Der Hexentöter von Blackmoor* (Sp / It / G 69) Jesús Franco *aka The Bloody Judge / Il giudice sanguinario / El juez sangriento / Night of the Blood Monster / The Trial of the Witches / Throne of Fire / Throne of the Blood Monster / The Witches' Trial / The Witch Killer of Blackmoor. The Brotherhood of Satan* (71) Bernard McEveety. *Hexen-Geschändet und zu Tode gequält / Le streghe nere* (G / It 72) Adrian Hoven *aka Curse of the Devil / Mark of the Devil Part II / Witch Torture. Stranger in Our House* (78 TV) Wes Craven *aka Summer of Fear. The Devonsville Terror* (83) Ulli Lommel. *Necropolis* (86) Bruce Hickey. *The Witches of Eastwick* (87) George Miller. *The Witches* (GB 90) Nicolas Roeg.

With-It-Movie *see* **YOUTH FILM**

Woman Prison Film *see* **PRISON FILM: Women's Prison Films**

Woman-in-Danger Film *see* **SLASHER FILM**

Woman's Melodramas *see* **MELODRAMA**

WOMAN'S PICTURE (Women's Film) A woman's picture concentrates on women's problems, fantasies or expectations, exclusively from a woman's point of view. If directed by a man, it attempts to approach the film's theme from a woman's angle, regardless of whether that approach is stereotyped or not.

A woman's or women's picture is a blanket term for several adjacent genres; they range through kitchen-sink drama, weepies, romantic drama, romances and soap opera to sheer melodrama and pot-boilers. Often, the term woman's film has had a pejorative connotation, but it need not be so, as its overall meaning covers not just escapist cinema, but "serious" dramas involving heroines as opposed to the heroes in male-oriented films or men's pictures. The woman's picture flourished during the thirties, forties and fifties, after which it suffered a decline. In the seventies, there was a revival of neo-woman's films.

On the subject of women's films, *see* Molly Haskell, "The Woman's Film," in *From Reverence to Rape* (New York: Holt, Rinehart and Winston, 1974), 153–88, and Andrea S. Walsh, "The Women's Film," in *Women's Film and Female Experience 1940–1950* (New York: Praeger, 1984) 23–48.[147]

The Wind (28) Victor Sjöström. *The Royal Family of Broadway* (30) George Cukor. *Frail Women* (GB 31) Maurice Elvey. *Emma* (32) Clarence Brown. *The Constant Nymph* (GB 33) Basil Dean. *Design for Living* (33) Ernst Lubitsch. *Queen Christina* (33) Rouben Mamoulian. *Alice Adams* (35) George Stevens. *Anna Karenina* (35) Clarence Brown. *Escape Me Never* (GB 35) Paul Czinner. *History Is Made at Night* (37) Frank Borzage. *Stella Dallas* (37) King Vidor. *Bringing Up Baby* (38) Howard Hawks. *Stolen Life* (GB 38) Paul Czinner. *Dark Victory* (39) Edmund Goulding. *Love Affair* (39) Leo McCarey. *The Old Maid* (39) Edmund Goulding. *The Women* (39) George Cukor. *Dance, Girl, Dance* (40) Dorothy Arzner. *Kitty Foyle* (40) Sam Wood. *The Letter* (40) William Wyler. *The Philadelphia Story* (40) George Cukor. *Back Street* (41) Robert Stevenson. *Penny Serenade* (41) George Stevens. *Woman of the Year* (42) George Stevens. *Laura* (44) Otto Preminger. *Brief Encounter* (GB 45) David Lean. *Mildred Pierce* (45) Michael Curtiz. *The Seventh Veil* (GB 45) Compton Bennett. *Beware of Pity* (GB 46) Maurice Elvey. *The Courtneys of Curzon Street* (GB 47) Herbert Wilcox *aka The Courtney Affair*. *Daisy Kenyon* (47) Otto Preminger. *The Loves of Joanna Godden* (GB 47) Charles Frend. *The Glass Mountain / La montagna di cristallo* (GB / It 48) Henry Cass, Edoardo Anton. *Letter from an Unknown Woman* (48) Max Ophuls. *Passionate Friends* (GB 48) David Lean *aka One Woman's Story*. *Madame Bovary* (49) Vincente Minnelli. *The Reckless Moment* (49) Max Opuls (Ophuls). *All That Heaven Allows* (55) Douglas Sirk. *Imitation of Life* (49) Douglas Sirk. *Jules et Jim* (F 61) François Truffaut *aka Jules and Jim*. *Belle de Jour / Bella di giorno* (F / It 66) Luis Buñuel. *Faces* (66) John Cassavetes. *Persona* (Sw 66) Ingmar Bergman. *Petulia* (US / GB 68) Richard Lester. *The Prime of Miss Jean Brodie* (GB 68) Ronald Neame. *Rachel Rachel* (68) Paul Newman. *En Passion* (Sw 69) Ingmar Bergman *aka A Passion / The Passion of Anna*. *Klute* (71) Alan J. Pakula. *Alice Doesn't Live Here Anymore* (74) Martin Scorsese. *A Woman Under the Influence* (74) John Cassavetes.   *Love Letters* (83) Amy Jones *aka My Love Letters.   Terms of Endearment* (83) James L. Brooks.

Women's Lib Picture, Women's Suffrage Films   *see*   **FEMINIST FILM**

Worker Film   *see*   **ARBEITERFILM;**   *see also*   **LABOR FILM**

Working Girl Film   *see*   **HOOKER FILM**

World War I Film, World War II Film   *see*   **WAR FILM**

WRESTLING FILM   Wrestling is an old sport which was already popular in ancient Egypt and Greece. It varies in style from Greco-Roman and Japanese sumo to the flamboyance of modern, all-in wrestling. In the world of make-believe that is present-day wrestling, dressing up for the part, with masked wrestlers galore, is essential for allowing the crowd to distinguish quickly between the good guys and the bad guys. Wrestling is mostly practiced by men, but lately female grapplers have also begun participating in the sport. Although not as popular on screen as boxing, wrestling has also been the object of screen presentations, if only occasionally.

The exception to this is Mexico where wrestling movies have emerged as a local genre. They have been popular amongst the aficionados since the fifties and their popularity did not decrease until the seventies. In that country, wrestlers with such appellations as El Santo (the Saint), Blue Demon and Mil Máscaras (a Thousand Masks) have soared to the status of popular heroes fighting real and supernatural villains when not in the ring. The films are a mishmash of forms and genres, in which wrestlers are pitted against criminals of all sorts, or ghoulish monsters, as the case may be.

Flesh (32) John Ford.   *Here Come the Co-eds* (45) Jean Yarbrough.   *Night and the City* (GB / US 49) Jules Dassin.   *Mr. Universe* (51) Joseph Lerner.   *Las luchadoras contra el medico asesino* (Mex 62) René Cardona *aka Doctor of Doom / Wrestling Women vs. the Aztec Ape.   Las luchadoras contra la momia* (Mex 64) René Cardona *aka Wrestling Women vs. the Aztec Mummy.   Santo contra la invasión de los marcianos* (Mex 66) Alfredo B. Crevenna *aka Santo Versus the Martian Invasion.   Santo y Blue Demon contra los monstruos* (Mex 68) Gilberto Martínez Solares *aka Santo and Blue Demon vs. the Monsters / Santo contra los monstruos de Frankenstein.   Santo contra el Doctor Muerte* (Sp / Mex 73) Rafael Romero Marchent.   *Mad Bull* (77 TV) Walter Doniger, Len Steckler.   *The One and Only* (77) Carl Reiner.   *Paradise Alley* (78) Sylvester Stallone.   *Take Down* (78) Kieth Merrill.   *Below the Belt* (74-80) Robert Fowler.   *All the Marbles* (81) Robert Aldrich *aka The California Dolls / The California Girls.*

Wu Xia Pian   *see*   **CHINESE SWORDPLAY MOVIE**

YAKUZA FILM (Yakuza-Eiga)   Yakuza is a Japanese term that translates as "gambler" and whose meaning has been extended to mean "gangster." The *yakuza-eiga* are contemporary Japanese gangster films, a new genre that appeared in 1964 with the film *Bakuto / Gambler*, acknowledged as being the first genuine *yakuza* film. The *yakuza* films evolved from the samurai films which are period films or *jidai-geki* as the Japanese designate them. The Japanese government banned in 1868 the samurai and the long sword, the characteristic samurai weapon; as a result, there were no representations of samurai in films set beyond that date. Hence there was a need for a modern fighter-hero. The *yakuza* fulfilled this need.

Yakuza movies are different from Western gangster films. The Japanese gangster film is a strictly regulated and formulaic genre, and the gangsters are motivated by a code of behavior which all too often is responsible for the internal conflict of the *yakuza*. He is a divided hero who has to choose between serving his boss or godfather faithfully as his code of duty dictates and his ingrained feeling for humanity, his other moral code. He finally has to make a choice when the cruelty of an evil godfather impinges on the *yakuza*'s sense of responsibility towards humanity. After having been extremely popular, the genre went into a decline in the seventies. For a good account of the genre, *see* Paul Schrader, "*Yakuza-eiga:* a Primer," *Film Comment* 10.1 (1974): 8–17.

Jinsei gekijo (J 58) Tai Kato *aka Theater of Life.* *Yuhini akai ore no kao* (J 61) Masahiro Shinoda *aka My Face Red in the Sunset.* *Gyangu domei* (J 63) Kinji Fukasaku *aka League of Gangsters.* *Kawaita hana* (J 63) Masahiro Shinoda *aka Pale Flower.* *Kanto mushuku* (J 63) Seijun Suzuki *aka Kanto Wanderer.* *Bakuto* (J 64) Shingehiro Ozawa *aka Gambler.* *Abashiri Bangaichi* (J 65) Teruo Ishii *aka Abashiri Prison.* *Kawaita Hanna* (J 66) Masahiro Shinoda *aka Pale Flower.* *Kyodai jinji* (J 66) Kosaku Yamashita *aka Family Obligations.* *Tokyo nagaremono* (J 66) Seijun Suzuki *aka Tokyo Drifter.* *Bakuchiuchi: socho tobaku* (J 68) Kosaku Yamashita *aka Gambling House: Presidential Gambling.* *Jinsei gekijo: Hishakaku to Kiratsune* (J 68) Tomu Uchida *aka Theater of Life: Hishakaku and Kiratsune.* *Socho tobaku* (J 68) Kosaku Yamashita *aka Big-Time Gambling Boss.* *Hanafuda shobu* (J 69) Tai Kato *aka Flower Cards Match* [from the *Hibotan bakuto / Red Peony Gambler* series]. *Jinsei gekijo* (J 71) Tai Kato *aka Theater of Life.* *Jingi kaki tatakai* (J 73-76) Kinji Fukasaku *aka Battle without Honor and Humanity.* *Matabi* (J 73) Kon Ichikawa *aka The Wanderers.* *The Yakuza* (US / J 75) Sydney Pollack *aka Brotherhood of the Yakuza.* *Black Rain* (89) Ridley Scott.

Young Czech Cinema *see* **CZECH NEW WAVE**

Young German Cinema, Young German Film *see* **NEW GERMAN CINEMA**

YOUTH FILM (Now Film, Youth-Genre Film, Youth-Oriented Film, With-It-Movie)   In the late sixties, with the success of *The Graduate* (1967) and, more specifically, of the low-budget *Easy Rider* (1969), the youth film caught on and a number of films were made highlighting the concerns of young people querying the Establishment, society and its values. Ironically, many were mostly establishment products, half-hearted in the views they pretended to espouse and meant solely to cash in on the youth film market. There were, however, exceptions to this, and some very good films came out of it. They were films made for the young centering on counterculture trends like the drug scene, dropouts, student contestation, university riots, anti-war manifestations, rock festivals and youths doing their own thing. The trend was shortlived but important.

The Graduate (67) Mike Nichols. *Greetings* (68) Brian DePalma. *Head* (68) Bob Rafelson *aka Untitled. Out of It* (68) Paul Williams. *Alice's Restaurant* (69) Arthur Penn *aka The Alice's Restaurant Massacre. Easy Rider* (69) Dennis Hopper. *Goodbye, Columbus* (69) Larry Peerce. *Hi, Mom!* (69) Brian DePalma *aka Blue Manhattan / Confessions of a Peeping John. John and Mary* (69) Peter Yates. *Last Summer* (69) Frank Perry. *Medium Cool* (69) Haskell Wexler *aka Concrete Wilderness. Midnight Cowboy* (69) John Schlesinger. *More* (Lux 69) Barber Schroeder. *Rain People* (69) Francis Ford Coppola. *Zabriskie Point* (69) Michelangelo Antonioni. *B.S. I Love You* (70) Steven Hillard Stern. *Getting Straight* (70) Richard Rush. *Joe* (70) John G. Avildsen *aka The Gap. The Revolutionary* (70) Paul Williams. *Up in the Cellar* (70) Theodore J. Flicker *aka Hi In the Cellar / 3 In the Cellar. Woodstock* (70) Michael Wadleigh *aka Woodstock I & II* [first of the rockumentaries, filmed in Multi-Screen]. *Happy Birthday, Wanda June* (71) Mark Robson. *The Last Movie* (71) Dennis Hopper *aka Chinchero. Making It* (71) John Erman. *Medicine Ball Caravan* (US / F 71) François Reichenbach. *My Old Man's Place* (71) Edwin Sherin *aka Glory Boy / The Old Man's Place. The Pursuit of Happiness* (71) Robert Mulligan. *Dealing: or The Berkeley-to-Boston Forty-Brick Lost-Bag Blues* (72) Paul Williams. *Drive, He Said* (72) Jack Nicholson.

Youth-Oriented Film *see* **TEEN MOVIE;** *see also* **YOUTH FILM**

Youth Picture *see* **TEEN MOVIE**

Youth Sexploitation Comedies *see* **TEEN MOVIE: Teen Sex Comedies**

Youth Street Film *see* **TEEN MOVIE: Teen-Violence Films**

Z PICTURE (Grade Z Movie) A low-budget, quickly produced feature, mostly meant for the youth market. American International Pictures paved the way with such genre films as horror movies, juvenile delinquent films, science fiction films, surf films and motorcycle films.

Zany Comedy *see* **ANARCHIC COMEDY**

ZOMBIE MOVIE Traditionally, zombies are corpses reanimated into a semblance of life by the magic of a voodoo priest. They are strong and powerful and obey unquestioningly their master's orders. Since they are already dead, they cannot be killed, but they can be destroyed by various means. They first appeared on screen in *White Zombie* (1932) with Bela Lugosi as the slave-master of a bunch of zombies. Not as glamorous, and certainly not as popular as the vampire but more popular than the mummy, their closest relative, zombies have become more frequent in pictures through the years and at present, voodoo trappings are no longer necessary to awaken the dead; any supernatural or pseudo-scientific method will do. The walking dead, this time converted into ghouls, made a momentous and far-reaching reappearance in *The Night of the Living Dead* (1967-68), a film in which the corpses are brought back by radiation to prey on the living. The zombie picture comes now in many forms and is a well-established subgenre of the horror film.

White Zombie (32) Victor Halperin. *I Walked with a Zombie* (42) Jacques Tourneur. *Revenge of the Zombies* (43) Steve Sekely *aka The Corpse Vanished*. *Zombies on Broadway* (45) Gordon Douglas *aka Loonies on Broadway*. *Voodoo Island* (51) Reginald LeBorg *aka Silent Death*. *Roma contro Roma* (It 63) Giuseppe Vari *aka Night Star, Goddess of Electra / War of the Zombies*. *I Eat Your Skin* (64) Del Tenny *aka Voodoo Blood / Zombie(s)*. *Cinque tombe per un medium / Terror Creatures from the Grave* (It / US 65) Ralph Zucker (Massimo Pupillo) *aka Coffin of Terror / Five Graves for a Medium / The Tombs of Horror*. *The Plague of the Zombies* (GB 65) John Gilling *aka The Zombie(s)*. *The Night of the Living Dead* (67-68) George A. Romero *aka Flesh Eaters / Night of Anubis / Night of the Flesh Eaters* [with *Dawn of the Dead* (78) and *Day of the Dead* (85) forms a trilogy]. *Dead People* (72) Willard Huyck *aka Messiah of Evil / Return of the Living Dead / Revenge of the Screaming Dead / The Second Coming*. *The Night Walk / Dead of Night* (Can / GB / US 72) Bob Clark *aka Death Dream / Le Mort-vivant / The Night Andy Came Home / The Veteran* [rel. in 74]. *Vudú sangriento / Loa Vudu / Voodoo Black Exorcist* (Sp / It / US 72) Manuel Caño. *No profanar el sueño de los muertos / Non si deve profanare il suono dei morti* (Sp / It 74) Jorge Grau *aka Breakfast at the Manchester Morgue / Don't Open the Window / Fin de semana para los muertos / The Living Dead at the Manchester Morgue / No se deberá profanar el sueño de los muertos / Open the Window / Zombi 3*. *Sugar Hill* (74) Paul Maslansky *aka Voodoo Girl / The Zombies of Sugar Hill*. *Dawn of the Dead / Zombie* (US / It 77-78) George A. Romero *aka Dawn of the Living Dead / Zombies*. *Zombie 2* (It 79) Lucio Fulci *aka The Island of the Living Dead / Paura / Zombie / Zombie Flesh Eaters / Zombies 2*. *Kiss Daddy Goodbye* (81) Patrick Regan *aka Revenge of the Zombie*. *Hard Rock Zombies* (84) Krishna Shah. *The Return of the Living Dead* (84) Dan O'Bannon. *Day of the Dead* (85) George A. Romero. *I Was a Teenage Zombie* (86) John Elias Michalakias. *The Serpent and the Rainbow* (87) Wes Craven.

References

1. The films are listed under their original title or titles (if co-productions); *aka* indicates alternative or English titles under which the films may also be known.
2. For a referential listing of film adaptations, *see* A. G. S. Enser, *Filmed Books and Plays*, rev. ed. (Aldershot, Hampshire: Gower, 1987).
3. A fifth brother, Gummo (Milton Marx, 1893–1977), left the brothers' musical team before it reached Broadway in 1924. Frenchie (Simon Marx, d. 1933), father of the Marx Brothers, featured briefly in *Monkey Business* (1931); it was his only film appearance.
4. Bruno Edera, in *Full Length Animated Feature Films* (London and New York: Focal Press, 1977), examines the development of the feature-length animated film; he includes a catalogue of 195 features.
5. The present range of computer animation is examined in the documentaries *Computer Animation Magic* (1986) by Geoffrey de Valois and *Computer Dreams with Amanda Pays* (1988) by Geoffrey de Valois. N. Magnenat-Thalmann and D. Thalmann's manual *Computer Animation* (Tokyo: Springer-Verlag, 1985) includes in "Appendix C" a list of 300 computer-generated films produced in the period 1961 to 1984.
6. If a film is controlled by its producer, it may be designated a *producer's film*; if the personality of the actor dominates, or is meant to fit his screen persona, the picture becomes an *actor's film* or a star vehicle.
7. For a description of the emergence and evolution of the B picture, *see* Charles Flynn and Rodd McCarthy's "The Economic Imperative: Why Was the B Movie Necessary?" in *Kings of the Bs: Working Within the Hollywood System* (New York: E. P. Dutton, 1975). A complete filmography for each of 325 American directors, compiled by Todd McCarthy, is found in the end section of the book. *See also* Robin Cross' *The Big Book of B Movies or How Low Was My Budget* (New York: St. Martin's, 1981) and Wheeler W. Dixon's *The "B" Directors: A Biographical Directory* (Metuchen, N.J.: Scarecrow, 1985).
8. For this latter category, *see* **Film à Clef.**
9. For a definition of the "black film" as a genre, *see* Thomas Cripps, *Black Films as Genre* (Bloomington: Indiana University Press, 1978).
10. Although mainly a playwright, Bertolt Brecht wrote, alone or in collaboration, a few screenplays. For his ideas on epic theater, *see* Bertolt Brecht, *Brecht on Theatre*, ed. and tr. by John Willet (New York: Hill and Wang, 1964). For his views on the film medium, *see* Martin Walsh, *The Brechtian Aspect of Radical Cinema* (London: BFI, 1981). There are also a few film adaptations of some of his plays.
11. *See* Jeffrey Richards, "The Cinema of Empire," in *Visions of Yesterday* (London: Routledge & Kegan Paul, 1973), pp. 1–220; a filmography of 92 films ("Films of Empire," pp. 360–67) is included in the "Appendix."
12. *See* **FEATURE FILM.** The earlier Australian narrative film *The Soldiers of the Cross* (1900), an evangelical film produced by the Salvation Army, cannot be said

393

to be the first feature-length film since it was shown not as a continuous narrative, but as a succession of short films accompanied by lectures, slides and music.

13. *See* Stuart M. Kaminsky's "Variations on a Major Genre: The Big Caper Film," in *American Film Genres* (New York: Dell, 1977), chapter 6, for a clear exposition of the caper film.

14. The following length definitions are in use: spot (10 to 60 seconds' duration), pocket cartoon/pill (50 seconds to 2 minutes), short (2 to 20 minutes), medium-length film (20 to 50 minutes), feature /full-length film (50 minutes or over).

Thousands of shorts are made yearly. Sometimes, a series of shorts are grouped together and presented as a feature; they are in reality compilation films linked by a common theme. Features are not very numerous. The *Guinness Movie Facts & Feats* by Patrick Robertson (London: Guinness, 1988), p. 216, puts at 436 the world's output (up to 1987) of feature-length cartoons, the longest being Osamu Tezuka's *Senya ichiya monogatari/A Thousand and One Nights* (1969), a Japanese erotic feature cartoon running for 2 hours and 30 minutes.

15. The Chinese term *wu xia pian* ("martial chivalry film") comprises both the Chinese swordplay movie and the Kung fu film which may be considered its subgenre. *See* Rosalind Coward and John Ellis, "Hong Kong–China 1981," *Screen* 22.4 (1981): 92–96.

16. Recently (as has been done with the samurai film), the Chinese swordplay movies have been compared to the American Western; *see* Ralph C. Croizier, "Beyond East and West: The American Western and Rise of the Chinese Swordplay Movie," *Journal of Popular Film* 1 (1972): 229–43.

17. *Cinéma vérité* was known by different names to different people. The authors mention some of these terms on page 7 of their book.

18. William F. Van Wert, in *The Theory and Practice of the Ciné-Roman* (New York: Arno Press, 1978), examines the work of Alain Resnais, Chris Marker, Agnès Varda, Henri Colpi, Armand Gatti, Jean Cayrol, Alain Robbe-Grillet, and Marguerite Duras, who directed or propounded the theory of *ciné-romans*.

19. *See*, for instance, William K. Everson's *Classics of the Horror Film* (Secaucus, NJ: Citadel, 1974) and *More Classics of the Horror Film* (Secaucus, NJ: Citadel, 1986); Anthony Slide and Edward Wagenknecht's *Fifty Great American Silent Films 1912–1920: A Pictorial Survey of 25 Films from 1913 to 1957* (New York: Dover, 1983); Anthony Slide's *Fifty Classic British Films: 1932–1982: A Pictorial Record* (New York: Dover, 1985) and *Fifty Classic French Films, 1912–1982: A Pictorial Record* (New York: Dover, 1987).

20. For the evolution of color processes, *see* Brian Coe, "The Development of Colour Cinematography," in *The International Encyclopedia of Film*, ed. by Roger Manvell (London: Rainbird Reference Books, 1972), 29–48.

21. The story of Technicolor has been printed in Fred E. Basten, *Glorious Technicolor* (South Brunswick and New York: A. S. Barnes, 1980). A filmography (pp. 169–94) includes a listing of Technicolor features and important shorts produced between 1917 and 1979.

22. Diverse trade-names for basically similar systems are: Agfacolor (Germany), Ansco Color (USA), CineFotoColor (Spain), Ferraniacolor (Italy), Fujicolor (Japan), Gevacolor (Belgium), Sovcolor (USSR). Metrocolor, Warnercolor, and DeLuxe are processes using Eastman Color stock. Even films labelled "Color by Technicolor" or "Print by Technicolor" may in fact be using Eastman Color negative with Technicolor being responsible only for the laboratory work of the final release prints.

References 395

23. *See*, for instance, Carlos Clarens, *Crime Movies* (London: Secker & Warburg, 1980).

24. The following reference works are useful on the subject of dance films: David L. Parker and Esther Siegel, *Guide to Dance in Film* (Detroit, MI: Gale Research, 1978); John Mueller, *Dance Film Directory* (Princeton, NJ: Princeton Book Company, 1979); Peter Kennedy, ed., *Films on Traditional Music and Dance* (Paris: UNESCO, 1970).

25. Maurice Yacowar, "The Bug in the Rug: Notes on the Disaster Genre," in *Film Genre*, ed. Barry K. Grant (Metuchen, NJ: Scarecrow, 1977), 90–107. A good article on the subject of real disaster, disaster films, and the appeal they offer to cinema goers and television viewers is Andrée Conrad, "Beyond the Panic Principle: Disaster and the American Imagination," *Book Forum* 4.2 (1978): 204–34.

26. Michael Starks in *Cocaine Fiends and Reefer Madness* (New York: Cornwall Books, 1982) has written an exhaustive history of the drug film. He mentions literally hundreds of films (see "Film Index," pp. 218–37) in a chronological rundown. However, his definition of the term "drug film" tends to be too broad; *see* his Introduction.

27. Starks devotes a whole chapter in his book to these films and lists well over 400 titles in his film index.

28. Two books examining Ealing Studios' film production and their comedies are: Charles Barr, *Ealing Studios* (Woodstock, NY: The Overlook Press, 1980), and George Perry, *Forever Ealing* (London: Pavilion, 1981). *See also* Ian Green, "Ealing: in the Comedy Frame," in *British Cinema History*, James Curran and Vincent Porter, eds. (London: Weidenfeld and Nicolson, 1983), 294–302.

29. The first acknowledged feature-length film, *The Story of the Kelly Gang*, dates from 1906. *See* FEATURE FILM.

30. In panoramic films, the camera moved or was carried on a moving vehicle (rather than remaining fixed and static) to show a wider or panoramic view of a well-known place, e.g., Niagara Falls, Paris. The panoramic film or panorama was a development of the actuality film.

31. A filmography listing 139 Yiddish films made in different countries is included in Eric A. Goldman's *Visions, Images, and Dreams* (Ann Arbor, MI: UMI Research Press, 1983), 173–205.

32. George Huaco in *The Sociology of Film Art* (New York: Basic Books, 1965) used the term "Expressive Realism" in referring to the Soviet avant-garde films of the 1920s.

33. Eisenstein's film *Oktyabr' / October* (1927), which had no formal plot and was a series of episodes extolling the revolutionary events of 1917, climaxing in the storming of Petrograd's Winter Palace, proved incomprehensible to the audience at large, and the Bolshevik government utilized the term "formalism" to describe in a derogatory manner the film's style.

34. Eighty-four times since 1898 according to Robertson's *Guinness* (1988 ed.), p. 25. The *Guinness* (1985 ed.) also includes a filmography (p. 31).

35. So far the best reference work on the subject of fantastic films is *Reference Guide to Fantastic Films: Science Fiction, Fantasy & Horror*, 3 vols., compiled by Walt Lee (Los Angeles: Chelsea-Lee Books, 1972–74).

36. *See* Tzvetan Todorov, *The Fantastic: A Structural Approach to a Literary Genre* (Cleveland: Press of Case Western Reserve University, 1973).

37. Some dissociate farce from comedy and consider it a separate genre. *See*, for example, Albert Bermel, *Farce* (New York: Simon and Schuster, 1982).

38. As referential sources on the subject of women and feminism, *see* Kaye

Sullivan, *Films For, By and About Women* (Metuchen, NJ: Scarecrow, 1980); Jeanne Belancourt, *Women in Focus* (Dayton, Ohio: Pflaum, 1974); Rosemary Ribich Kowalski, *Women and Film: A Bibliography* (Metuchen, NJ: Scarecrow, 1976); Marc Silberman, "Women Filmmakers in West Germany: A Catalogue," *camera obscura*, no. 6 (Fall 1980): 123–52.

39. *See* Martin F. Norden, "Women's Suffrage Films as Genre," *Journal of Popular Film and Television*, 13 (1986): 171–77.

40. James Robert Parish and Michael R. Pitts describe 287 films dealing with Hollywood in *Hollywood on Hollywood* (Metuchen, NJ: Scarecrow, 1978). *See also* Anthony Slide, *Films on Film History* (Metuchen, NJ: Scarecrow, 1979).

41. For a definition of its main characteristics, *see* Peter L. Valenti, "The 'Film Blanc': Suggestions for a Variety of Fantasy, 1940–45," *Journal of Popular Film* 6 (1978): 295.

42. Three good sources of reference for *film noir* are: *Film Noir*, ed. by Alain Silver and Elizabeth War (Woodstock, N.Y.: The Overlook Press, 1979). This work discusses in dictionary form 301 films belonging to the *film noir* body of films or marginally related to it. An interesting appendix studies the interrelationship that *film noir* has with some genres: the gangster film, the Western, the period film, and the comedy film. Robert Ottoson, *A Reference Guide to the American Film Noir: 1940–1958* (Metuchen, NJ: Scarecrow, 1981) has alphabetical entries for 215 films. An appendix lists an additional annotated filmography of 45 minor *films noirs*. Spencer Selby includes an annotated filmography of 490 items in his *Dark City* (Jefferson, NC: McFarland, 1984). He also lists off-genre *films noirs* and others in "Appendix A."

43. John S. Witney in "A Filmography of Film Noir," *The Journal of Popular Film* 5 (1976): 321–71, lists 108 films and classifies them according to four general headings: Bourgeois Crime, Crime, The Law, Private Detective /Adventurer.

44. For example, Universal's *Dracula* (1930) with Bela Lugosi as the vampire, directed by Tod Browning, and the simultaneously made Spanish version with Carlos Villarias Villar in the role of the Count, directed by George Melford.

45. Parker Tyler, *Screening the Sexes: Homosexuality in the Movies* (New York: Doubleday, 1973); Richard Dyer, ed., *Gays in Film* (London: British Film Institute, 1977); Vito Russo, *The Celluloid Closet*, rev. ed. (New York: Harper & Row, 1987); Richard Dyer, *Now You See It: Studies on Lesbian and Gay Film* (London: Routlege, 1990).

46. *Herschell Gordon Lewis "The Godfather of Gore,"* part of the British TV series *The Incredibly Strange Film Show* (1988) hosted by Jonathan Ross, features interviews with the filmmakers and clips from Lewis's films.

47. M. G. Lewis' *The Monk* (1795), Charles Robert Maturin's *Melmoth the Wanderer* (1820), Mary Wollstonecraft Shelley's *Frankenstein* (1818), and Bram Stoker's *Dracula* (1897) are some of its better known masterpieces. For English Gothic films, *see* David Pirie, *A Heritage of Horror* (London: Gordon Fraser, 1973).

48. In trade parlance, porno films are designated according to their length: a loop is a short of one reel or 400 feet of 16mm color film running about 10 minutes at 24 frames per second. The term loop also applies to an 8mm film of approximately 200 feet with a running time of less than 10 minutes. Sometimes, several loops are spliced together to form a feature. A short consists of 2 or 3 reels, or about 30 minutes' running time. A featurette consists of 4 reels; five-reel films are rare. Lastly, a feature runs for 60 minutes or longer; the average hard-core feature used to run from 70 to 75 minutes, but porno features that run 100 minutes or longer are not unusual.

49. According to Robertson's *Guinness* (1988 ed.), p. 57, the first theatrical release to feature a scene of non-simulated sexual intercourse was the Swedish film *Dom kallar oss mods / They Call Us Misfits* (1966–68). *Extase / Ecstasy* (1932), the famous Czech film starring Hedwing Kiester (Hedy Lamarr) in the nude, was the first film to portray an act of simulated sex in a film intended for commercial release. The underground Andy Warhol film, *Blue Movie* (1968), contains a long sequence of sexual coupling featuring underground superstar Viva.

50. On the subject of high school pictures, *see* Joseph W. Reed's "Let's Burn the School: The High School Picture," in *American Scenarios* (Middletown, CT: Wesleyan UP, 1989), 132–59.

51. *See* Jimmy McDonough and Bill Landis, "Hillbilly Heaven," *Film Comment* 21.6 (1985): 55–59.

52. Both horror and science fiction films were referred to in the 1950s as "weirdies" in the trade papers. The term also included fantasy and shockers.

53. On the subject of the Frankenstein monster, *see* Donald F. Glut, *The Frankenstein Legend* (Metuchen, NJ: Scarecrow, 1973) and *The Frankenstein Catalog* (Jefferson, NC: McFarland, 1984). For a Frankenstein filmography, *see also* Jean-Pierre Bouyxou, "La Saga des Frankenstein," in *L'Avant-Scène du Cinéma*, nos. 160/161 (1975): 43–58; no. 166 (1976): 56–58.

54. Denis Gifford divides his book *Movie Monsters* (London: Studio Vista, 1970) into three parts which he designates: Creation, Resuscitation, and Metamorphosis. The best filmography on the horror film (including fantasy and science fiction) is the three-volume *Reference Guide to Fantastic Films* (1972–1974), compiled by Walt Lee.

55. Many films (hospital dramas, country-doctor pictures, medical farces, psychiatric pictures, biographies) in which doctors have a prominent role are mentioned in Jack Spears, "The Doctor on the Screen," chap. 11 in *Hollywood: The Golden Era* (New York: A. S. Barnes, 1971), 314–32. The article also includes several films on nurses.

56. For a Tarzan filmography, *see* Robertson's *Guinness* (1985 ed.), p. 48.

57. *See* Mark Thomas McGee and R. J. Robertson, *The J. D. Film* (Jefferson, NC: McFarland, 1983). The authors include a filmography of 188 films.

58. The choreographed combat movements include high bounces, leaps and hops, with the kung fu hero either landing out of reach of his enemies or confronting them in midair with much thrusting, kicking, punching, slapping and agile maneuvering of limbs on both sides. These sequences have the properties of a dance or ballet ritual, and they have often been compared to the choreography of the dance film. *See*, for instance, Stuart M. Kaminsky, "Kung Fu Film as Ghetto Myth," *The Journal of Popular Film* 3 (1974): 129–38, and Richard Hyatt, "Haeee! Kung Fu Movies: A Primer," *Take One* 3.12 (1972; published in 1973): 8–9.

59. On the subject of film melodrama, see the special issues on melodrama in the following film journals: *Monogram*, no. 4 (1972), *Les Cahiers de la Cinéma-thèque*, no. 28 (1979), *Wide Angle* 4.2 (1980), *Movie*, nos. 29/30 (1982), *The Journal of the University Film and Video Association* 35.1 (1983). *See also* Marcia Landy, ed., *Imitations of Life: A Reader on Film & Television Melodrama* (Detroit: Wayne State UP, 1991).

60. For the origins and evolution of melodrama, *see* James Smith, *Melodrama* (London: Methuen, 1973). Smith identifies three general types of melodrama: the "melodrama of defeat" with an unhappy ending; the "melodrama of triumph" in which good triumphs over evil; and the "melodrama of protest" which focusses on some social injustice in order to arouse anger in its audience, and may end in defeat

or triumph. This last type of melodrama may also be open-ended or unresolved.

61. Roy Armes, *The Ambiguous Image: Narrative Style in Modern European Cinema* (London: Secker & Warburg, 1976).

62. For a sociological analysis of bike pictures in the sixties, see John L. Mason, *The Identity Crisis Theme in American Feature Films, 1960-1969* (New York: Arno Press, 1977).

63. Pierre Berton, "Perils of the Royal Mountie," in *Hollywood's Canada* (Toronto: McClelland and Stewart Limited, 1975), p. 112. The author puts at 256 the number of motion pictures in which Mounties have a significant role (p. 111). The book contains a useful list of Hollywood movies about Canada (pp. 247-70). Bernard A. Drew's *Lawmen in Scarlet* (Metuchen, NJ: Scarecrow, 1990) contains a section listing more than 200 Mountie movies.

64. Music videos have also been called band clips, pop clips, promotional clips (promo clips, promos), promotional videos, rock clips, rock promos, rock videos (rockvids), videos, video music, and video rock clips.

65. Other terms are "video singles" (several clips released on a video cassette of about 15 minutes' running time) and "video EPs" (cassettes lasting over 15 minutes). "Ambient video" or "video wallpaper" refers to jazz, MOR (middle of the road) or soft rock music accompanied by a background of animation, computer graphics, travel footage or extracts from films.

66. Rick Altman groups American musicals under three subgenres: the fairy tale musical, the show musical and the folk musical. See "Yearly Table of Musicals by Subgenres," in *The American Film Musical* (Bloomington: Indiana UP, 1989).

67. Robert C. Reimer, "Nazi-Retro Films: Experiencing the Mistakes of the Ordinary Citizen," *Journal of Popular Film and Television*, 12 (1984): 112-17. Robert Reimer and Carol Reimer, "Nazi-retro Filmography," *Journal of Popular Film and Television*, 14 (1986):81-92.

68. The term "neorealismo" was used as early as 1942 in the film review *Cinema* by the Marxist film critic Umberto Barbero.

69. Although the Liberal Party government of Prime Minister John Gorton approved the establishment of government-support schemes, it is to Prime Minister Gough Whitlam's Labor Party government that credit for the reality of a government-supported industry must go. His government also brought about a relaxation of the previous stiff censorship laws in order to bring them more into line with current trends overseas. See David Stratton, *The Last New Wave* (Sydney: Angus & Robertson, 1980) for an account of the changes that took place and for a description of how the movies of the New Australian Cinema came to be made. *See also The New Australian Cinema*, ed. Scott Murray (West Melbourne: Thomas Nelson Australia / Cinema Papers, 1980).

70. The Chinese film generational system comprises: First generation (film pioneers), Second generation (filmmakers of the 30s and 40s), Third generation (filmmakers of the 50s), Fourth generation (film students who graduated in the early 60s), and Fifth generation (1982 graduates).

71. Chinese film titles are in the pinyin transliteration system.

72. Besides narrative feature films, the New German Cinema includes TV films, underground and experimental films, independent films, documentaries and shorts. For information on the New German Cinema, see Thomas Elsaesser, *New German Cinema* (London: Macmillan, 1989); it includes a bibliography, a filmography of 427 films and a directory of New German Cinema directors. *See also* the special issue (Spring 1980) of *Quarterly Review of Film Studies*, 5 (1980); John

Sandford, *The New German Cinema* (London: Oswald Wolff, 1980); and Hans Günther Pflaum and Hans Helmut Prinzler, *Cinema in the Federal Republic of Germany* (Bonn: Inter Nationes, 1983).

73. India comprises 22 States and 9 Union Territories. The official languages number 16, and there are 1,652 dialects.

74. See "Faking the Early News Films," in *The American Newsreel 1911-1967*, by Raymond Fielding, chapter 5, pp. 37-45.

75. See "Newsreels" in Robertson's *Guinness* (1988 ed.), pp. 230-31.

78. The British *Faust* (1907), using a sound-on-disc process, directed by Arthur Gilbert, was the first complete opera to be filmed. *Music in Film and Television* (Paris: UNESCO Press, 1975) includes a directory of filmed opera works for the period 1964-1974. For a dossier on opera films plus filmography *see L'Avant-Scène Cinéma / Opéra* (May 1987).

77. For the importance of the partisan film in Yugoslavia, *see* Andrew Horton's "The Rise and Fall of the Yugoslav Partisan Film: Cinematic Perceptions of a National Identity," *Film Criticism* 12 (Winter 1987-88): 18-27.

78. For a filmography, *see* Patrick Brion, "Eléments de documentation pour la connaissance du peplum," *Dossiers du cinéma. Cinéastes-Recueil 2* (1971): 251-56.

79. For a Charlie Chan filmography *see* Ken Hanke's *Charlie Chan at the Movies: History, Filmography, and Criticism* (Jefferson, NC: McFarland, 1989).

80. The police detective film is included under the **POLICE FILM** entry. Some police detectives (e.g., Charlie Chan, the oriental detective of the Honolulu police force, Inspector Maigret of the French police) seem to have it both ways as they use the techniques and methods of the private eye and, at the same time, have the resources of the Police Establishment to back them up. Contrasting differences between the police detective and the private eye films are well-defined in Stanley J. Solomon, *Beyond Formula: American Film Genres* (New York: Harcourt Brace Jovanovich, 1976), chap. 5, "The Search for Clues," pp. 200-14.

81. *See* **CRIME FILM: Master Criminal Films** for other Arsene Lupin movies.

82. On the subject of film propaganda, *see* Leif Furhammar and Folke Isaksson, *Politics and Film* (London: Studio Vista, 1971).

83. The movies have not always made a clear distinction between psychiatrists, psychoanalysts, therapists, psychotherapists, analysts, and psychologists, who have at times been used indiscriminately performing each other's functions from picture to picture. For psychiatric movies, *see* Irving Schneider's "Images on the Mind: Psychiatry in the Commercial Film," *The American Journal of Psychiatry* 134 (1977): 613-20. For the portrayal of madness on the screen, *see* Michael Fleming and Roger Manvell's *Images of Madness* (London and Toronto: Associated University Presses, 1985).

84. Since 1983, the new categories of the British Board of Censors are: U (suitable for any age); PG (Parental Guidance); 15 (persons under fifteen will not be admitted); 18 (for audiences of eighteen years or over); 18R for porno and violent films shown in specialized cinemas.

The U.S. rating system was introduced by the Motion Pictures Association of America on November 1, 1968. As it stands at present, it consists of the following categories of ratings: G (suitable for general audiences of all ages); PG (parental guidance is suggested, but all ages can be admitted); PG-13 (introduced in 1984; it suggests that children be accompanied by a parent or guardian); R (restricted; those under seventeen must be accompanied by a parent or adult guardian); X (restricted to those over seventeen); NC-17 was introduced in 1990 by the MPPA to indicate no children under 17.

85. The Malignant Small Town film, the Couple film, the Hot-Car Road film, the Trucker film and the Lifestyle film.

86. Richard H. Campbell and Michael R. Pitts in *The Bible on Film* (Metuchen, NJ: Scarecrow, 1981) provide a useful checklist of biblical films.

87. Neil P. Hurley, in "Cinema Transfigurations of Jesus," *Religion in Film*, ed. by John R. May and Michael Bird (Knoxville: University of Tennessee Press, 1982), pp. 61–78, distinguishes between faith-inspired and humanistic renderings of the Jesus persona, between Christ figures and Jesus transfigurations (p. 64).

88. Robertson's *Guinness* (1988 ed.), p. 25, mentions 51 remakes of Marlowe's, Goethe's and Gunod's *Faust*.

89. *Guinness* (1988 ed.), p. 25, cites 84 productions of *Cinderella* between 1898 and 1988, and lists 58 titles in a *Hamlet* filmography (p. 35). A useful reference guide listing titles of remakes, etc., is James L. Limbacher, *Haven't I Seen You Somewhere?: Remakes, Sequels and Series in Motion Pictures and Television, 1896-1978* (Ann Arbor, MI: Pierian Press, 1979). *See also* Robert A. Nowlan and Gwendolyn Wright Nowlan, *Cinema Sequels and Remakes, 1903-1989* (Jefferson, NC: McFarland, 1989) and Michael B. Bruxman, *Make It Again, Sam* (Brunswick and New York: A. S. Barnes, 1975).

90. *See* Anand Patwardhan, "Guerrilla Film, Underground and in Exile: A Critique and a Case Study of *Waves of Revolution*," in *Show Us Life*, ed. Thomas Waugh (Metuchen, NJ: Scarecrow, 1984), pp. 444-64.

91. For a comparison between samurai films and Westerns, *see* Stuart M. Kaminsky, "The Samurai Film and the Western," *Journal of Popular Film* 1 (1972): 312-24. Alain Silver in *The Samurai Film* (Woodstock, N.Y.: Overlook Press, 1983) includes an extensive filmography (384 titles are listed for the period 1950-1982). David Desser's, *The Samurai Films of Akira Kurosawa* (Ann Arbor: UMI, 1983) distinguishes four subgenres within the Samurai film: the Nostalgic Samurai Drama, the Anti-Feudal Samurai Drama, the Zen Fighter Picture and the Sword Film.

92. The term science fiction (SF, for short) is universally accepted, but at one time or another, other terms have been proposed to categorize the genre, e.g., fantascience, science fantasy, scientific fantasy, scientific fiction, scientifiction, speculative fantasy, speculative fiction, structural fabulation, etc.

93. For science fiction in general, a good reference work is *The Science Fiction Encyclopedia*, ed. by Peter Nicholls (Garden City, N.Y.: Doubleday / Dolphin, 1979). The best filmography (along with fantasy and horror films) is found in the *Reference Guide to Fantastic Films (1972-1974)*, compiled by Walt Lee. *See also* James Robert Parish and Michael R. Pitts, *The Great Science Fiction Pictures; II* (Metuchen, N.J.: Scarecrow, 1972; 1990) and Donald C. Willis, *Horror and Science Fiction Films; II; III* (Metuchen, N.J.: Scarecrow, 1972; 1982; 1984). *Science Fiction*, ed. by Phil Hardy (London: Aurum Press, 1984) describes most of the science fiction films produced up to 1983.

94. The term "futuristic films" has been used to group together some of these categories (Dystopian, Political Extrapolation, SF Disaster Films, Space Travel, Time Travel, Future Barbarian movies) which comprise films dealing with or prophesying about the future of the Earth and its inhabitants.

95. For published material on the serial, *see* Larry N. Landrum and Jack Nachbar, "The Serials: A Selected Checklist of Published Materials," *The Journal of Popular Film 3* (1974): 273-76.

96. I. C. Jarvie, "Case Study—Films about Marriage." *Movies as Social Criticism* (Metuchen, N.J.: Scarecrow, 1978), pp. 45-81.

97. Georges Méliès' film *Après le bal / After the Ball* (1897) has been mentioned as the first in which an actress, Jeanne d'Alcy, appears nude. In fact, she has a flesh-colored leotard on as she stands in a tub with her back to the camera.

98. John Waters, *Shock Value* (New York: Dell, 1981). John Waters was called the Prince of Puke and is known to his fans as "the Master of Sleaze." The filmmaker and clips from his films are featured in *John Waters "Pope of Trash,"* part of the British TV series *The Incredibly Strange Film Show* (1988).

99. Azriel Bibliowicz, "Be Happy Because Your Father Isn't Your Father," *Journal of Popular Culture* 14 (1980): 479.

100. Robertson's *Guinness* (1988 ed.), p. 62, includes a soccer filmography of 92 films.

101. For Populist cinema, *see* Jeffrey Richards' "The Cinema of Populism," in *Visions of Yesterday* (London: Routledge & Kegan Paul, 1973), pp. 222–85.

102. Christopher Frayling in his study of the Italian Western, *Spaghetti Westerns* (London: Routledge & Kegan Paul, 1981), p. xi, mentions that the term "Spaghetti" started an onrush of food-related appellations for Westerns made in countries other than America. He lists: Sauerkraut Westerns (Germany), Paella Westerns (Spain), Camembert Westerns (France), Borsch Westerns (Russia), Curry Westerns (India) and Chop Suey Westerns (Hong Kong). He also points out that the Italians themselves preferred the term Macaroni Westerns rather than Spaghetti Westerns. Among Italian film critics, the terms *western-spaghetti, western makaroni, western all'italiana* and *western italiano* are in common use. For a filmography of 172 European Westerns (with some credits), *see* David Austen, "Continental Westerns," *Films and Filming* 17.10 (July 1971): 36–44.

103. There are three major varieties of special effects: special visual (optical) effects, special mechanical effects and special sound (audial) effects.

104. For the diversity of special effects and their many uses, *see* John Culhane, *Special Effects in the Movies* (New York: Ballantine, 1981).

105. On the subject of sports movies, *see also* Nora Sayre, "Winning the Weepstakes: The Problems of American Sports Movies," in *Film Genre*, ed. Barry K. Grant (Metuchen, N.J.: Scarecrow, 1977), pp. 182–94 and Ronald Bergan, *Sports in the Movies* (London: Proteus, 1982). This book has individual chapters on the major sports (boxing, football, baseball, horse racing, etc.) and groups many others under different headings.

106. The strong appeal and individuality of some of the better-known British comedians have made them the star of one-man comedy shows, e.g., *The Dick Emery Show, The Benny Hill Show, The Stanley Baxter Show.*

107. For an explanation of the term by a filmmaker involved in this type of film, *see* Peter Gidal, "Theory and Definition of Structural / Materialist Film," in *Structural Film Anthology*, ed. Peter Gidal (London: British Film Institute, 1976, 1978), pp. 1–21.

108. John Carpenter's *Dark Star* (1972–74) is another example of a successful student film which was expanded into feature length and to 35mm (from 16mm) for commercial release. It has attained cult status.

109. According to Robertson's *Guinness* (1988 ed.), p. 136, the longest sword fight sequence in a Hollywood movie was staged in *Scaramouche* (1952) and had a duration of six-and-a-half minutes. By contrast, the longest in a non–Hollywood movie was in the Hong Kong film *Beach of the War Gods* (1972); it lasted for 22 minutes.

110. Richard Staehling in "From *Rock Around the Clock* to *The Trip*: the Truth about Teen Movies (1969)," in *Kings of the Bs*, edited by Todd McCarthy and

Charles Flynn (New York: Dutton, 1975), pp. 220–51, sections teen movies into four main categories: musicals, wild youth films, mild youth films and beach films.

111. In a few countries the advertisements come before or after the program being broadcast. Commercials run for 10, 20, 30, 45, 60 (or over) seconds. Two 30-second ads together promoting different products from the same advertiser are known as "piggy-backs."

112. In alphabetical order the 37 plays comprise *All's Well That Ends Well* (GB / US 80), *Antony and Cleopatra* (GB 80), *As You Like It* (GB 80), *The Comedy of Errors* (GB 83), *Coriolanus* (GB 83), *Cymbeline* (GB 82), *Hamlet* (GB 80), *Henry the Fourth, Part One* (GB 79), *Henry the Fourth, Part Two* (GB 79), *Henry the Fifth* (GB 79), *Henry the Sixth, Part One* (GB 81), *Henry the Sixth, Part Two* (GB 81), *Henry the Sixth, Part Three* (GB 82), *Henry the Eighth* (GB 78-79), *Julius Caesar* (GB 78), *The Life and Death of King John* (GB 84), *King Lear* (GB 82), *Love's Labor's Lost* (GB 84), *Macbeth* (GB 82), *Measure for Measure* (GB 78), *The Merchant of Venice* (GB 80), *The Merry Wives of Windsor* (GB 82), *A Midsummer Night's Dream* (GB 81), *Much Ado about Nothing* (GB 84), *Othello* (GB 81), *Pericles: Prince of Tyre* (GB 83), *Richard the Second* (GB 78), *Richard the Third* (GB 83), *Romeo and Juliet* (GB 78), *The Taming of the Shrew* (GB 78), *The Tempest* (GB 79), *Timon of Athens* (GB 81), *Titus Andronicus* (GB 85), *Troilus and Cressida* (GB 81), *The Twelfth Night: or, What You Will* (GB 80), *Two Gentlemen of Verona* (GB 83), *The Winter's Tale* (GB 80).

113. *The Killers* (1964), a made-for-TV remake of the 1946 film of the same title, was rejected by NBC as too violent and released instead to the theaters. *The Man* (1972) is another example of a film, originally made for TV, first shown theatrically.

114. *See* Robertson's *Guinness* (1988 ed.), p. 226. Anthony Slide, however, in *The American Film Industry* (New York: Greenwood, 1986), p. 123, cites *The Three Musketeers* (1950) as the first feature-length made-for-TV film, followed a few weeks later by *The Pharmacist's Mate. See How They Run* (1964) is mentioned as the first made-for-TV movie in Leonard Maltin's *TV Movies and Video Guide* (New York: Signet, 1990). *See also* Gary Edgerton's "The American Made-for-TV Movie," in *TV Genres*, ed. Brian G. Rose (Westport, Conn: Greenwood Press, 1985), p. 156.

115. Some television productions are sometimes shown in syndication or abroad as TV movies when, in fact, they were originally broadcast in a different format or as part of a series. This television material includes: a) feature-length episodes of continuing series (for the 90-minute or 2-hour time slots), e.g., "Columbo," "McCloud," "The Name of the Game," "How the West Was Won"; b) two-hour specials in TV series such as "Police Story" and "Emergency!"; c) films made of episodes originally aired as part of a TV series. Some of these strung-together movies include: *The Spy with My Face* (1965), *The Last of the Powerseekers* (1969), *The Forty-Eight Hour Mile* (1970), *Slay Ride* (1972), *Back to the Planet of the Apes* (1980); and d) filmed dramas initially presented in two parts or episodes of television anthologies and subsequently edited into a single film, e.g., *Nightmare in Chicago* (1964), *Asylum for a Spy* (1967), *The Movie Maker* (1967), *Code Name: Heraclitus* (1967).

116. That is, television hours which take into account the insertion of commercials. The actual running time of the programs minus commercials may vary between 47 and 53 minutes' duration per hour.

117. NBC's *Mystery Movie* (1971-77) included at one time or another the following detective series: *Amy Prentiss, Columbo, Lanigan's Rabbi, McCloud, McMillan and Wife* (later just *McMillan*), *Madigan, Faraday and Company, The*

Snoop Sisters, Hec Ramsey, Tenafly, McCoy, Quincy, M.E., Cool Million, and *Banacek*. ABC's *The Men* alternated with *Assignment Vienna, The Delphiu Bureau* and *Jigsaw*.

118. There are four main categories of game and quiz shows: Greed Shows (*Let's Make a Deal, The Price Is Right*), People Shows (*The Newlywed Game, What's My Line?*), Hard Quiz Shows (*Jeopardy!, Split-Second*), and Celebrity Shows (*The Hollywood Squares, The Match Game*). *See* Neil Hickey, "What Do You Mean It's Only a Game," in *Television Today: A Close-Up View*, ed. Barry Cole (New York: Oxford University Press, 1981) p. 64.

119. Within Third World films, "First Cinema" defines the Hollywood-type films, "Second Cinema" applies to the indigenous national product of a country, and "Third Cinema" means the films made by progressive and militant filmmakers.

120. Previous to this feature film, the earliest public presentation of 3-D films took place in New York in 1915 and consisted of three one-reelers. The film *L'Arrivée du train* made by Auguste and Louis Lumière, shown in France in 1903, is credited as the first 3-D movie to be presented publicly.

121. There are several methods used to achieve depth in motion pictures. Six basic processes are: 1. Stereoscopic; 2. Anaglyphic; 3. Polaroid; 4. Raster (grid or lenticular); 5. Alternative view; and 6. Laser Holography. *See* Daniel L. Symmes, "3-D: Cinema's Slowest Revolution," *American Cinematographer* 55.4 (April 1974): 406.

122. For a history and extensive filmography of stereoscopic cinema, *see* R. M. Hayes, *3-D Movies* (Jefferson, NC: McFarland, 1989); *see also* Hal Morgan and Dan Symmes, *Amazing 3-D* (Boston: Little, Brown and Co., 1982).

123. For an appraisal of the thriller from the point of view of genre, *see* Charles Derry's *The Suspense Thriller* (Jefferson, NC: McFarland, 1988).

124. While all thrillers qualify as suspense films, a suspense film does not necessarily have to be a thriller. Suspense is a component of many films; for instance, it figures prominently in Westerns.

125. Theatrical trailers run for an average of two to three minutes; trailers meant for television run from 10 to 90 seconds.

126. The term travelogue originated with Burton Holmes who in Chicago in 1897, showed a view of St. Peter's, Rome, in a film of 50 feet.

127. Although film critic Manny Farber defined in 1957 as "underground" the films of a few lesser-known Hollywood directors, the word was used by Stan VanDerBeek in connection with a group of avant-garde and experimental filmmakers in his article-manifesto "The Cinema Dilemma: Films from the Underground," *Film Quarterly* 14.4 (1961): 5–15. The term "underground" was quickly adopted and became popular throughout the 1960s. It was later superseded by that of independent film.

128. The Western European countries which have been most productive in terms of underground films are: Britain, Germany, Italy, Austria, Switzerland, the Netherlands, Belgium and France.

129. Some collage films which incorporate footage from a diverse number of sources are also referred to as Found-footage films; *see* Michael O'Pray, "From Dada to Junk — Bruce Conner and the Found-footage film," *Monthly Film Bulletin* 54 (October 1987): 315–16.

130. Most cinema books dealing with vampires limit themselves to a chronological exposition of vampire films with little analysis. Two of the best examples of this type are David Pirie, *The Vampire Cinema* (London: Hamlyn, 1977), and Barrie Pattison, *The Seal of Dracula* (London: Lorrimer, 1975).

131. Ronald Borst, "The Vampire in the Cinema," *Photon* No. 19 (1970): 25–49; No. 21 (1971): 25–44 includes a "Vampire Film Checklist" detailing many vampire films.

132. For a list of these films, *see* pp. 56–57 of Patrick Robertson's *Guinness Movie Facts & Feats* (London: Guiness, 1991).

133. A good source for establishing the correlation between the fictional Dracula and the historical Vlad the Impaler is Raymond T. McNally and Radu Florescu, *In Search of Dracula: A True History of Dracula and Vampire Legends* (Greenwich, Conn.: New York Graphic Society, 1972).

134. Two previous white slavery films are *Den hvide Slavinde / The White Slave Girl* (1906) directed by Viggo Larsen and *Den hvide Slavehandel / The White Slave Trade* (1910) by Alfred Lind; *Den hvide Slavehandel II* (1911) by August Blom and *III* (1912) by Peter Urband Gad followed in the wake of the successful *Den hvide Slavehandel I*.

135. Another way of playing prerecorded items on television is the videodisc. However, it is not possible to record programs directly from the air onto a disc as with videocassettes.

136. Craig W. Campbell, *Reel America and World War I: A Comprehensive Filmography and History of Motion Pictures in the United States, 1914–1920* (Jefferson, NC: McFarland, 1985) includes several filmographies covering fiction and nonfiction World War I films for the period 1914–20.

137. For a filmography of 490 titles describing fiction and nonfiction, short and feature-length films connected with the Spanish Civil War, *see* Carlos Fernández Cuenca, *La Guerra de España y el Cine.* 2 vols. (Madrid: Editora Nacional, 1972), vol. 2, pp. 735–987.

138. Robertson's *Guinness* (1988 ed.), p. 63, cites *Kit Carson* and *The Pioneers*, copyrighted by the American Mutoscope and Biograph Co. on September 21, 1903, as the first Westerns. *The Great Train Robbery* was copyrighted on December 1, 1903. On the subject of early Westerns, *see* Daryl E. Jones, "The Earliest Western Films," *Journal of Popular Film and Television* 8.2 (1980): 42–46.

139. Michael R. Pitts, *Western Movies* (Jefferson, NC: McFarland, 1986) includes data on 4,189 feature Westerns; Les Adams and Buck Rainey's, *Shoot-'em-Ups* (New Rochelle, NY: Arlington House Publishers, 1978) has 3,339 entries for the period 1928 to 1977; Phil Hardy, *The Western* (London: Aurum Press, 1983) lists some 1,800 entries; and Brian Garfield, *Western Films* (New York: Rawson Associates, 1982) mentions about 1,500 films. For other reference sources, *see also* James Robert Parish and Michael R. Pitts, *The Great Western Pictures* and *The Great Western Pictures II* (Metuchen, NJ: Scarecrow, 1976; 1988) with 300 and 401 entries respectively, and Jack Nachbar, "Seventy Years on the Trail: A Selected Chronology of the Western Movie," *The Journal of Popular Film* 2 (1973): 75–83. For a bibliography: John G. Nachbar, *Western Films: An Annotated Critical Bibliography* (New York & London: Garland, 1975).

140. The seven-plot division was put forward by Frank Gruber who, in *The Pulp Jungle* (Los Angeles: Sherbourne Press, 1967), pp. 183–86, named them: the Union Pacific Story, the Ranch Story, the Empire Story, the Revenge Story, Custer's Last Stand or the Cavalry and Indian Story, the Outlaw Story and the Marshall Story.

141. The term horse opera (hoss opera) is also applied sometimes to films centered on a horse, with or without a Western context.

142. Robert Warshow, "Movie Chronicle: The Westerner," *Partisan Review* 21 (1954): 190–203.

143. *See Guinness* (1991 ed.), p. 71; the *Guinness* (1985 ed.) includes a Buffalo Bill filmography, p. 74.

144. For a subject category listing of film titles, *see* "Anatomy of the Indian," in *The Only Good Indian. . . The Hollywood Gospel* by Ralph E. Friar and Natasha A. Friar (New York: Drama Book Specialists, 1972), pp. 285–323. For published material on the subject of the Indian, *see* Gretchen M. Bataille and Charles L. P. Silet, "The Indian in American Film: A Checklist of Published Materials on Popular Images of the Indian in the American Film," *The Journal of Popular Film* 5 (1976): 171–82. *See also* Jack Spears, "The Indian on the Screen," in *Hollywood: The Golden Era* (New York: A. S. Barnes, 1971), pp. 361–96.

145. Besides wide-screen processes, 3-D films and various short-lived gimmicks [subliminal films (q.v.) with images which are supposed to work at a subconscious level and "smellies" or smell movies trying to convey odors, e.g., *Scent of Mystery* (60)] were also tried with the intention of luring audiences back to the cinemas.

146. Amongst the early wide-screen projection devices, Magnascope, introduced in 1924, continued to be used in some films until 1953 (e.g., *Niagara*). It was basically a device to enlarge portions of the screen image. In the early fifties when wide screen became fashionable, many film studios had a backlog of 35mm films which they converted into wide screen by the process of masking the top or bottom of the academy frame; this gave different aspect ratios: 1.66:1 (Paramount), 1.75:1 (MGM), 1.85:1 (Universal and Columbia). The studios also made a few films shot with wide-angle lenses, using masking devices installed in the theater projectors; some of the names for these systems include AMP-O-Vision, Metroscope, Paravision, Panoramic Screen, Photorama, Scenic-Scope, VastVision, Wide-Vision and comparable devices from other countries.

Multiple camera processes include the old Raoul Grimoin-Sanson's Cinéorama, a system that used ten projectors and ten films to show a panoramic view on a huge circular screen; Widescope, a 1921 invention which used a camera with two lenses; the French processes used by Abel Gance and Claude Autant-Lara, respectively named Triptych and Hypergonar; Vitarama, an eleven projector system introduced at New York's 1939 World's Fair by Fred Waller (1886–1954), which was later transformed into Cinerama in 1952, the number of projectors having been reduced to three. Five features were produced before Cinerama turned to films which were adaptable for showing in regular cinemas, and finally it discarded the three-camera, three-projector curved screen system for a 70mm wide film anamorphic process using a single camera and a single projector. After Cinerama, other processes attempting similar ventures with a greater or lesser measure of success have been Cinemiracle, Thrillarama, Wonderama, Kinopanorama (Russian), Quadravision, Walt Disney's Circle-Vision and Circlorama (a British circular film system).

The anamorphic processes took off in earnest after the successful public reception of CinemaScope's *The Robe* (1953). Other anamorphic systems include Cinema-Scope 55 (using 55mm negative), Naturama, Panavision, Panoscope, Superama, SuperScope, Technirama, Super Technirama 70, Techniscope, Ultra Panavision 70 (using 65mm negative), Vistarama, WarnerScope and scores of foreign systems compatible with CinemaScope: Franscope and Dyaliscope (France), Camerascope, MegaScope (Great Britain), Ultrascope, Superfilmscope, Supercinescope and Totalscope (Italy), AgaScope (Sweden), Sovscope (USSR), Starsea Scope (China), Shawscope (Hong Kong), Daieiscope, GrandScope, Nikkatsuscope, Tohoscope (Japan), etc.

Wide film systems comprise the 1920s German Tri-Ergon (42mm film), Natural

Vision (70mm film), Realife, Super Panavision 70 (65mm film), Panavision 70 (anamorphic 35mm negative into 70mm release print), Super Technirama 70, Todd-AO (65mm negative), VistaVision (35mm film, double-frame photography) and others using different sized gauges. Many of these systems are described in Robert E. Carr and R. M. Hayes's *Wide Screen Movies* (Jefferson, NC: McFarland, 1988).

147. Andrea S. Walsh, selecting films of the 1940s, analyzes three major varieties of women's films: maternal dramas, career woman comedies and films of suspicion and distrust. She also mentions two more categories: "woman in suffering" films, and "good woman / bad woman" films (p. 4; p. 26).

Index of Names

Aaron, Paul 177
Abbott, George 24, 192, 194, 197
Abbot, John William 286
Abbott and Costello 384
Abel, Alan 308
Abel, Jean 308
Abraham, John 208
Abrahams, Jim 22, 76, 109, 221
Abrams, Jerry 286
Adachi, Masao 160
Adair, Nancy 129
Adair, Peter 79, 129
Adams, J. D. 37
Adamson, Al 167
Adidge, Pierre 199
Adler, Lou 57, 84
Adolfi, John G. 196, 301
Adreon, Franklin 280
Afric, Vjekoslav 221
Agosti, Silvano 241
Agrama, Frank 161
Aguirre, Javier 358
Ahern, Charlie 158
Ahlberg, Mac 137, 304, 305, 306
Akerman, Chantal 110, 128
Akkad, Moustapha 250
Alaimo, Louise 80
Alazraki, Benito 36
Albertini, Bitto 307
Alda, Alan 283, 300
Aldrich, Adell 24
Aldrich, Robert 4, 21, 30, 35, 113, 119, 121, 128, 166, 175, 223, 226, 237, 242, 245, 248, 315, 327, 364, 370, 380, 383, 389
Alessandrini, Goffredo 53
Alexandrov, Grigori 71, 88, 99, 142, 372
Alexeïeff, Alexander 15
Algar, James 80, 350
Alk, Howard 74
Alk, Jones 74
Allégret, Marc 116, 191
Allégret, Yves 201
Allen, Corey 69, 76, 305
Allen, David L. 137
Allen, Irwin 18, 75, 76, 80, 277, 313, 352
Allen, Lewis 63, 119, 139, 209, 328

Allen, Steve 344
Allen, Woody 6, 30, 58, 107, 114, 144, 220, 221, 249, 261, 272, 275
Allio, René 33, 114, 143
Allouache, Merzak 346
Almendros, Nestor 78
Almodóvar, Pedro 109, 115, 266
Alter, Paul 343
Altman, Rick 398
Altman, Robert 7, 9, 10, 27, 57, 83, 91, 107, 123, 129, 157, 158, 229, 255, 274, 292, 367, 379
Alvarez, Santiago 239
Amadio, Silvio 89, 108
Amateau, Rod 141, 292
Amero, John 137
Amero, Lem 137
Amo, Antonio del 317
Amram, Robert 314
Anderson, G. M. 68
Anderson, John Murray 196
Anderson, Lindsay 9, 34, 122, 156, 167, 266, 315
Anderson, Michael 21, 30, 70, 107, 130, 269, 317, 368
Andre, Jacques 344
Angelopoulos, Theodore 114
Angelucci, Gianfranco 92
Anger, Kenneth 353, 354, 355
Annakin, Ken 8, 21, 64, 90, 103, 186, 188, 328, 367, 369, 370, 375
Annaud, Jean-Jacques 53, 200, 271, 299
Annett, Paul 377
Ansah, Kwan Paintsil 347
Anspaugh, David 10, 24
Antamoro, Giulio Cesare 251
Antel, Franz 92, 202, 308
Antoine, André 201
Anton, Edoardo 388
Anton, Karl 239
Antonio, Lou 75, 228, 248, 338, 362
Antonioni, Michelangelo 18, 54, 90, 179, 182, 183, 203, 348, 391
Apted, Michael 26, 70, 161, 166, 196, 200, 213, 215
Aravindan, G. 208
Arbuckle, Roscoe 293, 380

Arcand, Denys 114, 229, 252
Archainbaud, George 169, 180, 236, 290, 310
Ardolino, Emile 73
Arehn, Mats 229
Argento, Dario 130, 131
Arkush, Allan 141, 187, 259
Arledge, Sara Kathryn 354
Arliss, Leslie 64, 181
Arlych, Ralph 323
Armes, Roy 182
Armitage, George 29, 128, 307, 362
Armstrong, Charles 16
Armstrong, Gillian 197, 205
Armstrong, Michael 139, 387
Arnold, Jack 23, 26, 84, 147, 152, 163, 186, 215, 270, 273, 304 331
Arnold, Newt 153, 177
Arnoldy, John 132
Arnshtam, Lev 23
Arrabal, Fernando 19, 326, 373
Arroyo, J. F. 326
Arzner, Dorothy 193, 196, 388
Ascott, Anthony 131, 266, 312
Ashby, Hal 26, 27, 58, 175, 194, 266, 283, 372, 374
Asher, William 174, 198, 270, 292, 295, 324, 331, 332
Ashley, Ray 44, 158
Asquith, Anthony 7, 58, 315, 319, 365, 368, 373
Assonitis, Ovidio 153
Astaire, Fred 73, 191, 195
Astruc, Alexandre 214
Athens, J. D. 5
Attenborough, Richard 25, 31, 88, 353, 366, 375
Attias, Daniel 377
Audry, Jacqueline 7, 171
Auer, Gabriel 234
Auer, John H, 365
August, Bille 213
Aured, Carlos 151, 377
Austin, Ray 154
Autant-Lara, Claude 20, 27, 130, 173, 385, 386, 405
Autry, Gene 190, 382, 383, 384
Auzins, Igo 205
Avakian, Aram 39, 52, 126

407

Index of Titles

In this index, initial articles and most subtitles are dropped, lengthy titles are truncated, different films with the same title (e.g., remakes) are combined, sequels discussed together whose titles begin with the same words are combined, and alternate language titles that differ only slightly and that would appear next to the main title are dropped.

431